D1601914

HAYDN STUDIES

*Proceedings of the
International Haydn Conference*
Washington, D.C., 1975

HAYDN STUDIES

Proceedings of the
International Haydn Conference
Washington, D.C., 1975

EDITED BY

JENS PETER LARSEN

HOWARD SERWER

JAMES WEBSTER

New York · London

W · W · NORTON & COMPANY

Copyright © 1981 by W. W. Norton & Company, Inc.
Published simultaneously in Canada by George J. McLeod Limited, Toronto.
Printed in the United States of America.
First Edition
All Rights Reserved

Library of Congress Cataloging in Publication Data
International Haydn Conference, Washington, D.C., 1975.
  Haydn studies.

  At head of title: American Musicological Society.
  Includes bibliographical references and index.
  1. Haydn, Joseph, 1732–1809—Congresses. I. Larsen,
Jens Peter, 1902–   II. Serwer, Howard, 1928–
III. Webster, James, 1942–   IV. American
Musicological Society. V. Title.
ML36.I59593 1975   780'.92'4   80–15688
ISBN 0-393-01454-1

W. W. Norton & Company, Inc. 500 Fifth Avenue, New York N.Y. 10110
W. W. Norton & Company Ltd. 25 New Street Square, London EC4A3NT

1 2 3 4 5 6 7 8 9 0

Contents

v

Round Table

Problems of Authenticity—The Raigern Keyboard Sonatas
WILLIAM S. NEWMAN, *Chairman*

Free Papers

Authenticity, Chronology, Source Studies, Editorial Practice

Free Papers

Historical Context; Haydn's Relations to Others

PART THREE: PERFORMANCE

Preface

In 1972 the John F. Kennedy Center for the Performing Arts, Washington, D.C., initiated planning for a Haydn Festival, to include a series of concerts and an international conference devoted to Haydn. In the first stage of preparation a committee representing performers and musicologists was formed under the direction of Martin Feinstein, Executive Director of the Kennedy Center. It was agreed that Antal Dorati would serve as Music Director of the Festival, and Jens Peter Larsen as Musicologist-in-Residence at the Kennedy Center. The special planning committee for the Conference, formed later in collaboration with the International Musicological Society and the American Musicological Society, consisted of Jens Peter Larsen (chairman), Barry S. Brook, Alvin H. Johnson, Janet Knapp, Jan LaRue, Irving Lowens, and Alfred Mann. Howard Serwer functioned as Executive Officer of the Conference.

The Haydn Festival took place from September 22 through October 11, 1975, and the Conference, October 3–11. The musical performances were held chiefly at the Kennedy Center, and also at the Smithsonian Institution and the Library of Congress. The Conference had been scheduled for the Kennedy Center as well, but practical difficulties necessitated moving it elsewhere. Following a kind initiative on the part of the Division of Musical Instruments of the Smithsonian Institution, the facilities of the Institution were placed at the disposal of the Conference.

A generous grant from the National Endowment for the Humanities to the American Musicological Society made it possible to invite about sixty American and foreign scholars and musicians to serve as chairmen of sessions and to participate in panel discussions; their names and institutional affiliations are listed on pp. 561–63. In addition, qualified graduate students were invited to read papers, and it is a pleasure to be able to include these in the present volume. A number of musical performances of special interest to musicologists were arranged by the conference committee; most of these informal concerts and workshop-rehearsals took place in the Smithsonian Institution. The remarkable performances of Haydn's complete Masses as free evening concerts in the Grand Foyer of the Kennedy Center comprised one of the most outstanding features in the rich musical offerings of the Festival.

The Haydn Conference was of longer duration than is usual in gatherings of this type. It was organized around three broad topics, each of which could have been the subject of an entire conference of its own: Haydn documentation, Haydn performance problems, and problems of form and style in Haydn's music. Although these questions are all of primary importance, they have received varying degrees of attention in this century.

Haydn documentation has been widely pursued since the 1930s. In the Conference it proved possible—and meaningful—to survey the research tradition which has been established through international collaboration during several decades. A center of documentation has developed since 1955 in the Joseph Haydn-Institut in Cologne; it was fortunate that its entire research staff was able to participate in the Conference.

Much has been written about the performance practice of early eighteenth-century music, but the music of the later eighteenth century has been subjected to similar investigation only recently, and many problems concerning the performance of Haydn's music have not yet even been raised. Two round tables were dedicated to this subject; but above all, the six workshops comprised a forum for questions of performance practice. Unfortunately, it has not been possible to give a full account of them, because they centered around the performance of music—live and recorded—which could not be included in the report.

In the past, problems of form and style have been discussed rather extensively in relation to the somewhat fictitious concept of "Classical style," but problems relating to Haydn's music in particular still require much attention. Among the reasons for this are 1) even today, Haydn's works are not fully available; 2) it is difficult to establish an exact chronology for his compositions; and 3) the traditional tools for analysis and criticism were shaped chiefly to fit Beethoven's music, rather than Haydn's. Hence one would scarcely be justified in speaking of an established tradition in this field. Many valuable individual contributions could be named, but a general research tradition such as we enjoy in the field of documentation is still in the making.

A special problem in preparing the present volume was the necessity to abbreviate many of the papers and discussions. In the round tables and workshops these condensations have omitted very little of substance from the discussions among the participants, but for reasons of space many of the prepared statements delivered in these panels have had to be shortened, even though on their merits they should have been printed in full. The public lectures and the great majority of the free papers, on the other hand, appear here unabridged.

With a few exceptions, the round tables and workshops have been edited as follows: first, a tape of the proceedings was transcribed by the secretary. Based on this transcription, the chairman prepared a draft report, usually abridged, which was circulated to the panel members for their comments and eventual approval. The chairman then submitted a revised report to the editors. With the assistance of the Publications Committee of the American Musicological Society, the editors revised these reports further where necessary, and they supplied additional documentation and cross-references. These final revisions were submitted to chairmen and contributors once again for their approval.

In order to facilitate the coherence and utility of the present volume, some reorganization has been imposed on the order of events during the Conference. A program of the Conference appears on pp. 558–60. Books and other references are cited in abbreviated form in the notes; full titles and necessary cross-references are found in the List of Works Cited, on pp. 531–57.

The realization of the Haydn Conference and this volume was made possible through the assistance of a great number of institutions and individuals. The National Endowment for the Humanities provided the major financial assistance for the Conference. The American Musicological Society served as the sponsoring organization, and the Society has made available a most generous subvention for the production of this volume. The Kennedy Center supported the Musicologist-in-Residence during planning and execution of the Conference. The Danish foundations Carlsbergfond and Statens human. Forskningsråd provided travel and secretarial expenses. Facilities for the Conference were made available by the Kennedy Center and the Smithsonian Institution. The managements and staffs of all these institutions provided much kind assistance at every stage. Thanks are due further to the many colleagues who contributed to the Conference and to this volume by acting as chairmen of paper sessions and as chairmen and secretaries of the panel discussions.

The Editors

PART ONE: PUBLIC LECTURES

Haydn and His Viennese Background

KARL GEIRINGER

In order to set the stage for this lecture, I should like to play two brief recorded examples of Austrian music before Haydn. One, written about sixty years before Haydn's birth, illustrates the light and gay spirit of Austrian music and its leaning toward folk art. It is a serenade of Heinrich Biber, sung by a night watchman to the following text:

> Listen, The hour has struck ten.
> Tend the hearth,
> And praise God the Father,
> And our dear Lady.

The second, composed in 1734 when Haydn was two years old, exemplifies the highly significant role of Italian music in Austria, and it also illustrates the ruling classes' lively participation in the performance of music. This work was written at the command of the Austrian Empress. The two soprano parts were sung by her two daughters, the Archduchesses Maria Anna and the future Empress Maria Theresa. It is drawn from Antonio Caldara's *Il giuoco del quadriglio*. Four girls are playing cards, but they get bored and decide to dance instead; they sing this "ballo" as they do so.[1]

RECORDED EXAMPLES: Biber, from the *Night Watchman Serenade*
Caldara, from *Il giuoco del quadriglio*

[1] The Biber serenade was published by Paul Nettl as *Serenade für fünf Streichinstrumente (Nachtwächter-Bass) und Cembalo,* as No. 112 in *Nagels Musik-Archiv* (Kassel, 1934). It was sung by J. Staempfli on Musical Heritage Society recording MHS 938, *A Concert at Mirabelle Palace in Salzburg.* Caldara's *Giuoco* was published by Eusebius Mandyczewski and Karl Geiringer in DTÖ, Vol. 75 (Jahrgang XXXIX, 1932), 46–61. It was performed by the Società cameristica di Lugano on Nonesuch recording 71103.

3

Joseph Haydn was born in the eastern part of Austria, in a region which was inhabited predominantly by German-speaking people. However, the border was not far, and some Hungarians as well as Croatians had settled in the same area. Haydn learned neither the Hungarian nor the Croatian language, but from childhood onward he was familiar with a mixture of peoples.

At the age of eight Haydn moved to Vienna to become a choirboy at St. Stephen's, the capital's magnificent cathedral. In a way, the conditions he encountered there resembled those in his native province. Vienna was the capital of an empire in which Czechs, Poles, Croatians, Slovaks, Slovenes, Italians, Hungarians, and others coexisted with the dominant German population. From all corners of the Hapsburg lands people came to settle in Austria's commercial, political, and cultural center. Vienna thus provided a fusion of the most diversified ethnic elements, a harmonious synthesis which exercised a highly beneficial influence on Haydn's artistic development.

In the eighteenth century Vienna was a beautiful place. Following the destruction of large parts of the city during the siege by the Turks, magnificent churches and palaces had been built by such great architects as Fischer von Erlach and Lukas von Hildebrandt. An Italian traveler visiting Vienna in 1718 and comparing it with other European cities emphasized its similarity to the towns of his homeland, exclaiming enthusiastically that one seemed to breathe here something akin to Italian air.[2] Certain Northern features in the architecture, he added, did not reduce, but rather enhanced the city's attractions.

Considerably less enthusiastic was the verdict of the famous "Queen of the Bluestockings," Lady Mary Wortley Montagu, who had visited Vienna two years earlier. In a letter to a friend she wrote:

This town, which has the honour of being the emperor's residence, did not at all answer my ideas of it, being much less than I expected to find it; the streets are very close, and so narrow, one cannot observe the fine fronts of the palaces, though many of them very well deserve observation, being truly magnificent. . . For, as the town is too little for the number of the people that desire to live in it, the builders seem to have projected to repair that misfortune, by clapping one town on top of another, most of the houses being of five, and some of them six stories. You may easily imagine, that the streets being so narrow, the rooms are extremely dark; and, what is an inconvenience much more intolerable, in my opinion, the apartments of the greatest ladies, and even of the ministers of state, are divided but by a partition from that of a tailor or shoemaker. Those that have houses of their own, let out the rest of them to whoever will take them.[3]

[2] Niccolo Madrisio, *Viaggi per l'Italia, Francia e Germania* (Venice, 1718), as quoted in Hans Tietze, *Alt-Wien in Wort und Bild* (Vienna, 1924), 37.
[3] *The Letters and Works of Lady Mary Wortley Montagu, Edited by her Great Grandson, Lord Wharncliffe,* 3rd ed. by W. Moy Thomas, 2 vols. (London, 1861), I, 235–36.

Later in the same letter she remarks, however:

I must own, I never saw a place so perfectly delightful as the Fauxbourg [out-skirts] of Vienna. It is very large, and almost wholly composed of delicious pal-aces. If the emperor found it proper to permit the gates of the town to be laid open, he would have one of the largest and best-built cities in Europe.

Particularly interesting in this letter is the reference to the physical prox-imity between the residences of the nobility and those of the lower classes. An Austrian attitude seems to be reflected here. The unbridge-able gulf which existed in some countries between the high aristocracy and the common people was not nearly as much in evidence in Austria. The imperial family at times took part in popular festivities; it opened its parks to the citizens of Vienna. Emperor Joseph II is known to have vis-ited peasants and plowed a field. Music, in particular, helped to bridge gaps in social status. Though never oblivious of his humble origins, Haydn learned to move with a certain ease in circles of the highest aris-tocracy.

The narrowness and darkness of many city streets, which Lady Mon-tagu criticized, induced the Viennese to seek relaxation in the lovely landscape surrounding the imperial city. In the south and west were the green Vienna woods and the undulating foothills of the Alps, in the north the majestic Danube river, in the east the fertile plains leading to Hungary. Abbot Anselm Desing, who offered in 1741 a description of the Austrian capital, had this to report:

Inside the city the Viennese don't feel well; they love the open air. . . . Walking around and hiking is very common, and there is everywhere ample opportunity for so doing. The nobility at times rides in carriages to the Prater, which is an ex-cessively gay and clean little wood on an island of the Danube. Close by are ordi-nary walks for pedestrians.[4]

Thus, love of the outdoors was quite natural to the Viennese. Haydn acquired it, no doubt, in his youth, and the composer of *The Creation* and *The Seasons* still manifested it near the end of his life. Beethoven, too, was a great hiker who loved to tramp through the Vienna woods.

As we have said, music linked the various social strata. The imperial family took the lead in musical patronage. The achievements of the Hof-kapelle won fame throughout Europe. Most of the emperors were ac-complished performers, and some were also gifted composers. The aris-tocracy tried to emulate the imperial family. Several wealthy counts and princes engaged their own bands of musicians, and some of the patrons took active part in the performances. Love of music was equally great among the bourgeoisie. Most young persons learned to sing or to play an instrument, and domestic chamber music was generally cultivated. The French author Marcel Brion rightly stated: "In Vienna, music has always

---

[4] Anselm Desing, *Auxilia Historica* (Stadt am Hof, 1741); see Tietze, 43–44.

been something far more important than mere entertainment or even aesthetic enjoyment; it was a vital necessity."[5] And in the eighteenth century it was said that in Vienna even the stone angels carved over the doors seemed to be in song.

Haydn strongly felt the magic attraction of this city, to which he returned even after his triumphs won in London. The same is true of Mozart, Beethoven, Brahms, Bruckner, and Mahler, to mention only a few of the great musicians who were not born in Vienna, but who elected to live there.

Operatic performances were particularly enjoyed by the Viennese. Beginning with the works of Cavalli and Cesti in the mid-seventeenth century, a large number of operatic compositions, mostly by Italians in the employ of the Austrian court, were mounted on Viennese stages. The great librettists Zeno and Metastasio were active in Vienna as court poets, while the renowned architects Burnacini and Galli-Bibiena designed the lavish stage sets. Lady Montagu wrote to Alexander Pope of an operatic performance she attended in the garden of the imperial castle La Favorita. "Nothing of that kind," she wrote, "ever was more magnificent; and I can easily believe what I am told, that the decorations and costumes cost the emperor thirty thousand pounds sterling."[6] Significantly enough, nothing is mentioned in this letter about the drama or the music performed. We should not believe, however, that the imperial patron maintained an equally one-sided attitude. After all, the impressive operatic productions in Vienna during the first half of the eighteenth century laid the groundwork for the later climactic achievements of Gluck and Mozart, and indirectly for the work Haydn did for the stage in Eszterháza.

In the field of the spoken drama the Viennese showed special liking for comedy. Foreign visitors were shocked at times by the coarseness of the jokes to which elegant ladies and gentlemen listened with obvious enjoyment. Famous buffoons such as Stranitzky, Prehauser, and Kurz-Bernardon were the darlings of Viennese audiences. Simple, popular music was interwoven with the texts of these comedies, greatly adding to their attraction. Young Haydn wrote the music to two of Kurz-Bernardon's comedies. He may also have been the author of other pieces based on comedy texts which have been preserved without the composer's name: compositions in the famous collection *Teutsche Comoedie-Arien* in the Vienna National Library, from which Robert Haas and Eva Badura-Skoda have published interesting excerpts.[7] The peculiar combination of Italian elements with features of Austrian folk music, noticeable in this repertory, conforms to the style of many of Haydn's early compositions.

[5] Brion, *Vienna*, 58.   [6] Montagu, I, 237–39.
[7] Robert Haas, ed., *Teutsche Comoedie-Arien*, DTÖ, Vol. 64 (Jahrgang XXXIII:1, 1926); Badura-Skoda, "Comoedie-Arien."

So far we have attempted to offer a bird's-eye view of the general social and cultural conditions prevailing in the city where Haydn spent his formative years. Now we have to investigate the specific musical background against which the composer's artistic personality developed. The training which the young choirboy received at St. Stephen's was quite scanty; but in the cathedral, and more still in greater Vienna, he found the atmosphere and the models needed for his general intellectual growth.

The generation of composers active in the mid-eighteenth century attempted to supplant the majestic splendor of Baroque art by the graceful delicacy prevalent in the newly developed *style galant*. Instead of powerful unity of form they wanted unrestrained variety. Strict counterpoint was practically eliminated from their compositions. In instrumental music the Italian *sonata da chiesa* and the French *ouverture* were shunned, because they included polyphonic sections. Instead, the light and gay sinfonia and the colorful suite of dances enjoyed widest popularity. Combinations of these two forms were particularly successful. For orchestral compositions mixtures were mostly chosen in which the *sinfonia* element prevailed. On the other hand the divertimenti, notturni, and cassazioni written for chamber ensemble favored the suite form. An important feature was the gradual growth of the binary structures of individual movements into the highly developed sonata form, a process which went on throughout the whole eighteenth century.

These trends were more or less conspicuous in various parts of Europe. Haydn grew up with them in music of Viennese composers such as Georg Christoph Wagenseil, court composer and the music teacher of Empress Maria Theresa; Georg Matthias Monn, organist of the Karlskirche; Franz Asplmayer, composer of ballets; and others. He shared their efforts and eventually fulfilled their aims.

In the field of keyboard music, which in a wider sense includes the clavier trios, the influence of Viennese music on the fledgling composer is particularly noticeable. The suitelike character of these pieces, which use a minuet as middle or final movement and maintain the same basic tonality in all three movements, as well as the common heading "Partita," are typical features in South German and Austrian keyboard music, particularly of its most representative composer, Wagenseil. But Haydn's musical language was not limited to the light and graceful idiom of the *style galant*. In some early sonatas we already find features of passionate subjectivity which may point to the art of C. P. E. Bach. Without leaving his Austrian base Haydn extended his vistas beyond it.

What a shame that Haydn's early Viennese comedies are lost; we can only conjecture what they may have sounded like! In the works for the stage which he later wrote for Prince Esterházy, he followed traditions of the Italian opera. He embraced in turn its serious and its comic aspects, eventually combining the two features in his greatest dramatic works. Haydn must have first heard Italian operas during his stay in Vienna. He was personally acquainted with Metastasio, who lived for a time under the same roof as Haydn. Moreover, the young musician studied with and worked for the celebrated Neapolitan opera composer and singing teacher Nicola Porpora, who spent several years in the Austrian capital.

In the field of church music Haydn received invaluable practical training while working as a choirboy at St. Stephen's. Thus it was quite natural for him to utilize in his own work in this field the style of religious composition predominant in the capital at that time. Its stylistic features had likewise originated in Italy, but so long before that their origins had almost been forgotten. Solid textures combined with the antiphonal use of different sound groups were first employed in the sacred music of Venice and Rome. They were soon adopted by Austrian composers in an unbroken tradition beginning with the seventeenth-century Masses of Stadlmayr and Christoph Strauss and culminating in the works of the court composer Johann Joseph Fux, who was still alive when Haydn entered St. Stephen's. On the other hand elements of the Italian opera—the use of arias and duets, brilliant vocal coloratura, and the occasional overemphasis of purely musical devices—had likewise been adopted by composers of church music active in Vienna. We might only mention Antonio Caldara and Georg von Reutter, the Kapellmeister at St. Stephen's under whom Haydn had to sing. All these features are also to be observed in Haydn's church music, and we may safely state that it originally grew out of his daily occupation in the cathedral.

Let us now attempt to survey the works the young Haydn wrote before he entered the services of Count Morzin. This is no easy undertaking, as the composer's early works strikingly resemble those of his Austrian contemporaries and therefore often present puzzling problems of authenticity. Moreover, very few of the authentic early works can be securely dated. We must therefore be satisfied to state in the most general terms that Haydn wrote solo keyboard sonatas as well as trios for a keyboard instrument accompanied by violin and violoncello ("Basso"). There are string trios for two violins and cello, which some have interpreted as studies for the very important string quartets. The early quartets still clearly show the influence of the suite. They are always in the major mode and contain five movements, two of them minuets. The divertimenti for string and wind instruments may have been written for the fashionable serenades in which the young Haydn took part. It was the custom in Vienna to assemble a group of musicians in front of a fair lady's house to celebrate with music her name-day or birthday. This offered musicians an opportunity to earn a modest fee from the sponsor of such entertainment.

Among Haydn's early compositions is a keyboard concerto, Hob. XVIII:1 in C major, whose autograph has been preserved. The composer corrected it later and added the date 1756. It may serve as an example of the close affinity of Haydn's early works to those of his Viennese predecessors. I would like to play the finale of this concerto and the finale of a keyboard concerto in D major by Georg Matthias Monn, which was probably written a few years earlier. There is no direct connection between the two works—possibly Haydn did not even know the earlier concerto—but in style and content they seem very much alike. (Incidentally, in performances and recordings of these concertos you will sometimes hear a harpsichord performing the solo part, at other times an organ. Please disregard this difference. Haydn stated that the work could also be played on the harpsichord, and such exchanges were quite common at the time.[8])

RECORDED EXAMPLES: Haydn, Concerto in C major, Hob. XVIII:1, finale
G. M. Monn, Concerto in D major, finale

For the church, the young Haydn composed a *Salve Regina* (Hob. XXIIIb:1) for soprano solo, chorus, and organ, and one or two *Missae breves* (short Masses). One of these, the *Missa brevis* in F major, is certainly a work of Haydn, but the authenticity of the second one, known as *Missa Rorate coeli desuper* (Hob. XXII:3), is doubtful. The thematic beginning of the work is quoted in EK (however, entered about fifty years later); on the other hand, manuscript copies name Georg Reutter the Younger or the Vienna court organist Ferdinand Arbesser as the author. Once again it seems almost impossible to distinguish with certainty an early work by Haydn from those of his contemporaries. One argument for the attribution of the little Mass to Haydn is the fact that the work is marred by somewhat primitive and awkward progressions in the vocal parts. It seems quite possible that the fledgling composer was responsible for these shortcomings, but unlikely that a solid craftsman like Reutter or Arbesser could have written them.

As you know, in (or around) 1759 Haydn entered the service of the Czech Count Morzin as music director. When financial difficulties forced the count to dismiss his musicians, the composer quickly found a position as vice-Kapellmeister and soon afterwards as Kapellmeister of Prince Esterházy. Henceforth, up to 1790, Haydn had his residence in the country. But this does not mean that his ties to Vienna were severed. Count Morzin, who lived at his Bohemian castle Lukaveč, liked to spend the

---

[8] The score of the Haydn concerto was first published by Max Schneider (Wiesbaden, 1953). It was performed by E. Power Biggs on Columbia recording ML 6082. The Monn concerto for harpsichord was edited by W. Fischer in DTÖ, Vol. 39 (Jahrgang XIX:2, 1912), 92–106. It was performed by J. Sebestyen on Turnabout recording 34324.

winter months in the capital and may have taken some musicians along. When Haydn was subsequently active at the court of the Princes Esterházy in Eisenstadt and at the castle of Esterháza, visits to Vienna occurred from time to time. Although Haydn's duties at the Esterházy court were staggering, he found time to write a large-scale oratorio for Vienna. *Il ritorno di Tobia* was premiered in 1775 in the Vienna Kärntnerthortheater for the benefit of a charitable institution. Its great success may have been responsible for the request sent to Haydn in 1776 to write an autobiographical sketch for the publication *Das gelehrte Österreich,* a sort of Austrian *Who's Who.* This article is one of the most important biographical sources available to us. According to tradition (handed down especially by Dies) Haydn was also invited to write an opera for Vienna. He readily undertook this commission, but when he came to rehearse the new work, his competitors let loose such a flood of intrigues that he withdrew his score in disgust. *La vera costanza* was then premiered, like other Haydn operas, at the castle of Esterháza.[9] The composer also had disagreements with the charitable institution for which he had written *Il ritorno di Tobia,* but all this did not change his strong attachment to the city where he had grown up.

That attachment was further increased by the warm friendship between him and Mozart. The Salzburg composer had moved to Vienna in 1781. Haydn and Mozart established personal relations presumably in 1784 or 1785, and they even had the joy of playing chamber music together. We don't have to quote here the well-known praise of Mozart's work uttered by Haydn to Mozart's father, or Mozart's moving dedication of six quartets to his "beloved friend Haydn." More important still is the fact that in the 1780s the two composers independently—and yet quite often influencing each other—reached a classical maturity of style. In combining the light gaiety of the *style galant* with the tender subjectivity of *Empfindsamkeit,* adding some of the strictness of Baroque polyphony and imbuing the whole with elements of folk music, Haydn—and on a different plane also Mozart—established a classical balance of expression. Vienna, the city in which for centuries various ethnic groups had lived together and harmoniously blended, offered the inspiration for such a fusion of artistic elements. It is unlikely that a similar influence could have been exerted by any other city.

About 1780 a very significant practical tie was established between Haydn and Vienna in the form of a business connection with the important publishing house of Artaria & Co. This firm published more than three hundred editions of his works: string quartets, symphonies, the *Seven Last Words,* the late piano sonatas, and many other compositions. The lively correspondence testifies to the friendly relationship between

---

[9] On this subject see Horst Walter's Free Paper elsewhere in this volume. [Ed.]

Haydn and Carlo and Francesco Artaria, who were, of course, of Italian extraction. In 1785 Haydn joined the freemasonic lodge *Zur wahren Eintracht* in Vienna. This step was probably taken largely on the recommendation of Mozart. But Haydn, as opposed to Mozart, never had much contact with the world of freemasonry, and it seems doubtful whether the ideas of the order had any influence on his attitude as a loyal son of the Catholic church.

Towards 1790 probably the strongest attraction in Vienna was offered by visits to the home of Dr. von Genzinger, physician to Prince Esterházy. The doctor and his charming wife Marianne were ardent music lovers, and Frau von Genzinger, the mother of five children, was an excellent singer and pianist. In the Genzinger home Haydn found the congenial atmosphere never provided by his own wife, who took no interest whatever in her husband's work. The letters that Haydn wrote to Marianne von Genzinger, first from Esterháza and later from London, are warm, human documents free of the conventional stilted flourishes so often found in correspondence of the time.

Considering this strong attachment to the capital, it cannot surprise us that when Prince Nikolaus Esterházy died in September 1790, and his successor dissolved the Esterházy musical establishment, Haydn's instinctive reaction was to rush to Vienna. After three decades of service to the same family, the composer was suddenly relieved of his duties. But this state of affairs did not last long. Haydn received various offers, and he decided to go to London, where during two memorable visits his symphonic output reached its magnificent climax. We cannot accompany Haydn on his travels to England, but I should like to point out one characteristic feature of the works he performed there. The folkloristic element, which had always been strong in his compositions, is particularly emphasized in the last twelve symphonies. How natural and appealing, for instance, is the Andante theme from Symphony No. 94 in G major ("Surprise"), derived, as E. F. Schmid pointed out,[10] from a German nursery song. An Austrian rustic scene is conjured up in the following minuet, Allegro molto. We seem to witness Austrian peasants vigorously swinging their girls in a spirited folk dance. Austrian folklore, nurtured by the different nationalities of its inhabitants, is also encountered in other symphonies. No doubt the homeland, and with it the center and heart of Austria, were in the composer's mind when he wrote these symphonies intended for English music lovers. The situation was not entirely different a century later, when Dvořák composed his *New World Symphony*.

Between his two visits to England Haydn returned to Vienna. He used the newly won riches for the purchase and remodeling of a comfortable

---

[10] Schmid, *Haydn,* 302.

house in the Vienna suburb Gumpendorf. Obviously he intended eventually to retire to his favorite city.

I would like to mention a small, but not insignificant, incident from these years. In autumn 1792 Haydn was asked to provide music for a masked ball to be held at the imperial Redoutensaal (ballroom) for the benefit of artists' widows and orphans. Such a mixture of good fun with charity appealed to the composer, and he accepted the commission without pay (although he made up for it later by selling the music for twenty-four ducats to Artaria). Thus, on November 25, 1792, twelve minuets and twelve German dances newly composed by Haydn had their first performance. These enchanting pieces are far too little known, though they are remarkable for their thoroughness of workmanship and delicacy of orchestration. Haydn applied himself to all twenty-four pieces with a zeal which seems out of proportion to the modest task. While in his younger years he had dashed off dance music rather quickly, he now worked more carefully and deliberately. As a matter of fact, more than two dozen sketches for this work have been preserved. The feeling of responsibility, not least after the great successes he had won in London, and his desire to present himself in Vienna to best advantage, left their imprint even on so humble a composition as this tiny German dance.

RECORDED EXAMPLE: Haydn, German Dance, Hob. IX:12, No. 4.[11]

With Haydn's return to Vienna after his second visit to London the circle closes. Haydn now chose to reside in the city in which he had grown up. Artistically, he turned over a new leaf. After having achieved his greatest successes in the field of instrumental music, he now wrote chiefly vocal compositions. Elements of folk song and art music reached a magnificent, classical fusion in the song *Gott erhalte Franz den Kaiser,* composed in 1797. Haydn labored for quite some time on the perfection of this tune, and he made many sketches before it was completed. The result was a song that sounds familiar at first hearing and is never forgotten afterwards, despite—or perhaps because of—its unique melodic invention.

Haydn had always loved Vienna; now, at last, this love was fully reciprocated. The Viennese had learned to appreciate the beauty of his work. In particular, they were delighted by the decidedly Austrian character revealed in the last two oratorios, with their fine sense of humor and deep love of nature. When *The Creation* was heard in the Vienna Burgtheater in 1799 it drew the greatest crowd ever assembled in this theater. The Viennese were so excited about the treat offered to them that they hardly seemed to notice the Russian army under general Su-

[11] Haydn's *Deutscher Tanz* (Hob. IX:12, No. 4) was first published by Otto Erich Deutsch (Leipzig, 1931). It was performed by the Philharmonic Orchestra of Vienna conducted by Hans Gillesberger on Haydn Society recording HSLP 1022.

varov that was passing through the capital on the same day. Performances of *The Creation* and *The Seasons* which Haydn conducted in Vienna for the benefit of widows and orphans netted 40,000 florins for charity.

This brings us to the end of Haydn's career. But the impact of his work was felt in Vienna long after his death. Beethoven revealed in his string quartets and symphonies strong ties with Haydn's music. Schubert, Brahms, Bruckner, and Mahler received vital inspiration from the great old man's work. Even Vienna-born Arnold Schoenberg expressed admiration for the boldness of Haydn's modulations.[12] No doubt the atmosphere and culture of the Austrian capital exercised a decisive influence on Haydn's artistic personality, while his work, in turn, left its imprint on music created in Vienna by later generations.

[12] Schoenberg, *Structural,* 147–49, 167.

A Survey of the Development of Haydn Research: Solved and Unsolved Problems

JENS PETER LARSEN

Before I begin my discussion of Haydn research problems, I would like to say a few words about musicology and musicological problems in a more general sense. I still remember the British passport officer who, when I came to England twenty years ago to attend an international musicological conference in Oxford, said to me, "Tell me, what *is* musicology?" I believe that many people must still be asking this question during an event like this Haydn conference. And musicology may really seem to have so many faces that you cannot blame anybody for asking it. I will not enumerate all the various branches of musicology, such as acoustics, ethnomusicology, music sociology, knowledge about musical instruments past and present, the development of music theory, and so forth. I shall limit myself to some reflections on research in music history, and within this large field I have especially in mind problems concerning eighteenth-century music and concerning the study of an individual composer and his works. I would like to say something about the aims, the qualifications, and the approach of the musicologist who wants to contribute to research in these directions.

Research centered around a composer has two sides—according to one traditional terminology, the life and the works. You may want to concentrate on one or the other, but anybody doing serious work in either field will also have to be fully aware of the problems in the other one. Whichever you choose, the beginning of your work must consist of collecting material and facts, together with a study of all the relevant literature about your topic. It may be difficult to collect all the needed material. Besides a great investment of time and labor, it will demand a high standard of scholarly responsibility. Even at this preliminary stage the vulnerability of research in the humanities will become clear. Certain facts seem unshakable, but very soon the question will arise: is this particular piece of information really a *fact,* or is it to a certain extent an *interpretation* of facts, or even *guesswork?* We are not working with general physical laws, but with individuals and individual creations of the human mind. Let me name a few of the tasks we have to face, and let us see to what extent we can accomplish our work without introducing a measure of interpretation or guesswork.

14

Of course, collecting material for a biography of a composer will establish many definite facts, such as those about a composer's birth, education, positions held, and so on. But this material may be very incomplete—as for example in the case of Haydn's early years in Vienna. How much do we know in the way of immutable facts about Haydn's doings in the twenty years between c. 1740 and c. 1760? It will scarcely be possible to refrain from including features taken from much later sources, like Griesinger,[1] or relating to circumstances and events which, although characteristic of his surroundings, we cannot definitely connect with Haydn himself. The problem is of course very much enlarged when one proceeds from collecting material to working out a real biography. Not only will the author have to use material of problematic reliability, but he will inevitably have to interpret his material and to flesh it out in various ways. The difference between a "documentary biography" of the type we associate with the name of Otto Erich Deutsch, and any corresponding major biography, will largely depend on two conditions: it must be based on all the relevant facts, and it must provide a convincing interpretation of all supplementary material.

A list of the composer's works may be part of any biography, but for important and prolific composers, a thematic catalogue is a necessity. In Haydn's case this task has approached completion only in recent times. Anyone using the well-known catalogues of Mozart's, Beethoven's, or Haydn's works will know how much uncertainty is still—and will continue to be—associated with these compilations. Above all: the authenticity problem is not only a question of Yes or No, but often of Maybe. The time-consuming problems are just those where the interpretation of sources and music is our only means to approach a solution.

A third fundamental demand is a first-rate critical collected edition of a composer's works. Every responsible editor of such an edition can tell you how much interpretation is connected with work of this kind. If you look into the impressive list of sources in one of the critical reports from the Cologne edition of Haydn's works (JHW), you will see that the fundamental prerequisite for the actual editing is to evaluate the sources ("Quellenbewertung"). And in this process, many editorial problems must be solved through interpretation—a choice between two or more possibilities, each of which *might* be the right solution. A student who wishes to find the proper reading of a specific chord and consults the collected edition may accept its solution as the word of a supreme court. If only he could know how much trouble perhaps just this reading caused the editor, who eventually was compelled to make some decision, even if he himself was still in doubt!

I have talked about problems in the field of documentation, in which

---

[1] See the bibliography under Griesinger.

you would certainly expect to find rather objective criteria for research, and I have tried to point out how much, even in this field, our conclusions and results depend on responsible interpretation. When we move on to the evaluation of purely musical problems, as in analyzing and performing music, the degree of objectivity is even smaller. I will return to this point a little later. But first let me briefly discuss the qualifications and approach of the scholar whose work in research is to be of lasting importance.

I have stressed the question of interpretation rather strongly because I think it is a key problem, not only in Haydn research but in much research of our time. I believe that a certain "inflation" of the results claimed for research has taken place. Too many results are presented and accepted as facts, even if they are based more or less on interpretation or guesswork. I recall the nice old university official on whom I called after having finished my master's degree with a thesis on Haydn's early symphonies. I wanted to ask about the possibilities of getting a research grant, and he answered, smiling kindly, "You aren't a researcher yet, but you want to *become* one." Nowadays I sometimes get the impression that ordinary undergraduate or even high school papers are regarded as "research." (I do not mean that gifted students can never approach the level of scholarly work. There are quite a number of student papers at this conference. And of course there are studies, for example of a statistical nature, which are based on the collecting of facts to such a great extent that a talented student can do quite as well as a professor.) But the more closely we approach problems which can only be solved through interpretation, the more I feel that serious training in scholarly methods and traditions is required, such as one ordinarily receives from graduate work in good university departments. (I don't believe that such training is available *only* in a university, but this is the natural way, and the best way in most cases. Of course, some professional musicologists are fine teachers but have very little contact with serious research, and some learned, perhaps even self-taught, scholars who do valuable research have no connection with a university department. The line should not be drawn between professional and nonprofessional musicologists, but between valuable and worthless scholarly contributions, and between responsible and irresponsible approaches.)

Let me briefly summarize the essential qualifications for taking up scholarly work in our field:

1. A basic knowledge of music history and general methods of historical research, combined with more specialized knowledge of musical analysis, and of problems of notation, authenticity and chronology, and performance; and, built into all this knowledge, a permanent understanding of its changeability, a willingness to put the validity of supposed basic knowledge on trial.

2. Complete and up-to-date knowledge of relevant research in our own special area.

3. Balanced and well-trained judgment of problems within this field, including a strong tendency—and ability—to avoid fashionable doctrines and dogmas.

4. The determination—and again, the ability—to approach eighteenth-century music in terms of its relations to, of its having been conditioned by, what came *before* it, not what came afterwards; to compare Haydn to the Austrian music tradition of about 1750, rather than 1850 or 1950, and not to hold him responsible for neglecting nineteenth-century models of composition.

5. I hesitate to add two very simple qualifications, which some may find out of place today: *talent* and *experience*. I know it is an old joke that the musicologists are those who were not talented enough to become "real" musicians. And in some cases there may be some truth in this. But a bad musician does not by nature make a good musicologist. To be a good scholar is actually a question of talent, like being a good musician. Concert life is a constant sorting out, a comparison of artistic abilities. Research is judged as a demonstration of scholarly ability less often, perhaps, than it should be; a new book is accepted as valid information too often, perhaps, without reasonable reservations. In the long run distinguished scholarly work will hold, but the transmission of questionable information can blur the picture for many generations.

I have begun with this general statement of my musicological creed, if you will, to give you some background for my judgments and evaluations, which might otherwise seem casual or even arrogant. You may perhaps find my demands exaggerated and old-fashioned. Old-fashioned they are, in the literal sense that they are fashioned after old traditions, based on the principles of music history which my generation adopted from Guido Adler's *Methode der Musikgeschichte*.[2] This work is scarcely attractive reading for young people today, but it implanted in us a high regard for the quality, integrity, and seriousness of the principles of German-style "Wissenschaft"—traditions from an earlier period of Western culture. In the course of this brief survey of Haydn research, I shall try to show how far these demands have been fulfilled, to what extent we now have established traditions to work from, and how much has still to be done to create such traditions. I will begin with a general survey, and conclude by considering each of the three main topics of our conference: documentation, problems of form and style, and performance problems.

As in the case of other composers, the earliest stage in Haydn literature is the simple life-story, told immediately after Haydn's death, about

[2] Adler, *Methode.*

1810, by three different persons: Griesinger, Dies, and Carpani.[3] Although they tried, in a way, to find out something of Haydn's personal development, their books can hardly be regarded as research. Nevertheless, they are indispensable collections of raw material for research on Haydn.

The second half of the nineteenth century witnessed the rise of the monumental biographies of great composers, of which Jahn's *Mozart* and Spitta's *Bach* are rightly the most famous. These authors had both been trained in scholarly methods in other fields, from which they transferred their experience in such methods and their literary professionalism to musical biography. Jahn was also asked to write a Haydn biography, and it might have been better for Haydn research if he had done so. But he declined, suggesting instead the archivist of the Gesellschaft der Musikfreunde in Vienna, Carl Ferdinand Pohl; Pohl, who had already published a well-documented study of Mozart and Haydn in London,[4] agreed to do it. His unfinished Haydn biography appeared in two volumes (1875–82), leading up to the year 1790, when Haydn left for London.[5]

Anybody who has worked on the materials Pohl collected must admire his industry and his comprehensive scope. We are all in his debt, and he deserves to be honored by all Haydn scholars. But we must nevertheless admit that he cannot be ranked with Jahn or Spitta. Of course, he had a much tougher job than Jahn, if only in that Jahn could use Mozart's letters, which are numerous and are quite personal documents, whereas Haydn's correspondence is much more limited and bears much less the stamp of his personality. (There are years of Haydn's life from which we have scarcely any personal document of importance.) But unfortunately Pohl's judgment was also rather limited. For example, he divided the symphonies into various groups: one in which the whole symphony was said to be fine, another in which at least one movement was outstanding, and so on. And on the question of Haydn's predecessors, of the development of what was later to be called the "Viennese Classical style," he made an oft-quoted remark that Haydn failed to inform us of his real models, and then he merely listed a number of composers who might come under consideration. Spitta criticized this attitude in a review of Pohl's book, saying, "He paves the way for the historian, but he does not set foot on it himself."[6] In the second volume, Pohl gave a short thematic list of works belonging to the period covered by this volume, 1766–90. Though Pohl's biography did not reach the level of Jahn or Spitta, it was of course a great step forward, and there was no alternative to making do with it as the "great" Haydn biography.

During the following fifty years the picture did not change very much.

---

[3] See Griesinger; Dies; Carpani, *Haydine*.   [4] Pohl, *London*.   [5] Pohl, I–II.
[6] Spitta, "Pohl," 167.

A few articles of distinction appeared, like Adolf Sandberger's on the quartets (1900), Theodor de Wyzewa's on Haydn's "Crise romantique" (1909), and Wilhelm Fischer's fine article on the development of Classical style (1915).[7] But one important thing did happen: the first (attempted) collected edition of Haydn's works began to appear in 1907.[8] You will hear about the problem of a collected edition of Haydn's works in Dr. Feder's lecture, so I will limit my remarks about it to a few words. It soon became clear that this edition was based on much too limited source material. The publishers, Breitkopf & Härtel, started collecting material on a much broader scale, but World War I stopped further activities, and after the war the edition was continued so slowly that only ten or eleven volumes in all were published before World War II put an end to it.

Otherwise, nothing of importance appeared in Haydn research in the 1920s. But the celebration of the bicentenary of Haydn's birth in 1932 seems to have been responsible for a number of valuable contributions which appeared just before and around that year. Perhaps it would be natural to mention first the Haydn biography by Karl Geiringer,[9] at that time successor to Mandyczewski and Pohl as archivist in the Gesellschaft der Musikfreunde. Geiringer had not been active in the Haydn field before, and he had only a very limited time at his disposal. He did not attempt to produce a new "great" standard biography to replace Pohl, but he did write a very good survey. After moving to the United States, he published a completely new biography in English (1946),[10] and later still a third one (now again in German) in 1959.[11] His biographies have been useful introductions, which have served their purpose very well.

The English Haydn scholar Marion M. Scott wrote valuable articles about Haydn's quartets,[12] and she and Geiringer, independently of each other, published the early quartet Hob. II:6 in E-flat major, which until then had been omitted from the collected quartet editions. Friedrich Blume and Donald Francis Tovey also wrote interesting articles on the quartets, and Oliver Strunk attempted the first comprehensive survey of the baryton trios.[13] But perhaps the most important contributions of 1932 were Otto Erich Deutsch's article on Haydn's canons,[14] and E. F. Schmid's article on Haydn's music for a mechanical clock (his *Flötenuhr-stücke*).[15] Both were of rather limited scope, but at the same time each covered its field so well that it laid the foundation for any further work in

---

[7] Sandberger, "Streichquartett"; Wyzewa, "Centenaire"; Fischer, "Entwicklungsgeschichte."

[8] Haydn, GA.   [9] Geiringer, *Haydn*₁.   [10] Geiringer, *Haydn*₂.

[11] Geiringer, *Haydn*₃.   [12] For example, Scott, "Op. 2–3" and "83."

[13] Blume, "Streichquartette"; Tovey, "Chamber" (published in 1929); Strunk, "Baryton."

[14] O. Deutsch, "Kanons."   [15] Schmid, "Flötenuhr."

it. Another less conspicuous contribution of Deutsch's was a list of first editions of Haydn in the catalogue of a Vienna Haydn exhibition.[16] Based on the Hoboken collection of old editions (of which he was then the librarian) Deutsch's survey gave the first suggestion of his later work on music publishers' numbers. Although Deutsch and Schmid were almost as unlike personalities as you could possibly imagine, they shared untiring scholarly diligence, pleasure in discovering new facts, and the constructive power to produce scholarly work of lasting importance.

Two years later, Schmid published the first comprehensive study which definitively solved a problem concerning Haydn (insofar as we are entitled to say this in the never-ending field of research).[17] Schmid attacked an issue which had been discussed before, but never with full scholarly care. Seizing on the fact that Haydn was born and worked most of his life in a part of the Habsburg empire where various nationalities came into close contact, some had claimed that Haydn was a Hungarian, a Croatian, or even a gypsy. Based on extensive documentation, Schmid proved that Haydn was descended from German-Austrian peasant and artisan families. Although Schmid's book may be called a model of research in its field, and its conclusions are not likely to be challenged, it is obvious that, having solved its central question, it did not open up new paths for further research. But at the same time a problem was being raised in quite another corner of the Haydn domain which would occupy scholars until the present day, and will continue to do so even in years to come.

In late 1932 Adolf Sandberger, the distinguished old Munich professor, gave a lecture in which he suggested that he had found seventy-eight hitherto unknown Haydn symphonies. This created a sensation in the musicological world. If Sandberger had been a Mr. Nobody, there would scarcely have been so much talk about it, but since he was one of the pioneers in this field, a scholar and teacher of high reputation, it was not easy to ignore this claim, despite its fantastic character. In 1934, he began to publish "unknown masterpieces" said to be by Haydn. At the same time he published an article, based on a small thematic catalogue of symphonies and chamber music then in the Esterházy archives (called *das kleine Quartbuch* by Pohl), which he interpreted as a catalogue of Haydn's repertoire as Kapellmeister and a clue to his musical taste.[18]

Since I had studied Haydn's symphonies for some years and knew the source material—even in the Esterházy archives—it was clear to me that the whole story must derive from some curious mistake. I wrote an article disagreeing with Sandberger's interpretation of the *Quartbuch* and expressing doubt concerning the assertion of having found a great number of unknown Haydn symphonies.[19] Specifically, I showed that

[16] Reuther-Orel.   [17] Schmid, *Haydn*.   [18] Sandberger, "Haydniana."
[19] Larsen, "Quartbuch"; cf. Larsen, "Revisit."

the newly published "unknown Haydn symphony" was very probably by Vanhal. After that, Sandberger and I disputed these questions in print for two years. Nevertheless, this kind of polemic could not really solve the problem of the number of Haydn symphonies. (Of course, it originated primarily because there was still no thematic catalogue of Haydn's works corresponding to Köchel's Mozart catalogue.) Reluctantly, I set aside my research into stylistic development in Haydn's symphonies and took up the authenticity problem. The result was my book *Die Haydn-Überlieferung* (*The Haydn Tradition*) (1939), followed by an edition in facsimile of *Drei Haydn Kataloge* (*Three Haydn Catalogues*) (1941).[20] I consciously adopted the source-critical approach from general historical research. It had been used, for example, by Spitta, but for some time it had been little used in musicology. Moreover, in the years following World War I a new wave of style analysis had been fashionable enough to make any work with "unmusical" methods seem rather odious. But I saw no other possibility of finding my way to a secure foundation for judging the problems of authenticity.

Since my book is known to many people in the United States only indirectly through the first chapter of R. Landon's symphony book,[21] which may partly be regarded as a condensed (and amended) version of it, I may perhaps briefly point out what it meant to Haydn research. It introduced the concept of the critical evaluation of sources. Autographs, copies of various sorts, and the various printed editions were surveyed, not with the aim of achieving completeness (which I could not possibly afford), but above all of establishing their relative value as sources for solving the problem of authenticity. Of special importance was the analysis of Haydn's so-called *Entwurf-Katalog* (EK). I was able to prove that this was not a "draft" for the late catalogue (HV) from 1805 (as the designation might suggest), but rather Haydn's personal catalogue, laid out about 1765, and carried on more or less consistently for different groups of works in later years. This considerably altered the state of our authentic knowledge of the earlier (though not the earliest) years in Haydn's development. I believe that my book, supplemented by my edition of the three Haydn catalogues, put an end to a long period of uneasiness, of lack of enterprise in Haydn research, owing to the feeling that a secure foundation was lacking. As opposed to Schmid's volume, which opened up but also closed off a field of investigation, mine called for *more* research in the same field—but just at that time, around 1940, the curtain came down on all international collaboration.

The most important activities in Haydn research since World War II have certainly been the editorial achievements: the Haydn Society edition (Haydn, CE), the Joseph Haydn-Institut edition (Haydn, JHW), and the

[20]Larsen, HÜb; Larsen, DHK. [21]Landon, *Symphonies.*

many valuable editions by Landon. I have said something about this in the program book of our conference,[22] and Dr. Feder will say more about it in his lecture.

Two books of outstanding importance appeared in 1955 and 1960: H. C. Robbins Landon's *The Symphonies of Joseph Haydn* and Dénes Bartha and László Somfai's *Haydn als Opernkapellmeister*. Landon's very impressive book covers a number of different aspects. On the documentary side, the first chapter, as already mentioned, discusses the problems of sources and source evaluation, and the last part is a comprehensive (if not exhaustive) source catalogue for the symphonies, including a substantial number of spurious Haydn compositions. Much new information is also found in the section about Haydn in London. But the book has two other important sides. A chapter on performance practice reflects the author's experience with recordings, combined with numerous references to eighteenth-century theorists. And the central part of the book is a presentation of the stylistic development in the symphonies. The value of this book is beyond discussion; in English-speaking countries it has probably contributed more than any other book in recent times to the promotion of Haydn research. Its chief merit is its contributions to Haydn documentation, especially in the catalogue of the symphonies and the chapter on Haydn in London. I don't believe that Landon's studies in performance practice or his descriptive and analytical presentation reach the same level. (It seems to me that the whole situation of Haydn research is reflected in this unevenness: we have developed a solid tradition of Haydn documentation, but neither analytical studies nor studies in performance problems have arrived at a similar stage of established scholarly tradition.)

Bartha and Somfai's book on Haydn's activities as an opera conductor and (more or less) impresario is one of those rare contributions which open up completely new insight into a field everybody thought they knew about. As Eva Badura-Skoda hints,[23] Bartha's survey of these studies at the Budapest conference, 1959, left all the Haydn specialists present almost shocked by his amazingly revolutionary report. We came to know about activities of Haydn that were not only highly interesting in themselves, but also explained why Haydn had been less active in other fields of composition. Furthermore, the volume described a number of previously unknown compositions. In the book, presenting all this on a much larger scale, some particularly valuable sections of fundamental documentary value were added about Esterházy copyists and watermarks in the Esterházy sources.

In the field of documentation, Haydn research has enjoyed quite a few valuable new publications. Let me name only a few of the most impor-

---

[22] Larsen, *"Revival."*   [23] Badura-Skoda, *"Opera."*

tant ones: Haydn's letters, edited in translation by Landon,[24] and afterwards in the original by Bartha;[25] Brown and Berkenstock's bibliography of Haydn literature;[26] Irmgard Becker-Glauch's survey of Haydn editions;[27] and Laśzló Somfai's book on Haydn's life in pictures.[28]

But more than any other publication of this kind, the long-awaited thematic catalogue of Haydn's works by Anthony van Hoboken stands out.[29] Everybody working seriously on Haydn's music must be grateful for this contribution to Haydn documentation. But even if we acknowledge in full the value of this indispensable tool, a survey of solved and unsolved problems in Haydn research must mention its shortcomings. One obvious feature is the substantial amount of space given to bibliographical description and accounts of printed editions, in contrast to the often very scanty indication of old manuscript sources, which often are of much greater importance. Of course, this resulted in part from its simultaneous function as a catalogue of Hoboken's unique collection of editions (now in the Austrian National Library, Vienna). A future revised edition or a new catalogue will have to find a better balance in the quotation and description of sources. The Haydn specialist inevitably feels a certain imperfection in the many instances of a not fully scholarly approach: for example, in the lack of absolute exactness in the quotations of musical themes or titles of editions, in the rather casual references to the Haydn literature, in the lack of real motivation in decisions about authenticity, or in the often rather problematic chronological indications. All this is true especially for the first volume; the second volume is very much improved, I presume in part because collaboration with the Joseph Haydn-Institut strengthened its critical approach. If Hoboken is kept as a principal description and survey of printed editions, it should be possible, based on the substantial material in the Haydn-Institut, eventually to produce a more balanced, more exact, and (not least) more fully documented Haydn thematic catalogue. However, one should not undervalue the pioneering work represented by Hoboken's catalogue. Among other unsolved problems, to whose solution the Joseph Haydn-Institut should in time contribute, the most important is a documentary biography like those compiled by Deutsch for Handel, Mozart, and Schubert.

Compared to this substantial progress in Haydn documentation, research in problems of form and style has advanced much more slowly. I think the problems of the string quartets have received the most attention in recent years, through the valuable studies by Somfai, Finscher, and Barrett-Ayres.[30] But speaking more generally, I believe that we still are not quite prepared to conquer new territory. We are obtaining reliable edi-

[24] Haydn, *CCLN.*   [25] Haydn, *Briefe.*   [26] Brown, "Bibliography."
[27] Becker-Glauch, "Haydn."   [28] Somfai, *Bilder.*   [29] Hoboken, I–II.
[30] Somfai, "Kvartett"; Finscher, *Streichquartett,* I; Barrett-Ayres, *Quartet.*

tions of Haydn, but the background of his development—the music of his Viennese predecessors and contemporaries—is still largely unpublished and not easily accessible. And above all, we need a fundamentally new approach to the problems of form and style in the music of Haydn and his predecessors. We still use the concepts of form from traditional music theory books (or in recent times perhaps ideas of structure from 1975). But we have to abandon these traditional prejudices and find new concepts drawn from Haydn's music itself. Fischer's "Entwicklungsgeschichte" is almost the only study to date which abandons traditional concepts and attempts to work out an approach based on the music rather than on theory books. It is strange that this article has never appeared in English and that, on the whole, it has scarcely been followed up.

Here we have returned to the problem of facts, interpretation, or guesswork. To find an entry into form, the formation or the "growth" of a piece of music, you may use different approaches: attempt to find a certain accepted "model" behind it; make statistics of certain typical features in it, as compared to their appearance in related forms; or start out from an impression of the importance of specific features. Your analysis may look like a mathematical formula, or it may embody a more descriptive approach. You may attempt to avoid evaluation of the music, or you may consciously stress critical judgments. You may try to analyze a composition without direct comparison to others—though your analysis will certainly be based on some sort of comparison—or you may wish to emphasize its relations to other compositions. In any case, you must begin with a decision, an interpretation of what seems important for your analysis—and then you try to collect facts which may confirm or fail to confirm your opinion. One can spend much time and energy on analytical work leading to hundreds of facts, but giving no understanding of real importance. More attention should be given to developing our perception of formal procedures before we can expect reasonable progress in analyzing the formal constructions of actual compositions. In this I believe I agree with Jan LaRue, whose "guidelines" are familiar to all of you,[31] though I may tend to stress the historical factor in the analysis a little more than he does.

Time is too short for a real discussion of the problems of musical performance practice. But in this field too I think we need an adjustment of methods and views. Many musicians have followed the lead of some musicologists in taking any given written or printed "singing master" as gospel, instead of subjecting it to a critical interpretation. Specific interest has been given to sound qualities in old instruments, more or less ne-

[31] LaRue, *Guidelines*.

glecting equally important aspects of musical performance. (Of course, this is not a specific Haydn problem, but a general weakness in much interpretation of eighteenth-century music.)

A generation of Haydn scholars has had the privilege of working in a field of research, Haydn documentation, where there were many rewarding projects to be carried out. I do not believe there is a great deal left to be done in this area, but there is more than enough to do in analysis and in clarifying the lines of development in the music of Haydn and of his contemporaries. As far as performance practice is concerned, uniting the efforts of musicians and musicologists can give valuable inspiration to both parties, if each is willing to submit its material to serious, understanding, and *talented* critical interpretation.

The Collected Works of Joseph Haydn

GEORG FEDER

My topic will be the edition of Haydn's collected works (hereafter referred to as JHW) edited by the Joseph Haydn-Institut, Cologne, and published by the G. Henle-Verlag, Munich. Most of Haydn's works are now available either in the steadily growing JHW or in individual editions of varying type and quality. Haydn scholars still attach great importance to the completion of the collected edition. Our procedures may be of interest not only to the small circle of specialists, but to a larger audience as well.

I would like to begin by trying to define a collected edition. It should appear in print, it should be printed in full score, it should be printed correctly and according to the best sources, it should include all the composer's works and only this composer's works, and it should present them in systematic and chronological order and in a legible, uniform, and handsome format useful for musical performance. It also should include editorial comments.

I shall try to analyze some actual problems and historical implications of this definition. In doing so I shall sometimes use the term "critical edition." This term denotes not the collection of all the works in a single uniform edition, but the quality of their editing. Viewed in this light, a collected edition should comprise critical editions of all the individual works written by the composer.

It may sound like pleonasm to say that a collected edition should be printed. But there was a time when the printing of music was not normally considered necessary. It was not customary in Vienna before 1780. Most of Haydn's music prior to that year circulated in handwritten copies before it was printed in Paris, Amsterdam, Berlin, London, and other places. Authorized editions of Haydn's instrumental music were regularly published only after about 1780. However, the distribution of manuscript copies was generally continued after that date, and it was even considered normal for his vocal compositions with orchestral accompaniment.

Manuscript copies of a given work often differ in many details, even when they are written by the same professional Viennese copyist. Much of a modern critical editor's trouble is caused by copyists' errors. But it may even happen that different exemplars of the same printed edition from Haydn's time are not necessarily identical. One or more of the plates from which a small issue was printed could have been damaged and then replaced. One of a critical editor's tasks is to compare several copies in order to find a copy of the original impression of every important edition.

In a modern scholarly edition every copy of a given volume ought to be exactly the same as all the others. If alterations are made later, the publisher should state this fact on the title page. No alteration whatsoever has been made in the second printing of volumes in JHW.

Another desirable requirement for a collected edition is that all copies be available in sufficient number. They must be available in public libraries, and for sale in music stores and through booksellers. This detail of our definition excludes, for example, unprinted "published" scores of Haydn's operas which are available only in very limited numbers and only on a rental basis to conductors who plan a performance. The public is excluded from the study of these scores, and there is no certainty that all the copies are identical, especially since conductors usually enter their performance markings into the score.

But has the importance of a printed edition not been thoroughly reduced by the growing influence of records, radio, and television? It is marvelous that lovers of Beethoven's or Haydn's music can buy complete recordings of Beethoven's works or Haydn's symphonies. But even if different recorded performances are based on the same critically revised score, each remains a personal interpretation, and it must be so in order to be real music. A critical edition is something different. While it may not be definitive and may be replaced by a still better edition in the future, it is certainly more nearly objective than any performance based on such an edition. It may inspire performers to individual interpretations of the same original notes.[1]

Modern collected editions appear as scores. Most of us would probably say: quite naturally so. But again, this is the point of view of our age. The editions of Haydn's collected string quartets, selected symphonies, and (miscellaneous) keyboard music starting around 1800, such as Pleyel's, Simrock's, or Breitkopf & Härtel's, appeared in parts. For the piano trios, for example, all three parts were printed separately, whereas today even in nonscholarly editions the piano part serves as the score. Nonscholarly editions of chamber music without a piano are still often printed without a score, but today more publications of instrumental music include a score than used to be the case, and there must be a conductor's score for all orchestral works.

In Haydn's time, all kinds of music, operas and oratorios excepted, were normally distributed in parts only. A score was by no means con-

---

[1] See, for example, Sonya Monosoff's remarks in Workshop 3. [Ed.]

sidered essential for the performance of a Haydn symphony or Mass. In 1802, Haydn negotiated with the publishing house Breitkopf & Härtel about the publication of one of his Masses, Georg August Griesinger serving as an agent. In a letter to the publishers (January 13, 1802), Griesinger informed them of Haydn's proposal to print the Mass in parts so that it could be played immediately; students should write their own score from the parts, as Haydn had seen Mozart do with his (Haydn's) string quartets.[2] The scoring of music from parts was a centuries-old method of studying a composition, especially for beginning composers. After 1800, publishers began to feel that the scores of classical master-pieces were desirable for the public. Pleyel printed a selection of Haydn's string quartets in miniature scores; Le Duc, Breitkopf & Härtel, and Cianchettini e Sperati published a number of Haydn's symphonies in score. That was the beginning of a practice that gradually became the rule and is now considered indispensable for a collected edition.

It is another truism to say that a critical edition should be correctly printed and be based on the best sources. But when investigated more closely this turns out to be a complicated matter. The "correctness" of an edition was not always taken to mean that it should be identical with the original. It is most revealing to compare the judgments of the older editions of Haydn's string quartets reported by the British scholar Marion M. Scott. A devoted Haydn scholar, she said with respect to Pleyel's edition in parts: "It has definite authority." But she calls the edition of C. F. Peters "excellent," too, and quotes the French scholar Fétis to describe a selected edition published about 1820 by Janet et Cotelle of Paris as being more "correct" than Pleyel. She also quotes the German scholar Altmann, who described the edition published by Kistner of Leipzig as "the best."[3] Did any of these scholars try to find out what kind of sources this or that "best" edition was based upon? Probably not. The conception of "correctness" was purely musical: there were no misprints, and the edition was well suited to practical performance.

When we try to determine how the influential Pleyel quartet edition originated, we realize that, in every case which has been examined so far, it was not based on the original sources, and that its apparent correctness is often a matter of mere conjecture and added performance marks. The often grotesque alterations made by the publisher Johann Julius Hummel of Amsterdam and Berlin in some of his unauthorized early editions are reproduced in Pleyel's edition whenever the latter was based on Hummel's edition or a reprint of it. For example, one measure is lacking in all the nineteenth- and twentieth-century editions I have seen of the Quartet Op. 33, No. 4 in B-flat major, because their common source is Hummel,

[2] Thomas, "Griesinger," 82.   [3] Scott, "83," 206 [*sic; recte* 209], 211, 212.

who, feeling that the first nine bars of the trio to the menuet were odd, cancelled one bar to give this section its "regular" eight bars.[4]

Hummel's ideas about editing were not shared by many other publishers, fortunately. Some of them printed exactly what they found in the manuscript copies that came into their hands. Others preferred to edit the text, which might occasionally help to restore the original reading, but more often it led to an altered version. Even the apparent musical correctness of Breitkopf & Härtel's *Oeuvres Complettes* is due more to the clever editing by the Leipzig musician August Eberhard Müller than to Haydn's authority, despite his signature on the preface.

It is true that Haydn deplored the poor quality of some editions, but he was not a scholarly editor himself. When asked in 1802 to consent to an edition of his symphonies, he answered that he would like to have the editing done by his pupils and to take one ducat per symphony for overseeing their work. The project was not realized. How it would probably have been accomplished can be surmised when inspecting the edition of Haydn's string quartets Opus 20, composed in 1772. These quartets were republished in parts in 1800–01 by the Viennese publisher Artaria, who announced that this edition was the most correct ever published because the composer himself had taken a hand in the editing. My colleague Sonja Gerlach and I compared this edition with Haydn's autograph and with some early copies and printed editions. We became convinced that the "correctness" of Artaria's edition resulted from a purely musical editing, done apparently by one of Haydn's pupils, and without consulting the autograph (which was probably no longer in the composer's possession in 1800). You may read the details of the story in the critical commentary to JHW XII:3.

Modern scholarly editions are based on a different idea. An edition is considered correct today if, in principle, it agrees with the autograph or with other authentic sources. Musical correctness achieved by conjecture and by supplying plausible performance marks, on the other hand, is of only relative validity; each new generation, even each different editor, will find different musical solutions more persuasive. Such "correctness" is nonhistorical. The critical editor therefore strives primarily to achieve historical correctness in his musical text. He studies the primary documents. I need not go into the different kinds of sources such as autograph scores, original editions, copied parts corrected by the composer, and so on.[5] The loss of much original material, and in some cases the preservation of secondary material only, make the research for a critical edition more difficult. But in addition to approaching this subject from the "dip-

[4] On Hummel's disfigurements of Haydn, see Feder, "Eingriffe."
[5] These are discussed in the Round Table Source Problems, Authenticity and Chronology, List of Works. [Ed.]

lomatic" evaluation of existing sources, that is, by tracing their provenance and determining their authority, one can also attempt to establish a line of descent or "family tree" among the sources on the basis of their variant readings. This method, called "filiation," is an adaptation of the principle of textual criticism as developed by classical philology.

Diplomatic evaluation and philological filiation are often combined in JHW. The diplomatic method is sufficient as long as there is a clearly superior authentic source; but it must be supplemented if the original documentary form of the text is lost, and if the extant sources transmit a musical text of indifferent accuracy. Experience in evaluating manuscript copies of different provenance and early editions from different publishing houses helps an editor to select those which generally best preserve the original text. But such experience alone will not prevent wrong decisions where the readings are divergent at crucial points. Only the philological method can help reconstruct the lost original source or the so-called archetype, that is, the lost copy from which all the extant sources derive. Since many links in the chain of transmission from the lost original to the extant sources may be missing, the *stemma* (to use the Greek term) or family tree is often tentative, but it is helpful nevertheless.

The use of scholarly editorial methods has also been aided by progress in technology. The catalogues of the Joseph Haydn-Institut in Cologne list 10,000 contemporary manuscripts, including about 250 Haydn autographs, and 2,200 contemporary printed editions of Haydn's more than 900 authentic compositions and arrangements and his 400 settings of Scottish and Welsh songs, to say nothing of hundreds of doubtful and spurious works attributed to him. All this material is now distributed over more than 200 libraries and archives in Europe, North America, and Japan. Without the help of photography, and especially microfilm, we would not be able simultaneously to compare, for example, a manuscript preserved in the National Library of Hungary in Budapest and one preserved in the Library of Congress in Washington, D.C. Sometimes ten or twenty or even more sources from as many public libraries or private archives all over the world must be compared on microfilm in order to find the original version and the original reading of a composition by Haydn. Much of the perfection of modern critical editing was inconceivable when scholars had to rely on making notes, often without being able to check them later or to study the same subject from a new point of view.

I mentioned the critical commentary before. In my opinion it is an integral part of a critical edition, since it enables the reader or performer to verify the editor's decisions. This again seems to me a scientific attitude; editing is considered like an experiment; it is considered valid only if it can be repeated. The reader should be able to repeat for himself at least part of the editorial work, in order to see whether he would reach the same conclusions and eventually the same musical text.

Some people are surprised to find small differences in two or more critical or "Urtext" editions of the same work. There are both objective and subjective reasons for such differences. The objective reasons consist mainly of the ambiguity of many details found in the original text, and the discrepancies among the early manuscript copies and prints. The subjective reasons are the different methods used by different editors and the possibility of divergence in their decisions. The user of a critical edition will better understand such differences if a critical commentary is available—provided he makes the effort to study it.

Such study would be easier if every critical edition could be accompanied by a complete facsimile of the autograph or of the authentic set of copied or printed parts used as the primary source for the edition (when such an authentic source is preserved). I do not know whether owners of manuscripts and publishers of future critical editions would agree to this procedure. When several original sources are preserved, or when there is no authentic source extant but only secondary material, there might be some difficulty in selecting the right facsimile. JHW does not accompany its scores with complete facsimiles, but it follows tradition in issuing critical commentaries describing in words every significant observation, and offering musical examples where necessary, including a facsimile page as a specimen.

Efforts have been made by one or two publishing houses to avoid the costs of printing the critical commentaries by depositing a few typewritten copies in public libraries and by printing an abridged version only. This procedure has been supported by some scholars. I do not agree with them. In a discussion by thirty musicological editors held in Wolfenbüttel, Germany, in 1974, it was suggested that perhaps someday even the critically revised score, with its footnotes, editorial symbols, variant readings, and so on, would only be deposited at a few libraries. Since the conventional published scores would then appear neat and would be free of any critical apparatus, no trace of the editorial problems would remain to disturb the reader or conductor. This idea was unanimously rejected.[6] But how long will it be rejected if it is already favored insofar as the critical commentaries are concerned?

I think there is a better alternative. It has always been the policy of the Haydn-Institut to compose the critical commentaries in a concise style, concentrating on essentials, avoiding redundancy, and taking pains to make the text as comprehensible as possible—but nevertheless to print it. The critical commentaries of some of the published scores are still lacking, but I am confident that they will be issued too.

---

[6] See Feder, "Editoren," esp. 346.

There is also a general tendency today to abandon the use of such devices as parentheses and brackets, or smaller or oblique typefaces, to distinguish the additional performance marks suggested by the editor. I still consider it wise to use such typographical devices in some critical editions, including the Haydn edition. But I am aware of the inherent difficulties. We cannot, for example, easily indicate by typographical means original performance marks which the editor had to correct, because they seemed inconsistently or carelessly written by the composer. If we introduced more typographical signs in order to make such corrections immediately visible, the legibility of the score would be jeopardized. Such changes are mentioned in the critical commentary instead. In JHW the commentary, the editorial symbols in the score, the footnotes, the variant readings above the staff, and the preface constitute an integral unit, which is split up for technical reasons only. They should accordingly be consulted simultaneously.

The general opinion is that a critical edition should present a legible score which conforms to modern conventions and expectations. The most important shortcoming of a facsimile edition is its poor legibility, except to a specialist. Engraving or equivalent means is generally considered the best way of making a score legible to every musician. Especially in the collected editions, we are used to a technical and aesthetic standard of printing far superior to that which was customary in Haydn's time.

Modern musicians are also used to a modern score format and to a complete indication of all necessary performance marks. As for the latter, I have come to the conclusion that Haydn never intended to write all the details like staccato dots and strokes, slurs, and so on, with the kind of distinctness and completeness required by modern printing and performance standards. The ambiguity and incompleteness can often be corrected with some certainty by comparing similar passages in the same movement or in his other works. But such editorial work should, I think, always be restricted to the narrow limits of Haydn's general style of writing, as determined by study of his manuscripts.

Criticism has been raised against this policy of the Haydn edition. Some critics maintain that we should not only comply with the style in which Haydn intended to write, but with the style in which he intended the music to be performed. I believe that this demand could lead to excessively subjective interpretation, and to a text which represents the editor's wishes about performance rather than Haydn's. Guesswork is necessary for the performer, but it would be dangerous for the critical editor. I warmly recommend that performers study the critically revised scores and the commentaries, in order to become aware of the amount, as well as the limits, of uncertainty in the original text.

Most collected editions claim to be useful "for practical and scholarly purposes alike," or something of this kind. But I suspect that the claim implied by the word "alike" is more eagerly made by publishers than by editors. This problem has in part been solved for Haydn's music in a rather peculiar manner. Some more or less critically revised Haydn editions now on the market meet the needs of performers more immediately than JHW can do, and they are often better known, partly for that reason and partly because of the publicity made on their behalf. I am speaking mainly of the many individual editions appearing in Doblinger's series Diletto Musicale, in the Universal-Edition, and in the Haydn-Mozart Press. All these editions, especially the complete symphonies prepared by H. C. Robbins Landon,[7] have been published in scores and parts. There is relatively little description or diplomatic and philological evaluation of the sources in most of these, although they include a useful minimum of information. The editorial reconstructions are not always clearly marked. But Landon's editions are usually based on the best sources or at least on a reasonable selection of them, and they are far superior to most other practical editions on the market. In a sense, the scores and critical commentaries of JHW serve primarily a scholarly purpose, although I hope that the historically minded performer will not forego the opportunity offered by such an edition. Landon's scores and parts are more practically oriented, though scholars certainly will not pass up the opportunity to study them as well.

However, editions published primarily to serve the practical demands of musicians and the commercial demands of publishers would perhaps omit some of Haydn's special-purpose works. Most of his 126 baryton trios had not been printed before they appeared in JHW. The early cantata *Applausus,* the oratorio *Il ritorno di Tobia,* and many of the operas would perhaps never be printed in full score, if not in JHW.

The last aspect of collected editions I would like to comment on is therefore the seemingly self-explanatory attribute "complete." In Haydn's aforementioned discussion with Breitkopf & Härtel about the publication of Masses, he is reported to have advised against the printing of his early Masses, because they were no longer in accord with present taste (November 11, 1801).[8] And in the preface to Breitkopf & Härtel's *Oeuvres Complettes,* written by the publisher and signed by the composer, we read: "I will see to it that in this collection nothing will be included which until now has carried my name unjustifiably; or which, as a work of my early youth, would not deserve to be preserved in this collection" (December 20, 1799). The elimination of spurious works is still an essential task. Several Round Tables of this conference deal with this problem, which needs much study and perhaps will never be fully solved. But the rejection of Haydn's works no longer in accordance with modern taste or not yet written in a developed style would certainly be opposed by all

[7] Haydn, *Symphonies.*   [8] Thomas, "Griesinger," 79.

true scholars. A modern scholar is a historian; consequently he also wishes to see the works of supposedly minor importance and the rudimentary beginnings of a great master's career. Our historical interest has increased to such a degree that we are not content with a complete and chronological survey of all works; we also wish to have a documentation of the history of all the individual works.

Musicological editors more or less subscribe to the sometimes exaggerated theory that the shape of a historical composition is not precisely defined, and that we are not dealing with an *opus perfectum,* a work which (perhaps after several changes made by the composer) was eventually accomplished and definitely finished. According to the relativistic concept valid today, a work is a kind of process, every stage of which is more or less interesting, with no stage definitive. I doubt whether the concept of a definitive version, a *Fassung letzter Hand,* is really as outdated as some musicologists seem to think. But at least it is the intent of all musicological editors to document the process of a composition from the first sketch, through all corrections, variants, and versions made by the author, up to the final phase. There may be financial limits to such a project in the case of composers like Wagner and Schoenberg. Beethoven's sketches are so numerous that they need a collected edition of their own. Haydn's works do not normally offer so many versions, nor are there so many sketches that the collected edition is substantially enlarged by including them. The commentaries also list the corrections Haydn made in his original scores and in written copies; these corrections are more numerous and more interesting than usually thought.

As a concluding remark I would like to mention a more direct implication of the word "complete." Two earlier modern Haydn editions that were announced as complete editions ended up very incomplete indeed. The first was entitled *Joseph Haydns Werke: Erste kritisch durchgesehene Gesamtausgabe* (GA). It was begun in 1908 by Breitkopf & Härtel and ceased publication after eleven volumes had been published. The second attempt was entitled *Joseph Haydn: Kritische Gesamtausgabe—Joseph Haydn: The Complete Works: Critical Edition* (CE). It was published in 1950–51 by the Haydn Society of Boston and Vienna, but it ceased after four volumes. The collected edition of which I have been speaking is cautiously titled *Joseph Haydn: Werke.* It was begun in 1955, and in twenty years has issued forty-eight volumes and thirty-three critical commentaries. But it will perhaps be another twenty years before anyone can really speak of a "complete" Haydn edition.

Haydn in America

IRVING LOWENS[1]

The subject of Haydn in America is a bit more complicated than the casual music lover might think, and for this reason, I will confine my remarks to the extent of Haydn's popularity in this country during his lifetime. But first, a few words about the history of Haydn's reputation in more recent years might be appropriate. One of the best sources of information is John H. Mueller's excellent social history of musical taste.[2] The somewhat less excellent supplement to the late Professor Mueller's work by his wife, Kate Hevner Mueller,[3] attempts a history and analysis of the American symphonic repertory from the 1842–43 through the 1969–70 music seasons, and is also useful.

Professor Mueller claims that in 1951, when his study appeared, Haydn's works enjoyed "low but stable" currency. He states that in December 1842, when the New York Philharmonic played its first concert,

. . . the star of Haydn had been dimmed somewhat by the brilliance of the works of Beethoven. While three of the Beethoven symphonies were performed during the first Philharmonic season of three concerts, Haydn had to await the third and ninth seasons for the first two symphonic offerings. This marks his approximate pace down to the present day, almost always maintaining a sure and predictable position, but never crowding the leaders. More precisely, this trend shows a recession between 1875 and 1900, when most of the present orchestras were founded, but then takes a definite upward turn which continues to the present day. In 1926, the editor of *Musical America* could state that Haydn was "no longer a musical mummy," but had now again come to life. This ascent, unambiguous but by no means dramatic, roughly coincides with the centennial of his death (1909); the observance of the bicentennial of his birth (1932); the launching of a project for publication of his "complete" works (never completed) by Breitkopf und Härtel (1907), which gave the symphonies a new, chronological numbering); and a growing archeological and scholarly interest in his life and works. As a

[1] I would like to acknowledge the assistance of Richard Claypool (Moravian Music Foundation), Margaret Cook (Special Collections Division, Earl Gregg Swem Library, Williamsburg, Virginia [College of William and Mary]), Richard Crawford (University of Michigan), Theodore Front, John B. Hench (American Antiquarian Society), Cynthia Hoover (Smithsonian Institution), H. Earle Johnson (College of William and Mary), Karl Kroeger (Moravian Music Foundation), Jens Peter Larsen, Jan LaRue (New York University), Margery Morgan Lowens, Rodney Mill (Library of Congress), and Marie-Thérèse Robillard (Grosvenor Reference Division, Buffalo and Erie County Public Library).
[2] J. Mueller, *Orchestra.*   [3] K. Mueller, *Orchestras.*

result of this historical interest, nearly a dozen of his earlier symphonies have been performed for the first time in America.[4]

Compare this with what has taken place here in Washington during the last three weeks (September 22 through October 11), and it is perfectly plain that a decided change in the American musical attitude towards Haydn has occurred. Mrs. Mueller documents this change by pointing out that between 1890 and 1970, Haydn moved from the category of "low but stable" composers, a category which now includes Schubert, Mendelssohn, Handel, and Weber, to a position of composers with "ascending records" in the American symphonic repertory. Only two composers registered more spectacular gains during the last eighty years—Mozart and Mahler. Bach and Bruckner are also "ascending," but somewhat less rapidly than Haydn.[5]

Mrs. Mueller is not very illuminating when it comes to giving us convincing reasons for Haydn's "ascending record." There is little to explain it, she says, "except to note more symphonies introduced and many symphonies more often played. The recent publication of authentic scores has aroused new interest. . . . all orchestras have participated in his rise, more especially Boston, Buffalo, and Chicago."[6] She seems to be unaware of the advent of the long-playing record.

With this observation, I leave the present and turn back the calendar to the America of 1809. From the earliest publication of a Haydn composition in 1789 through 1809 I have been able to trace the existence of sixty separate editions of twenty-eight works published in this country, of which a total of 178 exemplars are extant in thirty American collections. Early American Haydn imprints must be characterized as rare, if not excessively rare. And beginning with the first public performance of a Haydn work on April 27, 1782, during the British occupation of New York City, I have been able to find 247 American concerts in which Haydn's name appears on the programs—68 in New York, 59 in Nazareth, Pa., 55 in Philadelphia, 19 in Boston, 11 in Charleston, S. C., 9 in Baltimore, 2 in Hartford, Conn., 2 in Salem, Mass., and 1 in Albany, N.Y.

The appearance of 28 compositions in print and 247 concerts in which Haydn's name is cited in the program between 1782 and 1809, the very years Haydn's name became a household word all over Europe, does not seem like a very impressive showing of strength. Furthermore, when one begins to look behind the cold statistics, the case for Haydn's popularity in America during his lifetime gets even shakier. Almost without exception, the twenty-eight published American Haydn compositions are slight, and frequently they are truncated. The most popular work

[4] J. Mueller, *Orchestra,* 211.   [5] K. Mueller, *Orchestras,* xxv–xxvi.   [6] Ibid., xxviii.

with Haydn's name on it published here before 1810 was the song *A Prey to Tender Anguish* (Hob. XXVIa:G1). The first American edition was brought out by G. Willig in Philadelphia between 1798 and 1804. No less than eleven editions had appeared by 1807. Unfortunately, the pretty little song is almost certainly spurious. An authentic Haydn item, *The Mermaid's Song* (Hob. XXVIa:25), was second in popularity. It was first published by B. Carr in Philadelphia between 1797 and 1799, and six editions had appeared in 1808. The record shows the publication of not a single symphony, not a single string quartet, on this side of the Atlantic during Haydn's lifetime. One complete piano sonata, Hob. XVI:21 (ChL. 36) in C major, did appear. It is plain that the early American record of Haydn publication is nothing to boast about.

Furthermore, the record of Haydn performances is also sadly incomplete. The single comprehensive and reliable source of information about concert life in eighteenth-century America remains Oscar G. Sonneck's classic study, now nearly seventy years old, and his picture is no more than a sketch for a comprehensive history.[7] He worked painstakingly, basing his research on newspapers which were accessible to him at the turn of the century, and he hardly can be blamed for not listing concert programs then lacking in the newspaper files. As early as 1910, Robert R. Drummond established the inadequacy of Sonneck's survey: Sonneck had been unable to locate a file of Philadelphia newspapers giving 1791 concert programs, but Drummond located one, and a detailed list of the 1791 programs may be found in his study.[8] Since Sonneck's day, a tremendous number of eighteenth-century newspapers unknown to him have turned up, yet no one has taken the trouble to read through them.

Incomplete though our knowledge of eighteenth-century musical life may be, things are far worse in regard to the early nineteenth century. Sonneck confined his research to eighteenth-century American concert life. With the exception of the work done by the Moravian Music Foundation, there has been no systematic attempt to survey American concert life during the first decade of the nineteenth century. One must rely on such secondary sources of information as Odell's record of the New York stage or passing references in H. Earle Johnson's account of Boston musical activities.[9]

The Moravian Music Foundation, under the guidance of Donald M. McCorkle, Ewald Nolte, and now Karl Kroeger, has made a determined effort to discover the reality of the eighteenth- and nineteenth-century musical worlds in which the "Moravians" (German immigrants) functioned. The tiny settlement of Nazareth in Pennsylvania, a dot on today's map, has more documented performances of Haydn through 1809 than

[7] Sonneck, *Concert.*   [8] Drummond, *Philadelphia,* 62–72.
[9] Odell, *Annals;* Johnson, *Boston.*

any other American cities except New York and Philadelphia. An unusually complete record of Nazareth Collegium Musicum performances
has survived in a ledger entitled *Verzeichnis derer Musicalien welche in Con-*
cert sind gemacht worden, dated October 14, 1796. This has been completely indexed by Kroeger through 1806 only, but it is reasonably complete through 1815 and rather spotty thereafter until 1845, when the
Collegium Musicum died a natural death. The Nazareth Collegium sessions were held weekly on Thursdays from mid-October to mid-March.
From 1797 to 1799 there was also a biweekly summer series. With such a
spectacular record for the small Collegium in Nazareth, one must assume
that Haydn was at least as popular in the larger Collegia in Bethlehem
and Old Salem; both were considerably more important musically. Unfortunately, no comparable record of Bethlehem and Salem performances exists. I have been able to find only 74 documented Haydn performances between 1801 and 1809, compared to 163 between 1782 and
1800. Obviously, this is not an accurate reflection of the true state of affairs. The apparent decline in Haydn's popularity in America from 1801
through 1809 is due more to lack of basic research in American music
history after 1800 than to any genuine neglect of his music—considering
the provincial nature of American musical life of the period.

At this point, the whole matter of Haydn in America can be placed in
sharper perspective by citing a few statistics, taken from tables compiled
by the U. S. Census Bureau for 1790, 1800, and 1810. In 1790, the total
United States population was 3.92 million; in 1800, 5.30 million; in 1810,
7.24 million. That sounds like a lot. But the picture changes radically
when you realize the nature of this population. In 1790, only 202,000
people (5% of the total) lived in urban areas, that is, in centers where the
population was at least 2,500. In 1800, 322,000 (6%) was the urban population; in 1810, the figure rose to 525,000 (7%). The remainder of the
population was classified as rural, and even today formal concert life in
towns of 2,500 or less is minuscule. To put it another way, in 1790, there
was not a single American city with a population larger than 50,000; in
1800, there were only two (New York and Philadelphia), neither of
which reached a population of 70,000; in 1810, neither of these cities had
yet reached a population of 100,000. In 1800 and 1810, only two additional American cities had populations between 25,000 and 50,000 (Baltimore and Boston), and neither of them exceeded 30,000.[10]
Compare this to the state of affairs in Europe, heavily urbanized for
centuries. Here are some comparable figures for cities in the Old World:
London (1801, 888,000; 1811, 1,010,000); Paris (1789, 524,100); St. Pe-

---

[10] J. D. B. DeBow, *The Seventh Census of the United States: 1850* (Washington, 1853), Table
XXXIV.

tersburg (1805, 271,100); Vienna (1800, 232,000; 1815, 250,000); Berlin (1806, 155,000; 1817, 188,400); Moscow (1811, 265,000); Dublin (1798, 182,000; 1813, 176,600); Amsterdam (1796, 217,000; 1809, 207,700); Cairo (1800, 263,000). New York, with a population of 96,373, was the largest city in the United States in 1810. At that time, in addition to those cited above, the following European cities were larger: Liverpool (103,000 in 1811); Glasgow (100,000 in 1811); Manchester (98,000 in 1811); Lyon (138,000 in 1789); and Copenhagen (100,000 in 1801).[11] Who knows anything about Haydn in Liverpool, or Glasgow, or Manchester, or Lyon?

Even these American population figures for cities are somewhat exaggerated, because they do not take into account the fact that almost 25% of our population between 1790 and 1810 was black, thus reducing the effective audience for concerts (essentially a white, upperclass phenomenon) by one-quarter. Nor do they take into account the variation by nationality of the white audience in various areas of the country. Thus in 1790, 82.0% of the population in Massachusetts was of English extraction, 4.4% Scottish, and 3.9% Irish. In Pennsylvania, on the other hand, only 35.3% of the white population was English, 8.6% Scottish, and 14.5% Irish, while no less than 33.3% was of German extraction. In New York, 52.0% was English, 7.0% Scottish, 8.1% Irish, but 17.5% was Dutch. In the light of these elementary facts of demography, one's view of concert life in the United States during Haydn's lifetime must take on a somewhat different complexion.

Another fact about the American musical world which even the careful student of our artistic scene often fails to realize is the lack of any direct correlation between the music *published* here and the music *publicly performed* here during the years under discussion—roughly 1782 through 1810. Two entirely different music consumer groups were involved— *Kenner* and *Liebhaber*, to use C. P. E. Bach's familiar phrase. The American music publishing industry before 1810 catered exclusively to *Liebhaber*, or amateurs. It supplied the demand for music in the home, and its products consisted primarily of songs and piano pieces (with occasional bows in the direction of the harp, guitar, violin, and flute, all considered appropriate instruments for ladies and gentlemen to play). What was printed by the Carrs, the Paffs, the Willigs, and other leading figures in the industry was music the gentry could perform without taxing their limited technical skill, music that was simple, pleasant, innocuous, trouble-free, and eminently suited to the genteel surroundings of an eighteenth-century home.

American publishers did not cater to the needs of *Kenner,* or profes-

[11] Ibid., Table XXXVI.

sionals. I know of no set of orchestral parts published in the United States before 1810. The Haydn "symphonies," "overtures," and "full pieces" that appeared so frequently in concert programs, as well as the orchestral works by other composers of the day, could only have been obtained from European sources, either by direct purchase or through hand copying.

Thus, the American records of publication and performance before 1810 are startlingly different. In terms of publication alone, by far the most popular composer in the United States was James Hook (1746–1827). I have been able to identify no fewer than 261 of his works published here before Haydn's death in 1809. In order, he was followed by William Shield (1748–1829) with 151, James Hewitt (1770–1827) with 125, Raynor Taylor (1747–1825) with 114, Charles Dibdin (1745–1814) with 114, Samuel Arnold (1740–1802) with 100, Alexander Reinagle (1756–1809) with 87, Benjamin Carr (1768–1831) with 75, Stephen Storace (1763–96) with 66, Ignaz Pleyel (1757–1831) with 60, William Reeve (1757–1815) with 53, Michael Kelly (1762–1826) with 53, George K. Jackson (1743–1822) with 36, and Victor Pelissier (fl. 1792–1811) with 33. Haydn, with a mere 28 compositions published in the United States during his lifetime, ends up a poor fifteenth on the list. There may be some consolation to be drawn from the fact that Mozart (25 publications) and Handel (21 publications) were even less popular among the American *Liebhaber* of the day.

The record of performance in concert is quite a different story. Using as a basis for comparison the number of times the names of other composers appeared in the programs of the 247 concerts in which Haydn's music was played, we discover that Pleyel, with 129 mentions, is far in front of Haydn's other competitors. If you add to this the fact that more than twice as much Pleyel as Haydn was available in print before 1810 in the United States, and if you take into consideration the frequent appearance of Pleyel's name in concerts when Haydn's name did not appear, the temptation to say that Pleyel outranked Haydn in popularity in young America is very strong. Other composers whose names appeared on Haydn concert programs ten times or more were (in order of frequency) Stamitz—probably Karl (1745–1801), although this is by no means certain—with 46, Johann Baptist Vanhal (1739–1813) with 22, Leopold Koželuch (1752–1818) with 21, Giambattista—better known as Padre—Martini (1706–84) with 18, Reinagle with 16, Karl Friedrich Abel (1723–87) with 13, Paul Wranitzky (1756–1808) with 11, André Grétry (1741–1813) with 11, J. C. Bach (1735–82) and Shield with 10. The distinction between the music for *Kenner* and *Liebhaber* could not be clearer.

If the separation between music in the home and music in the concert hall was thus quite distinct, there was a certain small overlap. The average American concert at the end of the eighteenth century tended to combine the talents of both professionals and amateurs, and its miscellaneous nature has been somewhat exaggerated. True, the concert seemed to be a rather lengthy, miscellaneous affair, and a casual glance at a typical program might lead to the belief that there was little logic displayed in the choice of selections. In point of fact, the public concert followed a fairly consistent form. Each part or act customarily began with an orchestral "overture" or "symphony" and concluded with a "finale" or "full piece." Between these overtures and full pieces, individual artists, both professional and amateur, had an opportunity to display their widely varying talents. A professional might play a difficult "concerto"; an amateur might sing a popular song or perform a simple "lesson."

The impresarios of the day were largely professional musicians such as Reinagle, Alexander Juhan (1765–1845), Henri Capron (fl. 1785–99?), John Christopher Moller (fl. 1790–1803), Hewitt, Jean Gehot (1756–1820?), Gottlieb Graupner (1767–1836), Mrs. Mary Ann Pownall (1751–96), Peter Albrecht Van Hagen (1750–1803), and many others. Many were associated with the professional theater. A few had rather distinguished musical pedigrees. Reinagle, for example, appears to have been a close friend of C. P. E. Bach. He must have been quite familiar with Haydn's music, since he spent much time in London and undoubtedly heard Haydn's symphonies performed at the Bach-Abel concerts there before he arrived in the New World in 1786. Others, such as Hewitt, Gehot, Bergmann, Young, and Phillips, billed themselves upon their arrival in New York in 1792 as "professors of music from the Opera-House, Hanover-Square and Professional Concerts under the direction of Haydn, Pleyel, etc., London."[12] A contingent of French professionals came over because of the French Revolution of 1793. Another group of skilled performers fled to this country in 1794 because of the massacre of whites at Fort Dauphin, in Santo Domingo, during the course of the black insurrection led by Toussaint L'Ouverture. Graupner, a Hanoverian oboist, went to London before 1791 and played in the "Salomon" orchestra under Haydn in 1791–92, arriving in Charleston, S. C. in 1795. Peter Van Hagen, Dutch-born but active in Charleston as early as 1774, appears to have returned to Europe for a time before he came back to the United States in 1789 with a brood of smaller musical Van Hagens and a musically gifted wife. He first gave luster to New York's concert life before settling in Boston in 1796.

Beginning in the 1780s, series of subscription concerts were presented in Philadelphia and New York during the winter season, while summer concerts, modeled after those of Vauxhall in London, made the warm evenings more pleasurable. These summer concerts were offered by some rather colorful figures, prominent among them a New York ca-

[12] Sonneck, *Concert,* 191.

terer, Joseph Delacroix, who was (according to Oscar Sonneck) "unrivalled for his delicious ice-cream, not then so common as now."[13] Delacroix began offering concerts at his Ice House Garden on Broadway in September 1794 with Hewitt as leader of the band. The first piece offered in Act I of the first Delacroix concert was an "overture" by Haydn, the closing piece in the same act was a "symphony" by Pleyel, and the final piece at the end of Act II was a "finale" by Stamitz. By 1797, the Ice House Garden, elegantly redecorated in "a new taste," had been renamed the Vaux Hall Gardens; by 1798, Delacroix's concerts—and ice cream—had won him such a large following that he rented a larger and more pleasant site for a term of several years. Still calling the establishment the "Vaux Hall Gardens," he continued his outdoor concerts, offering three (later four) concerts a week beginning in June and shutting down at the end of July beause of the oppressive heat of New York's August. He had competition from B. Isherwood's Ranelagh Gardens and from Joseph Corre's Columbia Garden, a pleasant spot adjoining his hotel, also a concert center. Isherwood and Corre both profited from the cooling breezes off the waters near the Battery. Corre offered some particularly distinguished programs from 1798 through 1800, complete details of which are given by Sonneck. Haydn's name appeared frequently in summer programs as well as in the regular winter subscription programs offered in the larger towns.

Which of Haydn's works were actually performed at these concerts? Disregarding for the moment the Moravian performances, a survey of the concerts in which his music was heard reveals that only six can be positively identified: one or more movements from Symphony No. 85 in B-flat major ("La Reine") were performed on December 1, 1792, in Philadelphia, repeated in that city on December 29, 1792, and in New York on January 23, 1794; one or more movements from Symphony No. 73 in D major ("La Chasse") in New York on March 25, 1793, and on January 23, 1794; the *Seven Last Words* in an instrumental version was performed, complete, in New York on March 25, 1793, and the "Earthquake" movement in the same city on April 1, 1794; one or more movements from Symphony No. 63 in C major ("La Roxolane") were performed in Boston on July 22, 1794; the *Stabat Mater* was performed complete in Charleston, S. C., on July 6, 1796; and the last movement of Symphony No. 45 in F-sharp minor ("The Farewell") was performed in New York on March 23, 1802. This is the complete list of identifiable Haydn works performed in the United States during his lifetime (excluding the Moravian performances).

We have documentation of the specific musical forces used in one of these performances. In presenting the complete *Stabat Mater* in Charles-

---

[13] Ibid., 208–09.

ton in 1796, Mr. Poiteaux (a refugee from Santo Domingo) advertised that

the solos, duettos and choruses and instrumental parts [are] to be filled up by the most eminent professors and amateurs in town, who have all offered their assistance for this singular occasion. Besides the vocal parts, the orchestra shall be composed as follows: one organ, twelve violins, three basses, five tenors [violas], six oboes, flutes and clarinets, two horns, one bassoon, and two pair kettle drums, in all 30 [*sic*].[14]

As for the rest of the references to Haydn during his lifetime, we are left with a miscellany of overtures, grand overtures, new overtures, symphonies, grand symphonies, full pieces, finales, sonatas, grand sonatas, trios, and what have you. The probability is that only a small number of works were utilized in our concert life, and that Haydn was more honored in reputation than in performance. Certainly the size of the American Haydn repertory did not approach that of Europe.

All of which brings us to the extraordinary music-making activities in that part of the country which was not dominated by settlers from Great Britain, that is, in the places where the Moravians established themselves. They founded and nurtured self-contained model communities, mostly in Pennsylvania and North Carolina, during the middle of the eighteenth century. It is not generally known that some members of the renewed branch of the pre-Reformation Unitas Fratrum, a branch of the Bohemian Brethren, arrived in Savannah, Georgia, as early as February, 1735. The settlement there failed, and the Moravians moved to Pennsylvania in April, 1740. During the spring and summer of 1741, seventeen men and women lived in a clearing in a temporary log house. In December of that year, they were joined by a small additional company of Moravians under the leadership of Nicholas Ludwig, Count von Zinzendorf, and on Christmas Eve, 1741, the settlement was named Bethlehem, inspired by the singing of a hymn by Adam Drese (1630–1718), in which one of the nine stanzas reads, in English translation:

> Not Jerusalem,
> Rather Bethlehem
> Gave us that which
> Maketh life rich;
> Not Jerusalem.[15]

By 1744, a Collegium Musicum had been established, at a time when its European prototypes were dying out under the impact of the development of public concerts. It was maintained until 1820, when it was absorbed by the Philharmonic Society of Bethlehem. Similar organizations were set up in Lititz, Pa., in 1765, Nazareth, Pa., in 1780, and Salem, N. C.

[14] Charleston *City Gazette,* July 2, 1796.   [15] Anon., "Moravian."

in 1786. All were extremely active, and "like their brethren in Europe, were musical offspring of the European pre-classical movement, and therefore drew their inspiration from the musical lights—the Grauns, the Hasses, the Haydns, the Stamitzes—of the period."[16]

Fortunately, a large portion of the music assembled by the various Moravian collegia is still extant. Their music libraries contained both manuscript and printed copies, some of which are virtually nonexistent in Europe today. The Moravians were great proselytizers (and great travelers too). They were also quite music-mad and, as an inevitable result, a great deal of very strange European music found its way to Pennsylvania and North Carolina. They considered all music-making, and not alone the making of sacred music, as an activity beloved in the sight of God. Hence a figure such as John Frederik Peter (1746–1813), born in Heerendijk, Holland, busied himself in the 1760s making dozens of copies of works by Stamitz, J. C. F. Bach, J. C. Bach, Abel, Boccherini, and Haydn, all of which he carefully dated and brought with him when he came to America in 1770. The earliest known copy of Haydn's Symphony No. 17 in F major, dated December 12, 1766, is in the archives of the Salem Collegium Musicum. A Peter manuscript copy (not listed in Hoboken) of the spurious symphony Hob. I:Es5, dated January 13, 1769, may be found in the same location.

Nor was Peter the only Moravian copyist. There was also the prolific Johannes Herbst (1735–1812), who assembled an enormous collection of manuscript scores and parts before he arrived in America in 1786, and continued to add to it after his installation first at Lancaster, Pennsylvania, and later at Lititz, Pennsylvania, amassing during the course of a fifty-year career more than 500 manuscripts containing approximately 1,000 anthems and arias with orchestral accompaniment, numerous extended choral works, and anthologies of miscellaneous compositions. A complete catalogue of the Herbst collection, edited by Marilyn Gombosi, was published in 1970.[17] Immanuel Nitschmann (1736–90) was another prolific copyist; his copy of the spurious string quartet Hob. III:F4, made for the Lititz Collegium Musicum, is unknown to Hoboken. A manuscript copy of the spurious string trio Hob. V:Es13, dated November 24, 1789 in Peter's hand, also belongs to the Lititz Collegium Musicum collection. (Hoboken lists no manuscript copies of this work.) The only copy known to Hoboken of the spurious divertimento Hob. II:B7 is in the hand of an unknown copyist who worked for the Salem Collegium Musicum. Other significant Peter manuscripts include those of the string quartets Hob. II:6, III:2–4, 7, 8, 12 (all written down before 1770); the spurious symphony Hob. I:B12 (October 27, 1767); the string trios Hob. V:3, 20, and (spurious) G2 (all written down before 1775); and

[16] McCorkle, *Moravian*, 2.   [17] Gombosi, *Herbst*.

the divertimento Hob. II:21 arranged for string quartet (Hob. III:9). The manuscript copies by Nitschmann include the quartets Op. 17, Nos. 1, 2, and 6, dated 1786. An unidentified Haydn "Notturno" in the hand of John Antes, whose travels took him (rather astonishingly) from Fredericks township, Pennsylvania (where he was born on March 24, 1740) to Bethlehem, to Herrnhut (Saxony), back to Bethlehem, and thence to London, Cairo, Leghorn, Bologna, Venice, Trieste, Vienna, Herrnhut, and finally to Fulneck, England in 1783, where he served as warden of the congregation for the next twenty-five years. This "Notturno" in the collections of the Lititz Collegium Musicum, otherwise unknown in the Haydn literature, is a string quartet scored for two violins, a viola, and basso, and it was probably copied after Antes's arrival in England.

There is, by the way, a persistent story that Haydn and Antes were in some way acquainted. Rufus A. Grider, writing in 1873, even went so far as to say that "in Vienna, Antes made the acquaintance of Haydn, who, together with other musicians, performed his compositions.[18] McCorkle, calling on Geiringer as further authority, states that none of this can be substantiated.[19] Yet there is clear evidence that the two men did meet in London. In an entry in Haydn's first London notebook, placed just before an item datable December 31, 1791, the following cryptic line appears: "Mr. Antis, Bishop and a minor composer."[20] There can be little doubt that the "Mr. Antis," who was a clergyman if not a "Bishop," and was certainly a "minor composer," was our John Antes. So there is at least one documentable connection between an American-born composer and Joseph Haydn.

Any discussion of Haydn in America would be incomplete without mention of Thomas Jefferson, perhaps the most musical of our presidents. Quite a few interesting Haydn printed editions and manuscript copies are located in the Monticello music collection (ca. 1775–1827), now held by the University of Virginia. Jefferson, born in 1743, is known to have been fairly proficient as a violinist before he enrolled at the College of William and Mary in 1760. According to Dumas Malone,

We have no information about his first music teacher, but it must have been before he went to Williamsburg and found new opportunities there that he learned to play. In the musical language of his time this was not by "rote or ear," but "by book according to the gamut." . . . He may have neglected his instrument for his books while he was at the College, but he afterwards reported that for 12 years after the Revolution he played no fewer than three hours a day. While he was a student at Williamsburg he found musical opportunities such as he had never had before, and which as a performer he was not to know again. . . . Jefferson was hardly proficient enough for the first violin part at the Palace;

[18] Grider, *Bethlehem*, 5.   [19] McCorkle, "Antes," 491.
[20] Haydn, CCLN, 266 (*Briefe*, 501).

he probably had the second part and may even have played on the cello, for he was a passable performer on that instrument at a later time.

Furthermore, his wife, Martha Eppes Jefferson,

was not only a "pretty lady" but an accomplished one in the customary ways, and her love for music was a special bond with him. She played on the harpsichord and the pianoforte, as he did on the violin and cello. The tradition is that music provided the accompaniment for his successful suit: his rivals are said to have departed in admitted defeat after hearing him play and sing with her. . . . By this time [1771] he had found opportunity to take violin lessons in Williamsburg from Francis Alberti, who had come to the capital as a player and had remained as a teacher. Martha is said to have taken lessons on the harpsichord from the same man. No doubt she shared Jefferson's enthusiasm when he induced the Italian to come to Monticello at some time after the wedding, and to continue to give instruction there.[21]

Jefferson's idyllic marriage was short-lived—his wife Martha died on September 6, 1782. He was virtually inconsolable, and one of the things he did in order to while away the hours was to compile a catalogue, dated 1783, of his extraordinarily extensive library, later to form the nucleus of the Library of Congress. Chapters 35, 36, and 37 are concerned with his musical holdings. Chapter 35 treats of theoretical works, and here as elsewhere, Jefferson followed the practice of placing a check mark before those items he actually owned. Those he later hoped to acquire were entered in the catalogue, but were left unchecked. Among the checked items in Chapter 35 are treatises by Holden, Jackson, Bremner, Burney, Geminiani, Heck, Pasquali, Zuccari, and Hoegi. Missing, but desired, were "Miss Ford's instructions for playing on the musical glasses." Chapter 36 was devoted to vocal music. He owned copies of works by Piccinni, Handel, Pergolesi, Daniel Purcell, Arne, Baildon, J. C. Bach, Heron, and Dibdin, among others. But Chapter 37, dealing with instrumental music, was by far the largest. It showed that he owned concertos by Corelli and Vivaldi, no less than sixty Handel overtures, and other compositions by Arne, Abel, Howard, Lampugnani, the Earl of Kelly, Pasquali, Humphries, Martini, Campioni, Humble, Boccherini, Gasparini, Kammel, Vanhal, Schwindel, Roeser, Godwin, Tessarini, Bezossi [sic; recte Besozzi], Battino, Figlio, Wodizka, Burgess, Felton, Stamitz, Bremner, Hardin, J. C. Bach, Arnold, and many others.

Where was Haydn? He was in the list, but all the Haydn items were unchecked. Jefferson wanted to acquire Haydn's "1st, 2nd, 3rd, 47th and 48th Sonatas," his "51st and 52nd Concertos," and his "9th Duet"— whatever these may be—but he did not own them in 1783. Almost all the Haydn at Monticello was the property of his elder daughter Martha (usually called "Patsy" in the family), who sailed with Jefferson for

[21]Dumas Malone, *Jefferson and his Time*, 5 vols., vol. 1, *Jefferson the Virginian* (Boston: Little, Brown & Co., 1948), 47–48, 78–79, 158–59.

France after his appointment as American commissioner to that country. The pair arrived in Paris on August 6, 1784, about two months before her twelfth birthday. There, among other things, Patsy studied music, and by a fortunate circumstance, her music master turned out to be a distinguished French musician, Claude-Bénigne Balbastre. Except for a few manuscript copies of songs and piano pieces in an unidentified hand, the Haydn prints at Monticello were undoubtedly chosen for the youngster by Balbastre. Some of Patsy Jefferson's editions of arrangements for keyboard of Haydn symphonies are quite rare. Her copies of Nos. 75, 53, and 73 are found neither in Hoboken nor in the BUC, although they are plainly genuine eighteenth-century editions published in London by H. Wright, J. Bland, and Longman & Broderip.

Undoubtedly Jefferson heard Haydn's music not infrequently—the "Paris" symphonies were premiered while he was there—but it is doubtful that he was especially fond of the master's handiwork. Indeed, there exists a document in Jefferson's hand which shows that his musical inclinations ran in somewhat different directions. In Folder 34 of the Monticello music collection is a thematic catalogue bearing the following inscription: "On this paper is noted the beginning of the several compositions of Campioni which are in possession of T. Jefferson. He would be glad to have everything else he has composed of solos, duets, or trios. Printed copies would be preferred; but if not to be had, he would have them in manuscript."[22] Such enthusiasm for the work of Carlo Antonio Campioni (1720–93) is not necessarily antithetical to a parallel enthusiasm for the work of Haydn, but such a catholic taste would have been quite unusual at the time.

To sum up, the picture of Haydn's popularity in America during his lifetime is by no means clear. He was performed, but how many works is unknown. He was published, but rather infrequently compared to the record of far less distinguished figures. Certainly, he was not appreciated at his true worth, as he was in England and on the Continent. Even *The Creation,* a tremendous success in Europe from its first performance in 1798, had to wait two decades before the Handel and Haydn Society of Boston gave it its first complete American hearing in 1819. J. F. Peter did copy a set of parts for the piece in 1811, and part of the oratorio may have been performed in Bethlehem some time that year. But the evidence for a complete performance in Bethlehem in that year comes from unreliable secondary sources,[23] and no complete Bethlehem performance can be conclusively documented until 1823.

We still know all too little about the history of music in our own country during the first decade of the nineteenth century, and we rely too

[22] Quoted in Cripe, *Jefferson,* 114.
[23] Walters, *Choir,* 18 for example; Lahee, *America.*

heavily on the pioneer work of Oscar Sonneck. The full story is yet to be told. After all, there were Haydn societies in New York in 1798, in Philadelphia in 1809, and even in tiny Cincinnati in 1819. It is high time for American scholars to proceed farther along the path cut through a wilderness of ignorance by Oscar Sonneck. It is high time for American scholars to find out what really took place in our own country while Joseph Haydn was still among the living.

PART TWO: DOCUMENTATION

Round Table

Background, Biography, Iconography[1]

DÉNES BARTHA, *Chairman*   WALTER PASS
GERHARD CROLL   LÁSZLÓ SOMFAI
KARL GEIRINGER   GÜNTER THOMAS
VERNON GOTWALS   HORST WALTER
C.-G. STELLAN MÖRNER   A. PETER BROWN, *Secretary*

BARTHA We don't intend to deal with general Haydn biographies today. Despite its great merits for its time, particularly in archival research, Pohl's basic work[2] is outdated. Professor Geiringer's eminently readable survey[3] is invaluable in teaching. But the long overdue great Haydn biography cannot be written until worldwide research into the documentary background has become better coordinated, and the results better assimilated. [At the time of this Conference, H. C. Robbins Landon's massive new biography had not yet begun to appear, and, as of this writing, it is still not complete. It is too early to attempt to assess its significance.–*Ed.*]

Repertoire and Ensemble

Remarks on Haydn as an Opera Conductor

BARTHA In 1960 my colleague László Somfai and I published our monograph on Haydn the opera conductor; a short résumé in English appeared later.[4]

[1] The text of this report was prepared by Dénes Bartha and James Webster.
[2] Pohl I–II.   [3] Geiringer₁₋₃.   [4] Bartha-Somfai; Bartha, "Repertory."

The monograph was based on the musical and documentary materials preserved in the Esterházy archives. Between the two world wars, these materials had been divided into two parts. One, consisting primarily of church music, remained in Austrian castles of the Esterházy family. The other, mainly secular music along with relevant documents, was transferred to the Esterházy palace in Budapest; from there, after surviving World War II (for the most part), it was later transfered to the National Széchényi Library.

Pohl, who around 1870 had access to all parts of the Esterházy collections, paid little attention to these operatic materials (except Haydn's own works); for the works of the other (mostly Italian) composers he contented himself with a cursory mention of titles, obviously taken from the librettos. (The libretto collection itself was lost to fire in 1945.) Thus Pohl was unaware of the countless revisions and additions—including entire new arias—which Haydn made in the operas of Anfossi, Righini, Paisiello, Cimarosa, and dozens of other Italian composers of the time. In the 1950s, Somfai located and identified more than 100 scores and sets of performing parts—some complete, many incomplete. Haydn's highly critical attitude toward Italian opera can be demonstrated in telling detail from those sources.

The first half of our book consists of a nearly complete documentation of opera performances, ensembles, players, and singers performing under Haydn's direction. The relevant documents had to be dug out from thousands of others; fortunately, a special group, *Acta Musicalia,* had been separated from the bulk of the other (nonmusical) documents before the war by Prince Esterházy's archive director, János Hárich. Although by no means complete, the *Acta Musicalia* were an essential aid in our research. Another fortuitous circumstance was the existence of a complete typewritten catalogue of the war-ravaged Esterházy libretto collection.[5] Unfortunately, when we began in 1957, Hárich had just left Hungary and was unavailable for collaboration. Furthermore, since the early 1950s Arisztid Valkó had been sifting the Esterházy Archives for Haydn documents.[6] Valkó was not a professional musicologist, and he was unable to judge the relevance of the various documents; wherever he saw Haydn's name, he transcribed and published the document. As Hárich later showed,[7] Valkó's selection was incomplete and his readings often unreliable. And since, under pressure of time, the documentation section of our book had to be based mainly on Valkó's publications, it too was, to an extent, incomplete. Nevertheless, our work, particularly Somfai's detailed musical analysis of the scores and performing parts, has opened a new perspective in our knowledge of Haydn's activities at Esz-

---

[5] Hárich, "Librettos."   [6] Valkó I–II.   [7] Hárich, "Repertoire."

terháza. Somfai also identified the handwriting of a special opera copyist, Johann Schellinger, not only in the many opera parts copied by him, but even in one important section of EK, Haydn's early thematic catalogue.

ALAN TYSON[8] I would like to ask one question about the singers. Are we certain who all the singers were for certain roles, and what their tessituras were? For Handel, Winton Dean was able to establish that certain singers could or could not have sung certain roles. Might this be a good thing to investigate for Eszterháza, or has it already been done?

SOMFAI Thank you for the idea. Recently, we have tried to find a younger musicologist to do this work, to go through all of the hundreds of arias to look for transpositions. Because of Haydn's own "insertion arias," we did it for Luigia Polzelli, but not for the other singers.

The *Comedia la Marchesa Nespola:* Some Documentary Problems

GEIRINGER The National Library in Budapest owns the incomplete original manuscript of a stage work by Haydn entitled *Arie per la Comedia Marchese.* Haydn also listed this work in EK with the title *Comedia la Marchesa Nespola.* The last name of the marchioness has caused some headache to scholars. Haydn's hastily scribbled entry was interpreted not only as "Nespola" but also as "Nepola" which, in turn, was associated with the city of Naples. Hoboken stated, however, that such a marchioness of Naples never existed, and he referred to Robert Haas's having encountered the name of a comic opera entitled *Il Conte Nespola* (1746) in a list of Venetian intermezzi.[9] This is not so very different from Haydn's *La Marchesa Nespola.*

When I consulted an Italian dictionary, I found "nespola" listed as the fruit of the medlar tree. This tree is common in Italy and Central Europe; its small, brownish, sticky fruit, which resembles a crabapple and is closely related to the American loquat, can be consumed only when it is overripe. "Nespola" also has comical connotations; "dare cento nespole" means to give a good hiding, and a person with a protruding chin and a speech defect is called a "succia nespole," a loquat sucker. In Austria, too, this not very appetizing fruit is considered amusing. Thus it seems appropriate to interpret Haydn's title as "The Marchioness of the Loquats," following an established *opera buffa* tradition documented in Venice.

Some of the characters in Haydn's little composition are borrowed from the Italian *commedia dell'arte:* Columbina, Sganarello, and Panta-

---

[8] From the audience.   [9] Hoboken II, 448, 440–41; Haas, "Komödie," 5–7.

lone. Perhaps the visit of a troupe of Italian comedians to Eisenstadt during May and June 1762 was responsible for this choice. An amusing
twist, however, is that the remaining characters are given ordinary first
names: Barbara, Leopoldo, and Augusta.

Bartha and Somfai suggest that the "Signora Barbara" of Haydn's
comedia might have been meant for the singer Barbara Fux, a valued
member of the Esterházy musical staff.[10] Similarly Haydn's "Leopoldo"
could have been intended for the newly engaged (1763) tenor Leopold
Dichtler. (Feder has recently stated that Pohl's dating 1762 might be due
to his misreading of the hastily written autograph date 1763—which may
have originally read 1762.)[11]

The third name, Augusta, is not so easy to place. No singer named
Augusta was in Eisenstadt at that time. But once again consulting my
trusty dictionary, I learned that Augusta signifies a majestic, grand,
noble lady. As the whole work is a musical spoof, it seems that Augusta
must refer to the Marchesa Nespola herself. She begins her aria with the
words "Se non son bella tanto, almeno ho il cor sincero." These words,
sung by a lady costumed as a rotund, overripe fruit, will have provoked
utmost hilarity in the audience.

Pohl claims that Haydn's comedy was performed in Eisenstadt during
a visit of traveling Italian comedians in May or June 1762; Hoboken asserts that it was presented on May 17, 1762, to celebrate the solemn entry
of Prince Nicholas into Eisenstadt. I cannot find any proof for either contention. On the other hand a performance in 1763 (the date on the autograph) seems most likely. On January 10, 1763, Prince Anton Esterházy, eldest son of the ruling Prince Nicholas, was married. The
magnificent festivities that took place at this occasion in Eisenstadt are
described in the *Wiener Diarium* (No. 9, dated Eisenstadt, January 20). A
solemn *Te Deum* was sung on the first day of the celebration; on the second day the "Festa teatrale" *Acide* was performed; and on the third day
an *opera buffa* was played, the castle illuminated, and a masked ball held.
The name of the *opera buffa* is not indicated, but it seems likely that it
was *La Marchesa Nespola*. It would have been appropriate, on the occasion of wedding celebrations, to have a comedy follow an opera seria.
Significantly enough Haydn listed *La Marchesa* immediately below *Acide*
in EK.

My conclusions are thus 1) that "nespola" was a traditional comic idea
based on the fruit of the medlar tree and that "Augusta" was a parodistic
name for the Marchioness Nespola herself; and 2) that this little comedy
was first performed not in 1762, but in January 1763, at the festivities following the wedding of Prince Anton Esterházy.

[10] Bartha-Somfai, 379.   [11] Feder, "Datierung," 52.

CROLL In Austria, the name Augusta, as far as I know, is used only in the context of the imperial family. Perhaps a daughter of Maria Theresa participated in this performance at Anton Esterházy's wedding. We know of several performances during these years where members of the imperial family sang in cantatas or little operas in Schönbrunn Castle, especially in connection with wedding festivities.

GEIRINGER I would be surprised if this were the case. The detailed report in the *Wiener Diarium* doesn't mention this.

Personalities in Haydn's Circle

Luigi Tomasini the Younger and "Demoiselle Croll"

CROLL Luigi Tomasini the Younger, as I shall call him, deserves our attention—and not only because he was the son of Haydn's friend Luigi Tomasini. In a petition on the younger Tomasini's behalf to Prince Nicholas, written probably at the end of 1803, Haydn notes "the *rare* genius of the petitioner," underlining the word "rare," and thus emphasizing his petition in an unusually forceful manner. But not only Haydn's special benevolence induced me to record several facts today—some of them new—about Tomasini's son and his wife. Personal reasons—family pride—also had considerable influence. For this, I beg your indulgence.

The identity of this young and apparently very talented Tomasini was the subject of puzzles, errors, suppositions, and polemics from Pohl and Botstiber, Csatkai, Brand, Valkó, Landon, Bartha, and Hárich. We need not mention the particulars. Even Hárich did not succeed in producing accurate information on young Tomasini's identity: he had to impute two mistakes to the registrar who functioned at Tomasini's marriage.

The young man whom Haydn described as a "rare genius" used the signature "Luigi Tomasini." Prince Nicholas called him "the young Luigi Tomasini." [12] He was born on July 10, 1779, in Esterháza. He was admitted officially into the orchestra as first violinist on January 1, 1796, receiving a wage of 450 florins. In the following years the young man received repeated signs of special favor from his princely master, but at the same time attracted his indignation because of "frivolous conduct" and disregard of princely instructions.

In the summer of 1807 a young singer entered into Esterházy's service:

[12] In order to distinguish him from his father Luigi, Hárich calls the younger Tomasini Alois [Basil Nikolaus] Tomasini.

Sophie Friederike Croll.[13] She was born on March 7, 1785, in Neustre-litz-Mecklenburg, where her father was a trumpeter and finally "court-fourier" (provisioner). She later traveled to the south, presumably pa-tronized by her sovereign, and as a singer found her way into Esterházy's service, probably in July 1807; her contract was for one and a half years.[14] She and Luigi Tomasini the younger evidently very soon came to terms: as early as autumn of the same year (presumably in September), Tomasini asked the prince for a marriage license. Connected with the request was a petition for amortization of his debts. If neither of the two were granted, he would seek his luck elsewhere. Prince Nicholas refused and had his "deserving father" teach Tomasini a lesson, and "Demoiselle Croll" was strongly warned by the Prince himself against the marriage.

But in the following weeks and months Luigi Tomasini the younger succeeded in attaining the amortization of his debts (the sum amounted to 594 florins). After a further written petition of February 16, 1808—in which he emphatically and with many exclamation marks asks for "per-mission" to marry, as well as for Sophie Friederike Croll to remain in service, calling this his "happiness on earth"—the prince gave his oral consent in February 1808, which was supposed to be put down in writ-ing within three months. But it never came to that.

When Luigi Tomasini the elder died on April 25, 1808, his son imme-diately requested to succeed his father as concertmaster, referring to an appropriate promise of the prince to his father. Again, Prince Nikolaus took his time.

At this point Tomasini proceeded to take action and, without written consent, married Sophie Friederike Croll on July 17, 1808, in Eisenstadt. Witnesses to the marriage were the princely privy counselor and central director Johann von Karner and the vice-Kapellmeister Johann Fuchs. (One could take this as a sign that the prince did not protest.)

The withholding of the written marriage license, however, destroyed Sophie Tomasini-Croll's hope of a widow's pension or even a further en-gagement. So the young couple took the consequences and gave notice. The princely attestations (of August 16, 1808) acknowledged Tomasini's fifteen years of service "with aptitude and special talent" as "first violin-ist and concertant (soloist) of our orchestra"; his wife was given for her

---

[13] The father of the then twenty-two-year-old lady (her Christian names were Johanna Sophia Christiane, as an artist Sophie Friederike) and her younger brother is my direct ancestor; the evidence of the genealogy was found in the legacy of my father, who died in 1972. For additional information, especially about Sophie Friederike Croll, I am indebted to the archive of the cathedral at Ratzeburg (F. W. Kock), the state archives in Schwerin, and to Dr. Dempe of the Öffentliche Wissenschaftliche Bibliothek of Schwerin (formerly Mecklenburgische Landesbibliothek).

[14] In the Hummel Catalogue (additions of January 1808), it is stated that a "Pianoforte von polirten Nussbaum von Ignaz Kober . . . ist bei der Sängerin Croll." See Hárich, "Inven-tare," 110.

thirteen months service as a "chorus and court singer" the predicate "with distinction." Thus, they departed in a benevolent atmosphere and explicitly "by their own request," "in order to perfect themselves in the realm of art." Hárich rightly contrasted this with Pohl's standing theory of a forced dismissal of Tomasini.

About the further destiny of the couple Tomasini-Croll little was known until now. On February 2, 1809, they went into service with Duke Karl of Mecklenburg-Strelitz; the combined payment was granted from Christmas 1808 onward. A daughter (Friederike) was born on April 5, 1810; a son (Carl) on January 26, 1813; and a second daughter, Louisa, on April 1, 1814. On November 12, 1825, Luigi Tomasini became concertmaster.

Together with his wife, but also alone, Tomasini made concert tours. In his ambitious repertoire one finds, besides short-lived, fashionable violin concertos (by Maurer and Cremon), as early as 1812 Beethoven's violin concerto, and as early as 1820(!) compositions of Paganini. In a concert on December 4, 1822, at Ludwigslust Castle of the Grand Duke of Mecklenburg-Schwerin, Tomasini began the program with an overture of his own composition. The concert also featured Tomasini as soloist in a violin concerto by Maurer and a "Pot-pouri" of A. Romberg; Sophie appeared as soloist in two arias, one by Weber, and one from [Rossini's] *Tancredi;* the conclusion was the overture to *Der Freischütz.* Tomasini was honored with 25 louis d'or.

At Neustrelitz, Madame Tomasini shared her husband's successes. An episode that took place in the winter of 1823–24 illustrates her status: the duke appointed her as traveling companion for a young singer under his patronage, whom he sent to Berlin for eight days to become acquainted with the grand opera there.[15]

Sophie Tomasini died on June 29, 1848, at Neustrelitz. Luigi Tomasini the Younger died on February 19, 1858, after half a century of service in the Neustrelitz court orchestra, more than half of this time as concertmaster. Their musical talent survived in their descendants: Their son Carl (1813–80) was concertmaster, their daughter Friederike (1810–86) court singer at Neustrelitz; brother and sister thus recapitulated the careers of their parents. A grandson of Carl Tomasini, named after him, also was a court musician of the duke of Mecklenburg-Strelitz.

Fredrik Samuel Silverstolpe: A Swedish Friend of Haydn's

MÖRNER In the literature, one reads of a Swedish diplomat by the name of Silverstolpe, whom Haydn befriended at the close of the eighteenth cen-

[15] This young girl was engaged to a brother of Sophie Tomasini. After her return from Berlin, she refused the duke's offer of a position as court singer; she left Neustrelitz in April

tury.[16] In Schreiber's biography (1928) of Joseph Martin Kraus, Court
Kapellmeister of Gustav III in Stockholm, one reads a German translation of excerpts from Silverstolpe's notes concerning his visits to
Haydn.[17] Silverstolpe's printed recollections from those years in
Vienna, published in 1838, were based on notes and letters from the years
1796–1802. Silverstolpe's memoirs thus represent our earliest account
of a friendship with Haydn; Dies and Griesinger knew him only during
the last decade of his life.[18]

Who was this Swede who succeeded in becoming friends with Haydn
and his pupils Neukomm and Struck, with Constanze Mozart, and many
others? Fredrik Samuel Silverstolpe was born in Stockholm on December 28, 1769. After studies at the University of Uppsala he entered
the civil service. In the 1790s he became a career diplomat and was appointed *chargé d'affaires* in Vienna from 1796 to 1802. The entire family
doted on music and especially valued Haydn's *Seven Words,* which in the
original orchestral version had already been performed in Stockholm.
Silverstolpe himself had studied both literature and art, but especially
music. He played the piano, sang, studied the theory of music, copied a
lot of fine music, and in his old age even composed songs.

On his arrival in Vienna in 1796 Silverstolpe devoted himself to cultivating all possible literary, artistic, and musical friendships, among
them Haydn, Salieri, and Albrechtsberger. During these years he sent
extensive reports on his musical experiences to his family and friends in
Stockholm. As a member of the nobility and a diplomat, Silverstolpe
was received in many prominent houses and musical circles; in 1797 he
attended the Easter Concerts in the palace of Prince Schwarzenberg, and
there he met Haydn personally for the first time, as he wrote in an unpublished letter:

Then I made Haydn's acquaintance, which I have kept alive through many a
"visite." He distinguishes himself through his modesty, and he doesn't like com-
pliments. His face is quite thoughtful, but not as much as you would expeʳ t. The
time spent with him is most agreeable. . . . Speaking of the *Seven Words,* Haydn
said: "I have never felt like boasting, but this very work is not without value et je
me flatte que c'est le meilleur ouvrage que j'ai fait. . . ."

In another letter from June 1797, Silverstolpe mentions Haydn's quartets
Op. 76 in such terms that we may draw the conclusion that they were
completed by this time:

A few days ago I visited Haydn once again. . . . He played for me at the piano the
string quartets commissioned by Count Erdödi at a price of 100 ducats gold, and
which are not to be printed until a certain period of years has elapsed. They are

1824 and went to Stettin, to marry "her Croll," as she wrote in her diary. This Croll was
my great-great-grandfather Carl Friedrich Wilhelm Croll, a merchant.
[16] Pohl-Botstiber, 119.   [17] Schreiber, *Kraus,* 69ff.
[18] The relations between Haydn and Silverstolpe are described in Mörner, "Haydniana."

more than great and full of new thinking. He told me to sit next to him while he was playing in order to be able to notice the way he had scored the different parts. He also sang a few arias to me which he intends to publish in subscription when they will have the number of 24. They are characterized by his usual rhythms and display many touches of genius and choice ideas.

A few days later Silverstolpe wrote to his mother that he frequently sees Haydn, who often spoils him, playing. Silverstolpe in turn invites Haydn to intimate chamber music evenings in his apartment.

At the end of 1797 Silverstope proposed to the Musical Academy of Stockholm to elect Haydn, Salieri, and Albrechtsberger as members. This was granted in 1798. In many of his later printed works, e.g., the subscription edition of *The Creation* (1800), Haydn liked to insert among other titles that of "Member of the Royal Swedish Musical Academy of Stockholm."

In his reminiscences, Silverstolpe tells about his impressions of *The Creation,* having made notes from both the last rehearsal and the première at Schwarzenberg's. He also writes the following:

When I entered Haydn's dining room I heard a parrot crying out: "Papa Haydn!" In one of the rooms to the right you could often see the unprepossessing figure of the great man rise from his work, sometimes staying at the table until the visitor was quite near. *There* it was that he showed me his aria in D from *The Creation,* which is supposed to picture the movements of the sea and the rising of the cliffs out of the sea. "Can you see," he said, very amused, "how the notes behave like waves, up and down they go? Look, you can also see the mountains rising out of the depths of the sea. You *have* to amuse yourself sometimes, after having been serious for so long." [19]

In the beginning of April 1800 Silverstolpe reported that Haydn was working on the *Seasons,* of which "Spring" was already finished.

Silverstolpe prepared the first Swedish performance of *The Creation;* his translations of the recitatives were checked by Haydn. Haydn's pupil Paul Struck was sent from Vienna to Sockholm to assist at the rehearsal; Struck presented the Musical Academy with the autograph of Symphony No. 49, once given to Struck by Haydn. Silverstolpe also helped get Haydn's permission to allow the recently deceased Swedish composer John Wikmanson's three string quartets to be dedicated to him.

During his subsequent stay as a diplomat in St. Petersburg, Silverstolpe revived his friendship with Haydn's pupil Neukomm and corresponded with Haydn. Through correspondence with Struck, Silverstolpe was kept informed about musical life in Vienna.

Silverstolpe's collection at Näs not only contains autographs and first prints but also copies of works by about 150 different composers, including Mozart, Kraus, Struck, and Neukomm. There are also several valuable authentic Haydn copies, among them an "insertion aria" from 1790,

[19] Quoted ibid., 26.

"Il meglio mio carattere" for soprano and orchestra, which is known nowhere else.[20]

When Silverstolpe collected material for his biography on Kraus, he entered into correspondence with the monk Roman Hoffstetter, the probable author of "Opus 3."[21]

Through his collections and his reminiscences Silverstolpe has a secure place in the history of music. The Haydniana from his estate are now available on microfilm at the Haydn-Institut in Cologne.

Gottfried van Swieten: Some Documentary Problems

PASS Among Haydn's acquaintances Baron van Swieten played a major part in his life. In recent years, important contributions about the baron and Haydn have come from Olleson, Holschneider, Riedel-Martiny, Thomas, Walter, and Stern.[22] Gerhard Croll recently discovered very important documents in the Schwarzenberg Archiv,[23] which give an interesting picture of the Baron's social importance in the Gesellschaft der Associierten in Vienna, and they also reflect the effect that Haydn's oratorios made on Viennese musical life.

But of van Swieten's life and his career we know relatively little. He was the head of the Kaiserliche Hofbibliothek and the son of the famous doctor of Maria Theresa. His career had begun as Austrian ambassador to the Prussian court in Berlin, a very delicate position. At the beginning of the reign of Joseph II, he reached the pinnacle of his career as the head of the Commission of Censorship. This was an important paid position of the Austrian Enlightenment, sometimes called the "Bloodless Revolution." Swieten supervised the elimination of the monasteries, the control of publications, and so on. Thus he influenced the Enlightenment.

Van Swieten's relationship with Haydn lasted quite a long time; he must have interested Haydn. Without doubt, he exerted a significant influence upon Haydn's development into a free, independent artist in the modern sense.

On Haydn's Pupils

WALTER Up to now there has been no comprehensive account of Haydn's pupils. Except for his relations with Beethoven and Sigismund Neukomm, there have been no individual investigations. The number of his students was considerable. His teaching extended over a period of almost pre-

[20] Silverstolpe, *Kraus.*
[21] See Feder, "Hoffstetter"; on Op. 3, see the Round Table elsewhere in this volume.
[22] Olleson, "Swieten"; Holschneider, "Bibliothek"; Riedel-Martiny, "Oratorien"; Thomas, "Griesinger"; Walter, "Textbücher"; Stern, "Schöpfung."
[23] Croll, "Schwarzenberg."

cisely 50 years, from his first piano lessons in 1753 (for which Haydn received 2 florins monthly) to a draft of a letter from about 1804 showing that Haydn was too weak to give lessons. "I am very sorry," he wrote to an unknown correspondent, "that in this short time I have not been able to give more than 30 lessons to your son, whom people here have robbed of the hope that he might ever learn how to compose. He is a good boy, I love him, and he has enough talent . . . to show the world quite the contrary."[24]

Griesinger mentions only "his best and most grateful pupils": Pleyel, Neukomm, and Lessel. Dies gives us more: "Haydn trained the following students . . .: Hoffmann, a Livonian; Kranz in Stuttgart; Anton Wranizky; Lessel; Fuchs, in the service of Prince Esterházy; Tomisch; Graf; Specht; Pleyel; Hänsel; Destouches; Struck; two brothers Pulcelli, of whom one died; the living one is in the service of Prince Esterházy; Neukomm."[25] For many of these names we look in vain in Haydn biographies; only Pleyel, Neukomm, and Polzelli appear regularly. To those are added, as a rule, Robert Kimmerling, who (with Abund Mikysch) was presumably Haydn's first student in counterpoint; Marianne von Martinez, one of his first and most talented piano pupils; Fritz and Edmund von Weber; Rebecca Schroeter; and, naturally, Beethoven. Some names (Graf, Hoffmann) remain unidentified even today.

One can categorize the students in different ways: as piano, singing, or composition pupils; as early or late ones; as Bohemian, German, English, or Polish students; as private pupils or as musicians of the Esterházy court. Today I will report on Haydn's instruction of the court musicians and on some little-known private students of the middle and late period.

To a certain degree all the instrumentalists and singers at the Esterházy court were Haydn's students. They were entrusted to his guiding hand, studied their parts with him, and profited by his instruction. As Burney writes, paraphrasing the oboist Johann Christian Fischer, Haydn's compositions "have the advantage of being rehearsed and performed . . . by a band of his own forming, who have apartments in the palace and practice from morning to night . . . like the students in the conservatories in Naples."[26] From Haydn's contract of 1761 we learn that he was obliged "to instruct the female singers, so that they should not forget in the country what they have learned in Vienna from distinguished masters." This concerned the singers in the opera ensemble at Esterháza as well as those in the church choir at Eisenstadt. In November 1777, for instance, Haydn seems to have taught singing to Elisabeth Prandtner and Elisabeth Griessler.[27] From a letter he wrote to Luigia Polzelli we know that he

---

[24] Haydn, CCLN, 231 (*Briefe,* 448).

[25] Gotwals, *Haydn,* 196 (Dies, 198; modern ed., 197).

[26] Burney, *History* IV, 601; modern ed., II, 959.

[27] Hárich, "Fideikommiss," 19.

himself went to the trouble of studying all her parts with her. Haydn's pupils in composition consisted of court musicians only in exceptional cases (Johann Baptist Krumpholtz, Anton Kraft, Johann Nepomuk Fuchs). Likewise there is little reason to believe that Haydn taught music to all those members of the Kapelle who were composers (Tomasini, Purksteiner, Friberth, Schiringer, Dietzl, Mestrino, Marteau, Lidl, Rossetti[28]).

Most of Haydn's pupils came from "outside"; they were private students. He considered Ignaz Pleyel his dearest and most accomplished student. Pleyel studied with Haydn from 1772 to 1777. Boris Steinpress has recently cited the Russian emigré violin virtuoso and composer Ferdinand Anton Titz,[29] who called himself Haydn's pupil on the title page of one edition. But this has not been confirmed; the claim "Élève d'Haidn" is found only on a publication of the Paris publisher Bailleux. And Titz's biography has undergone fantastic falsifications since Fétis, Schilling, and Eitner.[30] Steinpress names another possible pupil, the Moscow Kapellmeister Franz Kerzelli, who lived in Vienna at the beginning of the 1770s, where he supposedly was associated with Haydn.

Haydn seems to have taken a strong interest in teaching during the 1780s, when the number of private pupils begins to grow rapidly. More than a dozen students are documented, many of them by Haydn's own testimony, including, in the 1780s, Anton Wranitzky, Fritz and Edmund von Weber, Johann Friedrich Kranz, and Franz Seraph von Destouches; and, after 1790—besides Beethoven and a few English students—Peter Haensel, Pietro and Antonio Polzelli, Johann Spech (a Hungarian musician), Paul Struck (a Swedish composer), Sigismund Neukomm, and the Polish student Franz Lessel. Other names brought into connection with Haydn by Gerber, Dlabacz, or personal dedications cannot be properly documented. Again and again, unfamiliar names turn up. The famous Polish violinist Felix Janiewicz, for example, lived in Vienna in 1784–85, knew Haydn personally and had contact with his circle of pupils. The mulatto violinist George Polgreen Bridgetower, of "Kreutzer Sonata" fame, was introduced at his first public appearances in Germany and England (1786 and 1789) as a pupil of Haydn's.[31] And Bridgetower's father is documented as Prince Esterházy's valet, "Mohr [the Moor] August," between 1779 and 1784.[32] There the young George Polgreen could well have received his first musical instruction from Haydn.

---

[28] This Antonio Rossetti, (d. 1784), in Esterházy's service 1776–81, should not be confused with the well-known Franz Anton Rössler, also called Rosetti by Pohl (II, 104–05).
[29] Steinpress, "Oratorien," 80.   [30] See Mooser, *Annales,* II, 179ff.
[31] See Vernon Delves Broughton, ed., *Court and Private Life in the Time of Queen Charlotte: Being the Journals of Mrs. Papendiek,* II (London, 1887), 134ff., 153ff., 177ff.
[32] Radant, "Rosenbaum," 109.

We have hardly any documents that give direct evidence of Haydn's methods of instruction. Like Mozart, Albrechtsberger, and later on Beethoven, Haydn used Fux's *Gradus ad Parnassum* as the basis for contrapuntal instruction. The two manuscript sources which prove this have been described and edited by Alfred Mann: 1) Haydn's annotations to Fux's *Gradus;* 2) a fragmentary abstract made from the *Gradus,* entitled *Elementarbuch der verschiedenen Gattungen des Contrapuncts* (A Compendium of the Different Species of Counterpoint), dated 1789 and written by Haydn's student F. C. Magnus, a Livonian.[33] Nottebohm suggested that Haydn formulated a similar abstract for each of his students; we are now informed that, at the beginning of his studies with Haydn, Franz Lessel had also laid out an *Elementarbuch,* dated 1800.[34] But the counterpoint studies transmit only one side of Haydn's methods of teaching. Instruction in "strict style" was usually accompanied by exercises in "free style"; one lesson of the latter type is described by Silverstolpe.[35] It seems probable that this was also the decisive aspect of Haydn's influence on Beethoven.[36]

Around 1800 numerous artists, dilettanti, and students came to visit Haydn.[37] In 1802, Anton Reicha met Beethoven; he lived in Vienna until 1808 and also made friends with Haydn. "Haydn's door was always open for me," wrote Reicha later, "and though he was unable to give regular lessons any longer because of age, one got many useful hints, which did not remain fruitless."[38] Reicha thus profited from Haydn's informative talks, without any compendium or timetable. The English composer William Shield, who spent a few days with Haydn at Taplow in 1794, said that he had learned more about music on that occasion than from years of study.[39] Haydn also advised and encouraged several young composers who were not his pupils in the strict sense. Joseph Eybler (1789), Joseph Weigl (1794), Ignaz Seyfried (1799), and Anton Eberl (1801) received congratulations and praise after performances of their compositions, which Haydn had looked over before. As late as 1803–04 Johann Nepomuk Hummel, Anton Diabelli, Friedrich Kalkbrenner, and Conradin Kreutzer seem to have profited by his fatherly advice. That the young could count on Haydn's kindness and encouragement is confirmed by Carl Maria von Weber, who met Haydn in 1804 and wrote afterwards: "He is always cheerful and lively, likes to talk of his experiences, and particularly enjoys having up-and-coming artists about him. He is the very model of a great man."[40]

---

[33] Mann, "Critic"; Haydn, *Elementarbuch,* transl.
[34] Rudnicka, *Lessel,* 19, 77. This copy is now lost.   [35] Mörner, "Haydniana," 27.
[36] See Walter, "Beziehungen," 80–81; Solomon, *Beethoven,* Ch. 7. Cf. Alfred Mann's remarks in the Round Table Melodic Style Traditions. [Ed.]
[37] See Walter, "Beziehungen," 82.   [38] Ibid.
[39] Grove's Dictionary of Music and Musicians, 5th ed., VII, s.v. Shield.
[40] Ibid., 1st ed., IV, s.v. Weber.

Problems in the Documentation of Haydn's Life

On the Letters and London Notebooks

BARTHA As you know, the first modern edition of Haydn's letters was prepared and published by H. C. Robbins Landon in English translation.[41] In quantity and quality, Landon's edition was an enormous advance; all earlier editions covered only limited parts of the surviving material—unfortunately only a small fraction of what must have been in existence in Haydn's time—and suffered from faulty readings and inaccurate editing. (Only the old edition of the Genzinger letters by Karajan in 1861 was philologically accurate.[42]) Some years later, I was commissioned to prepare another edition in the original languages (mostly German, some French, Italian, and English), which is based primarily on the same sources as Landon's.[43]

In his (otherwise excellent) English translation, Landon glossed over the difficulties in reading Haydn's often nearly illegible handwriting. When I had to establish the correct readings of the originals, I often faced some difficult (occasionally rewarding) problems. An amusing example was Haydn's remark, in the first London Notebook, about the relative virtue of French, Dutch, and English ladies (supposedly originating in contemporary London gossip). Landon's version (p. 253) ends with, ". . . In England they stay proper all their lives"; Landon seems to have translated from an inaccurate (or bowdlerized) copy of the original German. But Haydn's concluding sentence reads ". . . they remain whores all their lives" ("bleibt sie allezeit hur"), an appropriately pointed conclusion to his gossipy statement.

I would like to mention two additional small matters. One is the question of ownership indications. There is no problem with public collections and libraries. But many Haydn letters are in private possession; their owners are difficult to locate, and the letters often change hands. In this respect, many indications in both current editions are already out of date. (Many changes in ownership and new discoveries are currently reported in *The Haydn Yearbook* and *Haydn-Studien*.)

The other question concerns the dividing line between letters proper and documents. I don't think that we will need a new edition of the letters in the future. What we need very badly is a documentary biography in the style established by the late Otto Erich Deutsch. I made a modest contribution toward this task by incorporating into my edition certain documents signed by Haydn which seemed important for Haydn's opera conducting activity at Eszterháza. In the strict sense of the term, they don't form part of Haydn's correspondence; but my principal aim was to

---

[41] Haydn, CCLN.   [42] In Karajan, *Haydn*.   [43] Haydn, *Briefe*.

call attention to the necessity of a comprehensive documentary biography. This important task can be achieved only by means of organized institutional teamwork, perhaps best undertaken by the Haydn Institute in Cologne.

WALTER In a Hans Schneider catalogue there is a letter from Haydn to Pleyel from 1801, unknown to Landon and Bartha.

CROLL I am planning to collect the correspondence of Michael Haydn. If anyone can help, I would be most grateful.

Contemporary Accounts, Diaries, and Journals

Discussion

BARTHA We do not need to discuss the well-known early biographies.[44] Excerpts from two contemporary diaries, of Rosenbaum and of Count Zinzendorf, have recently been published.[45]

CROLL Another edition of excerpts from Zinzendorf's diaries was published in 1973, for the Gesellschaft der Bibliophilen in Vienna. The editor, Hans Wagener, is a renowned historian. It is not for sale; to get a copy, one must ask a member of the society.

BARTHA Of course, there are many other memoirs related to Haydn. Brown's comprehensive Haydn bibliography[46] lists no fewer than thirty-five items under the heading "Anecdotes" (many of them of questionable authenticity), and ninety-one items under "Contemporary Accounts, Reminiscences, Tagebücher, etc.," among them such well-known names as Burney, Forkel, and Gerber. Pohl used many of these, but how comprehensively or critically is difficult to say. For example, he cites Framery[47] in his preface, but I don't recall substantial information on Haydn originating with Framery in Pohl's text. As you know, Alan Tyson drew important new information about the spurious piano trios Hob. XV:3 and 4 from Framery, because Pleyel, their probable author, was Framery's main source.[48] This detail illustrates once again how badly we need a comprehensive and critical documentary biography of Haydn.

The question of references to Haydn in contemporary periodicals also touches on a documentary biography. For Mozart and Schubert it was relatively easy for Deutsch to gather the limited number of newspaper

[44] Griesinger; Dies; Carpani, *Haydine.*
[45] Radant, "Rosenbaum"; Olleson, "Zinzendorf."   [46] Brown, "Bibliography."
[47] Framery, *Haydn.*   [48] Tyson, "Trios."

reports. But for Haydn, there will be a tremendous amount of material, especially in the later years. Not all of it is relevant. For example: should enthusiastic but superficial newspaper reports be included? Or might a simple bibliographical reference suffice?

GOTWALS When I was a graduate student, I discovered a number of stories about Haydn in the AmZ. I showed a few of these to Oliver Strunk, and he said, "Yes, that's very interesting, but most of it is moonshine." Perhaps such things should be included, but with a cautionary note.

BARTHA The *Pressburger Zeitung* is an important source.[49] In Haydn's time, Pressburg (now Bratislava) was an important cultural and musical center in the vicinity of Vienna. Haydn himself was in Pressburg many times.

WALTER These excerpts are not complete. At the Haydn-Institut we have abstracts from E. F. Schmid which go further.

PAUL BRYAN[50]   It is a problem for the historian when a series like that is done only partially. One can't tell what has been left out. Has the newspaper from Brno been transcribed?

WALTER No, the *Brünner Zeitung* hasn't been done. It's not as important as the *Pressburger Zeitung;* many of their dispatches were copied from Pressburg.

BARTHA Pressburg is much closer to Vienna and Eszterháza than Brünn is. Here is another example of a misleading contemporary newspaper report: When Haydn went to Buda (now part of Budapest) in 1800 to conduct *The Creation* in the royal palace there, a contemporary Hungarian newspaper reported that he would arrive from Padua! Of course, Haydn never set foot in Italy in his life. But we know that he arrived from Baden near Vienna, where he had been visiting his wife. Perhaps an oral report in Austrian dialect, in which "Baden" could have sounded like "Paden," accounts for this error.

TYSON Much of what one reads in these journalistic accounts must be "interpreted." The whole style of the reports on Haydn's London concerts was pitched in a most misleading tone. Unless you realize this—and you probably will if you read a lot of it—you'll misunderstand what took place. In other English newspaper announcements, concerts that were an absolute disaster were written up in the same enthusiastic tone. (We infer that they were disasters because the repeat concerts were canceled.) Or if a concert was canceled, often there is no announcement to explain this—unless the concert is rescheduled for a later date. But from the newspapers one would judge that concerts which had to be canceled actually took place. In these cases, the so-called documents in a documentary bi-

---

[49] See Pandi-Schmidt.   [50] From the audience.

ography need a great deal of critical explanation before they can be fully understood.

Contradictions in Haydn Biography

THOMAS I would like to describe some examples of problems in Haydn biography that arise when you check details long taken for granted in the literature. These remarks can be considered an appendix to Hoboken's lecture.[51]

Now and then one reads that after Haydn's termination as a choirboy at St. Stephen's Cathedral in Vienna, his first livelihood was playing dance music at inns and taverns. Referring to this period, Haydn himself mentioned only that he had "had to eke out a wretched existence for eight whole years by teaching young pupils". Griesinger wrote merely that Haydn "divided his whole time among the giving of lessons, the study of his art, and performing. He played for money in serenades and in the orchestras. . . ." But it was Pohl who first suggested that he played dance music—a conjecture which soon became an accepted "fact".[52]

In the *Jahrbuch der Tonkunst von Wien und Prag* for the year 1796 one reads that the musicians who played dance music in Vienna had their own guild, St. Nicolai's Brotherhood, up to 1782. And Friedrich Nicolai expressly informs us (in his report of a journey through Germany and Switzerland in the year 1781) that only members of that guild were allowed to play dance music in public. If Haydn played music for dancing, he ought to have been affiliated. The material relating to the brotherhood supposedly belongs to St. Michael's Church in Vienna, but when I looked for it there, it was said to be missing.

Now it is true that Dies wrote that Haydn composed dance-hall pieces which found much favor on account of their originality. But this too seems questionable; it may merely embellish a different anecdote of Dies's and Griesinger's (I quote the latter here):

Once when Haydn was going through the streets in Vienna with Dittersdorf, they heard some Haydn minuets being very badly played in a tavern. "We ought to have some fun with these bunglers," said one to the other. They went into the tavern, ordered a glass, and listened a while. "Who wrote these minuets anyway?" Haydn finally asked. They gave him his own name. "Ach, that's pretty miserable stuff!" he exclaimed. At this the musicians flew into such a rage that one of them would have broken his violin on Haydn's head if he had not speedily taken flight.[53]

In Dies's description, Haydn's words are even stronger. But Dies might have taken the story from Griesinger himself and embellished it. Dies ad-

[51] Hoboken, *Discrepancies*.
[52] Griesinger, 12–13 (modern ed., 11), as transl. Gotwals, *Haydn,* 11; Pohl I, 121.
[53] Gotwals, *Haydn,* 20 (Griesinger, 30; modern ed., 19–20); cf. 92–93 (Dies, 33–34; modern ed., 36–37).

mitted that he had used several articles in the *Allgemeine musikalische Zeitung,* the periodical in which Griesinger's *Biographical Notes* were first printed.

Griesinger gives no indication when the tavern episode occurred. He merely recounts the story along with several others from Haydn's earlier years. Dittersdorf's autobiography mentions friendly contacts with Haydn only at the beginning of the 1760s. As evidence of an earlier connection between the two composers, one reads that in 1755 Haydn played as a visitor in the court orchestra of the Prince of Sachsen-Hildburghausen, Dittersdorf's employer at that time. But the only source for this assertion is Griesinger. He reported that Porpora, who had given lessons in singing to the mistress of the Venetian ambassador, Pietro Correr, had gone with Correr to the baths at Mannersdorf and had taken Haydn with him. And Griesinger continued: "Here [Haydn] sometimes had to accompany on the clavier for Porpora at a Prince von Hildburghausen's, in the presence of Gluck, Wagenseil, and other celebrated masters, and the approval of such connoisseurs served as a special encouragement to him."[54] Dittersdorf is not mentioned, and the year is not given. Yet Pohl states that Correr represented his government in Vienna from March 1753 until May 1757.[55] Thus it is possible that Haydn met Dittersdorf in those years, but we have no documentary evidence.

Another example is the story about Haydn's oratorio *Il ritorno di Tobia* and the so-called Tonkünstlersozietät of Vienna. Griesinger's version is plausible:

The oratorio "Il Ritorno di Tobia" Haydn wrote in 1774 in order to be received into the Society for Musicians' Widows and Orphans in Vienna. His application was accepted upon payment of the prescribed amount; how great then was his surprise on being further informed the following day by the directors that he must also engage himself whenever requested to write cantatas, oratorios, symphonies, and the like for the Society. Prince Esterházy was so angry over this unreasonable demand that he ordered Haydn to reclaim his deposit forthwith.[56]

But Haydn's letter to the society of February 4, 1779, and the records of the society published by Pohl, demonstrate that the society did not commission the composition of "oratorios, cantatas, choruses, symphonies, etc." before January 18, 1779 (or November 18, 1778, when Haydn's petition to join was considered). And in any case this was nearly four years after the first performance of *Tobia* on April 2, 1775. It seems that Haydn's attempt to become a member of the Tonkünstlersozietät had little to do with the origin of his first oratorio—and that Griesinger confused two different events.

Perhaps the reverse should be considered with Pohl's moving story of the farewell between Haydn and Mozart before Haydn's departure for

---

[54] Ibid., 12 (Griesinger, 14; modern ed., 12).   [55] Pohl I, 171.
[56] Gotwals, *Haydn,* 18 (Griesinger, 25; modern ed., 17).

London in 1790.[57] According to Pohl, Mozart was present on the day of departure (Wednesday, December 15) as well as at a farewell dinner the day before. The story contains important quotations, above all Haydn's famous sentence "My language is understood all over the world." Pohl did not cite his sources. But it is obvious that they were Dies and Griesinger. Now Dies describes only the day of departure, December 15; whereas Griesinger reports only "a happy meal with Salomon," without giving a date! Dies writes further that on the departure day Mozart never left his friend Haydn and had "dined with him" (!); and finally Griesinger asserts that Mozart would have taken Haydn's place in Salomon's concerts in 1794 if he had not died prematurely in 1791.[58] How then did Pohl know of a farewell dinner the day before Haydn's departure, or of Salomon's and Mozart's agreement at this dinner that Mozart should come to London on similar terms after Haydn's return to Vienna? Perhaps he simply interpreted these accounts rather freely. (In the Mozart literature, one reads that Mozart was to go to London in the next winter season; this is merely a false inference from Pohl.) I fear that there was no farewell dinner at all on December 14.

In the summer of 1808 the Czech composer Wenzel Johann Tomaschek visited Haydn. In Tomaschek's memoirs we read: "A plaster bust which I saw as I entered the room prompted me to ask Haydn whom it represented. The poor man, bursting into tears, moaned more than spoke: 'My best friend, the sculptor Fischer. Oh! why dost Thou not take me to Thee!' "[59] A person whom Haydn called his best friend is worthy of our interest. But it cannot have been the then famous Viennese sculptor Johann Martin Fischer, who did not die until 1820. More probably it was the sculptor Anton Grassi, well known to us for his busts of Haydn. Since Grassi died on December 31, 1807, Haydn's exclamation "Warum nimmst mich nicht zu Dir!" can readily be understood. Now there is no bust of Grassi cited in Haydn's *Nachlass;* only a bust of Haydn by Grassi. And it is hard to imagine that Tomaschek could have asked about a bust of Haydn himself. Nevertheless, it was Grassi who introduced Dies to Haydn. Dies mentions Grassi's "long-standing acquaintance" with the composer. And Griesinger writes that Haydn took Grassi's death very hard, and he too refers to Grassi as Haydn's friend. So we may safely assume that "Haydn's best friend" was not the "Bildhauer Fischer" but Anton Grassi.

From these examples it is clear that there still remain many problems to solve before we can achieve a documentary biography of Haydn worthy of the name.

[57] Pohl II, 250–51.
[58] Gotwals, *Haydn,* 22–23 (Griesinger, 35–36; modern ed., 22); 119–21 (Dies, 75–77; modern ed., 78–80).
[59] Tomaschek, "Memoirs," 246 (Pohl-Botstiber, 260).

Remarks on Iconography

SOMFAI I think that the era of a single person doing meritorious scholarly work on a complex topic like Haydn iconography is over. I was glad to do what I could.[60] But the situation has completely changed. We have the Haydn-Institut in Cologne. Although their main task is to publish Haydn's music, their knowledge and documentation on Haydn-related areas is more extensive than that of any other institution or individual. Furthermore, we finally have the *Répertoire international d'iconographie musicale,* a new international effort to collect iconography on music. There is now a center where all new data can be collected, and where interested scholars can study it.

No existing iconography has anything to do with social history in the eighteenth century, which is part of the background to Haydn's life and music. This will require collaboration between specialists in other areas and music historians. But two areas of iconography are left for us. One is strict, scholarly iconographic documentation, as was done by Deutsch for Mozart. This is what must be undertaken by an institution. The other one, which will require a specialist in iconography, is the study of Haydn's physical appearance, that is, a comparative study of Haydn's physiognomy.

The criticism I received from Professor Larsen was very constructive.[61] It pointed out that in London, as in every great city of that time, there were markedly manneristic tendencies in the execution of portraits. It used to be said that Haydn's favorite portrait was the Dance drawing, and that therefore we should like it in the same way. But when one sees many Dance portraits, as in the Portrait Gallery in London, one realizes that he had a certain style, and an established technique, which he applied to each of his sitters. It may be realistic as far as the line goes, but not beyond that. So, we do need more help from specialists. Our whole meeting today indicates that one-man biographical work is a thing of the past. We must have an institutionally researched biography.

Existing Lacunae in the Publication of Haydn Documents

BROWN Unfortunately, the many contributions to Haydn documentation that have been mentioned here do not signify that control and retrieval of all relevant Haydn materials have been attained. Indeed, in some areas of utmost importance to our understanding of Haydn biography, we have ·today little more than the material that Pohl collected more than a century ago. As mentioned, perhaps the most baffling period of Haydn's life is the decade following his dismissal from St. Stephen's before his official

---

[60] Somfai, *Bilder.*   [61] Larsen, "Bildnisse."

association with the Esterházy family: unless some new cache of material is discovered, only speculation seems in order. Yet for other periods there are a number of extant documents which, if made more accessible through publication, could have a significant effect on Haydn biography.

First, a high priority should be given to the inventories of the musicalia owned by the Esterházy family and those of Haydn's musical library and other personal possessions. The publication of the former—that is, Hummel's inventory of 1809, the Zagitz catalogue dating from the mid-nineteenth century, and Leopold Nowak's list of musical materials remaining in Eisenstadt after the war and presumably still housed today in the castle archives—would provide new and valuable direction in defining the repertoires of chamber and church music with which Haydn was familiar. Concerning the latter, there are two as yet unpublished inventories prepared by Haydn himself or under his supervision: a holograph catalogue of librettos—now owned by the Wiener Stadtbibliothek and as late as 1973 on exhibition in the Vienna Haydnhaus—and the so-called *Haydn-Bibliothek-Verzeichnis* in the hand of Johann Elssler—owned by the British Library.[62] Also unpublished are Haydn's *Nachlass-Verzeichnis*, consisting of lists of *Musicalia* and *Kupferstiche*—prepared by Schatzmeister Sauer—and non-music books and household effects, which are contained with other records of Haydn's official transactions with the city of Vienna in a single folder in the Archiv der Stadt Wien.[63] It is surprising that these repositories of information have not yet played a more central role in biographical and stylistic studies, as they shed important light on the music Haydn personally owned and his preferences in literature. A critical edition of these sources would perhaps be of greatest use if presented with a complete description of each item that has survived from Haydn's estate.

Second, of great utility for our work are the early published references found in contemporary newspapers, periodicals, reminiscences, and *Reisebücher*. Although the documents for the London years and relevant notices from the *Pressburger Zeitung* have been republished,[64] some of the most important reviews, announcements, and news items remain to be collected from the *Allgemeine musikalische Zeitung* (Leipzig), *Allgemeine musikalische Zeitung* (Vienna), *Musikalische Korrespondenz der Teutschen Filharmonischen Gesellschaft,* and the *Wienerisches Diarium/Wiener Zeitung*. This task is not insurmountable: the three music journals have their own indices, and the *Wienerisches Diarium/Wiener Zeitung* can be accessed by the Portheim files in the Wiener Stadtbibliothek.

More difficult to collect, because of poor bibliographic control, is a third category of documents: unpublished materials such as diaries and

---

[62] Haydn, "Librettos"; Haydn, HBV.   [63] Haydn, HNV.
[64] R. Landon, *Symphonies,* Ch. XII; Pandi-Schmidt.

correspondence of those who knew Haydn or observed firsthand the man and his music. The publication of excerpts from the Griesinger correspondence[65] and the *Tagebücher* of Rosenbaum and Zinzendorf[66] has provided revealing, if at times parochial, observations. Fortunately, further such material relevant for Haydn research may come to light in the publications of the *Wiener Bibliophilen Gesellschaft,* the *Kommission für neuere Geschichte Österreichs,* and the *Institut für österreichische Kulturgeschichte.* Although perfect bibliographic control of this type of material may be an unattainable goal for the near future, in the meantime, archivists and librarians should be encouraged to provide us with catalogues organized not only by author, title, and subject, but also by place and date.

A fourth group of materials that should be evaluated and selectively republished is the flood of prose—bibliographic and at times memorial in tone—that appeared in 1809 or shortly thereafter. Special consideration should be accorded to that which emanated from Haydn's students themselves or sources close to them. Of primary need is a modern annotated edition of Carpani's biographical letters; for however we may question his facts and disparage his fictionalizations, one cannot deny that *Le Haydine* contains some astute aesthetic observations on the music itself.

The ideal situation, of course, would be a comprehensive collection, between two or more covers, of documents—such as I have described—in chronological order with judicious annotations, as Deutsch has provided for Handel, Mozart, and Schubert. However, Mozart, Schubert, and even Handel had a definable audience, whereas Haydn's audience encompassed all of Europe by the 1780s and was further expanded by the two London visits. Thus, Haydn scholars are confronted with a problem of control which is both multinational and multifaceted in scope.

Accepting the fact that such documentary control could possibly be achieved, I would like to touch upon a few aspects which perhaps deserve consideration. First, students of the period known as Viennese Classicism must be encouraged to deal with not only the more than a hundred virtually unexplored *Kleinmeister,* but also the history of musical institutions and musical history of nonmusical institutions. From this type of activity, pieces of the Haydn puzzle will come to light and perhaps eventually fit together. For example, incidentally to his history of music at Melk Abbey, Robert N. Freeman was able to isolate when Robert Kimmerling studied with Haydn (c. 1760).[67] This finding in turn adds credence to the theory that Haydn may have had a period of unemployment between his dismissal by Morzin and his engagement by Esterházy. Other examples can also be cited: the discovery of Haydn's in-

[65] Thomas, "Griesinger."   [66] Radant, "Rosenbaum"; Olleson, "Zinzendorf."
[67] Freeman, "Melk."

terest in Christoph Sonnleithner's music,[68] and a new document found by Christa Landon in the course of her Schubert research.[69]

More emphasis also needs to be placed on communication with students of cultural, theatrical, legal, political, and intellectual history, as well as journalism and bibliography, so that we become aware of not only new facts but also new possible avenues of investigation.

Third, the scope for the selection and presentation of the documents themselves must be broad enough to prevent the exclusion of valuable material and to make collation possible. For example, the policy adopted by Valkó for publication of the Budapest documents[70]—i.e., that Haydn's signature or name must be present—surely resulted in the exclusion of pertinent data. Even though Harich adopted a more comprehensive scope,[71] a collocation of these two publications of documents would not necessarily result in a complete set of the Esterházy materials relevant to Haydn.

And lastly, we must carefully evaluate both newly discovered and already known documents with the same scrutiny that scholarly editions of the music require. For just as the identification of authentic works and sources has been a central problem to those editing Haydn's music, compilers of the documents will be haunted by the plagiarism and unacknowledged parody practiced by not only critics and journalists, but also those who reminisced for their own amusement about the leading contemporary musical personage of the era.

---

[68] Wurzbach, Lexikon, s.v. Sonnleithner.   [69] C. Landon, "Dokument."
[70] Valkó I–II.   [71] Hárich, "Repertoire"; Hárich, "Dokumenta."

Round Table

Source Problems, Authenticity and Chronology, List of Works

GEORG FEDER, *Chairman*	LÁSZLÓ SOMFAI
IRMGARD BECKER-GLAUCH	ALAN TYSON
SONJA GERLACH	JAMES WEBSTER
EUGENE HELM	ELLWOOD DERR,
JAN LA RUE	*Secretary*

Introductory Statement

FEDER Our discussion will be divided into three sections.

Authenticity: by far the greater part of what is generally performed as Haydn's music needs no discussion. On the other hand, there are many works falsely ascribed to Haydn, but most of them are not generally known. Between these extremes lie many works which have been proved neither authentic nor spurious. These are labeled doubtful. Some of them are often performed. It is especially with respect to the doubtful works that we will discuss the different kinds and degrees of evidence.

There are two ways to approach these questions. The first method is to examine the external evidence offered by the different kinds of documents that more or less convincingly attribute a work to Joseph Haydn. While this method is generally agreed to be the fundamental one, the second is problematic. It consists in the attempt to use musical criteria. They are normally called stylistic, but they may be aesthetic criteria as well.

Related versions of the same work: some of Haydn's early works are lost. But a lost work may have been preserved in disguise; for instance, in an arrangement for other instruments, or in a so-called parody, in which a sacred text is substituted in a piece that was originally secular. The methods of research applied to such cases will be shown by examples.

Chronology: there are about 250 autograph manuscripts by Haydn. The greater part of these are dated with the year of composition. But there are more than 1,000 works and arrangements preserved only in mostly undated manuscript copies or in generally undated early editions. There does not yet exist a chronological list of Haydn's works like those by Köchel, Einstein, and others for Mozart. Anthony van Hoboken's Haydn catalogue is a systematic one ordered according to genres: first the symphonies, then the divertimenti, and so forth. In some of the groups the single works are listed in a rough chronological order, in others they are not. Many of Haydn's works still lack a precise dating.

To summarize: The questions of authenticity and chronology are of primary importance to a Haydn worklist. They are most important for the comprehensive edition of Haydn's works, too. Previous research has not yet solved all these problems.

Authenticity

External Criteria for Determining the Authenticity of Haydn's Music

WEBSTER The problem of authenticity has long been the most important issue in Haydn scholarship.[1] The reason is simple: there are nearly as many doubtful and spurious works attributed to Haydn as there are genuine ones. Indeed in many important genres, including the symphonies, string trios, string quartets, ensemble divertimenti, and Masses, there are many more nonauthentic works than authentic ones. In this situation, how do we establish the canon of Haydn's music?

Any work attributed to Joseph Haydn makes a claim: "Haydn wrote me." An authentic work is a genuine work; that is, a work for which this claim is true. The work is what it is represented to be—a composition by Joseph Haydn.

We identify authentic works on the basis of authentic sources. These two terms are not identical. An authentic or genuine work is one that Haydn did, in fact, compose. The opposite of an authentic work is a spurious work—one that he did not compose (but which is attributed to him). An authentic source is a musical source or document which derives from Haydn himself. Its opposite is simply a nonauthentic source—one not deriving directly from Haydn. An authentic source is thus a witness; it testifies that the work it transmits or documents is genuine. Such works are said to be authenticated.

We must distinguish between direct and indirect authentication. Direct authentication is provided by Haydn's own handwriting or unambiguous documentary testimony. Four types of sources fall into this category. First, we have Haydn's autograph manuscripts, nearly always signed and dated with the year of composition.[2] Second, we have two

---

[1] See Larsen, HÜb; R. Landon, *Symphonies,* Ch. I–II; Geiringer, *Haydn* 2, 2d ed., 213–22; JHW, *passim.*

[2] *Larsen,* HÜb, Ch. II; Hoboken, *passim;* Geiringer, *Haydn* 2, 2d ed., 401–06; Feder, "Überlieferung."

thematic catalogues that Haydn made or instigated.[3] The earlier of these, the so-called *Entwurf-Katalog* or EK, is relatively complete only for the main genres and the baryton pieces, and only until 1775 or so (through the 1780s for the symphonies). On the other hand, with perhaps a single exception, EK is absolutely reliable.[4] The *Haydn-Verzeichnis* or HV, compiled by Haydn's amanuensis Johann Elssler toward the end of the composer's life, is far more comprehensive than EK, but it is not wholly trustworthy. Third, we have manuscript and printed sources which Haydn signed or otherwise approved in his own hand, for example by altering or supplementing the musical text. Finally, many works are directly authenticated by autograph letters, or by other documents such as those in the Esterházy archives.[5]

A second class of sources is indirectly authenticated. Most important here are the numerous authentic manuscript copies written by persons other than Haydn.[6] These copies are presumed to be authentic—kindly note the qualification—because of features which imply that they were written under Haydn's supervision or, at least, with his approval. Such manuscripts include those written by Elssler or by Haydn's other colleagues at the Esterházy court; those whose paper was produced at the private Esterházy paper mill; and those whose provenance testifies to their authenticity. In addition to manuscripts in the Esterházy archives and Haydn's effects at his death, the latter group includes other collections. One example is the so-called Fürnberg manuscripts, some of which bear the *ex libris* of the son of the man who, in Haydn's own accounts, commissioned his earliest string quartets.[7] The status of these authenticating criteria depends on their prior identification in directly authenticated sources. Once established, however, these criteria are then customarily accepted as independent guarantors of authenticity in their own right.

Printed editions are most often authenticated by correspondence, contracts and business records, and the like.[8] One must distinguish carefully between authentic prints—those engraved from sources supplied by Haydn; that is, from authentic sources—and mere authorized prints, which Haydn may have approved in one fashion or another, but in whose production he played no direct part. Examples of the latter are Artaria's late (1800–01) edition of the string quartets Op. 20, as well as

---

[3] Larsen, HÜb, Ch. VI–VII; Larsen, DHK.

[4] The exception is the *Missa Rorate coeli desuper* (Hob. XXII:3); cf. R. Landon, "Haydniana," 199–200; Becker-Glauch, "Kirchenmusik," 172; and the discussion in *Kongress Graz:1970*, 84–85.

[5] For the letters, see Haydn, *Briefe* and Haydn, CCLN. Extensive publications from the Esterházy archives can be found in Valkó I–II; Bartha-Somfai; and all the publications by Hárich cited in the worklist.

[6] Larsen, HÜb, Ch. III; Feder, "Überlieferung"; JHW, *passim*.

[7] See Pohl, I, 180–84; Feder, "Überlieferung," 16–17; Webster, "Chronology," 36–37.

[8] Larsen, HÜb, Ch. IV; Pohl, II, 32–35, 169ff.; Hoboken, *passim*.

collected editions like Breitkopf & Härtel's *Oeuvres Complettes* and Pleyel's eighty-three string quartets. The latter two collections, in fact, contain nonauthentic works.[9]

Indirectly authenticated sources fade off imperceptibly into the so-called good sources. These comprise manuscripts and prints which are similar to the best secondary (nonauthentic) sources for authentic works. The two most important categories of "good" sources are 1) early, Viennese and Austrian manuscripts and catalogue entries of the sort which exist for early genuine works; and 2) printed editions from Vienna after 1780, and from London in the first half of the 1790s, that is, originating when and where Haydn could have exercised some kind of control over them. It is necessary to emphasize that as unsupported evidence for authenticity, "good" sources are insufficient.

The thousands of mediocre and poor sources (late or peripheral manuscripts, North and West European prints, and so forth) are worthless as witnesses for authenticity. Works transmitted only in sources of this kind do not ordinarily concern us further.

How do we identify all the authentic works, and only those? If we accept authenticated works only, we guarantee ourselves "Haydn, and nothing but Haydn," but we will almost certainly fail to obtain "the whole Haydn." Each type of authentic source testifies only to a fraction of the entire body of authenticated works. It is therefore almost certain that some genuine works, especially from the early years and in the "occasional" genres, have not survived in any authentic sources. These works cannot be authenticated today. If, on the other hand, we accept any work attributed to Haydn whenever it suits us, we may hope to acquire "the whole Haydn," but at the certain cost of including a good deal that is not Haydn at all. No evaluation of "good" sources and no critical analysis of style is an infallible means of determining authenticity. In cases like the Ordoñez symphony Hob. I:A6 and the Albrechtsberger string quartet Hob. III:D3, even sophisticated postwar scholars at first attributed spurious music to Haydn.[10]

In principle, neither genuine works (those which have been authenticated) nor spurious works (those which have been authenticated for other composers) present any problem. But the remaining works attributed to Haydn, some 1,000 of them, are "doubtful"—they have not been authenticated for any composer. To determine which of these

[9]Larsen, HÜb, 138–51, 292–93. Pleyel's inclusion of the spurious "Opus 3" [cf. the Round Table below—Ed.] is only the most egregious error perpetrated by these editions. On Op. 20, see JHW XII:3, critical report, 28–29.

[10]See R. Landon, "Authenticity," 31–36; Feder, "Streichquartette," 135–36. On the general issue, see Larsen, "Echtheitsbestimmung." The extent to which Hoboken, vol. 1, is unreliable on doubtful works is still not appreciated outside the domain of technical Haydn scholarship.

works might be genuine, two principles apply. First, a given piece must be transmitted in "good" sources. But not any "good" sources will do; they should be as similar as possible—in provenance, character, and textual integrity—to the best secondary sources for the authentic works in the same genre from the same period.[11] Second, as soon as a source with a conflicting attribution turns up, any work must be critically reevaluated. This criterion corresponds to our expectation that, in case of doubt or fraud, Haydn's name will normally have been substituted for that of the true author, not the other way around. And in fact, while "plausible" works are continually being authenticated for Michael Haydn, Albrechtsberger, Ordoñez, Vanhal, and so forth, few sources for authentic works bear attributions to other composers. On the other hand we must distinguish between an authentic source for another composer, like Albrechtsberger's autograph to Hob. III:D3, and an ordinary source. The former makes the work spurious (as far as Haydn research is concerned); the latter, strictly speaking, does not remove the work from the "doubtful" category.

A work attributed to Haydn which passes both of these tests is still technically "doubtful," but naturally we will be very interested in it. It will not hurt to call these works transmitted in appropriate "good" sources without conflicting attributions "plausible," to distinguish them from the very much more numerous ordinary "doubtful" ones.

Discussion

LA RUE Aren't there three "doubtful" categories—plausible, uncertain, unlikely?[12]

FEDER If you have to make a catalogue, and especially if you have to make a collected edition, it is difficult to apply so many categories. Printed music is black notes on white paper, not different shades of gray.

TYSON What is the purpose of trying to divide the "doubtful" category after it has been settled by definition? This simply leads to a new set of dilemmas. It is as if you were a sentry, and the password is a kind of cheese, and today it is "Emmenthal." Now supposing somebody says "Gruyère." Do you let him pass? He seems to know the password, but he's a bit wrong.

[11] The dozen or so MSS for the Albrechtsberger quartet Hob. III:D3 seem impressive at first glance, but they compare unfavorably with the average of forty sources for the authentic early quartets (see JHW XII:1, critical report, 9). On the other hand, the authentic windband divertimenti have fewer than half a dozen extant sources apiece, and several divertimenti authenticated by EK are lost. Hence, evaluation of "good" sources may vary markedly, depending on the type of work in question.

[12] Compare the similar categories in Larsen, HÜb, 15. [Ed.]

WEBSTER But we must nevertheless make some kind of distinction between the mass of ordinary doubtful works and those which may be genuine—for example, those which we may wish to include in a complete edition.

TYSON But isn't this simply the distinction between better supported works and worse supported? Once you say "plausible," you must make the decision, is this work "plausible" or not? Yes or no? The distinctions become blurred.

HELM I don't think music behaves that way. There's a big difference between "plausible" and "very doubtful"—it's like comparing Limburger with Cheddar.

FEDER If we include within a given genre those works which seem to be plausible, we may err in one or two cases, but we may succeed in giving a complete idea of that genre. On the other hand, if we exclude all the plausible works, this will limit the number of Haydn's works in some early genres considerably.

WEBSTER Supposing that a complete edition does include some plausible works, should they be put in an appendix? Should they have a footnote saying that the authenticity of this work is not certain? Should there be merely a remark in the foreword?

FEDER Previous attempts at establishing lists of Haydn's works, for example in the genre of keyboard concertos, started from the fully authenticated works, but also included the plausible ones. This has also been the procedure of JHW. But there are various degrees of authentication, and there is often some kind of interpretation inherent in evaluating sources. Dr. Tyson determined that, although a manuscript copy of the Piano Trios Hob. XV:3 and 4 is signed by Haydn, they are more probably by Pleyel. Or take the unsigned autograph of the song *Trust Not Too Much* (Hob. XXXIc:17). Is it a composition by Haydn, or is it a copy of a composition by another composer, or is it an arrangement (as Hoboken believes)? The interpretation starts right with the autograph. The same is true of some "insertion arias" Haydn supplied for other composers' operas, for example the textless aria Hob. XXIVb:4.

SOMFAI There were four stages of the composition of this aria: 1) Haydn wrote the two violins directly in parts (lost); 2) he had Schellinger copy the two parts in score and filled in the other parts; 3) his copyists copied the parts of these instruments; 4) Haydn made cuts in the score and in the parts (new violin parts by Schellinger).

Though the dated manuscripts are unsigned and the score lacks the words for the singer, there is no doubt of its authenticity.

PAUL BRYAN[13]   Is there no question at all about this aria? If it is not signed, is it conceivable that it might have been by someone else and that Haydn copied it down some way?

FEDER   It's a matter of interpretation, and if you studied the same material, you would possibly come to a different conclusion.

[At the request of the chairman, Helm made comparative remarks about his Carl Philipp Emanuel Bach research in respect to authentication.]

LA RUE   I've been concerned with stylistic authentication for a number of years and have felt extremely frustrated by it. Whenever I think I have found something characteristic of Haydn, then I find it in Galuppi, perhaps. At any rate, any single thing that you look at seems to be a very poor way to authenticate a work by Haydn or anybody else. So we must find ways of correlating and coordinating observations. We must look at melodies, rhythm, harmonies together in order to find anything powerful enough to solve these difficult questions.

One solution is what I call "activity analysis." Melody and harmony and rhythm are all concerned with the activity of the music. If in some way we can represent this activity, we can pull these three things together. The method I am using to represent the activity is to assign a rather simple number system to it, and I can then at any moment in the piece, but particularly on a particular beat or bar, make a quantification. In the Round Table on "Op. 3," I will illustrate with a short activity analysis.

FEDER   There is a common opinion opposing all kinds of stylistic analysis. In this view, no correspondence proves much, because we don't know the work of Haydn's contemporaries. It is true that one can never be certain that the same features do not occur in works by a contemporary composer, because it is virtually impossible to know them all. I think it would help if those who oppose stylistic arguments in favor of an attribution would demonstrate that the features which are claimed for Haydn actually appear in other composers.

LA RUE   "Activity analysis" is an attempt to identify the metabolic rate of a composer. It yields what I call a "beat ecology"; each beat in the composition has a certain amount of activity in it, and the variation is enormous. Each composer has a different kind of ecology.

BARRY S. BROOK[14]   What this method can do is to provide negative evidence to begin with. It may demonstrate that a given piece could not be by

---

[13] From the audience.   [14] From the audience.

Haydn. Later, when you amass profiles of hundreds of composers, you will be able to operate more positively.

BRYAN There remains always the problem of chronology. If we are relating something by Haydn to something by Vanhal, there is the difficulty that you can't date the Vanhal.

FEDER Professor LaRue, do you think that qualitative features are at all valuable?

LA RUE My method is sheerly quantitative. The qualitative approach is the most subtle; it requires the most experience, judgment, musicality; it is the most open to criticism, to disagreement. I want to see if by this simpler and less sophisticated method of quantitative approach some useful results can be produced.

Related Versions of the Same Work

Remarks on Versions and Arrangements

SOMFAI There are at least three kinds of different versions of the same work in Haydn's music.

1. Truly independent versions (*Werkfassungen*), using the same composition for a work in a different genre. Examples are Haydn's using the orchestral version of the *Seven Last Words* for the oratorio versions, or a movement from the lyre concerto Hob. VIIh:3 for the slow movement in the "Military" Symphony.
2. Arrangements in a different scoring (rather than substantially new versions), for example, the string quartet version of the *Seven Last Words*.
3. The same work preserved in two states of composition, for example, (a) when there are additional trumpets and drum parts; (b) when Haydn later added essentially new performance marks, as in the C-minor Sonata Hob. XVI:20 (ChL. 33).

Particularly interesting are Haydn's unsigned (but authentic) rearrangements of arias by other composers, made for performances he conducted. They exhibit five different procedures:

1. Haydn allowed the other composer's first section to stand and substituted his own new second section. Both versions should be printed in a complete edition.
2. Haydn added wind parts or rewrote the first violin or did something similar. These arias, too, should be included in a complete edition, with

the new first violin part perhaps printed as an *ossia* above the original violin part.

3. Haydn cut sections of arias. I think these should also be printed in their complete form, using "Vi–de" signs to indicate what Haydn found superfluous.

4. Haydn extended and/or embellished the singer's part by writing new coloratura sections. A complete edition should print both versions in *ossia* format.

5. Haydn made such substantial changes in other composers' arias that it was necessary for him to write new scores. A complete edition should print both versions.

The Apparently Authentic Version of the *Motetto de Sancta Thecla* (Hob. XXXIIIa:4)

BECKER-GLAUCH   Among the manuscripts belonging to the cathedral of St. Martin in Eisenstadt are the parts of an unpublished *Motetto de Sancta Thecla . . . del Sigre Giuseppe Haydn.* The end of the "Violone" part is signed by Haydn himself. Therefore this work is undoubtedly authentic.

According to the title, the work is composed for soprano solo, four-part choir, strings, and organ. The composition consists of a secco recitative, followed by a coloratura da capo aria, and finally a chorus. Thus, the so-called *Motetto* is in fact a small cantata.

First, I should like to give a short summary of the Latin text. The recitative "Quis stellae radius" praises the splendor of the star which gladdens the pious heart. In free translation the contents of the aria "Aurora ridet post atra nubila" are as follows: "Aurora, the goddess of dawn, is smiling after dusky clouds have gone. The monsters of the lower regions still are grudging. Do not be afraid of these threats, since God stands up for you." Later it says: "The pure spirit is rising when grief calms down." The closing chorus proclaims the praises of virtue.

We see that the text is not a sacred one. Instead of the St. Thecla named in the title, the allegorical figures Aurora and the "averni monstra" are cited. Therefore, the text is secular. Yet it does not show its originally secular form completely, because there are some sacred details, such as the word "Deus" in its singular form; this is unusual in an allegorical context.

Examination of surviving manuscript parts demonstrates that:

1. there is no part labeled "Organo";

2. the part labeled "Basso" was written by an Esterházy copyist and is apparently the original harpsichord part of the secular cantata;

3. in the recitative this "Basso" part contains figures and the soprano solo part with the apparently original text;

4. all the instrumental parts are original;
5. the vocal parts were recopied with the extant text—the original vocal parts are lost;
6. the original text of the recitative is identical to that of the later soprano part.

The text of the aria is preserved in the soprano part. It consists of two verses. The words of the second verse seem to be mostly original:

> Cor pergit amare perfecto amore,
> Mens sobria surgit sedato maerore.
> Non sentit dolores zelosus ardor,
> Qui escit in Deo nunc castus amor.

On the other hand, the text of the first verse, with only three lines instead of four, seems to have been altered considerably:

> Aurora ridet post atra nubila.
> Fremant iam licet averni monstra,
> Non cura has minas, stat Deus pro te.

In comparison with the second verse the first one is a clumsy poem with an uneven meter and without rhyme. Moreover, in the text underlay there are senseless repetitions. For example, after the words "Si Deus stat pro te" (Since God stands up for you) there is a small interlude, after which only the word "ridet" (smiles) follows. Another blunder is the false musical accentuation of the word "Deus" by an ascending sixth. Thus, it is obvious that the first verse cannot be the original text.

The same must be said of the text of the chorus:

> Sic virtus coronatur lauro decora,
> Encomium laudis est corona.

Moreover, in the composition this curious text often shows parlando-like repeated notes (see Example 1). But if we omit some of the eighth notes, it is possible to reconstruct the same poetic meter as it is presented in the second verse of the aria. This meter occurs in some sacred versions of the same composition outside of Eisenstadt (see Example 2). Perhaps the first verse of the aria and of the chorus are preserved somewhere in fragments.

Example 1

Allegro

Sic vir - tus co - ro - na - tur lau - ro de - co - ra

Example 2

Allegro

Tri - um - phum can - te - mus in ju - bi - lo

On the basis of some details with which I will not bother you, I dated Haydn's cantata at "1762 at the latest."[15] But for what occasion did he compose the cantata? The fundamental idea of the text is that immediately after sad events there follows a solemn occasion which is to be celebrated. Such contrasting events happened in the Esterházy family within the spring of 1762. Prince Paul Anton died on March 18; on April 24, his and Prince Nikolaus's mother Maria Octavia died. The entry of Prince Nikolaus Esterházy into Eisenstadt took place on May 17, 1762. I would suggest that Haydn composed this cantata for that important occasion.

The Reconstructed Original Version of Haydn's Baryton Trio Hob. XI:2

GERLACH How to trace a lost version of a work may be demonstrated by Haydn's baryton trio Hob. XI:2. (An overview of the many different versions of this work and their relationships is given in Table 1.) Hoboken lists two different versions: No. 2 and No.2[bis]. No. 2 is a four-movement version in A major, consisting of a set of variations, a slow movement, minuet, and finale. It must be considered as authentic, judging by the sources, though the use of four movements is a bit odd, since all the other trios—except Nos. 1 and 97—consist of only three movements.

No.2[bis] is listed by Hoboken as a three-movement version in G major, scored for cello instead of baryton. Its first movement is the slow one of No. 2, which was clearly originally a middle movement, since its key is the subdominant; the second movement is an otherwise unknown tempo di menuet which is a typical finale; the third movement consists of the variations of No. 2, plus one more variation. This order of the movements is apparently wrong, and therefore this second version is a spurious arrangement. But the music of the unknown tempo di menuet and the additional variation in 2[bis] may well have been composed by Haydn.

Bearing this in mind, another arrangement in D major, using the flute instead of the baryton, gains our interest, though it has survived only in one manuscript copy. It consists of the three movements of No. 2[bis], but in the more reasonable order: variations, slow movement, tempo di menuet. The existing sources of the cello arrangement show no trace of dependence on the flute arrangement, nor the reverse. Therefore, the most likely origin of No. 2[bis] was neither the cello nor the flute arrangement, but an unknown ancestor of both. If the ancestor was an authentic version, it was most probably in the key of A major and scored for baryton, as in the authentic version of No. 2.

[15] Cf. Becker-Glauch, "Kirchenmusik," 179–80.

Table 1   The Versions of Haydn's Baryton Trio Hob. XI:2 and XI:2[bis]

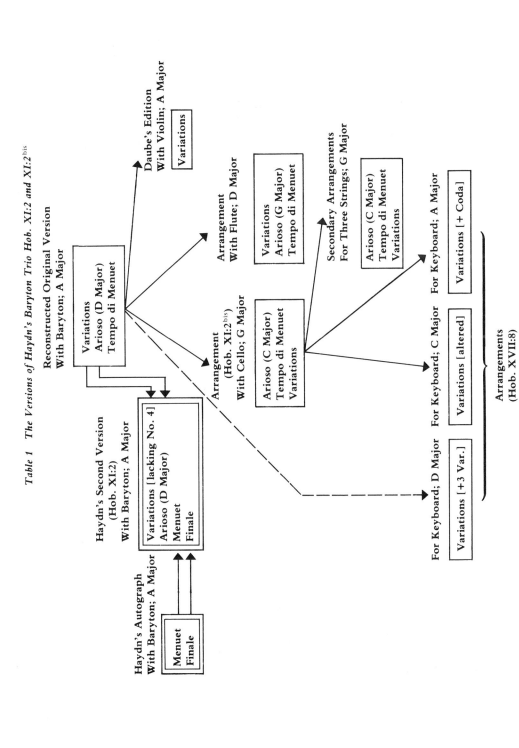

There is a hint that such an A-major version did indeed exist, since Johann Friedrich Daube printed the variations in A major in 1770.[16] The variations correspond exactly to the authentic No. 2 version, but contain the additional variation of No. 2bis.

Another hint is provided by comparing the other early baryton trios. In examining their sources one finds family trees similar to that of No. 2bis, descending from a cello arrangement and a flute arrangement, each independent of one another, and each coming directly from the original baryton version, if extant. This is quite clear in the case of No. 6, where there are about a dozen sources, of which one transmits the original version with baryton.

To what extent the analogy to the other trios is convincing can be judged by the following:

1. All extant cello arrangements from the baryton trios Nos. 1–6 (Nos. 1, 2bis, 3, 4, and 6; No. 5 is a secondary G major descendant scored for two violins and bass) are transposed to G major.

2. None of the surviving arrangements from Nos. 7–12 (Nos. 7–11 survive) is transposed.

3. All extant flute arrangements (which are apparently independent of the cello arrangements) are in D major; the ones from Nos. 1–6 (Nos. 1, 2bis, 3, and 6) are scored for violin in the second voice.

4. All flute arrangements from Nos. 7–12 (Nos. 7, 9, and 11 survive) require the viola in the second voice.

This distinct grouping is even more remarkable since the extant sources do not show any grouping of this kind. Most of them are single copies, and if there are collections, they assemble various pieces.

Therefore, the chances are that the cello arrangements as well as the flute arrangements are primary arrangements, both made from the original baryton trios at a time when they were still assembled in their original orders of Nos. 1–6 and 7–12. (This order is confirmed by Haydn in EK.) If that is true, among them there was No. 2bis or, more exactly, the unknown original A-major version of No. 2bis, which is the ancestor of the extant arrangements.

Under these circumstances, one wonders why there are two authentic versions of a single trio: No. 2 and the A-major ancestor of No. 2bis. The latter must have been Haydn's first version. After it had slipped out of his hands together with the other trios from Nos. 1–6, Haydn replaced the tempo di menuet by the menuet and finale of No. 2 and canceled the additional 2bis variation. (These changes may have been requested by the princely baryton player. We know from Haydn's letter of December 1766 that there were indeed some trios altered at the Prince's request.)

---

[16] Daube, *Dillettant* I, 69–72. On these sources, see JHW XIV:1, critical report.

Moreover, Haydn's autograph of the menuet and finale of No. 2 clearly shows that these movements were composed separately, for the autograph begins with some final bars of another work, following which the menuet begins with the designation "menuet of the second divertimento."

Since two new movements take the place of one tempo di menuet, the first movement of the original 2bis version would have sufficed to complete a three-movement trio. But our sources contain its first and second movements, and that is why the new version No. 2 contains the unusual number of four movements.

Finally, there is a surprising conclusion referring to the keyboard variations Hob. XVII:8. The three independent sources cited by Hoboken are in fact three different compositions; all three of them are based upon the variations of the baryton trio No. 2bis. Stylistic aspects, as well as the fact that there is only one source known for each of the keyboard arrangements, suggest that none of them has anything to do with Haydn. Two of them show evidence of being secondary descendants from Hob. XI:2bis, because they preserve a characteristic mistake found in the cello arrangement of the baryton trio. Therefore Hoboken's number XVII:8 should be canceled.

Chronology

Remarks on the Importance of Accurate Datings

TYSON Why is the subject of chronology of importance to us? Far beyond anything else we are interested in the chronology of the music itself—the date at which each piece was composed. And that is largely because we recognize that, so long as chronological inaccuracy or uncertainty prevails in regard to the dates of composition, our notions of any composer's stylistic changes and aesthetic development are likely to be blurred. After all, our views of Haydn's aims, resources, and attainments as a symphonist can only be more confused if (for example) we insist on believing that Symphony No. 72 was written at the same time as Symphonies No. 71 and 73 rather than some fifteen or more years earlier. So we are grateful for any help that we can get in determining the composition date of a piece of music.

The catalogues of his works made by Haydn himself or under his supervision provide one obvious source of help here, though not necessarily an easy one to use. Another source is Haydn's correspondence. A third kind of help, the one that most people will think of first, is afforded by the autograph scores. After 1760 Haydn usually, though not invariably, wrote a date on these, and we believe that in general he did so when he started or finished the score, and not at a later time. For obvious reasons the date of the autograph, and the date *on* the autograph, is taken to be the same as the date of composition; so that in most cases, where the autograph has survived, we have a composition date provided by Haydn himself. Methods have also been devised for determining the dates of those autographs which the composer neglected to date, or which are only fragmentary and have lost the information provided by the composer.

Next, we are likely to be interested in the date at which a work was first performed. This of course gives us a *terminus ante quem* for the work's composition date; but it may also tell us something about the composer's relations with his patron, his fellow-musicians, his supporters or natural audience, and the wider public.

Our interest in the dates of nonautograph manuscript sources is of various kinds. Where the autograph is absent they may be our only sources; determining their dates may therefore provide a *terminus ante quem* for the composition date. But more probably, a precise estimate of the dates of manuscripts is of help in predicting their probable textual worth, especially in relationship to other, similar manuscripts. This is no doubt an area in which watermarks could be especially useful.

Finally there are the published editions. Why should we want to date these precisely? Again, in some cases the first printings may provide a *terminus ante quem* for the composition date, as perhaps with the piano sonata in A-flat major Hob. XVI:43 (ChL. 35). But the interest is more likely to be a textual one: a comparison of the publication dates of several editions of the same work is likely to suggest which are the sources that are closer to the composer, and which are the more obvious *Nachdrücke*. For the dating of editions, newspaper announcements and advertisements, publishers' catalogues, and copyright deposit entries (such as those at Stationers Hall in London) are likely to prove particularly valuable.

FEDER There is the case of the organ concerto Hob. XVIII:1 in C major, which was originally undated; one can see from the autograph manuscript that Haydn wrote the date 1756 with a different ink. There is also a manuscript copy of Haydn's first Mass, the *Missa brevis* in F major, written in parts, with the autograph date 1749. But this date may not be precise, since many years had intervened.

Some Remarks about the Dating of Haydn's Settings of Scottish Songs

BECKER-GLAUCH In the years 1792–1839 almost 400 British folk songs (Scottish, Welsh, and Irish) were published with remarks like "The Harmony by Haydn" or "With Symphonies and Accompaniments by Haydn." The publishers were William Napier in London, and George Thomson and William Whyte in Edinburgh. In recent years thematic catalogues of these arrangements have been made by Cecil Hopkinson and C. B. Old-man, by Karl Geiringer, and finally by Anthony van Hoboken.[17] According to Hoboken, there are all in all 427 arrangements, at least 23 by Neukomm.[18]

All scholars have based the chronology of their catalogues mainly on the editions. But the publishers dealt with Haydn's arrangements according to their own ideas; quite a number appeared only after his death. A complete edition of Haydn's works should be based on a different principle. For JHW we have sought to determine the chronology of Haydn's arrangements, and the contents of his own groupings of them.

There is no problem as far as the arrangements for Napier are concerned. It is different concerning the arrangements for Thomson and Whyte. Two larger fragments of autographs have been preserved, as well as some smaller fragments and almost all the *Stichvorlagen* (engravers' copies) for Thomson. Furthermore we have the comprehensive Thomson correspondence, receipts of payments, and other documents.

Our task is to combine the musical sources with the other documents. Hoboken took a first step in his introduction to Haydn's arrangements in his catalogue. In a chart of the music manuscripts he places the authentic copies in different groups, not chronologically but in the order in which they were bound together in different volumes. Hoboken's introduction also gives a chronology of the other documents (letters, etc.) with a brief summary.

Only in a few cases does Hoboken combine the music manuscripts with the other documents, usually (but not always) correctly. Yet, by evaluating all the facts and every detail, it is possible to sort out the arrangements for Thomson chronologically in groups and to get a more accurate chronology for the arrangements for Whyte.

I should like to give an example of how to determine, from the letters, the first group of songs that Haydn arranged for Thomson. In the beginning of February 1800, Alexander Straton, secretary of the British legation in Vienna, received a letter from Thomson, dated November 30, 1799, with an enclosed packet for Haydn. The packet was supposed to contain thirty tunes. In the postscript Thomson writes: "I have sent but Sixteen of the Thirty Airs—the rest will be sent afterwards." On February 9, 1800, Straton acknowledges receipt of the parcel to Thomson and writes: ". . . I lost no time in sending to Haydn the letter which you had intrusted to my care, as well as the Airs that it contained. . . ." Thomson notes on the back of Straton's letter: ". . . & sent my letter with the 15 [*sic*] Airs to Haydn."

[17] Hopkinson-Oldman, "Haydn"; idem, "Thomson"; Geiringer, *Catalogue;* Hoboken II, Group XXXI.
[18] See Angermüller, "Neukomm."

In his next letter to Thomson (February 16), Straton also mentions the number 15 rather than 16: "Haydn called here yesterday and mentioned that he had . . . begun the composition of the accompanyments to the Scotch airs (15 in number) that you had sent him through me." No letter sent by Thomson with "the rest" to Vienna has been preserved. In a letter of June 18, 1800, Straton writes to Thomson: "I avail myself of the opportunity of a Messenger who is going to London, to transmit 32 Scotch Airs, which Haydn put into my hands a few days ago. . . . I have paid him 64 Ducats. . . ." We can therefore conclude that, in the period between February and June 1800, Haydn arranged thirty-two airs for Thomson and received two ducats for each song.

In the British Library in London a volume is preserved which contains a score with thirty-two Haydn arrangements copied by Elssler. The manuscript consisted originally of two halves with sixteen airs each; the last page of each half is empty.[19] Elssler numbered the arrangements of the first half from 1 to 16. Haydn signed the first page of the second half "Organyzed by Dr. Haydn," and Elssler started again with No. 1. He continued up to 13 (or 14), but then changed the numbers into 17–29 (or 30); the last two received the numbers 31 and 32 directly. Elssler, having almost finished copying the second half, must have been instructed to number its airs continuing from 17 to 32.

Hoboken has not dated this score. But it is highly probable that this manuscript of thirty-two airs is the one mentioned in the letters quoted above, and that it originated between February and June 1800.

Watermarks

TYSON I want to say something about watermarks, especially as they relate to Haydn research. (Most of the work that I have done with watermarks has been in the autograph sources of Beethoven, and to a lesser extent Mozart. So what I say may need some modification when applied to Haydn, though I doubt if the modification is very great.)

First of all, I find the descriptions of most watermarks in the Haydn literature—whether in Landon, *Symphonies,* or in Bartha-Somfai, or in some of the earlier critical reports in JHW—unsatisfactory. (And the NMA can also share the blame.) They are unsatisfactory for my purposes, at any rate! For I take it that there is some intention of enabling the reader to identify a watermark, and it is really not good enough to describe a few of the features found on some of the leaves in a score. After all, many watermarks have three moons, or REAL, or the letters GF or GFA or W or CS and the like, and crowns or baldachins; but it is the precise combination of these, and usually their sizes or shapes, that is important.

[19] Hoboken II, 457 cites this MS as *a1* and *a2*.

It seems clear to me that there should be an agreed way of describing watermarks. This requires the adoption of certain conventions, which must be to some extent arbitrary—in the same way that the convention that, in describing the size of a manuscript, we state its height before stating its width is an arbitrary convention. (I hope we all use it.)

1. Describe watermarks in terms of the whole sheet and not in terms of the individual leaf of paper. This is common sense.

2. When tracing or describing watermarks, view the watermark from the mold-side of the paper, not from the felt-side (even if that results in some of the letters, etc. reading "backwards"). This is an arbitrary convention, to ensure standardization.

3. Identify and distinguish the two ("twin") forms of every watermark. There will be differences between them. This again is common sense; if one doesn't do this one will trace "hybrid" forms, and one will not have complete control of the watermark.

4. Label the watermarks of the individual leaves with reference to the sheet watermark (of which they will be parts). Here again, the *way* that these are labeled will be an arbitrary convention.[20]

If these rules, or similar agreed ones, are systematically followed, then it is possible to see whether the watermark of one manuscript is identical with that of another—but not, I think, otherwise. And it is surely this identity that is important: mere similarity will not do, unless we are interested merely in distinguishing, say, Haydn's Eszterháza paper from his "Viennese" (or North Italian) paper, or from his English paper. This is indeed *something,* but surely we can take matters a bit further today.

But when we identify a particular watermark with some precision and then try to assign a date to it, it seems we are in trouble. May I illustrate here the sort of dilemma that arises? Everyone who has looked at Viennese watermarks of this period is familiar with one particular pattern: on one side, the letter W; on the other, three moons over the world REAL, and the letter A underneath that. But the trouble is—if we are using watermarks for purposes of chronology—*that* watermark continues for far too long. It is found in Haydn's *Orlando Paladino* (1782) and in various of Mozart's "Haydn" quartets dating from 1782 (K.387) to 1785 (K.464); in the autograph of *Don Giovanni* (1787); and even in two Beethoven autographs of the mid-1790s. Obviously, if this is all the same watermark, it is valueless for chronology. But *is* it the same? If one takes the trouble to trace it one soon finds that there are at least two forms: an earlier one in which the letter W is placed roughly between two chain lines (in both its "twin" versions) and a later one in which a chain line runs through the

[20] The conventions outlined here are described in greater detail in Tyson, "Leonore," 332–34.

middle of the W. Despite their overall similarities, these are clearly two (or more) completely distinct watermarks, and from a chronological point of view there is nothing to be said for assimilating them. From study of Mozart watermarks I have gained an impression that the changeover from one to the other may have taken place in the fall of 1784.

Students of manuscripts are expected to look at two other features: the makeup and format of the manuscript, and the rastrology. The makeup is simply the way that the individual leaves or (more likely) bifolia were put together or grouped in gatherings (*Lagen*). Rastrology is the study of the *Rastrierung,* or the way in which the leaves on each page were ruled with a *rastrum* (Latin for "rake"; in German, *Rastral*) to produce the staves.

In Vienna neither Mozart nor Beethoven found any difficulty in getting paper ruled by machine with twelve or even sixteen staves (before 1800, at any rate, the eighteen-stave paper is ruled by machine, nine staves and then nine more). But when they went to Prague or Berlin or Munich this could not usually be done; instead, the staves were ruled by hand singly or in pairs with one-staff or two-staff rastra. Thus this hand ruling is a sign of provincial or out-of-town provenance. Moreover the rastra have their own individual characteristics by which they can be identified, as Bach scholars know.

I should like to illustrate these points by referring to the autograph of Haydn's Symphony No. 40 in F major, in the British Library, dated by Haydn 1763. This is an upright score (*Hochformat*), not oblong (*Querformat*). The autograph is made up of three gatherings. In the first, of "three moon" paper (i.e., North Italian, i.e., "Viennese"), the twelve staves are ruled all at once by machine. In the second, which has two types of non-Italian paper, the twelve staves are ruled one at a time by hand. The third gathering (the finale) has the Esterházy leaping stags watermark; here the staves are ruled in pairs with a two-staff rastral with a span of 36.5 mm.

These facts might imply that the first movement was written in Vienna and the rest at Eszterháza. But the format of the first movement makes me uneasy. The way that sheets of Viennese paper were normally folded yielded an oblong format—as in most of Haydn's later scores, or as in the autograph of Symphony No. 7 in C major ("Le midi"). But this Viennese paper was evidently ruled and folded in a way to make an upright format—the most natural format for the differently shaped Esterházy sheets. Thus it looks as though Haydn, in arranging for the ruling and folding of the Viennese paper, anticipated that it would be joined by Esterházy paper.[21]

[21] The autograph of Symphony No. 7 is available in a facsimile, ed. László Somfai (Budapest: Editio musica, 1972). The first pages of the autographs of Symphonies Nos. 7 and 40 appear in R. Landon, *Symphonies,* facing 241, 272.

I should be interested in learning what other autograph scores of this time were ruled with a single-staff or a two-staff rastrum.

A small final point about makeup. In a score of Mozart or Beethoven, the intrusion of a bifolium of alien paper—recognized by its watermark—into an otherwise homogeneous manuscript will suggest that we are dealing with a substitute bifolium, a replacement. This will lead to the suspicion that an earlier version has been suppressed: the offending bifolium has been withdrawn and another offered in its place. I see no reason why such ripples beneath the surface, which have been detected in these other composers, should not be found in Haydn as well. Thus watermarks and makeup can be used to expose compositional layers and revisions as well as to illuminate chronological points.

LA RUE If you reproduce watermarks, please reproduce them full size. If you don't have the money to do that, a practical suggestion I made some time ago is to give measurements, in millimeters, of the figures or letters or whatever you find in watermarks.

On the Chronological Correlation of Haydn's Scoring and the Esterházy Musicians

GERLACH Whenever Haydn wrote a work with an unusual scoring, he had in mind the musicians who were to perform the work. In order to date a composition, we can work in reverse and try to determine when the musicians who played the instruments needed in that composition were available in the Esterházy ensemble.[22]

To begin with a rather simple example: during the 1760s, the use of a flute in addition to two oboes depended on the presence of the flautist, Franz Sigel. He was a member of the orchestra from April 1761 until September 13, 1765, when he was abruptly dismissed for having caused a fire by shooting a gun. This implies that Symphonies Nos. 30 and 31 in C major and D major, which are dated 1765 and use the flute, were composed no later than September 13. Sigel joined the band again in February 1, 1767, and stayed through the beginning of the 1770s. This is of interest with respect to Symphony No. 41 in C major, which therefore could not have been composed before February 1767. (The latest possible date is 1770, according to dated manuscript sources.)

Judging from Haydn's dated compositions, our list of Esterházy musicians seems to be rather complete with regard to all instruments except trumpets and timpani, which, therefore, must be left out of consideration.[23] To what extent that list may be trusted can be seen from the concerto-like Symphony No. 7 in C major, "Le midi," dated 1761. Haydn's score has thirteen different parts, and our list from June through the year 1761 shows—apart from Haydn himself—exactly the thirteen necessary

[22] See Gerlach, "Ordnung."   [23] See Gerlach, "Orchestermusiker."

players. Perhaps Haydn had some help from the church musicians or other extras when performing "Le midi," but if so, they only doubled the strings and had no obbligato parts of their own.

Another piece with a similarly "tailor-made" scoring is the undated divertimento fragment Hob. II:24. Its eleven parts require eleven of the Esterházy musicians (the twelfth and thirteenth being the viola and one of the violins). The choice of exactly eleven participating instruments can scarcely have happened by accident and, therefore, Hob. II:24 may have been written for the Esterházy ensemble. The dating "1760–1762," based on external evidence,[24] may therefore be made more precise: May, 1761–1762.[25]

[24] See Feder, "Datierung."

[25] The dating "vor 1775" found in Hoboken is based on a dubious criterion and is no longer relevant in view of the results established here.

Round Table

Problems of Authenticity—"Opus 3"

LÁSZLÓ SOMFAI, *Chairman*
REGINALD BARRETT-AYRES
LUDWIG FINSCHER
JAN LA RUE

ALAN TYSON
JAMES WEBSTER
HUBERT UNVERRICHT,
    Secretary (assisted by Alan Tyson)

SOMFAI With the exception of H. C. Robbins Landon and Georg Feder, our panel includes all the scholars who have made significant contributions to the problem of the authorship of "Opus 3," the six string quartets Hob. III:13–18. I suggest that our discussion should address itself to three questions:

1. Is Haydn the author of "Opus 3"?
2. If not, is Hoffstetter the author?
3. If Hoffstetter did not write all six quartets, which ones are by him, and which are by another composer or composers?

Most of the panel members are in agreement over the answer to the first question; Haydn did not write any of the "Opus 3" quartets. Some of the reasons for this conclusion, which one panel member contests, will be given later. The justification for my being named chairman of this panel is that I published the first article seriously questioning Haydn's authorship.[1]

I should now like to call on the Isidor Saslav Quartet to play certain movements from "Opus 3," to call attention to features that are uncharacteristic of Haydn's style in the genuine quartets of the earlier years: in No. 1/iv, mechanical repetitions and symmetrical phrase rhythm; in No. 3/iii, certain folklike features; No. 4/i and ii comprise a two-movement piece without common tonality and with atypical tempo and meter combinations. In my view, the quartets of "Opus 3" are "à la Haydn," but they are not by Haydn.

PERFORMED EXAMPLES: "Opus 3," Nos. 1, 3, and 4 (excerpts)

Bibliographical Observations on Bailleux's Edition

TYSON The first edition of the six "Op. 3" quartets was published by Bailleux of Paris, probably in 1777, as "Œuvre XXVI" of "G. Hayden." The edi-

[1] Somfai, "Kvartett"; cf. Somfai, "Op. 3."

tion exhibits a number of curious features, some of which have never been properly described. I think it will be helpful if I list them here, and if I leave it to others for the most part to comment on their significance.

1. The music is engraved by two different engravers, one being responsible for the first two quartets and the other for quartets 3–6. The engraver of quartets 3–6 is the Madame Annereau named on the title page of Bailleux's edition ("Gravés par Mme. Annereau"). She engraved a number of other works for Bailleux (for example, a keyboard concerto in E-flat major by J. C. Bach, published by Bailleux as Op. 14, and Antonio Lolli's eighth violin concerto), and her engraving style—that is, her freehand lettering and her engraving punches—is readily identifiable. The engraver of the first two quartets—let us call him, or possibly her, "Engraver X"—has not so far been identified. The words "écrit par Ribiere" are also found on the title page of this edition, and on the title pages of certain other editions published by Bailleux; they are also found on the catalogue of Bailleux's publications in the first violin part of this edition. It is clear that they apply to those pages only (title pages and catalogues); Ribiere is not Engraver X.

2. In all the four parts the first line of music of the first quartet is preceded by the words "QUATUOR I." Some other words originally stood there but have been deleted; and in certain copies the deleted words can still be read. (This is sometimes the case in copies printed from worn plates; what had first been engraved on the plates and had then been erased as a correction may become visible in late copies printed from the worn plates.) In the second violin, viola, and basso parts the original words were:

> Quartetto
> del Signor
> Hofftetter N.º 1

In the first violin part a longer superscription ran across the page, above the music, as well as in the place where "QUATUOR I" was later engraved. The wording appears to have been:

> Quartetto per due Violini *Alto e Basso* del Signor Hofftetter
> Violino Primo
> N.º 1

(The words italicized by me are the only ones that cannot be read clearly, but there is not in fact much doubt about them.)

3. In a similar way, at the beginning of the second quartet, where "QUATUOR II" now stands, some words have been deleted. These are harder to read than in the first quartet, but appear to be (in all parts, with minor differences in the layout):

> Quartetto del
> Sig.ʳ Hofftetter
> N.º 2

There is no evidence of deletions in any of the other quartets. Thus it is only the first two quartets that *ever* had the name of "Hofstetter" on them.

4. The fact that the first two quartets were engraved by the same hand and were formerly numbered "N.º 1 and N.º 2" suggests that they originally belonged together. Two small differences may, however, be noted:

a. In the first quartet the number of bars is indicated at the end of each section (as Hoboken points out), but not in the second (or in any other quartet).

b. In the second quartet the viola part is headed "Viola," but in the first quartet (and in all the others) "Alto Viola." (The title page refers to "une Quinte.")

5. None of the earlier catalogues of Bailleux or of any other French music publisher of the time reproduced by Cari Johansson[2] contains quartets by "Hofstetter." The origin of the plates of the first two quartets is therefore at present a mystery. Since the composer's name was originally given at the beginning of each quartet, the possibility should not be ruled out that they belonged to a set made up of works by different authors ("vari autori"), as was not rare at this period.

6. Naturally enough, I have scrutinized the edition for any other clues to the identity of Engraver X or to the origin of the plates of the first two quartets. The most promising approach is surely to identify the punches used by Engraver X, but that has not so far been successful. We might also ask: Was the engraver French? In the "Fantasia con Variazioni" movement of the second quartet, the notes of the basso part are the same throughout the theme, the five variations, and the theme da capo at the end. After engraving the basso part of the theme, Engraver X writes: "Rep. 6. F. à la 3.ᵉ Pizzic." This suggests to me that the engraver was French or was following a French source. Certain idiosyncrasies of spelling may possibly be of relevance. The Fantasia movement just referred to is described as "Fantasia con Variation," and the Andantino of the first quartet is described as "Andantino Gratioso"; this last is a common misspelling by French engravers of the period. I do not think there is much significance in the form "Baßo" at the top of the basso part of the second quartet, but others may have different views.

7. For the sake of completeness, and to avoid any possible false trails, let me add that in addition to deleting the references to "Signor Hofstetter" in the first and second quartet and substituting "QUATUOR I" and "QUATUOR II," Mme. Annereau touched up a few of the plates of the first two quartets. In the first violin part, for example, she added "Con Sordini" at the start of the Andantino grazioso movement of the first quartet, and a few dynamic signs in the "presto" finale of the second

[2] Johansson, *Catalogues.*

quartet (Mme. Annereau's *f* punch has a cross-stroke that extends both sides of the vertical stroke; in Engraver X's *f* punch the horizontal stroke is only on the right of the vertical stroke). In the viola part Mme. Annereau added "Replica 2 fois" after the Fantasia theme—somewhat unhelpfully, since the theme was to be repeated da capo only after the five variations had been played. If the plates of the first two quartets were used elsewhere before they were used by Bailleux, as seems to me a rather likely possibility, this earlier printing will not show these small additions by Mme. Annereau. More strikingly, of course, it is likely to have Hoffstetter's name at the head of the music in a clear form and not in a half-obliterated one.

Summary of Documentary Facts Relevant to the Question of Haydn's Authorship

UNVERRICHT   The sole primary source of Op. 3, as Feder has recently demonstrated,[3] is the edition of Bailleux, published in Paris in 1777. On the plates of this edition, at the head of the first and second quartet, originally stood the name of Hoffstetter. But the title page bears the name "G. Hayden." Pleyel used this edition for his edition of Haydn's "83," which Haydn in turn allowed his amanuensis, Johann Elssler, to use as the basis for the 1805 thematic catalogue of his works (HV).[4] (Haydn does not refer to these works in EK, the only catalogue of his that dates from the time that Op. 3 must have been composed.) As early as 1939, Larsen had noted the lack of secure documentation,[5] and in 1960 Somfai cast serious doubt on their authenticity, based primarily on stylistic and other grounds.[6] Nevertheless, Op. 3 continued to be generally regarded as genuine until Tyson's and Landon's demonstration that Bailleux's edition had originally named Hoffstetter as the composer of the first two quartets.[7]

There remained the task of checking whether Hoffstetter's authorship could be confirmed. There were two composers surnamed Hoffstetter in the second half of the eighteenth century: Pater Roman(us) Hoffstetter and Johann Urban Alois Hoffstetter.[8] Only Roman Hoffstetter need be considered: he was the only one to write string quartets, and their easily graspable melodies point to him as the author of Op. 3. Barrett-Ayres has nevertheless continued to argue that they might be by Haydn,[9] while Finscher uses stylistic evidence to argue that Roman Hoffstetter is the likely author of Op. 3.[10]

Apart from the original superscription in the Bailleux edition and the

[3] Feder, "Streichquartette," 125–31.   [4] Larsen, DHK, 80.
[5] Larsen, HÜb, 150; [2] 1979, xvii, xxxv.   [6] Somfai, "Kvartett"; Somfai, "Op. 3."
[7] Tyson-Landon.   [8] Unverricht, *Hoffstetter*.   [9] Barrett-Ayres, *Quartet,* 39–56.
[10] Finscher, *Streichquartett* I, 168–90.

similarities with the style of Roman Hoffstetter's quartets, there is no direct and unequivocal evidence—otherwise there would be no need to discuss the authorship of Op. 3 any further. An extra piece of evidence for Roman Hoffstetter's probable authorship is that Hoffstetter admitted to Silverstolpe that he had taken Haydn as a model.[11]

For final confirmation that Roman Hoffstetter wrote the Op. 3 string quartets, the following expectations would have to be fulfilled:

1. There would have to be manuscript copies of the quartets naming Roman Hoffstetter as the author, which would have also to be, if possible, independent of the Bailleux edition, or Roman Hoffstetter's autographs of these six quartets would have to be discovered; or

2. There would have to be proof in the form of a letter or receipt that showed conclusively that Roman Hoffstetter was the author of these quartets.

To date neither document has come to light. It has not even been possible to identify with certainty any musical autograph of Hoffstetter's, because his posthumous papers and the contents of the library of the monastery of Amorbach disappeared as a result of its dissolution in 1803.

The other string quartets by Roman Hoffstetter have come down to us for the most part only in printed editions; but Quartet No. 1, which was not published in the eighteenth or nineteenth centuries, survives in manuscript, and a copy of No. 11 dating from the eighteenth century, which is independent of the published editions, is extant.[12] All other string quartets of Roman Hoffstetter are known only from contemporary printed editions: the original edition of Op. 2 and the (probably) original edition of Op. 1. The transmission of "Op. 3," accordingly, fits into the picture that applies to the string quartets of Roman Hoffstetter.

Relations Between the Documentary and the Stylistic Evidence

WEBSTER Technically "Op. 3" is a "doubtful" work. It has been attributed both to Haydn and to Romanus Hoffstetter. I wish merely to indicate the nature of the documentary and the stylistic arguments that have been made up to this point, and the relationships between them. These considerations will suggest one or two directions for future research.

Consider first the documentary evidence. If we apply the criteria for "doubtful" works developed in the Round Table on Source Problems, Authenticity and Chronology, List of Works, Haydn's authorship of

[11] Feder, "Hoffstetter."
[12] These numberings for Hoffstetter's quartets are taken from Unverricht, *Hoffstetter*.

"Op. 3" appears completely implausible. The first criterion was that to be considered seriously, a doubtful work must have "good" sources comparable to the better secondary sources for genuine works of the same genre and period. On this score, "Op. 3" fails miserably.[13] Like any other North or West European print, the Bailleux edition, in itself, is worthless as evidence for authenticity. But every other one of the peripheral, late sources, including Pleyel's edition and, hence, the entry of "Op. 3" in HV, derives directly from Bailleux.[14] The comparison with the genuine early quartets is even less flattering: the latter average forty extant sources per quartet, including authentic sources for seven of the ten, numerous "good" manuscripts, and many additional catalogue entries.[15]

The second criterion, the absence of a conflicting attribution, is violated by the original attribution to Hoffstetter in two quartets from the Bailleux print, as Dr. Tyson has just described. The circumstantial evidence is also damning: both Bailleux himself and his business partner Mme. Bérault published spurious works, some of them, indeed, clearly from Hoffstetter's pen.[16] On external grounds, the attribution to Haydn is as weak as it is possible to be, without actually being disproved.

The attribution to Hoffstetter is also not completely convincing. Bailleux in Paris, though useless as a witness for Esterházy's kapellmeister, is not too much better a witness for a South German monk. But of course the name "Hoffstetter" was the original one in the edition, and "Haydn" seems much more likely to have been the choice for a deliberate forgery. And as Prof. Unverricht has described, Hoffstetter is known as the author of two other sets of quartets published in Paris between 1770 and 1780. In this respect too his authorship is plausible enough.

In turning to the role of stylistic investigation in questions of authenticity, I will paraphrase Professor Larsen's recent discussion of this problem.[17] When, as in the present case, the documentary evidence is not conclusive, the much broader and more varied resources of stylistic comparisons offer our only hope for fresh insights. And stylistic evidence can often persuade us that Composer X *may* have written a given work. But it can never prove that he *must* have composed it. Such an assertion would claim that *nobody else* could *possibly* have been the composer—not Composer Y, not Z, and not even W. None of us is in a position to risk this assertion, which would imply that we have scrutinized the music of every relevant eighteenth-century composer in exhaustive detail, and that our stylistic judgement is unfailingly accurate. On the other hand,

[13] Feder, "Streichquartette," 125–31.
[14] It is well to recall that the reliability of HV does not necessarily go beyond the reliability of the sources from which it was compiled. Cf. Larsen, HÜb, 258–59, 317–21.
[15] See JHW XII:1, critical report.
[16] Unverricht, *Hoffstetter,* 48–52; Feder, Streichquartette," 130–31.
[17] Larsen, "Echtheitsbestimmung."

these reflections show that we should be comparing "Op. 3" not only to Haydn and to Hoffstetter, as has already been done,[18] but also to the string quartets of every other French and German—perhaps even Austrian—composer whose works could have fallen into Bailleux's hands in the 1770s. Not only is this step necessary on the grounds of principle just stated, but the very process of searching out Hoffstetter's contemporaries and bringing their music into the discussion would increase our knowledge of French and German chamber music in the 1770s—something we very much need to do in any case.

One possibility which Larsen does not explicitly mention is the attempt to prove, not that Composer X must have written a given work, but that Composer Y *could not* have written it. This assertion would imply merely that we had compared this work with the *oeuvre* of a single man. I can well imagine a stylistic demonstration that Haydn could not have composed "Op. 3." To be sure, this project implies a more profound knowledge of his early chamber music than we now possess. But the insufficiency of past studies of this sort is no valid objection, because in comparison with the documentary and stylistic knowledge of his early music we now have (or can achieve), they have been carried out almost literally in the dark.

In considering stylistic studies, it will be well to recall three of Larsen's methodological principles. One is that any study of "doubtful" works requires a body of genuine works as a basis for comparison. The latter may not be chosen at random; they must be in the same or related genres, and from the same period. I am not certain whether Hoffstetter's Op. 1 and Op. 2 provide such a foundation, especially in view of Finscher's demonstration of their considerable stylistic diversity. Second, the concepts animating a stylistic comparison must be relevant, unbiased, and historically appropriate to the repertory at hand. On this basis it would be silly, for example, to deny Haydn's authorship on the grounds of the failure of a sonata-form movement from the 1750s to recapitulate the first theme in the tonic, but less silly for one from the 1770s. On the other hand, it is highly suspicious that Op. 3, No. 4 consists of only two movements not in the same key; no Haydn instrumental composition (except Op. 103!) is so constructed. Third, the similarities and differences of the works under comparison must be properly interpreted. Many similarities reflect merely the shared stylistic resources of an age, and so do not imply the same author for different works. On the other hand some similarities betray the influence of one author on another—in which case they certainly do not establish an *identity* of authorship! Conversely, we may not assume that one or more striking differences necessarily exclude a common authorship.

[18] Finscher, *Streichquartett* I, 168–81.

A more reliable indication that different works stem from different authors might be the accumulation of many "unconscious" differences of detail in many varied aspects of style. Once again, it is precisely this kind of reliable, detailed, unbiased stylistic investigation that, so far, Haydn (let alone his contemporaries) has not enjoyed. We should devote a major scholarly effort to investigations of just this kind.

Remarks on Activity Analysis

LA RUE   I would like to describe a possible method of using style analysis as a test of authenticity. The method employs a type of numerical activity analysis already used to study the authenticity of an early Mozart symphony.[19] The general idea can be summed up as follows: if we assign numerical values to activity in melody, rhythm, and harmony for each bar, various patterns emerge that reflect important interactions in a composer's style. Ignoring adjustments for special situations, the melodic activity is assumed to be the sum of the melodic intervals used; the rhythmic value is the total number of impacts per bar; and the harmonic activity can be represented as 3 for root-movement by fourth or fifth; 2 for movement by second; and 1 for movement by third or over a pedal. Table 1 shows the results for three similar themes: in an early quartet and Op. 9 by Haydn, and Op. 3. It immediately strikes the eye that Haydn's basic pattern is a surge of activity on the first, third, and following odd bars, with

Table 1   Activity Analyses of Variation Themes

Haydn, Adagio, Op. 2, No. 6

```
M: |10| 5 |16| 3 /  15 12 19  2      16  4 20 10 ;  8 6 /  6 18  2  7 18 2
R:   6 4   7  2 /   7  4 11  2  :||:  8  9  4  3 ;  4 3 /  6  8  7  7 11 3
H:   4 7   8  4 /   4  5 12  5         4  9  5  5 ;  4 4 /  4  0  5  4 11 5
```

Hoffstetter?, Andante, Op. 3, No. 2

```
M:  7 6 |17| 2 /  7  6 |10| 2       6 8  8 8 ;  6 2 / 10 6 17 2
R:  5 6   8  5 /  5  3   7  3  :||:  6 8 11 5 ;  4 3 /  5 6  8 5
H:  1 4   9  8 /  4 12   7  5        5 9  6 5 ;  5 6 /  4 4  9 5
```

Haydn, Poco adagio, Op. 9, No. 5

```
M: |15| 5 |18| 9 ;  15 18 14  2      16  5 10  6 / 15  7 18  8 / 13 6 10 2
R:   4 5   4  5 ;   4  4  4  3  :||:  4  4  4  2 /  4  4  4  4 /  4 4  4 3
H:   4 5  11  5 ;   4  5 11  5        4  7  6  4 /  0  5 11  5 /  4 8  6 5
```

[19] LaRue, "Mozart." [The method is also used in the Free Paper by Lester S. Steinberg elsewhere in this volume.—Ed.]

markedly lesser activity in the second, fourth, and following even bars. The numbers for Op. 3 show quite a different pattern, rising toward each third bar of the four-bar phrases. This is even more striking if we study the combined totals (Table 2). Despite its negligible size, this small sample shows some promising possibilities: the idea of assigning numerical values to activity definitely opens a way for studying interrelationships between melody, harmony, and rhythm in the style of any composer.

Table 2   Combined Totals from Table 1

Op. 2, No. 6: (20) 16 (31) 9 / 26 21 42 9 :‖: 28 22 29 18 ; 16 13 / 16 26 14 18 40 10:‖
Hoffstetter?: 13 16 (34) 15 / 16 21 24 10 :‖: 17 25 25 18 ; 15 11 / 19 14 34 12:‖
Op. 9, No. 5: (23) 15 (33) 19 ; 23 27 29 10 :‖: 24 16 20 12 / 19 16 33 17 / 21 18 20 10:‖

Comments on Style

[Finscher's remarks concentrated not on stylistic details but on stylistic generalities. First, he pointed to the "popular" minuets of "Op. 3," found also in quartets known to be by Hoffstetter. Secondly, he drew a contrast between a) the combination of simple formal patterns but sophisticated detail found in Haydn's Op. 1 and Op. 2, and b) the combination of more elaborate forms but coarser detail found in "Op. 3." Third, he stressed that the technique of many minor composers of the 1760s and 1770s—including Mozart—was to place 2-bar, 4-bar, and 8-bar sections in a row, sometimes adding a bar, or changing the order of sections. This is found in "Op. 3" and often elsewhere, but never in Haydn from Op. 9 onwards. Finally, the possibility, suggested by the bibliographical evidence in Bailleux's edition, that "Op. 3" was not by one composer but by two or even several should be taken very seriously.]

SOMFAI Our quartet will now play an exposition of a sonata movement by Hoffstetter as a musical introduction to Mr. Barrett-Ayres's remarks.

> PERFORMED EXAMPLE: Hoffstetter, Quartet Op. 2, No. 3, first movement, exposition

---

"Not Proven"

BARRETT-AYRES   I have no idea who wrote "Opus 3." But I am suspicious about Hoffstetter, and I am also suspicious—very suspicious—about Haydn, for the reasons that have been given by my colleagues here.

There is a legal term in Scots law which states that a case is "not proven," meaning that although the circumstances may be extremely suspicious, no direct ruling can be made by the judiciary for or against the sides in a dispute. I feel that this case is "not proven," and I should like to say one or two things in favor of Haydn's authorship of "Op. 3"—not that I believe it, but I think the case should be put.

These are the points in favor of Haydn's authorship:

1. The "Op. 3" quartets appear both in the first complete edition of the quartets issued by Ignaz Pleyel (very doubtful because he only saw printed copies), and in the Elssler HV catalogue.

2. There is documentary evidence in the form of two letters to prove Haydn's approval of the Pleyel edition, but of course at that time Haydn was a very old man and it is very possible that he did not examine the set with care or understanding.

3. Pohl relates how he heard from Artaria that Haydn had told Artaria's father that he wished his quartets to be remembered starting at number 19. If he did not write "Op. 3," how did he get 19 quartets prior to Op. 9, No. 1?

4. Professor Larsen has reminded us that modern scholars should not ignore, for example, Sandberger, Marion Scott, or Donald Tovey. I believe that we can base later scholarship on their work. Tovey had no doubts as to the authenticity of "Op. 3." Nor does Marion Scott cast any serious doubts on the authenticity of "Op. 3." In fact she gives a reasonable explanation of how they could have come to be published by Bailleux: She suggests that perhaps Haydn received a commission from Bailleux, and being extremely busy, had dispatched six works begun at various times. Two of these, Nos. 2 and 4, were not even finished. This explanation, though possible, is not wholly convincing, of course.

5. "Op. 3" contains many of Haydn's "thumbprints."

   a. Op. 2, No. 1, slow movement and the presto finale of "Op. 3," No. 1 open with a slow introduction and close with the same.

   b. A solo violin is used *con sordino* with pizzicato underneath in Op. 1, No. 6, slow movement and in "Op. 3," No. 1, slow movement.

   c. The texture is often broken down to three parts in both sets. Examples can be found in Op. 1, No. 3, first movement, Op. 1, No. 6, second trio, Op. 2, No. 2, Adagio, "Op. 3," No. 1, first movement, "Op. 3," No. 3, minuet.

   d. Dialogue between one instrument and the other three can be found in "Op. 3," No. 5, and of course there are plenty of examples in Haydn's early quartets.

   e. The trio sonata style is also present in the early quartets and in "Op. 3." Compare Op. 1, No. 3, first movement with "Op. 3," No. 6, second movement.

   f. The harmonic structure remains the same in the variation movements. The bass is thus constant in "Op. 3," No. 2, and in Op. 2, No. 6.

With this in mind, I should now like to play some examples that show that Haydn *may*—for I am as skeptical as all my friends—have been the composer of "Opus 3."

> RECORDED EXAMPLES: Op. 1, No. 6, slow movement; a serenade by Hoff-
> stetter; "Op. 3," No. 5, serenade; "Op. 3," No. 1, slow move-
> ment; Hoffstetter, Op. 1, D major quartet, minuet and trio; "Op.
> 3," No. 1, minuet

Hoffstetter's examples by and large do not show the standard of musical craftsmanship found in "Op. 3." No matter what our decision about the authenticity of "Op. 3," I hope we shall continue to play these quartets.

Discussion

SOMFAI I suspect we have retreated from the question of authentication to questions of compositional quality and whether we feel a work is good or poor. There was of course a trend to imitate Haydn's manner.

WEBSTER Nothing in Sandberger, Tovey, or Scott weighs much against the evidence that has come to light since the 1930s. Concerning Pohl's story about Haydn and Artaria, we have no way of knowing whether the incident is authentic (although Carpani reports something similar). Even if it were, Haydn would not have referred to "Number 19"; this would merely have been *Pohl's* paraphrase of the anecdote, based on what had become a "canon" of works in the meantime. Finally, Miss Scott's hypothesis about Haydn and Bailleux is wholly incredible. There is no evidence of a relation between the two or between Haydn and any other northern or western European publisher before 1780. It is also incredible to suppose that Haydn would have sent incomplete works for publication.

FINSCHER It is inconceivable that Haydn would send pieces like "Op. 3" to a French publisher after the publication and dissemination in manuscript copies all over Europe of Opp. 9, 17, and 20. The hypothesis was ingenious but untenable.

BARRETT-AYRES   Considering Haydn's behavior in the case of the *Seven Last Words,* I would not be surprised if he did what Marion Scott suggested.

WEBSTER If, as you argue, Op. 3 are early works, then you must explain why there is not a single source for Op. 3 that is earlier than the Bailleux print. Nor was there anything untoward in Haydn's dealings with the *Seven Last Words* or most of his other works, by eighteenth-century standards.

[From the floor, Victor Meyer raised doubts as to whether Bailleux, in passing off another's work as Haydn's, would have failed to delete Hoffstetter's name. Tyson pointed out that Hoffstetter's name was not intended to be seen—indeed, it had escaped detection till 1964—and could be made out only in certain copies of Bailleux's edition and even then only with difficulty. Somfai stressed the danger of applying modern views about copyright and piracy to French publishing in the 1770s.

[Daniel Brantley described his computer analysis of the style of Hoffstetter, based on Hoffstetter's published Op. 1 and Op. 2 quartets. The results have been applied to "Op. 3."[20] Finscher called attention to a difficulty: there were profound stylistic differences between Hoffstetter's Op. 1 and his Op. 2, and these might blur the results. He regarded Hoffstetter's Op. 2 as being influenced by the second generation of Mannheim composers.

[Dénes Bartha reminded the meeting that Bailleux's opus number had not been "Op. 3" but "Op. 26." The "Op. 3" derived from Pleyel's edition. Webster clarified this point: it was not a true opus number but meant simply "third set of quartets"; the quartets that Pleyel printed on the pages immediately following were labeled "fourth opus—Op. 9."

[Øivind Eckhoff argued the case against Haydn's authorship of "Op. 3," stressing their stylistic crudity, lack of imagination, and poverty of harmony (with the exception of No. 5) and the blunders in the part writing. Somfai replied that the presence of such blunders did not necessarily disqualify Haydn's authorship. In summarizing the discussion as a whole he regretted that much of the detailed stylistic evidence presented in Finscher's book had not yet come in for a full evaluation. In general the discussion had not changed the minds of the panel members. Feder's view, that the authenticity of "Op. 3" as Haydn's work was not established and that the quartets were probably not authentic, represented the general opinion. As for Hoffstetter's authorship—that would have to await further research.]

[20] Brantley, "Authorship"

Round Table

Problems of Authenticity—The Raigern Keyboard Sonatas

WILLIAM S. NEWMAN, *Chairman*   CARSTEN E. HATTING
A. PETER BROWN   CHRISTA LANDON
GEORG FEDER   ROBERT LEVIN, *Secretary*
SONJA GERLACH

NEWMAN Two keyboard sonatas in E-flat major attributed to Haydn were discovered by Georg Feder in 1961. They are now usually referred to as the Raigern sonatas, Nos. 1 and 2; or, respectively, by the fictitious "Hoboken numbers" XVI:Es2 and Es3 (in English, E-flat 2 and E-flat 3). (They are not cited in Hoboken because his first volume, 1957, had already appeared before their discovery.) In 1962 Feder presented arguments for the authenticity of these sonatas,[1] which were generally accepted. They were published in JHW XVIII:1 as Nos. 8 and 9 in the group "Neun frühe Sonaten," and in the first volume of the two-volume Henle selection of Haydn sonatas drawn from JHW; and they were also published in Volume 1 of Christa Landon's edition in the *Wiener Urtext-Ausgabe* (ChL. 17 and 18).

Ten years later, however, Carsten Hatting found another source for the second Raigern sonata (E-flat 3), attributing it to Mariano Romano Kayser.[2] This source also contains a hitherto unknown finale for this sonata.

After a survey of the sources for these two sonatas, the panel will try to wrestle with the tough questions of stylistic congruity and incongruity.

The Sources of the Two Disputed Raigern Sonatas

FEDER I shall try to evaluate the sources for the two Raigern sonatas, and then I shall add a few remarks about the sources for Haydn's early keyboard works in general.

There are three manuscript copies: (1) the Rutka manuscript; (2) the Roskovszky manuscript; and indirectly (3) a Viennese manuscript. The Rutka manuscript, from the Rajhrad (Raigern) monastery in Moravia, was found in Brno in 1961 and contains five works titled "Parthia": Piano Sonata Hob. XVI:14 (ChL. 16) in D major, authenticated by EK;

[1]Feder, "Zwei Sonaten"   [2]Hatting, "Haydn?"

107

Piano Sonata Hob. XVI:13 (ChL. 15) in E major, not fully authenticated, but not doubted since Haydn's time; Piano Sonata Hob. XVI:2 (ChL. 11) in B-flat major, not authenticated, but not doubted since Karl Päsler published it from a different source in 1918 (it bears no attribution in the Rutka manuscript); and, in fourth and fifth place, the two disputed sonatas in E-flat major, titled "Parthia 4ta del Sig Haydn" and "Parthia Vta J:Haydn."

Matthäus Benedict Rutka was an organist at Raigern and began work as a copyist and collector of musical manuscripts not later than 1774, the date on a signed manuscript (Brno, A 12482, organ part). He was still alive in 1824 (manuscript biography in Vienna, Gesellschaft der Musikfreunde). He copied or signed his name on at least ten early compositions by Haydn,[3] some early works generally considered authentic,[4] on the doubtful string quintet Hob. II:A1, and on three spurious string quartets.[5] Therefore, although he owned or copied a remarkable number of authentic Haydn works, the latest dating from the 1770s, Rutka can no longer be considered a fully reliable witness.

Pantaleon Roskovszky, a Franciscan monk, lived in Slovakia and Hungary from 1734 to 1789 and served as organist and choirmaster at several different monasteries. Roskovszky's manuscript, now in Budapest, is a collection of miscellaneous keyboard music from about 1742 to 1766. The collection does not mention Haydn's name, although it includes the minuet from Haydn's early divertimento Hob. XIV:4 in C major for keyboard, two violins, and bass, without title, attribution, or accompanying instruments. It also includes the second of the two disputed sonatas, a fact presumably first discovered immediately preceding Dr. Hatting's publication in 1972. The sonata begins at the top of a left-hand page, without title or author. But at the bottom of the preceding page is written: "Seque Divertimento pour le Clavecin Cembalo Solo. Del Sig.re Mariano Romano Kayser. Si Volti." The connection of this title with the music on the following page is plausible, if not absolutely certain.

Nothing is known of Kayser. The volume also attributes a canzona, an aria, and possibly the following allegro to this composer. The fascicle containing these pieces is dated 1759.

The volume consists of several fascicles apparently not all written at the same time and not bound in strictly chronological order. Among the earliest compositions are the sonatas Op. 1 by Platti, printed in 1742 but certainly copied here much later. The earliest fascicles are dated 1757 and 1759 and are found at the end of the volume. As mentioned, one fascicle contains the minuet from Hob. XIV:4, dated 1764 in the autograph. Still

[3] Hob. I:10, 32; II:2; III:12; XI:123, 124, 126; XVI:14; XVIII:1; the Great Organ Mass.
[4] Hob. XV:34; XVI:2, 13; XVIII:5.
[5] Hob. III:C15 (deest; see Feder, "Streichquartette"), D3, B9.

another includes Wagenseil's divertimenti [keyboard sonatas], Raccolta I, advertised by Breitkopf in 1763. The fascicle with the second Raigern sonata also includes a sonata by Štěpán (Steffan), a manuscript copy of which was advertised as a symphony by Breitkopf in 1766.[6] I am not persuaded by Mr. Hatting's suggestion, based on another collection by Roskovszky from these years, that this fascicle was written between 1771 and 1774, because the paper is not the same in the two collections. I believe rather that the fascicle was written earlier, possibly around 1766.

How trustworthy are the two witnesses? Rutka wrote hastily, not very accurately, and with abbreviations and slips. Roskovszky was more careful with the music, but he wrote "Suite de Preces" and "Svite D. Reces" for "Suite de Pièces." (Could he possibly have written "Kayser" for "Haydn"?) He also playfully wrote such tempo indications as "Con poco Spirito e Smanioso. Andante" and "Lamentevole Amante Pietoso" and he sometimes added an "Adio" or "Adieu" above a final movement. His tempo indications for the first movement and minuet of the second Raigern sonata are "Allegro pietoso" and "Largo," respectively.

Two hypotheses to explain the conflicting attributions are possible: either Roskovszky copied a sonata by Haydn who was perhaps still unknown to him and substituted the name Kayser, known to him from the other pieces in the collection; or Rutka misread the name of Kayser, possibly unknown to him, and substituted the name of Haydn, whose works were already familiar to him. Since neither copyist knew Haydn personally, as far as we know, either hypothesis may be right or wrong.

The Roskovszky source of the second Raigern Sonata is more complete and more carefully written. Its highest note, eb^3, is always replaced by some lower note in the Rutka manuscript, possibly to avoid exceeding d^3, normally the highest pitch in Haydn's early keyboard music. The pitch eb^3 appears in the authentic Divertimento for piano trio and two horns in E-flat major, Hob. XIV:1, advertised in 1766 by Breitkopf. The pitch e^3 appears in the harpsichord part of his cantata "Qual dubbio" of 1764. In general, eb^3 would be unacceptable in Haydn's earliest sonatas, but perhaps acceptable in a sonata dated no earlier than 1764. More problematic is the f^3 of the first movement in the Roskovszky version, in a five-bar section written one octave higher than in the Rutka source. Haydn apparently did not use this note in his keyboard music much earlier than 1771.[7] As our sonata cannot be assumed to have originated later than Haydn's Piano Sonata Hob. XVI:45 (ChL. 29) in E-flat major of 1766, the use of f^3 argues against its authenticity, provided the note is correct. However, this is not certain, since the prominent sound of this

[6] Šetková, *Štěpán,* 175, No. 79.
[7] See Feder, "Klaviersonaten," 101–02; Feder, "Klaviertrios," 308; JHW XVIII:1, foreword, ix–x.

high section finds no counterpart in the rest of the sonata even where f³ might have been introduced (for example, bar 142; cf. bar 48).[8]

Though indirect, a third source is a manuscript in the archives of the Gesellschaft der Musikfreunde in Vienna (VII 27713) that contains miscellaneous keyboard music copied perhaps in the 1760s. The collection includes the Haydn sonatas Hob. XVI:14, 13, 2 (ChL. 16, 15, 11), in the same order as the first three sonatas in the Rutka manuscript. No. 2 lacks the author's name and No. 13 lacks the trio of the minuet; these omissions correspond to the Rutka manuscript. But several divergent readings attest to the independence of the two manuscripts. Both probably derive from a single lost source. That source may have arranged the movements of Sonata No. 2 differently from a manuscript copy now in Berlin—the only one that ascribes the sonata to Haydn. The order there and in modern editions is Moderato—Largo—Menuet; the order in the Rutka manuscript is Moderato—Menuet—Largo, and in the Viennese manuscript Moderato—Menuet, followed by a very different movement in G minor and other unconnected movements. I conclude that both Rutka and the unidentified Viennese copyist followed the lost common source beginning with No. 14 and continuing through the second movement (Menuet) of No. 2; then they went in different directions, Rutka copying the third movement (Largo), the Viennese copyist turning to other musical sources. It is an open question whether Rutka continued to follow the lost common source when he went on to copy the two Raigern sonatas that follow Sonata No. 2.

The result of these new investigations of the sources—some of them unknown to the present writer in 1961—seems to be that the authorship of the disputed sonatas is now to be considered more or less doubtful.

Of Haydn's early keyboard music in general, there are quite a few fully authenticated works. However, the sources for a considerable number of other works traditionally believed authentic are not fully convincing. A useful rule of thumb developed by the Bach-Institut in Göttingen states that if a source appears reliable but one has doubts about the attribution of a work in that source, the burden of proof is on him who would contest its authenticity; whereas if one wishes to credit attribution in a poor source, the burden of proof is on him who believes that it is genuine.[9] By this principle, the following early keyboard compositions require further proof of authenticity:

the twelve minuets Hob. IX:8

the concertos Hob. XVIII:5, 7, 8, 9, 10 (No. 7 is an arrangement of the piano trio Hob. XV:40; No. 9 may well be unauthentic)

---

[8] Cf. the present writer's revised edition of this sonata, including the finale, in Haydn, *Sonaten* (1972), I.
[9] Cf. *Erbe*.

the concertinos Hob. XIV:12, 13, XVIII:F2
the divertimentos Hob. XIV:C1, C2
the piano trios Hob. XV:40, and C1
the sonatas Hob. XVI:1, 2, 16, G1; XVII:D1

The list might even be longer if one included works whose authenticity rests chiefly on Haydn's indirectly reported approval in 1803, when he may not have been sure what he had written nearly half a century before.[10]

Haydn's Keyboard Idiom and the Raigern Sonatas

BROWN In restudying the two Raigern sonatas in terms of keyboard idiom, I was struck not so much by their similarities to other Haydn keyboard works, as by their impression of redundancy and resulting lack of thrust, which seems to segregate them from other keyboard works attributed to Haydn from the late 1760s. For this discussion I would like to consider briefly the control of thrust in these two sonatas by reexamining—at the risk of some redundancy—the interactions of various rhythmic parameters, the placement and strength of articulatory weight, and phrase morphology.

The initial statements of both sonatas have the same basic structure (E-flat 2, mm. 1–11; E-flat 3, mm. 1–12): a series of three phrases made of the same musical material, with the central phrase in E-flat 2 and the beginning of the third phrase in E-flat 3 moved to a different pitch level. With the exception of the Partita in F major for keyboard four hands (Hob. XVIIa:2)—a work of questionable paternity—no other Haydn keyboard sonata before 1788 utilizes a tripartite structure for the opening statement. Furthermore, these repetitions are only ornamentally or otherwise minimally varied; in E-flat 2 the impression of redundancy is strengthened by the plethora of cadences and the stationary bass line. In both sonatas the texture remains essentially constant, and the shape of the melodic curve offers little directionality. Although E-flat 2 has three-measure phrases, E-flat 3 has an almost too regular architectonic structure.

In comparison, the initial statement of the first movement of the supposedly chronologically neighboring authentic sonata in E-flat major, Hob. XVI:45 (ChL. 29; 1766), manifests a more focused control (see Example 1). More specifically, the two-measure modules for the first three subphrases are established by the behavior of the harmonic rhythm, surface rhythm, melodic motion, and texture, and then the module is lengthened for the terminal subphrase, creating a sense of anticipation.

---

[10] This refers, e.g., to the following keyboard compositions: the piano trios Hob. XV:1, 36–38, 41; the sonatas XVI:5, 7–13 (ChL. 8, 2, 1, 3, 6, 5, 12, 15); XVII:7.

Note should also be made of the subtle distinction in the weight of the cadences, which carefully define the two phrases of the statement: the first resolves on a weak beat and the second on a strong one.

Example 1. Hob. XVI:45 (ChL. 29), opening

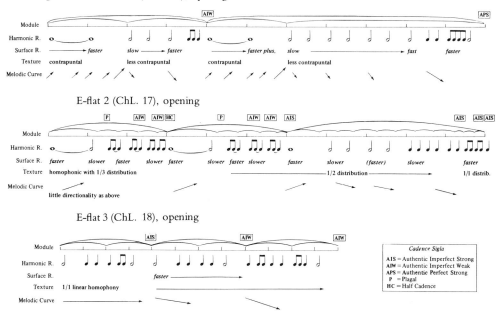

E-flat 2 (ChL. 17), opening

E-flat 3 (ChL. 18), opening

The final measures of the primary section of E-flat 2 (mm. 8–12), as Dr. Feder pointed out in first reporting on those sonatas, provide two of the more convincing parallels to authenticated Haydn works: the end of the primary section (mm. 14–18) of the first movement of Hob. XVI:19 (ChL. 30) in D major and the closing cadence (mm. 39–41) of the first movement exposition in the String Quartet Opus 9, No. 2, in E-flat major. For Sonata No. 19, the similarities are readily apparent: three eighth notes following an eighth rest in the accompaniment, and a similar repetition and resulting melodic contour, as seen in Example 2. Yet if one plots the rhythmic interactions of the two phrases, different levels of structural control are readily discernible. In the excerpt from E-flat 2, the surface rhythm briefly quickens in m. 9 but only ornamentally and not dynamically, and the lengths of the subphrases are one measure and then a half measure; furthermore, these phrase lengths are correlated with the harmonic rhythm. On the other hand, in mm. 14–18 of the first movement of Sonata No. 19, the acceleration of the harmonic rhythm is intensified by kinetic recurrence, the surface rhythm accelerates dynamically, and the module of activity increasingly diminishes; furthermore, here there is an overlapping of activity. It should also be noted that in the

D-major sonata the rhythmic aspects are further intensified by the rising melodic outline.

Example 2. E-flat 2 (ChL. 17), mm. 8–12

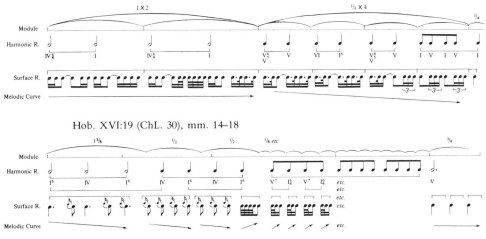

Hob. XVI:19 (ChL. 30), mm. 14–18

The parallel with the closing cadence from Op. 9, No. 2, points to a characteristic more incongruous to Haydn's keyboard idiom: while both have triplet cadential formulas, the placement of such a cadence at the end of the primary section in E-flat 2 reduces the forward thrust of the entire exposition and, in my experience, is quite foreign to Haydn's keyboard style. Indeed, the placement of cadences in a keyboard sonata exposition is one of the few parameters in which Haydn is predictable: as shown in Example 3, a diagram of the exposition of the first movement of Sonata No. 45, the placement and strength of articulatory weight is manipulated so that within the primary area the tonality is at first confirmed and then weakened in order to prepare for the transition and establishment of the secondary key area, while the greatest cadential strength is reserved for the final portion of the exposition. As can be seen in Example 4 (page 114), E-flat 2 does not conform to this pattern. In addition, there are almost three times as many cadential progressions, even though the exposition is only half as long.

Example 3. Hob. XVI:45 (ChL. 29), Exposition, Cadences [for abbreviations, see Example 1]

The transition sections of both Raigern sonatas are remarkably similar: a D-flat to C resolution is girded by a I_4^6-V progression within a transition section. As in the primary sections of these two sonatas, there is a

Example 4. E-flat 2 (ChL. 17), Exposition, Cadences

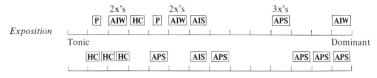

number of repeated one- and two-measure modules without the directionality afforded by the use of sequence, and—perhaps more remarkable for a transition section—an overall lack of forward thrust, which is further underlined in E-flat 3 by the thick left-hand texture in mm. 27–34.

Although more of my comments have been directed against Haydn's authorship of E-flat 2, E-flat 3 also has traits incongruous to Haydn's style. A tabulation of varied and exact melodic repetitions in the first-movement expositions of Sonatas Nos. 14, 19, 45, E-flat 2, and E-flat 3 (ChL. 16, 30, 29, 17, 18) shows that E-flat 3 has a significantly higher percentage of exact repetitions.[11] Nevertheless, in E-flat 2, though the redundancies are fewer, they are more immediately audible, because of other stylistic components, while in E-flat 3 the greater percentage of exact melodic repetitions is veiled by the more linear texture and lighter articulations.

In both first movements perhaps the strongest case for authenticity can be made in the rather impressive development sections; particularly striking is the extended repetition of materials in mm. 32–35 of E-flat 2 and mm. 79–93 of E-flat 3. Although the exposition and recapitulation in E-flat 3 are practically identical—perhaps too much so for Haydn—the recapitulation in E-flat 2 is disturbingly abbreviated: the entire transition is replaced by a trill, accompanied by three eighth notes, and an ascending flourish culminating in a fermata on B-flat.

The slow movement of E-flat 2, like the first movements of both sonatas, is also remarkable for its extended repetitions (mm. 9–18, 32–35, and 41–45). Indeed, there seems to be a noticeable lack of invention with regard to melodic continuation and texture, especially when compared to the melodically similar slow movement of Symphony No. 37 in C major—a work written perhaps as many as seven or eight years earlier. In the orchestral movement one is impressed by the variety of textures used to extend the melodic materials, whereas the more monochromatic keyboard setting, which seems to require even more frequent changes of texture, lacks the needed contrast. Most telling, however, is the tonal structure of the first part: with nearly equal strength three separate key areas—C minor, G minor, and B-flat major—are established. Not only is the articulation of three tonal areas nonexistent in Haydn's keyboard music, but so is a section ending in VII.

---

[11]See the identical approach used by LaRue, "Gniezno."

Concerning the minuet of E-flat 3, the syncopation in nearly every measure of the trio is not uncharacteristic of Haydn and is often found in triple-metered movements by his Viennese contemporaries. However, the first part of the trio in the Sonata Hob. XVI:12 (ChL. 12) in A major—a presumably much earlier movement—shows a more ingenious approach.

The evidence as a whole seems to indicate that the two sonatas contain enough parallels to have in all probability stemmed from the same pen. Unfortunately, our present control over the dating and chronology of Haydn's keyboard music up to about 1766 and the available sampling of Kayser's output are not sufficient to validate all stylistic observations; the existence of several serious source questions makes the sword of skepticism a double-edged one.[12] If indeed these two sonatas are from Haydn's hand, they do not convincingly exemplify either his keyboard style or his high level of craftsmanship.

Remarks on the Structure and Harmony of the Raigern Sonatas

GERLACH I believe that both Raigern Sonatas may be dated before c. 1766 (cf. Dr. Feder's paper at the beginning of this Round Table). I would therefore like to limit my comparisons to early Haydn works.

The types of structure and harmony used in Sonata E-flat 2 are found in some early sonatas and symphonies by Haydn.[13] Sonata Hob. XVI:14 (ChL. 16) in particular shows several similarities in detail (see below). However, two details in E-flat 2 are not common in Haydn. The first is the immediate repetition in the dominant key of the theme of the first movement, without any suggestion of contrapuntal style. After the repetition the movement continues in the tonic. A theme other than a fugato theme that is repeated in the dominant by another instrument appears only once among Haydn's authenticated string trios (Hob. V:6), and once among the early keyboard trios (Hob. XV:36)—both in E flat. The second unusual detail is the sequence of keys in the second movement of E-flat 2. The C minor movement goes first to G minor and then to B-flat major. The progression from the tonic minor to VII in an exposition is very uncommon. These two details might be explained as the clumsiness of a less experienced though gifted composer. If Haydn were indeed the

[12] Neither Raigern sonata is listed in EK; the source for E-flat 3 under Kayser's name is textually superior to the Raigern source; the latter may not be as unified a collection as has been asserted; and the entry for this collection in the eighteenth-century monastic inventory of musicalia seems to have been inscribed during the last decades of the century.

[13] Cf. the corresponding harmonies in the trios of E-flat 2 and Haydn's Sonata Hob. XVI:6 (ChL. 13); cf. Symphony No. 37 in C for a theme corresponding to the Andante; cf. Symphony No. 18 in G for corresponding form, and Symphony No. 19 in D for a corresponding development section in a slow movement; cf. Symphony No. 32, third movement, m. 65, for the rest corresponding to E-flat 2, first movement, m. 53.

composer, this sonata must then be a forerunner of his authenticated sonatas.

The structure and harmony of the E-flat 3 sonata are very similar to
Sonatas Hob. XVI:14 in D major, 6 in G major, and 2 in B-flat major
(ChL. 16, 13, 11). (Two of these sonatas are authenticated Haydn works,
and the third has never been doubted.) In particular, the structure of all
the first movements is nearly identical, and similar cadences are used in
corresponding places. The trios of the minuets are in the tonic minor
(note especially the E-flat minor and B-flat minor in Sonatas E-flat 2 and
Hob. XVI:2, respectively). There are also some similarities with other,
smaller Haydn sonatas of the period.[14] One detail of E-flat 3 is not found
in any of the three comparison sonatas. At the end of the development
section of the finale the tonic chord seems to arrive one bar too early (m.
85), with the result that the tension of the dominant is resolved before the
recapitulation begins. However, this detail appears in other early works
by Haydn, such as Symphonies No. 108 in B-flat major, finale, and No.
36 in E-flat major, first movement; and the Sonata Hob. XVI:G1 (ChL.
4) (believed to be authentic), first movement.

To illustrate the similarities between E-flat 3 or E-flat 2 and Sonatas
Nos. 14, 6, and 2, I shall refer to four types of cadences. The first type
has a well-placed subdominant (i.e. IV or II⁶, or both combined) and a
short ⁶₄ chord before the dominant, and may be either a half cadence or
full cadence. Both the bass line and melody are very similar in E-flat 2, i,
21–22, 25–26, and No. 14, i, 26–28, 34–36; to a lesser extent also in No.
6, iii, 9–10; No. 2, ii, 24–25; E-flat 3, i, 18–20.

The second type of cadence is related to the first with its long subdominant, but in this type the subdominant occurs before the real cadence begins. The actual cadence, 3–4–5–1 or 6–4–5–1 in the bass, contains one more short subdominant. This cadence occurs in E-flat 3, i,
42–45, 147–51; No. 6, i, 13–14; with an extremely long subdominant in
E-flat 3, i, 53–57, and No. 2, i, 43–48.

The third type is a half cadence using the raised fourth degree in the
bass or, in other words, the dominant of the dominant. This type occurs
in several different forms in both major and minor, and begins with the
weighty subdominant or tonic. Examples are found in E-flat 2, i, 14–16,
ii, 40–41; E-flat 3, i, 20–22, 114–16; No. 2, i, 108–09; No. 6, i, 7–8,
35–36; No. 14, iii, 70–71.

The fourth type of cadence is a special derivative of the third type. It
contains the raised fourth in the bass line but consists of an entire phrase
with a chain of trills on descending chromatic steps in the melody and a
pedal point in the bass.[15] It occurs only twice: in E-flat 3, i, 30–34; and in

[14] Especially Nos. 13, 10, and G1 (ChL. 15, 6, 4), all of which are considered to be genuine,
though only No. 10 is authenticated.
[15] Feder notes this cadence, together with other remarkable similarities to Haydn works, in
"Zwei Sonaten."

No. 6, i, 10–12—in both cases, in the middle of the second group of the exposition.[16]

Finally, let us look at the "Aria" attributed to Kayser for any possible parallels with E-flat 3. In this aria there is no lengthy subdominant and no half cadence with a raised fourth in the bass line. Furthermore, the $\frac{6}{4}$ chord is very rare and seemingly avoided in every full cadence, quite in contrast to E-flat 3 and Haydn sonatas. In fact, none of the types of cadences found in the Raigern sonatas and Haydn sonatas are found in this aria. Instead, two other types of full cadence are found. The first has the bass line 1–4–5–1 (or 3–4–5–1), similar to bass lines found in the sonatas, but preceded by a weighty dominant (see Example 5) instead of a tonic. The second type begins on the tonic, but has a weighty dominant and no subdominant at all (Example 6). This type does not occur in the Raigern sonatas or in Haydn sonatas. It is found, however, in the *Notebook for Anna Magdalena Bach,* in both major and minor contexts (Example 7).

Example 5. M. R. Kayser, Andante

Example 6. M. R. Kayser, Andante

Example 7. *Klavierbüchlein für Anna Magdalena Bach von 1725* [BWV 515, *Neue Bach-Ausgabe,* V:4, No. 20a]

[16] Similar cadences (though without the characteristic chain of trills) are also found elsewhere, but usually at the beginning or perhaps the end of a large section, not in the middle. See, for example, Sonata No. 14 (ChL. 16), iii, 44ff, and Symphony No. 36 in E-flat major, iv, 51ff. In both cases the cadence occurs at the beginning of the development section.

Aspects of the Texture of the Two Raigern Sonatas

HATTING Asked to investigate the question of texture in the two Raigern sonatas, I must report that I was unable to find any details for which I could not also find parallels in authentic or traditionally accepted Haydn sonatas. For example, the rather heavy texture of the opening of E-flat 2 finds a parallel in the first movement of the D-major fragment Hob. XIV:5 (ChL. 28) and the third movement of XVI:6 (ChL. 13), as well as in the first movement of E-flat 3.

Instead of citing other details I should like to sketch my analytical procedure.[17]. It rests on three roughly differentiated types of texture found in Haydn's keyboard music. The first or "nonidiomatic" type includes a melody accompanied in one of three ways: by repeated chords, by a more or less regular "walking bass," or by chords in a three- or four-part harmonization. Hermann Abert pointed out that the repeated-chord and walking-bass patterns are found in much contemporary chamber or orchestral music and are very common in Haydn sonatas up to 1770.[18] (Accompaniment by three- or four-part chords is found throughout Haydn's production of keyboard music, and it is no more idiomatic than the other two accompaniment patterns in this group.) The second type of texture is melody accompanied by repeating broken-chord figurations of four, three, or two notes, of which the "Alberti bass" is the most familiar. The third, less common type may be called a "broken chord" texture; it is distinguished from the second by its lack of a clear and independent melody.

These three types of texture are too general to characterize any one composer's personal style. However, they may be used to identify typical examples in the authentic or near-authentic works of Haydn. But the problem then arises of deciding how much similarity is required to support, or dissimilarity to refute, common authorship. Each Haydn sonata has its own individual as well as typical traits. Therefore, the question is one of the degree of deviation allowed from the typical.

Nearly all the authentic Haydn sonatas contain a variety of textures. Both Raigern sonatas, including the finale to E-flat 3 attributed nowhere to Haydn, also contain such textural variety. Since the textures of sonatas by Haydn and by his contemporaries are so much alike, my analytical procedure does not produce the degree of distinction necessary to solve the problem of authenticity.

Discussion

LANDON It is usually those pieces of lesser musical importance that give us the most difficulties. A second point is that it is terribly difficult to study

[17] This methodology is described in detail in Hatting, "Satz."
[18] Abert, "Klavier," Part 1, 565–66.

anything by inner criteria, since we know so very little about Haydn and about keyboard music of his time. In reference to Mr. Hatting's remark about the chords at the beginning of E-flat 2 and the parallel in the D-major fragment, I find the context of the examples too different; the D-major example is from the middle, while the E-flat 2 example is a beginning, a very primitive beginning where nothing moves. The parallel with the Adagio of No. 6 is also too different, as the effect is so different at a slow tempo. It is also unusual that E-flat 2 takes so long to settle on the dominant. The theme of E-flat 3, on the other hand, is unstable. Also the figure in bar 3 is unlike Haydn, though I know very little about the keyboard trios. As Peter Brown said, the amount of repetition in both sonatas is also peculiar. Also, many new ideas are introduced without leading anywhere. But most striking in E-flat 3 is the finale, with its repeats and its ending in three registers, which is unusual in Haydn. If I were to do another edition I would have reservations about E-flat 3, and omit E-flat 2 and the finale of E-flat 3. They don't "lie" well for the hand—especially E-flat 3. I would also omit Hob. XVI:5, 11, and the F-major version of 47 (ChL. 8, 5, 57).

NEWMAN One problem that keeps confronting me is how much of what we talk about seems to be "in the air," and not particular to any one composer. About twenty-five years ago, Charles Cudworth wrote about cadences of the sort discussed by Miss Gerlach, pointing out that they seem to be universal.[19] Particularly in the early phases of a composer, it is very difficult to determine authenticity. It's hard for me to believe that Haydn, even at this early stage, was not original enough to do one of these things in just this one sonata—he had all sorts of odd turns that might have turned up later or not at all.

FEDER The manuscript that attributes the E-flat 3 sonata to another composer does make things look different. If its theme were not in EK, even a fully authenticated work such as the keyboard concerto Hob. XVIII:2 could come under suspicion, since it is attributed in one Berlin manuscript to Galuppi. Also, in early compositions by Haydn you can find stylistic details that confirm or even add to what we already know of this composer, but you can also find things that seem strange at first glance. We should also take into consideration the comparison made possible by the inclusion of the aria by Kayser in the manuscript.

HATTING I think it is useless, because all three compositions attributed to Kayser are so different.

LANDON The attributions in the Budapest manuscripts are not always reliable. We have no idea who Kayser was or whether he flourished there. We know there are pieces wrongly attributed to Handel. I don't think there's any

[19] Cudworth, "Cadence"

point in comparing the two pieces, because we can't prove that Kayser or Haydn composed them. Also, Haydn was becoming quite famous in the 1760s, and one usually changes an attribution to a more famous composer rather than a lesser-known one.

BROWN What is the date of the Raigern source?

FEDER About ten years later than the Roskovszky manuscript; in the mid-1770s.

BROWN With regard to its placement within the Raigern catalogue itself, could it not be as late as 1790?

FEDER We have several manuscripts by Rutka with little change in the handwriting among them. The catalogue may have included this manuscript later than it was written.

BROWN But the catalogue seems to be in chronological order, with these sonatas placed toward the end of the eighteenth century. The fact that this source is textually inferior as well as being later than the Budapest source casts doubt on its reliability.

FEDER I cannot believe it was written as late as 1790. Frau Landon, about Hob. XVI:47 (ChL. 57) that you regard as doubtful, aren't the last two movements the same as the E-minor sonata (JHW XVIII:1, 108; ChL. 19)?

LANDON Yes, but I was referring to the F-major version, and its first movement, as the doubtful ones.

FEDER The oldest source of that movement is in a manuscript copy of the Sonata in G minor, Hob. XVI:44 (ChL. 32). Why it appears in this manuscript and why it has the transposition is not clear. That the E-minor version is the original one is clear from the use of the "short octave" in one of the movements.[20] That is such a special feature that any publisher in 1787 or 1788 would probably have altered it.

LANDON But there are copies of the F-major version in Kremsier, also titled "erstes Stück" and "zweites Stück." I believe this was put together in a copyist's workshop and then given to Artaria.

BROWN In its early E-minor version this sonata shows a great deal of musical unity.

[20] Cf. Horst Walter's paper in Workshop 2; JHW XVIII:1, foreword. [Ed.]

Free Papers

Authenticity, Chronology, Source Studies, Editorial Practice

Regarding the Authenticity of the "Haydn" Keyboard Concerto Hoboken XVIII:F3

SHELLEY DAVIS

Apart from Jens Peter Larsen's 1939 account in *Die Haydn-Überlieferung,* there were relatively few dependable reference works regarding Haydn's keyboard concertos prior to the 1950s. Renewed emphasis on Haydn research then began illuminating the lesser-known works, and editions by Michael Schneider, Ewald Lassen, Horst Heussner, Horst Walter, and H. C. Robbins Landon, among others, as well as articles by Heussner and Georg Feder, have subsequently added depth to our knowledge of the concertos.[1]

However, one concerto for which thorny problems of potential authenticity linger is Hob. XVIII:F3, hereafter abbreviated F3. No autograph has surfaced, and its connection with Haydn results from a single attribution in an incomplete copy at Kloster Einsiedeln, Switzerland.[2] This version, hereafter referred to as "Einsiedeln," consists only of the string parts. Two other copies, not mentioned by Hoboken, have survived. One, a print of keyboard arrangements in the King's College Library at Cambridge,[3] was issued in or before 1775 by the London firm of Longman, Lukey, & Company. In it, the concerto comes last in a set of six attributed to Johann Stamitz. (This version will hereafter be

[1] The principal editions include the following: Hob. XVIII:1 in C major, by Michael Schneider (Wiesbaden: Breitkopf & Härtel, 1953); XVIII:3 in F major, by Ewald Lassen (Mainz: B. Schott's Söhne, 1958); XVIII:4 in G major, by Karl Schubert (Hannover: Verlag Adolph Nagel, 1932) after Boyer's edition of c. 1784, and by Bruno Hinze-Reinhold (Leipzig: C. F. Peters, 1958); XVIII:5 in C major, by Horst Heussner (Cassel: Nagels Verlag, 1959, 1969); XVIII:6 in F major, by Helmut Schultz (Leipzig: Musikwissenschaftlicher Verlag, 1937, reissued Cassel, 1959), and by Paul Bormann (London and New York: Boosey & Hawkes, 1954, based on the copy then at the Westdeutsche Bibliothek at Marburg); XVIII:8 in F major, by H. C. Robbins Landon (Vienna: Verlag Doblinger, 1962); XVIII:10 in C major, by Horst Walter (Munich-Duisburg: G. Henle-Verlag, 1969); the many editions of XVIII:11 in D major include one by Kurt Soldan (Leipzig: C. F. Peters, 1931). Other recent editions of concertos attributed to Haydn include that of Hob. XVIII:F2 (a divertimento type more closely related to the works in Hoboken's Group XIV than to the concertos proper) by Landon (Vienna: Verlag Doblinger, 1969). Feder, "Klaviersonaten," 102, n. 31 was the first to raise doubts regarding the authenticity of XVIII:9 in G major. Among other significant articles are Feder, "Orgelkonzerte"; Heussner, "Konzert."

[2] Reference number 200,11.   [3] Reference number Rw. 31.145(4).

121

referred to as "Longman/Lukey 6.") The other source is a handwritten
copy presently in the Staatsbibliothek Preussischer Kulturbesitz in West
Berlin.[4] This version, hereafter referred to as "Berlin," is the most complete of the three: all parts survive, including those for two obbligato
horns. The attribution is to the Bohemian violinist Johann Georg Lang,
concertmaster at Ehrenbreitstein, who evidently wrote at least twenty-
eight keyboard concertos, several of which were issued by the firms of
Johann André at Offenbach and William Forster and Longman & Broderip at London.[5] The Lang attribution gains support from a listing in
the 1766 Supplement to the Breitkopf Catalogue.[6] But any neat determination of authenticity for F3 is complicated by widely variant readings
among the sources. To avoid ambiguity, only those early Haydn concertos that are believed authentic and, like F3, clearly in concerto style,
will be compared with it here; unless otherwise stated, these include
Hob. XVIII:1–3, 5, 6 (with violin), and 8.[7]

Various errors in Einsiedeln suggest that the copyist was nonprofessional. While the origin of this version is still cloudy, the appearance of
the paper does not exclude an early date: the incomplete watermark,
employing a variant of the savage-man-with-club motif, together with
the letters LCVSE, may have come from an eighteenth-century Austrian
paper mill.[8] In any event, the Einsiedeln monastery probably did not
acquire the manuscript before 1835, since the inventory for that year did
not yet list it.[9] A formal reconstruction shows that Einsiedeln is the most
primitive of the three versions—and the one least likely to be by Haydn.
It is the shortest; its first movement being only 86 bars is considerably
shorter than those of Haydn's concertos. Furthermore, the internal pro-

[4] Reference number Mus. Ms. 12510/12.

[5] André issued prints of two Lang concertos in D major in 1776 ("Opera IV," and a *Concerto
pastorale* as "Opera V"), and both Forster and Longman & Broderip issued prints of an
E-flat major Lang concerto around 1785. Lang's keyboard concertos were written over a
period from the early 1760s to the early 1780s. Further on Lang, see Davis, "Lang."

[6] Page 54. On the same page, the incipits of Haydn's concertos Hob. XVIII:6–8 and the first
concerto (by Stamitz) in the Longman/Lukey print, mentioned above, appear as well.

[7] Hob. XVIII:11, in a more modern style, may nevertheless antedate its appearance in the
1782–84 Supplement to Breitkopf. Seemingly related stylistically to No. 11 is XVIII:4;
could it have originated later than around 1770, the date Larsen suggests for the entries of
this work in EK (HÜb, 233)? XVIII:10 and F2 are in divertimento style; XVIII:7 is an arrangement of the Piano Trio XV:40 in F major (see Feder, "Klaviertrios," 300–01). In the
recent Haydn literature, XVIII:9, F1 (ed. by Gustav Lenzewski [Berlin-Lichterfelde: Vie-
weg, 1927]), and Es1 have become increasingly suspect with regard to their authenticity.

[8] The figure-with-club motif was long favored in the Lower Austrian paper mills, especially at Rannersdorf, near Schwechat, and at Sankt Pölten, Lower Mill on the Traisen; see
Eineder, *Watermarks,* Nos. 827–50.

[9] The writer is grateful to Pater Kanisius Zünd of the Musikbibliothek, Kloster Einsiedeln,
as well as to Dr. Karl-Heinz Köhler, Abteilungsdirektor at the Deutsche Staatsbibliothek,
and to Dr. Heinz Ramge of the Staatsbibliothek Preussischer Kulturbesitz for supplying
him with information regarding the manuscripts discussed in this paper.

portions of the first movement invert Haydn's solo-to-tutti relationship: the opening tutti is longer than any of the three solo sections, while in Haydn's concertos each of the solo sections is longer than its respective opening tutti. (The only partial exception is the development of the later concerto Hob. XVIII:11, which equals its opening tutti, both 48 bars.) Also, each solo section begins on the third beat in a common-time movement. Such half-bar displacement, when it does on rare occasion occur in Haydn's concertos, more often affects a tutti than a solo entrance, and it never occurs for an entrance of the solo exposition or development. The other movements of Einsiedeln are also unusually short and correspondingly primitive in design.

Beyond its approximate date, the Longman/Lukey print is a puzzle. Only one surviving keyboard concerto by Stamitz has been authenticated. In the Breitkopf Catalogue, two keyboard concertos by Stamitz appear: the authenticated D-major work and a C-major concerto.[10] The D-major incipit is that of the first concerto in Longman/Lukey, hereafter referred to as Longman/Lukey 1. This concerto appears in the J. J. and B. Hummel Catalogue of 1767, and copies of Hummel's edition survive at Amsterdam and Berlin.[11] The C-major concerto is not in Longman/Lukey. A possible corroboration for it appears in La Chevardière's advertisement that Cari Johansson dated as 1762 or 1763, or in La Chevardière's subsequent 1765 listing of two clavecin concertos by Stamitz, a listing that may dovetail with the two concertos appearing in Breitkopf.[12] Against this sparse backdrop, no less than six keyboard concertos attributed to Stamitz suddenly appear in the Longman/Lukey print. Suspicion regarding the reliability of the Longman/Lukey attributions increases when we find that Longman/Lukey 4 was attributed to Johan Agrell by Breitkopf in 1763.[13]

Regarding the music, Longman/Lukey 6 is the only source with 2/4

---

[10] Page 54 (1766); page 29 (1768), respectively.

[11] A full copy in the Deutsche Staatsbibliothek (Thulemeier coll., Th. 229), and a copy of the cembalo part in the Toonkunst Bibliotheek at Amsterdam. The orchestral parts, without Horn II and the title page, survive also at the Library of Congress (reference number M 1010.S755, Op. 10, Case). For references in the Hummel catalogues, see Johansson, *Hummel*, II, facs. 4, as well as the incipit that appears in III, T. 13.

[12] Johannson, *Catalogues*, II, facs. 48, 50. Another possible Johann Stamitz keyboard concerto is a D-major work arranged for keyboard solo ("A Favorite Concerto for the Harpsicord [*sic*] or Piano Forte") printed at London by John Rutherford (before c. 1784) and presently in the New York Public Library (reference number Drexel 5967, No. 9); this concerto was then reissued by the London firm of Samuel, Ann, and Peter Thompson (before 1793), and a copy of this print appears in the Boston Public Library (reference number ★★M.420.100). The attribution is to "Stamitz," possibly Johann. There is also a G-minor concerto in the Universitetsbiblioteket at Lund (reference number Kraus 224, dated 1767), probably misattributed to "Stamits." The writer is grateful to Eugene K. Wolf for bringing these concertos to his attention.

[13] Part IV, p. 17 (C minor).

meter in the first movement. Neither keyboard concerto in Breitkopf employs 2/4; of forty other concertos for sundry instruments attributed to Stamitz, only two have 2/4 meter for their first movements, and both have more active first measures than that of Longman/Lukey 6. The finale also differs from Berlin and Einsiedeln in that it is a straightforward concerto-sonata movement without central repeats. Despite a veneer of sophisticated keyboard writing involving changes of register, Longman/Lukey 6 seems uncertain in other ways with sudden jolts resulting from asymmetrical phrase groupings. The overall effect is a patchwork structure, with a small-dimension emphasis uncharacteristic of Stamitz's symphonic forms.

While no proof of an early date exists for Berlin, the appearance of the paper and indistinct watermark do not exclude a date of c. 1800. The watermark is probably a cartouche or coronet over the letters B and V plus an indistinct third letter.[14] The paper may thus be of Italian origin and date from the eighteenth century. The manuscript reveals the regular hand of a professional copyist, and despite frequent occurrence of ink seepage from the undersides of the folios, the music is easily read and relatively free of mistakes. The attribution to Lang, at variance with Einsiedeln and Longman/Lukey 6, agrees with Breitkopf. While Einsiedeln and Longman/Lukey 6 differ strikingly from each other, Berlin shares important material with both and spans several gaps between them. The tuttis in the first movement of Berlin agree with those of Einsiedeln, while the disproportionate tutti emphasis in Einsiedeln is obviated by longer solos in Berlin. Likewise, the identity and sequence of themes in Berlin agree with Longman/Lukey 6, while the thematic repetitions indigenous to Berlin are absent in Longman/Lukey 6. Thus, Berlin is longer than either Einsiedeln or Longman/Lukey 6, yet closer to both than they to each other. Similar relationshps occur in the other movements, and again Berlin's slow movement and finale are longer than those of Einsiedeln and Longman/Lukey 6. On the basis of these facts, Einsiedeln seems least likely as Haydn, Longman/Lukey 6 is questionable Stamitz, and Berlin emerges as a double mystery, since it shares material with both Einsiedeln and Longman/Lukey 6.

F3 is uncharacteristic of Haydn's keyboard concertos. In all of them, the slow movement is in a contrasting key or mode, while in F3 all three movements are in F major. In Lang's eighteen surviving concertos, nine—no less than half—have the same key and mode for all three movements. The finale of F3 is formally primitive by Haydn's standards; even the Berlin version is shorter than any of the finales in Haydn's concertos, and well below Haydn's average length.[15] Its 111 bars, however, are

---

[14] For a possibly related type of watermark, see R. Landon, "Authenticity," 52.
[15] The lengths of Haydn's early concerto finales average over 215 bars.

about average for Lang's concertos of the 1760s. In the first movements, Haydn's developments are significantly longer than the solo expositions, with the notable exceptions of Hob. XVIII:4 and 11, both doubtless of later date. In all three versions of F3, however, the developments are almost the same lengths as the expositions, agreeing with the proportions in Lang's concertos before c. 1771. Also in the developments, Haydn's concertos reveal unchanging patterns of chord rhythm over relatively long periods, while in the development of F3 the chord rhythm is comparatively fast and irregular, with quickly changing patterns, which is characteristic of Lang's early concertos. Melodically, the background shape of the primary theme, a steady horizontal line with small descending patterns above it, differs from the graceful rise-fall curves in most of Haydn's early concertos. Moreover, the opening repeated notes and phrase punctuation by falling line are characteristic of Lang, in whose works they occur so frequently as to become melodic clichés. Also, as Feder points out,[16] most of Haydn's early concertos (Hob. XVIII:1, 2, 5–8, 10) were written for organ, and the tessitura does not exceed c^3. In F3, however, the keyboard reaches d^3 in both the first movement and finale. This pitch occurs relatively often in Lang's concertos of the 1760s. Thus, the music indicates that while F3 is exceptional for Haydn's early concertos, it comfortably fits the stylistic norm of Lang's early concertos.

Turning to a comparison of Lang and Stamitz, significant formal differences arise between F3 and Longman/Lukey 1, especially with the lack of clear ritornello structure in the first movement of the latter. However, no single work is reliable as a basis for comparison, since it may be exceptional, and a deeper probing will remain largely inconclusive, since no other keyboard concerto attributed to Stamitz has yet been authenticated. But one point may be made: the extremely stable opening of F3 is rare for Stamitz, appearing in only one other concerto attributed to him. With Lang, however, three of his first seven concertos, all written before c. 1771, reveal an opening melodic shape similar to that of F3. While these data are insufficient to exclude Stamitz, to some extent they thus support the Breitkopf attribution to Lang.

Berlin is certainly the most credible source. It is carefully copied in a professional hand, and it is the most complete of all the versions. Musically, the balanced repetitions are consistent with Lang's treatment in other concertos. Though Breitkopf does not cite the two obbligato horns, their structural treatment is consistent with Lang's handling of them elsewhere, and otherwise Berlin agrees totally with Breitkopf. Einsiedeln is a deficient source, both with regard to the missing solo part and the numerous mistakes in the viola and violone parts. Musically, the

---

[16] "Orgelkonzerte," 442.

first-movement proportions and the third-beat entrances for all solo statements occur nowhere else in the keyboard concertos of Haydn or Lang or for that matter, in Longman/Lukey 1. Perhaps it is a faulty copy of a primitive version that was later revised into the version represented in Berlin. The Longman/Lukey print is suspect, since it contains only one authenticated Stamitz concerto, the other five arising rather mysteriously from unknown sources, one of them, No. 4, most probably by Agrell. Further, the patchwork effect of Longman/Lukey 6 contravenes the symphonic sweep found in the larger works of Haydn, Lang, and Stamitz. The retention of Berlin's asymmetrical themes, without the balancing repetitions but with some changes of melody and register that add variety, occasionally at the expense of proper voice leading, suggests that Longman/Lukey 6 is a reworking of the source on which Berlin is based. Of course, it is quite possible that some as yet unidentified person adapted a Lang original to the specific requirements of a publisher.

In short, the composer of Hob. XVIII:F3 is most probably Lang, and the most reliable of the three versions is very likely Berlin.

Haydn's Works for Musical Clock (*Flötenuhr*): Problems of Authenticity, Grouping, and Chronology

SONJA GERLACH

Most of what we know about Haydn's works for musical clock or *Flötenuhr*—a special kind of music box—was unearthed by Ernst Fritz Schmid at the beginning of the 1930s.[1] He published thirty-two pieces under Haydn's name. Hoboken lists them as *Werkgruppe* XIX, with some reservations about the authenticity of a few of them.

I consider only about eighteen or twenty of these pieces to be genuine Haydn works, including the arrangements made by Haydn himself, but excluding the arrangements of Haydn's music which are thought to have been made by others. I shall try to sketch the main facts and my own views concerning the authenticity, classification, and chronology of the thirty-two pieces. My investigation is based on the information and material collected by the Joseph Haydn-Institut, Cologne, including that of the late Ernst Fritz Schmid.

Let us first consider the sources. Thirteen of the thirty-two pieces are preserved in Haydn's autograph. The other nineteen pieces should be considered doubtful. Six of these have survived in a manuscript copy. The remaining thirteen are known only from the cylinders of three musical clocks which together play thirty of the thirty-two pieces and are said by oral tradition to play only music composed by Haydn. Nevertheless, each of the clocks plays at least one spurious piece.

---

[1] Schmid, "Flötenuhr"; Schmid, "Funde."

Two of the clocks are signed and dated by Primitiv Niemetz, a clock builder who was employed as a librarian at the Esterházy court. One is dated 1792, the other 1793. Each plays twelve pieces.

The third clock is not signed; perhaps, therefore, it was built not by Niemetz himself but by his apprentice Joseph Gurck. It plays sixteen pieces. According to oral tradition, it was built as early as 1772, but in fact it plays a fugue composed no earlier than 1789. Moreover, it was probably built as late as 1796, to judge from the (somewhat hypothetical) dating of a spurious piece it plays.[2] It therefore seems to be the latest of the three clocks, not the earliest.

The clocks themselves must be considered as documents of eighteenth-century performance practice, though unfortunately they do not play exactly as they once did. Above all, the original clock spring that is responsible for the speed has been replaced, and therefore nobody knows the original tempo of the pieces. That the pipes were retuned several times and may therefore no longer have exactly the original pitches is not so important, in my view, since after all there cannot be much difference in pitch. Some of the pins that open the valves of the pipes are bent or have been replaced, but despite these defects it is still possible to estimate approximately how the original performance sounded, especially the intentions with respect to the articulation.

The original grouping of the works is not the same as that given by the clocks. In order to find out which of the pieces could have been composed for a particular clock, we have to compare their ranges: since each clock has a specific assortment of pipes, each piece is based on a corresponding set of pitches. I discovered that there are four significantly different sets of pitches (17, 25, 29, and 32 different notes; see Table 1).[3]

To judge from the pieces preserved in autograph Haydn used all the available pitches in most of the pieces, including the arrangements. There are only a few pieces in which one or two pitches are not used. On the other hand, in several doubtful and spurious pieces (Hob. XIX:4,26) from four to as many as nine pitches are missing. The absence of many pitches suggests that these works may not be authentic. In combination with stylistic and other types of evidence it serves to divide the doubtful pieces into those that are probably genuine and those that are probably spurious (see Table 1).

The group that falls into Range I consists of at least four and probably

[2] Hob. XIX:4, which seems to have first become known in Vienna as a dance from a ballet performed in 1796. It was evidently popular, since Beethoven used the same melody as the basis of a set of variations (WoO 71) in the same year. A similar case occured in 1793, when Niemetz transcribed a piece first known from an opera performed in Vienna in that year (Hob. XIX:26) onto the cylinder of the 1793 clock.

[3] A few negligible differences concern one or two pitches. It would seem that Haydn did not keep in mind the precise range determined by the first piece in a given group when composing later pieces in the same group.

Table 1   Haydn's Works for Musical Clock

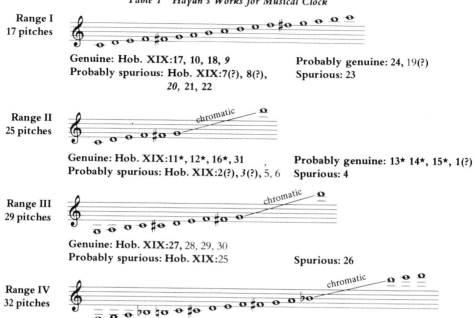

Range I
17 pitches

Genuine: Hob. XIX:17, 10, 18, *9*   Probably genuine: 24, 19(?)
Probably spurious: Hob. XIX:7(?), 8(?),   Spurious: 23
        20, 21, 22

Range II
25 pitches

Genuine: Hob. XIX:11★, 12★, 16★, 31   Probably genuine: 13★ 14★, 15★, 1(?)
Probably spurious: Hob. XIX:2(?), *3*(?), 5, 6   Spurious: 4

Range III
29 pitches

Genuine: Hob. XIX:27, 28, 29, 30
Probably spurious: Hob. XIX:25   Spurious: 26

Range IV
32 pitches

Genuine: Hob. XIX:32

Works given in lightface are arrangements of a work by Haydn.
Works given in italics are apparently influenced by another Haydn work.
★With a second version for Range III.

five genuine pieces. These are contained in the 1792 clock, which has a corresponding set of pipes. But it is tuned in F major instead of C major, so that the pipes are tuned a fourth higher than the written notes. Mainly because of this transposition, I have concluded that the 1792 clock is not the one for which Haydn composed these pieces. If that is true, there are two consequences: 1) the value of the clock in establishing authenticity is diminished; 2) the genuine Range I pieces were probably not composed in 1792 but earlier, perhaps before Haydn's first journey to England; more precisely, between 1788 and 1790. To judge from the datable arrangements that the clock plays, 1788 is the earliest possible date.[4] Among the seven pieces known only from this cylinder, one piece is a literal transcription of a Haydn song. This arrangement (Hob. XIX:19) might have served for increasing the unusual number of five genuine works to the usual six. The remaining six pieces on the clock, I suspect, are spurious, to judge from the music. But so far only one has been proved spurious (Hob. XIX:23).

[4] Hob. XIX:9 is an arrangement based on the minuet of Haydn's String Quartet Op. 54, No. 2 in C major (1788).

The Range II group is that of the fugue Hob. XIX:16, dated 1789. From the title of a manuscript copy we learn that this fugue was part of eight so-called sonatas composed by Haydn and transcribed onto the cylinder in December 1789. Since the copy now contains only the fugue, and there is no clock of 1789 available, we cannot determine which pieces the other seven sonatas are. The chances are that six of them are identical to Hob. XIX:11–15, 31 (preserved in another copy) for, with the exception of XIX:31, they also appear on the cylinder of the unsigned clock, which uses the same Range II and which also contains the fugue. The unsigned clock, of course, is not the one of 1789 for which Haydn composed his eight sonatas, because it contains sixteen pieces, not eight, among them four in the smaller Range I (XIX:7–10) which we already know from the 1792 clock. Probably it was built much later. Three other pieces on this clock are arrangements; Hob. XIX:4 is spurious, and 5 and 6 are probably spurious. We are left with three pieces on the clock which are doubtful in every sense of the word. Among them may be hidden the eighth sonata of 1789. To judge from the style, Hoboken's No. 1 may, in fact, be that sonata and a genuine Haydn work, though some doubts remain.[5]

Range III is the one of the 1793 clock, which is very likely the clock for which Haydn composed his Range III pieces. The clock was Haydn's farewell gift to Prince Anton Esterházy on the occasion of his departure for England in January 1794. Seemingly, Haydn was too busy with other preparations for his journey to spend much time on the clock, for eleven of its twelve pieces are arrangements! Two arrangements, moreover, are spurious (Hob. XIX:25,26). Three were made by Haydn from other works, and six are adapted from the so-called sonatas of 1789 by enlarging their ranges.[6] The twelfth piece (Hob. XIX:27) is the only original composition Haydn wrote for this clock and range, and together with the arrangements may be dated to 1793. It is one of Haydn's most splendid and typical pieces for the musical clock.

Finally, there is only a single Range IV piece extant. It is an arrangement made by Haydn from Symphony No. 99 in E-flat major of 1793 and probably made in the same year, or possibly later. A clock with that range is not known. Haydn noted all the pitches of the piece as a scale, beneath the following words (which seem to have been instructions for a pupil): "The key of this scale is F. But it is possible to write pieces in C [major], G [major], and D minor, for the sake of variety."[7] With this advice, Haydn apparently ceased to compose works for musical clock.

---

[5] Especially since it is not in the same key as the other sonatas.
[6] Some evidence indicates that Haydn knew about the Range III versions but did not make the changes himself.
[7] The autograph is preserved in Vienna, Gesellschaft der Musikfreunde.

Text and Performance: The Treatment of *Ossia* Variants in Haydn Critical Scores

MAKOTO OHMIYA

Joseph Haydn's six Scherzandi (Hob. II:33–38) first appeared in the Breitkopf Catalogue for 1765, titled "VI Scherzandi," and scored for two oboes, two horns, two violins, and bass, with an added flute solo in each Trio. Of these works, only one, No. 6 in A major (Hob. II:38), appears in EK, at the top of the first surviving page; it is labeled "Sÿnfonia Ex A."

There are no surviving autographs or authentic manuscripts, but there are eleven sets of eighteenth-century manuscript copies. Conducting the Haydn Ensemble Tokyo, I made the first complete recording of the scherzandi in 1975 in Paris. As texts, I used the critical scores edited by H. C. Robbins Landon (Diletto Musicale, Nos. 71–76). Two of the eleven eighteenth-century copies were unknown to Landon, however: one in the National Museum, Prague (Waldstein archives), and one in the Gesellschaft der Musikfreunde, Vienna.

The Waldstein manuscript was first reported by Georg Feder.[1] It contains substantial variants in the flute solos in the Trios of Nos. 5 and 6. The two chief variants in No. 5 (see Example 1) are the transposition to the upper octave in both halves of the Trio, and the addition of staccati and slurs in the first three bars of the second half. In No. 6 (see Example 2), transposition to the upper octave appears in most of the first half, and in the return of the theme in the second half. One could adopt these variants as *ossia* bars in a critical edition. But even so, the performer would have to choose which version to use. Obviously, the octave transpositions make a considerable difference.

Variants in critical editions occur mainly in two contexts: when the autograph and the other authentic sources contain different readings, and when there is no surviving authentic source. The performer's attitude must be different in these two cases. When all the variants come from the composer, he can choose the one he prefers according to his own musical preference. But when they depend on an editor's interpretation, he must study the sources himself if he wishes to reach an informed conclusion.

In the Diletto Musicale edition of the scherzandi, the evaluation of the sources is not sufficiently detailed to permit an intelligent interpretation of the Waldstein variants in the Trios. I was therefore compelled to study the sources independently. They fall into four categories, according to their instrumentation:[2]

[1] Feder, "Überlieferung," 22.
[2] For detailed descriptions of these and other manuscript sources for the Scherzandi, see JHW VIII. [Ed.]

Example 1. Scherzando No. 5 (Hob. II:37) in E major, Trio

Example 2. Scherzando No. 6 (Hob. II:38) in A major, Trio, First Section

A. Fl, 2 Ob, 2 Hr, 2 Vln, B.
   London (Moravian Archives); Berlin; Prague (Pachta)

B. Fl, 2 Vln, B [oboes and horns omitted]
   Vienna (Musikfreunde); Salzburg (with locally added horns and viola)

C. 2 Ob, 2 Hr, 2 Vln, B [flute omitted; Vln. I substitutes in the Trios]
   Modena; Český Krumlau [formerly Schwarzenberg]; Kremsmünster

D. [As in A, but with additional violas]
Waldstein; Seitenstetten; St. Florian
(On the basis of variant readings in the added viola parts, it seems possible that Waldstein is the "archetype" of these three sources. Another indication that they are closely related is that the flute part in No. 5 in St. Florian has the same variants as Waldstein.)

The viola parts in Waldstein double the bass at the octave. This accords with Landon's statement that a copyist never omits a viola part in a Haydn work, but that viola parts were added locally from time to time. Although the Waldstein viola parts are not authentic, its readings in the other instruments are always close to those in the sources of category A. But these added violas and the variant flute readings suggest that Waldstein originated relatively late. Hence I omitted the flute variants in the Trios of Nos. 5 and 6.

The critical scores published in the Diletto Musicale series are conscientiously edited and also intended for practical performance. But as noted above, they do not offer detailed studies of the sources. The volumes in JHW, on the other hand, are accompanied by critical reports, which supply these studies. But even they do not give all the particulars relating to *ossia* variants in the text. Even here, the performer must select the reading which best satisfies his musical sense.

The Haydn Ensemble Tokyo has toured with Haydn's Violin Concerto No. 1 in C major in its repertoire. For the musical text, I used JHW III:1. There is no authentic source extant; the score in JHW has no fewer than thirty-one measures with *ossia* readings, some of these in several parts simultaneously. In the critical report, the editors merely list general principles which govern the *ossia* variants printed.[3]

The performer's choice of *ossia* variants is made first on the basis of parallel passages, which are also used for the addition, where necessary, of slurs and staccati. But it is not easy to do this when the passage in question and the parallel passage exchange the "main" reading and the *ossia* reading.

In the first movement, for example, the first variant, in the viola part, m. 3, has no parallel passage. The next variant is found in m. 12, in the solo and orchestral violins. The editors have added the *ossia* reading by analogy with m. 265, where, however, it appears as the main reading. According to the critical report (p. 12), the *ossia* reading in m. 265 (which is the same as the main reading in m. 12) appears in only one source in the principal violin; and it does not appear in any source for the first orchestral violins. In the second violin—as in most of the *ossia* variants in this concerto—the sources in which the *ossia* reading appears are not speci-

[3] See JHW, III, critical report, 12.

fied. The critical report merely makes the summary statement (p. 12) that they do not appear in the main source, but rather either in two (of the three) secondary sources, or in one secondary source and at least one tertiary source. The reader or performer who might wish to know these details from the sources cannot find them, even though they could easily have been supplied by the editors.[4]

A third example from the first movement is found in m. 55. The *ossia* for the second violin corresponds in rhythm—but not in pitch—to the main reading in m. 216, and (except for an octave shift) to all three parts in m. 202. On the other hand, the main reading corresponds to m. 135; there, however, the reading in the principal violin corresponds to the *ossia* reading of the second violin in m. 55 and, in effect, to m. 202.

If a critical report included all the relevant readings for *ossia* variants and also took parallel passages into account (as I have done here), it would aid the performer by enabling him to avoid complex independent study of the sources when choosing the readings to use in performance.

The Chronology of the Early Piano Sonatas of Joseph Haydn: A Comparative Study of Three Editions

JANE BOSTIAN PRICE

About one-third of Haydn's piano sonatas show stylistic features which suggest that they were composed prior to 1771, the year of the C-minor Sonata Hob. XVI:20 (ChL. 33). The lack of dated autographs or systematic cataloguing of these works, along with the lack of general knowledge about Haydn's activities in the early years, makes impossible a definitive chronology of these works. This paper presents some observations and conclusions drawn from a comparative study of the three twentieth-century editions of these sonatas which have attempted to give them a chronological arrangement.

The earliest of these editions, by Karl Päsler, published in Haydn, GA (1918), includes among its fifty-two works fifteen of the sonatas to be considered here. Päsler's chronology is based on entries found in the Breitkopf catalogues (in which No. 5 [Hob. XVI:5, ChL. 8] in A major appeared as early as 1763) and on orderings and numberings of these works in manuscript copies known to him.

In JHW (XVIII:1–3, 1966–70), Georg Feder does not attempt a strictly chronological ordering. Instead, he arranges the eighteen works which he considers to date from before 1765 in two categories, according to stylistic features representing the kinds of functions Haydn may have

---

[4] Although JHW often gives summary descriptions of insignificant deviations in articulation markings and other performance indications, its use of the procedure described here for actual textual variants in the musical substance is unusual. Perhaps it was motivated by the unsatisfactory character of the sources for this particular work. [Ed.]

meant the pieces to fulfill. One group, called "Nine small early sonatas,"
Feder considers to have been written for Haydn's students, or for performance by amateurs or dilettants. These works are technically and formally limited. A second group, "Nine early sonatas," he considers to be
works written for the professional musician. They are more demanding
technically and on a larger scale, and their broader range of experimentation suggests that in them Haydn was testing his capacities as a
composer. Feder claims that, although Haydn may have written both
types contemporaneously, the orderings within his two categories in
JHW XVIII:1 reflect increasing musical sophistication, and therefore he
implies that they may represent Haydn's chronological development.

The eighteen works in Feder's two categories have served as the basic
list of works to be considered in this study. This arbitrary limitation does
not do justice to the thoroughness of Christa Landon's edition (ChL.),
published in the mid-1960s. A comparison of the treatment given to
Feder's eighteen works in all three editions may be seen in Table 1.

The juxtaposition of these three chronologies reveals numerous points
of contradiction. Feder and Landon presumably deviated from Päsler's
ordering on the basis of sources not available to him. But it is not possible to evaluate these decisions at this writing (1975), because neither set
of critical notes has been published. The focus of this study will therefore
be upon the musical substance of the works in question. Selected features
of style and form have been examined in an effort to establish evidence of

Table 1   Haydn's Early Sonatas (Roughly to 1765) in Three Editions

Feder (*JHW XVIII:1*)	*Päsler (Haydn, GA)* [=Hob. XVI]	*C. Landon* (Haydn, Sonatas)
Nine Small Early Sonatas		
1st	1	10
2nd	7	2
3rd	8	1
4th	9	3
5th	10	6
6th	——	4
7th	——	7
8th	3	14
9th	4	9
Nine Early Sonatas		
1st	16	——
2nd	5	8
3rd	12	12
4th	13	15
5th	14	16
6th	6	13
7th	2	11
8th	——	17
9th	——	18

systematic employment or development of these elements. Subsequently, the particular ordering of the sonatas in each chronology has been examined for ways in which the order might reflect an evolving style or technical approach in the work of the young Haydn.

Since space does not permit a thorough exposition of the data of the study, close examination of one problem and the import of selected data for evaluating that problem will illustrate the general approach. The placement in each system of Päsler's Sonata No. 1 (Hob. XVI:1, ChL. 10) in C major will serve as an illustration. This work appears in Feder's system as the first of the "Nine small early sonatas," which implies that he finds it a somewhat unsophisticated work. In Christa Landon's arrangement, it does not appear until No. 10. Three of the stylistic features examined for the repertory as a whole have particular significance for this sonata.

The first is the presence of a slow movement. We might also observe the character of such a movement. Table 2 shows the location within each chronology of those sonatas in which the second movement is a slow movement. In Päsler's chronology, sonatas with slow movements as middle movements occur more often in the earliest works. In both Feder's and Landon's systems, these sonatas occur more often among the later works. Our sonata, however, is an exception to this trend in Feder's arrangement. Moreover, in Feder's and Landon's systems, generally speaking, those slow movements of greater length and gravity occur relatively late, while in Päsler's they are very early works. In Landon's edition the tempo marking for the second movement of our sonata is Adagio, rather than Andante as in Päsler and Feder. This makes of it a movement of greater gravity, and the sonata of which it is a part occurs, significantly, in the latter half of her chronology. While these are insufficient grounds to compare the Päsler and Landon systems for internal consistency, the inconsistency in Feder's system here makes Landon's arrangement seem more convincing in this respect.

Data relative to a second feature corroborate this evidence. All these sonatas have a Menuet/Trio movement. Those sonatas which have a slow movement as middle movement (that is, those listed in Table 2)

Table 2   *Slow Movements in Second Position*

	Päsler [*Hob. XVI*]	*Landon*	*JHW XVIII:1*
Andante, 9 mm.	8	1	"9 Small," No. 3
Andante, 17 mm.	1	10 [Adagio]	"9 Small," No. 1
Andante, 56 mm.	———	17	"9 Early," No. 8
Andante, 63 mm.	11	5	[Appendix]
Andante, 79 mm.	3	14	"9 Small," No. 8
Adagio, 25 mm.	6	13	"9 Early," No. 6
Largo, 54 mm.	2	11	"9 Early," No. 7

have the Menuet/Trio as last movement. All other sonatas included in the study have the Menuet/Trio as the second movement.

The third feature examined, perhaps the most significant one, is whether the first movement is in sonata form. The criterion used to establish the presence of the form in this study is the presence of a recapitulation of the opening material in the tonic. In many cases, the second group in the dominant is also recapitulated, but this element has not been considered essential in this context. Conversely, it is not itself sufficient to establish sonata form. Table 3 shows the disposition in each chronology of those works whose first movements are in sonata form.

Table 3   First Movements in Sonata Form

Päsler [Hob. XVI:] 2, 4, 7–10, 12–14
Landon: 1–4, 6, 9, 11, 12, 15, 16, 18
Feder: "9 Small": 2–6, 9; "9 Early": 3–5, 9

In Feder's system, sonata form predominates in the "Nine small early sonatas," but it occurs in fewer than half of his group of larger sonatas. In his preface he suggests that Haydn devoted a greater degree of inventiveness and experimentation to the "nine early works." The statistical summary just presented helps to corroborate this point of view: the strict adherence to formal outlines is abandoned in favor of other techniques in these larger sonatas.

According to Päsler's arrangement, the majority of pieces with sonata-form first movements occurs in the middle third of the group, between numbers 6 and 12. Possibly, according to this arrangement, Haydn's earliest efforts at sonata composition did not adhere strictly to the basics of what was to become the standardized form, nor do the latter works of these years incorporate the form strictly; but for a time in between, Haydn employed the form more consistently. Landon's chronology, on the other hand, suggests a tendency to use rudiments of the form at first, then to relax this strict adherence (in approximately the middle third of her chronology), and then to return to more consistent use of it. While neither of these chronologies is completely consistent in this respect, the juxtaposition of the two permits one to focus on the problem being considered here.

The first movement of Päsler's Sonata No. 1 (ChL.10) is not in sonata form, a trait less typical of the "small" sonatas, to which it belongs, than of his other category. In both Päsler's and Landon's systems, it is located in an appropriate portion of the chronology to reflect the tendencies described above in each system, making a comparative evaluation of these two systems on the basis of this feature alone impossible. However, when the evidence discussed above relative to the presence and character of the slow movement of this work is considered as well, Landon's system seems to accommodate this particular sonata more appropriately than either of the others.

Although Landon's arrangement is more convincing in the case of this sonata, in others Feder's system seems to make more sense. Because both editors claim to have made judgements on the basis of materials unknown to Päsler, more critical attention has been given to a comparison of the two recent editions. Feder's arrangement by category is a useful and in many cases quite convincing means of ordering the works in question. At some points of difference, the internal evidence seems to support Landon's arrangement. No final decision about the merits of either edition in these respects can be rendered, however, until the source materials and other historical documentation on which they are based can be examined.

The Breitkopf & Härtel *Oeuvres complettes de J. Haydn*

LAURIE SHULMAN

The late eighteenth and early nineteenth centuries did not share our modern insistence upon accurate texts in music. Accessibility of the music was more important. If a publisher could produce an inexpensive, attractive, and well-printed volume comprising a substantial amount of music, he was certain to have a market—especially for a popular composer like Haydn.

Breitkopf and Härtel were aware of the possibilities for prestige and financial success in producing an edition of Haydn's works on a large scale. In April 1799, Christoph Gottlob Breitkopf wrote Haydn asking for a piece from *The Creation;* in the same letter he submitted to Haydn a plan for a complete edition of Haydn's keyboard compositions.[1] At this time, Breitkopf and Härtel were well under way with their *Oeuvres complettes de Mozart,* which they had begun in 1798. This edition was doing well enough to predict success in a similar venture with Haydn.

The firm had been trying to take over Artaria's role as Haydn's principal publisher since the early 1790s. By 1798 they had succeeded in publishing only two first editions of Haydn's music.[2] They were still interested in procuring new and unpublished music, and the proposal for the new edition was ambitious. Breitkopf realized that Haydn's consent was essential to the success of the project. A major edition authorized and approved by the composer, and advertised as such, would sell more individual copies and subscriptions to the series than a pirate reprint.

It appears that Haydn did not react to Breitkopf's suggestion. At any

[1] Hase, 16.

[2] Larsen, HÜb, 138 cites the sonata Hob. XVI:48 (ChL. 58) in C major, which appeared in 1789 in Breitkopf's *Musikalisiches Potpourri,* and separately as "Op. 89" in 1798; and the trio Hob. XV:30 in E-flat major, printed c. 1796 as "Op. 88."

rate, Gottfried Christoph Härtel, Breitkopf's younger partner, asked Georg August Griesinger to inquire personally of Haydn about the venture. (This was the origin of the contact between Haydn and Griesinger to which we owe so much biographical information about Haydn.) Griesinger's letters to Härtel testify to his success with Haydn. One dated May 25, 1799 reads:

> Your projected edition of his keyboard works has his complete approval, and I have specific instructions to assure you of this approval. However, there is much music published under his name of which he is not the composer, so he would like to receive from you a list [*Verzeichnis*] of the compositions which you intend to publish.[3]

Härtel lost no time in advertising Haydn's cooperation. The public announcement for the forthcoming edition, date May 1799, read in part:

> We believe that we are fulfilling the wishes of all lovers of excellent—and especially of Haydn's—music in announcing a complete, tasteful, and extremely attractive edition of the complete works of this great man, and first of all of his keyboard compositions—in our publishing house, under agreement and authority of the composer himself. The so-often-deceived public has nothing whatever to fear that any spurious work will be admitted, nor any which Haydn himself has not acknowledged as worthy and authentic. . . .[4]

Breitkopf and Härtel went out of their way to make the Haydn edition as desirable and attractive as possible. Griesinger was able to report to Härtel on June 12, 1799 that Haydn was completely satisfied with the written copy of the announcement.[5]

Shortly prior to the appearance of the first volume, Härtel drafted a preface for the Haydn edition which publicly reaffirmed Haydn's collaboration with and approval of the forthcoming volumes.[6] This preface tells us much about the twelve-volume series which kept Breitkopf & Härtel busy from New Year's Day of 1800 through December 1806. It is intended to give the impression that Haydn took an active interest in planning the edition, if not in formal supervision of the text preparation, and that everything included was authentic. Despite its title, the edition can in no way be considered complete, even for the keyboard works. Whether Haydn ever planned to compose new works so that the *Oeuvres complettes* would not be a total reissue of "old favorites," as the preface implies he hoped to do, is uncertain.

Several questions the preface does *not* answer. First of all, precisely what works were included? And—related, of course—what was *not* in-

---

[3] The letter appears in part in Hase, 16–17; in fuller quotation in Pohl-Botstiber, 138–39 and Thomas, "Griesinger," 55–56.
[4] Translated from Hase, 18–19.
[5] Pohl-Botstiber, 139–40; Thomas, "Griesinger," 57–58.
[6] The text of this preface is quoted in Hase, 17; by Päsler in the foreword to Haydn, GA, XIV:1, xviii; and elsewhere.

cluded? Were all the works included published in their original form, or were they arranged for other combinations of instruments? Were any new, previously unpublished works added? To what extent, if any, did Haydn revise any of the proofs? How accurate is the musical text; is it consistent throughout all twelve volumes? Were any works included which have been subsequently shown *not* to be by Haydn? We shall endeavor to deal with all of these problems.

Breitkopf and Härtel were not concerned with a critical complete edition in the modern sense, but rather a "Haydn's Greatest Hits" series. Larsen likens the venture to a modern anthology of a prominent writer's principal works. The publishers were aiming for as wide an audience as possible; works for keyboard were most suitable. Of the twelve volumes, three are exclusively solo piano works, and one more contains only one work not for piano solo. Two volumes are solo and polyphonic songs with piano accompaniment. Five are piano trios and piano sonatas with spurious added violin parts. Only one volume—significantly, the last one—contains a mélange: three piano sonatas and one Adagio for solo piano, two violin sonatas and three piano trios. We shall discuss the peculiarities of this last volume later. A survey of the edition's contents is given in Table 1.

Table 1   *The Contents of the Breitkopf & Härtel* **Ouevres complettes de J. Haydn**

Cahier I.	**Sonatas Hob. XVI:52, 34, 49, 44, 45, 46, 19, 18**	**(Early 1800)**
Cahier II.	**Sonatas Hob. XVI:35–39, 20**	**(November 1800)**
	One-movement works Hob. XVII:6, 4, 1, 5, 3	
Cahier III.	**Piano trios Hob. XV:24–29**	**(1801)**
Cahier IV.	**Sonatas Hob. XVI:40–42, 48**	**(May 1802)**
	Piano trio Hob. XV:32	
	Sonata Hob. XVI:47	
	Arietta Hob. XVII:2	
	Piano trio Hob. XV:15	
Cahier V.	**Piano trios Hob. XV:6–8, 14, 16**	**(October 1802)**
Cahier VI.	**Piano trios Hob. XV:21–23, 10, 17**	**(May 1803)**
Cahier VII.	**Piano trios Hob. XV:18–20, 11–13**	**(June 1803)**
Cahier VIII.	**Lied Hob. XXVIa:45**	**(June 1803)**
	Duets Hob. XXVa:1, 2	
	Part-songs Hob. XXVb:1, XXVc:4, 3, 2, XXVb:3, XXVc:8, 9	
	Lieder Hob. XXVIa:31–35	
	Arianna auf Naxos **(Hob. XXVIb:2)**	
Cahier IX.	**Lieder Hob. XXVIa:46, 22, 21, 24, 36, 4, 3**	**(June 1803)**
	Part-songs Hob. XXVb:4, XXVc:5, 1, 6, 7	
	Lieder Hob. XXVIa:36, 17, 6, 13, 25–30, 23, 14, 11, 10, 5, 7, 14, 8, 15, 12	
Cahier X.	**Piano trios Hob. XV:31, 30, 9, 2, 1**	**(June 1804)**
	Sonatas Hob. XVI:24–26 [added violin parts supplied by Charles Burney]	
Cahier XI.	**Sonatas Hob. XVI:27–32, 21–23, 51, 12, 13**	**(180–)**
Cahier XII.	**Sonatas Hob. XVI:33, 6, 14, 50/ii**	**(December 1806)**
	Sonatas Hob. XVI:43bis, 15 [with added violin parts]	
	Piano trios Hob. XV:3–5 [Hob. XV:3, 4 probably by Pleyel]	

Ascertaining what was omitted from the *Oeuvres complettes* is far more problematic. None of the concertos or music for piano four-hands appears. Neither does the edition include any of the piano–cum–accompaniment works in Hoboken's group XIV. Of the fifty-two piano sonatas in the 1918 Päsler edition, the following sonatas are absent: Hob. XVI:1–5, 7–11, and 16 and 17 (the former is probably, the latter certainly, spurious). All of these are early works, from 1767 or earlier. Their exclusion falls in line with the statement in the preface that early, youthful works had been left out. A parallel situation exists with the trios: no work from before 1766 was included.

Five of the piano sonatas appear as violin sonatas. The piano sonata Hob. XVI:50 (ChL. 60) in C major is represented only by its slow movement, an Adagio in F, which appears in Volume 12. In 1794 the single movement appeared in an Artaria print,[7] but the reasons for including the Adagio alone in the *Oeuvres complettes* are unknown. Evidently the movement acquired sufficient popularity on its own, perhaps through fewer technical demands than the outer two movements, to merit its inclusion independently.

A complete list of Haydn's solo and polyphonic songs not included in the *Oeuvres complettes* lies beyond the scope of this study. Though many which are included appear in two languages, the original language of the text is not always represented. For example, the songs on texts by Anne Hunter, originally published by the composer in 1794 as *Six Original Canzonettas,* appear only in German in Volume 9. Presumably this made the songs palatable to a greater number of purchasers in Germany and Austria.[8] The policy is inconsistent with, for example, the presentation of the two *Duetti: Nisa e Tirsi* in both Italian and German in Volume 8.

These two duets for soprano and tenor are noteworthy in that they are among the few works in the *Oeuvres complettes* which had not been published previously. In addition to these duets, Larsen cites the following works as appearing for the first time in the *Oeuvres complettes:* the piano sonatas Hob. XVI:12–14 (ChL. 12, 15, 16) in Volumes 11 and 12; the solo songs *Ein kleines Haus/Un tetto umil* in Volume 8 and *Antwort auf die Frage eines Mädchens* in Volume 9; and the entire group of three- and four-part songs.[9] The musical text in the two volumes of vocal works is significantly better than that of the instrumental music.

Whether Haydn was directly involved with the preparation and revision of the *Oeuvres complettes* may never be ascertained. There is evidence both for and against his personal involvement. For instance, the selection of works for new volumes, and particularly the "separation of early,

---

[7] Cf. Hoboken, I, 777.

[8] Hoboken, II, 256 indicates that the *Ouevres complettes* text was taken from the Artaria print of 1794.

[9] Larsen, HÜb, 144.

youthful works" alluded to in the preface, was attended to by the firm and not by Haydn. However, we know from Hase that Breitkopf & Härtel complied promptly with Haydn's request for their catalogues of his works.[10] They sent him a long list of his earlier works, with the request that he mark those which were authentic and nonauthentic, and attempt a rough chronology of those which he had indeed written. According to Päsler, Härtel made written entries on the returned handwritten thematic catalogues for the first seven volumes, that Haydn had reviewed and approved the contents.[11] Päsler also states that another document notes a great number of sonatas that were sent to the composer for revision on December 11 (1802?). Clearly, Haydn received the catalogues to begin with, and he worked actively with the publishers at least for seven volumes. But we have no way of knowing precisely in what capacity he worked with them. Larsen points out that in all likelihood Haydn gave no more than cursory supervision to the catalogues, as his weakened memory was providing the principal support.

As Larsen has shown, Haydn apparently did not directly contribute to the last volumes in the series.[12] Hence it is hardly surprising that they suffer from problems: textual errors, rearrangements, inclusion of spurious works, and inconsistent groupings of musical genres. Two works in Volumes 11 and 12 have since been shown to be nonauthentic: the two piano trios Hob. XV:3 and 4. Originally published by Forster as Opus 40 (along with the authentic trio Hob. XV:5), they were for many years thought to be by Michael Haydn, on stylistic grounds; more recently, Alan Tyson has argued convincingly for Pleyel's authorship.[13] In either case, the inclusion of these spurious works implies the the publishers were devoting less careful attention to the edition in the later volumes. Volume 11 has serious flaws in the musical text. Päsler asserts that the unauthorized 1777 Hummel edition of the sonatas Hob. XVI:21–26 (ChL. 36–41) was used as the model for the *Oeuvres complettes* for those works.[14] He enumerates so many problems with this Hummel edition that it is painfully easy to speculate about the number of errors transmitted into the *Oeuvres complettes*.

The Haydn *Oeuvres complettes* are an object lesson in explaining the problems of nineteenth-century editions to twentieth-century musicians. The Haydn and Mozart editions were important forerunners of the homage and tribute editions of the later nineteenth century and, of course, of the first *Gesamtausgaben*. But this Haydn edition also condemned the nineteenth century to its belief that Haydn wrote only thirty-four piano sonatas; Breitkopf & Härtel either published the others as violin sonatas or trios or omitted them. It was not until 1895, when Hugo Riemann

[10] Hase, 17; cf. Larsen, HÜb, 140.   [11] Päsler in Haydn, GA, XIV:1, iii.
[12] Larsen, HÜb, 298–99.   [13] Tyson, "Trios."   [14] Päsler in Haydn, GA, XIV:1, xiii.

edited Haydn's sonatas for Augener, that some other early sonatas were published for the first time. If the *Oeuvres complettes* were regarded as Haydn's last will and testament with regard to musical text, the nineteenth century must be forgiven some of its transgressions, as it were, against our twentieth-century delight in the *Urtext*.

A Study of Editions of Haydn's Piano Sonata Hob. XVI:52 (ChL. 62) in E-flat Major

JEANETTE TAVES

Haydn's Piano Sonata Hob. XVI:52 (ChL. 62) was composed in London in 1794. Within the next decade it appeared in three important editions: the first edition published by Artaria in Vienna in 1798, the first English edition published by Longman & Clementi in London in 1799, and the reprint in the *Oeuvres complettes* published by Breitkopf & Härtel in Leipzig in 1800. Of these three, only the Longman & Clementi can definitely be said to have been engraved from the autograph. There are directions for the engraver in English in Haydn's hand on the autograph, and the edition follows the autograph almost exactly. The present study, made with the aid of a facsimile of the autograph, is a comparison of these early editions, some nineteenth- and early twentieth-century editions, and recent editions made after the rediscovery of the autograph, which is now in the Library of Congress, in the 1930s.

The other editions under comparison are the Hallberger publication from Stuttgart, edited by J. Moscheles (mid-nineteenth-century); Haydn, GA, XIV:3, edited by Karl Päsler (1918); the C. F. Peters edition, edited by Carl Adolf Martienssen (1937); the Henle edition, edited by Georg Feder (1966); the Universal edition, edited by Christa Landon (1963); and portions of the Doblinger edition, edited by Paul Badura-Skoda (1958). In this edition Badura-Skoda indicates the variants between the autograph and the Artaria first edition. In the present study, this edition was used as the source for information on the Artaria edition.

By means of a few select examples two types of editorial problems will be pointed out: first, the problems that occur when successive editions are based on previous editions, as opposed to the autograph; and second, differences that appear even when editions are based on the autograph.

The first problem for study, and one which is unique to this sonata, is that of the arpeggiated chords. In the first movement, mm. 1–2, in the autograph the only arpeggiated chord in these two measures is the initial chord in the left hand.[1] In fact, this is the only arpeggiated chord indicated by Haydn in the entire first movement. However, Artaria's edition

---

[1] The passages from the first movement discussed in this paper can be seen in the facsimile of the first page of the autograph on the frontispiece of JHW XVIII:3.

was responsible for a tradition of indicating arpeggiation on many of the block chords in this movement. The chords to be arpeggiated vary from edition to edition, except, of course, in those editions based on the autograph.

A second example, from mm. 9–10 of the first movement, constitutes an error in harmony. The problem chord is found on the first beat of m. 10. In the autograph the bass note is f. The *Oeuvres complettes* indicate e♭ as the bass note. While this could be explained as a continuation of a tonic pedal, it is clearly lacking in the autograph. Moscheles, Päsler, and Martienssen perpetuate this error.

In mm. 14–17 we find two problematic points. One is the dynamic indications in mm. 16–17. The decrescendo to *piano* in m. 16 is omitted in the *Oeuvres complettes*. Martienssen took the liberty of suggesting his own dynamic marking: a crescendo at the beginning of m. 16 leading to the *forte* in m. 17, which produces exactly the opposite effect of the one Haydn intended. The second problem is the curved line between the successive bass notes on f. Artaria, the *Oeuvres complettes,* and Feder agree that in the first two measures the line indicates a phrasing for the tenor voice, and that in m. 16 it is a tie. Christa Landon, however, indicates all three lines as ties, a conceivable interpretation. However, I would agree with the interpretation of a phrase marking, because, given the rate of decay of sound even in a modern piano, by m. 16 f would be inaudible.

The final problem is a most fascinating one: mm. 40 and 48 of the second movement.[2] Each of these measures appears to contain an extra beat. Compared with the initial arpeggio figure of m. 48, the notes which make up the four beats do not appear to be written in such a way as to indicate that the passages are "ornamental" or rhythmically free. Editors have attempted various feats to make these passages rhythmically "correct." The *Oeuvres complettes* suggest that in m. 40 the last three arpeggiated notes (in the right hand) overlap with the left-hand figure, but the autograph seems to indicate that these figures are to be played successively. In m. 48, this edition indicates a triplet over the first three descending thirty-second notes, but still winds up with three beats plus three thirty-seconds. The edition ignores what appears to be a dot on the eighth-note value of beat two. Christa Landon writes the arpeggiated passages as ornamental notes. Badura-Skoda indicates an editorial 4/4 at the beginning of each of these measures and then follows the autograph. Feder changes note values to make the measure fit into 3/4 time: in m. 40 he makes the second beat a double-dotted eighth note instead of double-dotted quarter, and the following thirty-second notes he changes to sixty-fourths. Similarly in m. 48 on beat two the dotted eighth becomes

[2] The passages from the second movement discussed here can be seen in the facsimile of a page from the autograph on the frontispiece of the *Wiener Urtext Ausgabe* (Haydn, *Sonatas*), Vol. 3.

a dotted sixteenth, and some of the following thirty-seconds become sixty-fourths. These are certainly all editorial interpretations of the score.

From this brief discussion of a few examples from various editions, two main points become apparent. First, before the autograph was redis-covered, mistakes in earlier editions, some minor and some very major, were kept alive and often compounded in later editions. Second, the three recent editions based on the autograph are all quite plausible, yet very different from each other. Even when the autograph is available, some aspects of the notation will always be unclear and therefore subject to individual interpretation.

Observations on *Il mondo della luna*

GÜNTER THOMAS

Georg August Griesinger reports in his *Biographical Notes Concerning Joseph Haydn* that Haydn said, "Instead of the many quartets, sonatas, and symphonies, he [Haydn] should have written more vocal music. Not only might he have become one of the foremost opera composers, but also"—I am not sure if this was intended as a joke—"it is far easier to compose along the lines of a text than without one."[1] Haydn, a foremost opera composer! This image does not suit him very well. But an utter-ance like this one might show that Haydn did not consider his operas oc-casional works which were easy to write. An example in support of this hypothesis is provided by the surviving material of *Il mondo della luna* (The World on the Moon). Numerous variants and versions have come down to us. Haydn's efforts to achieve the best possible setting for this music can be very well demonstrated by means of the different versions of the three cavatinas of Buonafede, along with their instrumental ritor-nelli and patter recitatives, in the first act. Here and elsewhere in this opera each new version is a result of Haydn's attempts to produce the most satisfactory piece of music possible.

Following *Lo speziale* (The Apothecary) and *Le pescatrici* (The Fisher-women) *Il mondo della luna* was the third and last of Haydn's operas based on a book by Carlo Goldoni. It seems that Haydn was the sixth com-poser to set this text to music.[2] His predecessors were Baldassare Galuppi (Venice, 1750), Pedro Antonio Avondano (Lisbon, 1765), Nicola Pic-cinni (Milan, 1770), Giovanni Paisiello (Naples, 1774), and Gennaro As-taritta (Venice, 1775). (Pohl and later Landon wrote that Avondano's opera had *preceded* Goldoni's version and had been produced at Naples in 1732. One can also read about an opera of Florian Leopold Gassmann of the same title, produced at Venice in 1765. But these may be errors.[3])

[1] Gotwals, *Haydn,* 63 (Griesinger, 118; modern ed., 63).
[2] See, e.g., Pohl II, 80; Sonneck, *Librettos;* Goldoni, *Opere,* X, 1291; Manferrari, *Opere;* Loewenberg, *Annals;* R. Landon, "Mondo," vii.
[3] See Donath, "Gassmann," 129.

One of the last operas based on Goldoni's book was probably that composed by Marcos Antonio da Fonseca Portugal (Lisbon, 1792).[4]

There are some discrepancies in the reports on the first performance (apparently the only contemporary performance) of Haydn's opera. According to the libretto,[5] it was performed on the occasion of the marriage of Count Nikolaus Esterházy, son of the reigning Prince Nikolaus Esterházy "the Magnificent," to Countess Maria Anna Weissenwolf in the summer of 1777.[6]

Unfortunately no documents concerning the wedding solemnities are known at present. Concerning the preparations of the first performance, too, only a few documents are known. Pietro Travaglia worked ten hours each day on the scenery from July 6 until August 2.[7] And according to an undated bill which Prince Nikolaus Esterházy ordered to be paid on August 25 and which was settled four days later, Leopold Dichtler, the singer, copied 508 folia of this opera.[8]

According to Pohl, the marriage was celebrated on August 3, 1777.[9] I do not know where Pohl obtained this date. (The libretto speaks only of the summer of 1777.) If Pohl's date is correct, there would appear to be a contradiction: according to the libretto,[10] Ecclitico and Lisetta were sung by the married couple Guglielmo and Maria Jermoli, but in the salary lists of that year the names of these singers are to be found only from March till June.[11] It is true that other records show that on July 24 Guglielmo Jermoli received their salaries for the months from July to October as well.[12] But in the so-called Conventionale of 1773 it is made clear that the couple has quitted its service "Ende July" (at the end of July).[13] Thus on August 3 the two singers were probably no longer available. If the opera was performed on that date, the identity of the singers of their parts is unclear.

Nevertheless, this matter may help us to recognize the purpose of the new version of the role of Lisetta. Apart from musical claims, there were

[4] Vieira, *Portuguezes* II, 197, 215. The libretti to several of these operas are in the Library of Congress; cf. Sonneck, *Librettos* I, 772–73.

[5] Somfai, *Bilder*, 74, No. 122.

[6] In R. Landon, *Haydn*, 48, one reads that this son of Prince Nikolaus had later become Nikolaus II. That is not correct. The later Prince Nikolaus II was a grandson of Nikolaus "the Magnificent" and a nephew of the bridegroom of 1777. *This* Count Nikolaus Esterházy (1741–1809) was the second son of Prince Nikolaus "the Magnificent" and his wife, Princess Maria Elisabeth, *née* Countess Weissenwolf. And the bride was his cousin: Countess Maria Anna [sometimes also called Franzisca] Weissenwolf (1747–1822) was a niece of the Princess Esterházy. See Pohl II, 79; Wurzbach, *Lexikon*, LIV, genealogical table facing 178; Eszterházy, 126–27, genealogical table facing 136.

[7] By courtesy of Dr. Johann Hárich. Cf. Harich, *Textbücher*, 40.

[8] Hárich, "Dokumenta," 4th installment, 159–60.   [9] Pohl II, 79.

[10] Somfai, *Bilder*, 74, No. 123.

[11] Bartha-Somfai, 168, 170; Thomas, "Mondo," 123.

[12] Budapest, National Széchényi Library, Acta musicalia, Nos. 1005–6.

[13] Cf. Hárich, "Dokumenta," 4th installment, 101; Hárich, "Opernensemble," 7, 38.

also practical motives for writing new versions of a number of pieces. Above all, three parts of this opera have come down to us in two different registers: the parts of Ecclitico and Ernesto in both alto and tenor clef, Lisetta in both soprano and alto clef.

In his edition of the opera in 1958, Landon claimed that the part of Ernesto had originally been composed for an alto castrato.[14] Bartha and Somfai showed that it was just the other way around.[15] Exploring the large autograph fragment in Budapest they came to the conclusion that there were two versions of the opera:

1. an earlier one with
   Ecclitico—alto
   Ernesto—tenor
   Lisetta—soprano
2. and a later one with
   Ecclitico—tenor
   Ernesto—alto
   Lisetta—alto

—and that constitutes a problem which has not yet been solved. How did these different versions come about?

Further performances of this opera are unknown to us in Haydn's time. The somewhat strange modern notion that there was a revival for marionettes[16] arose from a misunderstanding. Pohl, immediately after he had concluded his summary of this opera, continued, "The marionette opera mentioned above. . . ,"[17] and that was erroneously understood as referring to *Il mondo della luna*. But he was referring not to this opera but to the marionette opera *Genovevens vierter Theil,* which is said to have been presented, like *Il mondo della luna,* at the wedding festivities in 1777.[18]

Griesinger's report that in 1788 the Viennese publisher Johann Traeg had purchased *Il mondo della luna* and three other Haydn operas from the legacy of Count Erdödy[19] has also not yet been explained. In any case, Traeg advertised copies of the opera for sale as early as May 16, 1789.[20] It is assumed that the two copies of the opera in the Österreichische Nationalbibliothek in Vienna and in the Moravské Muzeum at Brno in Czechoslovakia are copies made by Traeg.[21] But this hypothesis cannot be proved. On the other hand, the copy in the Bibliothèque du Conservatoire Royal de Musique in Brussels (the third act of which is lost) is clearly proved to be a Traeg copy by its number "1/28."—which agrees with the number of this opera in Traeg's 1799 catalogue.[22] That copy is

[14] R. Landon, "Mondo," viii.   [15] Bartha-Somfai, 188ff.
[16] Wendschuh, *Opern,* 77; R. Landon, "Mondo," viii.   [17] Pohl II, 81.
[18] See especially R. Landon, "Marionette," 183.   [19] Hase, 49n, Pohl-Botstiber, 214.
[20] Hoboken II, 379.   [21] R. Landon, "Marionette," 135–36.
[22] Traeg, *Verzeichnis,* 202 and 201.

especially valuable to us because it was made from an autograph, or at least from a direct copy. For those sections of the opera for which the autograph is lost the Brussels copy is by far the best substitute.

Several numbers from *Il mondo della luna* lived on in other works.[23] Besides the overture, which was used as the first movement of Symphony No. 63 in C major, the most famous example is the aria of the cavaliere Ernesto in the second act, which became the source of the Benedictus in the *Mariazellermesse,* composed in 1782. In 1782 or 1783 the small instrumental number at the beginning of Scene 11 of Act II appeared as a part of the third movement in the symphonic version of the overture to *La vera costanza* (Hob. Ia:15). The Presto section which concludes the duet between Clarice and Ecclitico in the third act is similar to the corresponding section of the duet in *Armida,*[24] composed in 1783. And five of the six trios for two violins (or flute and violin) and cello which were sent by Haydn to William Forster in 1784 (Hob. IV:6–8, 10, 11) are based in part on pieces from this opera, among them the aria of Flaminia in the second act.

An arrangement of the same aria is also found in the later version of *Philemon und Baucis,* preserved in the only extant copy of this marionette opera, originally composed in 1773.[25] But this seems to have as little to do with Haydn himself as the combination of three pieces from *Il mondo della luna* to form an overture (Hob. Ia:12). One of these pieces is the aria of Ernesto mentioned above. Further arrangements were the adaptation of the opera for a string quintet (a common practice of the time) in the so-called Kaisersammlung in Vienna and, finally, piano reductions of four pieces in a collection published by Johann Traeg in 1805 and 1806.[26]

The opera as a whole was almost forgotten until 1932 when—in celebration of the bicentenary of Haydn's birth—an adaptation by the composer Mark Lothar and Wilhelm M. Treichlinger, then first assistant to Max Reinhardt, was given at the Mecklenburgische Staatsbühne in Schwerin. (The first part of this performance is said to have been broadcast by seventy-six American broadcasting stations.)[27] Landon's piano-vocal score appeared in 1958, and the first edition in full score is scheduled to appear as JHW XXV:7.

Haydn and Franklin: The Quartet with Open Strings and Scordatura
HUBERT UNVERRICHT

In his Haydn biography C. F. Pohl mentioned as a curiosity a quartet "nur auf losen Saiten zu spielen (Non tangendo digitis cordas)" for three violins and violoncello attributed to Joseph Haydn, without studying the

[23] Cf. Hoboken II, 369ff.   [24] Feder, "Similarities," 186–87.
[25] Cf. J. Braun's foreword to JHW XXIV:1, viii.   [26] Cf. Hoboken I, 805.
[27] Reinhard, "Schwerin"

question whether this work is doubtful or spurious.[1] Karl Geiringer says in his book about Haydn in 1932[2] that this quartet is possibly an authentic composition. Hoboken takes over this remark in his thematic catalogue of the works of Joseph Haydn,[3] but he gives this work the number II:F10 only, implying that he did not believe it to be authentic. Geiringer does not say anything concerning this quartet with open strings in the later revisions of his book about the life and works of Joseph Haydn (1959).[4] Perhaps one reason was that H. C. Robbins Landon had stated two years earlier that this quartet attributed to Haydn probably had been composed by the American statesman and philosopher Benjamin Franklin: a second composition, also for open strings and found in Göttweig (Austria) "is known to be by Franklin."[5]

The staff of the music division of the Library of Congress in Washington made some skeptical annotations about the problems of the authorship in connection with the edition of the quartet attributed to Benjamin Franklin at that time.[6] Later Richard S. Hill, Chief of the Music Division, suggested that perhaps the philosophical and special idea for this composition for four instruments went back to Benjamin Franklin and that Franklin himself might have composed this quartet with open and tuned strings.[7] But an eighteenth-century remark,[8] unknown to Hill, shows that these ideas were very common indeed and not the special concern of a philosopher. After a comprehensive study of the sources of these two quartets with open strings, W. Thomas Marrocco pointed out[9] the confusing masquerade in the traditions of these amusing compositions: "This writer expresses his deepest regrets for depriving our great statesman-inventor of the authorship of this singularly unusual composition."[10]

The filiation of the different sources, given here for the first time, will bring us further instructive information concerning the authorship of both quartets. In 1792, Kunzen and Reichardt include in the *Studien für Tonkünstler und Musikfreunde*[11] a reference to quartets of this character in their *Kunststück-Verzeichnis Magia harmonica*. As numbers 11 and 12 they mention the two following works:

Quartetto auf die Violin eingericht, welches, ohne auf dem Instrument zu fingern, von vier Personen gespielt wird. Von Martinez.

Ein zweites Quartetto von eben dieser Art. Von Roller.[12]

---

[1] Pohl II, 301, n. 23.   [2] Geiringer, *Haydn*₁, 77.   [3] Hoboken I, 349–50.
[4] Geiringer, *Haydn*₂ and *Haydn*₃   [5] R. Landon, "Quartets," 220.
[6] Benjamin Franklin, *Quatuor pour trois violons et violoncelle*, ed. by Guillaume de Van (Paris; 1946); materials in the Library of Congress, Washington, D.C.
[7] *Ibid*   [8] Reichardt, *Studien*, 167 (December 1792).
[9] Marrocco, "Franklin." I thank Sonja Gerlach for bringing this article to my attention.
[10] *Ibid.*, 483.   [11] See footnote 8.
[12] Quartet for the violin that is to be played on open strings and performed by four persons, composed by Martinez. A second quartet of the same kind, composed by Roller.

A composer named Roller is mentioned only in this source, and is otherwise unknown. In spite of the intentional hoax of using the name Martinez—Marianne Martinez was a famous musician and composer in Vienna in those years—both names seem to be pseudonyms.

So far the following sources have been located:

1. Quartetto Armonioso / Senza digiti / Per / Tre Violini & Violoncello / del' Signore / Ferandini / Milanese / 36 X. / in Augusta / Presso Gombart et Comp: / 255
   Announced: *Frankfurter Staatsristretto,* 9.2.1799, price 36 kr.
   Review: *Allgemeine Literatur-Zeitung* [Jena], June 1799 p. 783f.
   Remarks: Printed parts. The edition, to be found in the Library of Congress, Washington, has different numeration of the pages from the issue in the Bayerische Staatsbibliothek München; Ernst Ludwig Gerber noted the review of 1799 in his article Ferandini Milanese in NL.

2. Qvartetto / Del Sig: Ignatio Pleyel / Per il Tre Violini / Violoncello
   Remarks: Manuscript parts, 3rd violin and violoncello only, around 1810, in the National Museum, Prague. Watermark according to the information of the National Museum in Prague:
   ANTON   HELLER
CASDORF
   between the names a coat of arms with crossed keys(?). It appears that the name Pleyel was added later by the same writer.

3. Neugebohrnes musikalisches Gleichheitskind, / ein / QUARTETT / für 3 Violinen und Violoncell, / welche ohne Fingersetzung blos mit leeren Saiten gespielt wird und / doch eine schöne Harmonie bildet. / Prag bey Haas. Jesuitengasse. N. 186.
   Remarks: Printed parts. According to Robert Eitner[13] this issue was published around 1810. The copy in the Gesellschaft der Musikfreunde in Vienna was used.

4. 2 Quartetti / Autor(es): / Incerti / Numer.: / 109.
   Remarks: Manuscript parts around 1815 in the Stift Göttweig (Austria). Watermark: fleur-de-lys.
   Formerly this manuscript was in the possession of a monk, later in the library of the monastery (according to information of Fr. W. Riedel, Mainz).

5. Quartetto / a / 3 Violini / con / Violoncello / Del Sig.re Benjamin Francklin.
   Remarks: Manuscript score in the notation for playing with open strings around 1815 in Bibliothèque Nationale Paris.
   Watermark: three half moons with MA (Information supplied by H. Schneider, Mainz).

---

[13] Eitner, *Musikalienhändler,* 93.

A Viennese copy, At the top of the score is to be read: Accord von einen jeden.

6. Harmoniae ohne Finger zu kreifen / in. Quartetto: / a / Violino Primo: / Violino Secondo: / Violino. Tertzio: / Baßo: [later]: Aloys Weiß
Remarks: Manuscript parts from around 1810 in the Gesellschaft der Musikfreunde in Vienna. In the handwriting of Dr. Mitringer at the top of the title it is marked "Ferrandini."
Watermark according to information from Gernot Gruber in Vienna: fleur-de-lys.

7. Quartetto / pour / Violino I$\underline{\underline{mo}}$ II$\underline{\underline{do}}$ III$\underline{\underline{tio}}$ / con / Violoncello. / Composés / par / J. Haydn. / man tangendo digitis mordas.
[recte: non tangendo digitis cordas.]
Remarks: The stamp in the cover of the manuscript parts advertises that the merchant Exner of Zittau (German Democratic Republic) formerly owned this copy. Manuscript parts around 1820 of the Christian Weise-Bibliothek in Zittau, now in the music library of the Sächsische Landesbibliothek Dresden.
Watermarks of the cover: double headed eagle with the letter Z on the breast (watermark of the paper mill in Zittau); watermark of the pages: coat of arms in the form of a bell with a crown.

The manuscript of the monastery St. Florian in Austria has been lost. According to Hoboken's notice[14] this quartet is attributed to Pleyel in the thematic catalogue of this monastery. Perhaps it was identical with the source in Prague (source 2). C. F. Pohl copied the manuscript of Zittau by scoring the parts in "sound notation" now kept in the Gesellschaft der Musikfreunde in Vienna.[15] A facsimile and edition of the manuscript in Paris was published by John Kirkpatrick in 1958 after Guillaume de Van edited the Parisian manuscript, which bears the name of Benjamin Franklin, in 1946.[16] The quartet of Benjamin Franklin, cited in RISM,[17] is this edition of Guillaume de Van and not an issue of the eighteenth century. Roger Paul Phelps edited this Parisian edition from 1946 in his dissertation.[18]

A hypothesis of the filiation of these sources is shown in Table 1. (Lost sources are written in parentheses. The datings were determined by the constitution of the paper, the handwriting, and so forth.)

A collection of the various scordaturas in the separate parts can be seen immediately following Table 1.

[14] See footnote 3.
[15] IX 41.139^b with the title: Quartetto / pour Violino I^{mo} II^{do} III^{tio} / con / Violoncello / composé par / Joseph Haydn. / Man tangendo digitis mordas.
[16] See footnote 6.
[17] RISM A/I/3, p. 111; School of Music Library, Indiana University, Bloomington, Ind.
[18] Phelps, "Chamber"

Table 1   *Haydn or Ferandini*

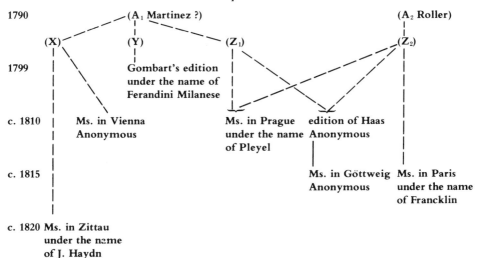

Source	Part	Scordatura			
1, 3–7	1st violin	c′	g′	c″	f″
1, 3, 4, 6, 7	2nd violin	a	f′	b♭′	e″
1–7	3rd violin	a	e′	a′	d″
1, 2, 6, 7	violoncello	C	F	c	g
5	2nd violin	b♭	f′	b♭′	e″
3, 4	violoncello	B₁♭	F	c	g
5	violoncello	B₁	F	c	g

The scordatura of the "Franklin" quartet may be corrected in the second violin into: b f′ b♭′ e″. Perhaps the lowest note was tuned to b♭ because of the use of this accidental in the second chord. Possibly the scordatura C F c g would be better for the violoncello. The writing of the scordatura in the issue of Gombart seems to be correct, but it is possible that the lowest string of the violoncello should be B♭, and not C, in this "Ferandini" quartet.

Haas collected two works of the same kind and printed them in a single edition. They gave the same scordatura for both quartets, which confused some details of the texture, and Haas also made some mistakes. The manuscript of Prague omitted the first movement of the "Franklin" quartet and numbered the movements from one to seven; for the last movement there is no number. For the manuscript of Göttweig probably the "Stichvorlage" of the Haas edition (or the edition itself) was used as the original copy; in the second quartet, the Göttweig manuscript restored one missing bar in the first violin of the second minuet lacking in the Haas edition, but in all the other movements it is identical to Prague. In Paris, only this second quartet is transmitted. In this "Franklin" quartet the one missing bar was added with other notes; it has more mistakes than in the "Prague," the "Haas," and the "Göttweig" ones. Gombart may have chosen the name of Ferandini because the dead master of chamber music Giovanni Ferrandini of Munich was popular in the south of Germany at that time. The reference "Milanese" may have been an intentional deception. The manuscripts of Vienna and of Zittau have some connections with the edition of Gombart; and perhaps they stem from the same original source. Zittau gives an arrangement in which the minuet is the fifth and a new minuet is the third movement. A finale with trio and coda has been added. In this source there are six movements altogether, and if the coda is numbered separately, then this composition has seven movements, as Pohl says.[19] The manuscripts of Prague, Vienna, and Zittau have the same scordatura as the Gombart issue. The author of the two added movements in the source of Zittau may have used this scordatura; there is no question that the lowest string must be tuned to C, and not to Bb_1 as in the remaining sources. The additional movements avoid the confusion of two-, three-, or four-measure groups of the original movements; they prefer distinct eight-bar periods. The arranger employs more rhythmic and dynamic differentiations and the use of two strings sounding simultaneously. Therefore it seems likely that these movements were attached to the original four movements some time later. The following table summarizes the groupings of these eleven movements into larger works:

1) Attr. Ferandini (Sources 1–4)	1. Marche 2. Allegro 3. Menuetto and Trio 4. Rondo (Moderato)
2) Attr. Franklin[20] (Sources 2–5)	5. Allegro (lacking in Source 2) 6. Menuetto (without Trio) 7. Capriccio (Allegro) 8. Menuetto (without Trio) 9. Rondo (Finale)

3) Attr. Haydn (Sources 6–7)	1. Marche
	2. Allegro
	10. Minuet and Trio
	4. Rondo
	3. Menuetto and Trio
	11. Finale: Presto
	       Trio
	       Coda

[19] See footnote 1.   [20] Marrocco, "Franklin," 484 f.

Movements with the same number are nearly identical. Altogether eleven movements have been handed down.

All of the extant sources were written or edited in South Germany or Austria around or after 1800. The similar constitution of the two pieces suggests that they were composed—as Landon supposed[21]—by one person, who liked the different combinations of single movements and also the amusing and confusing masquerades. The composer tried to achieve the correct resolution of the harmonies simply by crossing the parts. But he overlooked errors such as parallel fifths. The ordered scordatura causes some harmonically "countrified" chords as in the *Musical Joke* by Mozart (K. 522). Articulations and dynamics are very rare. The composer of these two quartets was of only the third or fourth rank. Joseph Haydn and also Ignaz Pleyel would have taken greater care and would have given us a much better composition, especially because these two pieces originated not earlier than 1790. It is well known that Benjamin Franklin died in that year in Philadelphia. These two quartets with open and tuned strings are a musical joke, a curious idea, a clowning; they are not to be criticized as a serious composition of the period. The review—possibly by J. Fr. Reichardt—in the newspaper *Allgemeine Literatur-Zeitung Jena* of 1799 takes the "Ferandini" quartet in the Gombart edition too seriously. The author of this review says[22]

Das Beywort *armonioso* hingegen scheint ein Schreib oder Stichfehler zu seyn; denn wir finden diese erbärmliche Arbeit, worin noch überdies an eine nur leidliche Melodie gar nicht zu gedenken ist, sehr unharmonisch und äusserst unrein im Satze. . . . Ueber die Modulation und den Rhythmus wollen wir kein Wort verlieren, denn bey einer solchen Stümperey lohnt dies die Mühe nicht. . . . Welche unangenehme Wirkung übrigens ein Tonstück, auf lauter blossen oder unbedeckten Saiten gespielt, hervorbringen muss, kann jeder nur mittelmässige Violinist leicht berechnen, da man sonst bekanntlich die blossen Saiten so viel als möglich zu vermeiden sucht.[23]

This last sentence is notable for its statement that the violinist takes the fourth finger and not the open strings.

These decades fostered such curious, amateurish, clumsy pieces of work attributed to the great composers, such as the *Musikalischen Würfelspiele* (musical games of dice) and a quintet *Glockenspiel* with six movements for violin in scordatura, three glasses, and bass—"ein vielleicht

[21] See footnote 5.   [22] ALz, 1799, No. 201 (June 25) = Vol. 2, col. 783–84.

[23] Freely translated: The adjective *armonioso* seems to be a mistake or a typographical error, for we find this wretched work, in which there is not even a good melody, very unharmonious and flawed in its composition. . . . We won't waste any words on the progressions or the rhythm because such bungling is not worth the trouble. . . . Morever, even a mediocre violinist can easily figure out what a disagreeable effect is produced on the open strings since everyone knows they should be avoided as much as possible.

unbekanntes Curiosum von Haydn"[24]—and other compositions in the *Kunststück-Verzeichnis* of Reichardt and Kunzen. These compositions with open strings are jokes, funny games, sometimes used for glossing the political tendency of those years, as in the title of the edition in Prague (source 3).

To summarize, it must be concluded—I am sorry to say—that the one quartet with open and tuned strings is not by Joseph Haydn nor the other by Benjamin Franklin. The different editions of the "Franklin" quartet by Kirkpatrick in 1958 and some time later by Arcady Dubensky,[25] based on the manuscript in Paris, are insufficient grounds for accepting his authorship, because this source has been corrupted in some details and constitutes only one of the several inconsistent traditions. These two (or three?) works in an outmoded style were probably composed by an unknown minor South German musician around 1790, even if they are attributed to great composers and persons of that time. Because of the various occasional attributions to famous names and the other pseudonyms for these two quartets it seems likely that the composer preferred to remain unknown. Only by chance would one be able to guess his name.

On the History of the Composition and the Performance of *La vera costanza*

HORST WALTER

The problems concerning the origin of Haydn's opera *La vera costanza,* the circumstances of its first performances, and the version which has come down to us have hitherto been answered inadequately, if not indeed quite falsely. In the literature the prevailing view is that the opera was composed in 1776 for the Viennese court.[1] But it is well known that the first performance took place in 1779 in Eszterháza, and that the autograph which is preserved in Paris is dated 1785. The attempt to separate truth from conjecture is complicated by the double compositional history of the opera, and by the scarcity of documentary reports on the lost original version compared to those on the reconstructed revised version.

It was C. F. Pohl who proposed 1776 as the year of composition: "In this year Haydn was asked to compose a new work for the Imperial Court to open the Italian opera season in January 1777."[2] What happened next we can read in the report of A. C. Dies, who supposedly learned the

[24] NrMZ, VIII, (1860) 54.
[25] Editions in the Music Division of the Library of Congress, M45.4.F72 in F major (1958), M1160.F84.Q43.583.
[1] With the exception of Hoboken II, 386f.   [2] Pohl II, 77.

story from Haydn himself, and whose remarks fueled all the subsequent speculation:

> Haydn undertook the work with pleasure and set to music *La vera costanza,* Dramma giocoso. The opera was completed. As a matter of course Haydn had weighed the capabilities, likewise the vocal range, of each singer and arranged the voice parts accordingly, so they would be suitable. How great then was his astonishment to see his distribution of the parts overruled and to be informed that he had no right to assign parts according to his own opinion. They wished now to impose upon him another distribution. Haydn replied, "I know *what* and for *whom* I wrote," would not be imposed upon, and took his case to the Monarch. Emperor Joseph understood Haydn's rights, sought to mediate, but found unbelievable opposition so that Haydn declared that he would sooner not have the opera produced than struggle any longer against the cabal. Haydn concluded today's account with the words, "I did not give the opera. I packed up, went home to my Prince, and told him the whole story. The Prince did not condemn my course of action but had the opera given at Eszterháza in 1779."[3]

Among the operas that spread Haydn's fame, Dies mentions *Il mondo della luna* from 1777. Consequently Haydn would have received the commission from the Court between 1777 and 1779, not in 1776. But in determining the date, Pohl had to consider that Pasquale Anfossi's setting of *La vera costanza,* premiered 1776 in Rome and also performed the same year in Florence, Turin, Bologna, and Venice, *was* performed in Vienna in January 1777. Pohl conjectured rivalry between Haydn and Anfossi, and so devised the year 1776 as the date of the commission. But, to anticipate the conclusion of this investigation, Haydn composed his opera in 1778, for Eszterháza, in full knowledge of Anfossi's existing work.

How does this relate to Dies's assertions? His story, which at first sounds authentic in its circumstantial detail, actually awakens serious misgivings. It seems unlikely that there was any Viennese commission for an opera from Haydn in the 1770s. The account in G. A. Griesinger, Haydn's other early biographer, tends to support this position. Eschewing all anecdotal elaboration, Griesinger reports:

> The Emperor [Joseph II] wanted to hear his [Haydn's] opera *La vera costanza,* but because of intrigues the roles were so badly assigned that Haydn took his score back again.[4]

That is, Griesinger speaks of a performance in Vienna, not a commission from Vienna, and this is more plausible. Another statement from around 1802, cited by Botstiber without giving a source, sounds like a commentary on Griesinger:

> We hear that about this time Salieri asked Haydn for the rights to perform his *Vera costanza*. Haydn refused, because Salieri had intended to give the leading

---

[3] Gotwals, *Haydn,* 107f. (Dies, 57; modern ed., 59–60).
[4] Gotwals, *Haydn,* 36 (Griesinger, 62–63; modern ed., 35).

part to [Signora] Tomeoni, but in Haydn's view this role [Rosina] could only succeed if performed by an innocent girl like [Therese] Saal.[5]

The conjecture that Haydn wrote *La vera costanza* with the Esterházy company in mind, rather than for Vienna, is confirmed by closer examination of the sources.

1. In 1778–79 the necessary personnel was at hand. Barbara Ripamonti, the prima donna for this opera, was engaged for Eszterháza in April 1778; in June of that year Andrea Totti, the male principal, joined the company.[6] (As Dies states, Haydn knew for whom he wrote.) Therefore, it is not surprising to find copies of one aria headed, "Scrita per la Ripamonti L'anno 1779 à Esterhaz." Furthermore, the 1785–86 revival was evidently considered only after the return of Ripamonti and the *primo buffo* of the first performance, Benedetto Bianchi, in the summer of 1784, following an absence from the troupe.

2. A special observation concerning the orchestral scoring of that time may help fix the period of composition more closely. My colleague Sonja Gerlach has determined that between April 1778 and the end of 1780 the Esterházy *Kapelle* had only one bassoonist.[7] Since a few numbers which can be shown to belong to the original version of the opera differ from the revised version in being scored for only one bassoon, it can be assumed that the original version came into being after April 1778. This corresponds quite well with the engagement of the two singers mentioned above.

3. No documents about the preparations for the first performance had hitherto been known. A recently published Esterházy order form indicates that by November 8, 1778 *La vera costanza* was finished to the extent that special music paper for copying the parts had to be bought.[8] The period of composition can therefore be placed roughly in the second half of the year 1778.

Only with the revival of *La vera costanza* in the 1785–86 season did the opera prove to be a great success. At Eszterháza it was given no fewer than twenty-one times.[9] Pressburg, Budapest, Vienna, Paris, and Brno repeated the opera. The extant manuscript sources from the years around 1790, with copies of the whole work (today in Bologna, Brno, Brussels, Graz, Vienna, Weimar, Zurich) as well as single arias, demonstrate the wide interest in this opera.

In the 1780s Haydn restored to the Esterházy repertoire a few earlier works whose performance material had been destroyed by fire in Eszterháza in November 1779. The reason may have been the reengagement

[5]Pohl-Botstiber, 196f.   [6]Hárich, "Opernensemble," 5–7, 25–26.
[7]Gerlach, "Ordnung," 52f.   [8]Feder-Gerlach, 99.
[9]Hárich, "Repertoire," 62, 69.

of Ripamonti and Bianchi, who had sung in the premiere. In 1785, for instance, Haydn produced an opera by Anfossi that had not been given since 1778, and he had the vocal and orchestral parts copied from the extant score.[10] For the revival of his own *La vera costanza* apparently not even a score was available. How else could the existence of the 1785 partly autograph full score, which is now in Paris, be explained? Evidently this score represents a reconstruction of the lost version of the first performance. With the assistance of three Esterházy copyists Haydn recreated the whole work in perceptible haste. Concerning the sources which he took as a basis we can offer some conjectures. The five single numbers written out by the copyists may well derive from sources which were sold commercially, or perhaps owned by Haydn. Among them is the scena for the Count in Act II which, strange to say, was not composed by Haydn but—in his 1776 opera of the same name—by Anfossi! We must assume that, for whatever reasons, Haydn himself inserted it in 1785. That the original version of Haydn's opera contained his own setting of the same scena is proved by a sketch which has survived.

By far the greater part of the Paris score was written by Haydn himself, with often rather hasty corrections. Here the sources that he used, if indeed there were any, must have been very inadequate, and at any rate unsuitable for copyists: sketches, a short score, a few vocal parts? Differences in the color of the ink (especially in the introduzione and in the finale to Act I) clearly reveal Haydn's procedure of composing the musical parts "horizontally," one after the other. He apparently filled in the vocal staves first of all (in lighter ink, along with the scoring indications, key and time signatures); the orchestral staves were added in a second stage, with darker ink; there were many corrections. The introduzione is informative in another respect: the overture was published by Artaria in 1782, not in two movements as an opera sinfonia, however, but rather as a three-part concert version, in which the third movement was essentially borrowed from the introduzione. Now in 1785 Haydn could reverse the process: he drew the beginning of the introduzione from the finale of the overture. Again the colors of the ink tell the particulars. Incidentally, Haydn seems to have composed all the recitatives anew. In no respect do they correspond with the extant sketches of recitatives. The concerted numbers, on the other hand, agree for the most part with the surviving sketches.

Finally, I should like to draw attention to the preface and the critical report to this opera in JHW.[11]

[10] Bartha-Somfai, 297.
[11] Full score JHW XXV:8 (1976); critical report (1978).

Historical Context; Haydn's Relations to Others

Joseph Haydn and C. P. E. Bach: The Question of Influence

A. PETER BROWN

The problems of influence, causation, and origins have traditionally been of central concern to historians. Although in the recent past it has no longer been especially modish to concern oneself with such matters, we have nonetheless accepted many of the theses developed from such an approach. One of the central explanations for the development of Haydn's style during the mysterious period from his dismissal from the choir school at St. Stephen's around 1749 to his recorded employ with the Esterházy family in May of 1761 has been his relationship with the leading musician of North Germany, Carl Philipp Emanuel Bach. Today, it is still common to read of Haydn's playing C. P. E. Bach's sonatas at a well-worn clavichord on the sixth floor of the Michaelerhaus in the cold of winter.

The association of Haydn and C. P. E. Bach is admittedly an appealing thesis from many traditional viewpoints: for the evolutionist, it provides a line from Johann Sebastian Bach to the so-called Viennese Classical School; for those who view history in the Carlylian manner as the product of interactions of great men, it provides a link between two of the most imaginative minds of the eighteenth century; and for the nationalists, it emphasizes the joining of Protestant and Catholic, North and South—albeit both German. The result, however, has been a rather indistinct view: instead of attempting to clarify, define, and corroborate—or even doubt—certain aspects of the ubiquitous association, there has been a tendency to synthesize and obscure. This is unfortunate, since a return to the origins of the idea with consideration of corroborative evidence tends to cast doubt on those very aspects of the relationship between C. P. E. Bach and Haydn that have been most fully exploited.

The earliest statement concerning Haydn and Bach appeared in the October 1784 issue of the *European Magazine, and London Review,* an influential publication in intellectual circles in England and on the continent. This 1784 issue contained a biographical "Account" as well as a review of Haydn's keyboard sonatas Hob. XVI:21–32 (ChL. 36–47). The statements concerning Haydn and Bach included a reference to a feud between the two, which was subsequently denied by Bach in a letter published by a Hamburg newspaper. Although the veracity of the author (or authors) can therefore be questioned, the sketch and review, which I quote here in extract, provide the earliest and most specific reference to a stylistic relationship.[1]

An Account of Joseph Haydn, a Celebrated Composer of Music.

With these advantages, it is no wonder if we now behold Haydn outstrip all his competitors. And as envy never fails to pursue merit, the masters in Germany were so jealous of his rising fame, that they entered into a combination against him in order to decry his works and ridicule his compositions; nay, they even carried it so far as to write against him; and many pamphlets in the German language appeared in print to depreciate him in the public esteem, alledging his works were too flighty, trifling, and wild, accusing him at the same time as the inventor of a new musical doctrine, and introducing a species of sounds totally unknown in that country. . . .

Amongst the number of Professors who wrote against our rising author was Philip-Emanuel Bach of Hamburgh (formerly of Berlin); and the only notice Haydn took of their scurrility and abuse was, to publish lessons written in imitation of the several stiles of his enemies, in which their peculiarities were so closely copied, and their extraneous passages (particularly those of Bach of Hamburgh) so inimitably burlesqued, that they all felt the poignancy of his musical wit, confessed its truth, and were silent.

This anecdote will account for a number of strange passages that are here and there dispersed throughout several of the sonatas that have been reprinted in England from the German copies, of which we shall point out the few following passages by way of illustration. Among others, Six Sonatas for the Piano-Forte or Harpsichord, Opera 13 and 14, are expressly composed in order to ridicule Bach of Hamburgh. No one can peruse the second part of the second sonata in the thirteenth opera, and the whole of the third sonata in the same work, and believe Haydn in earnest, writing from his own natural genius, and committing his chaste and original thoughts upon paper. On the contrary, the stile of Bach is closely copied, without the passages being stolen, in which his capricious manner, odd breaks, whimsical modulations, and very often childish manner, mixed with an affectation of profound science, are finely hit off and burlesqued. [P. 253]

Impartial and Critical Review of Musical Publications.
Six Sonatas for the Forte-Piano . . . Opera 13. . . .

Although these Sonatas abound with great variety of thoughts, and a vast fund of invention, yet they are not so free and so generously open as most of this happy composer's works are generally found to be: some of them are confined, and others pedantick; but then it should be known they were intended to burlesque the manners of some German musicians, who, either from envy or ignorance, had entered into combinations against our author, and criticised his works with great severity in periodical pamphlets. Instead of answering them, however, in their own way, he composed and printed three or four sets of Sonatas, in which, without announcing it to the public, he took them all off in so artful a manner, that each one beheld his own stile held forth in a ridiculous light, and yet none of them could claim one bar of the music!—It would be endless to particularize every passage throughout this work; but we cannot pass over the minuet to the fifth Sonata, in which Haydn had Bach of Hamburgh in his eye, whose compositions now and then are somewhat in the old stile, often consisting of "imitations" and "fugues." This minuet that we are now pointing out being a regular

[1] For further commentary and an annotated presentation of the "Account," see Brown, "Biography."

canon, the answer of which is in the "unison"; in the first part the treble takes the lead, in the second part the bass begins, and the treble follows. This minuet is not a very pleasant one, because it is bound down by the rigid fetters that must encircle that species of music called a canon; so that for what we lose of the pleasantry of the air, ample amends is made by the contrivance and ingenuity of the art. [P. 303]

This review specifically refers to the canonic minuet found in Haydn's sonata Hob. XVI:25 (ChL. 40) in E♭ major as an imitation of Bach. While minuets represent an important Viennese tradition, in Bach's sonatas they are rarities and canonic minuets are nonexistent. The "Account" is more general.

Georg August Griesinger's biography has been the most frequently quoted source:

> *Haydn was dismissed from the Choir School in his sixteenth year because his voice had broken.* He could not expect to make his own way by his talent alone. *In Vienna he moved into a wretched little attic room without a stove* (in the house at No. 1220 in the Michaelerplatz) *in which he was scarcely sheltered from the rain. Innocent of the comforts of life, he divided his whole time among the giving of lessons, the study of his art, and performing. He played for money in serenades and in the orchestras, and he was industrious in the practice of composition,* for "when I was sitting at my old worm-eaten clavier, I envied no king his lot." About this time Haydn came upon the first six sonatas of Emanuel Bach. "I did not come away from my clavier till I had played through them, and whoever knows me thoroughly must discover that I owe a great deal to Emanuel Bach, that I understood him and have studied him diligently. Emanuel Bach once made me a compliment on this score himself."
>
> *In the same house in which Joseph Haydn was quartered dwelt also the celebrated poet Metastasio. The latter was educating a Fräulein Martinez.*[2]

Based on a series of visits to Haydn, Griesinger's material was apparently rearranged into a chronological continuity. The question here then is not *whether* Haydn had an encounter with C. P. E. Bach's sonatas, but rather *when.* If one compares Bertuch's account of Haydn's early years originally published in 1805 in the *Journal des Luxus und der Moden*—which Bertuch himself later confirmed as based on Griesinger's not yet published material (indicated by the italicized passages in the Griesinger excerpts)—with the final presentation in 1809, one can hypothesize that the entire C. P. E. Bach episode was inserted by Griesinger at a later date:

> In his sixteenth year Haydn was dismissed from St. Stephens because his voice had broken. In great want, he now endured a number of years in Vienna. He lived on the sixth floor, his living place had neither a window nor a stove; his breath froze in the winter on his bedcover and the water which he had to fetch in order to wash, by the time of his arrival in the higher region, was often already changed to a clump of ice. Haydn gave lessons, he played in orchestras—when he was able to earn something, his poverty isolated him from humanity, and he found his happiness at an old worm-eaten clavier. He composed with abandon, his genius permitted him no rest. He taught singing and keyboard playing to a

---

[2] Gotwals, *Haydn,* 11–12 (emphasis added) (Griesinger, 12–13; modern ed., 11).

Fräulein Martini [*sic*], who was associated with Metastasio, and received in return free board for three years.[3]

That is, I suggest that the portion of Griesinger's paragraph ending with ". . . 'when I was sitting at my old worm-eaten clavier, I envied no king his lot.' . . ." and the following reference to C. P. E. Bach were recounted by Haydn during different conversations with Griesinger. Griesinger himself provides a caveat with the lead-in "About this time. . . ." How confining is "About this time . . ." when stated perhaps almost half a century after the fact?

What Haydn meant by ". . . the first six sonatas of Emanuel Bach" also requires comment. Pohl and nearly everyone after him had assumed that Haydn studied the first print of Bach's keyboard sonatas, the so-called "Prussian" Sonatas (Wq. 48). Since the Prussian Sonatas are not designated as Opus 1 on their title page, this is a slippery hypothesis. At least two prints of Bach's keyboard music with the indication Opus 1 were sold in Vienna: (1) an unauthorized print (Wq. 62/8, 13; 65/9–10, 18, 22) published in Paris by Huberty in 1761, which was available through Huberty's Viennese agent Van Ghelen, who incidentally lived in the Michaelerhaus and sold a number of other works Haydn owned, including those of Marpurg, Mattheson, and Kirnberger; and (2) the *Six sonatas . . . l'usage des dames* (Wq. 54), published by Hummel around 1770. In addition, consideration should perhaps also be given to the first collection of Bach's *Kenner und Liebhaber* Sonatas (Wq. 55), published in 1779, a dozen copies of which Haydn's friend Baron van Swieten and his publisher Artaria each subscribed to.

The only early Haydn source to refer to Bach's *Versuch über die wahre Art das Clavier zu spielen* is Albert Christoph Dies:

> Haydn was pleased to see the improvement in his situation. What lay closest to his heart, though, was to do something with the important discovery I mentioned above, and enable himself through a serious study of theory to bring order (which he loved above all, as we already know) into the outpourings of his soul. He decided to buy a good book. But what? That he could not tell, and he had reasons for not asking advice. Since he did not know how to choose, he left it almost to chance, planning first to leaf around in the book a little and size it up before uselessly spending perhaps the income of an entire month for it. Haydn ventured to walk into a bookstore and ask for a good textbook of theory. The bookseller named the writings of Carl Philipp Emanuel Bach as the newest and best. Haydn wanted to look and see for himself. He began to read, understood, found what he was seeking, paid for the book, took it away thoroughly pleased.
>
> That Haydn sought to make Bach's principles his own, that he studied them untiringly, can already be noted in his youthful works of that period. Haydn wrote in his nineteenth year quartets that made him known to lovers of music as a profound genius, so quickly had he understood. As time went on, he procured

---

[3] As translated from Bertuch, *Reise,* I, 185–86. For the Griesinger acknowledgment, see II, 53.

Bach's later writings. In his opinion Bach's writings form the best, most basic and useful textbook ever published.[4]

In contrast to Griesinger's, Dies's biography had a limited impact during the nineteenth century and was somewhat maligned by Pohl for its loquacity. Dies's biography is also based on his own visits, but with apparently no attempt at chronological rearrangement of the material. Still, this reference to Haydn and C. P. E. Bach is not without confusion: the factuality of the statement on the early string quartets from Haydn's nineteenth year has been labeled as highly improbable by both Finscher and Webster.[5] However, the remainder of the statement seems clear: Haydn bought a book by C. P. E. Bach. A number of commentators have tried to place this incident during the 1750s, as the first part of the *Versuch* appeared in 1753; but from the context Dies seems to be referring to a compositionally oriented theoretical work. Since the first part of the *Versuch* is primarily a manual of performance, it sounds as if Haydn was referring to Part II, which could not have been available in Vienna until after 1762. That neither part of the *Versuch* is listed in the HBV or HNV can perhaps be explained by the various fires of the 1760s and 1770s at Eisenstadt and Eszterháza.

The most completely satisfying first-hand statements regarding the Bach–Haydn relationship derive from Haydn's friend Abbé Maximilian Stadler. His version has been made known primarily through the introduction to an essay on Bach by Friedrich Rochlitz.[6] Stadler's own statements can be found in his little-known *Materialien zur Geschichte der Musik unter den österreichischen Regenten,* which is in the manuscript collection of the Austrian National Library:

> As a boy gifted with genius, he had the opportunity to study singing and instruments. The learned masters, among them Reutter, Porpora, and the books of Fux, Mattheson, etc., willingly imparted instructions to this diligent pupil. He heard with interest the masterpieces of Holzbauer, Wagenseil, [and] Hasse, which then were improving the musical tastes of the time, and many other composers of Vienna, who were, so to speak, his predecessors; he himself began to compose early, and whoever possesses and examines his first keyboard sonatas and violin divertimenti will easily see that he had modeled himself after Wagenseil and his kind. Later he took in hand the foreign "products" such as those of C. P. E. Bach, etc., studied them, and while remaining faithful to his own special tastes, through this study he still molded more and more the realization of his own ideas, among which his quartets with figues can serve as examples.[7]

Stadler gives the distinct impression that Haydn's early stylistic development can be viewed in two phases: 1) a period during which Haydn absorbed the style of his Viennese predecessors, including works by Holz-

[4] As translated in Gotwals, *Haydn,* 95 (Dies, 37–38; modern ed., 40).
[5] Finscher, *Streichquartett* I, 138–44; Webster, "Chronology," 38–44.
[6] Rochlitz, *Tonkunst* IV, 273–77.   [7] S. n. 4310; mod. ed., 127–34.

bauer, Wagenseil, Hasse, and others, which were models for his early keyboard sonatas and "violin divertimenti"; and 2) a somewhat later period during which he studied the "products" of foreign composers, among them C. P. E. Bach. Stadler also informs us that the study of Bach was not unfashionable in Vienna at this time. He specifically cites two musicians associated with Haydn: his lifelong friend Georg Albrechtsberger, and Robert Kimmerling, a Haydn student (c. 1760) who later became *Regens chori* at Melk. (As evidence to support this statement, Kimmerling's library today survives at Melk with at least one work in which he inscribed that it was recommended to him by Haydn, and C. P. E. Bach's Sonatas Wq. 51, 54, and 55, none of which were available before 1760.)

It is perhaps also of value to consider those early sources where one might expect mention of Haydn and C. P. E. Bach, but finds none. As examples, why are both composers discussed but no relationship drawn by Junker in his *Zwanzig Componisten?* Indeed, why are there no sources referring to a Bach–Haydn relationship prior to the 1780s? More significantly, why is Bach omitted from Haydn's autobiographical sketch of 1776, which otherwise seems to be one of the most explicit documents concerning his early years? Furthermore, why does the first authentic report of Haydn's acknowledgement of his indebtedness to Bach date from his London visits?[8]

From the sources extant today it therefore appears that the statements found in the *European Magazine, and London Review* and the Dies and Griesinger biographies have provided the kernels for three distinct traditions: 1) Haydn played, studied, and admired the keyboard sonatas of C. P. E. Bach; 2) Haydn studied the *Versuch;* and 3) Bach influenced Haydn's stylistic development, presumably the keyboard sonatas, in one way or another. In contrast to the picture offered by modern biographers, it is my belief that Haydn's contact with Emanuel Bach's works probably did not take place until at least the 1760s for the *Versuch,* and perhaps even later for the "first six sonatas." Such a hypothesis germinates from a reexamination of the texts of Dies and Griesinger and is not contradicted—perhaps it is even supported—by Stadler. The publication date of Part II of the *Versuch* and the identification problem of the "first six" Bach sonatas also tend to buttress this supposition.

Space does not permit me to deal adequately with the most widely disseminated view—that Bach's sonatas had a significant and observable stylistic impact on Haydn—but I would like to offer a few comments.

Modern scholars have tended toward two approaches to this stylistic question: 1) the citation of parallel passages, and 2) the attempt to establish similar compositional processes. Concerning the former, such ex-

---

[8] See Brown, "Biography," 353.

amples as cited by E. F. Schmid (Hob. XVI:22 [ChL. 37] in E major
with Wq. 78) and H. C. R. Landon (Hob. XVI:19 in D major with Wq.
49/3) are not especially convincing; in fact, both Schmid and Landon
themselves tacitly admit this by stating that the parallel is one of
"spirit."[9]

The similar stylistic features which have been cited—such as colorful
harmonic language and the varied reprise—do not hold up under closer
scrutiny. By way of example, Bach's and Haydn's concepts of the varied
reprise in a sonata-form movement differ markedly: 1) Haydn never
adopts Bach's written-out repeats of both of the two parts; 2) while Bach
at times changes the bass line in a manner which obscures the structure
(e.g., Wq. 50/3), Haydn always leaves the bass line intact, preferring register changes and limited variation of the melodic material; and 3)
Haydn's varied reprises normally affect the *second* phrase or *second* part of
a phrase, so that the listener can more fully confirm points of structural
downbeat, whereas Bach's normal practice affects both parts of the
phrase or subphrase equally.

Perhaps a more convincing approach to this question of influence
would emerge if one were to refrain from joining the search for similarities in the works of Bach and Haydn, but instead examine statements in
Bach's *Versuch* for indications of certain practices found in Haydn's output after the early 1760s. For when one reads Bach's final chapter, in
which he offers perceptive comments on cadential articulation and modulation (*Ausweichung*), with special emphasis on the beauty of surprise
changes in tonality, we are led to concur with Dies "that Haydn sought
to make Bach's principles his own. . . ."

The Liturgical Basis of Haydn's Masses

KARL GUSTAV FELLERER

Haydn ceased composing Masses from the *Mariazeller Mass* of 1782 until
the *Mass in Time of War* of 1796. Similarly, Mozart's Mass compositions
concluded in 1783 with the incomplete C-minor Mass (K. 427 [417a]),
followed only by the Requiem of 1791, which, as is well known, was the
result of a commission. In the case of both masters, the decade beginning
around 1780 saw no major sacred works. This simultaneous interruption
in the composition of church music on the part of Haydn and Mozart indicates a change in the concepts and regulations for church music around
1780, as a tendency of the Enlightenment.

In the year 1749, Pope Benedict XIV issued his encyclical concerning
church music, which became the liturgical basis for the church music of
the era. His letter to the bishops of the Papal States sought to promote an

[9] Schmid, "Bach," 303; R. Landon, "Sonatas," 53–55.

exemplary form of religious service for the Holy Year 1750. Gregorian chant was emphasized at the expense of *cantus musicus;* nevertheless, the encyclical spoke at length of figural music, both with and without instruments. Music in the theatrical manner was rejected on the basis of the Tridentine *nihil profanum,* and orchestral accompaniment of the voices was restricted to strings. The papal regulations summarize the customary aspects of contemporary church music, except in regard to its limitations on the use of instruments. The essential aspect was the exclusion of secular and particularly operatic style.

Because of the extensive treatment of church music and its liturgical basis in the papal document, it became a code of liturgical musical practice in the eighteenth century. But it is an open question how extensively it was so understood in the Catholic world outside of Italy, particularly since eighteenth-century efforts toward national churches, especially in Germany, greeted decrees of the Roman Curia with considerable skepticism.

Nonetheless, there is no doubt that the papal regulations concerning church music formed part of a general ecclesiastical tendency of the time, concerned with limiting the excessive splendor (and the concomitant financial burden) of Baroque divine service. Furthermore, the Roman practice of church music was widely disseminated not only by diplomatic means but also through the pilgrimages made to Rome in the Holy Year 1750. Viennese ecclesiastical authorities eagerly seized on the papal decree as the opportunity to install a reform of church music and liturgy that, in the spirit of the Enlightenment, went even a step further by promulgating a rationalistic divine service in the vernacular, restricted to singing by the congregation.

Toward this end, the aim of both ecclesiastical and secular authorities in various German dioceses, the first step was to establish limitations on the orchestra. An Imperial decree of 1754 expressly forbade the use of trumpets and drums both in church and in processions within the Habsburg Empire. Even when in 1767 Cardinal Migazzi petitioned that trumpets and drums be permitted in a service of thanksgiving for the Empress Maria Theresia's recovery of health, a dispensation was issued only under special precautionary regulations.

To be sure the populace were hardly agreeable to this limitation on the customary orchestral sound in church. Whenever possible the Imperial decree was ignored, as in the festal service for the Caecilian Brotherhood, and yet the prohibition against instruments was made even more severe. In 1782, the reforms of Emperor Joseph II restated the restriction against orchestrally accompanied divine services, eventually prohibiting them altogether, emphasizing instead services in German with the singing of school songs as the ideal form of worship. Prince Kaunitz, the Austrian Chancellor, fostered the replacement of the Latin High Mass, with its orchestral accompaniment, by congregational singing in German; he commissioned a collection of appropriate German hymns from Abbé Michael Denis, who as early as 1774 had published a German hymnal for St. Stephen's in Vienna.

The basis for these restrictions on church music lay in Enlightenment notions of liturgical simplicity and comprehensibility, together with the trend towards national churches, but most of all in the intent of using the funds freed by the renunciation of art for educational and social purposes.

It is notable that after the death of Joseph II in 1790, when Cardinal Migazzi resumed his efforts to have the orchestral prohibition rescinded, it was relaxed in such as way that church music with instruments was permitted, "provided the church's resources are sufficient to meet the cost," in the words of the decree by Emperor Leopold. Because the state oversaw the church's endowment (and had often expropriated it), this declaration was in the main rhetorical; yet it initiated a gradual easing of the restrictions on Viennese church music, as demonstrated by Haydn's Masses composed from 1796 to 1802.

Once again the financial resources for church music could be increased so as to provide the orchestral Masses so popular with the people. Following Francis II's assumption of the throne in 1792 and after renewed appeals by Cardinal Migazzi, instrumentally accompanied Masses were once again permitted.

In the year 1782, at the time of Joseph II's reinforcement of the liturgical rules within the Empire, Archbishop Hieronymus Colloredo, on the occasion of the 1200-year Jubilee of his bishopric, had also renounced "unnecessary religious expenditures" for his Salzburg realm in the spirit of the moral and virtuous ideas of the Enlightenment, indicating the preferability of the German hymn. In Salzburg too there was opposition to this limitation on church music. The author of an anonymous attack in 1783 opposed what he called "naked divine service" as the ideal of an "enlightened" concept of the liturgy. To be sure, a rebuttal appeared in the *Abfertigung der sogennante gründliche Anmerkungen* (Vienna, 1783), but the populace still preferred the splendid Baroque form of the Mass with its rich use of instruments.

The opposition to orchestrally accompanied church music became general toward the end of the eighteenth century as part of the Enlightenment, on the part of secular as well as ecclesiastical authorities. The idea of the "feast," the worship of God with the highest artistic means in the church as the Great Hall of God, just as a secular prince was richly honored in the great hall of a palace, was suppressed in favor of rationalistic religious instruction in the spirit of virtue and morality. Thus artistic development had to be abandoned in favor of simple, understandable song; the effects of the artistic perfection of soloists, chorus, and orchestra typical of the time, in favor of comprehensible communal singing in the vernacular. There are obvious parallels to these manifestations of the Enlightenment in present-day attitudes toward church music.

Apart from the economic arguments favoring pedagogical and social undertakings, this movement arose from the rationalistic thinking of the age. Obermeyer based his rejection of the great musical art of the church in his *Bildergalerie katholischer Missbräuche* (1784) on these very grounds, just as these ideas were emphasized in the prefaces to songbooks for schools and churches and in the pastoral theological writings of the time. When the *Vossische Zeitung* (Berlin) reported from Vienna in 1782 that "the previous church music" of the Imperial Chapel has been done away with and "except for the very important feasts, figural music is now entirely" banned from the church, we have confirmation of the results of this aspect of the Enlightenment.[1]

An Imperial decree of February 23, 1783 ordered a simpler divine service in general and established the precise ritual for the common service (*Volksgottesdienst*). In *Vorderösterreich,* instrumental music in church was generally prohibited in 1784, and Mass with German hymns was prescribed.

In this context, despite the resistance of the populace to this development, which was reaching its climax in the 1780s, the interruption of Haydn's and Mozart's compositional activities for the church in the last two decades of the eighteenth-century becomes understandable, as does the special nature of the artistic evolution of Haydn's great Masses from 1796 to 1802 (*Missa in tempore belli* [*Paukenmesse*] and *Missa St. Bernardi* [*Heiligmesse*] of 1796, *Nelsonmesse* of 1798, *Theresienmesse* of 1799, *Schöpfungsmesse* of 1801, *Harmoniemesse* of 1802). In comparison to the sacred music composed up to 1783 they show a new development. The declamation, the relationship between voices and orchestra, and the intensity of the cyclic organization of the various movements achieve new standards.

The intense confrontation with text and music, especially in the *Missa St. Bernardi* (*Heiligmesse*), is typical of the new attitude. Haydn began this work in 1796, but he did not complete it until the following year, after various changes and additions. The effect of contrapuntal activity, intensified in the *Nelsonmesse,* in conjunction with affective melodic writing is already clear. Text declamation forms the basis of the treatment of the vocal parts. We find a deeper understanding than in the musically determined declamation of the Masses before the pause.

In the *Little Organ Mass* of 1775, most of the text of the Gloria is divided among the four voices and performed simultaneously, so that the entire movement runs only thirty-one measures. Similarly the Credo is

---

[1] VZ, October, 1782, p. 948; November 2, 1782, p. 1022.

abbreviated to only eight-two measures; only the "Et incarnatus" can be understood, in that its text is presented in all voices homophonically, or by the solists, in a thirty-six-measure section. The reason of this polytextuality, which ignored comprehensibility or correct musical projection of the text, was the oft-stated demand for a short service. It is clear that the musical form alone determined this church music, not a musical interpretation of the significance of the text.

Even though Haydn's Masses from before 1783 do distinguish sacred from secular style in the sense of Fux by their increasing use of counterpoint, in the later Masses the contrapuntal structure is deepened and combined with expressive orchestral accompaniment. Instead of external drama, the musical interpretation of the liturgical text conditions the inner unity of the composition by symphonic means. In the *Missa in tempore belli (Paukenmesse)* and in the *Nelsonmesse,* at the words in the Credo "et iterum venturus est *cum gloria* iudicare," Haydn recalls the theme of the Gloria itself; the symbolic intent is clear. This represents a new mode of the expression of feelings.

The Enlightenment's rejection of the orchestrally accompanied Mass had, after a fourteen-year interruption, evoked an intensification of form and sound in Haydn's Masses, which grew both out of Haydn's own artistic development and also from a reaction to the externally rationalistic concept of the liturgy during the Enlightenment, as manifested by the Josephinian decrees.

In the consistency of its projection of emotion, Haydn's church music evolved into a liturgical art in conformity with the requirement of the encyclical of 1749, in which, as Pope Benedict XIV stated, "fidelium animos ad devotionem et pietatem excitat" and "ab iis hominibus libentius auditur," thus conforming to the striving for both piety and sensual pleasure in music.

Haydn's church music is to be understood not only in terms of its artistic development, but also in terms of the liturgical principles that determined its form and expression. The liturgical decrees not only caused an interruption in Haydn's compositions for the church, they also necessitated an inner confrontation with the problems of church music, just as the interruption of his production of string quartets from 1772–81 may have resulted from the struggle to achieve a new artistic style. Haydn's Masses composed after 1796 make clear the change in his approach to church music.

Josephinism and the Josephinian Reforms Concerning Haydn

WALTER PASS

The wealth of literature about Josephinism in relation to the Josephinian reforms in most cases takes a position either for or against Joseph II. It is therefore very difficult to grasp the actual situation in Haydn's time. In most cases this influence of the Austrian Enlightenment, which was under State control and the strict standards of the emperors and high officials, may help to explain the great pause in Haydn's Mass composition from 1782 to 1796. Still unclear, however, remains the question how far Haydn himself was affected by the Enlightenment and this environment. Little is known of his actual relationship to the court: for example, to his brother-in-law, the court officer Joseph Keller, or to the Genzinger family. Nor are we better informed about his relationship to Baron van Swieten, who was director of the *Zensurkommission* (censorship office) under Joseph II, a key position in the Josephinian movement. Finally, it would be very interesting to investigate how much the total process of "enlightened" thoughts, or even the so-called *Vulgärjosephinismus,* may have made itself felt in Haydn's life and works. On the other hand, the Enlightenment seems unquestionably to have been very important for Haydn's development as a free artist in the modern sense.

Joseph II's policy affected church music especially, if not exclusively. The emphasis on "rationalistic" standards also pertained to secular musical life, and so they affected secular music, at least indirectly. Here we can specify:

1. a ban against theater music and balls on special days and in special places;
2. the elimination of the musicians' guild (*Spielgrafenamt*), that for hundreds of years had enjoyed great freedom, and which now came under control of the State;
3. the use of student scholarships as an instrument of policy, for example, restricting the support of choirboys to those in courts, cathedrals, or cloisters (but not ordinary religious establishments);
4. the allocation of funds, which altered and reduced the activities of previously active musical societies;
5. smaller changes such as those regarding street songs (*Gassenlieder*), which had to be submitted to the State for approval.

All of this reflects a new outlook, based on a new and modern *Zeitgeist* and a sense of progress in human life which influenced many important people. The climax of this development was the role of the Emperor as the "first servant of the State," a point of view scarcely found in other countries. One could call this a contradiction in itself. But actually it was an extreme expression of the Enlightenment and, at the same time, the beginning of the end of a hierarchical attitude toward the structure of the State, a process which was supposed to culminate in total loyalty to and identification with the Hapsburgs and their highest symbol, the emperor.

In the center of these reforms stood the reform of church music. This was in fact one main purpose of the entire reform of the Church, which consisted in the elimination of most of the 500 monasteries in the empire. It also consisted in the reorganization of the individual parish churches and the official order of the service. It was the last great reform or reorganization in the Catholic Church before the liturgical reforms of our own century. In accordance with his personality as a peace-loving person on excellent terms with the papacy, Joseph's reforms did not concern the liturgical books established after the Council of Trent. (We may recall that the emperor of the Holy Roman Empire was the official protector of the Roman Catholic Church.) Rather, they affected the form of the church service itself. Since the chief aim was "enlightenment" of the people, the partly exaggerated, somewhat showy piety of the Baroque was replaced by a liturgical service conceived as a devotion toward God, and as a tool for inculcating virtue and morals in the people. Muratori's desires, as represented by his pamphlet *Wahre Andacht des Christen,* were thus finally realized.

Joseph II's decision about church music was established through the decree of February 25, 1783, and it took effect on Easter Sunday of the same year. It was to a considerable degree the work of the emperor himself. According to the church-service order:

1. In every parish church one "Segenmesse mit Volksgesang" was permitted daily.
2. At St. Stephen's, one "Choralmesse" was allowed with or without organ, but *without* instruments.
3. On Sundays and holidays instrumental music was permitted in the high services of every parish church; but where qualified instrumental forces were not available, the singing was to be "choraliter" (monodic chant).
4. In the afternoon Vespers could only be "choraliter," on high-feast days with organ accompaniment, but always without instruments. These were reserved exclusively for the "Pontifikalvesper" of twelve high-feast days.
5. All other music was forbidden in the church service.

The second important decision affecting musical life was the introduction of church service restrictions in Lower Austria by court decree of February 6, 1786. The instigator was Landmarschall Anton Count Perger. The decree consisted of restrictions (similar to those listed above) on all *Stadtpfarreien* (local parishes) with at least three or more priests.

After the death of Joseph II, the bishops of the empire were given the opportunity to present grievances and complaints to the emperor. One of the Josephinian bishops, Anton Gall of Linz, claimed that the greatest fault of church services was monotony, and that a more solemn service should be permitted in towns and villages, which sometimes enjoyed not only a greater population, but also better musical forces, than churches where music was permitted; on this account they felt themselves victims of discrimination. Other bishops also made similar complaints and asked for permission to have concerted music in church. In order to calm this discussion, Leopold II finally permitted the restoration of instrumental music in parish churches in 1791, although only for Masses on Sundays and feast days.

On this basis the church service policies for Lower Austria were reorganized. The radical limitations on church music under Joseph II could not last, and within a few years they were in fact mostly eliminated. But Joseph II's reform policy, it should be remembered, was not changed as a whole until 1850.

Haydn and his Czech Contemporary Antonín Kammel

ZDEŇKA PILKOVÁ[1]

Antonín Kammel was one of the many eighteenth-century musicians from Bohemia who worked in musical residences and centers abroad, and who contributed to the formation of Classical style. Some of these musicians, like J. V. Stamic [Stamitz], J. [Georg] Benda, and others, composed in a very characteristic and personal manner; others helped the new style to crystallize in a more general way. I shall concentrate here on the relation of Antonín Kammel's works to those of the early Haydn. The music of both composers from the 1760s and 1770s shares many common features, and a few works of each composer circulated under the other's name.

If we survey Kammel's life and work, one circumstance seems to stand out. His works were often performed, and most of them were published in his lifetime, in London, Paris, Amsterdam, The Hague, and Berlin. After 1786 his works appeared in print but rarely, however, and he was soon almost completely forgotten. Nor, despite many recent attempts to explain the genesis of Classical style in greater detail and the rediscovery of many forgotten personalities from this period, has modern musicology devoted much attention to Kammel, as one sees at once from the inadequate treatment of him in the most recent musical encyclopedias and in general works devoted to the Classical period.

Let us briefly review Kammel's life, for certain errors are still found in standard reference works. He was born in Bělec, Bohemia, and was baptized on April 21, 1730. His father was a forester on the Wallenstein estates. From 1746 to 1751 Kammel studied at the Patres Piares Grammar School in Slaný, where he received the thorough musical education that was customary in Piarist schools in those days. He then studied at the University in Prague—philosophy, apparently, from 1751 to 1753, and

[1] Translated from the Czech by Joy Moss-Kohoutová.

law from 1753 to 1754. But Kammel's striking musical talent determined his future career. At an unknown date Count Vincent of Wallenstein sent him to Italy; in Padua, he was a pupil of Tartini. He then returned to Prague, but only for a brief period. (Further details of this period in his life are not known.)

By 1764 (not 1774) he was in London: he is mentioned as a musical personality there in Leopold Mozart's diary from that year. He published his first compositions in London in 1766.[2] His first recorded public appearance as a performer was on May 6, 1768, at one of the Bach-Abel concerts in "Almack's Rooms."[3] That Kammel had close ties with these musicians is indicated by the programs of their concerts in the following years, and perhaps also by an edition, in one volume, of works by J. C. Bach, Abel, and Kammel.[4] Apparently, Kammel was not a member of the royal orchestra—his name does not appear in the relevant documents—but he often played at court in chamber ensembles, as both violinist and violist.

The traditional stories of Kammel's marriage to a rich lady do not seem to be based on fact. On January 20, 1768, he was married by special license to Ann Edicatt, who was not of age and could not write.[5] They lived in Half-Moon Street, in the parish of St. George. In 1787 Kammel's name ceases to appear on the list of tenants, and the same year saw the remarriage of Ann Kammel.[6] So it may be assumed that Kammel had died by that year.

Kammel wrote instrumental music exclusively. (The reports of Masses from his pen have not been confirmed.) His compositions are chiefly for strings: violin sonatas, duos, string trios, quartets, and violin concertos, as well as symphonies and divertimenti, in which he also used wind instruments and harpsichord.

In the early 1770s Kammel's works were often performed and advertised for sale together with those by Haydn, in both London and Paris. In prints of Kammel's compositions at this time, we often find advertisements for Haydn's works, and vice versa. For example, in a print of Kammel's Six Divertimentos for Harpsichord (London, Preston), both

---

[2] *Sei Trii di violino e basso, at Author's expence.* London, Welcker, c. 1770.

[3] *The Public Advertiser,* London, May 3, 1768.

[4] *Six Sonates for two violins and a violoncello, with a thorough bass for the harpsichord, composed by Messrs. Bach, Abel and Kammell.* London, Welcker, c. 1780.

[5] The Harleian Society, Vol. XLVIII: *The Register of Marriages of St. Mary le Bone, Middlesex, 1754–75,* Part II (London, 1918), p. 78.

[6] The Rate Books for the parish of St. George (now in the Westminster Local History Collection, Westminster Public Library), list Anthony Kammel as a rate payer in Half-Moon Street from 1771 to 1786. *The Register Book of Marriages belonging to the Parish of St. George, Hanover Square,* ed. by John H. Chapman (London, Harleian Society, 1886) lists the marriage of Ann Kammel to Richard Tanner on December 12, 1787.

Haydn's Quartets Op. 9 and Kammel's Quartets Op. 7 are advertised. On the title page of Welcker's edition of Haydn's Op. 9 (1775), we find an advertisement for Kammel quartets (most probably Op. 7, which Welcker published in 1775). These connections imply that a stylistic comparison of the two composers may not be out of place.

Since their works appeared together, Haydn and Kammel must have been linked in the minds of English and French consumers of music in the 1770s. An interesting bit of evidence is provided by the pamphlet published anonymously by Karl Ludwig Junker, *Zwanzig Componisten* (1776). Among the twenty composers treated were Haydn and Kammel. The author was favorably inclined toward the Mannheim School; Haydn, on the other hand, comes in for sharp criticism, and so does Kammel.

On the only occasion that Kammel published foreign compositions, he included Haydn's Symphony No. 35 in B-flat major, along with works by the Czech composers Stamic, Vaňhal, and Mysliveček.[7] Haydn's symphony dates from 1767, Kammel's print from 1773; the symphony had already appeared in Paris (Venier) in 1771. We do not know what source Kammel used for his edition. There are several copies of this symphony in Czech archives; most of these date from the 1780s, and only one from the 1770s.[8] According to the critical report in JHW I:6, there are no surviving manuscript copies in England.

That Kammel's and Haydn's works from around 1770 could be mistaken for one another is evidence of their stylistic similarity. Of course, the entire question of authenticity is unusually difficult in this period. In the doubtful cases to be discussed now, too, the external evidence is usually insufficient to suggest a clear answer. (But internal evidence is also unreliable, especially during these earlier phases of the Classical period, when individual styles were less highly developed than they were to become later. Furthermore, the two composers themselves were still both relatively young. For both reasons, stylistic characteristics common to the period as a whole may outweigh personal traits.)

In three cases, works bear conflicting attributions to Haydn and Kammel.[9] One involves three string trios for two violins and bass, Hob. V:Es12, F2, F6. They appear in the Breitkopf Catalogue for 1781 as Nos. 4, 1, and 5 of the series "VI Trii da Ant. Kammel op. XVII Parigi."[10]

---

[7] *Six Ouvertures in eight parts by the following composers: I Stamitz, II. Vanhall, III. Mislevecheck, IV. Princess Royall of Saxony, V. Hayden, VI. Vanhall. The whole collected by Antonio Kammell.* London, Welcker, 1773.

[8] Frýdlant, Clam-Gallas Archives (now Prague, National Museum).

[9] Poštolka, *Haydn,* 106ff., was the first to point out these cases of conflicting attribution (Hoboken's raw data aside).

[10] Breitkopf, col. 716.

However, they had been published in Paris in the "Six Trios . . . di Giuseppe Hayden op. XXIII," also as Nos. 4, 1, and 5.[11] The confusion is compounded by Bailleux's use of the same opus number, 23, in an advertisement for six Haydn "Sonates"; these, however, are probably the duets Hob. VI:1–6.[12]

The trios, whose incipits are given in the Breitkopf Catalogue as Op. XVII by Kammel, were published by Chevardière in Paris under that composers name. Hoboken mentions that the other three trios of this volume appear nowhere under Haydn's name. This could lead to the conclusion that all six trios were probably written by Kammel. Three of them might have been brought out by the anonymous publisher of the print "Six Trios . . . di G. Heyden Op.XXIII" together with three trios by Haydn or some other composer altogether. (Haydn's claim to authorship appears nowhere but on the print itself.) Or, conversely, Chevardière might have published three trios by Haydn together with three trios by Kammel under the latter's name. We know approximately the year of Chevardière's print (1777), but not the year of the anonymous print bearing Haydn's name. My thematic catalogue of Kammel's compositions still lacks some prints from archives abroad. So it may yet be possible to confirm the citation in Breitkopf. For the moment, however, the authorship of these trios remains uncertain.

Another conflicting attribution appears in the duo for two violins Hob. VI:G1. It is listed under Haydn's name in the Breitkopf Catalogue, with the remark "laufen in Mspt. unter dem Namen Kammel" ("circulating in MS under the name Kammel").[13] It was published by Hummel as a work of Haydn's, together with five other Haydn duos.[14] Contemporary catalogues—Ulrico Ringmacher (1773) and Godefried Dunwalt (1770)—also list it as a work of Haydn. Only Westphal's catalogue (1783) states, "sind in Paris unter dem Namen Campioni Op. IX erschienen" ("have appeared in Paris under the name Campioni").[15] According to Hoboken, no manuscript of this duo with Haydn's name is known. Among the sources for Kammel's works that I know, there is also no such duo. The external evidence therefore speaks more strongly for Haydn, although the case is not conclusive. But one interesting detail can be added. There is a Kammel violin sonata preserved in Czech archives whose incipit is almost identical to Hob. VI:G1, but it differs in key and instrumentation.[16] The violin part is quite characteristic of Kammel. Un-

---

[11] See Hoboken, I, 497, 499, 500.   [12] See Hoboken, I, 499.

[13] Breitkopf, col. 385.   [14] Six Sonates, opera VI.

[15] The data on the catalogues are taken from Hoboken, I, 518. (Whether "Campioni" is simply an Italianized form of "Kammel" is not known.)

[16] "Sonata à Violino Solo con Basso Del Sig^re Kammel," Pachta Archives, now Prague, National Museum, XXII D 176.

fortunately, I did not have Humel's edition of the duo (attributed to Haydn) at my disposal when preparing this paper.

The third conflicting attribution affects the String Quartet in C major Hob. III:C11, which is attributed to Kammel in a number of sources. As Hoboken notes, it was also attributed to Haydn. In this case, the evidence at hand seems sufficient to resolve the question. This quartet is given as Kammel's work not only in the Breitkopf Catalogue of 1771,[17] but also in the Dunwalt catalogue of 1770.[18] It is the first quartet in the set Op. 4, published under Kammel's name around 1770 by Welcker in London and by Huberty in Paris.[19] Furthermore, this quarter has survived in Czech archives (the only one in this set to do so), in a contemporary copy, also attributed to Kammel.[20] The entire opus was very popular, as is evident from the surviving copies and arrangements. In Dresden, for example, there is a copy of all six quartets, probably made from Huberty's edition,[21] along with an arrangement for two harpsichords.[22] All these sources bear Kammel's name.

The musical contents of this quartet support this conclusion. Although the character of the themes and the overall structure exhibit a number of typical features of early Classical style, which we also find in early Haydn, it has one characteristic which is peculiar to Kammel, namely detailed dynamic markings. These are not found in Haydn's quartets before Op. 20. All in all, I believe that the quartet Hob. III:C11 can be attributed to Kammel without question.

This raises the problem of Haydn's and Kammel's similarity of structure and style. I can present only a brief summary of my results here. They were based chiefly on analysis of the doubtful works which were available to me, or (in the case of Haydn's string trios and duos) of works from the same period using the same instruments. In addition, I compared Haydn's Op. 9, published about the same time as Kammel's Op. 4. Of Kammel's works, I chose for comparison the violin duos Op. 2 and the sonatas for two violins and bass Op. 3. (Unfortunately, the quartets Op. 7 were not available for comparison.)

Kammel persisted in writing three movements in each work, and occasionally only two movements, with a minuet as the concluding movement. Haydn, on the other hand, regularly used the four-movement cycle from Op. 9 on. In many Kammel works from the early 1770s, the

---

[17] Breitkopf, col. 419.　　[18] Hoboken, I, 444.

[19] Six Quartettos for two violins, a tenor and a violoncello obligato. London, Welcker, c. 1770.

[20] "Quarteto in C . . . Del Sigre Kammel." Doksy Archives, now Prague, National Museum, XX E 51.

[21] Dresden, Sächsische Landesbibliothek, Mus. 3440/P/1.

[22] Ibid., Mus. 3440/P/2: "Quartetti accomodati per due cembali di Kammel."

movements in sonata form contain a clearly differentiated second theme, and often even a third theme. In Haydn's sonata form during these years, the second theme is not always clearly differentiated; the entire movement is often built on a single theme.

But the most important differences, as suggested above, are found in the dynamics. Kammel usually elaborated the dynamic markings in great detail in all the parts, not merely in the first violin. We find not only the customary *forte* and *piano,* but other indications such as *ff* and especially *pp.* often with added signs like *pp dolce.* Aside from *mf,* he also uses *mezza voce, un poco f, cresc, rinf,* and others. From this point of view his compositions were considerably more elaborate than those of many of his contemporaries around 1770, including Haydn.

We also find other differences. Kammel was an outstanding violin virtuoso, and he placed greater stress on sonority than did Haydn in these years. His inventive scoring for string suggests a conscious striving for original sonorities. We even find an effort to obtain sound effects like those used by the Mannheim School. Although the first violin clearly predominates and is often technically demanding, the other parts are frequently written very carefully and exhibit considerable independence, frequent solos, and so forth.

Kammel's works vary in their degree of difficulty, from compositions intended for amateurs to works containing difficult concertante passages. The structure of his works is consistently homophonic; we do not find imitation or polyphony, as we do in Haydn. The originality or individuality of Kammel's compositions is uneven, varying widely not only from work to work but among the individual movements within a single work. For example, the first movement of the doubtful quartet Hob. III:C11 is fairly interesting, especially in structure, but the other two movements are routine. Such cases may perhaps be found in early Haydn, but very rarely in Op. 9 or thereafter. This seems to me to be one of the chief differences between composers like Kammel and great personalities such as Haydn. Here, too, is the answer to our opening question: how can a composer who was so popular in his time have been almost completely forgotten as soon as he died?

Like many composers of this period, Kammel matured quickly. A number of his early compositions, such as the duos Op. 2 and the quartets Op. 4, are mature in many ways—in their use of sonata form, in dynamics, and in instrumental stylization. In some of these respects they are more mature than some of Haydn's works from the same years. However, like many of his contemporaries, Kammel developed no further. The great differences among his compositions would seem to have resulted primarily from the specific purposes for which they were written (for amateurs or for concert performance). We do not find that unfailing and constant organic growth which one observes in Haydn's artistic development. Kammel matured quickly to a certain stage, characteristic of the last phase of the early Classical period, but he never moved beyond this stylistic boundary. For this reason, as Classical style reached its culmination in the 1780s, Kammel's music rapidly became outmoded and lost favor.

Even within these limitations, Kammel ranks among the most interesting personalities of the early Classical period. The cases of "mistaken identity" between him and Haydn demonstrate the quality and popularity of his music. As a remarkable personality in the London musical scene during the 1770s, he deserves greater attention and study than has been devoted to him in the past.

Two Unknown Pupils of Haydn; Two Unknown Haydn Sources

MILAN POŠTOLKA

In the first part of this paper I would like to mention two of Haydn's pupils who are not generally known: Smrček and Tomeš. In a book published fifteen years ago,[1] I tried to give a general outline of the mutual relationships between Joseph Haydn and Czech musical culture of his time. Subsequently, I have had opportunities to reconsider many of the problems involved while working on relevant articles for MGG and Grove 6. There is still much to be investigated about those composers who, in the broadest sense, were Haydn's pupils.[2] I do not refer to composers who enjoyed considerable renown and popularity in their own time, for example Pavel Vranický (Wranitzky), his brother Antonín, Jan Křtitel (Baptist) Krumpholz, or Antonín (Anton) Kraft, but rather to musicians who, though artistically less important, were in some respects very characteristic of their times.

Both of my subjects were born in Bohemia: Smrček in Nové Město nad Metují (Neustadt an der Metau), Tomeš in Úpice (Eipel). Like Primitivus Němec and Abundius Mik[y]sch, fellow Czechs who are better known from biographies of Haydn, both Smrček and Tomeš were members of the Barmherzige Brüder. According to the baptismal registers of Nové Město nad Metují, Smrček was born on December 28, 1751 and baptized Josef. He joined the Barmherzige Brüder in Prague in 1773, assuming the monastic name Blasius. From his youth he studied organ, violin, and singing, and he served as choirmaster in churches belonging to the order, first at Prague and later at Valtice (Feldsberg) in Moravia. A remarkable document of Smrček's activity at Valtice has survived in the

---

[1] Poštolka, *Haydn*
[2] Cf. Horst Walter's paper in the Round Table *Background, Biography, Iconography.* [Ed.]

form of an inventory of music and musical instruments written around 1780, a microfilm of which is at the museum in Brno. The inventory includes much secular music, for example more than eighty symphonies, sixteen of them attributed to Haydn, twenty-three to Vanhal, fourteen to Pichl, and seven to Dittersdorf. Unfortunately all the items listed seem to be lost.

The main source of biographical information about Smrček is a manuscript account titled *Nachrichten von Tonkünstlern aus dem Orden der Barmherzigen Brüder,* written in 1796 in Prague by Vinzenz Kneer, a member of the order, and obviously commissioned by Dlabač, who used it in his *Künstlerlexikon.*[3] Kneer's report is now found in the Strahov Library in Prague as part of a volume titled, in Dlabač's hand, *Manuscripta varii argumenti a variis conscripta, collecta autem per me Godefridum Joann. Dlabacž* (shelf no. D.D.II.3). Kneer gives Smrček's monastic offices as "Bohemian province procurator" and "subprior" in Prague, and "convent procurator" in Vienna, the latter being, in 1796, "ein neuangetretenes Amt." He states that Smrček, in addition to these offices, devoted himself to teaching music, especially piano, and that he also composed, specifically mentioning Smrček's piano music and sacred works. According to Kneer, Smrček's piano compositions were highly regarded by "Kapellmeister Joseph Haydn," especially his arrangements of Haydn's symphonies and other works. From this I deduce that Haydn and Smrček were in contact in Vienna, most probably after Haydn's return from England. Dlabač goes a step further in his *Künstlerlexikon* (1815), claiming that Smrček studied composition with Haydn: "Als er zu Wien lebte, nahm er den Unterricht in der Kompozizion von Joseph Heyden [sic] und bald darauf machte er einige Symphonien und Konzerte für das Pianoforte, so wie auch einige Kirchensachen bekannt."[4] Though this could, of course, be simply a misinterpretation of Kneer's report, it is also possible that it is based on later information from Smrček himself, for Smrček died on August 19, 1813, in Vienna, about seventeen years after Kneer's report was written.

As indicated, Dlabač states that Smrček wrote not only church music but also several symphonies and piano concertos. I have been able to locate only Smrček's sacred compositions. The latter survive in manuscript copies owned mostly by the National Museum in Prague and the Moravian Museum in Brno. They include four Requiems, two offertories, one motet, one Te Deum, two Marian antiphons, two Rorate settings, two Advent arias, and a Vespers setting—fifteen works in all. Some of the copies bear only his monastic name, Blasius. These works exhibit few clearly defined stylistic traits which could be attributed to Haydn's influence. For the most part they combine the formulae of a

---

[3] Dlabač, *Lexikon,* s. v. "Smrček"   [4] Ibid.

cultivated *galant* speech with simple melodic ideas in the manner of the Catholic hymn. Some of them employ a concertante organ. On the whole, Kneer's characterization of Smrček's style as "modest and agreeable" ("sein modester angenehmer Kirchen Stylus") is justified.

Tomeš (Tomich, Tomisch, Thomish)—like Smrček, Němec, and Mik[y] sch—is also included in Kneer's report. Kneer (and Dlabač following him) give his birthdate as 1756 and his birthplace as Úpice (Eipel). According to the baptismal registers of Úpice, however, he was born three years later, on October 12, 1759, and baptized František Václav. Tomeš studied music (piano, violin, cello, and viola d'amore) at the Wrocław (Breslau) foundation of the Barmherzige Brüder and later joined the order, assuming the name Flosculus. Afterwards he studied pharmacy at the University of Vienna and served as apothecary at various monasteries of his order. Kneer's report of 1796 contains no further details about Tomeš's life and career. Dlabač's *Künsterlexikon* makes only minor additions.

In the early 1790s, however, compositions began to appear in print bearing the name "Tomich" in various forms (Tomish, Tomick) as composer. They were published in London, Paris, Amsterdam, Offenbach, and later Munich and Vienna. These prints give the composer's Christian name as Francisco or François, or they abbreviate it. Haydn's first London notebook lists, in 1792, "Tomich" as a composer active in London.[5] Later Haydn mentioned "Tomisch" when naming his pupils to Dies.[6] The question of identity inevitably arises, and for the time being the evidence is hardly conclusive.

The following prints survive:

1. Three sonatas for piano or harpsichord with violin and violoncello, dedicated to Joseph Haydn. They were first published in 1792 in London by Longman & Broderip, and subsequently in 1794 in Offenbach by André, and much later in Vienna by Chemische Druckerey. Curiously, the same sonatas in a version for piano and violin appeared as "Op. 94" by Joseph Haydn. The Fürstlich Hohenlohe-Langenburgische Schlossbibliothek at Langenburg owns a copy of this edition, published in 1799 by Falter in Munich. According to Gerber, these sonatas were printed under Haydn's name in the same year by Gombart in Augsburg, but this edition seems to be lost.[7] Though Falter was soon forced to admit his error in a statement in the AmZ,[8] he continued to advertise these sonatas in the following volume of the journal as Haydn's works.

[5] Haydn, CCLN, 263 (*Briefe,* 498).
[6] Dies, modern ed., 197 (original ed., 198; Gotwals, *Haydn,* 196).
[7] E. L. Gerber, "Haydn," 587–88; cf. E. L. Gerber, NL IV, 371.
[8] AmZ, I (1798–99), *Intelligenz-Blatt,* col. 57.

2. A sonata for the pianoforte with accompaniments for the violin and violoncello, without opus number, was printed in London for the composer with a dedication to a Miss McArthur. It is dated "c. 1795."[9]

3. Three sonatas for piano with violin or flute accompaniment, Op. 3, were printed for the composer by Longman & Broderip in London and reprinted in Amsterdam by J. Schmitt.

All of these duets and trios were written in a late *galant* style with occasional song- or dance-like themes of Haydnesque character. In fact, they are very easy keyboard sonatas with only a modest role for the violin, and with the cello doubling the keyboard bass.

Tomeš also arranged works of other composers. His arrangement of Mozart's Clarinet Trio K. 498 was published by N. Simrock at Bonn in 1802; the Preussische Staatsbibliothek, Berlin, owned a copy, but it seems to have been lost during World War II. Three string quartets by Ignaz Pleyel in Tomeš's arrangement as piano duets, and two Pleyel symphonies arranged for piano with violin accompaniment, were published by Longman & Broderip and are now in the British Library. According to H. C. Robbins Landon, Tomeš also arranged many of Haydn's symphonies for piano.[10] I have not been able to verify this. The list of single printed works by Joseph Haydn compiled by Irmgard Becker-Glauch attributes no such arrangement to Tomeš.[11]

One remarkable circumstance remains to be mentioned. In 1791, the "historical ballet" *Orpheus and Euridice* was performed at the King's Theater in London. A libretto, printed in that year by Hammond and now in Wolfenbüttel, gives "Thomish" as composer of most of the music, some of which survives as *The Celebrated Opera Dances for the Year 1791 . . . composed and adapted for the piano-forte, violin or flute by F. Tomich,* published in London by G. Smart. It is somewhat puzzling that the ballet with Tomeš's music was performed, whereas Haydn's opera *L'anima del filosofo,* on the same subject and written for the King's Theater in the same year, was not staged at all. One wonders whether there was some connection between these facts.

In the second part of this paper, may I call your attention to two previously unknown Haydn sources in the National Museum, Prague. The first is a printed libretto of *The Seasons,* not listed in Hoboken. It consists of thirty-two numbered pages in octavo, the title page reading

Die / Jahreszeiten / nach Thomson. / In Musik gesetzt / von / Joseph Haydn, / Doktor der Tonkunst, der Königl. Schwedischen musikalischen / Akademie Mitglied und Kapellmeister in wirklichen Diensten / Sr. Durchlaucht des Fürsten Esterhazy.

[9] In BUC II, 1015.   [10] Haydn, CCLN, 264 (*Briefe,* 498–99).
[11] Becker-Glauch, "Haydn," 239–79.

This libretto was printed in Prague by Johann Diesbach and bears the date 1803. It was published on the occasion of the Prague performance of *The Seasons* on December 25, 1803, organized by the Prague Musicians' Society (Tonkünstler-Sozietät), probably the public premiere of this work in Prague. Václav Praupner conducted, as he had at the earlier performance of *The Creation* on April 10, the inaugural concert of the Tonkünstler-Sozietät. For that performance, however, the Viennese libretto, printed by Mathias Andreas Schmidt in 1799, was used. These two libretti and seventeen others are bound together in a volume which belonged to Gerlak Strniště (1784–1855), choirmaster of the Premonstratensian monastic church at Strahov in Prague. Haydn's two oratorios were frequently performed and consequently well known in Bohemia in the early nineteenth century. The same was not necessarily true of Haydn's symphonies, however, as the following example may show.

The second source, call number II D 42 in the National Museum in Prague, is a manuscript copy of a symphony in G major, described on the title page as "del Sig. Vogel." In fact the work is the "Surprise" Symphony, No. 94 in G major, by Haydn. The copy consists of thirteen separate parts and a cover with title page. The name of the first owner and probably its copyist, Emanuel Pacha, is written on the lower right-hand corner of the title page and on most of the parts. Some of the parts, moreover, bear two other names, Joseph Schön and Franz Orban. I have not succeeded in identifying these three men. The copy was written, as stated at the end of the second clarinet [*sic*] part and on several others, in 1806 at "Böhmisch-Pettersdorf" (Petrovice), a small village in East Bohemia in the district of Ústí nad Orliá. The paper has a distinct watermark with the name J. HADAUN, which I have been unable to find in F. Zuman's *České filigrány*, the standard work on Bohemian watermarks. The copy differs from Haydn's original scoring in that clarinets are used instead of oboes, and two horns are added. But the most surprising fact is that one of Haydn's most popular symphonies could have been attributed to another composer fourteen years after its first performance. Could this imply that Haydn's symphonies were far less known in early nineteenth-century Bohemia than his oratorios?

PART THREE: PERFORMANCE

The panel discussions in this section are ordered in such a way as to present a coherent development of this complex topic. The opening Round Table offers a discussion of general problems affecting the performance of Haydn's music in his time, not limited to any particular genre. The six workshops, each uniting performers and scholars in consideration of the music in actual performance, focus on individual genres, in some cases on limited selections from a genre. In Workshops 1 (Church Music), 4 (Symphony), and 5 (Opera), the performers discuss problems primarily affecting a modern performance; on the other hand Workshops 2 (Keyboard Sonatas), 3 (String Quartets), and 6 (Piano Trios) give considerable attention to the use of "original" instruments and to historical performance practice. The concluding Round Table then surveys the entire issue, focusing on the problem of achieving a modern performance—not a historical recreation—that is faithful to the spirit of Haydn's music.

Round Table

Performance Problems in Haydn's Music: Historical Performance Conditions and Traditions

BARRY S. BROOK, *Chairman*
PAUL BRYAN
ROBERT N. FREEMAN
ROBERT LEVIN

CHRISTOPH-HELLMUT MAHLING
CHARLES ROSEN
VERA SCHWARZ
NEAL ZASLAW, *Secretary*

BROOK   Until recently Haydn and his performance traditions have been poorly served by historians. This is glaringly evident if one compares the scholarship on Bach, Beethoven, or Mozart—or, for that matter, on many lesser composers—with that on Haydn. Many still believe, for example, that Haydn wrote fifteen more string quartets than he actually did. If, as Collingwood put it, we have only a limited quantity of evidence concerning any historical question, our skepticism regarding our knowledge of Haydn must remain very great indeed. But if our job as historians is to establish the facts, as far as possible, our job as musicians is to help interpret these facts for the present.

This Round Table will attempt to clarify the performance traditions of Haydn's time in various places and for various functions and genres. Three topics have been designated: orchestral or symphonic sonority; the role of improvisation in Haydn performance, including the use of continuo; context and function in the performance of Haydn's works.

185

Orchestral (Symphonic) Sonority[1]

The Size and Composition of European Orchestras, 1775–1795

ZASLAW The following remarks are based on a comprehensive survey of eighteenth-century accounts and documents, as published in the modern musicological literature.[2] The orchestras studied performed in churches, courts, operas and theaters, public concerts, and private gatherings. Hence they varied widely in size, makeup, purpose, repertory, long-term stability, and economic status.

There are difficulties with interpreting the information that has come down to us. Often, only the total number of violinists is given, so that we know nothing about the proportion of first violins to seconds. Many orchestral musicians played two or more instruments: violin and double bass, flute and oboe, and so forth. A superfluous wind player might take a seat at the back of the second violins. In payroll documents, a musician might be listed for many years according to the instrument he played when first hired, even if he had long since mastered another in the meantime. The permanent rolls were often augmented by part-time players—amateurs, dilettantes, apprentices, students, waits—whether to increase the size of the whole ensemble on grand occasions, or to supply an instrument not normally present. Or they could be reduced in size by illness, musicians absent on tour, or musicians executing other duties for which they were concurrently liable. Hence in many respects the documents give an incomplete or even misleading picture of the actual conditions of performance.

Certain instruments pose particular problems. Chief among these is the viola. According to the published data a number of orchestras had no violas. But the vast majority of works from this period require violas; they must have been used. The explanation is simply that most violin players also played the viola, and that the term "violin" itself was occasionally used generically, for the entire violin family.

Clarinets were still rather rare; slightly more than half the orchestras can document clarinet players. Trumpets and timpani were usually on a different payroll—that of the stable rather than the *Kapelle*. Eighteenth-century writers like Forkel or Cramer were sometimes misled by mention of ten or twelve trumpets. These players were usually brought in only two or three at a time when needed.

The presence or absence of keyboard continuo players offers an even more difficult problem. Adam Carse did not report keyboard players,

---

[1] On this subject see also Workshop 4. [Ed.]
[2] For a full discussion, see Zaslaw, "Orchestra."

lute players, and other players of chordal instruments, because he did not consider them germane to his discussion of the eighteenth-century orchestra.[3] Furthermore, often the maestro himself was the keyboard player, but he was listed only as maestro.

As for the balance among the instruments and sections: eighteenth-century musicians preferred a relatively heavy bass line—cellos, double basses, and bassoons—with a light viola part.[4] The winds were much stronger in comparison to the strings than they are today. After reaching a combined total in all string sections of approximately twenty to twenty-five, it was considered necessary to double the woodwinds, and perhaps the brass as well.

There was no consistent growth from 1775 to 1795 in the size of the orchestra. The developmental idea based on an evolutionary model, showing growth from the small orchestra, to Mozart's and Haydn's, to Beethoven's, and finally to Wagner's, does not appear to work within a span of only twenty years.[5] Orchestras grew and shrank, particularly in response to the changing taste of princes and audiences and to fluctuating economic conditions. On the other hand, one can relate the size of eighteenth-century orchestras to the social origins of the groups. Private (not court) orchestras in the households of wealthy people averaged six violins in all, church orchestras averaged eleven, court orchestras twelve, opera and theater orchestras eighteen, and concert orchestras nineteen. The other instruments almost always remained in proportion.

Political subdivisions also played a role in the number and size of orchestras. In highly centralized countries like England and France there were fewer orchestras but larger ones. In Germany, and presumably in Italy (for which data are lacking), there were more orchestras but smaller ones. According to Koch, a normal string section included four or five each of first and second violins and two or three each of violas, cellos, and double basses, for a total of fourteen to eighteen instruments.[6] My investigations confirm these figures for medium ensembles.

Finally, many of our statistics have often been repeated in the literature without critical evaluation. It is misleading to represent an orchestral membership as static. To understand the size of an orchestra, it must be studied over a period of time rather than in isolated instances. A few studies have dealt with the matter properly: János Hárich meticulously explains the practices that determined who was available to play at Eszterháza; Professor Mahling points out in great detail why certain

[3] Carse, *18th-century,* 28.

[4] In 1768, however, Haydn stated (*Briefe,* 60; CCLN, 10–11) that he preferred one cello, one double bass, and one bassoon to three cellos and six double basses, "because [the bass line] is difficult to hear clearly" in the latter scoring. [Ed.]

[5] This contradicts received opinion; for example, Carse, *Orchestra,* 18.

[6] Koch, *Lexikon,* s. v. "Begleitung"; "Besetzung."

figures must not be taken at face value—for example, the orchestra pits in some surviving eighteenth-century opera houses were not big enough to accommodate the entire *Kapelle*.[7] The skepticism regarding historical facts that Professor Brook mentioned in his opening remarks is certainly appropriate in respect to our knowledge of the eighteenth-century orchestra.

Discussion

ROSEN I take it, Professor Zaslaw, that your "average" figures represent standing orchestras on regular salary rather than ones brought together for particular performances, such as the performance of Mozart's Symphony in C major K. 338 with forty violins, quadruple winds, and sixteen double basses.

ZASLAW That is correct. I also eliminated the occasional grand spectacular performances of Haydn's *Creation* or Handel's *Messiah*. My averages are day-to-day norms.

ROSEN How many of the concerts that would be given, say in Vienna in the 1780s, would have been by regular orchestras, and how many by orchestras hired for the occasion?

ZASLAW In Vienna there were no regular, public, concert-giving orchestras. In London, Paris, and Leipzig, however, there were standing public orchestral organizations.

SCHWARZ The smaller orchestras in Austria in Haydn's time were maintained chiefly by the nobility. There is still much research to be done in this area. Prince Lobkowitz, for example, had three different groups in his castle in Augnitz (Czechoslovakia): a string ensemble, a so-called *Harmonie* (wind band), and a Turkish band. The leader of the orchestra proper, Anton Wranitzky in Vienna, also trained these ensembles, which played much music by Haydn. Wranitzky arranged Haydn's *Creation* for string orchestra, with winds playing the vocal lines. After 1810 the nobles could no longer afford their big orchestras, but they kept the *Harmonie*. So they made wind-band arrangements of all this music.

The Composition of the Orchestra in Haydn's Time

MAHLING I should like to limit myself to a few problems, questions, and observations. The importance of personnel lists for orchestras is unquestionable. Yet these catalogues and personnel lists can only give us clues as to the

[7]Hárich, "Orchester"; Mahling, "Orchesterpraxis" and *Orchester;* cf. the excellent longitudinal study based on archival sources in Schiedermair, "Kapelle."

makeup of any orchestra in actual performance. In this connection Professor Zaslaw has indicated that almost every musician could play several instruments, and that this created the possibility of altering the composition of an orchestra *ad hoc.*

The difference between personnel and the actual performing forces is obvious in the case of trumpets. Though there were often a considerable number of court trumpeters available—ten or twelve was not unusual—only the so-called musical trumpeters come into question for participation in the orchestra. As a rule there were only two of these. It follows that there were rarely more than two trumpets used in the performance of a Haydn symphony. To this, a timpani player was always added. Moreover, trumpets and timpani comprised a consistent unit in the eighteenth century. This leads to a further question, whether timpani were used if there is a trumpet part but no timpani part, as we find, for example, in the Symphony in G Major, K. 318, by Mozart. Related to this is the question whether in the eighteenth century there was (still?) a related improvisatory practice for timpani—that is to say, if trumpets were used, whether a timpani part was automatically added *ex proviso.*

Another difference between personnel and performing forces arises in the performance of solo concertos. We know both from Haydn and from Dittersdorf that their court orchestras in the 1780s comprised a total of about twenty-five musicians. In each, about twelve of these were solo players.[8] As a rule, the Kapellmeister evidently assigned the solos in accordance with a consistent plan. Nevertheless, Dittersdorf reported that the soloists in his orchestra had to be ready to perform a solo concerto at any time, as determined by the Kapellmeister. In turn, this could change the instrumentation as a whole. Particularly with the small court orchestras of the eighteenth century, we must reckon with great flexibility in instrumentation, especially in the case of solo and tutti players.

In larger courts the difference between personnel and performing forces is even clearer. If on one hand the latter were determined in part by the size of the various rooms at the disposal of the orchestra and in which it performed, on the other it was also determined by service schedules. The court orchestras of Dresden and Munich, each of which boasted of a strength of from sixty to eighty musicians, are examples. But a number of contemporary reports complain that neither orchestra performed at full strength. For the reasons given above, however, such a "mass" presentation was neither necessary nor possible. We must remember, for example, that the pit in the Munich Court Theater had space for not more than thirty-five musicians. Moreover, we have printed service schedules—precisely for the Munich Court Orchestra—which establish that in every case only a part of the entire group was used. Thus it would

[8] Dittersdorf, *Lebensbeschreibung,* mod. ed., 141, 143 (original ed., 138, 144).

be amiss to try to draw conclusions about the actual performing forces of an orchestra from the personnel list applicable to any given occasion. From this arise certain problems in research into eighteenth-century performance practice. In our concern for suitable performance practice and appropriate size and proportions of the orchestra, we must therefore not only consider the known historical circumstances but also the composition, the work itself.

Another important question is the doubling of wind instruments. It is important not only for the eighteenth century, but above all for the nineteenth century, during which the string section of the orchestra was steadily enlarged. Even here no generalizations can be made or norms established, such as, for example, that in the nineteenth century orchestras performed exclusively with enlarged string sections and doubled winds, or that symphonies by Haydn or Mozart were performed with sixteen first violins. Concerning the historical consciousness of the nineteenth century with respect to the performance of eighteenth-century works, I find a report in the first volume of the *Neue Berliner Musikzeitung* of 1846/7 of some interest. It speaks of the sixth "Symphonic Evening" of the Royal Orchestra in which, among other things, Haydn's "Farewell" Symphony (No. 45 in F-sharp minor) was performed as follows: "In accordance with the nature of the piece, the orchestra comprised only six first, six second violins, etc.; and nevertheless it was able to throw the main features of the composition into sharp relief."[9] This then is a record of historical consciousness, that recognized that Haydn's composition could only be made to sound successfully in the appropriate orchestral setting. Today this point of view is all too often neglected.

Haydn's Alto Horns: Their Effect and the Question of Authenticity

BRYAN One of the most attractive aspects of recent recordings of Haydn symphonies is provided by their high horn parts. In addition to those parts actually marked *alto* (or *hoch*) by Haydn, those in many other works in B-flat or C, where Haydn makes no such specification, have been additionally so interpreted.[10] (So-called *alto* horns performed in the same octave as trumpets; "Basso" horns performed an octave lower than written.) H. C. Robbins Landon has vividly described the special timbre thus created as "intoxicating."[11] And Landon believes that almost all of Haydn's orchestral compositions in C major were conceived in the same way; therefore:

[9] NBMz 1 (1846–47), 22.
[10] A full account of the topics discussed in this paper appears in Bryan, "Horn."
[11] R. Landon, *Symphonies*, 340.

[in my edition of the symphonies] *alto* was added to all C-horn parts used in conjunction with trumpets and timpani. Whenever we have an autograph or authentic parts for these C major symphonies (i.e., for Nos. 41, 50, 56, etc.) *alto* is always specified, and there is no reason to suppose that the others (Nos. 20, 32, 33) are different.[12]

This statement, repeated throughout Landon's symphony edition, has helped create the impression that the authentic use of *alto* horn parts in C and B-flat is settled. It is not.

C major will be considered first. Authentic sources for several of Haydn's compositions indicate horns in C *alto:* Symphonies No. 41 (before 1771), 48 (before 1773), 50 (1773), 52 (before 1774), 56 (1774), 60, 82, 90, and the operas *L'infedeltà delusa, Philemon und Baucis, L'isola disabitata,* and *La vera costanza.* Significantly, of these works only Symphony No. 56 also originally called for trumpets. The majority were written from c. 1770 to 1774, *before* Haydn's orchestral wind section was expanded from the quartet of two oboes and two horns by the addition of two bassoons. That is, they date from a period where he sought to increase the utility of the horns. The combination of *alto* horns and timpani enabled him to derive both horn and trumpet-and-timpani functions from the same players. Support for this premise is provided by the Elssler parts for Symphony No. 41 which, like the ones for No. 48, include horns in C *alto* but lack trumpets and timpani. Together with No. 52 and its single C *alto* horn paired with a horn in E-flat, these appear to be Haydn's earliest works specifying *alto* horns.

The indication "Clarini e Corni" is uncommon. Especially enigmatic, therefore, is the indication "Clarini / e Corni in / C alto" found in the final chorus of *Philemon and Baucis.* Jürgen Braun, the editor of this work in JHW, eliminates the trumpet parts. To the excellent discussion in his critical report I can only add that *e* ("and") is very similar to *o* ("or"), which is normally found in this context. The only source which unquestionably specifies horns in C *alto* with trumpets is the autograph of Symphony No. 56. Although the trumpet parts in the first movement are complementary and effective, Haydn never used this instrumentation again. In Symphony No. 90, on the other hand, Haydn's substituting the *alto* horns for trumpets suggests that he may have decided to perform it at Eszterháza before sending it to Paris. The use of trumpets and *basso* horns in Paris seems assured, because the authentic parts at Harburg, with Haydn's corrections, include horns (not *alto*), trumpets, and timpani. Of the other post-1774 symphonies in C major with similar scoring, Nos. 63, 69, 95, and 97, none uses *alto* horns.

Concerning B-flat horns, Landon frankly states that "Haydn never bothered to write 'alto' or 'basso' on B-flat horn parts," which "leads [to the] conclusion that only one type of instrument was in common use"

[12] R. Landon, in Haydn, *Symphonies,* I, xxi.

before Symphony No. 98—i.e., B-flat *alto*.[13] But W. A. Mozart, Michael Haydn, and Gluck apparently took *basso* for granted, because when they did specify, it was always *alto*. Mozart apparently first specified *alto* horns in his Cassation in B-flat K. 99, probably from the summer of 1769, and he often did so thereafter. His earliest composition in B-flat with horns labeled "basso" seems to be the aria "Barbaro oh dio" from *Il rè pastore* of 1775. Regarding Michael Haydn, according to Charles Sherman (in a letter to the author), "the evidence . . . goes directly contrary to [Landon's] assertion. . . . In such symphonies as Perger 51 (n.d.) the horns can only be Basso, the autographs for Perger 9 (15 June 1772), 24 (28 Sept. 1786) clearly specify Basso. . . . Perger 18 (12 March 1784) specified Alto, and Perger 52 (n.d.) uses 4 horns: 2 B-flat Alto and 2 B-flat Basso." Gluck, in *Il rè pastore* of 1751, includes parts for both B-flat (unspecified) and B-flat *alto*.

[Here followed a series of recorded excerpts and a discussion of distributed music examples to illustrate the difficulty and illogicality of using the B-flat *alto* horn in specific instances.][14]

A final piece of evidence that the B-flat *basso* horn existed comes from a study of the horn maker Antoine Joseph Hampel, which informs us that the B-flat *basso* crook was in use some years before Anton Kerner, who served the Esterházy orchestra for many years and who made horns for them in 1773 and 1780, raised Hampel's horn to B-flat *alto*.[15] This relates nicely to Mozart's apparent initial use of B-flat *alto* in 1769 and Haydn's initial use of C *alto* in Symphony No. 41, from roughly the same time. Since Haydn continued to specify C *alto* thereafter, he would probably have called for B-flat *alto* horns had he desired their employment.

The Role of Improvisation in Haydn Performance

The Role of Organ Improvisation in Haydn's Church Music

FREEMAN From a historical standpoint the study of improvisation seems to present unique problems. Improvisation cuts against the grain of the methodology which has been carefully built up over the last fifty years for seeking out and assessing notated musical sources. It is precisely the absence of such sources, combined with other secondary evidence, which can imply a flourishing practice of improvisation. This seems to be the case with the organ literature of Haydn's time.

The relatively small extant repertory for unaccompanied organ in

[13] R. Landon, *Symphonies,* 124.   [14] Cf. Bryan, "Horn," 224–25, 227.
[15] Ibid., 226 and n. 111, 248.

eighteenth-century Austria contrasts sharply with what we know of the role this instrument played in Austrian life. Good organists and organs were everywhere. Haydn himself was active as a part-time organist as early as his Viennese free-lance period in the 1750s, and for some seventeen years he fulfilled the winter organist's duties in Eisenstadt, where he was surrounded by organs.

Yet the surviving Haydn compositions for the instrument are few indeed. The organ serves as part of the continuo section in the Masses and smaller liturgical works, and in a few of these it is given an obbligato part. If we accept Georg Feder's theory based on keyboard ranges, at least three and perhaps as many as seven of the keyboard concertos were intended for organ.[16] This disparity between activity as an organist and paucity of notated compositions is just as great among Haydn's contemporaries, such as Albrechtsberger or Michael Haydn, who were even more closely associated with the instrument. This discrepancy can be explained only by the existence of an intense tradition of improvisation.

What types of extemporization could have been demanded of eighteenth-century Austrian organists? First, church players would have had to improvise at least well enough to realize the figured-bass parts which continued to be included in Classical church compositions. Figured-bass tradition itself may have been perpetuated partly because organists were still adept in the art of improvisation. Second, concerto cadenzas would have been another area in which an organist could have been expected to improvise. (It appears, however, that cadenzas were frequently written out before they were played. A number of Haydn's keyboard concertos are preserved in copies with cadenzas spelled out in the solo part.) A third type of improvisation which became important toward the end of the century comprised the "partimento" pieces, fragmentary compositions which served as the basis for improvisation. In Austria these often went under the older name of "verset." Finally, free impromptu playing, referred to as *Spiel aus dem Stegreife* or *Präludieren,* differed from figured bass, cadenza, and the partimento in that it was divorced from any precomposed context. At the abbeys like Melk, for example, precise liturgical moments of *Präludieren* were designated in instruction manuals for the cloister officials. Mozart and Albrechtsberger were known as the greatest artists in this type of organ playing. Diaries, travelogues and similar sources leave little doubt that all these categories of improvisation could have been heard throughout Haydn's Austria where they played an integral part in the church services.

Toward the end of the century the publication and circulation in manuscript form of collections of independent organ pieces intended for church services increased remarkably. Perhaps there had been a decline in

---

[16] See Feder, "Orgelkonzerte."

the art of organ improvisation, which is implied particularly by the pro-liferation of partimento-type verset collections. Nevertheless, these late notated examples offer some clues as to the specific function of the earlier improvised practice. The organ pieces were produced under a variety of collective titles—*Praeludien, Versetten, Fugen,* and *Kadenzen*—and often contained liturgical designations in their individual titles. One by Al-brechtsberger carries the title *Präludium nach dem Sanctus, zur Joseph Hay-dens Mess ex G,* probably referring to the *Missa Sti. Nicolai* of 1772.

Bringing together the literary descriptions and the liturgical designa-tions contained in the titles of the extant preludes, a tentative composite picture of the role of organ improvisation, at least in the Mass, can be constructed. *Präludieren* could take place: 1) at the beginning of the Mass between the ringing of the church bells and the Introit; 2) between the Gloria and the Credo, before or after the Epistle or in place of the Grad-ual; 3) between the Sanctus and the Benedictus, during the Elevation; 4) before the Benediction; and 5) at the end of the Mass, as exit music.[17]

Discussion

LEVIN By Haydn's time the continuo was on the wane. Its presence here or there may be the result of habit, not the preference of a composer. Also, the continuo is several things, and some people tend to stress one func-tion at the expense of others. The harmonies supplied can give either mere vertical support, or they can unify. In the trio sonata, the keyboard player not only supplies the middle of the texture, but creates a certain homogeneity for the ensemble.

A continuo part is by nature improvised, which means that the player can perform either in exclusively chordal, predominantly chordal, or rather contrapuntal fashion. In Haydn's instrumental output harmonic support for its own sake becomes less and less important. The keyboard instrument used merely to complete the harmonies eventually becomes irrelevant; in the London symphonies it is unnecessary. But it would be an oversimplification to justify the continuo solely on the need for har-monic support. Sonority is also involved. The continuo is not needed in Bach's Brandenburg Concertos 90% of the time, and yet it's there.

In vocal works, especially where recitative occurs and the keyboard in-strument is present as a matter of course, its participation will probably not be limited merely to the accompaniment of recitative.

I would like to put in a word for those keyboard players, such as myself, who improvise when they play continuo and do not play block chords. In doing so the texture is enlivened, particularly in slow move-ments, in a valuable way. From this we may guess that perhaps one reason that the keyboard continuo survived was that it enabled the maes-

[17]See Kellner, *Kremsmünster* 530; Freeman, "Melk," *passim.*

tro, who was often the composer, to retain some kind of personal prerogative in performance even after he had given his piece out to be played.

MAHLING I would like to add three points:

1. In the symphonies there is certainly little opportunity for improvisation by the continuo player. Recently Mr. Dorati experimented along these lines in his recording of the slow movement of Haydn's Symphony No. 20 in C major.

2. Doubtless the continuo players in opera and oratorio were allowed great freedom in the performance of their parts. But this applies to the cellists as well as to the keyboard players (harpsichord, organ). In the eighteenth century and into the nineteenth, continuo practice included the cellist improvising in the manner of the harpsichordist—that is, with arpeggios, double stops, etc. It appears that J. S. Bach fixed and wrote down this customary practice in some of the obbligato parts for cello or gamba in his cantatas and passions (e.g., the *St. Matthew Passion*). But we have no indications that this practice would have been approved by Haydn. At the end of the eighteenth century, for example, on the death of the solo cellist of the Mannheim orchestra, it was discovered that none of the other cellists was qualified to play the continuo properly.[18]

3. In this connection there is the further question: To what extent did singers, say in Haydn's oratorios and operas, still "improvise" or ornament their parts, that is, use procedures perceived as obvious to an extent that we today are no longer able to imagine? How long such practices remained common can be seen in an account from the year 1824, in which it is stated that in a performance in Berlin of Mozart's *The Magic Flute,* Sarastro's aria "In diesen heil'gen Hallen" *at long last* had not been ornamented, and the singer had added no embellishments (*Schnörkeleien*).[19] Whether and how improvisation and ornamentation took place, of course, depended in the main on the abilities of the individual singers.

JAMES WEBSTER[20]   The evidence in the sources regarding the continuo in Haydn's orchestral music is really very scanty. The idea that a continuo is needed in Haydn's early orchestral music is not based on documentary evidence; it derives from the belief that it is historically related to Baroque music and the presence of many passages in thin texture. I don't find either of these arguments persuasive. The entire question must be subjected to critical examination.

SCHWARZ I would like to point out the problem of fermatas in Haydn's keyboard sonatas, and also in the trios. We do not know whether these fermatas

[18] AmZ 6 (1804), 221–22; cf. 11 (1809), 597–98.
[19] A. B. Marx in AmZ (Berlin), 1824, 322.   [20] From the audience.

were an indication for an improvised cadenza, or merely a fermata in the modern sense. In addition I would like to point out a peculiarity of the late keyboard works, that Haydn composed cadenzas in them but notated them in a "free" measure inserted between the barlines, so that it is often difficult for performers to recognize them; instead they play these cadenzas as if they were part of the actual composition. Thus it would be important to know at what places cadenzas should have been improvised.

LEVIN This question depends on the composer involved. For instance, in Mozart I would say that, most of the time, when a fermata appears in a piano concerto or in a divertimento, a cadenza, or an *Eingang* or *Atempause* (a brief elaboration of a given sonority), is to be played. In Haydn I think it is more difficult to be certain. Haydn was not the keyboard virtuoso that Mozart was.

ROSEN It makes no difference whether Haydn was himself a virtuoso or not. In certain places with a fermata you must have a cadenza. For example, in the A-flat Sonata Hob. XVI:46 (ChL. 31), in the slow movement, measure 77, there is a six-four chord; you must play a cadenza there whether or not the composer was a virtuoso. It depends in many cases on the placing of the fermata.

LEVIN A fermata on a dominant seventh implies an *Eingang*.

MANFRED BLUM[21] This *Atempause* fermata occurs in Haydn's String Quartet Opus 20, No. 6 in A major. In the second movement, the first fermata in measure 47 is written out as an *Eingang*. The second place toward the end (measure 72) is not written out, but a cadenza should be performed. Türk suggests this, by the way, in his *Klavierschule* (pp. 308–19).

FREEMAN Some copies of Haydn's time include cadenzas. There is also some evidence that Haydn's attitude towards improvisation changed somewhat. As is shown in Bartha-Somfai, for instance, around 1784 Haydn scratched out the fermata and some of the coloratura passages in opera arias. This seems to indicate a desire for greater control over improvisation in his later works.

EVA BADURA-SKODA[22] There are two little-known cadenzas in the Gesellschaft für Musikfreunde that bear the name of Haydn, but they have not been authenticated. In vocal music, cadenzas and embellishments of fermatas are more important than in instrumental music.

ROSEN I doubt that there is any evidence that anybody played continuo parts in secular instrumental music in a contrapuntal fashion after 1770.

ZASLAW The surviving examples of realized continuo are textbook examples, or cases where people who were afraid to improvise wrote out their own in

[21] From the audience.   [22] From the audience.

advance. Therefore the sources misrepresent the possibilities. We could only document contrapuntal realizations by looking to accounts of actual performances.

ROSEN There is a written-out continuo for one of the Mozart concertos. Characteristically, it has the continuo playing when the orchestra is *forte,* in which case it is doubtful that you would have heard the piano!

ZASLAW But one had to conduct the orchestra.

ROSEN But it is not certain that the orchestra was conducted by playing chords in sections where the music was *piano.* The music critics in London reported that Haydn's gestures were extremely beautiful while directing the orchestra. This must mean that he stopped playing continuo and waved his hands—certainly in the sections marked *piano* in the orchestra.

ZASLAW I would have assumed that the *piano* sections are played by the good players as chamber music; only the tuttis require the coordination of the chords.

BRYAN There are moments in Haydn's slow movements where there is no fermata, but the six-four chord is so strong that a cadenza seems required.

BROOK The evidence for improvisation and cadenzas is not so scarce in early Haydn, but it becomes very sparse indeed by the late period.

Context and Function in the Performance of Haydn's Works

Changing Contexts of a Work in the Composer's Lifetime

ROSEN One problem of eighteenth-century performance practice is the change in the context or the function of a work that occurs during the lifetime of the composer, especially when related to the gradual development of public concerts. Vienna lagged behind many other European cities in this respect. The first public concert in Vienna is said to have taken place in 1771; the first public concert that was not centered around an opera or oratorio in 1777.[23] On the other hand, some private concerts at the homes of wealthy and aristocratic patrons were to a certain extent semi-public, and they were described in newspaper articles. They therefore enjoyed some measure of publicity like that given to public concerts in other more advanced cities, such as Paris, London, New York, and Boston.

Certain problems relate to the increasing frequency of public performance of works originally intended for private hearing. These difficulties

[23] Chrysander, "Conzertwesen," 219, 234 (reviewing Hanslick, *Concertwesen*).

include the choice of instrument and, in earlier Haydn sonatas, the problem of the ornamented reprise. In examining the traditions and musical style of the 1760s, it is apparent that the reprise was often ornamented; some Haydn sonatas from that period take ornamentation and variation extremely well. The C-minor Sonata Hob. XVI:20 (ChL.33) of 1771, containing some written-out ornamentation, seems to cry out for more decoration in performance.

In ornamenting the repeat of the exposition, as in sonatas "mit veränderten Reprisen," you create the problem of balancing the recapitulation with it. In the recapitulation of the C-minor Sonata, Haydn recasts the opening theme in a quite different and more dramatic structure; the addition of ornamentation here would spoil this effect. At the same time if the repetition of the exposition is ornamented (as the style seems to require), the unornamented recapitulation becomes lighter and less forceful in comparison. Problems such as these gradually arose from composers' building the expressive values of music into the structure, rather than allowing them to depend upon ornamentation in performance.

We should not restrict our study of performance practice to the exact moment at which a piece was written. With radical changes in musical style, such as those for which Haydn was particularly responsible, the original performance tradition may have lagged behind. (This is one reason why contemporary accounts and theories of performance practice are often misleading.) Certain Haydn sonatas were apparently written for harpsichord, yet they include dynamic indications that make sense only on the piano.[24] The changes in style of Haydn and his contemporaries were thus actually responsible for many later modifications in performance practice. (And so the best instrument for performing Haydn may be the one created in response to his music, not the one he wrote it for.) Continuo, ornamentation, and improvisation must all be considered within this changing context of style and function.

Discussion

MAHLING Of course, style in the narrower sense is not changeable, but what pertains to style is always changeable. For example, this includes even the sound; and in turn the latter depends, among other things, on the performing forces. There is also the problem of compositions for particular persons, particular ensembles and orchestras, or particular musicians in an orchestra, etc. This situation probably applies to Haydn more than Mozart; Mozart himself mentioned, when sending several piano concertos to Donaueschingen, the possibility of playing the works with an

---

[24] On these points cf. Workshops 2 and 6 and the paper by A. Peter Brown in the Round Table on the Raigern Sonatas. [Ed.]

orchestra in which some of the required instruments were not available—for example, if there was no second clarinet it would be possible to play its part on a viola.[25] In Haydn's case we find explicit remarks of this kind scarcely at all. He was uneasy if he did not know for what musicians or for what orchestra he was composing.[26]

We should also remember that some orchestras and choruses in the eighteenth century had become accustomed to particular styles. For example, it was reported around 1788 that Prince Wallerstein's court orchestra in Germany "is proficient mainly in the works of four composers, namely Haydn; Rosetti, who imitates Haydn; Beecke, the present concertmaster at the court at Bonn; and Reicha, who formerly trained and directed this orchestra. . . ."[27] I believe that the relationship between style, manner of composition, and the identity of the performers for whom a piece was written is very close, and that therefore style may have something to do with performance practice after all.

BADURA-SKODA   The dates 1771 and 1777 as the occasions for the first public concerts in Vienna, which Professor Rosen took from Chrysander's review of Hanslick, are uncertain. After many years of research I would still hesitate to give any date for the first public concert. As early as 1763, an account book from the Hofkammer-Archiv in Vienna documents payment to Johann Baptist Schmidt for performing a concerto on the "Fortipiano" in the Burgtheater.

ROSEN Do we know that this performance was not merely the *entr'acte* of an opera?

BADURA-SKODA   It might have been. I brought this up more for its comment on the use of the fortepiano. During Lent, instrumental music was not only performed between the acts of operas or oratorios, but there were concerts in which instrumental works alternated with single arias. I believe that Chrysander's 1777 concert was of the latter type.[28]

The Function of Haydn's Instrumental Compositions in the Abbeys

FREEMAN The significance of the Austrian monastic archives, with their rich store of Haydn compositions in early copies, has long been recognized. The monasteries seem to have been particularly interested in Haydn's in-

[25] Mozart, *Briefe*, III, 590 (September 30, 1786)

[26] For example, in the oft-cited *Applausus* letter (*Briefe*, 60; CCLN, 11): "If I have perhaps not guessed the taste of these gentlemen, I am not to be blamed for it, for I know neither the persons nor the place, and the fact that they were concealed from me really made my work very difficult (*hat mir in wahrheit diese arbeith sauer gemacht*)."

[27] MRz 1 (1788–89), 52.

[28] Cf. also Gerhard Croll's references to 1758 concerts in the Round Table on *Classical Period and Classical Style*. [Ed.]

strumental music, which they assiduously collected from the early 1760s on. Göttweig, for example, owned copies of Symphonies Nos. 3–5 as early as 1762, while Seitenstetten had possession of the undated, but probably very early autograph of the orchestral minuets, Hob. IX:1. Interest in Haydn at Melk dates back at least to November 1760, when the abbot sent him his nephew, Robert Kimmerling, for instruction in composition.

In order to understand how Haydn's instrumental music fit into everyday life at the abbeys, one must recall that in many respects their social atmosphere resembled that of aristocratic establishments. To the extent affordable, the prelate was surrounded with musical trappings commensurate with his rank. In charge was a Kapellmeister or *regens chori,* who was either a layman or a priest who, like Kimmerling, had been specially trained for the position. Under his command were placed musical monks, professional musicians and, at abbeys that maintained schools, a group of choirboys. Like courtly orchestral players, the abbey lay musicians could even be outfitted with uniforms.

Certain duties of the *regens chori* were not unlike those stipulated in Haydn's contract with Esterházy. Witness the following provision:

so offt Ihro G. H. Prälath zu Mölckh anwesent extra clausuram thuet speisen, soll er Regens Chori sich mit allen Khnaben bald anfangs der Tafl praesentiren und auf sein Begehren ein musicalische Distraction zu machen, in Beraitschafft sein.[29]

A wide variety of traditions such as this one accounted for much of the demand for Haydn's instrumental compositions. Secular music was performed as entertainment for visitors, for the many celebrations in honor of the abbot, for the monks during *Fasching* (carnival), and for everybody during the biennial periods of therapeutic bleeding. At Melk, for example, trios and quartets were prescribed for the afternoons and evenings on the first two days of bleeding, while symphonic works could be performed on the last day. Other traditional celebrations, such as the New Year, anniversaries and jubilees of ordinations and namedays, feasts for local patron saints, and recreation days for the monks and students, required instrumental music. A typical description of dinner music for a recreation day comes from the Melk prior's diary in 1762:

In prandio facta e[st] musica ex fistulis et tubis clangentib[us] plane absurda et offendens poti[us] aures, quam recreans. In coena autem Musica ex solis fidibus suavissima et artificiosa a quatuor Musicis producta. . . .[30]

---

[29] Prälaten-Archiv, Melk Abbey, "Instruction pro Regente Chori mellicensis, 1681," in "Instructiones für weltl. Beamte," scrin. 41, fasc. 1, leaves 107 ff.: "Everytime His Grace, the prelate, is present at Melk and dines outside the clasura, the *regens chori* shall present himself with all of the Sängerknaben at the beginning of the meal and be prepared to produce a musical distraction upon order."

[30] Ibid., "Priorats-Ephemeriden," July 12, 1762: "At lunch, music was produced by clangorous flutes and trumpets which sounded entirely absurd and offensive rather than

Less is known about the extent and functions of Haydn's instrumental music inside the Austrian abbey churches and in churches across the continent. The available evidence suggests that such music could range from the "rude and barbarous flourish of drums and trumpets" heard by Burney at the Elevation during Masses in Augsburg and Antwerp,[31] to Mozart's elegant "Epistle" sonatas, which probably functioned as substitutes for the Gradual in the Salzburg liturgy.

In Spain, where the instrumental version of the *Seven Last Words* was commissioned for a church service in Cadiz, the guitarist Fernando Sor recalled his days as a choirboy at the abbey of Montserrat around 1790. He describes a morning Mass in which the introduction and first movement of a Haydn symphony in D major was performed during the Offertory, the Andante during the Communion, and the finale at the Gospel.[32] Since none of the three-movement symphonies in D major begins with a (slow) introduction, the reference must be to a four-movement work with the minuet omitted. This practice might explain the occasional monastic source which survives without minuet, such as the Melk copy of Symphony No. 28 in A major. A comparable account comes again from Burney, who heard a festive High Mass at St. Stephen's Cathedral in Vienna where "several symphonies for instruments only, composed by M. Hofman . . . were . . . well executed, except that the hateful sour organ, poisoned all whenever it played."[33] The function of Haydn's instrumental music in the abbey churches is an area deserving further exploration.

Discussion

MARTIN CHUSID[34]   We have a bit of evidence in the form of Haydn's famous letter of 1768 concerning "Applausus," in which he calls for the performance of a fast movement and a slow movement of a symphonic work, but he says not to play the finale since he will supply an independent finale with chorus.

FREEMAN   We also have Dittersdorf's comments concerning his own "Applausus" for the Bishop of Grosswardein (around 1765). He speaks of "grand symphonies" which were played for the performance. We also know that symphonic movements were used in this way for opera performances.

---

pleasing to the ears. At dinner, however, a most delightful and artful music was presented on solo stringed instruments by four musicians."

[31] Burney, *State,* 2nd ed., I, 326 (1st ed., 322).

[32] Sor's description is translated in part in Newman, *Classic,* 58.   [33] Op. cit., I, 117–18.

[34] From the audience.

BROOK In closing this session, I might refer to the important recent research by my colleagues Professors Freeman, Mahling, and Zaslaw.[35] Further explorations of this kind are essential; the more we establish the available historical facts, the closer we will come to authentic performances. But the very diversity of eighteenth-century performance practices implies that for many questions there can be no single correct answer.

[35] Freeman, "Melk"; Mahling, *Orchester;* Zaslaw, "Orchestra." Cf. also the additional literature cited in note 7 above.

Workshop 1

Church Music

ALFRED MANN, *Chairman*
IRMGARD BECKER-GLAUCH
KARL GUSTAV FELLERER
KARL GEIRINGER
J. MERRILL KNAPP

WALTER PASS
ROBERT RICKS
MOGENS WÖLDIKE
CHARLES SHERMAN,
Secretary

Introductory Remarks

PASS At the International Congress held in Vienna in 1909 and coinciding with the Haydn Centennial, a remarkable statement was presented. Including among its signers Peter Wagner, the distinguished scholar of church music, and Vincent Goller, the editor of a "liturgical arrangement" of Haydn's *Heiligmesse,* it called for a return to seventeenth-century church-music practice "in view of the deplorable decadence of eighteenth-century sacred music." It represented the climax of a century-old argument for and against the value of Haydn's church music. This dispute at least established the existence of a specifically Austrian church-music tradition reaching back to the Renaissance, of which eighteenth-century liturgical practice there was a natural outgrowth. The sacred music of Haydn's time can be fully understood only in this context.

This tradition was founded in the imperial court music, especially the Hofkapelle serving the imperial household in Vienna, which set a standard for all other musical establishments. During the Baroque, the Mass service had become increasingly concentrated upon the action of the priests and ministrants. The congregation, remaining in silent prayer, appreciated the meaning of the ritual as a whole, rather than distinct sections. This unity was reflected in musical settings oriented towards what we might call a *Gesamtkunstwerk.* In the early nineteenth century a composer was still expected to write Masses in various categories, determined by the occasion (praise, supplication, mourning).[1] An example of such a type is the pastoral Mass, which can be readily recognized in Haydn's *Missa Sti. Nicolai.*

The increasing importance of individual artistic expression led to seeming conflict with this order. Yet despite their strong expressions of his artistic personality, Haydn's last six Masses belong to the first type described by Glöggl—the orchestral Mass written for a festive occasion

---

[1] See Glöggl, *Kirchenmusikordnung.*

203

and suggesting homage as well as divine praise. The last manifestation of Haydn's orchestral art, these works are still today the finest representatives of an Austrian tradition that extended throughout the entire Danube territory and from the sixteenth century well into our own.

Problems with Performing Forces

Remarks on the Early Masses

GEIRINGER I should like to submit three questions dealing primarily with the young Haydn.

1. Austrian church music in the early eighteenth century was usually scored for two violins, bass, and organ continuo—but no viola. This scoring is found in Haydn's first Mass, the *Missa brevis* in F major, and in the *Great Organ Mass* and the *Little Organ Mass;* and also in the settings of the *Salve Regina* in E major (Hob. XXIIIb:1) and G major (Hob. XXIIIb:5),[2] the *Ave Regina* in A major (Hob. XXIIIb:3), and the first *Te Deum* (Hob. XXIIIc:1). Other early compositions, however, include violas: the *St. Caecilia Mass,* the settings of the *Salve Regina* in E-flat major (Hob. XXIIIb:4) and G minor (Hob. XXIIIb:2), the Offertory *Ens aeternum* (Hob. XXIIIa:3), and the motet *Quis stella radius* (Hob. XXIIIa:4). In the *Missa Sti. Nicolai* Haydn combines the two approaches: an independent viola part is prescribed in the *Incarnatus* and *Benedictus,* but there is no sign of it elsewhere. In contrast to the independent viola parts of the string quartets, all of Haydn's vocal music up to the 1780s includes sections in which the viola merely doubles the bass at the octave (for example, in *Orlando Paladino*). There were relatively few violas in the eighteenth-century orchestra, their ratio to the violins being 1:4, 1:5, or even 1:6. In the Eisenstadt orchestra the viola players were always listed as violinists; their precise number remains unknown.[3] *Should Haydn's sacred works omitting the viola parts be performed without violas today, or should a viola part be added? In the* Missa Sti. Nicolai, *should the viola double the bass at the octave in the other movements, or should it be omitted?*

2. Following a venerable tradition, only male singers were employed at St. Stephen's while Haydn was there; the same was true at the Hofkapelle. Accordingly, Haydn's *Missa brevis* in F major must have been written for two boy soprano solos. But what about later works? The *Little Organ Mass,* probably written for the Order of the Brothers of Mercy in Eisen-

---

[2] The latter work may not be authentic. Cf. Becker-Glauch, "Kirchenmusik," 176. [Ed.]
[3] Cf. the remarks by Neal Zaslaw and Christoph-Hellmut Mahling in the preceding Round Table. [Ed.]

stadt, has been recorded by Mogens Wöldike and Ferdinand Grossmann using only male singers, which seems historically correct. But Grossmann has also used an all-male group in fine recordings of the *Missa Sti. Nicolai* and the *Theresienmesse,* which were composed for the Esterházy ensemble which, as far as I know, employed women as the sopranos and altos. The use of boys seems historically questionable. *Shall we be guided by aesthetic or historical principles in choosing between boys and women, or a combination of the two?*

3. Haydn's organ solo parts are usually gentle and delicate. To my knowledge, he indicated the registration only once ("flauto" in the *Incarnatus* of the *Creation Mass*). When the organ sounds against a solo voice, as in the *Little Organ Mass,* it can be clearly heard. But Haydn also employed an organ solo in the full ensemble of voices and instruments. In the *Benedictus* from the *Great Organ Mass* as recorded by Theobald Schrems, it cannot be heard. *Is a performance of this kind adequate, or should the organ be made audible by recording techniques or possibly by altering the tempo?*

Remarks on the Viola in Haydn's Church Music

FELLERER A central question of orchestration in the church music of the seventeenth and eighteenth centuries is the balance between strings and winds. The lowest vocal parts are regularly doubled by trombones or violas, which fill out the trio-sonata scoring (two violins and organ continuo). This *colla parte* doubling, which goes back to the sixteenth century, was gradually discontinued. In Haydn's performance instructions for *Applausus* (1768), the violas are said to emphasize the independence of the middle voice rather than double the bass. In the same source Haydn insists on the precise execution of phrasing and dynamics (asking copyists to complete the latter if they are not consistently marked in the score), and he states as his preference that his obbligato bass should be performed by one bassoon, one cello, and one double bass.[4]

Trio-sonata scoring of the strings, without violas, is the rule in Haydn's early church works, even when winds are added, as in the *Great Organ Mass.* The organ part is often obbligato, even in later works such as the *Creation Mass.* But here it is joined by a full string orchestra with divided violas. Different phases of the transition from Baroque trio-sonata texture to the Classical orchestra are marked by differing uses of the violas. In the *Mariazellermesse,* the viola is used both as a reinforcement of the bass and independently, especially in the *Benedictus* where the strings play *senza organo;* this parallels the *Missa Sti. Nicolai.* Even in the more or less Classical instrumentation of the *St. Caecilia Mass,* including oboes, bassoons, trumpets, and drums, the viola is at times *colla parte.*

[4] Haydn, *Briefe,* 58–60, §§ 4–6, 10 (CCLN, 9–11).

But the strengthened independent middle part and the development of the orchestra were fully realized during the first period of Haydn's Masses, up to 1782. In the last six Masses they were taken for granted.

Remarks on the Late Church Music

BECKER-GLAUCH   The question of balance between soloists and chorus in Haydn's time can be reduced to the question of the size of the choir. These remarks refer to the six late Masses, and they are based on the texts in JHW. The authentic performance parts for all six are preserved in the Esterházy castle in Eisenstadt. For the five Masses from 1796 to 1801 there are two copies each of the soprano and alto ripieno parts, one each for tenor and bass; for the *Harmoniemesse* of 1802, four each for soprano and alto, and three each for tenor and bass. The parts for the soloists also contain the ripieno sections—the soloists were probably placed near the choir, unlike modern practice. Thus we have a total of ten parts for the ripieno voices in the five Masses through 1801, and eighteen in the *Harmoniemesse*. (That is, the ensemble was enlarged between the time of the *Creation Mass* and the *Harmoniemesse;* in fact, one additional ripieno part for each vocal part was later supplied for the five earlier Masses.) Thus the contrast between solo and tutti was not as pronounced in Haydn's time as it is today. On the other hand the Esterházy singers were probably professionals, whereas modern choirs consist principally of laymen.

An interesting example of divergent readings for solo and tutti occurs in the second section of the *Benedictus* from the *Creation Mass* (beginning at m. 68). All editions before JHW, beginning with Breitkopf & Härtel in 1804, show *solo* for the four vocal entries, but the autograph and the original performance parts indicate *tutti*.

> The two versions were illustrated by recordings based on the traditional editions (*solo*) and JHW (*tutti*).

The sources for the winds generally offer more problems than those for the strings. A classic example for the study of additional wind instruments is, of course, the *Nelson Mass*. Here we can distinguish two versions: the earlier one, in which Haydn supplied an obbligato organ part to take the place of the woodwinds (which were unavailable at that time); and the later one, not by Haydn himself but supposedly approved by him, which substitutes winds for the organ. But in some cases, for example the flute part in the *Gloria* of the *Mass in Time of War* and the horn parts in the *Heiligmesse,* it is not clear whether added winds are authentic.

H. C. Robbins Landon included three trombone parts in his edition of Haydn's second *Te Deum* (Hob. XXIIIc:2; c. 1798–1800). To judge from three authentic sets of performance parts written by Elssler and other Esterházy copyists, however, these trombone parts—more or less doubling alto, tenor, and bass—are not authentic. They were added later; some of them are even marked "ad libitum." The addition of trombone parts seems to have been a common practice in Viennese churches.[5] For example, the performance material of the Vienna Hofkapelle contains trombone parts doubling the alto and tenor of the *Nelson Mass,* the *Theresienmesse,* and the *Creation Mass.* Doubling with trombones is also familiar from Mozart's church music. But it is not at all characteristic of Haydn.

Oboes were added to the score of Haydn's first *Te Deum* (Hob. XXIIIc:1; 1762 or 1763), originally scored for the so-called church trio (two violins and bass) with trumpets and timpani. Despite their unquestionably inauthentic status—they appear only in later sources—they are included in Landon's first edition of 1966. Two oboes were also added later to Haydn's *Cantilena pro adventu* in A major, *Ein' Magd, ein' Dienerin* (Hob. XXIIId:1), for soprano solo.

Haydn's *Quatuor responsoria de Venerabili Sacramento* (Hob. XXIIIc:4), a composition regarded as lost until 1964, contains in its only source two horn parts in addition to the two violins and bass. I included these horn parts in the first edition (1965) of the work, much to my regret, for I realized later that the sources of the smaller sacred works—this one among them—contain many wind parts that were added subsequently.[6] It may seem odd that horn parts should have been added to so small an ensemble. But the sources of Haydn's time prove it. The explanation may lie in the relatively mild dynamic strength of the horns in Haydn's day, compared to our own.

Problems in Interpretation

[Ricks outlined the typical range of problems which face modern interpreters of Haydn's church music, under the headings Tempo, Tempo Modification or Pacing, and Dynamics. As a basis for discussion, five recent recordings of the *Mass in Time of War* were chosen, conducted by Leonard Bernstein, Hans Gillesberger, George Guest, David Willcocks, and Mogens Wöldike.[7]]

[5] Biba, "Kirchenmusik," 70–71. On this *Te Deum,* see Becker-Glauch, "Te Deum."
[6] See Becker-Glauch, "Kirchenmusik," esp. 206.
[7] In the order named: Columbia M-32196; Turnabout 34138 (originally Haydn Society HSL 2027); Argo ZRG-634; Angel S-36417; Vanguard HM-28 (originally Vanguard/Everyman SRV-1535D).

Tempo

WÖLDIKE In about 1920, Carl Nielsen, then my teacher in theory, remarked to me
that "of all musical elements, tempo is the most important; when the
tempo is right, everything else will be good, too; but if the tempo is
wrong, nothing will be right." The tempo problem was to prove of
crucial importance in my work on Haydn's Masses (of which I have performed nine). I must say at the outset that, as regards tempo, my old
recordings are not always in agreement with my point of view today. It
stands to reason that the tempo of both fast and slow movements will
vary somewhat according to the acoustics of the halls and the number of
performers. Nevertheless it came as a shock to me, in comparing various
recordings, that, for example, the *Creation Mass* is celebrated in forty-one
minutes in Vienna, whereas in nearby Salzburg it takes fifty-five—one-
third again as long.

The slow movements pose the greatest problems. Largo—apparently
Haydn's slowest tempo indication—is found only twice in the Masses. In
the *Kyrie* introduction of the *Mass in Time of War,* it recalls the
typical slow introduction in the late symphonies, and (in the interest
of the fine ornaments in the oboe parts) it calls for a certain elated calm.
The eighth notes in the strings should be considered as representing the
beat.

Adagio appears twenty-nine times, while Andante, again, appears
only twice. Thus, Adagio is Haydn's principal indication for slow movements, and a closer examination of the twenty-nine Adagios might
throw some light on the tempo problem. There are six in common time,
four in *alla breve,* and nineteen in triple meter, among which we might
include one in 6/8. The slowest movements are those written predominantly in quarter notes, usually short settings of the *Sanctus.* These
require a very poised, deliberate pace, so that the three choral "Sanctus"
invocations may unfold fully, and the orchestral themes and ornaments
may attain their appropriate *espressivo* character. Essentially, the beat
should be on the quarter note, although the tempo might at times be so
slow that it would be useful to indicate every eighth beat. In the *alla breve*
movements, the beat is on the half note; the tempo is usually twice as
fast. There are exceptions, however; the *Qui tollis* of the *Mass in Time of
War* cannot represent a normal *alla breve.* I imagine Haydn marked it so
in order to caution against too slow a tempo. Yet one can easily feel the
eighth note as the beat.

As I see it, the tempos in the triple-meter Adagios are usually a little
faster than those in movements with four beats to the bar. Good examples are the two triple-meter Adagios of the *Little Organ Mass,* in
which neither the vocal parts nor the string parts with their steady
eighth-note motion can bear a slow tempo. The nature of these pieces is

more suited to a flowing Andante, as is that of the *Et incarnatus est* in the *Mass in Time of War*.

The Italian term "adagio" means "comfortable," "at ease." It thus describes character rather than tempo. It seems that a post-Beethovenian tradition of invariably interpreting "adagio" as "very slow" is haunting us. A comparison of the *Agnus Dei* from the Gillesberger recording (♪ = 60) and the one by Willcocks (♩ = 54–55) shows that the eighth-note beat of the former makes the music lose its natural flow. The trumpets and timpani lose their militant spirit, and the vocal parts their sense of declamation. In the flowing tempo of the English performance all this is restored. I might add that fast tempos pose the same problem in reverse. Even a slight exaggeration may be dangerous. Past a certain limit, the piece may sound elegant and dashing, but at the same time hectic and mechanical.

Luther's famous words about Josquin, "He is the master of the notes; they must do as he wills; the other composers must do as the notes will," may be applied to our problem. If the music is hurried, the performers can do no more than "hang on." Given time, the running sixteenth-note passages in the violin parts, which are the life and color of this music, will retain flexibility and rhythmic freedom, and the singers' diction can render the meaning of the significant words in their wondrous musical setting.

Tempo Modification or Pacing

[Ricks introduced five examples each in discussing pacing and dynamics. Eighteenth-century sources quoted in the following commentaries are C. P. E. Bach, *Versuch;* L. Mozart, *Violinschule;* Quantz, *Verusch;* and Türk, *Klavierschule.*[8]]

RICKS 1. *Ritard in approaching a recapitulation* (*Mass in Time of War, Qui tollis* [*Gloria,* mm. 157–58]). The illustrations chosen from the recordings ranged from little ritard (Gillesberger) to considerable (Bernstein). Türk (chapter on performance, § 63) gives a list of typical instances where either an accelerando or ritard is recommended. In § 69 he mentions that a ritard is called for in approaching a principal theme.

2. *Ritard as an "affective" rendering of a special portion of the verbal text.* Willcocks and Bernstein vary considerably in the passage on "mortuorum" (*Credo,* mm. 179–84). While C. P. E. Bach's remarks on the "affections" are of a general nature, Türk is specific on this point. In § 68 of the same chapter he says: "A tenderly touching passage between two lively, fiery ideas can be performed somewhat haltingly, provided one takes the tempo in this case not little by little, but immediately slightly slower."

[8] The passages from Türk quoted here were drawn from a translation by Robert Dumm, whose permission to reproduce it is gratefully acknowledged.

3. *Ritard before a fermata.* At the close of the *Crucifixus* (*Credo*, mm. 92–93) Gillesberger keeps in tempo almost to the very end; Bernstein makes a noticeable ritard. Both C. P. E. Bach and Türk advise a slight broadening. Türk (§ 67) extends this also to diminuendo and sforzando passages.

4. *Ritard at cadences not marked by a fermata.* All five conductors agree on this point in the final cadence of the work, Willcocks being the most pronounced in his rendering. C. P. E. Bach confirms this practice. Türk (§ 12) says that in such cases the musicians should follow the practice of a speaker reading poetry.

5. *Release of a fermata.* The recordings differ on this point at the fermata on the word "pacem," twelve bars before the end of the Mass. C. P. E. Bach's remark that the fermata must be held "as long as required generally by the nature of the composition" suggests that considerable prolonging of a fermata like this one is an important element of performance. Leopold Mozart states that "the tone of the instrument must be allowed to diminish and die away entirely before beginning to play again" (Ch. I, Section ii, § 191).

Dynamics

RICKS 1. *Echo effects.* Both Guest and Willcocks provide an "echo" interpretation of the word "passus" near the end of the *Crucifixus* (*Credo*, mm. 76–77). Türk gives the following comment in § 31:

> It is, unfortunately, impossible to define each single place which must be played a little louder or softer than the foregoing and following. If an idea is repeated, one usually plays it softly the second time, that is, if it had been played loudly before. In the opposite case, one plays a repeated section louder when the composer has enlivened it by variation.

The passage in question, however, is not "enlivened by variation."

2. *Terraced dynamics versus crescendo.* At the conclusion of the *Kyrie* introduction, m. 8, Gillesberger gives a literal reading, while Willcocks makes a gradual crescendo to the *forte* in m. 9. Quantz and C. P. E. Bach link the use of crescendo and diminuendo to the use of dissonances. Türk, § 29, adds to this sudden modulations—which seems to apply to this case and supports the crescendo interpretation.

3. *Crescendo leading to a forte marked in the middle of a syllable.* In the *Et incarnatus est* (Credo, m. 63), the singers are asked to produce a *subito forte* in the middle of a single syllable. Each of our five conductors finds a different solution! Perhaps Haydn had a particular effect in mind of which we are not aware.

4. *Dynamic levels inferred from the text or from the needs of vocal technique.* In the *Crucifixus*, Willcocks allows a decrescendo from the *forte* in m. 78 to

the *piano* in m. 82. Could Haydn have "assumed" that the choir would lose volume in descending, or that the text and the musical "picture" would automatically dictate a decrescendo?

5. *Dynamic level of soloists.* In the Agnus Dei, mm. 57–68, Guest is very loud, Bernstein quite soft. Haydn wrote *ff* in the orchestra, but nothing for the soloists.

With one final example, the *Benedictus,* we return to the question of tempo. All the conductors take this rather slowly except Willcocks, who is much faster. These differences are interesting when considered from the points of view expressed in Türk's §§ 4, 43, 45, 46, 47, which combine considerations of 1) general character of the composition, 2) tempo marking, 3) meter, and 4) note values involved. Türk's remarks suggest that the staccatos in the violas and basses beginning at m. 24 may have more than casual significance. They imply a faster, lighter interpretation than traditionally adopted.

Discussion

BECKER-GLAUCH   A comparison of recordings shows a marked discrepancy in the *Qui tollis* of the *Creation Mass.* This section begins (mm. 152–60) with a quote from *The Creation* ("Der tauende Morgen, o wie ermuntert er"). In spite of its reference to the fascimile edition of the autograph, one recording (Musica sacra; L. Schwann, Düsseldorf; conducted by Ernst Hinreiner) includes a most curious ritard before the solo bass entrance, which is nowhere justified in the sources.

KNAPP   Brand remarks that the tempo of the *Sanctus* from the *Mass in Time of War* should be Adagio *alla breve,*[9] whereas H. C. Robbins Landon says in an edition of the work, "By all means it should be Adagio 4/4." This point indicates the difficulty of attempting hard and fast decisions on what are really questions of interpretation. A marked ritard may be an exaggeration; the conductor must remain responsible for understanding and interpreting the proper context. The composer's changes in dynamics, pauses, or long-held notes may in themselves suggest a slowing down.

Similarly, the use of echo effects is a question of subtle interpretation. The echo effect was more characteristic of the early eighteenth century than of Haydn's late years. Caution is also advised on crescendos. Haydn is explicit in indicating the contrast and juxtaposition of *forte* and *piano;* the drama and surprise conveyed by his dynamics should remain sufficiently marked in interpretation. Logically, his distinct orchestral dynamics should also be observed by the singers. It is the conductor's re-

[9] Brand, *Messen,* 250–51.

sponsibility to have these dynamics entered into the vocal parts and to carry them out in performance.

CHARLES WARNER[10]   In his book on conducting, Scherchen states that the composer frequently "builds in" crescendos. This seems to apply to one of the examples under discussion, in which the orchestral volume grows through addition of winds to the strings.

RICKS With no crescendo marked in the strings, is the intended effect one of terraced dynamics or crescendo?

MANN Is it not rather an unavoidable effect of crescendo that emerges?

In closing our session, may I quote from one of Professor Larsen's essays on performance practice:

A short time ago I had a letter from an elderly gentleman, keenly interested in Haydn's music and its revival. He sent me a quotation from an old book, containing reminiscences and observations of a once rather well-known German musician. The father of this musician had been in contact with Haydn, and as my correspondent's father had in his turn known the said musician well, he felt that he himself was in possession of a sense of tradition from Haydn's own world.[11]

With delightful objectivity, Larsen goes on to discuss the shortcomings of such "source study" in performance practice. While we lack his correspondent's direct lineage, this discussion may have brought us closer to a "sense of tradition from Haydn's own world."

[10] From the audience.   [11] Larsen, "Interpretation," 38.

Workshop 2

Keyboard Sonatas[1]

WILLIAM S. NEWMAN, *Chairman*	ROBERT LEVIN
EVA BADURA-SKODA	CHARLES ROSEN
MALCOLM BILSON	VERA SCHWARZ
CHRISTA LANDON	HORST WALTER

Instruments

Haydn's Keyboard Instruments

WALTER The problem of authenticity arises in connection with Haydn's keyboard instruments as well as with his compositions.[2] Which instruments have been falsely attributed to Haydn, and which did he actually own? (We concern ourselves here with fortepianos,[3] harpsichords, and clavichords, not with the organ.) A harpsichord by Shudi and Broadwood (1775) and a square piano by Johann Schanz (c. 1790–1800), both in the Vienna Kunsthistorisches Museum, and a fortepiano by Johann Jakob Könnicke (1796) in the Vienna Haydn-Museum have traditionally been regarded as Haydn's. But their supposed connection with him cannot withstand critical scrutiny. There are only four instruments whose authenticity is certain: a clavichord by Johann Bohak; and three fortepianos, one by Wenzel Schanz, one by Erard, and one by Longman & Broderip. Of these, only the clavichord is extant, in the Royal College of Music in London. Built in Vienna in 1794, it has a compass of five octaves, is *bundfrei* (unfretted), and has black naturals and white sharps. The case is plain, and the stand is copied from a clavichord of 1767. It is not playable at this writing but is to be restored. Haydn owned it during his last years at Eisenstadt. In 1803 he gave it to the father of Demetrius Lichtenthal for his son, telling him that he had composed most of *The Creation* on it, a well-documented story. Like Mozart, then, Haydn continued to compose on the clavichord even toward the end of his life. Though most popular in North Germany, this instrument was also widely used in Austria for composing and instruction.

[1] The text of this report was prepared by James Webster.

[2] For a full discussion, see Walter, "Klaviere," and Walter, "Tasteninstrument."

[3] In this report the term "fortepiano" is used to denote eighteenth-century pianos, in distinction to more recent and modern pianos. It is perhaps also worth noting that the term "Klavier" ("Clavier") was the generic term for "keyboard instrument," and it did not necessarily denote any particular instrument, while "Cembalo" denoted the harpsichord. [Ed.]

In October 1788, Haydn, then at Eszterháza, requested Artaria to advance payment for a fortepiano to use in composing the piano trios Hob. XV:11–13.[4] The Viennese piano builder most highly regarded by Haydn was Wenzel Schanz. Although this is Haydn's first reference to the fortepiano, he probably owned or at least used a hammer–action piano earlier. The word "fortepiano" occasionally appears on his manuscripts from 1784 on, in place of the earlier "cembalo" or "clavicembalo." In a letter to Marianne von Genzinger, to whom Haydn dedicated his *Sonata per il Fortepiano* (Hob. XVI:49 [ChL.59] in E-flat major), he writes:

> It's a pity that your Grace doesn't own a Schantz [*sic*] fortepiano, on which everything is better expressed. I thought that your Grace might turn over your still tolerable harpsichord [*Flügel*] to Fräulein Peperl and buy a new fortepiano for yourself. . . . I know I ought to have composed this sonata in accordance with the capabilities of your clavier, but I found this impossible because I was no longer accustomed to it.

And in a further letter:

> I should like your Grace to try one made by Herr Schanz; his fortepianos are particularly light in touch and mechanism very agreeable. A good fortepiano is absolutely necessary for your Grace, and my sonata will gain double its effect by it.[5]

Unfortunately, we have no date for Haydn's piano and no knowledge of its location, since he sold it for 200 ducats a few weeks before his death. Its compass was probably five octaves (F_1 to f^3), the standard range of Viennese pianos at the time. It was probably equipped with damper raising and with *Pianozug* (a felt strip laid across the strings to achieve a softer sound), both operated by knee levers.

Haydn preferred Schanz pianos to those of Anton Walter, whose instruments were particular favorites of Mozart's. Some years later, after Johann Schanz took over his brother Wenzel's workshop, we read: "The tone of Schanz pianos was not as strong as those of the Walter productions, but as clear and mostly more gentle. In addition, they are easier to play because the touch is not so deep."[6] In the same publication one reads that Schanz pianos were a cheaper copy of Stein-Streicher instruments.

Haydn became acquainted with English grand fortepianos in 1791. In London he played a Broadwood instrument, with its heavier action, deeper touch, and fuller tone than the Viennese pianos. In his English sonata Hob. XVI:50 (Ch.L.60) in C major, Haydn exploited the wider range and unusual pedaling of those instruments. He also expressed interest in a Stodart design for an upright grand piano.

Haydn's *Nachlass* (HNV) lists two pianofortes: an Erard and a Long-

---

[4] Haydn, *Briefe,* 195 (CCLN, 79).
[5] Cf. Haydn, CCLN, 106, 107, respectively (June 27 and July 4, 1790) (the translations in the texts very slightly altered) (*Briefe,* 242, 244).
[6] *Jahrbuch,* 1796, 89.

man & Broderip. These instruments, both lost, had the powerful English-type action and tone-coloring pedals; their range was five-and-a-half octaves, which Haydn, however, did not exploit in his compositions. Friends who visited Haydn in Vienna after 1797 mentioned these pianos only incidentally. Griesinger reports that, around 1803, "[Haydn] had to get for his composing a clavier that was very easy to play because the touch of an old pianoforte which he had used for many years already strained his nerves too much."[7] This "old" piano, "the priceless treasure," as Dies called it,[8] was without doubt the Wenzel Schanz of 1788. The Longman & Broderip grand "at which Haydn sat down from time to time to improvise"[9] is known only from the HNV and a report by Vincent Novello in 1829, who found it in the possession of Abbé Stadler. The French piano was presented to Haydn in 1801 as a gift by the Frères Erard in Paris. Beethoven's often-described Erard of 1803 and his description of the shifting pedal for an *una corda* effect on Haydn's piano give us an idea of Haydn's instrument.[10]

Haydn's compositions for "cembalo" fall in the period of transition from harpsichord to pianoforte, but the majority of them were undoubtedly for harpsichord. The few documents on the instruments at Eszterháza, all concerning repairs and maintenance, reveal that in the 1770s only harpsichords were available. The compositions themselves provide some information. In general, the keyboard range does not indicate a particular instrument, but the conservative range (less than F_1 to f^3) in Haydn's keyboard music before 1767 implies that he used or owned an Italian harpsichord during this period. Three compositions from around 1765, the "Sauschneider-Capriccio" Hob. XVII:1, the Variations Hob. XVII:2, and Sonata Hob. XVI:47 (ChL.19) in E minor, must have used a harpsichord with a "short octave."

Haydn's dynamic indications also help to determine which instrument was used. The autograph fragment of the Sonata Hob. XVI:20 (ChL.33) in C minor of 1771 shows surprisingly subtle dynamic gradations, though the composition is an exception among the works of that period. Not until the 1780s do Haydn's piano works regularly contain graduated dynamic marks. Did Haydn in 1771 really write for the piano and not for the clavichord? Harpsichord and fortepiano were interchangeable into the 1770s, and coexisted even up to 1790, since piano playing remained a private affair. After 1790, the harpsichord was replaced in preeminence by the fortepiano. Between 1788 and 1790 Haydn committed himself to composing in a style suited to the fortepiano. He had clearly become

[7] Gotwals, *Haydn,* 42 (Griesinger, 76; modern ed., 42). This instrument must have been a table fortepiano or a clavichord; cf. Walter, "Klaviere," 281.
[8] Gotwals, *Haydn,* 134 (Dies, 97; modern ed., 99).
[9] Gotwals, *Haydn,* 47 (Griesinger, 87; modern ed., 48).
[10] See Walter, "Klaviere," 282–83.

interested in the development of the piano and its advantages much earlier, even assuming them in some of his keyboard works, but until that time he had not yet explicitly differentiated the two instruments. The development of an idiomatic piano style took place gradually, and independent of his actual choice of instrument.[11]

Discussion

BADURA-SKODA   Thus a question as to the keyboard instrument arises mainly in connection with Haydn's sonatas of the 1770s and early 1780s. In Vienna, a "fortepiano" was used in the Burgtheater as early as 1763 (on which I will report in an article soon scheduled for publication). Haydn may thus have become acquainted with a fortepiano as early as the 1760s, and certainly before the end of 1771. The C-minor Sonata, composed in 1771, has a remarkable symphonic scope; the autograph crescendo markings imply that it was intended for the fortepiano rather than the clavichord. But I agree that this sonata is rather exceptional; afterwards Haydn may well have written sonatas intended for performance on the harpsichord. (During the 1770s Prince Esterházy seems to have preferred harpsichords.)

The absence of references to the fortepiano in the few surviving documents does not necessarily prove that there was none at Eszterháza in the 1770s or 1780s. Although Haydn may not have had a fortepiano at his disposal during the 1770s, with regard to the early 1780s I believe the contrary. His letter to Artaria which Dr. Walter cited speaks of "a new fortepiano"; this could mean that he had already owned a fortepiano before 1788, which had to be replaced by a newer one. (The delicate action of Viennese fortepianos of the 1770s, surprisingly simple in comparison to those of the 1780s, did not last long, and the instruments were not expensive.)

SCHWARZ The so-called Auenbrugger sonatas, Hob. XVI:35–39 and 20 (ChL. 48–52, 33), were published by Artaria in 1780 as *Sei sonate per il Clavicembalo, o Forte Piano*. Perhaps the instrument is still uncertain for some earlier sonatas. The crispness of sound and the distribution of lines between two manuals in the Raigern Sonata No. 2 (ChL.18) seem to imply the harpsichord.

BILSON But the same kind of figuration is found in such sonatas as the C minor Sonata, which is very probably not a harpsichord piece.

[11]Further on these questions see Workshop 6; the Round Tables on *Present-Day Haydn Performance* and on *Turning Points;* and the Free Papers by Edwin M. Ripin and Leslie Tung. [Ed.]

ROSEN It is also found in the clavichord music of C. P. E. Bach. Some of his pieces are as symphonic in style as the Haydn C-minor Sonata, but nevertheless are for clavichord. But as Professor Helm has pointed out, Bach probably preferred the piano to the clavichord beginning in the 1750s and 1760s. In any case his figuration is more suited to the clavichord or fortepiano than to the harpsichord. The finale of the Haydn C-minor Sonata begins like a minuet, but it soon becomes quite brilliant and free. To play it on a modern piano can destroy the minuet quality.

BADURA-SKODA Nevertheless, the presence of dynamic markings and the symphonic scope call for the fortepiano.

LESLIE TUNG[12] In view of the liberal performance practices of the time and the acceptability of interchanging instruments in the decade before 1775, one must beware of categorically assigning certain types of passage-work to a particular instrument. Some passages may just be part of a general keyboard style of the time. Also, it is difficult to imagine the sound of a fortepiano by extrapolating "down" from the modern piano. With the lighter and clearer tone of the fortepiano the minuet effect of the last movement of the C minor Sonata might easily be achieved.

SCHWARZ Some people have mentioned the possibility of a harpsichord with Venetian swell shutters, which Haydn is known to have owned. But in the C minor Sonata this seems improbable for technical reasons.

BILSON But there was a keyboard style of writing "in the air." During the transitional decades in the change from harpsichord and clavichord to fortepiano, could one not have still been writing for performance on the harpsichord, but already "hearing" crescendos, diminuendos, and accents?

ROSEN In the mid-eighteenth century one did not necessarily make a distinction between the kind of music written for fortepiano and the kind written for harpsichord. For example, J. S. Bach wrote the six-voice ricercar from the *Musical Offering* in association with the early fortepiano, the instrument preferred in Frederick's court, and yet nothing in the style of the music tells us it was specifically meant for this instrument. We also know that Mozart's Concerto in E-flat major K. 271 was performed on the harpsichord, and yet it contains dynamic indications.

LEVIN Does it make sense to suppose that, in an age of *Gebrauchsmusik,* a composer would have written for any other instruments than the ones at hand?

BADURA-SKODA Many of Haydn's earlier sonatas may doubtless be played on either keyboard instrument.

[12] From the audience.

Sonata in G major, Hob. XVI:40 (ChL. 54), First Movement: Comparative Performances and Discussion

LANDON This work was probably written in 1783, and it was published in 1784. The first movement is headed "Allegretto e innocente," and it has many dynamic markings. There are significant differences in articulation and dynamics between the ChL. and JHW editions. [See also Example 1.)

> PERFORMANCES
> Bilson: fortepiano; takes repeats; embellishments
> Schwarz: fortepiano; no repeats or embellishments
> Levin: modern grand; takes repeats; embellishments

Tempo

LANDON Mr. Rosen told me that this is a joke piece. I don't agree: it is full of *esprit,* but I don't think it's a witty piece, and certainly not a "joke." Mr. Bilson's tempo (which I thought too fast) emphasized its witty aspects; Vera Schwarz and Mr. Levin played it more *empfindsam,* which is more its proper character.

BILSON We seem to differ somewhat on what we think "Allegretto e innocente" means. I don't think *empfindsam* and "innocente" go together.

ROSEN None of the performances sounded innocent to me! In the twentieth century we have all eaten the apple.

LANDON Why can't a piece be played "innocently" and still be expansive? I don't believe these moods necessarily contradict each other.

SCHWARZ The G-minor part reminded me of Pamina's aria in *Die Zauberflöte.* This aria is always sung very slowly. But Mozart wrote, "Das ist das gepresste Herz—man muss diese Pause sehr lang verlängern." My other consideration was to keep to two accents in a measure. So I couldn't play it any more slowly.

BILSON But Pamina's aria is Andante. The Schwarz and Levin performances seemed slow to me, because they were in a work marked Allegretto.

SCHWARZ But the aria has the same sighing figure and the same expression.

BADURA-SKODA   A word in front of the piece is not as important as the character of the music. Mozart calls the Rondo in F major K. 494 Andante, but when the same piece becomes the finale of the Sonata K. 533, it is Allegretto.

ROSEN It is an Andante because it is a piece by itself; to make it the finale of a sonata changes the context entirely. Mozart adds an enormous cadenza at the end. I would play K. 494 more slowly and expressively than the finale of K. 533.

LEVIN I had difficulty reconciling the indication "Allegretto" with the thirty-second notes; they kept sounding clipped and uncomfortable, so I ultimately decided on a slower tempo.

BILSON I think that difficulty on a modern piano illustrates the advantages of the fortepiano! This movement is a bit slippery—why else would we get such different interpretations? I wouldn't want to put all my Allegrettos on one side and all my Andantes on the other, and say that none can cross the line.

LANDON Only one other sonata movement is marked "innocente," I believe: the first movement in the Sonata in E minor, Hob. XVI:34 (ChL.53). But it is marked Presto.

BILSON I admit, although the slow movement in the Piano Trio in E-flat major, Hob. XV:29, is marked "Andantino et innocentemente," it is very *empfindsam*. All these movements are in 6/8 meter.[13]

Articulation and Dynamics

BILSON I believe that one must take the articulation markings very seriously, but the differences between the ChL. and JHW editions create problems. (See Example 1.) For example, in m. 3 ChL. extends the first slur to the third note, as in m. 1, but JHW cuts it off at the second note, like the second slur in the same bar. This difference affects not only the motivic meaning of the third note in m. 3 and the change from legato (m.1) to differentiated three-note groups (mm. 3–4), but also the interpretation of the characteristic place in m. 4, where a two-note slur leads to a staccato stroke. In any case, on the fortepiano I hardly ever use the pedal, because I would hate to pedal through these slurs, and the articulation is so much clearer than on a modern piano.

Example 1. Sonata in G major, Hob. XVI:40 (ChL.54), i, 1–5

LANDON The extant sources for this sonata are very poor; that is why the editions are so different—each editor must make many difficult choices. Another problem is the dynamics: the use of *f* and *fz* is utterly inconsistent.

[13] Haydn also wrote "Andante ed Innocentemente" over the first movement of the String Quartet in D minor Op. 42. (But originally the first word read "Allegretto"!) The movement is in 2/4. [Ed.]

ROSEN Beethoven was completely inconsistent about the staccato dot [*Punkt*] and the stroke [*Strich* or *Keil*]. We have a problem of this kind in Example 1 too.

LANDON Early Haydn used strokes primarily. Later, he used both, and it is not always easy to distinguish them in his autographs.

SCHWARZ Another problem is crescendos. If there is an offbeat *sforzato,* as we see in m. 4 of Example 1, one must make a crescendo to it even if none is marked.

Embellishment

LANDON I would like to ask Mr. Bilson and Mr. Levin why they decorated the repeats. I'm a great believer in repeats and in embellishment, but this movement is a theme with variations, and I would not decorate.

BILSON Mr. Rosen states, "The music of Haydn after 1775 cannot be ornamented."[14] Here, it seems the most natural thing in the world.

SCHWARZ I did not decorate because Haydn decorates himself all the time. To change little notes into more little notes would be wrong.

NEWMAN But there is a precedent in C. P. E. Bach's "veränderte Reprisen" sonatas only a few years earlier.

LANDON Yes, but this is a variation movement—the theme is being altered all the time as it is.

ROSEN Do you spoil the variations if you embellish the repeats in the theme itself?

LANDON I think so.

LEVIN I have a problem with any recurrent theme to a set of variations. There is a general tendency in the eighteenth century to vary something when it returns—the veiled contradiction of asymmetrical symmetry. The return in this piece (m. 92) is built in, whether you decorate it or not. To debate the details of a particular decoration is to miss the point.

ROSEN But there is a great deal of eighteenth-century music in which the repeats are not varied at all—for example, symphonic music. At this time, Haydn is beginning to blend symphonic style into his solo music, as in the last movement of this sonata. There is such a tremendously dramatic effect at mm. 90–92 of the first movement that neither decoration nor an *Eingang* on the fermata, nor for that matter the repetition of the last section, can be justified.

BILSON I try not to decorate repeats. I try to achieve a natural performance, so that when I'm decorating I feel as if I were making it up. But the question

---

[14] Rosen, *Style,* 101.

of taking a repeat seems much more important. This theme is simple, and yet Haydn includes a turn in the very first measure.

ROSEN If you decorate the theme at the return in m. 92 you ought to choose a decoration that does not recall the first variation.

BILSON This is particularly important for the performer nowadays who makes recordings, for these things will haunt him.

LEVIN To improvise is not only to do nice things. It's to take risks.

LANDON In sonatas where the exposition of the first movement is repeated, would you decorate?

BILSON In Sonata Hob. XVI:49 (ChL.59) in E-flat major, I would not; it's too "characteristic." But it's not always easy to decorate even in a variation movement, such as the one in the Piano Trio in E-flat minor, Hob. XV:31.

[MAN IN AUDIENCE] To take every repeat in a piece such as the *Goldberg Variations* would be impossible for us in live performance today. Is it thinkable that Haydn didn't necessarily want every repeat?

NEWMAN You have to find out what you can about a composer's intentions and the practices of his time. Beyond that, it may be a matter of taste. I am convinced that the late Beethoven wanted all his repetitions to be observed.

A. PETER BROWN[15] After 1767, when Haydn repeats a phrase, he keeps a careful hierarchical relationship: although the middle may be varied, the beginnings and the endings—the structural places—are frequently preserved in the purest form possible. For example, in the Sonata in C major, Hob. XVI:48 (ChL.58), the purest form of the melodic material does not occur until the middle of the piece (mm. 73–76). Therefore, to decorate variations may destroy certain structural aspects of the piece.

KONRAD WOLFF[16] I would like to ask the three performers if they think it would be wrong to avoid all embellishments, in the manner of Artur Schnabel.

BILSON Schnabel doubtless felt that his prime duty was to be faithful to what he conceived as the composer's intentions. But he did things that nobody would do today. He played potpourris, paraphrases, and improvisations—in concerts. His generation hardly knew what a good edition was.

ROSEN No, there were always two kinds of musicians: those who did anything they liked, and those who paid attention to details. And the *Urtext* is not a twentieth-century invention.

BILSON It is not "wrong" to play without alterations. It is important that people play what is inspired and beautiful, not just what is correct or not correct.

[15] From the audience.   [16] From the audience.

Workshop 3

String Quartets[1]

LUDWIG FINSCHER, *Chairman*
REGINALD BARRETT-AYRES
DAVID D. BOYDEN
EDUARD MELKUS
SONYA MONOSOFF

ISIDOR SASLAV
LÁSZLÓ SOMFAI
JAMES WEBSTER
HUBERT UNVERRICHT,
Secretary

Problems of Instruments

The Evolution of the Bow During Haydn's Lifetime

BOYDEN It goes without saying that the character and quality of the instruments and bows are fundamental considerations in the performance of Haydn's string quartets.[2] During the period of nearly fifty years in which Haydn wrote his quartets, from the late 1750s to 1803, significant changes took place in the construction of the bow, which greatly affected the sound, the idiom of writing, and—often forgotten—the ease or difficulty for the player. (These remarks are limited to the violin bow, but they apply generally to the viola and the cello bows as well.)

In one typical bow from the first part of the eighteenth century—for sonatas and concertos about the time of Corelli—the snakewood bow stick is convex, curving *away* from the hair. The hair is held at fixed tension, and cannot be loosened or tightened. This bow is perhaps an inch shorter overall than the modern bow, and has nearly three inches less of playing hair. It is also lighter and has a different balance point and playing properties. A later bow possibly by Stradivari has a bow stick made of pernambuco wood which is virtually straight. The upper two-thirds of its length is fluted, combining lightness with strength. The hair is adjustable by means of a screw nut. This bow is also about an inch shorter than the modern bow, but its playing hair-length is only about two inches less. A remarkably balanced bow, its balance point is closer to the frog.

The modern bow, often called the "Tourte" or "Viotti" bow, was perfected by François Tourte around 1785. But there were transitional forms between the Baroque bows just described and the modern bow. One example, stamped FORSTER on the ivory frog and the bow stick, dates from about 1775. The bow stick is concave, curving *in* toward the

---

[1] The text of this report was prepared by James Webster.
[2] For a fuller, illustrated discussion of this topic, see Boyden, "Geigenbogen."

hair, which makes a difference in the bow action. The concave stick also requires a raised bow head to prevent the hair from hitting the bow stick in the middle. The hair is adjustable by means of a frog and screw nut.

There is no good name for these "transitional" bows, one reason being the numerous forms they take. If there is any single constant feature, it is the concavity of the bow stick. However, the heads and frogs vary greatly. The so-called Cramer bow, depicted and so styled by Woldemar about 1800,[3] was also transitional, with a slightly concave stick. Woldemar, a French violinist, says that this bow was "adopted in Cramer's time by the majority of Artists and Amateurs." This would seem to mean from about 1770 to 1795.

The modern bow has a bow stick more deeply concave than the transitional bow, a hatchet head, and an adjustable frog. The standard bow is generally longer, heavier, and stronger than earlier ones. It also has a wider ribbon of hair, and the hair is held in place by a ferrule and slide.

The modern bow was first available to play Haydn's quartets about the time that Op. 42 appeared. But it is unlikely that it was adopted immediately and exclusively. More likely, the Tourte bow and the best of the transitional types were both used well into the early years of the nineteenth century, as the familiar Begas portrait of Paganini (c. 1830) suggests. It is no wonder that the Cramer bow was highly satisfactory, since the best of the transitional bows were made by master bow makers.

It is probable that in the early 1770s Cramer, Forster, and Tourte *père* designed bows with an eye to the performance of such pieces as Haydn's quartets and Mozart's violin concertos. Or *vice versa:* that in the early 1770s Haydn may have been busy exploiting the new Cramer bow. Haydn's motivation for his sudden intense cultivation of the quartet between about 1770 and 1772 is unknown.[4] Perhaps the answer lies in the possibilities of the Cramer bow. Perhaps something similar happened in the early 1780s; perhaps Op. 33 was written in a "new and special manner" partly to explore the possibilities of the new Tourte (i.e., modern) bow. In any case, Haydn and Forster had extensive relations; Forster published 129 works of Haydn between 1781 and 1787.

In eighteenth-century bows, when the bow hair is brought in contact with the string, it yields more under the pressure of the player's hand than is the case with the modern bow hair. The yielding hair of these early bows requires a small "take-up" or "give" before the tone emerges—what Leopold Mozart called a "small softness." By contrast, the concave stick of the modern bow makes the hair tighter and less yielding, producing the tone practically at once. The modern bow can produce a good sforzando easily, even a true biting martelé, and so can the transitional bow (to a lesser extent). Both *sf* and martelé are much

[3] Woldemar, *Méthode*   [4] Webster, "Chronology," 30.

more difficult to produce with an old bow. Hence it is not surprising that *sf* is uncommon in music written before 1750.

In the old bow, the "small softness" and the relatively light head combine to produce a basic non-legato stroke which, in turn, is the basis of a brilliantly clear articulation in rapid passage-work and string crossing, especially in the upper third of the bow. The action of the transitional bow is partway between the old bow and the modern bow. While it lacks the strength and tension of the modern bow, it seems to produce a *piano* or *pianissimo* of good or even luminous quality more easily than the modern bow. It also produces double stops without scratching, and nuances of tone or delicate changes of bow strokes demanded by mixed bowings more easily.

These points were demonstrated by Sonya Monosoff.

The Development of the Violin during Haydn's Lifetime

MELKUS The Baroque violin, from the early seventeenth to the early eighteenth century, had a straight neck and a short fingerboard set at an angle, which automatically produced a much smaller sound than the modern violin. At the beginning of the eighteenth century, and still more in the 1730s, the neck began to be set farther back in, reducing the angle of the fingerboard; the neck was also lengthened somewhat, and the bass bar (inside the instrument) was widened and lengthened. The resulting instrument changed little until 1830 or 1840. The modern violin then set the neck of the violin much farther back, and made the modern fingerboard much longer, parallel to the body of the instrument.

The reasons for these changes in the early eighteenth century were the increasing demands of expression, the economics of the time, and the rise in pitch, which demanded fortification of the neck (previously the neck had just lain against the body). Of course it broke off occasionally and damaged the body of the instrument. So putting back the neck and increasing the tension of the strings reduced this danger. The resulting instrument, which served during an entire century—the century of the greatest development of violin playing, from Tartini to Paganini—should really have its own name and not be considered merely a "transitional" violin. I would like to call it the "Classical violin." Examples of this instrument include Mozart's own concert violin at the Mozarteum in Salzburg; and the Paganini violin in Genoa, which still has a somewhat shorter fingerboard and neck than the modern violin.

The same is true for the bow. What Dr. Boyden called the "transitional" bow and the Tourte bow coexisted for decades. One could play on the Classical violin with the Tourte bow, and vice-versa. And so it would be oversimplifying matters to use only soft strings and low pitch in "historical" performances, or to execute a *forzato* only with a Tourte bow.

Op. 20, No. 2 in C major: Comparative Performances and Discussion

PERFORMANCES: Haydn, Quartet in C major Op. 20, No. 2, first movement, exposition:

1. Isidor Saslav, Adrian Semo, Thomas Dumm, Paula Virizlay (modern instruments, steel strings, modern concert pitch, nineteenth–twentieth-century musical text)
2. Sonya Monosoff, Carol Lieberman, Cynthia Kitt, John Hsu (eighteenth-century instruments, gut strings, low pitch [A-415], text based on Haydn's autograph [JHW XII:3])

FINSCHER Miss Monosoff and Mr. Saslav: how much are your interpretations affected by the instruments themselves?

MONOSOFF The lightness and fleetness of the bow and the instrument encourage me to take slightly faster tempos, and of course that affects the interpretation.

BOYDEN Miss Monosoff, in my own experience there is a sort of luminous quality about these old instruments, even in the hands of amateur players. Would this be affected by playing slower or faster, especially slower?

MONOSOFF I think that one is so affected by the instruments that the difference in tempo is actually implied. Another thing is that you can't use so much vibrato with these instruments, especially at low pitch and with gut strings, because you get an awful wobble in the sound.

SOMFAI In the 1800–1801 Artaria edition of Op. 20, the tempo of this movement was changed from Moderato to Allegro Moderato. (This is not the only case in which the tempo was accelerated in late editions.) Do you think that the meaning of the terms Moderato and Allegro Moderato changed from 1772 to 1800, or that the new heavier bow instigated a decrease in speed, so that composers felt obliged to specify "faster" tempos in order to obtain the same actual speed? The first performance, just now, with the modern instruments, seemed "automatically" slower.

MONOSOFF It seems that in the late-nineteenth-century tradition slow movements in particular must be played very slowly in order to be "expressive." The light eighteenth-century bow and violin cannot produce that big, luscious, vibrato-filled, pressed-bow tone which fills large concert halls. So the concept "expressivity" must have been quite different in the minds of eighteenth-century composers and performers.

BARRETT-AYRES   It seemed to me that the greatest change came from the cello. The cello was much less important in the historical ensemble than in the modern one, and the viola much more important. Did the viola and the cello change as much as the violin?

MELKUS   I don't think so; I think that this was a personal interpretation. For example, the Classical viola was much smaller than the modern viola. Often it was just a second instrument for the violinist. So the small viola sound must have been more typical for the string quartet. It's true that the more nasal sound of the old instruments affects the lower voices, especially the cello, more than the violin. On the other hand, Mr. Hsu has here a Baroque bridge of the Stradivarius type, which sounds more like the early eighteenth-century than the Classical period. Also, Stradivarius's last instruments were those of an old man—he just continued building the old way.

FINSCHER   Mr. Boyden and Mr. Melkus: Do we have a "transitional" violin in the late eighteenth century, or do we have a well-defined "Classical" violin? Could you either come to an agreement or state your disagreement clearly?

BOYDEN   Well, the bow underwent a period of change from about 1760 to about 1830, but the modern bow came along as early as 1785. So, from about 1785 to about 1830 you had different kinds of bows. Some of the Paganini caprices are more easily played with the "transitional" bow than the Tourte bow.

   As far as the violin is concerned, I do not feel quite so confident about what happened as Mr. Melkus. It's very difficult to pin down what happened to the violin. My own feeling is that the violin developed more slowly than the bow. The full potential of the modern bow was not realized until after 1800, because its inherent power can only be exploited by a stronger violin. And this was sociologically necessary, because at the end of Haydn's life we have, in effect, the rise of the commercial concert. The new violin and bow accompanied visiting artists like Paganini who traveled around and played for high fees, so that you had to fill a hall with 3,000 people. That meant a big violin sound and a bow to produce it.

MELKUS   If Mozart's violin and Paganini's violin were nearly the same, then within this period there was "an" instrument. As far as the bow is concerned, an early Italian bow which once belonged to Tartini proves that what Professor Boyden calls a "transitional" bow was used shortly after 1700.

BOYDEN   We should also remember that different developments took place at different cities at different times. Paris was a leader—the violin was often said to have been changed "in the manner of Paris." This undoubtedly means the modern violin.

ROBERT N. FREEMAN[5] At Melk, violin strings were purchased from various parts of Europe, mostly Italy. How much difference was there in string quality, say in Italy itself, say between Florentine and Roman string? Do we know much about the effect that these different kinds of string would have on the playing of the time?

BOYDEN There are theoretical documents which mention that you should get the first string from Rome, the second string from Milan, and so on; that certain makers specialize, and so on.

MELKUS The production of gut strings was a specialty. You had to get special sheep which had been raised in an especially dry climate. The sheep had to be slaughtered in the spring, at a certain age, so that (with the heavy digestion and so on) the gut would be strong but thin. This meant that the strings could be used just as they were, without trimming larger strings from the outside in order to produce the desirable small diameter. It was always recommended, for example by Leopold Mozart, that you should get a strong E string, to produce a manly, good sound.

The production of gut strings has suffered terribly since World War II. They cannot be produced any longer, because the right gut can't be obtained. So to use gut strings is not necessarily historically accurate.

MONOSOFF I don't agree. I have had the same problems with gut strings as everyone who has done historical performance. The E and A gut strings work quite well, but I have never yet found a D string which is true. But a metal E string changes the instrument so completely and gives such a "twangy," modern sound that I can't justify using it. But the gut strings do have to be played at lower pitch—I use A-415 to A-423.

MELKUS A good instrument shows its quality whether we tune it high or low.

Problems in the Sources

WEBSTER Miss Monosoff and I would like to demonstrate some of the difficulties that performers encounter who play from original sources or from editions based on original sources. These sources and editions don't look entirely like traditional modern editions. The two most striking differences are, first, there isn't as much articulation in eighteenth-century sources. Hence the performers must learn to create much more of the articulation themselves, from indications given in the sources and their own musical

[5] From the audience.

judgment. Second, eighteenth-century sources are often inconsistent in the way they articulate a given figure throughout a movement. In this respect, too, the performers must clarify for themselves how they are going to deal with such passages.

When the performance indications are different, of course, they can seriously change the character of a piece. One example has to do with tempo. A characteristic tempo in Haydn is the Adagio *alla breve*. An example is the Largo from the Quartet in D major Opus 76, No. 5. The beat should perhaps be felt on the half note rather than the quarter note.

MONOSOFF: Demonstration—cf. Example 1

Example 1. String Quartet in D major, Op. 76, No. 5, ii, 1–2

SASLAV In the middle of the eighteenth century there were two meanings of the *alla breve* sign: it could mean "in two," but it could also mean merely slightly faster than common time. This latter meaning has fallen into obscurity, but it was actually more widespread.

WEBSTER Another example has to do with the fugue subject in Op. 20, No. 2. In the traditional modern editions we have slurs on the groups of three notes in 6/8, whereas the autograph gives two notes slurred and a single staccato, suggesting perhaps a sprightlier performance.

MONOSOFF: Demonstration—cf. Example 2

Example 2. String Quartet in C major, Op. 20, No. 2, iv, 1–3

Our last example is in the minuet of Op. 20, No. 2, where, after the first theme, there is a rising sequence, with turns in two measures but not in the intervening measure. (In traditional modern editions a turn or some other kind of ornament is added.) The performers must decide whether they should supply such an ornament or not.

MONOSOFF: Demonstration—cf. Example 3

Example 3. String Quartet in C major, Op. 20, No. 2, iii, 10–15

MONOSOFF The way it's written, some measures that have the turn have no slur, and some that have no turn have a slur.

MELKUS I would say that Haydn was just avoiding uniformity. A chief principle of eighteenth-century music is to supply continual variation.

MONOSOFF The problem with all of this is that there are so many inconsistencies that the performer has to make his own edition. I find it very refreshing to be able to go to an edition which is not cluttered with somebody else's interpretation so that I can clutter it with my own.

GEORG FEDER[6]   As a musicologist I can only applaud this use of a critical edition! It gives a new stimulus for our own work.

SOMFAI Performers not only need direction how to play from eighteenth-century texts, they need to differentiate between early autographs and late autographs. Haydn wrote at least three kinds of autographs. Op. 17 and Op. 20, for example, are written copies of the finished compositional statements. But they assume that the performer was familiar with the style and will know how to interpret the articulation marks. For example, the slur was intended mainly to direct that a motive be played legato; but whether, say, the upbeat or the last note was also to be played on the same bow is often not specified. The slurs usually stop at the barline.

Secondly, some string quartet autographs from the 1780s, for example Op. 54, Nos. 1 and 3, are short-hand scores, including interesting abbreviations for certain passages.

The third type is the late string quartet autographs, specifically Op. 77. The differences between the autograph score, the Elssler copy, and the authentic edition (not to speak of the corrupt modern editions) are quite large. I would like to illustrate this by one point: the meaning of a slur. A slur does not only mean "Play legato." A long slur above the staff means *una corda;* in the finale of Op. 77, No. 1, in G major, you have to go up to d² on the G string (mm. 46–53, 223–30). Another way of indicating how to phrase a motive is to give fingering. In this example from the slow movement of Op. 77, No. 1, the different fingerings create an upbeat phrasing of the sixteenths.

SASLAV: Demonstration—cf. Example 4

Example 4. String Quartet in G major, Op. 77, No. 1, ii, 22–24

[6] From the audience.

Perhaps Haydn made these innovations in string-quartet scoring be-cause these nuances in his style were no longer as well understood in the late 1790s as they had been in the 1770s—perhaps he realized this while he was in London.

Now, we would like to play the main theme of the Adagio from Op. 77, No. 1 as Haydn wrote it in the autograph (see Example 5). You will see at least two very interesting markings. One is in mm. 2 and 6: an in-verted accent or marcato sign. As far as I know, Haydn used marcatos only after his London experience. The point seems to be to create an accent, but one which is less heavy than the *fz* in m. 4.

Example 5. String Quartet in G major, Op. 77, No. 1, ii, 1–8, Autograph

The other interesting notational device is the slur from the last note of m. 2 through m. 3. It's not a later correction—we have the staccato strokes as well as the slur. It cannot be *una corda,* because it also appears in the second violin. It is not a portato, because Haydn wrote staccato *dots* with slurs for portato. It can have only one meaning: on the "ground floor" of the articulation, so to speak, you have staccato, but "above" that you must make a single phrase. I don't know whether Haydn intended a single bow, or a more general suggestion to perform one long phrase.

> DEMONSTRATION: Saslav Quartet was asked to *differentiate* between the third bar and the seventh bar. They were also asked to try to keep the bow going in the same direction in bars 2–3. [Demonstration.]. Somfai remarked on how marvelously detailed and innovative Haydn's late autographs are. These details are missing from Artaria's and all later editions to this date.

FINSCHER Are there other instances of this seeming differentiation between *articulation* on the "first level" of interpretation, and *phrasing* on the "second" level? And do they come only in slow movements or also in fast ones?

SOMFAI They do come elsewhere—in the scherzo of this same quartet, for example. In fast movements, however, you have portato in the accompaniment, while the melody has staccato strokes with slurs above it. This is really a question of phrasing, not merely articulation. It comes only in the late quartets—from Op. 76 on.

MONOSOFF You played mm. 1–2 with divided bow. Could the "marcato" sign possibly just mean an upbow? If you played it really as it's written in one bow that's where you'd come out.

SASLAV It seems inconceivable; it's absolutely backwards for the nature of the bow. . . . Let's try it. [Play]

BOYDEN I don't believe you played a true marcato at m. 2. But I'd like to raise the question of portato. Can you play mm. 2–3 all on one bow without going off the string?

SOMFAI I thought Haydn's intention was to play the notes shorter but with the bow in one direction.

MELKUS It could just mean to emphasize the notes, to play expressively like a portato, but with rests. It might even be a partial *return* of the bow. . . . [Plays] [Quartet plays]

BARRETT-AYRES I seem to remember seeing this kind of notation in Opus 20.

SOMFAI I don't think this kind of phrasing is characteristic of early Haydn.

BOYDEN It's in Quantz and Leopold Mozart.

GERHARD CROLL[7] Might it be possible to play the first two bars differently, with the first bar an *upbeat* of the second? [After several trials, the performers mastered this interpretation, which was greeted with spontaneous applause.]

[7] From the audience.

MIRIAM BERGAMINI[8]   Mr. Somfai, you said that in measures 2 and 3 it could be either a bowing or a phrase mark. But if mm. 2–3 is a bowing, what are the real slurs in mm. 3–4?

SOMFAI   It may not be a bowing in mm. 2–3. It may be a direction for style, as Mr. Melkus showed with his *affetuoso*. The other three slurs in mm. 1–4 are bowings.

KONRAD WOLFF[9]   Perhaps we don't know exactly what portato meant at any given time. In Moscheles's edition of Beethoven's sonatas from about 1840 he claims that notes with slurs plus dots are to be held three-quarters of their full value. I would read it simply as a portato, implying long-held eighth notes.

SASLAV   Even in his earliest years, Haydn was interested in experimental writing for the violin. (Some of these effects have only now come to light with the new critical editions in JHW.) In one string trio, the trio of the minuet is entirely in artificial harmonics. In the Quartet in D major Op. 1, No. 3 (Hob. III:3), the trio of the first minuet opens with the violin in dialogue with itself, the melody arco and the bass pizzicato (Example 6). In Op. 2, No. 2, the second minuet opens with a kind of *bariolage* (Example 7).

Example 6. String Quartet in G major, Op. 1, No. 3 (Hob. III:3), ii, 21–24

Example 7. String Quartet in E major, Op. 2, No. 2 (Hob. III:8), iv, 1–4

Even the later quartets harbor fantastic surprises in their authentic texts. In Opp. 64 and 71–74, which I helped to edit for JHW, we found, first of all, an entire missing trio for Op. 64, No. 6 in E-flat major. Haydn marks it "Trio per la seconda volta"—apparently implying that the minuet is to be played three times in all, with the trio alternating twice. But the publisher Koželuch apparently suppressed the *first* version of the trio in the Viennese edition (both appear in the London edition), so that the version we have always known had only one trio, as usual—the one he originally intended to come the second time around.

[8] From the audience.   [9] From the audience.

Quartet plays minuet and trios in original version.

There are many other surprises in JHW XII:5; compare, for example, Op. 64, No. 1 in C major, first movement, mm. 40–44, or the first violin part in Op. 71, No. 1 in B-flat major, m. 151, with the traditional modern texts. The changes in articulation, which Dr. Somfai has already discussed, alter the character of the music almost as much as if the notes had been changed.

WOLFF Could Haydn really have meant the same trio in Op. 64, No. 6 to be played twice?

SOMFAI Perhaps it was an optional variation, so to speak.

SASLAV The autograph says "per la seconda volta." It doesn't say as an alternate version.

LAWRENCE BERNSTEIN[10] Dr. Somfai: In the last movement of Op. 76, No. 2 in D minor, there seems to be the hint of a *glissando* in m. 8. . . .

SOMFAI Yes, there are many glissandos in Haydn's string quartets.

Problems of Scoring

The Instrumentation of the Lowest Part in the *Divertimento à Quattro*

UNVERRICHT The question of the scoring of the lowest part in the *divertimento à quattro* was first raised by L. Somfai à *propos* observations of freely attacked (that is, without preparation) six-four chords produced by the crossing of the viola and bass parts.[11] This issue, which can now be better differentiated from a stylistic point of view, nevertheless cannot be solved using this approach alone. There are, in brief, the following additional considerations.

As Bär and Webster have emphasized, the term "Basso" denotes the lowest part or foundation, but says nothing about the instruments used in performance.[12] Only from about 1770 on did Haydn distinguish between cello and double bass; this, however, did not prevent him, even in some of the London symphonies (a different genre, of course), from still writing "Bassi" or "Bassi continui" for the lowest part. This indicates that here he counted on the presence of a keyboard instrument, in accordance with the practice in London. Among the documents concerning

---

[10] From the audience.   [11] Somfai, "Opus 3," 159–60.
[12] Bär, "Basso"; Webster, "Chamber," 236–42, 246–47.

Haydn's performance practice in the *divertimento à quattro,* there is, until Griesinger (a work which cannot claim to be documentary in nature), scarcely any secure information about the instrument used in the bass part. Haydn's remarks and notes from around or after 1800 cannot be considered unequivocal evidence about the situation between 1740 and 1765 or 1770. Contemporary theory treatises suggest that, even as late as 1780, a double bass may have been used in the *divertimento à quattro.* [13]

By about 1775 at the latest, Daube and Riepel had characterized the six-four chord as a compositional *gaucherie* to be avoided; that is, it had become merely a compositional problem. Perhaps, however, this problem itself implies that two or three decades earlier—or even one decade earlier—composers counted (perhaps mostly unconsciously) on a double bass as part of the bass. [14] According to Finscher's account, Haydn's six-four chords are to be considered only a compositional problem, not one of performance practice. He offers an enlightening interpretation of Haydn's individual compositional tendencies, but he includes little general historical information. [15] It is certainly true that a separate, written-out double bass part for a *divertimento à quattro* is a decided rarity, and so it carries scarcely any weight in answering the question as to whether doubling of the bass part could have been intended in Haydn's time. On the other hand, the fact that it is rare does not constitute negative proof.

The six-four chord was used even later, if not as often. It could be used for various musical functions, as Somfai and, after him, Finscher and Webster have shown. [16] I refer here to the oft-cited beginning of the last movement of the C-major Quartet, No. 3 from Haydn's Op. 33. In this case it is difficult even for well-trained listeners to hear the six-four chord as such: the double stops in the second violin and, in particular, the interval of the sixth in the viola generate for the listener the difference-tone c (an octave below middle c), providing the root of the harmony; the fourth between the cello and the viola therefore almost sounds covered. Whether "Hungarianism" could also play a role cannot be further elucidated here. The first measure of Beethoven's String Quartet Op. 59, No. 1 in F major can be considered an extraordinarily refined and altered derivative of this kind of beginning for a movement. By means of c (an octave below middle c), the cello creates something that remotely recalls a six-four chord. The movement is in F major. The pitches a and c′ in the viola and the second violin belong to both A-minor and F-major harmony, and since the interval a–c′ is heard as root and third, measure 1 appears to be in A minor. Yet if the key of the piece is taken as F major, a

[13] Petri, *Anleitung;* similarly L. Mozart, *Violinschule;* Riepel, *Anfangsgründe.* These passages are quoted and interpreted in Unverricht, *Streichtrio,* 151–3, 181–7; Finscher, *Streichquartett* I, 106–16.
[14] Unverricht, *loc. cit.*   [15] Finscher, *Streichquartett* I, 181–90.
[16] Somfai, loc. cit.; Finscher, loc. cit.; Webster, "Bass Part," 402–20.

six-four chord occurs. In this instance Beethoven consciously exploited tonal ambiguity; only in the course of the movement is the beginning of this motive fully clarified harmonically.

Webster's interpretation of "covered" six-four chords arising from the previous sounding of the relevant root by the cello is further proof that such harmonies in the *divertimento à quattro* are not decisive in determining how the bass in these works was performed until about 1770, either generally or in Haydn's case. According to theoretical and documentary sources it could be played variously with cello, with double bass, or with both instruments; even participation by the harpsichord is not entirely out of the question, even though the compositions no longer require it. Finscher sees the Classical string quartet, with its standardization of four instruments, developing from the divertimento, and he classifies the latter as a predecessor of the string quartet.[17]

The Scoring of Haydn's Early String Quartets

WEBSTER   The precise scoring of Joseph Haydn's early string quartets has never been established.[18] Even the new critical edition hesitates on this point.[19] The problem involves two distinct but related issues. First, were Haydn's early quartets written for obligatory performance by soloists (as opposed to *ad libitum* orchestral performance)? Secondly, assuming soloistic performance for the ensemble as a whole, was the instrumentation of the bass part a solo violoncello, a solo double bass, cello and double bass together, or a basso continuo with keyboard? While the history of Haydn's string quartets is well documented from Op. 33 on, we know little or nothing about the circumstances under which Haydn composed his earlier quartets or how they were performed.[20] Insofar as it is precisely these works whose status as "true" string quartets has been doubted, the extant evidence bearing on this question must be described as scanty.

In the main, secular Viennese chamber music in this period was performed soloistically.[21] Haydn's quartets fit well into this general picture. For each chronological group through Op. 33, there is at least one authentic or eyewitness account of soloistic performance. According to the authentic biography by Georg August Griesinger, Haydn's first quartets were written for soloistic performance by four players, with solo violoncello on the bass part.[22] The next period, covering Op. 9 through

[17] Finscher, *Streichquartett* I, 89–105.
[18] A fuller version of this material, with music examples, appears in Webster, "Bass Part."
[19] See JHW XII:1, viii; /2, vi; /3, viii.
[20] See JHW XII:1–3, forewords; Webster, "Chronology."
[21] W. Kirkendale, *Fuge und Fugato,* 83–95; Webster, "Chamber," 231–35, 238–39, 244–46.
[22] Griesinger, 14 (modern ed., 12; Gotwals, *Haydn,* 13).

Op. 20, enjoys a precise account from Dr. Burney, who witnessed a performance of Haydn quartets in Vienna in 1772. The cellist was Joseph Weigl, who had been the principal cellist at Esterházy under Haydn himself from 1761 to 1769.[23] A similar performance of Op. 33 was described in the newspapers: On this occasion Haydn was present, accompanied by his concertmaster Tomasini, who played the first violin; Weigl still held down his old post on the cello.[24]

Every authentic source for Haydn's string quartets gives instrumental designations in the singular, never in the plural. No authentic source is transmitted with *Dubletten*. Likewise, no authentic source calls for the continuo or gives figures.[25] Furthermore, the entire European journalistic tradition agrees with these indications, and the anecdotal testimony just described, that Haydn's string quartets were soloistic chamber music from the beginning.

The titles on the authentic sources through Op. 33 read "Divertimento" for the most part; in the early quartets we also encounter "Cassatio" and "Notturno."[26] These titles conform to general practice in early Classical Austrian chamber music: the titles "Quartetto" and "Quadro" hardly ever appear, and the customary title for a string quartet is "Divertimento à quattro." Haydn first used the title "Quartetto" in the famous letters offering Op. 33 for sale by subscription; but even for these works, the only authentic manuscript reads "Divertimento à quattro." Thus Haydn did not use the title "Quartetto" exclusively until the late 1780s. On the other hand, the general absence in Vienna of the title "Quartetto" and the well-documented use of "Divertimento" for high-class soloistic chamber music render untenable the old argument that these titles imply orchestral performance.

Haydn's title for the bass part in his early quartets is "Basso." This term was the general designation for the bass *part,* which could imply any bass scoring. In particular, the term "Basso" was often used when the actual scoring was the solo cello.[27] Haydn first specified the cello in the autographs to Opp. 17 and 20; from Op. 33 on, the authentic manuscript sources use "Violoncello" exclusively. Once again, Haydn's usage parallels general Austrian practice.[28] But for the early quartets and Op. 9, the authentic sources give merely "Basso." We must therefore turn to the stylistic evidence.

The common notion that solo cello parts can easily be distinguished from doublebass parts by features such as relatively high notated range, use of the tenor clef, melodic activity, rapid or difficult figuration, regis-

[23] Burney, *State* I, 290 (2d ed., I, 294). On Weigl see Pohl I, 264–65.
[24] Quoted in Pohl II, 185; Pandi-Schmidt, 182.
[25] JHW XII:1–3 and critical reports; Webster, "Chamber," 233–34, 243–44.
[26] JHW XII:1, viii.   [27] Bär, "Basso"; Webster, "Chamber," 236–42, 246–47.
[28] Ibid.

tral mobility, participation in contrapuntal passages, *thematische Arbeit,* or a registral "gap" between the bass and the upper parts is untenable. An active and widespread school of double-bass virtuosos flourished in Austria from around 1765 to around 1800. The music written for these performers included not only concertos and *concertante* sonatas for double bass, but also many bass parts in soloistic chamber music. The extant music shows that in every respect just mentioned, these double-bass parts could be virtually indistinguishable from solo cello parts from the same time and place.[29] Hence the presence of these criteria is not sufficient to establish solo cello scoring.

On the other hand the lower tessiture of bass parts ought to be a workable criterion to distinguish the cello from the double bass. The Austrian double bass, called the "Violone," was usually tuned to contra F', notated F, as the lowest pitch. But the cello, of course, often goes below notated F; indeed it characteristically exploits the open C string to good musical effect. The bass parts whose scoring is specified generally agree with these twin criteria. Hence we can use them to help determine the bass scoring for those works whose sources give merely "Basso."

Consider first the clear evidence *for* the cello in Op. 20. In five of the six quartets, and thirteen of the twenty-four individual movements, the lowest note is low C. The lowest pitches appear prominently in crucial passages: for example, the beginning of Op. 20, No. 4 in D major, with its mysterious six-bar phrases; the pedal point at the climax of the fugue in the F-minor quartet Op. 20, No. 5; or the recapitulation of the first movement of Op. 20, No. 2, in C major, where low C is carefully withheld until the final note. Elsewhere, the low pitches are emphasized in other ways: they may follow large leaps from high registers, or be introduced with a *subito piano.* Such registral sophistication is a worthy companion to the more spectacular examples of modern quartet scoring in Op. 20: the extension of the upper tessitura to d^2, the long, expressive melodies in tenor register, and the "radical equality" among the parts created by the fugal finales in Nos. 2, 5, and 6.

In the ten early quartets, the bass parts are quite different in character. Although they are quite active and occasionally participate in *thematische Arbeit,* they are restricted for the most part to harmonic support, and in very few movements do we find low C. On the other hand, every quartet goes below F at least once; the pitch E flat is an integral part of the bass tessitura. These E flats are fairly strong evidence against solo double-bass scoring. Taken together, these features suggest that the bass part might have been performed by solo cello *and* solo double bass. A few passages, however, seem to demand solo cello. Three passages in the slow movement of Op. 2, No. 1, in A major (mm. 1, 35–38, 68–69) exploit low D.

---

[29] Meier, *Kontrabass;* Planyavsky, *Kontrabass;* Webster, "Violoncello."

Another comparable passage is the "pulsing" sixteenth-note idea at the end of the slow movement of Op. 2, No. 2, in E major (mm. 40–42). But the most impressive of these passages is the mysterious neighbor-note figure C–D♭–C towards the end of the slow movement of Op. 2, No. 4, in F major (mm. 79–81). These passages imply that the early quartets were written for solo cello.

The basses in Op. 9 demand the cello much more strongly. In four of the six quartets, the lowest pitch is C. Almost every occurrence of the lowest register is exposed or calculated: in No. 1 in C major, for example, first movement, mm. 7, 57–58, 71–72; minuet, mm. 1–4; Adagio, mm. 55–57; finale, mm. 138–42. Other occurrences are equally prominent. The use of the cello in Op. 17 is similar, but with a sharper profile and bolder use of the lowest register. Moreover, Op. 17 brings the first real tenor-register cello melody in Haydn's quartets: the tune in the finale of No. 1 in E major, mm. 43–50 and 168–75—a harbinger, it would seem, of the frequent significant cello melodies in Op. 20. Thus Haydn steadily increased the extent to which he realized the potentialities of the solo cello from the earliest quartets to Op. 20.

One specific stylistic feature in Haydn's string quartets which has received considerable attention comprises the passages in which the notated bass crosses over another part.[30] Often these passages appear to violate modern rules of part writing. But the argument that they imply double-bass scoring is easy to refute.[31] Passages of this kind occur at least twice in every opus Haydn wrote, right through Op. 103. Since it is certain that Haydn's mature quartets were written for solo cello, the presence of these part-crossing passages even in the early quartets does not constitute evidence for or against any particular scoring of the bass.

In sum, although the scoring of the ten early quartets is not documented, the evidence strongly suggests that these works were written for the same ensemble that is documented from Op. 17 on (and which is overwhelmingly likely for Op. 9): soloistic quartet with solo cello on the bass part.

Discussion

FINSCHER As far as I see, these were two different approaches to one controversial topic. Prof. Unverricht stated that in terms of historical performance practice nearly everything might be possible and probably has been done. And this would imply that when a double bass was used, it was up to the performer to deal with passages that went below the range of his instrument by transposing up an octave. On the other hand, Prof. Web-

[30] Somfai, "Op. 3," 159–60; Unverricht, *Streichtrio,* 153–55, 181–87; Unverricht, *Hoffstetter,* 16–17.
[31] See Finscher, *Streichquartett* I, 181–90; Webster, "Bass Part," 402–20.

ster makes a very strong stylistic case for the violoncello in Haydn's early quartets.

Without mentioning the famous phantom of the *Bassetl,* I'm not sure whether the Austrian double bass was restricted to low F. Koch states that the double bass—presumably in German speaking countries—is built with low E flat and even low D.[32] So there may have been a development with the aim of making use of the lower pitches for the double bass.

WEBSTER The question of the double basses is very complicated. Double basses were subject to a considerable degree of variation from one place to another, and possibly from one kind of music to another in the same place. But Albrechtsberger in 1790, who is more relevant for Haydn than is Koch, described the double bass as having F as the lowest pitch.[33] And there is a great deal of other documentation of this kind of five-string double bass, summarized in Meier, *Kontrabass.*

FINSCHER And there is Planyavsky's study too. It is unfortunate that Mr. Meier and Mr. Planyavsky are not here—their volumes differ in many of their conclusions.

UNVERRICHT Meier informed me that the principle of determining the lowest string in this manner, in his opinion, is very difficult.

MELKUS The five-string double bass was the common instrument for Viennese practice. But I thought its tuning was uncertain. And Leopold Mozart says that the *Bassetl* was tuned an octave lower than the cello.

WEBSTER That's quite different. The *Bassetl was* the cello—that was simply the term the Austrians used for the cello.[34]

FINSCHER I think it must still be emphasized that these matters are not considered settled. Now as far as the six-four chords are concerned, Mr. Webster stated that they are to be found up to Opus 103. This is true, but still I think that the number, the types, and the employment of six-four chords in the early quartets differ from their use in the later quartets. As you know, I have a chapter in my book about this.

WEBSTER I would agree. My chief aim here was to prove that they shouldn't be used as evidence for the scoring. I would be delighted to settle the question of scoring on documentary grounds alone; it's just that the evidence is insufficient.

The problem I was trying to solve was the *authentic* scoring of Haydn's early quartets—Haydn's own compositional intentions and the performing traditions he supervised or approved of. I don't believe that the vari-

---

[32] Koch, *Lexikon,* s. v. Contra-Violon.   [33] Albrechtsberger, *Composition,* 421–22.
[34] See Webster, "Violoncello," 413–18.

ety of musical practices which Prof. Unverricht described is relevant, because nobody has shown any reason to suppose that that variety applied to Haydn.

Problems in Recording

BARRETT–AYRES   The problems which face those who would record all the Haydn quartets are innumerable. The set on which I assisted, as a musicological consultant, was performed by the Aeolian Quartet and will be released by Argo Records. A performing musical text was made especially for the occasion by H. C. Robbins Landon and myself; this text is as close to an *Urtext* as possible.

We started in 1965, and we have now finished—a period of ten years. The first ten quartets were recorded in 1967. The Aeolian Quartet were astonished to find that many of the notes were different from the older editions with which they were familiar.

A church in the West End of London was selected with a good acoustic—not too lively, and yet far from dead. Much time was taken up finding a suitable place in the church for the recording and placing the microphones in positions where they could pick up the sound of the instruments faithfully. When these quartets were written—that is, up through Op. 64—they were written for the player; they were played in large drawing rooms, and interested parties were normally present. There was no idea of a real concert. This does not mean that an acoustic should be found similar to that in an eighteenth-century drawing room; early recordings of the Haydn quartets often had this somewhat "boxed in" feeling.

While the Quartet make themselves accustomed to the positions by playing a movement or two through, the technical team retire to another room, where they listen to various sounds coming from the Quartet and discuss the placement of the microphones and other technical matters. When it is time to begin, the Quartet tune to an A which has been previously prepared on a loop tape. This loop is used through the entire recording of the series, so that we maintain the same A. The movement in question is then recorded on a trial run, while the director marks questionable passages. The Quartet then listens to the result, considering the director's comments. (Here is where arguments take place.) I was often called upon to give judgment concerning tempo, performance of ornaments, cadenzas, and so on. I think that it is fair to say that one is never entirely satisfied. The recording of one movement—perhaps a minuet and trio—might take two days.

Compared to earlier recordings, ours have a host of changes. In the first place, the works themselves are often different. The tempos are often quite different—the minuets especially are often faster—and there is greater rhythmic impetus. In the slow movements, cadenzas and "lead-ins" were extemporized wherever appropriate. And so on.

Therefore, in the recording studio, the musicologist's advice touches many issues: the location of the recording, historical facts, the degree of reverberation required, editing the score for staccato marks, dynamic marks, indications of speed, the method of playing ornaments, and so on. But the historical point of view should always be considered equally with purely musical considerations.

FINSCHER I think this is a very good example of cooperation between musicians and musicologists, in trying to cover both the musicological conscience, the musical conscience, and creativity in reproducing historical music. This is one kind of recording of the future. At the same time I think that this note of cooperation is an appropriate conclusion to our session.

Workshop 4

The Paris Symphonies: Symphony No. 85 in B-flat major ("La Reine")

BORIS SCHWARZ, *Chairman*

BARRY S. BROOK

PAUL BRYAN

ANTAL DORATI

NEWELL JENKINS

JAN LA RUE

CHRISTOPH-HELLMUT MAHLING

MOGENS WÖLDIKE

NIELS KRABBE,

Secretary

Musical and Historical Context

Size of the Orchestra

MAHLING When we hear symphonies by Haydn and Mozart in a concert hall, we take for granted that the orchestra must be reduced in size, because we know that eighteenth-century orchestras were considerably smaller than modern ones. Norms have developed which one follows, regardless of the characteristics of individual works. Performance practice which is historically oriented, however, cannot be satisfied with this kind of simplification of the enormously complex problems of work and performance. Symphony No. 85 is one of the Paris symphonies, which Haydn composed in 1785–86. I should like to report on a few problems regarding the size and instrumentation of the orchestra for this symphony.

As in earlier centuries, it was usual in the eighteenth century to take account of the technical and musical capabilities of the performers for whom a work was intended. This held true not only for singers and instrumental soloists but, to an equal degree, for chamber music ensembles and orchestras. Haydn had the good fortune at Eszterháza always to have at his disposal an orchestra whose qualifications he knew very well and with which he could experiment.[1] From his utterances, we know that Haydn was reluctant to release a work to persons about whom he knew little. Referring to the Paris symphonies, Pohl pointed out that Haydn had to acquaint himself with an unfamiliar orchestra and with the taste of an equally unfamiliar audience, and he may have received suggestions with respect to instrumentation and the qualifications of the soloists, together with requests concerning individual movements.[2] Similarly,

[1] Cf. his well-known "and so I was forced to become original" (Griesinger, 24–25; modern ed., 17; Gotwals, 17).

[2] Pohl, II, 273–74.

242

Landon states: "It is quite obvious that Haydn wrote most . . . of these symphonies with the Parisian orchestra—reports of whose size and virtuoso standards will surely have reached his ears—and the French audience in mind."[3]

Landon assumes that the orchestra of the Concert de la Loge Olympique, which had succeeded the Concert des Amateurs in 1780–81 and in whose hall the concerts were performed, consisted, apart from other instruments, of forty violins and ten double basses.[4] Landon also believes that these facts are clearly documented by the Paris symphonies. These particulars, however, seem doubtful, especially since the Concert de la Loge Olympique was a private organization, and none of the comparable Parisian orchestras has the number of players Landon names. For example, the Concert Spirituel in 1773 had twenty-four violins (thirteen and eleven), four violas, ten violoncellos, and four double basses. The orchestra of the *Opéra* in 1773 had at its disposal twenty-two violins, five violas, nine violoncellos, six double basses; and in 1790 twenty-six violins, six violas, twelve violoncellos, and five double basses.[5]

There is also the question whether, in such large orchestras, all the musicians played at any given time. For instance, the musicians of the very large Munich Court Orchestra had an exact schedule of performance duty as early as the eighteenth century, and this orchestra hardly ever played with its full complement. The same is true for the Dresden Court Orchestra. Was it different in Paris?

If we compare the style of Symphony No. 85 with one of the London symphonies, which are scored for large orchestra,[6] and with one of the symphonies written around 1760, for example Symphony No. 14 in A major,[7] it appears that "La Reine" was in fact written for an orchestra like Haydn's at ?Esterháza in 1780. This orchestra comprised twenty-five musicians,[8] a large number for a court of that size; court orchestras usually had between ten and twenty musicians only.[9]

Support for this hypothesis comes from the scoring. For long passages, particularly in *forte,* the violins are in unison, as are the violas and basses. The frequent double stops, especially in the second violins, produce the impression of a larger orchestra even with small numbers. The

[3] R. Landon, in Haydn, *Symphonies,* vol. 9, xvii.

[4] R. Landon, *Symphonies,* 401. Brook, *Symphonie,* I, 340–41 writes merely: "Le Concert de la Loge Olympique . . . était aussi 'rempli indépendamment des professeurs par les plus habiles amateurs de Paris' "; he does not give details of size or instrumentation.

[5] Becker, "Orchester," tables X and XI following col. 192.

[6] R. Landon: "We do not know the exact size of Salomon's orchestra; but the London newspapers inform us that 'The Orchestra [of Viotti] will consist of more than Sixty Instrumental Performers, besides the Solo Players.' " (Haydn, *Symphonies,* vol. 12, xv.)

[7] Ibid., vol. 2.   [8] Hárich, "Orchester," 5.

[9] The larger court orchestras had between forty and fifty members. Cf. the Round Table on *Historical Performance Conditions.* [Ed.]

many solo wind passages, particularly in the oboe and the bassoon, could also imply that the string section of the orchestra was not large. This in turn could imply that despite the variation movement, Haydn did not write this symphony especially for Paris. In any case, it seems very unlikely that he expected the symphony to be performed with forty violins and ten double basses.

If, on the other hand, one assumes that the symphony was performed by a large orchestra, it would seem likely that one would have distinguished between the professional musicians at the first desks, and the *Ripienisten,* or tutti players. If so, soft passages or passages with solo wind instruments, and even certain whole movements, would have been performed with reduced strings. (This would be analogous, in reverse, to doubling the winds.) In Symphony No. 85, such a differentiation could easily be realized. With the exception of works like the London symphonies, it would seem adequate for most of Haydn's symphonies to take his orchestra at ?Esterháza as the norm, particularly since his manner of composing may have been influenced considerably by the sonorous possibilities of that particular orchestra. Thus for a symphony from the 1780s the following disposition should not be exceeded or reduced to any great extent: four to five each first and second violins, two or three violas, two violoncellos, and two double basses, assuming no doubling of the other instruments.[10] Normally this music was played in rooms much smaller than today's concert hall. If we increase the size of the orchestra because of the size of our concert halls, this should be done according to eighteenth-century practice: if the string section is enlarged beyond a certain size, the wind instruments must be doubled too, to maintain the proportions of winds and strings.[11]

The Commissioning of the Symphonies

BROOK Let us review a few specifics about the commissioning of these symphonies. The Concert de la Loge Olympique was a large semi-masonic group that included many amateurs. The figures of forty violins and ten double basses may represent the total number of members who played those instruments. But in any particular concert they may well have used fewer whenever it was appropriate. Claude-François-Marie Rigoley, comte d'Ogny, the chief patron of the organization, was a passionate music lover, and he owned an extraordinary collection of music. The commission given Haydn, according to Barbedette writing in *Le Ménestrel* in 1874, awarded Haydn more money than he had ever earned for any group of six pieces. For this reason I would dispute the assertion that

[10] In the 1760s and 1770s the Esterházy orchestra was smaller. Cf. Gerlach, "Orchestermusiker" and "Ordnung." [Ed.]

[11] Cf. the Round Table on *Historical Performance Conditions.* [Ed.]

perhaps these symphonies were not written with Paris in mind. Everyone in Europe knew that Paris was the musical center where one could make great fame and fortune. As Landon has suggested, Haydn may have had a couple of symphonies in his desk and included them in the group of six, or he may have taken the first two and dressed them up a bit. I believe that the six symphonies of the Paris group represent an important step forward in sonority, breadth, and maturity, and I think part of the reason was that Haydn had received a commission from that fabulous place which was Paris. He must have had Paris in mind.

Performance Problems

Some Specific Problems in the First Movement

SCHWARZ Before playing four recorded excerpts from Symphony No. 85, I should like to mention what you can expect in terms of problems. The exposition of the first movement consists of an Adagio introduction of eleven measures, followed by a Vivace of 100 measures (up to the repeat sign at m. 111). The entire exposition lasts less than three minutes. Yet, within this short segment, there are a surprising number of problems to be faced by the conductor.

The introduction is Adagio *alla breve.* Yet, among the four performances we are to hear, two are obviously conducted in four beats to a measure, the other two apparently in eight. Measured with a metronome, the tempos vary from $\quad = 63$ to $\quad = 84$. Many conductors have wondered how to interpret *alla breve* in a slow tempo. (The overtures to *Don Giovanni, Così fan tutte,* and *Die Zauberflöte* also begin slowly *alla breve.*) Obviously they cannot be conducted in two—it must be in four. Speaking of Haydn, Landon says:

> For some reasons, modern editions, beginning with Simrock and the old Breitkopf & Härtel scores, consistently omit the "alla breve" sign in Haydn's slow movements. This is a great mistake, since Haydn was very particular about the use of ¢. In quick movements, ¢ means literally that one should beat two-in-a-bar instead of 4, while in slow movements ¢ probably means that one should beat four-in-a-bar and not 8, i.e. that the centres of gravity should be in quarters and not in eighths; or perhaps that the musician should even think in terms of only two "heavy points" per measure. Of the "Salomon" Symphonies beginning in 4/4 time, all except No. 104 start with ¢ in Haydn's manuscripts. . . .[12]

The next problem in the introduction is the dotted rhythm which appears in every measure. The upbeat is a sixteenth note, and thereafter we

---

[12] R. Landon, *Symphonies,* 131. [On this point cf. Workshops 1 and 3 and the Free Paper by Isidor Saslav.—Ed.]

have the consistent pattern of dotted eighth followed by a sixteenth
(♪♫). Is the practice of double-dotting, so prevalent in the Baroque, still
applicable to Haydn? Some say yes, others deny it. The precepts of
Leopold Mozart's *Violinschule* of 1756 may be relevant:

> There are certain passages in slow pieces where the dot must be held rather longer
> than [is usually the case] if the performance is not to sound too sleepy. For ex-
> ample, if [in Example 1] the dot were held its usual length it would sound very
> languid and sleepy. In such cases dotted notes must be held somewhat
> longer. . . .[13]

Example 1. L. Mozart, *Violinschule*, trans., 41–42

(This example coincides with the beginning of Haydn's Violin Concerto
in C major, Hob. VIIa:1, which indeed sounds sluggish if played as notated. Even though it is an Allegro, Landon suggests double-dotting this
passage [Example 2].[14])

Example 2. Violin Concerto Hob. VIIa:1, opening

In slow tempos, such double-dottings may also be advisable. Landon
cites Symphony No. 86 in D major, particularly the Capriccio-Largo
(second movement):

> On the basis of the comments made by C. P. E. Bach, Leopold Mozart, and
> Quantz, one would be inclined to alter the first notes of the flute, 2nd oboe, 2nd
> violin, and viola in bars 15 and 16 from ♪· ♪ to ♪·· ♪. . . . While it would be in any
> case stylistically correct to apply the rules of these theorists to the passages in
> question, a confirmation of an even more authentic nature comes to us in the par-
> allel passage, where Haydn writes out the alteration (mm. 64–65). A more con-
> vincing argument for the necessity of rhythmical alteration could scarcely be
> found.[15]

Applied to the introduction of Symphony No. 85, this principle would
mean playing the sixteenth notes as thirty-seconds and double-dotting
the preceding eighths (cf. Example 7, p. 251). Of our four recorded performances, only Bernstein plays exactly as printed—and to my ears it
sounds heavy and sluggish. Ansermet's and Jochum's quicker initial
tempo makes the question of double-dotting less important.

The upbeat sixteenth at the very beginning (cf. Example 7) is an inter-

---

[13] Mozart, *Violinschule*, transl., 41–42 (1st ed., 39–40).
[14] R. Landon, *Symphonies*, 166–67.   [15] Ibid., 165–66.

esting problem for the string player. If it is played as a sixteenth (♪|♩), there is an audible separation between up-bow (V) and down-bow (⊓); if however it is played as a thirty-second (♪|♩), up-bow and down-bow flow into each other without separation.

Haydn often uses the tempo indication Vivace (in place of Allegro) after 1780. In general, he was careful in selecting his tempo indications and the qualifying adjectives, and occasionally he changed his mind. In Quantz's *Versuch* we find elaborate instructions as to how to arrive at the "right" tempo, using the human pulse as a sort of metronome. Based on Quantz's instructions, Dolmetsch set up a table which yields ♩ = 120 for Vivace.[16] Our recordings vary from ♩ = 126–32 to ♩ = 160. But an interesting detail is generally overlooked: in distinction to the traditional scores, which have no expression marking, JHW and Landon's *Complete Symphonies* place *cantabile* in the violins at the opening of the Vivace; this certainly should dampen the initial briskness of any conductor. Three measures later we meet the next obstacle—the articulation of the first quarter notes. In JHW and Landon they are slurred; in traditional modern editions there are two staccato dots below the last two quarter notes; JHW includes only the latter staccato (Example 3). Since this phrase occurs repeatedly throughout the movement, one must arrive at some consistent articulation. I don't know whether these two dots are worth getting excited about, but the *cantabile* is certainly significant. Bernstein's interpretation is more in keeping with it than the others.

Example 3. Symphony No. 85 in B-flat major, i, 12–15

A slight tightening of the tempo at m. 42 is noticeable in all renditions, and rightly so. In JHW and Landon's edition we find staccatos above the first scale in sixteenths (m. 23), which indicate a certain crispness (though possibly not the spiccato effect produced by the modern bow). The modern bouncing bow is particularly noticeable in Bernstein's interpretation of the closing theme (m. 96), where the groups of four sixteenths produce a veritable machine-gun effect. The Eulenburg score "resolves" the appoggiatura and places the group under a slur (Example 4).

Example 4. Symphony No. 85, i, 96–97

16 Dolmetsch, *Interpretation*, 35–44, esp. 42.

The following three recordings of Symphony No. 85, first movement, were played:

Antal Dorati, Philharmonia Hungarica, London STS 15232
Leonard Bernstein, New York Philharmonic, ML 6358 or MS 6948
Ernst Ansermet, L'Orchestre de la Suisse Romande, London CM 9335.

Discussion

WÖLDIKE I was very happy to learn that such lovely music would have been performed by a reduced ensemble instead of that huge Paris orchestra. I think that the ?Esterháza forces would be just right. If I were Bernstein I would have double-dotted it all, because it was so heavy; but if I were Dorati, I should think I would *not* do so, because it was light and flowing in itself.

I agree that the *alla breve* is very important in this kind of piece. Not on the half note—that wouldn't work: Haydn simply means, "Please, not too slowly." In the Vivace, I always feel that the four-bar phrases suggest the tempo; the quarter notes must be very light. It must be in a fast tempo; it must flow in long phrases.

SCHWARZ In other words, you would let the players feel a four-phrase bar—*quattro battute*.

JENKINS I agree wholeheartedly. People often confuse the term Adagio with "slow," but the Italian word is *ad-agio,* "at ease." This does not mean "slow." If you then see *alla breve,* this means either two or four pulses to the bar if you are to be "at ease." As far as the Vivace is concerned, I believe that there is a strong pulse relationship between the slow section and the fast, a relationship respected here only by Ansermet. The question of double-dotting becomes secondary. If you have a light performance, you don't have to worry about this—it will be done by the musicians almost instinctively. If it is not light enough for you, then double-dot!

The basic relationship of two or four bars in the fast section becomes extremely important when you get to the harmonic shifts. These harmonic shifts will also tell you the speed at which the fast section can go. In almost every piece of any length, there is a passage that determines the tempo of the entire piece. Find this passage, and you find the perfect speed. In this movement it is mm. 96–99. The earlier bars can take various tempos, but these bars—to me—are the ones which will give you the perfect tempo.

MAHLING In principle, the slow movements of this period were certainly performed faster than they are today, and conversely the fast movements were performed more slowly. It must be chiefly modern traditions of performance when, as in this case, Haydn is played as if he were Bach. In performing Baroque music one plays ♪♩ ; but the "correct" performance in music of the Classical period must be ♪♩ . But if, so to speak, we perpetuate the Baroque tradition of performance—not the Italian, but the French—then naturally ♫ will be performed ♫ —whereby the short note is understood as an upbeat to the next note: ♪♪ .

NEAL ZASLAW[17]   What sort of evidence does Professor Mahling have for this statement? Though Leopold Mozart wrote a little early for the interpretation of late Haydn symphonies, Türk's *Klavierschule* (1789) still talks of double-dotting. Also, there is ample evidence from mechanical instruments surviving from the second half of the eighteenth century to show that the convention was still in use.

MAHLING   In my opinion, Leopold Mozart's and Quantz's remarks must be understood in a retrospective sense; that is, they describe a practice which prevailed until 1770 or so. Türk's *Klavierschule* appeared in 1789, but even in this case I am not certain whether he describes precisely what was customary in his time. According to theory, of course, it would be correct not to play ♪♩ . But if you are a string player, a violinist, and have grown up in nineteenth- and twentieth-century traditions of performance, then you are apt to play ♪♩ as ♪♩ —not least because of its greater precision.

BRYAN   Türk was active in Halle, not Paris or Eszterháza. Perhaps local practice is something to be considered. Sometimes I think some performances turn out the way they do because the musicians play them that way best. Dorati started almost with dotted eighths and sixteenths and then ended up as thirty-seconds.

DORATI   There is the Baroque approach where we use short notes, and there is the other approach where we don't. I employ a third one where I make the sixteenths just a little bit more tense, but I do not double-dot them. I have found this the most satisfactory way.

BRYAN   Mr. Jenkins's point about the relationship of the tempo of the Vivace to that of the introduction is interesting. But should not the introduction be darker and richer, to set up what follows? Why does it have to be in a certain tempo relationship?

JENKINS   It does not *have* to be, but you will get in trouble if you don't do it. I think the piece will fall apart, as we heard in some of the performances today, if this is not observed. But if the relationship is not important to you, and you can make it work without it, then go to it.

BRYAN   This is a symphony in B flat. Two of the three performances we heard today used horn in B-flat *alto*. At m. 70, if the horns are in B-flat *basso*

---

[17] From the audience.

they fill in the octave between the oboes and bassoons, which I consider normal scoring (Example 5). On the other hand mm. 212–14 might be more effective in B-flat *alto* (Example 6). Haydn never specified horns in B-flat *alto* as far as I know; but Landon likes the sound of high horns and so he always specifies them.

Example 5. Symphony No. 85, i, 70

Example 6. Symphony No. 85, i, 212–19 (cf the initial statement, shown in Example 8.)

*Notation of pitch for B-flat alto horn. If *basso* were used, this part would be more effective.

DORATI For the most part I have accepted Landon's view.

LA RUE For me, the unity between the slow introduction and the rest of the piece is one of an unusual amount of activity followed by an unusual amount of rest. The contrast within the introduction is very strong, and this is reproduced in the Vivace as well. The symphony starts off with a two-bar module, repeated B flats followed by active, rising, dotted patterns (Example 7a). Then the module speeds up to single-bar size, reversing the activity pattern; rapidly rising scales lead to more repeated B flats (Example 7b). But in the Vivace the action–rest pattern occurs simultaneously on two levels of the texture. The bass produces activity and then rest; the upper part simultaneously produces rest and then activity (Example 8). This forms a special kind of four-bar module of activity–rest, two plus two. All through this Vivace Haydn is working out the activity–rest idea of the introduction.

DORATI My performance and recording are based on the very same idea. Our recordings were made in a small church and the orchestra was small throughout: basically eleven first violins, nine second, seven violas, five

Example 7. Symphony No. 85, i, 1–5

Example 8. Symphony No. 85, i, 12–15

cellos, and three double basses, with small changes from work to work. I increased these forces for some—not all—of the London symphonies. In the twentieth century, of course, we have much larger halls than in eighteenth-century Austria—especially in America. I would like to use orchestras that will fill the hall.

MAHLING In that case, even with the number of strings you had last night, you should have doubled the winds, at least in the tuttis: two first flutes, two second flutes, two first oboes, two second oboes, and so forth.

DORATI I don't necessarily agree. I will use anything; but I am a thoroughly practical musician, and I will do nothing at all for a theory.

SCHWARZ Let us now listen to a recording advertised as using "original instruments" and recorded in a small hall in a castle. This recording is done by six or seven violins, two violas, two cellos, and one double bass. Do you think that this very group and the "original instruments" are important to the enjoyment, to the authenticity of the musical sound?

FRANZ JOSEF MAIER, Collegium Aureum, Harmonia Mundi KHB 20340.

MICHAEL FELDMAN[18] I think that much depends on the recording technique, and the hall is extremely important in playing old instruments.

SCHWARZ Do we know anything about the Loge Olympique?

BROOK The Loge Olympique had its own hall; it was a theater in structure.

SCHWARZ On the other hand the *Concert Spirituel* took place in the *Tuileries,* and I can imagine that the acoustics were quite live.

[18] From the audience.

ZASLAW A recording like the one we just heard has little value as a historical document. There is no use taking players with the technique formed on modern instruments and having them refurbish in a week or a month. The players are good players struggling along with unfamiliar instruments, but the engineers have done their best to disguise the fact that this is a small string section. They recorded in such a way as to make it sound "symphonic" in the nineteenth-century sense. It is very difficult to get matched instruments and players who are willing to put aside the instruments by which they make their living and commit themselves to playing instruments which at the moment have little commercial possibility.

MAHLING The question whether one uses "old" or "modern" instruments may not make a great deal of difference for the strings, although there are certainly differences in timbre and sound quality. But it certainly does make a difference whether one uses a modern valve-horn or a natural horn—to give only one example. In fact, there is a greater degree of blending with the strings if one plays with natural horns. Other aspects of performance, as for example the size of the hall in which the music was heard, can be "reconstructed" today only in exceptional cases. As far as recordings are concerned, you are quite right: they can be controlled and manipulated at will. For example, there is no problem whatever in using technical means to make three violins "sound like" sixteen.

SCHWARZ The question of Tourte bow versus old bow is very important. The string instruments which are the bulk of the orchestra *were* played differently—with a different bow with less tension, with gut strings, with different fittings, and with a shorter neck. They had a different sound.[19]

WÖLDIKE I would be very sorry if in the future every time we listen to a Haydn symphony we hear it on old instruments, half a tone lower than normal, and played in quite another manner. But the *study* of these recordings—for me—has been a very good thing. What I learn through listening to recordings with old instruments I can carry over to playing on our instruments.

BROOK I like Professor Zaslaw's word about commitment. Old music requires a whole apparatus, a whole school of old-instrument players and old-instrument builders to obtain a proper result. It is great to hear performances of the same work on old instruments and then on modern ones and to learn from each. Both must proceed side by side; we cannot assert that one is better than the other.

[19] Cf. Workshop 3. [Ed.]

Workshop 5

Opera

BARRY S. BROOK, *Chairman*	J. MERRILL KNAPP
EVA BADURA-SKODA	ANDREW PORTER
ANTAL DORATI	GÜNTER THOMAS
GEORG FEDER	HORST WALTER
MICHAEL FELDMAN	BRUCE MAC INTYRE,
KARL GEIRINGER	*Secretary*

BROOK We are fortunate to have a large panel that includes conductors, producers, translators, critics, editors, and scholars.

In the acceptance of Haydn's operas there is a basic prejudice to overcome, a prejudice engendered in part by Haydn himself when he—even if only once—compared his own operas unfavorably to Mozart's, in the well-known letter to Roth in Prague. We tend to forget his proud statements about his own operas on other occasions. We all have had great difficulties with editions and performance materials on the one hand, production and performance problems on the other. We may hope that we stand at the threshold of an extensive Haydn opera renaissance.

Haydn as an Opera Composer

A Survey of Haydn's Operas

FEDER Haydn's activity as an opera composer was part of his duties as Kapellmeister to the princely house of Esterházy. But it had started as early as 1751 or 1753 in Vienna with *Der krumme Teufel.* Also his last opera, *Orfeo ed Euridice,* was not composed for the Esterházy stage; Haydn wrote it in 1791, his first year in London.

Haydn composed five different types of operas.[1] The first was the German *Singspiel,* that is, spoken dialogue with inserted musical numbers. As a young man of about twenty, he composed an often mentioned, but unfortunately lost, comic Viennese *Singspiel* called *Der krumme Teufel* (*The Crooked Devil*). Whether *Der neue krumme Teufel,* for which the music is also lost, was another composition or merely a new version of

---

[1] A tabular summary of Haydn's operas may be found in Feder, "Opern," 114–18.

253

Der krumme Teufel is an open question. Haydn's later contributions to the *Singspiel* were destined for the marionette theater of Prince Nikolaus Esterházy in the 1770s. Most of this music is also lost, but most of the librettos have been preserved. The titles of the four best authenticated marionette operas are *Philemon und Baucis, Hexenschabbas (Witches' Sabbath), Dido,* and *Die bestrafte Rachbegierde (Punished Vengefulness). Philemon und Baucis* is perhaps the only one for which the music is preserved, but without its farcical prelude usually called "Der Götterrat" ("The Council of the Gods"). What is left of the music has been published, together with the complete text, in JHW XXIV:1. It is doubtful whether the "Opéra comique vom abgebrannten Haus," mentioned in EK, was a marionette opera, and whether it was identical to the music of *Die Feuersbrunst,* a German *Singspiel,* published by H. C. R. Landon in vocal score in 1963 (Schott).

Hardly more has survived from the second group of Haydn's works composed for the stage: Italian comedy with inserted arias. Haydn listed four such comedies in EK, probably composed in the early 1760s before he began to write real *opere buffe.* The titles read: *La Marchesa Nespola, Il dottore, La vedova,* and *Il scanarello.* Some arias from the first of these are apparently preserved in an autograph of 1762 or 1763. The still unpublished manuscript is entitled "Arie per la comedia Marchese."[2] A published aria of Dorina (Hob. XXIVb:1) followed by an unpublished recitative of a person named Podagroso may be another fragment from one of these comedies.

The third, fourth, and fifth groups constitute what we may consider Haydn's main contribution to opera: *opera buffa, opera semiseria,* and *opera seria.* As was the custom of his time, all of them are based on Italian librettos. Among the authors whose librettos Haydn set to music were Pietro Metastasio, famous for *opera seria,* and Carlo Goldoni, renowned in *opera semiseria.* Most of the librettos Haydn set were originally written for Italian composers like Galuppi, Piccinni, Anfossi, or Cimarosa. Somebody in the Esterházy opera house took a copy of such a libretto originally printed, say, in Venice and made cuts or partial substitutions of newly written or borrowed text. This revised libretto Haydn set to music, not without carefully considering the individual abilities of the singers engaged at the Esterházy opera house.

Haydn composed three *opere buffe: La canterina* (1766), *Lo speziale* (1768), and *L'infedeltà delusa* (1773). The libretto for the last of these was by Marco Coltellini, who also had a hand in the libretto of Mozart's *La finta semplice.* The text of *Lo speziale* was originally an *opera semiseria* by Goldoni, but the serious roles were deleted in the libretto given to

---

[2] Cf. Karl Geiringer's remarks in the Round Table on *Background, Biography, Iconography.* [Ed.]

Haydn. The full scores of all three *opere buffe* are available in JHW XXV:2,3,5.

The *opera semiseria* introduces two or more "serious" characters into a comic libretto. Haydn's operas of this type begin with *Le pescatrici* (1769), on an essentially unaltered text by Goldoni. Part of the music is lost, as is unfortunately the case with *Lo speziale*. Next comes *L'incontro improvviso* (1775), an Italian *opera semiseria* based on the French text Gluck had set to music as *La rencontre imprévue* about twelve years earlier. There followed *Il mondo della luna* (1777), based on Goldoni's *dramma giocoso,* in which the serious roles seem less essential to the plot than do those of the *opere semiserie* which follow. These comprise *La vera costanza* (1779), rewritten in 1785, based on a libretto by Francesco Puttini; *La fedeltà premiata* (1780), on a libretto by Giambattista Lorenzi; and *Orlando Paladino* (1782), on a libretto by Carlo Francesco Badini and Nunziato Porta. Five of these six *opere semiserie* are available in full score in JHW XXV:4,6,8,10,11. Of *Il mondo della luna* a vocal score is available (Bärenreiter, 1958); the full score of the first act appears in JHW XXV:7^1, and the remaining acts will follow in JHW XXV:7^{II,III}.

The first and last Italian operas Haydn composed were *opere serie: Acide* (1762, revised 1773), based on a small libretto by Giovanni Ambrogio Migliavacca, and *L'anima del filosofo ossia Orfeo ed Euridice* (1791), based on a libretto by Badini. Two other *opere serie* are *L'isola disabitata* (1779), on a libretto in two acts by Metastasio, and *Armida* (1783), whose full-fledged, three-act libretto was compiled for Haydn from several earlier *Armida* librettos. The full scores of *Armida* and *Orfeo* have already appeared in JHW XXV:12,13. The music of *Acide* is partly lost and is unpublished, except for the overture and one aria. A vocal score of *L'isola disabitata* is now out of print.

The most developed and most completely preserved of Haydn's operas are those beginning with *L'infedeltà delusa* of 1773 and ending with *Armida* of 1783 (or *La vera costanza,* if we take into consideration the 1785 version). We cannot be certain if *Orfeo* is complete, since the libretto is not preserved apart from the music. Thus it seems that Haydn's activity as an opera composer achieved its peak between 1773 and 1783 (or 1785). By then Gluck had already composed most of his "reform" dramas, which, except perhaps for *L'isola disabitata,* exerted no more influence on Haydn than on other contemporary composers of Italian operas. On the other hand, Mozart's mature masterworks, i.e., *Figaro, Don Giovanni, Così fan tutte,* and *Zauberflöte,* were not yet written. Haydn acknowledged them as superior to his own *opere semiserie,* which among his operas resemble them most, and which may perhaps be considered as his most fortunate contributions to opera, especially *La vera costanza, La fedeltà premiata,* and *Orlando Paladino.*

Discussion

BADURA-SKODA   It is clear that Haydn had talent as an opera composer. "Odio, furor, dispetto" from *Armida* is a great dramatic aria.

> Taped performance: Cologne, Westdeutscher Rundfunk; Gundula Janowitz

But it is still necessary to fight the 170-year-old prejudice that this or any other great aria is only an isolated example, that Haydn had no real dramatic gifts, and that he was far greater as an instrumental composer. We simply have not heard enough performances of Haydn's operas—certainly not enough good performances, without cuts, without distortions, sung by singers who understand the traditions, the tempos, the embellishments—to judge his operas. Haydn had the bad luck of being a contemporary of the greatest opera composer of all time: Mozart. But Haydn was born twenty-four years—a generation—earlier. This made a big difference. If Mozart had not lived, I would say that Haydn, not Gluck, was the greatest opera composer of the second half of the eighteenth century. Gluck had marvelous dramatic ideas, but Haydn wrote better melodies.

PORTER   Haydn's operas show little sense of theatrical timing or theatrical situation. An example that comes readily to mind is in *L'incontro improvviso*. We need only contrast the moment when the two long-lost lovers meet at last with the similar place in Mozart's *Entführung*. There, a dramatic and touching situation flowers into music. All that happens in Haydn is a few phrases of recitative, and at once the heroine embarks on a little comic character aria impersonating the pirate chief who captured her and puffed tobacco in her face and made her feel seasick—an unromantic thing to recall at what should be the dramatic highpoint of the opera.

But I do not mean that Haydn's dramatic music lacks character. Certainly his arias have great *musical* character; and in the theatrical sense there is nearly always a very vivid sense of characterization. Each of the five personages in *L'infedeltà delusa,* for example, is very sharply drawn. Besides that, there is character of another kind. As we go through the operas, we begin to discover the vocal personalities and the temperaments of the singers in Haydn's company, especially the resourceful and versatile Maddalena Friberth, Karl Friberth, and Leopold Dichtler. One begins to feel one knows what these people were like when one has looked through several operas written for them.

Haydn's intentions were different in kind from those of his contemporaries Anfossi, Cimarosa, Paisiello, Sarti, whom he performed at Eszterháza. It is often said that his operas are different from Mozart's because they were written for a cultivated princely audience. In fact, Haydn himself said so in the well-known letter of 1787 or 1786 in praise of Mozart.[3]

---

[3] On the date of this letter cf. Badura-Skoda, "Opera," 31.

It is sometimes forgotten that his basic repertoire at Eszterháza was that of other theaters of the day. But even there his own operas were an exception, because his intentions were to add to the proven devices of Anfossi & Co. his own ideas about richness of instrumental texture, variation, development, and large-scale aria forms, which are based on very firm harmonic foundations. His operas seem to be a series of extended and often adventurous movements—well varied and superbly designed to show off and employ the skills and expressive powers of the voices and personalities of the singers in his company.

LUDWIG FINSCHER[4]   It is nice to see musicologists become enthusiastic about music, but I disagree heartily with the prevailing enthusiasm here. (My knowledge of Haydn's opera pertains only to the available published scores rather than to staged productions.) Haydn has to compete with Gluck's music drama and with Mozart's opera, which, as Professor Badura-Skoda pointed out, combines music and text in a way found neither before nor afterwards. Mozart's opera is greater than the sum of its musical and textual parts. I think this competition of Gluck and Mozart is impossible for most of the Haydn operas, excepting perhaps some of the *opere semiserie.* Certainly the aria from *Armida* we just heard is a very beautiful piece of music, but is it a piece of good musical drama?

PORTER If you judge Haydn's operas by Mozartian or Gluckian criteria, they cannot stand up to that competition. What I have been trying to say is that they are something *sui generis;* they offer rewards which are quite different in kind.

GERHARD CROLL[5]   Haydn appreciated Gluck's qualities as a dramatic composer. As he indicated in his letter of January 8, 1791, from London to Prince Anton Esterházy, Badini's libretto to *Orfeo,* which he had not yet received, "is supposed to be entirely different from that of Gluck."[6] I believe he felt that it would be impossible for him to compose a work to the same text, because he grasped Gluck's qualities as a musical dramatist. Metastasio would have said, "Gluck has a *fuoco manieroso ma pazzo.*" We are all afraid to perform Gluck on the stage with a *fuoco manieroso e pazzo.* This is music for a drama, dramatic music. Nobody has the courage to play Gluck as he is, as an incomparable dramatic composer.

CHRISTOPH-HELLMUT MAHLING[7]   Perhaps there is also a sociological aspect—namely the question of for whom (that is to say, for what group, for what public, and for what occasion) did Gluck and Mozart compose their operas on the one hand, and Haydn on the other? Naturally Haydn *also* composed opera, but he probably never considered himself primarily an opera composer, despite a certain inclination for the genre. Otherwise he

---

[4] From the audience.   [5] From the audience.
[6] Haydn, CCLN, 113 (*Briefe,* 253).   [7] From the audience.

surely would have applied himself more intensively to opera. In addition, as Kapellmeister at Eszterháza, he had a different role in the society of his time than Gluck or Mozart, and as a result he had different responsibilities. For the most part he composed his operas for the Court and for courtly society, for the immediate requirements of Eszterháza. I believe that this produced for Haydn a different relationship to opera. For him, composing opera was no absolute necessity, it was not a "calling." Unlike Gluck or Mozart, he never felt compelled to participate in the public musical life of the day as an opera composer, let alone to succeed in it. This is reflected both in the form and the design of his operas, as well as in the types of opera he preferred.

BROOK I disagree. On several occasions Haydn revealed his pride in his operas. In 1781 he wrote to Artaria:

> They have not yet heard anything. If they only could hear my operetta *L'isola disabitata* and my most recent opera, *La fedeltà premiata,* I assure you that no such work has been heard in Paris up to now, nor perhaps in Vienna either; my misfortune is that I live in the country.[8]

FEDER The improvised encounter between Ali and Rezia in *L'incontro improvviso* that Mr. Porter mentioned is indeed very different from the one in Mozart's *Entführung.* But was that not the responsibility of the librettist? Haydn simply set to music what the librettist gave him.[9]

PORTER That is really my point. In the last resort, a composer is responsible for his libretto.

BADURA-SKODA Gluck wrote:

> Between two works of a different nature there can be no comparison. If, for example, Piccinni and I had both composed a *Roland,* then people would have been able to judge which was the better; different libretti must necessarily produce different compositions, each of which might be the most beautiful of its kind; in any case *omnis comparatio claudicat* [all comparisons are odious].[10]

That is, when Gluck heard that Piccinni was composing a *Roland,* he refused to set the same libretto. It is not usually noticed that the libretto of Haydn's *L'incontro improvviso* is quite different from that of Mozart's *Entführung* or Gluck's *La rencontre imprévue.* The comparisons are invalid from the beginning. I agree it was Haydn's fault not to make more of this scene, by forcing the librettist to expand the text, or altering it himself.

PORTER The dramaturgy of Haydn's operas can be very fortuitous. For example, in the first act of *L'infedeltà delusa* the tenor, Nencio, goes offstage, be-

---

[8] Haydn, CCLN, 28 (*Briefe, 96–97;* May 27, 1781). For other comments by Haydn on his operas see the autobiographical sketch of 1776 (printed in Haydn, *Briefe;* here, 77), and the letter of May 18, 1784. Cf. Badura-Skoda, "Opera."
[9] Cf. Feder, "Dramatiker"
[10] Gluck, *Correspondence,* 85. This letter to Bailli du Roullet dates from the summer of 1776.

cause the plot requires him to go out of the action for a bit. But five pages later he is singing in the final section of that number, because his voice is required for musical purposes. Again and again Haydn puts musical considerations before good, strong dramaturgy.

STEVEN PAUL[11]   Why were no Mozart operas performed at Eszterháza? It has been suggested that this casts some doubt on the relationship between Mozart and Haydn.

LÁSZLÓ SOMFAI[12]   There is an "insertion aria" by Mozart in an Anfossi opera, I think it is, which was given at Eszterháza, but they did not perform this aria; it was cut. We don't know why.

GEIRINGER Do we have to compare Haydn and Mozart? When people asked, "Who is greater, Goethe or Schiller?," the Goethe family replied, "Let us be glad that we have two such figures and try not to compare them." I think this also applies to Haydn and Mozart.[13]

Problems of Production and Performance Practice

Practical Considerations in Modern Production

PORTER I have seen about twenty different productions of Haydn operas in the last dozen years, and I was closely connected with two of them—*L'infedeltà delusa* and *L'incontro improvviso*—both as translator of an English version and in helping to decide which music should be sung and which music should be left out.

For some fifteen years Haydn's principal activity was running a very busy and distinguished opera company, and he was very familiar with the works of the successful opera composers of his day—Cimarosa, Anfossi, Paisiello, and Sarti were prominent in his repertory at Eszterháza.[14] But as I said earlier, in his own operas he added his own ideas about richness of instrumental texture, about musical form and development, and he constructed them as a series of extended movements designed to show off the skills and personalities of his singers.

Now, where most modern productions of Haydn operas seem to go wrong is that instead of rejoicing in this musical richness, they regret it. The modern director tries to cut them down to the much lower level of the contemporary operas around Haydn's. The arias are nearly always

---

[11] From the audience.   [12] From the audience.
[13] For further discussion of the relationships between Haydn and Mozart, see the concluding Round Table in the section Form and Style. [Ed.]
[14] Cf. the fundamental study Bartha-Somfai, and the revisions and corrections to it in Hárich, "Repertoire." [Ed.]

cut; whole sections are left out. In that way the special, individual glories of Haydn's operas are destroyed; the pieces are mutilated. At the same time, because people feel guilty about cutting what they call the "music," they also cut the recitative—even more severely, to the bare bones of what will explain the plot. (I plead guilty to doing exactly this— but it was ten or twelve years ago; I realize my mistake now.) This further upsets the balance: the theatrical balance, because it does not give the actors the chance to act; the musical balance, because it brings the elaborate numbers too close together, so that the texture does not have the variety of the original. I do not believe that Haydn's operas will appear in their full splendor until they are integrally presented, and until audiences accept them for what they are and not what some modern director thinks they ought to be.

Two practical points come out of this. If the recitative is going to be sung *in extenso,* it has to be given in the language of the audience, for two reasons: it is rather dull to listen to screeds and screeds of dialogue that you cannot understand; but equally important, it does not give the actors the chance to act that they can get only when working in their own language before an audience that understands them.

The other point is that anyone who wants to do a Haydn opera along these lines today pretty well has to make his own performing material. You can't use the stuff available on rental. The Universal edition of *L'infedeltà delusa* gives no German or English versions of the recitatives, just much-abridged spoken dialogue. The Bärenreiter material for *L'incontro improvviso* incorporates all the cuts made by whoever first prepared the material. When we performed that opera, we had to do an enormous amount of copying out and inserting of whole sections of arias to get even a halfway acceptable performing edition.

Discussion

BADURA-SKODA   In the production of *Armida* from which I played an aria there were many disturbing cuts.

FELDMAN   I have been working with several colleagues, including Joel Kolk, on the preparation of a performing edition of *La vera costanza.* Since the only available edition by Schwalbe-Zimmer is in German and has no recitatives, it could not serve for an American performance. We decided to make our own performing edition based on the Paris autograph of 1785.

From the dramatic point of view, the autograph presents a serious problem since the third act appears to be truncated. In Haydn's opening recitative of the third act there are references to things which seem to have been eliminated. Schwalbe and Zimmer could not find a solution to the third act and changed the plot altogether. The published libretto for the 1779 Eszterháza performance coincides with the Paris autograph, but it differs from the libretto to the Anfossi opera of the same name, which is a large-scale work with a full-length third act. As it stands, the third act of the Eszterháza libretto does not really make sense. We are attempting to solve this problem by adding clarifying elements from the Anfossi libretto while changing Haydn's text as little as possible.

During the spring semester of 1975 we had a Haydn Seminar/Festival at the City University of New York under Professor Brook's supervision.[15] At our final session, we performed the scintillating finale to Act I of *La vera costanza* in a new translation by Robert Hess.

TAPED PERFORMANCE: *La vera costanza,* Act I, finale

WALTER I have edited *La vera costanza* for JHW (XXV:8).[16] I am delighted now to see Mr. Feldman's edition too—and to hear part of this magnificent finale.

The libretto that Haydn set was written by Francesco Puttini; it was printed in Vienna in 1779. It represents a shortened version of the original text, which had been set by Pasquale Anfossi and produced in Rome in 1776. The chief differences in the Esterházy libretto are severe cuts, not only in Acts I and II, but especially in Act III, where the first seven scenes have been excised. The author of this adaptation is unknown; it could have been the librarian Bader, who wrote libretti for marionette operas, or the theater-painter Travaglia, who is cited in the Haydn literature as coauthor of the libretto (but this idea derives from an ambiguous remark of Pohl's). Anfossi's setting of *La vera costanza* was very popular; in 1776 alone it was produced in Rome, Florence, Bologna, and Venice. Each time, a new libretto was printed; it appears that none of these is identical either to the original or to any of the others. Some of the cuts in the Esterházy version appear in the libretto printed for the Venice 1776 production. But it was not possible to determine the model for Haydn's text.

In the third act, the Count and Rosina enter, holding letters that the Baroness has forged. In the uncut version, the audience would have been aware since the opening scene of the third act that they were forgeries. But in the shorter version, the action here will seem incomprehensible at first.

All the musical sources for Haydn's *La vera costanza,* incidentally, agree with the shorter text found in the 1779 libretto and in Haydn's 1785 autograph for Paris. Rearrangements and additions did not enter the picture until *Laurette,* the French arrangement for Paris in 1791.

GEIRINGER *Orlando Paladino* also has a "used" text. Haydn bought the sets and costumes of the Guglielmi opera of the same name and apparently decided

---

[15] Cf. MacIntyre, "Seminar"

[16] This volume has appeared in the meantime. Cf. Dr. Walter's Free Paper elsewhere in this volume. [Ed.]

he might just as well set it himself. In one or two cases he employed the first words of the original Guglielmi libretto and then crossed them out and substituted a different text.

BADURA-SKODA   While I was a professor at the University of Wisconsin, I hoped to get Haydn operas performed. But it is impossible for a university to pay the rental fees which Bärenreiter and Universal demand. They treat Haydn as if he were a modern composer—although they do not have to share royalties with him! Fortunately, we can buy the scores from JHW. But without the parts it is a disaster; either we have to spend time, effort, and money to make our own material, or we have to fall back on the old arrangements, which are inadequate.

FELDMAN   The operas that have been recently published by Universal cannot solve the problem either. They translate the arias but not the recitatives. More recently, they don't translate anything at all.

BADURA-SKODA   I agree with Mr. Porter that the *opere buffe* will gain tremendously if they are performed in the language of the audience. This was the eighteenth-century tradition anyway: Haydn's *buffa* operas were widely performed in German in his lifetime. Whether the *opere serie* should be translated is a more difficult question. The extensive *accompagnato* recitatives are very hard to translate.

GEIRINGER   Haydn's operas were performed a great deal in his own lifetime. More than a dozen productions of *Orlando Paladino* were given in his lifetime, most of them in German, with spoken dialogue in place of recitatives. Haydn approved this. The National Library in Budapest owns a score of *Orlando Paladino* in German with his own corrections of the translation.

   Much of the delight of the performance of *Philomen und Baucis* by Mr. Feldman's troupe yesterday would have been lost had it not been in English. As long as Haydn is not universally accepted as a first-rate opera composer, we ought to perform him in the language of the audience, and with spoken dialogues instead of recitatives. Later on, for romance, we might have perfect performances with the original Italian recitatives.

   I might add that when I was a child in Vienna, all the Mozart operas were done only with German texts, often with spoken dialogue. Today, of course, this would be frowned upon.

FINSCHER   Regarding translation, there is a problem. If you translate the libretto, you automatically put the accent on the drama and less so on the music, but if you have the original version performed in a country speaking a different language, you have merely a concert in costumes, as in the case with Handel.

PORTER   I disagree that undue emphasis would be thrown on the drama by translation. I do not believe the arias to be dramatic in a conventional theatrical sense at all. All the drama should be carried on in the recitative, and one cannot have "undue" emphasis on the whole drama.

KNAPP What about Haydn's cuts and revisions? Were these for the better? Every eighteenth-century opera has this problem. The changes that Handel made were often very much for the worse. He was forced to make these changes because he was dealing with a whole new set of singers every season.

BADURA-SKODA   If the singers are good, there should be no cuts; if they aren't, then it would probably be better not to give the opera at all.

GEIRINGER We should constantly keep in mind that Haydn wrote for a small princely theater. There was an unhurried atmosphere. The recitatives could unfold the action, and arias could develop the musical materials. When we perform Haydn today, we need a small ensemble, a small hall, and plenty of time.

DÉNES BARTHA[17]   Haydn did make cuts, but they were in operas composed by other people. I would not dare to comment on how he would have felt about similar cuts in his own operas.

SOMFAI From Haydn's own experience with the singers and the audience, he would cut this aria or that section after one or more performances. And additions or "insertion arias" came into the body of the opera only when it was the premiere or a revival some years later. That is, the operas became shorter and shorter during successive performances. So my proposition would be: at first, make a full or long performance, and then listen to the audience and, step by step, make more cuts. That was Haydn's practice.

NEWELL JENKINS[18]   If you have a small theater and you find yourself swamped with more music than the stage director can possibly use and the action of the drama is going to be held up, you must cut to a certain extent. On the other hand, if you find yourself with more space to cover in the theater than you have music, perhaps you have to repeat a section. But these are practical cuts; they have nothing to do with musicology or with ideals. If your production is going to appeal to the public, you have to cut judiciously, in collaboration between the stage director and the conductor.

PORTER It seems to me dangerous to suggest that a score should be sacrificed to the conception of a stage director, to make an effective "spectacle." The stage director should be the servant of the score, and do the best he can to mount the work as originally conceived.

JENKINS I take this for granted. Otherwise we would hire another stage director.

[17] From the audience.   [18] From the audience.

SOMFAI It is too great a responsibility to make your judgement before the opera is staged. If you begin with a full performance, then you can see how cuts will affect it.

FELDMAN We made a cut in the duet of *Philomen und Baucis,* because our experience from some eighty performances convinced us that, dramatically speaking, it seemed to run long.

DORATI In recording *La fedeltà premiata,* the first in our new series of the complete Haydn operas for Philips, we made no cuts whatsoever in the set numbers. We did shorten the recitatives, but we retained the sense. In the set numbers a miracle occurred: the finales are like a second *Figaro.*

FEDER I agree that it is not good to cut sections out of arias. But these operas are fairly long, and perhaps one should cut certain whole arias, instead of sections of all of the numbers. This would be especially wise in *Armida,* where not all the arias are of such dramatic effect as Armida's "Odio, furor, dispetto," which we heard earlier.

BADURA-SKODA They all have dramatic effect; there is not one bad aria in the whole opera. Even some of Mozart's arias are less dramatic, but they are still beautiful.

FEDER I did not mean that these arias are not beautiful, merely that they are not all as dramatic as "Odio, furor, dispetto."

SOMFAI In Haydn's day, the cuts never damaged the kind of sonata-like principle in an aria. The recapitulation sections, or such sections which created the balance of the form, were never cut. Only shorter sections were removed.

FEDER But there is another problem: coloraturas. Modern singers are not used to singing so many and such long coloraturas as occur in some of Haydn's arias.

PORTER In England, people are brought up singing Handel, who has even longer coloraturas. So these present no difficulty.

DORATI Our singers had no difficulty with the coloraturas.

BROOK If we had a market in this country for Haydn operas with the coloratura, talented performers would spring up from everywhere.

THOMAS I should like to mention a problem in performance practice relating to *Il mondo della luna.* When Haydn composed this opera (1777), he had to write one of the roles for a castrato, the alto Pietro Gherardi, who was engaged at Eszterháza from February, 1776 to January, 1778. Originally Haydn planned the role of the false astrologer Ecclitico as an alto, but then changed his mind and assigned Gherardi the role of Cavaliere Ernesto, who had been a tenor in the first draft. Thus the roles of Ecclitico and Ernesto exist in two different versions: one each for alto and tenor. We can only speculate as to why Haydn exchanged these voice ranges, though I believe that the new versions must have been based on purely artistic considerations. (An external reason might also be seen in that the principal tenor role in the opera was to be given to Guglielmo Jermoli, who had been engaged in March 1777. Two years earlier in Venice, Jermoli had created the role of Ecclitico in an opera by Gennaro Astaritta on the same libretto.) I would also like to raise the problem of how a part that was composed for a castrato should be handled today, that is, what range ought to be substituted for such a part? Does it make sense, for example, in the case of *Il mondo della luna,* to change an alto role into one for baritone?

DORATI I would look at each role individually from the stage-worthiness point of view. You can't make rules. Also, I would consider who is available to sing.

BADURA-SKODA   It is a problem not only in *Il mondo della luna* but also for Volpino in *Lo speziale.* That is a soprano part and can be sung today only by a soprano.

FELDMAN In the long run, we on this panel are not the ones who will decide on the viability of Haydn's operas. I have been overwhelmed by the response of audiences. *Lo speziale* has been compared by some to *Così fan tutte;* people have said that individual arias are among the most extraordinary musical statements they have ever heard. Certainly Mr. Dorati's recording project—stating with *La fedeltà premiata*—is a wise idea because he is starting right in the middle of Haydn's greatest group of operas.

DORATI We were so much impressed by what happened at our recording of *La fedeltà premiata* that now we are working with redoubled energy. Not only we musicians but the recording company has "caught fire" and wants to speed up. We are now doing two or three operas per year. They are recorded in Lausanne, at the small theater, using the Lausanne Chamber Orchestra, one of the orchestras of the Suisse Romande.

SOMFAI In a genre like Haydn's operas, where the complete material is not available in edited form, and where there are problems like those mentioned by Dr. Thomas as well as unfinished acts, and so on, is it possible to make this kind of fantastic effort without the help of specialists? Musicologists should do as much as they can to inform people not only about Haydn's operas, but about the problems in them. Probably one should begin by criticizing recordings that are already available. If we speak up from many directions, the recording companies will, without much ado, agree to use our assistance. It is not too late.

BADURA-SKODA   We should also urge conductors to buy JHW and study these operas. It is so very important to have them performed, even if they are not done well at first. It makes a big difference even for us musicologists. And even Maestro Dorati did not become really enthusiastic about Haydn operas until after performing one.

FRED HEUTTE[19]   I think that there will soon be a great abundance of performing groups in this country that will be able to handle Haydn's operas. In Washington, D. C., within the last couple of years, Catholic University and the University of Maryland have both staged the *Magic Flute*—each school with two separate casts! So there *are* students who can handle this material. What we are still waiting for are the practical editions.

FELDMAN   Ultimately we will reach a point in our knowledge of eighteenth-century opera where Haydn will not have to "compete" with Mozart. At that time we will have a much clearer appreciation of Haydn's contribution. This appreciation will not come solely from people looking at scores in collected editions but also from people hearing performances in English, in French, in German, and in Italian, and loving the music. I think we are going to see this in the next ten years.

[19] From the audience.

Workshop 6

Piano Trios [1]

DONALD J. GROUT, *Chairman*   CHRISTA LANDON
EVA BADURA-SKODA   EDUARD MELKUS
MALCOLM BILSON   SONYA MONOSOFF
GEORG FEDER   VERA SCHWARZ
DINA KOSTON   MARIE ROLF, *Secretary*

Historical Instruments

BILSON   Those of us who are interested in historical performance practice don't
think that "our" way of playing Haydn (or anyone else) is the only
right way. We can't even agree among ourselves! But we would all agree
that using old instruments doesn't guarantee a good interpretation. Some
people who play old instruments haven't the slightest idea how to play
the music, and others who have no idea about old instruments play
marvelously. What old instruments do offer is a way to find out more
than we used to know about Haydn's music.

It is not necessarily true that one should always use the "most highly
developed" instrument of a given type. It's not true that since Mozart
and Haydn and everyone after them wrote for "the" piano, you should
use the modern piano for them. The eighteenth-century fortepiano is not
a "primitive" instrument.[2] Indeed I would say the opposite. Mozart and
the fortepiano had a specially intimate marriage, which you can only
compare to Couperin and the harpsichord, or Chopin and the nineteenth-century piano. The fortepiano influenced Mozart's whole keyboard thinking, partly *because* it was a consummate instrument.

About using old keyboard instruments: if we stick to the instruments
in museums, we won't get anywhere. The only way to make historical
performances of Haydn and Mozart viable will be the proliferation of
good new copies, such as has taken place with the harpsichord. The
harpsichord has become a standard concert instrument since World War
II because people are building new harpsichords all the time; indeed,
harpsichord building is probably the most vital kind of instrument building today. My own copy of the fine 1795 Dulcken fortepiano here in the
Smithsonian Institution has been criticized for "only" being a copy. But
Haydn and Mozart never heard their keyboard music played on 200-

---

[1] The text of this report was prepared by James Webster.
[2] The term "fortepiano" is used in this report to designate eighteenth-century pianos.

year-old instruments! Keyboard instruments sound very different when they get old. Now no important changes have been made to the modern piano since about 1870, but even so, few pianists would want to play concerts on a 100-year-old Steinway.

BADURA-SKODA   Another special type of Viennese fortepiano, which is preserved in an example owned by Paul Badura-Skoda and myself, by Schneider from about 1782, has a percussion stop—a drum attached underneath. Haydn's "Gypsy Rondo," the finale of the piano trio Hob. XV:25 in G Major, and Mozart's "alla turca" finale from the A major sonata K. 331, were meant for this type of instrument. [Example on tape] But an English Broadwood from about 1795, perhaps the very instrument which Haydn played in the Hanover Square Rooms, sounds very different. [Example on tape]

Not every old instrument is a good one. Many instruments by famous makers are inferior to others by relative unknowns, like the Schneider we just heard. So I am also in favor of copies—if they are good ones. The best makers, of course, like the harpsichord builder Skowroneck, don't just copy; they are artists in their own right.

MONOSOFF   The problems with violins are even worse. For example, the Amati that I use as a "modern" violin was first built in the 1670s, but has been modernized; while my "historical" violin dates from 1749. It's difficult to get old string instruments restored properly, because very few extant instruments have not been modernized, so nobody knows what "properly" means. And there are great differences among old violins. One person in England makes new violins to "eighteenth-century" proportions, but his models are either a Stradivarius or a Stainer, which have completely different shapes. And we have the same problems with the bow, as discussed in Workshop 3. So it isn't easy to say whether restored instruments or modern copies are better. And finally, we don't know exactly what kind of instrument was used by Composer X in the year Y.

MELKUS   I have found it difficult to get new violins built on Baroque models. It is hard for any modern builder to match the best violins of Stradivarius. I think the best choice is to restore an old instrument. If you find a modernized old violin that sounds good, it will certainly still sound good after it has been restored to its original state.

As far as bows are concerned, it's just a matter of money. You have to use first-class wood. You can get an excellent new bow modeled on an original one, if you are willing to pay for it.

LANDON   What about the problem of keeping old keyboard instruments in tune?

BILSON   It's true that the fortepiano has a thin, rather delicate soundboard. But it isn't necessarily true that they don't stay in tune. My instrument sometimes stays in tune for weeks, even while I transport it; and other times the sun hits it and it's out of tune in five minutes. You don't expect a violin to stay in tune like a modern piano; why should a fortepiano stay in tune like a modern piano?

LANDON Do modern copies stay in tune better than restored instruments?

TOM WOLF[3] You can never tell. Some restored instruments stay in tune beautifully. And the hardest instrument I ever had to take care of was a harpsichord that I had built myself. It depends on the situation, the players, changes in temperature. . . .

HAROLD ANDREWS[4] When I heard Haydn trios on "original" instruments, I was struck by the importance of the cello. The problem with getting these trios performed is finding a cellist to "sacrifice" himself for them. Yet because the bass of the fortepiano doesn't project like a modern piano, the cello suddenly becomes more bass-like. The balance is completely different; the difference is much greater than the difference between modern and historical string quartets. In the trios, the original instrumentation is basic to the entire contents.

BILSON That means that when playing this music on a modern piano, you must keep the bass much lighter than usual.

KOSTON Another difference is in the damping mechanism. The damping on a modern piano is much quicker and sharper. And low thirds in the bass sound much clearer on the eighteenth-century instruments.

MELKUS Balance is a problem even in nineteenth-century chamber music before the "final" stage of the modern piano—even in Schumann or the Brahms piano quartets.

"Rhetorical" Performance

SCHWARZ "Historical" performance is not just a question of instruments. It's also a question of sensibility and the nature of musical education. Many modern performances mechanically follow the notated musical text. But eighteenth-century theory, for example Marpurg's *Kritische Briefe über die Tonkunst* (1763), conceived of rhythm as including not merely "grammar," but also "rhetoric." By "grammar," they meant the structural aspects of rhythm which inhere in the notes—cadences, phrases and periods, and so on. But by "rhetoric," they meant the expressive aspects of rhythm. This approach was derived primarily from vocal recitative, but it also applied to concerted vocal music and instrumental music.

[3] From the audience.   [4] From the audience.

Marpurg proposes three types of rhetorical signs as an aid to the performer's understanding of the expressive content. The exclamation point signals any unusual expressive effect. The question mark is used whenever a "searching" effect or the illusion of a "question" is desired. (As we know, Haydn often provides a different "answer" from the one his "question" seems to imply.) The dash signals a pause, the effect of exhaustion, or a transition to another "subject."

In ordinary musical notation, these rhetorical effects can only be indicated by rests. Therefore, the performer must determine the correct rhetorical interpretation of the rests in the music. In some of these cases, it may be correct to suspend the meter temporarily.

In Haydn's early keyboard music, rests of this kind, and similar signs like fermatas, are uncommon; later they appear more frequently. (But this doesn't necessarily mean that he didn't want expressive performance of his earlier music.) A performance which systematically follows these rhetorical principles is more meaningful than one which merely reproduces the notated values.[5]

MELKUS Mattheson's *Der vollkommene Capellmeister* (1739) states that music should express all the feelings of the heart, without words. The listener should react to music as he does to a speech. This too applied to instrumental as well as vocal music. Mattheson includes an entire chapter on the "prosody" of music—analyzing it in terms of spondees, trochees, dactyls, and so on. Tartini provided many of his compositions with epigraphs, some of which could actually be sung to the opening theme.

The connection between Mattheson and Haydn is C. P. E. Bach. Precisely this rhetorical spirit informs his music. And Beethoven shared this attitude. Schindler portrays Beethoven as saying that prosody is the basis of all music; that it governs all durations and accents; that without it, one cannot achieve a proper performance. Beethoven taught music to his nephew Karl according to poetic feet. If C. P. E. Bach and Beethoven belong to this tradition, we may assume that it also applied to Haydn.

GROUT Have we any information about how public speakers in this period interpreted and realized the counsels given them by theorists?

SCHWARZ There are discussions of oratory even in musical treatises, for example Koch's *Musikalisches Lexikon* (1802).

BADURA-SKODA I had always been puzzled by the idea that C. P. E. Bach influenced early Haydn. Haydn's earliest sonatas show no trace of his style. What Haydn learned from Bach was expression—from pieces like the "Prussian Sonatas" which make sense only in "rhetorical" performance. In some middle and late Haydn sonatas, a "free" performance is also required.

[5]For a fuller account of this rhetorical interpretation of Haydn's keyboard music, see Schwarz, "Missverständnisse."

SCHWARZ In this period, texts were often used to "interpret" instrumental music. Momigny supplied a text for a Mozart string quartet, and for other Classical instrumental works. And we can understand the expressive content of instrumental music better when we compare it to vocal music.

GROUT Has anyone investigated this kind of "interpretation" with respect to *Lieder* texts? There, the composer has given us his own view, so to speak.

BADURA-SKODA This has been done for Schubert, but not for Haydn.

LUDWIG FINSCHER[6] There are sociological and methodological problems with this approach to expression. You cannot uncritically apply Mattheson or Marpurg to Haydn—to C. P. E. Bach, yes; perhaps to Beethoven, who was trained in this tradition by Neefe in Bonn. But we don't know of a similar tradition in Viennese music before Beethoven came there.

BADURA-SKODA What about Haydn's praise of C. P. E. Bach as his only model?

FINSCHER It's not good enough. We have no theoretical treatises of this kind from Vienna. It begs the question to say that Bach influenced Haydn. That doesn't mean that Haydn's music should be performed the way Bach's should be performed. Marpurg doesn't apply to music outside his own tradition. There are many different traditions in eighteenth-century music; you can't simply equate them.

Let me make three suggestions. First, with respect to accentuation and so on, study the strong neoclassical movement in Viennese literature in the 1780s and 1790s. We know something about Gluck's relations to this tradition, but nothing of Haydn's. Second, look for a musical *potpourri* from late-eighteenth-century Vienna. And third, as Professor Grout suggested, try to find analogies to vocal music in instrumental music. One starting point would be the "recitative–aria" slow movements in Haydn's string quartets.

BADURA-SKODA There were differences between Berlin and Vienna. In the first half of the eighteenth century, Viennese music was mainly Italian. But still, the Viennese were a Germanic people. And there was actually a lot of music theory, especially singing treatises, most of which are preserved only in manuscript. But these treatises discuss many of the same topics as the North German theorists.

Performance Markings in the Autographs

FEDER So far, we have heard about two kinds of evidence that bear on historical performance practice: original instruments, and the writings of theorists

---

[6] From the audience.

and composers. There is a third kind, however: autograph manuscripts, in this case Haydn's autographs. Any conclusions about performance that we draw from this evidence will be free from the methodological problems that Professor Finscher has just raised.

Modern musicians who expect complete performance marks are disappointed with Haydn's autographs. I believe that Haydn took special pains only with unusual markings, which a performer of his own time might not have taken for granted. For example, the Piano Trio Hob. XV:27 in C major begins with three staccato chords, followed by a longer chord; over this last chord, a slur begins.

Example 1. Piano Trio in C major Hob. XV:27, i, 1–2

No modern performer would dream of playing this fourth chord staccato. Nevertheless, Haydn added the express indication "tenuto." I can only suppose that he feared a performer might have continued to play staccato. On the other hand, many markings which are necessary from our viewpoint are lacking in the original sources. The performer must therefore figure out how to articulate all the music, not merely those passages where Haydn has helped him out.

Another example occurs later in the same movement:

Example 2. Piano Trio in C major Hob. XV:27, i, 48–51

[Bilson plays.] Mr. Bilson played this passage with a ritardando; but I'm not sure that's right. Haydn often uses repetitions of a short motive before a return, but you can never be certain that they will be followed by an immediate re-entry of the main theme. The fermata itself is therefore a surprise. But this surprise is lost if you play a ritard.

LANDON Haydn wrote very few performance indications, far fewer than Mozart. His markings are devoted primarily to unusual or exceptional effects. The problem, therefore, is how to perform the "ordinary" passages. That is also a problem for the editor and the student of this music.

GROUT That is an important question in all editions of Baroque and Classical music. For Haydn, part of the problem must be that he worked most of his life in a situation where, if something wasn't clear, he could just tell his colleagues how to play it.

BADURA-SKODA It's also a matter of different generations. Haydn was a full generation older than Mozart. Mozart wrote more complete articulation partly because he grew up at a later time.

MELKUS Before, Mr. Bilson played the first measures of the C-major trio quite lightly. But this tenuto on the fourth note could imply a more expressive performance. It seems to me characteristic of Haydn's late music, almost as if he had reacted to the French Revolution. This late style is more nearly *pathetisch,* akin to Beethoven's increased expressivity. [Plays Piano Trio Hob. XV:28 in E major, beginning.]

Another question is how to play the *Striche* (staccato strokes) on the first three chords. They don't necessarily mean a staccato; they can imply accents (wedges). In the contrapuntal coda in the finale of the "Jupiter" symphony, Mozart wrote *Striche* over the theme, which is in whole notes. This can't mean a staccato, so it must mean accents.

BILSON But here we have short notes—eighth notes and eighth rests. If Haydn had wanted accents, wouldn't he have written quarter notes with *Striche?*

LANDON For the question of accent, it's irrelevant.

BILSON I agree with what Dr. Feder said in this sense: I'm interested in the score. I'm not as interested in what people said about it. But Haydn's scores do lead to great frustration. I can't assume that I should make a ritard only where Haydn notated one. And there are terrific irregularities in the articulation. The best edition of the late trios presently available, by H. C. Robbins Landon, is full of inconsistencies. Are they really in the sources?

FEDER The reliability of any edition depends primarily on the reliability of the sources upon which it is based. Except for slight alterations, it cannot be made more consistent without falsification. I am confident that Mr. Landon made this edition carefully.

BILSON But what should I do about the inconsistencies?

FEDER You must think about them. Perhaps it was not in Haydn's style to be "consistent."

BILSON Well, after thinking about it, I play a ritard in Example 2.

MELKUS It goes further than that. When a performer is on stage, he must *perform.* A concert performance can never be repeated. That's why a good live performance is better than any record.

Articulation

KOSTON   The whole problem of articulation is a rhythmic problem. Some aspects of Haydn's rhythm are different from Mozart's. For example, Trios Nos. 27 and 28, the first movements, have very long measures—4/4, Allegro Moderato—not a true Allegro like Mozart's. The beat is much slower. In this rhythmic context, it's much easier to achieve an expressive rhythm. It's a little like the difference between recitative and aria, or between speech and music. When Mr. Melkus played the opening of Trio No. 28, for example, he lengthened the first quarter note more than you could in Mozart.

What do we know about the pulse in this kind of music? Is there a historical tradition for this kind of instability?

BADURA-SKODA   I'm not sure we should make such broad generalizations about Haydn's rhythm and Mozart's rhythm.

KOSTON   I didn't mean it quite that way. In Haydn's E-minor piano sonata, No. 34, the first movement is a Presto in 6/8, but the second movement is an arioso Adagio in 3/4. Not only the tempo, but the kind of pulse will be different. In the Adagio, you can have a lot of rubato within the beats, even if the beats themselves are quite regular.

BADURA-SKODA   In the eighteenth century, vocal music was considered primary. Instrumental music strove to be as expressive as vocal music—as speech. You didn't try for a constant rhythm, at least not in German-speaking countries.

SCHWARZ   Beethoven once added, in addition to the metronome mark, the sentence "The expression has its own rhythm" ("Die Empfindung hat auch ihren Takt"). Mozart was more Italian, with a different rhythm; Beethoven and Haydn are more rhetorical, like C. P. E. Bach.

MONOSOFF   You have to have freedom as a performer. You must keep the pulse freely, so to speak. And even after we've all read the same treatises, we still play quite differently. What Dina Koston calls "rhythm," though, I would call "accents."

BADURA-SKODA   It's also dynamic. Leopold Mozart says that you have to shorten the second of two notes, and to accent the first note.

BILSON   Both agogic and dynamic accents are part of expression.

MELKUS   There's a danger in searching for the "ideal" performance. A movement is a dramatic development; a symphony or a sonata is a three- or four-act drama. This drama has to develop in the performance. Otherwise, we haven't moved beyond grammar.

Round Table

Problems of a Present-Day Haydn Performance

JENS PETER LARSEN, *Chairman*   PAUL HENRY LANG
BARRY S. BROOK   NEWELL JENKINS
LUDWIG FINSCHER   CHARLES ROSEN
DONALD J. GROUT   JERALD C. GRAUE, *Secretary*

The Question of a "Relevant" Modern Performance

[The discussions in this Round Table were based on the following introductory statement sent by the chairman to the panel members in advance.]

Introductory Statement

After discussions of historical performance traditions [see pp. 185–202] and of specific problems of single groups of works in the workshops, the object of this Round Table will be a general discussion of a present-day Haydn interpretation aiming at a relevant performance on "normal" terms, i.e., without using old or reconstructed instruments. Obviously this performance situation—the normal one in concert and private music making—is characterized by a need for some compromise. Music based on eighteenth-century traditions of style and expression, sonorities and performance, is played 1) on instruments stamped by nineteenth–twentieth-century instrument traditions, 2) by artists trained in correspondingly late performing traditions, and 3) for an audience whose approach to music may vary considerably between "conservative" and "modern" tendencies.

To the artist facing this situation various solutions may present themselves. The easiest—and, I am afraid, rather common—way is to stick to "normal" performance traditions, i.e., the concert hall traditions of the post-Beethoven epoch, consciously or unconsciously ignoring the basic problem of interpretation. **But if the artist—conductor, pianist, violinist—is aware of the problem, how shall he try to solve it?** Can he use the (from a "modern" point of view) somewhat limited performing traditions of the eighteenth century alone as his guiding principle, or must he adjust (more or less) to performance traditions of the nineteenth and twentieth centuries as regards the style of orchestral playing, pianistic traditions, etc.?

If the artist wants to come as close as possible to "unmodernized" per-

275

formance, he will have to face a twofold problem: 1) What was the original performance style like; and 2) how far is it possible to "translate" this performing style into present-day performing, taking into regard the changed performing conditions and approach, but trying not to change the character of the music? **Are there features in the music itself and in performance traditions which may be regarded as rather unchangeable, and others which may be less unchangeable?** In what respect may changed sonorities make some change in performance acceptable or even advisable? And furthermore: is it desirable—or necessary—to try to accomodate to a "present-day approach"?

One more general remark: Changing performance traditions concerning Haydn's music are not just a problem of before and after Beethoven, even if that is the primary problem when we want to compare a present-day Haydn performance to a performance in Haydn's own time. Between the performance traditions in Vienna in Haydn's early years, the 1740s, and his late years, around 1800, is certainly a world of difference which we can only mention here. It needs to be stressed that any evaluation of original performance style must take into regard when, where, and under what conditions the single composition or compositions in question were written.

After discussion of these general questions, the second part of our session should be directed towards specific questions of style and performance. The following list of topics should give problems enough, presumably more than we can manage to take up, but of course further special problems may be added.

The following three basic features may condition and reflect the changes in performance perhaps more than any others: 1) sonorities, 2) dynamics, and 3) relations of tempo and motion (activity). Of course it must be admitted that our knowledge about changes in these factors is limited. Musical notation gives approximate and relative, not exact indications about them; there is an amount of guesswork in our perception, leaving room for rather different interpretations.

May I suggest that we give preference to two domains of Haydn's music: symphonies (orchestral sonorities) and keyboard sonatas, which may serve well as the basis for a discussion of our problems. May I further suggest a small list of works which may serve as examples of the various stages in Haydn's development; of course I don't want to suggest that all of these works should be discussed; they are only meant to help us in narrowing down a basis of characteristic examples.

Symphonies: 3 / 39, 47 / 64 / 88, 104.

Keyboard sonatas: Hob. XVI: 6, 13 / 46 / 21, 36 / 50 (ChL. 13, 15 / 31 / 36, 49 / 60).

Sonorities. a) *Symphonies.* Problems arise from the difference in sound qualities between eighteenth-century instruments and modern instruments, and from the differences in size between Haydn's own orchestra in Eisenstadt and Eszterháza, the orchestras in Paris and London, for which his late symphonies were composed, and modern orchestras of different types (full symphony orchestra, chamber orchestra). **Is it possible in our day's big concert hall and for an audience accustomed to the acoustic conditions of such a hall, to reintroduce a "Haydn orchestra"; and if not, how do the larger dimensions of hall and orchestra influence the impression of the music?** Is it possible to save the more intimate character, the finer details, or will the modern orchestral style tradition change the impression of the Haydn symphony?

b) Keyboard sonatas. Problems arise from the difference in sound qualities between the various types of eighteenth-century keyboard instruments (harpsichord, clavichord, "Hammerklavier") and the modern pianoforte. It is scarcely possible to decide which sonatas were written for one, and which for another instrument, though the changeover to the pianoforte, occasionally around 1770 but more consistently from about the mid-eighties, may become rather evident in various cases. Obviously the modern pianoforte will work well in the case of sonatas like Hob. XVI:35 in C (ChL. 48), with the broken-chord accompaniment which is more characteristic of the popular style at that time (1780) than of Haydn. But in the case of the more linear style in many sonatas, partly with a Baroque flavor, and less dependent on chordal texture: **will it be possible to transfer this style to the modern pianoforte, and how much can be saved of the linearity, the melodic clarity as opposed to the chordal fullness?**

Has the nineteenth-century tradition of pianoforte playing (Beethoven, Chopin, Brahms) raised a barrier between eighteenth- and nineteenth-century performing, or is it possible to find a way to play Haydn—like C. P. E. Bach and others—in a manner rather different from the nineteenth-century expressive style but expressive in its own way, not sensed as "underdeveloped" by the professional pianist?

Dynamics. In eighteenth-century music dynamics serve partly or mainly as a framework for the structural design. A basic dynamic unity, or an immediate dynamic contrast between parts and periods is a prevailing feature. About 1750 "graduated dynamics" (*Übergangs-Dynamik*), like crescendos and diminuendos, appear increasingly, as well as single dynamic effects (*fp, fz,* etc.). In the nineteenth and twentieth centuries a graduated dynamic development becomes normal, with dynamics partly contrasting as effect, partly stressing the design; a basic dynamic unity becomes absurd, unsound (as illustrated in Czerny's edition of J. S. Bach's *Das wohltemperierte Klavier*). A special feature in orchestral dynamics is the impressive collective crescendo in all instruments (Beethoven's *Leonore Overture No. 3*). A performance based on a "modern" approach to dynamics will tend to change the stable dynamic character of a Haydn symphony or sonata into a fluctuating character with added or exaggerated crescendos and diminuendos; and furthermore with added dynamic accents. **How far is it possible to preserve the impression of a "classical," balanced musical development in such a performance?** Is it possible to play even late Haydn symphonies in a "Beethoven tradition" without giving a false picture of the music?

Tempo, Motion. In eighteenth-century music it is normal to use a limited number of tempo types, and—parallel to dynamics—to regard the tempo as a fixed concept, not subject to individual shadings, often still with reminiscences of "tactus" traditions. In the nineteenth century the choice of tempo becomes a means of expression to be administered at will by the performer. In principle the rubato performance (in the sense of the nineteenth century) becomes the standard performance type, with tempo changes whenever desired. **Is it acceptable to have Haydn's music subjected to a performance of that kind?** It is certainly not acceptable in movements based on an unbroken rhythmic motion (like the first movement of Symphony No. 101, "The Clock"). But even in movements of a rather free nature (like certain slow introductions, or a few slow movements with "capriccio" character) it scarcely adds to, but rather goes against Haydn's idea of the musical character.

Another feature to be discussed is the problem of exaggerated tempos. The late Romantic tradition—as practiced still in the early twentieth century—tended to make the fast movements very fast and the slow movements very slow. In recent years this tendency seems to be rather prominent again, not least expressed in a rather fashionable "drive" in the finale which seems to reflect a not very "classical" approach. **Can this be accepted—or even praised—as a relevant Haydn interpretation, or does it represent rather a questionable concession to present-day fashion?**

Behind our discussion, as behind any performance of music, especially music from former times, there is to be found a confrontation, sometimes a conflict, which we are not going to discuss: the dualism of composer and performer. In a way it may be maintained that the work is finished, a definitive work of art, as put down on paper by the composer. But it makes sense also to say that it is only realized as a work of art when performed, when interpreted. The interpretation, the reproduction, makes music a living art. The performing artist will always need free-

dom, but what is called freedom for the artist is often to a great extent
freedom to follow traditions with which he grew up, on which he depends, though he may tend to regard them as born out of his own inspiration. It may seem a threat to the artist's freedom to ask him to put his
own deeply rooted traditions on trial, but in the end it may give him the
feeling of greater freedom, of a less traditional, more timeless approach.

Discussion

LARSEN   The first part of our discussion should deal with a general question.
Music from the eighteenth century—and in our case specifically Haydn's
music—was played originally on instruments partly rather different from
their modern counterparts (e.g., harpsichord and clavichord as against a
modern piano), and the performance was based on performance traditions more or less different from nineteenth- and twentieth-century traditions. Today some specialists try to come close to the original performance, using old or reconstructed instruments, and adopting
eighteenth-century performance traditions as far as possible, but in most
cases Haydn's music is played on instruments of our time, and according
to generally accepted, "normal" performance traditions. Referring to my
introductory remarks, I would like to raise the question of an
"unmodernized" performance, i.e., a performance which, even if not
aiming at a reproduction of the original performance style (including the
use of original instruments), is based on an understanding of the specific
character and style of the music in question, and which consequently
tries to avoid changing its character through later established traditional
performance manners, rooted in music of a rather different nature. How
far is it possible—and desirable—to arrive at such an "unmodernized"
performance?

LANG   Well, do we know how it was done in Haydn's time? That is, isn't this a
sort of a mirage? We can reconstruct old instruments, and we can find
excellent data in contemporary treatises, but we still have to make that
music live somehow, because we still don't know how they played on
those instruments. Today we should play a Haydn symphony, as far as
the instruments are concerned, with a modern orchestra. If we look at
the stylistic questions, that is quite another set of problems. And also, the
ardent champions of historical accuracy in performance practice usually
leave out of consideration the socio-economic factors which are so enormously important. A Haydn quartet on old instruments, that's lovely in
a tiny auditorium, but it won't do in a moderate-sized auditorium for a
larger public.

GROUT   Do you mind if I approach this from the sidelines, from an unpleasant
angle? I object to the use of the word "problem" in such discussion as

this. As Dorothy Sayers pointed out some twenty or thirty years ago, as soon as you say something is a problem you are either consciously or (probably) unconsciously making four assumptions. You are assuming: 1) that the data are all given; 2) that there is an answer; 3) that there is one, and only one, right answer; and 4) worst of all: you are assuming that once you've found the answer the problem is over. Now not one of these conditions holds in any such subject matter as we're discussing today; even used in a figurative sense, the word "problem" is misleading. As to the data: we don't know everything about how these things sounded in Haydn's time, and I don't see how we can ever be sure we know exactly how they sounded, partly because they were sounding in the ears of eighteenth-century people, and those ears are not the same as ours. Suppose we did know. If we could reproduce absolutely accurately what was done in Haydn's time, is that the right answer? Is that the only possible answer? Or are there other possibilities for which arguments could be made just as convincing as for the one of so-called perfect historical fidelity? There is another element in this business of Haydn. He is no longer to us what he was to his contemporaries. Famous in his own time, his reputation went down immediately after his death; Schumann found him not very interesting any longer (1841). Now he is more interesting to us, partly because he is antique. Because our age is an age interested in antiquity, musicologically and musically speaking. And this is part of the "problem." The situation is not as simple as the listing of the data would suggest. That is all I wanted to say now; this is a matter of general warning and skepticism for the whole thing.

ROSEN Regarding the word "problem": I don't think a general answer can be made to such questions. It is only possible to discuss certain works and how they should be played, or perhaps *if* they should be played. Some early Haydn piano sonatas, for example, were not intended for public performance, and the change from private to public performance is as much of a distortion as the change from an old instrument to a modern one. In other words, to go from performance in a room for just a few people to a large auditorium alters the nature of the work. This kind of question, however, can only be answered for a very specific problem, like the pedal indications in the C-major Sonata (Hob. XVI:50; ChL. 60), where the composer has twice written "open pedal" for several measures; in one of these passages, all of the notes are in low register. You can try on the modern piano to reconstruct the sonority of the old piano as much as possible, but that seems to me a makeshift solution. The way to solve such passages is to ask oneself what is the function of the pedal, what the pedal is supposed to be doing, what it is there for in the piece, and then to try to reconstruct that function on the modern piano. In other words, it is the same problem that you get even in famous passages of Beethoven pedaling such as the ones in the last movement of the "Waldstein" Sonata. Is the pedaling there to produce a blur or to hold a long note for a pedal point? The Beethoven pedal is there in order to provide a pedal point over which the rest of the music must go; but Haydn wants a blur. Therefore I think he should be given a small amount of a blur, although certainly not the exaggerated blur that a modern instrument would make. I think it's only for such very small points that these problems can ever be discussed; similarly with the string quartet, where there are still problems in the changeover from ancient instruments to modern ones.

LARSEN I think what Professor Rosen said is very much to the point, but we might perhaps rather come back to some of these questions of detail later.

FINSCHER I came here with the firm intention of being skeptical myself, but after so much skepticism I feel a strong urge to steer in another direction. There are certainly different ways to hear and perform old music, and various degrees of certainty in solving our difficulties. We may reconstruct an original concert of the eighteenth century (original surroundings, instruments, number of listeners, etc.), but as a historical reconstruction for the sake of reconstruction it doesn't really go beyond the surface, because we can't change our ears and minds, our own conditions into which we fall back totally the moment we leave the concert room. On the other hand there are a number of performance traditions and conditions which must be regarded as necessary for the historical understanding of the work—and others which are not. I think old instruments are only necessary to the degree by which the music would be changed if we used modern instruments, and this can only be determined for one work at a time. The baryton trios, with a special sonority and special limitations, may serve as an example, since the baryton has no modern counterpart. I'm not so sure about any instrument which has changed since the eighteenth century but remained essentially the same instrument, which has changed in detail, perhaps in parts of the sonority, but not in principle. And to this I think even belong the violins, even after the splendid demonstration of Miss Monosoff's quartet in Workshop 3.

BROOK I may be taking issue with some of the basic precepts enunciated here, and I will do so by using Professor Grout's four requirements for a problem as a scaffold. I don't care whether you call it a problem or a question about how Haydn's music may be performed today, but you spoke of data, you spoke of whether there is an answer or not, whether there is only one answer, and whether if you have it, is the problem over. I would like to suggest that we look at these four elements from the point of view of the historian. The historian's job is to gather and establish the facts. As I said in the previous Round Table, quoting Collingwood, we have only a strictly limited quantity of evidence concerning any historical question. Therefore, we have an answer: it is never complete. The answer that we have is the answer based on those facts that have been gathered and established up to that time. We must never give up our skepticism—that is part of what the definition of a historian must include. Now coming to the question of one answer or more than one answer. There is no one answer; there are no single answers to questions such as these. In one of the prior panels I said something to the effect that it is immensely useful, valuable, and lovely to hear the same works performed under appropriate acoustical conditions by musicians who are committed to old instruments and have lived with them for long enough to make them part and parcel of their very being, and to hear them play the same piece that may be done in a large hall with steel strings and nine-foot Steinways and so on. Both have their validity; both can learn from one another. On the question of whether or not the problem is over: the problem is never over; history doesn't work that way. And the question of how to perform Haydn is never over; we are constantly attempting to learn more, to improve, to polish, and to end up as each generation comes with perhaps some closer understanding of how it may have been played in the past on the one hand, and how better to adjust contemporary performances on the basis of what we have learned by greater exploration of the earlier music on the other.

JENKINS Well, I think virtually everything has been said that can be said about this "problem." The only thing that I can add is from the standpoint of the performing musician. The musician's responsibility to the score is to be as faithful as is physically possible. It is his job to listen to his betters and his more educated colleagues in the musicological field and learn from them, throwing out whatever they may hand him if it doesn't fit in with his own convictions. He must be convinced by them, but he must follow his own direction. He must take into consideration not only that he is performing for a group of scholars or a group of colleagues, such as we all are here today, but he must also remember that he's playing for a greater audience. He must consider the time in which he's playing; and if he can fulfill his function as a performer by satisfying his own innermost, soul-searching need as a performer to do the very best he can by the composer, then he has made one step in the right direction. And he should never stand at that one point for more than ten minutes. He should keep on growing all the time. And I beg my performing colleagues to consider this. I also beg the musicologists to help us reach this goal.

LARSEN May I make a few remarks to sum up after these introductory statements by the panel. Until now our discussion has dealt primarily with the problems concerning an "original" performance style. I think we all agree about the limitations of possibilities here; we cannot accept an advertisement of concerts telling us: "you will hear this music exactly as it was played in Haydn's time." However, I think most of us are aware of the importance of the work carried out by musicians specializing in "original" performance style. We may not agree in the evaluation of such concerts, which to some of us seem very interesting, to others apparently "historical" in a bad sense, but we probably all agree that it is helpful for the artist who performs eighteenth-century music under present-day conditions to know—as far as possible—how the composer expected it to be performed. In which ways this may influence his own performances is just the problem this Round Table is about.

LANG I'd like to join Professor Finscher in his definition. I think that all instruments that have reached their final development, like the harpsichord or the recorders, should be used. But I would use the violin family as it is constituted today. Unless there is an essential difference in the quality of an instrument, I would always use the modern version. But you can't use a guitar for a baryton.

ROSEN I don't think that is a tenable proposition. Historically speaking it puts the later history of an instrument and the change in sonority on a purely mechanical basis; it projects the future history of the instrument back into the eighteenth century, which seems to me a mistake. The difference in sonority between the violin in the middle of the eighteenth century and the violin in the nineteenth century is perhaps not very great. But the difference between the pianos and the harpsichords of the 1760s is not very great either. They both have a certain clarity and lightness and lack the heavy bass of a modern Steinway. I am not for a moment questioning the value of performances on old instruments. I merely thought that the discussion was to be directed to what you do on modern instruments. I cannot agree with the distinction between instruments that change and instruments that do not change.

FINSCHER I don't think we will be able to get any further with this question. For me the principal problem is, since we are concerned with bringing music to life, which instruments are necessary for the music itself? And I think there is much more necessity to use old instruments for sixteenth- and fifteenth-century music than for eighteenth-century music. But I would advocate playing the piano works of Debussy on a French instrument of his time, because here the sound of the instrument is an integral part of the composition itself. Wherever this is not the case, I'll say, just take those instruments which are easiest to play. These are certainly not the historical instruments in many cases.

LARSEN Professor Rosen was quite right in stressing that my idea with this Round Table was not so much to discuss these differences in character of the instruments but to face the fact that many pieces of music composed for old instruments will be played on modern ones; how far should we go to adjust our way of performing them to the modern instrument, knowing that the way they sounded formerly may have been rather different? To Professor Finscher's words about the sound of the instrument as an integral part of the composition one additional remark only: I don't think you can get really close to C. P. E. Bach's keyboard compositions without knowing the clavichord.

BORIS SCHWARZ[1]   If you listen to some performances made as recently as between forty and fifty years ago (Mengelberg, Thibaut), they sound totally antiquated to us. And these belong to our own century. It is much more problematic to suppose that you are reconstructing Haydn's kind of playing on these old instruments with the old bows. Is our modern equipment of the violin not capable of playing Haydn lightly and in an extremely elegant way? I must say as a violinist: it can be done, it is being done.

ROSEN   Those recordings of Mengelberg and Thibaut are already beginning to seem less old-fashioned today; in fact, they have a lot of admirers.

Specific Problems of Performance Style

Sonority: Symphonies

LARSEN   After our discussion of more general questions, we should proceed to specific questions of style and performance. Our first point of discussion should be the question of sonorities concerning the symphonies. Haydn's music hall in Eszterháza seats something like 150 or at most 200 people, I think, and here in the Kennedy Center we have a concert hall with 2750 seats. The acoustics are fine. You can play a quartet, you can play a symphony, and it comes out very nicely. But still the acoustic surroundings are very much changed. Haydn's late symphonies were composed with an orchestra in mind which might comprise 40 or 50 or even a few more players, but all the other symphonies (until about 1785), not just the very early ones, were written for an orchestra with scarcely more than about twenty people. How does it work when we put them up in the big concert hall? Should we prefer a full symphony orchestra of 80 or 100 players? Or shall we replace it with a small chamber orchestra, even if the hall is much more spacious than Haydn's hall, and acoustically quite different? May we perhaps put this question first to the conductor in our panel, Newell Jenkins?

[1] From the audience.

JENKINS I've toured extensively with a chamber orchestra in Europe and in this country. To the question: is it possible to use a Haydn orchestra in our day's big concert halls? The answer is absolutely yes, without a shadow of a doubt. It depends completely upon the acoustics of the hall, not on its size. And to the second question: is it possible to save the more intimate character and the finer details if you use a larger orchestra? No matter how finely trained the orchestra is, these finer subtleties will be lost. If we can approach as closely as possible, as far as we know, the size of an orchestra as used by Haydn, and use the most superlative musicians we can find, we probably will come up with a very satisfactory solution.

BROOK The situation and the musicianship of the director should provide the answers to all these questions. As Mr. Dorati said in the symphony workshop: I don't go by theories; I examine the situation and try to solve it in the best interests of the music. If you have a notion of what the music should sound like, and you go after it with the best intentions, I think that's the only solution in today's changing concert scene.

LARSEN I am always a little alarmed when I hear a good musician say that what has to decide is musicianship. We all know that behind it is to a great extent the tradition he grew up with, and what is felt as the musician's inner voice is largely the reflection of a tradition, which he depends on in a positive or negative sense.

BROOK There's a lot I was presupposing: an awareness of the theorists, of the early instruments, of possible articulation and sonority problems, and that I would take for granted. And then the musician—the conductor—has to do the best with what he has.

FINSCHER I agree with Mr. Jenkins that the intimate character of early or middle Haydn symphonies is linked to the sound of a small orchestra; but what are the finer details which are lost if a large orchestra is used, and are they really necessary for an adequate impression of the symphony?

JENKINS I think with the preponderance of a very heavy bass, and a thick string sound, you are going to lose some of the delicacy, the precision, the color, the sound. I have yet to hear a performance of such a large orchestra that is completely satisfactory. It may sound very beautiful, but it is not the sound I am looking for, and if one is looking for one particular kind of sound as a musician, one must know how to go about getting it.

FINSCHER Certainly, but is this specific quality of sound you are looking for really essential to the composition?

JENKINS I might answer by referring to two performances we have heard during this conference: the *St. Nicholas Mass* by a college choir and orchestra, and *The Seasons* by the National Symphony and a large chorus. What you liked and what you didn't like is perhaps a question of your own personal taste.

LARSEN May I add a remark to this discussion. I think that Dorati's recordings of Haydn's symphonies are so satisfactory not least because he had an orchestra of medium size, not a big orchestra, and not a very famous one. I've been to one of the recording sessions, and it was a great pleasure. If Mr. Karajan had made these performances with his Berlin orchestra, they would undoubtedly have been superior in some ways, but perhaps almost too perfect. The smaller and certainly less prominent orchestra impressed me, because they played with such enthusiasm and understanding, serving the music, not making the music serve the orchestra.

ROSEN May I stress what I said before, that it depends entirely on the given symphony, but it is not just a question of what orchestra Haydn had when he wrote the symphony. Haydn once said that he wanted only three bass instruments: one violoncello, one bassoon, and one double bass for the performance of his symphonies.

LARSEN That's not quite correct. He said that he would prefer one cello, one bass, and one bassoon to six basses and three cellos because the sound comes out with more clarity. But he didn't mean to say that was his ideal. (And he did not really talk about symphonies but referred to his cantata *Applausus* [1768].) He stressed his preference for a clear bass.

ROSEN He would surely not have said that about his late symphonies, written for a much larger orchestra. There are even some earlier symphonies, the more brilliant ones, particularly those in C with trumpets, which would certainly benefit from an orchestra larger than the one Haydn had in Eszterháza; I don't think we should just play the London symphonies with an orchestra like the Salomon orchestra, but think more in terms of the Viotti orchestra, which was much larger and more satisfactory. However, it really is a problem for each given symphony and cannot be decided mechanically by following the original performance. It goes still on the basis of the style of the symphony.

LARSEN I think there was a close connection between the style and the size of the orchestra. In Eszterháza it was something between a real orchestra and large-scale chamber music. But when he wrote for London he had orchestral sonorities in mind.

ROSEN Haydn's ideas are certainly—as stressed by Professor Mahling—clearly related to the orchestra he had, but a larger orchestra would no doubt have been welcome for a number of pieces.

LARSEN You refer to the "intrada symphonies" in C major with trumpets, but I think they sound beautiful also with a small orchestra: the church music tradition would very often have a small ensemble with trumpets and drums, and I don't think the trumpets point to orchestral sonorities as a latent intention.

CHRISTA LANDON[2]   I think great music cannot be destroyed by any wrong performance. But in the early symphonies, where you have the special eighth-note bass in fast movements, you cannot use more than at most two basses, otherwise you have a disgusting sound. And since you still need a harpsichord, I think you cannot use a big orchestra if you want a typical texture. With the later symphonies it is completely different. I am not at all a purist, but I think it would just ruin the music.

LANG   Two basses and four cellos will support quite an orchestra. But I miss a definition. What is a "Haydn orchestra"? The twenty-one or -two gardeners and horsegrooms (and a few professional strings) that made up Haydn's orchestra at Eszterháza—it's not a norm. He had to put up with it.

LARSEN   No, he had a very good orchestra; he had some players who would be in the first rank anywhere in Europe. The gardeners were before his time. He weeded them out.

LANG   But at the same time the *Hofkapelle* in Vienna was much larger than Haydn's, and there were many good-sized orchestras elsewhere.[3] I don't advocate a sizable orchestra for those early symphonies, but certainly one that is bigger than twenty-one.

ROSEN   In very big orchestras you do not necessarily lose fine details; it depends on the performance. You may lose a great deal else, but I still remember that the only performance of the Jupiter Symphony in which I can remember hearing every note of the bassoon was Toscanini's.

SCHWARZ   If, perhaps, Haydn would have thought of performing any of his earlier symphonies in London (which I think he did not), would he have used a larger orchestra to perform his old works? Is there any evidence that he ever returned to earlier symphonies?

LARSEN   Apparently he was not very interested in taking up earlier works again. There is the case of Symphony No. 60, composed c. 1775, which the empress wanted to hear some twenty-five years later, about 1800. Haydn of course took it up, but not without expressing a certain discontent with this old stuff, "den alten Schmarn." He would certainly not have performed it again except for this special reason.

IRVING LOWENS[4]   I would like to touch for just one moment on a point that Mr. Jenkins made, his definition of the role of the performer in relation to musicologists: the performer's duty is to play the notes, the right

[2] From the audience.
[3] Cf. the Round Table on *Historical Performance Conditions and Traditions.* [Ed.]
[4] From the audience.

notes, to learn from the musicologist. The type of assemblage that we have here is at any rate potentially a very important one because it enables the musicologist for the first time to circumnavigate the generation or two generations that it takes before the knowledge which he assembles painstakingly in libraries finally gets to the practical musician. When you put the musicologist together with the performer in the same environment, and you give the two an opportunity to discuss the same work together, you can circumvent this and you have a flash of electricity. Normally there is a separation between the performer and the musicologist, and a conference of this sort enables us, to a certain extent, to do away with that separation for a short time. Especially when it has a sharp focus, such as we have here on the problems of Haydn.

Sonority: Keyboard Sonatas

LARSEN Our next topic is the question of original and present-day performance of the piano sonatas. As far as I see, there are at least three principal points to discuss: 1) the types of keyboard instruments used by Haydn; 2) the stylistic variation in Haydn's sonatas viewed in connection with the various types of instrument; 3) the difference in performance style between Haydn's time and our time. A careful examination of the keyboard instruments used by Haydn has been made by Dr. Horst Walter. It would seem as if the clavichord has played a very modest role in his music performance; rather it may have served as a working tool for him when composing. The real problem is the difference between harpsichord and pianoforte style. How far is it possible to distinguish between works intended for one or the other of these two types of instrument? Let me name two features which may count in this respect. The very characteristic dynamic indications in the C-minor Sonata No. 20 (1771) seem to point to the pianoforte (Hammerklavier), but the two series from 1773–74 and 1776(?) don't follow this lead, and only the sonatas from about 1780 and later might seem to indicate a final turn to the pianoforte, confirmed by Haydn's letter to Artaria about his acquisition of a Schanz pianoforte in 1788. And as a second characteristic feature: the texture characterized by broken-chord accompaniment in the left hand (No. 35 in C and No. 37 in D [both 1780]) also seems to reflect the pianoforte style rather than the harpsichord tradition. I am afraid many piano players and teachers stick to these and a few other sonatas which come closer to traditional pianoforte style, as known from Mozart's sonatas, and neglect many very fine Haydn sonatas, stamped not least by a two-part setting and a more linear character. In these sonatas the use of a modern instrument will present more of a problem, because the modern piano favors the chordal more than the linear texture. And to this difference in style of composition comes a difference in performance style.

The pianist of our time will—more or less consciously—follow a number of performance traditions, based on nineteenth- and twentieth-century expression, but mostly considered obligatory for all pianoforte playing. Is this performance style the right one also in the case of the more characteristic Haydn sonatas?

ROSEN As far as I'm concerned there's no problem in playing any of the Haydn sonatas on a modern piano. Of course, you have to be careful of the sonority in a few places. I don't find it difficult to play two-part writing on the piano; at least I don't find it disagreeable to hear that kind of thin texture on the piano. The only two problems that you have with Haydn piano music are dynamics—which should come up later—and the balance of instruments in the piano trios. In the eighteenth century the clear and slightly metallic sound of the piano cuts through the much less brilliant sound of the violin, whereas in the nineteenth and twentieth centuries the violin cuts right through anything the piano is doing, if the piano is not very loud.

LARSEN I don't think I can agree about the keyboard sonatas as presenting no problems. If you compare the performance of one of the sonatas in a rather linear style on the clavichord and on the piano, there is a striking difference. On the clavichord (or harpsichord) such a two-part texture stands out as a self-contained community. But played on the piano, it is not quite sufficient.

ROSEN The damping of the sound is very much less efficient on the old instruments than on the piano; there is a kind of sonority that after the notes have been released continues to chase itself around inside the instrument, and which is quite audible. But if you play it dryly on the piano, it is rather disagreeable because piano dampers cut the note off immediately; for this reason one must use the pedal constantly, avoiding a blur, but realizing an adequate resonance from the instrument itself.

LARSEN That is one side of it, but not the whole thing. If you take, e.g., the Sonata Hob. XVI:19 in D (ChL. 30), the slow movement, with the changes between high and low register, the contrast comes out clearly on a clavichord, but much less pronouncedly on a piano. There is a fine characterization of the individualities of the two parts, which cannot be given the same way on the piano.

ROSEN Well, that suggests only that the individuality of part-writing on the clavichord is achieved by the instrument, whereas the pianist today has to provide it by balancing the voices himself.

LARSEN Yes, but it will not be quite the same. It has to do with overtones, too, I believe. To my ear something gets lost in the modern instrument.

ROSEN But something gets lost in all Haydn piano works, even in the late sonatas.

LARSEN At least I am very glad to hear you say you play them without problems on a modern instrument.

ROSEN Without anxiety, anyway.

[A question from Boris Schwarz gave rise to a discussion of the meaning of the term "clavier" in the eighteenth century. It was agreed that the word must be taken to mean keyboard instrument in general, not specifically the clavichord. At the same time it was stressed that very many indications of instrument on title pages of printed editions are rather misleading, especially the indication "cembalo (o pianoforte)" at a late time, when only pianoforte could be intended (Beethoven, Op. 27).]

Dynamics

LARSEN Our next question is about dynamics. Haydn's fifty years or so as a composer coincide with the development of a previously unheard-of stressing of dynamic effect, leading from the rather static use of dynamic graduation in late Baroque to the "modern," much more expansive and much more dominating dynamics in Beethoven's orchestral style. Do we serve Haydn's music well if we take this "modern" orchestral style for granted in the performance of Haydn's symphonies?

LANG It all depends on what we call Beethoven's tradition, which we know as little about as we know of Haydn's tradition. If the way Mengelberg played Beethoven was the Beethoven tradition thirty or forty years ago, then ours is a totally different one. And one point more: we are told by almost every theorist to try to let the instruments imitate the human voice. If that is so, graduated dynamics were known since times immemorial, and I think that the whole terraced dynamics idea is just a fable.

LARSEN But what about the harpsichord and the organ, where you have such contrasting dynamics?

LANG I know, but I am speaking now of instrumental music.

LARSEN It is certainly not my invention that a piece like *Leonore Overture No. 3* represents a new dynamic approach. What you experience in the first part of the Allegro is not melodic structure, but a dynamic development, quite different from anything in Haydn's orchestral style.

LANG Well, I don't know, but you will find it in Mozart, which is the same period.

LARSEN Not anything like that.

ROSEN Not on that level, but I think the problem is that there is very little of that in Haydn, mainly because in this particular sense (and in this sense alone), one could say that Haydn does not think on as large a scale as Mozart. There are a number of places in Mozart's piano concertos and in his operas where there is an obvious tendency of that kind, as in the famous examples in the D-minor Concerto K. 466, or the last page of K. 450, the B-flat-major Concerto. A crescendo is a very natural thing, but it is true that there is almost nothing of that sort in Haydn.

LARSEN I think you are right, but don't forget that there is almost a generation between Haydn and Mozart. Haydn never gave up having inside himself some Baroque feeling. We are here just to try to find out about the specific Haydn tradition.

ROSEN But where have you heard, say, a conductor impose a huge crescendo of that sort on a Haydn symphony?

LARSEN Not quite as much, but to some extent a crescendo for the sake of the crescendo. In his late works Haydn would certainly go further in the way of a dynamic expansion, yet still be very far from Beethoven's effect. In his early works he would almost never use a dynamic effect of that kind; in Symphony No. 1 he apparently imitated Stamitz once, and found out that that was a bad idea, so he did not do it again.

JENKINS I don't think we find in Haydn any long passage with one huge crescendo running through it, but I think it is absolutely true that the crescendo exists in Haydn. It exists in a much smaller way, and it is mounted distinctively. The actual crescendo takes place only over a very few notes, and the phrasing is the principle, the articulation is the main thing, which gives you the impression of a crescendo, not the fact that the steamroller is running down the track, pushing a bulldozer, pushing everything ahead of it.

LARSEN There was in Haydn no doubt some sort of crescendo–diminuendo on a small scale, but not as an intentional building up, a dynamic expansion. Crescendos and diminuendos are there to contribute to the general expressiveness; they are servants, not masters.

[The discussion changed to the question of dynamics in the keyboard sonatas.]

LANDON I think musical notation is a very primitive means of putting down music. The connection between one note and the other one is terrifically important. What makes music alive is this breathing relationship; the free interpretation is up to the artist, certainly, but it is within the music and can't be put down on paper anyway. Otherwise, I might make some sort of addition in an edition, but it would be very difficult be-cause I would change from one day to the next. Different interpretations are all right, I think, if they are convincing.

FINSCHER I think the implication of what you said was that to a certain extent Haydn intended to leave the question of dynamics open.

LANDON Certainly.

FINSCHER To leave it to the performer. And this may be further suggested by string-quartet traditions: a very distinct and complicated, complexly no-tated phrasing and articulation is even in Haydn's string quartets not the rule, the rule being some level of interpretation consciously left open to be filled in by the performance.

ROSEN Is it left open or is it perhaps obvious? Or would have been obvious? Surely, some part of what is being left open is fairly obvious and would have been interpreted in a relatively conventional way by everybody.

BROOK And some are very contradictory in parallel passages. This is true in a number of Haydn autographs, which present a different side of the pic-ture, it seems.

LANDON Also Mozart and Schubert.

ROSEN And in fact every composer.

LARSEN I think you are expressing now the specific views of the performer: there should be no binding rules, and everybody who plays shall do it his own way. I don't think that is right.

BROOK In the question where you have contradictory information about articu-lation and dynamics, etc., you examine it very carefully; you come to a conclusion that makes reasonable sense with the evidence at hand, and you apply your musicianship not in a free, emotional way to what you see in front of you, but to the facts as they exist. I think that's a perfectly reasonable solution.

LARSEN It sounds so, but once again: the musicianship we apply today is one that has gone through the nineteenth century. The musicianship Haydn used was quite another sort, and I think all possible crescendos and the like were on a much smaller scale.

BROOK I agree, but there is also an informed musicianship, an intelligent applica-tion of knowledge of eighteenth-century performance traditions.

LARSEN There certainly is, but in general I think one must still warn against the unreflecting application of nineteenth-century performance traditions.

ROSEN Professor Larsen, you are really, without realizing it, I think, pleading for the use of the eighteenth-century instruments!

LARSEN No, no.

ROSEN You complain about exaggerated dynamics. I would like to make the opposite complaint. Many pianists are quite conscious now that a *fortissimo* in the eighteenth century is not nearly as loud as later, and I have heard a performance of a Mozart sonata in which a *fortissimo* would at no time go above the level of what I would consider a *mezzo-forte*. When Mozart wrote *fortissimo* he meant that the pianist should play as loud as he could at that time, but if you play a piece by Mozart or Haydn as loud as you can on a modern Steinway, it sounds terrible. So we must try to make it sound as if we are playing as loud as we can, but actually we must secretly hold back. On a piano of the eighteenth century *fortissimo*, of course, presents no difficulty at all; you just bang.

LARSEN I think Mozart stopped when it sounded awful. If you try a real *fortissimo* on one of these wonderful old instruments, such as the Walter pianos from Mozart's time in the Music Instruments Collection in Vienna, you will find that there is a limit of loudness, if beautiful sound is aimed at. Mozart had a great sense of beauty, and I don't think he would overstep that limit.

ROSEN I don't know enough about these eighteenth-century instruments, but I am very skeptical about the ones that have lasted; I wonder whether the power and the range of sound has not varied, or at least slightly diminished over two centuries. I'm not exactly sure whether anybody could answer that.

PAUL HELM[5] I was just wondering: we are taking the modern Steinway as something absolute, but from practice we know it is not. Recently my institution (McGill) bought two new nine-foot Steinways off the assembly line, and they are as different as night and day. One of them is the most beautiful, quasi-eighteenth-century-sounding instrument I've heard. It has a very soft bass, very malleable, very subtle, and perfect for this repertoire. The other is completely different. It's good for Bartók or something like that. We can't take the modern instruments as something absolute. There are incredible differences between them.

Tempo and Motion

LARSEN Our last point of discussion should concern problems of tempo and motion. I think we agree that this is a very important question, but unfortunately we have very little fixed, objective knowledge to start out from. Quantz has often been quoted almost as a gospel in this field, but what he says about tempos seems to me rather theoretical and too much simpli-

[5] From the audience.

fied, and I think many ill-founded conclusions have been drawn from it. It has been a pleasure for me to get to know Isidor Saslav's fine dissertation about tempo problems in Haydn's quartets, which demonstrates a most valuable combination of musicianship and scholarship.

As far as I see, the problems of tempo in a present-day performance of Haydn's music must be discussed from two angles: 1) the possibility of fixing a more or less relevant speed (metronome number) for Haydn's own general tempo indications (Allegro, Moderato, Largo, etc.); and 2) the question of using tempo rubato (in a nineteenth-century sense) in performances of Haydn's music.

It was stressed just before by Professor Lang (in connection with our discussion of dynamics) how much orchestral performance had changed in the course of thirty or forty years. I have experienced similar changes in tempo traditions in about fifty years of concertgoing. In my youth Late Romantic traditions were still at work, leading to very pronounced contrasts in tempo between quick and slow movements. Then after World War I, or more specifically around 1930, in connection with the renewed interest in Baroque music, I believe (and probably also as a reaction to the Late Romantic tradition), a sense of more balanced, less exaggerated tempos arose, which was certainly more in accordance with traditions from Haydn's time. In the last ten or fifteen years, however, it has often seemed to me as if tempo traditions have once again become like those of around 1920, not least with a tendency to speed up the finale beyond reason. You end up with a performance which does not give you a clear picture of the musical development and details, but rather an impression of speed for speed's sake.

GROUT *À propos* all these questions, I think we tend to forget that the eighteenth century was primarily a century of song. The famous artists of the eighteenth century were the singers. Therefore the ideal of performance must be marked by moderation in dynamics, by moderation with regards to extremes of tempo, by all these things. Instruments can play terrifically fast, but there was a limit to the speed with which even an accomplished castrato singer could sing a coloratura passage, and similarly with regard to dynamics. It seems as though we could get some kind of an intuition about a good many of these subjects, even in the case of instrumental music, by considering that simple fact.

LARSEN I think that what you say goes along with a statement allegedly made by Haydn on occasion: if you want to know whether a melody is good, sing it.

FINSCHER I would subscribe to this in general terms, but with one limitation: the influence of rhetorical traditions on instrumental music. The best-documented examples of this are the two "Malinconia" movements of the early Beethoven (slow movements of Op. 18, No. 6, and Op. 10, No. 3); at least for the pianoforte movement, Beethoven wanted it to be played with seven tempo changes, according to the rhetorical character of the sections of the music. Obviously, it ought to be played in this fashion, though the general tempo description is Adagio, nothing more.

ROSEN Largo—Largo e mesto. Actually Beethoven said: You must make seven tempo changes but none of them should be audible to the average listener; only the connoisseur must know that they have been made. That remark has often been cited as an excuse for the most outrageous tempo changes in a piece of Beethoven, though he wanted them to be perceptible only to the connoisseur.

FINSCHER Another point is the famous reported remark of Haydn: "Ich habe öfters versucht, in meinen Symphonien moralische Charaktere darzustellen." I think this is only understandable against the background of the rhetorical tradition; and so I am not quite sure whether we can really say—what you said, Professor Larsen—that we ought to regard tempo as a fixed concept. I believe that there are movements in which the rhetorical influence can be detected, and where we have to reckon with a kind of tempo rubato, as another exception to the rule.

LARSEN Could you give examples of what you are thinking about?

FINSCHER Well, for instance, some slow movements in string quartets, which are built up like an operatic scene, and other forms analogous to vocal forms, of which I think there are a lot; in movements of this type we should be aware of the possibility of a kind of tempo rubato.

BROOK I would like to raise the question of general tactus for the length of a piece. In the discussion of "La Reine" in Workshop 4 there was a good deal of feeling that there was a clear-cut tactus, or that there should be a relationship between the introduction and the fast section. Perhaps one can go still a little further. It has appeared to me, and certainly to many others as well, that one can look at many eighteenth-century multimovement pieces, perhaps in particular those of Haydn, as having a tactus relationship from one movement to the next, making the unity of an entire piece that much more powerful.

JENKINS I do not believe that there is a tactus relationship between the various movements of a symphony, but between a slow introduction and a succeeding allegro there very definitely and almost invariably is. You will find it similarly in Masses of Sammartini, and even down to Cherubini. So I think this is a basis we could say started sometime in the early eighteenth century and goes on even in the early nineteenth century.

LARSEN We will have to end our discussion now, though I am afraid we did not arrive at any definitive solutions of the difficult and complicated problems we have discussed. However, the idea of this conference was not that we should be forced to present premature solutions, but that we might survey the field of Haydn research and try to help delineate the work which has to be done. I hope that our discussions have contributed to this general task.

Free Papers

Performance Practice in Haydn's Works for *Lira organizzata*

CHRISTOPH-HELLMUT MAHLING

In December 1790, Haydn delivered a collection of notturni for two *lire organizzate* and other instruments (Hob. II:25–32) to Ferdinand IV, King of Naples, on the occasion of the latter's visit to Vienna. The composer probably received the commission no later than 1788, after having already composed (likewise for Ferdinand) five concertos for two *lire organizzate* in 1786 (Hob. VII:1–5). The Austrian Ambassador, Norbert Hadrawa, had succeeded not only in awakening the king's enthusiasm for this instrument, but in encouraging him to play it himself. Hadrawa himself taught the royal pupil, and he played the second part in works for two *lire organizzate*. We may also have his initiative to thank for the fact that composers like Adalbert Gyrowetz, Ignaz Pleyel, Johann Sterkel, and Joseph Haydn as well composed concertos and divertimenti for this rather curious instrument.[1]

The *lira organizzata* was a kind of hurdy-gurdy, whose guitarlike body was substantially deeper than usual, because it had to accommodate not only the wheel, but also a bellows, which could be operated either through the turning of the wheel or by means of a leather strap wrapped around the right foot of the player. The bellows

was connected to two rows of pipes, one next to the other, on the surface; the pipes are graduated like panpipes. When the player stopped the melody strings, apertures in the corresponding pipes were opened by the tangents that had been depressed. Because the pipes were coupled to the tangents of the melody strings, they had the same range as the normal hurdy-gurdy, two octaves. The melody strings produced the same pitches as the pipes in the lower of the rows. The other row was tuned an octave higher, so that the sounding of a string and a pipe always produced notes an octave apart. . . . The player could make strings and pipes sound simultaneously, but he also could silence either pipes or strings. In the latter case the strings were moved away from the wheel by means of a lever that could be activated without interrupting the performance.[2]

---

[1] See Hadrawa's letter to Sterkel of October 12, 1785, printed in Scharnagl, *Sterkel,* 84. In this letter Sterkel was asked to compose "three concertos for two *lire organizzate* for the King of Naples, one in the key of C, the second in F, and the third in G."

[2] Bröcker, *Drehleier,* I, 164.

Besides the melody strings, there were, of course, also drone strings, as on the hurdy-gurdy. The performer could thus choose between a "tutti" registration (strings and pipes), a "string" registration, or an "organ" registration (pipes only). If the hurdy-gurdy, technically improved and used as a solo instrument, was no longer the instrument of the folk musician but rather a fashionable instrument for dilettantes and virtuosi, this was particularly true of the *lira organizzata*. Neither in the manner of composition nor of performance did one seek to imitate the original countrified or "folk" ambiance for which the hurdy-gurdy had mainly been used, and which one otherwise evoked by its use.[3] Hurdy-gurdy and *lira organizzata* were now solo instruments, treated no differently from any others. This is also demonstrated by Hadrawa's instruction to Sterkel "to arrange the tunes for the *lire* or the melodies in the manner of the oboe."[4]

Ernst Fritz Schmid, H. C. Robbins Landon, Harry R. Edwall, Makoto Ohmiya, and Marianne Bröcker have dealt with Haydn's works for *lira organizzata*,[5] to some extent in great detail. The limitations of the instrument have determined the form and organization of these compositions, especially their simple harmonic structure. Nonetheless, it was entirely possible to perform quick eighths, sixteenths, or thirty-second runs, as is demonstrated in the arrangements for hurdy-gurdy of Vivaldi concertos by Nicolas Chédeville.[6] Thus Edwall is only partly correct when he writes, "The difficulty in fingering rapid passages involving both white and black keys is the most likely reason for the principal keys being limited to C, F, and G."[7] The limitation to these keys and their relative minors, as well as the infrequent modulation (and then only to related keys), is rather to be associated with the drone strings, which determined these limitations. The sounding of the drone strings was assumed and therefore not specially notated. Even in the case of Haydn's works we cannot assume out of hand that the drone strings were eliminated.[8] On the contrary, the sustaining of individual pitches through several measures, not only in the solo part but also in the accompanying instruments, appears to argue not only for the sounding of the drones, but even for their reinforcement by other instruments such as the horns. For example, one may note passages in the second movement (Allegro) of Notturno No. 1 in C (Hob. II:25), mm. 44–48 and in the last movement

---

[3] Cf. Mozart in the second of four minuets, dances, K. 601; or in the third of the four German dances, K. 602, in the trio. Both dances are in C major. See also Mahling, "Volkinstrumente," especially 41–42.

[4] Scharnagl, *Sterkel,* 84.

[5] Schmid, "Drehleier;" R. Landon, *Symphonies;* Edwall, *Lira;* Haydn, JHW, VII; Bröcker, *Drehleier.*

[6] Cf. also Bröcker, *Drehleier,* I, 319 f.   [7] Edwall, "Lira," 194.

[8] See Bröcker, *Drehleier,* I, 323.

(Allegro con brio) of No. 2 in F (Hob. II:26), mm. 17–24. Such doubling of the drones is also found in compositions by Mozart and others.[9]

With respect to the performance of works for the *lira organizzata,* Bröcker has indicated that there are no difficulties with pieces in the keys of G and C, but that those in F either were played without the pipes— which is improbable—or "instruments tuned in F" must have been used, whose range "slightly exceeded two octaves," since g[3] is needed as the highest pitch.[10] The parts for the *lire* were often written in parallel thirds and sixths, and they were often doubled by the violins and violas at the octave. Whether Edwall is correct in asserting that "the lira parts are very difficult when played on the instrument for which they were written"[11] seems unlikely, particularly in view of other compositions and arrangements for the hurdy-gurdy. On the other hand, I agree entirely with his observations that "all other parts are technically simple, for Haydn took pains to see that they did not overshadow the *lira* in degree of virtuosity."[12] With respect to performance practice in Haydn's works for *lira organizzata,* the following questions arise, among others, related to instrumentation:

1. With which instruments are the *lira* parts to be performed?
2. Are clarinets or violins to be used in the notturni?
3. Which instruments are to be used as "Basso?"

As to the first question, both in the concertos and in the notturni Haydn arranged the "tunes for the *lire* or the melodies in the manner of the oboe" and thereby certainly fulfilled the expectations of both Hadrawa and Ferdinand. Yet it was possible to play these parts without great difficulty on other melody instruments, in which case the choice was determined first of all by the tessitura required. On the other hand, the general harmonic plan of these compositions is determined by the *lire* and the manner in which they were played, that is to say, as a rule extensive modulations are found only in passages during which the *lire* rests. On the other hand, the characteristic sound of the instrument will certainly have compensated for many "weaknesses" of the composition. As is well known, in 1791–92 Haydn himself presented performances of some of the notturni at the Salomon concerts, arranged for the occasion as "New Divertimenti" and scored for flute and oboe or two flutes in place of the *lire,* and for violins in place of the clarinets.[13] Only in the program for the concert of May 20, 1791 do we find the title "New Concertino,"[14] which could mean that rather than one of the notturni, one of

[9] See the dances mentioned in note 3.   [10] Bröcker, *Drehleier,* 322–23.
[11] Edwall, "Lira," 196.   [12] Ibid.
[13] Among others, see the programs quoted by R. Landon, *Symphonies,* 450 ff.
[14] Ibid., 455.

the concertos was performed. Above all, Haydn may have been grateful to be able to perform these works in 1792, because in that year he had publicly obligated himself to present a new composition in each of Salomon's concerts, just as his pupil Pleyel had done in the "Professional" concerts.[15] Since we know that Haydn always arranged the form of his compositions, as well as the performance and instrumentation, according to the situation and the available resources,[16] the "London" scoring must surely be regarded only as one possibility for an alternative to performance with the *lira,* not the only one. Perhaps this could be confirmed by Haydn's offer to the publisher William Forster in London on April 8, 1787 (if we assume that it concerned not the Divertimenti Op. 31 but rather "a partial transcription of the *lira* concertos for the King of Naples"): "Item, I have in addition three entirely new charming Notturni for a violin obbligato, but not at all difficult, a flute, cello, two ripieno violins, two horns, viola, and double bass."[17] It would follow that in this instance the *lira* parts were to be played by flute and violin.

To be sure, these alternative scorings named or authorized by Haydn by no means constitute *carte blanche* authority for any conceivable arrangement, certainly not if we are concerned with historically correct performance practice. Attempts to perform the *lira* parts with instruments which, either by their construction or by the particular method of playing them, approach the sound of the *lira* as closely as possible, cannot be regarded as successful, insofar as they onesidedly consider only the "organ" registration (the pipes); the melody and the drone registrations are completely ignored. This is true both for arrangements with electronic organ (falsely labeled *lira* on some recordings!—in its place, moreover, they could have used positive organ just as well) and for recorder. Although the performance of the *lira* parts on recorder presents no technical problems, there remains the question whether such a scoring is appropriate from a historical point of view. Haydn himself would scarcely have used this instrument, since at the time of the composition of these works it was hardly in use any longer. Settings with flute and oboe or with two flutes can be considered more correct historically, because they correspond to the alternative settings used by Haydn himself. At the same time these alternative settings do not justify enlarged complements of the remaining instruments. Since by their nature the *lira* concertos resemble concertinos, the notturni divertimenti, we should think of only in terms of small, mostly soloistic settings of all the instruments, especially because doublings would lead to the danger of covering the sound of the *lire,* which are not particularly loud. We

---

[15] Haydn, *Briefe,* 280 (CCLN, 132).
[16] Also see, for example, the letter accompanying the cantata *Applausus* (Haydn, *Briefe,* 58 ff.) (CCLN, 9 ff.).
[17] Haydn, *Briefe,* 162, 163 (n.6) (CCLN, 59–60).

should keep the sound of the hurdy-gurdy in mind, to which we should add the sound of the pipes for the *lira organizzata.*

There are further problems in the instrumentation of the *lira* parts. One is the choice of the correct tempo, particularly for the quick movements. In general we can say that in the eighteenth century slow movements were probably played faster than today, but fast movements slower. In particular, however, the technical possibilities of each particular instrument must be considered when chosing a tempo. Virtuoso playing was possible on the *lira organizzata,* but certainly not such rapid performance as in the case of the flute or oboe. In any case, a historically accurate performance of these works will only be possible if the *lira* parts are played on original instruments. Because two of the three extant *lire organizzate* are still in playable condition (Brussels and Berlin), this ought to be possible, and it ought to be attempted, analogous to the use of the hurdy-gurdy in works by Mozart.

Concerning the use of clarinets and violins in the notturni: the fact that Haydn's London arrangements of the notturni not only set the *lira* parts for two flutes or flute and oboe, but at the same time arranged the clarinet parts for violins, and the further fact that this "alternative" setting was specified in the second version of the notturni, should not lead to the indiscriminate substitution of clarinets and violins for one another. Clarinets must be considered the "original" instrumentation even when the *lira* parts are given to other instruments, not least because the clarinets blend better both with the other wind instruments and with the violas. If violins are used, then the bass part must be correspondingly reinforced; that is, cello and double bass must be used, just as Haydn did in the second version of the notturni. The result will be to emphasize their symphonic character at the expense of serenadelike features (cf., for example, the style and instrumentation of Haydn's early symphonies).

Not from a historical point of view, but from the point of view of sonority, we should also inquire whether, when using violins, the *lira* parts ought perhaps to be scored for flute and violin or two violins. Obviously the situation is different in Notturni Nos. 7 in F and 8 in G (Hob. II:27 and 28), in which Haydn intended violins from the beginning, the parts are conceived violinistically, and the violins are entrusted with a leading role within the part writing. In this case the strings form a unity, while the *lire* and winds are clearly separate and play a rather subordinate role. This leads to the question—one which we cannot discuss in this context—as to whether these two works might not better be classified as belonging to a different genre.[18]

The setting of the "basso" part in the works of the Viennese classical composers and their contemporaries has often been treated in the litera-

---

[18] See also the Foreword to Haydn, JHW, VII, vii, and the critical commentary.

ture.[19] In the case of Mozart's serenades, Carl Bär in particular has tried to demonstrate that "Basso is always to be equated with double bass."[20] Adolf Meier has pointed out in this connection that when the double bass is specified, it does not absolutely follow that the cello was absent.[21] Furthermore, he showed that around 1780 the cello displaced the double bass "from these genres of chamber music of the early classical period related to the divertimento" but that the double bass kept its position in chamber works with larger numbers of parts.[22] Landon, in writing about Haydn's symphonies, indicates as one of the "important changes in Haydn's orchestral structure" around 1790 among other things "the emergence of the violoncello as a fifth voice in the four-part string orchestra."[23] This observation can be confirmed in that the second versions of the notturni originating at this time likewise show a clear separation of the cello and double bass parts. If we consider the notation, position, and tessitura of the bass parts as well as the fact that the double bass sounds an octave lower than written (16-foot register), we may conclude that in those

which go below F 𝄢 in the bass, the "Basso" part can be assumed to

have been played by the cello and not the double bass. A comparison of measure 25 ff. of the Andante of Notturno No. 3 in C (Hob. II:32) with measures 21 ff. of the second version illustrates this. In line with this result, the bass parts of the *lira* concertos, like the lower parts of the first versions of the notturni that are marked "Basso," are also to be played on the cello. Finally, use of the violone (the Viennese double bass) for the "Basso" would be conceivable; yet for these works it cannot be assumed.[24]

Only a few problems concerning the performance practice of Haydn's works can be discussed here in the context of his works for *lira organizzata*. In order to achieve the most "historically correct" performance of Haydn's music, further investigation is essential. It is to be hoped that the results of research will be observed by musicians and realized in performance.

Haydn and the Keyboard Instruments of His Time[1]

EDWIN M. RIPIN

The limited space available has made it necessary for me to circumscribe my treatment of Haydn's rather complex relationship to the keyboard in-

[19] Bär, "Basso"; Meier, *Kontrabass,* especially 44 f.; Webster, "Violoncello."
[20] Bär, "Basso"
[21] Meier, *Kontrabass,* 45.
[22] Ibid., 53.
[23] R. London, *Symphonies,* 427
[24] Concerning these questions see also Webster, "Violoncello," especially 429–30, 432.
[1] The author's untimely death shortly after the Conference prevented the editors from discussing this paper with him. Rather than a purely scholarly interpretation of the available

struments of his time, especially if I were to hope to add anything to the published findings of Horst Walter and Vera Schwarz in this area.[2] Accordingly, I will limit myself to a small number of general points and only a few of the specific matters that these points can serve to illuminate.

Haydn is, of course, a very special composer. Of all the important eighteenth-century composers of keyboard music, Haydn alone was not himself a virtuoso performer writing in large part for his own use as a soloist; a corollary of this point is that more of his late keyboard music was written with the primary intention of publication than is true for many of his contemporaries. Moreover, Haydn is an unusually eclectic composer of keyboard music; some of his sonatas display an extraordinary variety of styles and idioms brought together in a single work. Finally, Haydn is the only major composer whose music truly documents the transition from the harpsichord and clavichord to the piano and who was, in addition, completely at home with both Viennese and English pianos.

For all these reasons, the unraveling of Haydn's relationship to the keyboard instruments of his time is a complex task. It will not be my principal purpose to attempt to assign specific sonatas to the clavichord, the harpsichord, or the piano. Rather, I would like to offer a few reasons why such an endeavor is bound to fail in most instances; and to suggest (and this is hardly new) that, when it fails, it does so because the choice of instrument matters very little either in theory or in practice. This is the case both because of the facts about Haydn as a keyboard composer mentioned above and because of the nature of the instruments and the conditions of performance in the second half of the eighteenth century.

Viewed from our perspective, the great revolution in the field of keyboard music during this period was the triumph of the piano over its predecessors. Viewed from the perspective of eighteenth-century Germany and Austria, however, this development had few of the attributes of a revolution. In fact, it was a very gradual affair, in which the clavichord, harpsichord, and piano all coexisted until the end of the century, and in which a number of composers, of whom the most prominent is C. P. E. Bach, never really came to terms with the piano at all. Moreover, even composers who did make a whole-hearted change to the newer instrument—including Haydn, Mozart, and even Beethoven—

---

evidence, in many respects it is polemical and even (in his own words) "heretical" in intent. Haydn was a fully accomplished keyboard player and almost certainly composed the vast majority of his keyboard works for his personal performance (occasionally for the use of others). The clavichord was primarily a North German instrument and, as far as we know, was little used for performance in Austria. (The clavichord belonging to Haydn mentioned in fn. 3 was not acquired until 1795.) Although he may well have used such a instrument while drafting compositions in many scorings, he decisively turned to the piano for his actual keyboard works no later than the early 1780s. [Ed.]

[2] Walter, "Klaviere"; Walter, "Tasteninstrument"; Schwarz, "Cembalo."

owned and presumably played clavichords long after they had begun composing for the piano.[3]

This coexistence of the three instruments was possible in part because, as they then existed, they were remarkably equivalent to one another. The piano was far less loud than the modern instrument and thus—especially in the rectangular form that was most common in domestic use—was far more similar to the clavichord than one might think. Indeed, the clavichords made in the last third of the eighteenth century have a different sound and touch from earlier instruments, which makes them rather more suitable for playing what we now think of as piano music than earlier ones. To be sure, the clavichord could not play as loudly as the piano, but its dynamic range from an all but inaudible *pianissimo* to a quite considerable *forte* was as wide as or wider than that of the piano of the period. Since most solo sonatas for keyboard were not intended as "public" music to be played in large halls, the small sound of the clavichord might not have been thought of as an obstacle to its use in performing them.

Similarly, the harpsichord was no longer the same instrument as in the time of Couperin, Bach, or Handel. Beginning in the late 1750s—at a period when the piano was still all but unknown—pedals and knee levers were being added to harpsichords to permit them to imitate crescendos and decrescendos.[4] Moreover soft-leather plectra were introduced in the 1760s to provide a modicum of touch sensitivity. C. P. E. Bach mentioned a harpsichord with a crescendo pedal in the second part of his *Versuch,* published in 1762;[5] Mozart played a harpsichord with such a pedal during his visit to London in 1765,[6] and he encountered another in Naples in 1770.[7] Thus, by the time that crescendo markings make their appearance in Haydn's keyboard music around 1770, harpsichords capable of producing the required crescendo effects were already in existence. For this reason, it is not the appearance of a crescendo mark in Haydn's great C-minor Sonata Hob. XVI:20 (ChL. 33), that suggests that the work would not have been conceived for the harpsichord but, rather, the *forte* and *piano* marks on individual notes written into the autograph al-

---

[3] A clavichord owned by Haydn is in the Donaldson Collection, Royal College of Music, London; one by Mozart in the Wohnhaus, Salzburg; and one by Beethoven in the Conservatoire National Supérieur de Musique, Paris.

[4] These mechanisms are described in detail in Ripin, "Devices."

[5] Bach, *Versuch,* II, 245. Translation (368–69): "The fine invention of our celebrated Holefeld which makes it possible to increase or decrease the registration by means of pedals, while playing, has made the harpsichord, particularly the single-manual kind, a much-improved instrument, and fortunately, eliminated all difficulties connected with the performance of a piano. If only all harpsichords were similarly constructed as a tribute to good taste!"

[6] *Salzburger Zeitung,* August 6, 1765; quoted in Pohl, *London,* 127.

[7] Leopold Mozart to his wife, May 19, 1770 (W. Mozart, *Briefe,* I, 348).

ready in 1771. Although I do not lightly disagree with the many authorities who have stated that this work was conceived for the piano, this belief seems to me to arise from a lack of first-hand experience with the great capabilities of good clavichords dating from the last third of the eighteenth century. In the hands of an accomplished performer, there is no problem in doing this sonata justice on the clavichord, especially when one considers the dramatic character and the dynamic markings found in a number of works by C. P. E. Bach—works that also contain *Bebung* indications, permitting one quite definitely to assign them to the clavichord.[8] Even hand-crossings, specifically cited by H. C. Robbins Landon,[9] are found in a C. P. E. Bach work of this kind, Wq. 63/6, one of the *Probe-Stücke* composed as a supplement to the *Versuch* and published in 1753.

In short, the clavichord, the harpsichord, and the piano were tolerably similar in character and capabilities in the latter part of the eighteenth century, and may have been far more interchangeable in the performance of solo keyboard music than the modern partisans of one or another instrument are likely to concede. This is one reason why internal evidence of a work's being specifically conceived for only one of the three instruments is particularly hard to find in solo sonatas and, I think, particularly suspect when one thinks that one has found it. Furthermore, if I might add another heretical note, I would like to suggest that the history of music has two quite distinct components: on the one hand, what composers might have had in mind and, on the other, what actually occurred in performance. Clavichords and, especially, harpsichords were made side by side with pianos by some instrument builders during the last third of the eighteenth century. Their purchasers may be presumed to have played all the latest music on them, whether the composer really wanted this or not. Thus, the superscription "per clavicembalo o fortepiano" on many of the title pages of the period does not only represent publishers' attempts at increasing sales; it also represents performance practice of the period, and it certainly represents a practical performance possibility in terms of the capabilities of the contemporary instruments. Thus, even Haydn's C-minor Sonata can be played on the harpsichord—if one pretends that the smaller-scale dynamic marks are not there and conceives one's performance in harpsichordistic terms. (Although C.P.E. Bach can be adduced as an authority for this,[10] I am not recommending it, except perhaps as an experiment, but I am sure that it was done quite frequently in the eighteenth century, especially on the post-

[8] For example, Sonata in F major (H. 130, Wq. 55/2), i; Fantasia in C minor (H. 75, Wq. 63/6), iii.

[9] Landon, "Sonatas", 60.

[10] Bach, *Versuch,* I, 131 (transl., 164) states that on a two-manual harpsichord one should not change manuals to distinguish *f* and *p* on individual notes, but only on longer passages.

Baroque harpsichords with their touch-sensitive leathered registers and their crescendo devices of various types.)

With these thoughts in mind, I would like to return to Haydn and his special place among keyboard composers. Haydn's keyboard works seem to me to lack that specific appropriateness to a particular instrument that is characteristic of Mozart's keyboard music. This very quality probably made Haydn's works more suitable for publication, where appropriateness to only a single instrument would tend to limit sales.

Haydn's extraordinary eclecticism of style can compel a similar conclusion. In a single sonata he may employ idioms of C. P. E. Bach (pointing to the clavichord), those of Alberti or even Scarlatti (pointing to the harpsichord), and a frankly pianistic style that seems to prefigure Beethoven.[11] Since only one instrument can be used in any given performance, Haydn must have conceived of these idioms not as being exclusive but, rather, as appropriate to keyboard instruments in general.

For all these reasons, the question of when Haydn first came to know the piano remains baffling. It could have been as early as the 1760s or as late as the 1780s. Whenever it was, it seems to have produced no immediate and clear-cut change in his keyboard writing. But since (as I believe) he was never writing specifically for any particular instrument, one should not expect it to. Instead, one would expect that Haydn's music would continue to be tailored to the instruments possessed by his dedicatees or to being useful to the widest possible circle of buyers of published editions.

Having said all this, one must add that eventually Haydn transfered his allegiance from the clavichord and harpsichord to the piano. But for the reasons already given, the date of this transfer cannot be established with certainty. The piano trios Hob. XV:5 and 6 (1784) and the Concerto in D major Hob. XVIII:11 (c.1783–84) contain dynamic markings suggestive of the piano, and the lack of any very great change in the style of the keyboard writing between that in these works and that of the trios of 1788 Hob. XV:11–13, in connection with which Haydn bought "a new fortepiano" made by Wenzel Schanz,[12] suggests that this instrument may have replaced an earlier piano rather than a harpsichord. This impression is reinforced by Haydn's well-known letter to Marianne von Genzinger of two years later in which he implies that he was by then completely unaccustomed to the harpsichord.[13] All in all, I think that the date of Haydn's change of allegiance to the piano probably falls around 1780. The group of sonatas published by Artaria in that year (Hob. XVI:35–39, 20 [ChL. 48–52, 33]) has all the mixture of styles one would expect of a group of pieces brought together at a time of transition. Not only does it

---

[11] An outstanding example is the Sonata Hob. XVI:32 (ChL. 47) in B minor.

[12] Haydn to Artaria, October 26, 1788 (Haydn, *Briefe,* 195; CCLN, 79).

[13] Ibid., 242. [Quoted in Workshop 2. —Ed.]

include the C-minor Sonata, which dates from 1771, it also contains the D-major Sonata Hob. XVI:37 (ChL. 50), which seems to many people so unpianistic that it has long been part of many modern harpsichordists' repertory—even for those playing instruments without pedals—as well as works that might very well have been conceived with the sound of the piano rather than that of the clavichord in mind.

In any event, all uncertainty vanishes very abruptly in 1788, with the composition of a number of works explicitly conceived in terms of particular instruments, above all with a nearly unique example of a keyboard work written by Haydn for his own public performance. The former are the trios Hob. XV:11–13 alluded to above. These are followed by the sonatas Hob. XVI:48, 49 (ChL. 58, 59) in C major and in E-flat major, the latter dedicated to Frau von Genzinger, which, as Haydn's letters make clear, was conceived in terms of Schantz's instruments.[14] Finally, the most personal of all Haydn's tributes to the Viennese piano is the alternately lyrical and dramatic accompaniment to the canata *Arianna a Naxos* (Hob. XXVIb:2), composed for his own performance shortly before leaving for his first trip to England and played by him almost immediately after his arrival in London.

Haydn's next group of compositions with prominent keyboard parts, written only during his second trip to England, shows in the clearest possible way his reaction to the rather different capabilities of the English piano. This may be seen at once by comparing the accompaniments in the English canzonettas with that in *Arianna a Naxos*. The accompaniments in "Pleasing Pain," "Fidelity," and the "Sailor's Song" (Hob. XXVIa:29–31) are far showier and make different technical demands, including hand-crossings and, most significantly, repeated chords in the highest register and right-hand octave passages in rapid tempo. These are difficult to execute on the Viennese piano with its feather-light action, but are enormously effective on the English instrument with its somewhat thicker tone and its greater key resistance. There is nothing quite like them in Haydn's keyboard writing except in a second group of keyboard works specifically connected with England—the last three sonatas Hob. XVI:50–52 (ChL. 60–62) and the trios XV:27–29, all but one of which were written for Theresa Jansen. In contrast, other trios written at the same period in London, but dedicated to Esterházy princesses (Hob. XV:18–23), are still entirely suited to the possibilities of the Viennese instruments.

Haydn clearly was impressed with English pianos—he brought one back with him after his second London sojourn[15]—but he retained his fondness for the Viennese piano and, as shown by the stylistic differences

---

[14] Ibid., 242–44. [Likewise—Ed.]

[15] This instrument, by Longman & Broderip, was still in Haydn's possession at his death; cf. Walter, "Klaviere," 280, 283, 284.

among the late trios, never lost sight of the need to write somewhat differently for the two instruments. It is noteworthy that Haydn's writing for the English piano in the canzonetta accompaniments did not extend to the point of using the wider keyboard range available on English pianos. Since he planned to offer these works for publication on the Continent,[16] he restricted the range of their accompaniments to the five octaves available on Continental instruments. In fact, he exceeded this range only once: in the Sonata Hob. XVI:50 (ChL. 60) in C major, iii, 27, 74–79, dedicated to Theresa Jansen (Bartolozzi), to whom he had given exclusive rights of publication, with the result that possible sales to musicians on the Continent might have been of less concern to him then usual.

Thus, to conclude, we have seen that Haydn's relationship to the keyboard instruments of his time was a complex one shaped by a variety of factors. Some of these factors were unique to Haydn, in part reflecting his intense practicality; others relate to the equally special nature of the keyboard instruments themselves at the critical time at which Haydn was composing for them.

The *alla breve* "March": Its Evolution and Meaning in Haydn's String Quartets[1]

ISIDOR SASLAV

When discussing Haydn's string quartets I use the term *"alla breve march"* to refer to a particular group of movements. Usually first movements, they are characterized by the time signature ¢ , by dotted eighth- and sixteenth-note rhythms, and also usually by passage-work in eighth-note triplets. These triplets represent the smallest subdivision of the quarter note used for such passage-work, in this case ¢ ♪♪♪ .[2] The tempo is marked Allegro or Allegro moderato; and the whole effect is of a sharply rhythmic, marching character. Good examples are Op. 55, No.

---

[16] Both collections were subsequently published in Vienna.

[1] The information here is drawn from Saslav, "Tempos," where a full discussion with documentation is given. The metronome markings are my own estimates.

These studies are based on Haydn's autographs and other authentic sources. Widely circulated editions of Haydn's music, such as the Eulenburg miniature scores and the Peters parts, cannot be trusted as guides to Haydn's notation.

I am grateful for the assistance of Dr. Georg Feder, of the Joseph Haydn-Institute, Cologne. The editions of Haydn's quartets in JHW, of which at this writing XII:1–3 and 5 have appeared and XII:4 is scheduled for publication shortly, are the first in which the matters discussed here are reproduced accurately.

[2] In the formulations of this type used in this study, the first sign gives the time signature; the second gives the value(s) of the dominant passage-work in the movement; usually these values are a division of the quarter note.

2 in F minor, ii; Op. 64, No. 1 in C major, i; and Op. 77, No. 1 in G major, i.

This type of movement forms part of a larger category for which I use the symbol: Haydn ¢ ♪♪♪(♪♪ ♪♪♪♪). Within this larger category there are a number of other movements which, with some imagination, might also be considered marchlike. While these lack both the triplet eighth notes and dotted rhythms of the first group and display passage-work in eighth notes rather than triplet eighths, they nevertheless exhibit fanfarelike themes and flourishlike embellishments which likewise impart a martial flavor to the proceedings. The tempos here are Allegro or Allegro spiritoso, Vivace, and Presto, and the rhythmic scheme is ¢ ♪♪♪♪. Good examples are Op. 55, No. 1 in A major, i, and Op. 74, No. 2 in F major, i.

Movements in still a third group within the Haydn ¢ show even less marchlike character, for while they retain the triplet eighths they lack the dotted rhythms. They are usually Allegro or Allegro ma non troppo, and the rhythmic scheme is ¢ ♪♪♪. Examples of this group are Op. 50, No. 1 in B-flat major, i; Op. 54, No. 3 in E major, i; and Op. 76, No. 1 in G major, iv.

These three groups, each belonging to Haydn ¢, stand in contrast to another category of movements all of which are in C rather than ¢, which contain virtually no dotted rhythms and no eighth-note triplets, in which the passage-work is in sixteenth notes, and whose tempos are Allegro or faster, such as Allegro con brio or Allegro con spirito. This second large category of movements represents the conception known generally as the "Classical sonata-allegro," which I call Mozart C ♪♪♪♪. I use it in this case not only because it is characteristic of many of Mozart's first movements (such as K.387 in G major and K.465 in C major), but also because its initial appearance in Haydn's quartets came only after Haydn got to know Mozart's music, specifically after his receipt of Mozart's six quartets dedicated to him.

Both of the large categories of movements described above represent a rather late development in Haydn's quartet composition, and both make their initial appearance simultaneously in Op. 50 (1787)—namely, the Haydn ¢ in Op. 50, No. 1 in B-flat major, i; and the Mozart C in Op. 50, No. 6 in D major, i. Indeed the appearance of both these new categories of tempo notation forms one dividing point between pre-Classical and true Classical style in Haydn's quartets. It must be noted that what was new in Op. 50/6/i was the combination of the rhythmic scheme C ♪♪♪♪ with the unmodified tempo word Allegro. Previous examples of this rhythmic scheme in Haydn's quartets, not numerous in any case, were always marked Allegro di molto, thus perhaps M.M. ♩.=160, after Quantz (for example, Op. 20, No. 3 in G minor, iv). Also not to be confused with the new notation were those older movements, likewise in 𝄴 , but with tempo markings slower than Allegro and subdivisions of the quarter note even smaller than the sixteenth note (very common from Op. 9 to Op. 33). It is the purpose of the present paper to show how the new notations evolved from the older ones, what their inherent tempos were in relation to each other, and the light shed on this process by the type I have called the *"alla breve* march."

The evolution of the Mozart 𝄴 [♫♫♫] in Haydn's first movements can be described as follows: In Opp. 9, 17, and 20 he employed the tempo Moderato 𝄴 [♫♫], M.M. ♩ = 80–90; in Op. 33, this became Allegro moderato 𝄴 [♫♫], M.M. ♩ = 90–100; and from Op. 50 on we find Allegro 𝄴 [♫♫♫], M.M. ♩ = 120–130. (I remind the reader that these metronome markings are my own estimates; there are none in eighteenth-century sources for Haydn's music.) The Haydn 𝄵 is also descended from the old Moderato 𝄴 , in the form Moderato 𝄴 [³♫♫], [♫], [♫♫♫], M.M.♩ = 80, as well as the Allegro di molto 𝄴 [♫♫♫] , M.M.♩ = 80, but in this case there was a direct transformation into Allegro 𝄵 [♫♫], [³♫], M.M.♩ = 80, which we find from Op. 50 on. The triplet sixteenths and dotted figures associated with Moderato 𝄴 in the preceding sentence represent not the fastest notes—those are still the thirty-seconds, of course—but the values out of which the characteristic triplet eighths and dotted eighths and sixteenths in the later Allegro 𝄵 derive. (This relation is illustrated by the paired passages from the Opp. 9–17–20 period and from the Opp. 50–54/55–64 period shown in Examples 1 and 2. Many others could also be cited: for example, Op. 9, No. 4, i, 28–29 vs. Op. 77, No. 1, i, 19–21; Op. 17, No. 1, i, 31–32 vs. Op. 54, No. 3, i, 32–35; Op. 17, No. 5, i, 29 vs. Op. 50, No. 1, i, 8–10; or Op. 33, No. 2, i, 25–28 vs. Op. 55, No. 1, i, 44–48.) On the other hand, there is no passage-work in sixteenths in the Allegro 𝄵 , which could have derived in analogous fashion from the thirty-seconds of the earlier tempo; passage-work in sixteenths was reserved for the Mozart 𝄴 category.

If my suppositions concerning tempos are correct, then why did Haydn need to cast his old tempo (M.M. ♩ = 80) into a new notational form (M.M. ♩ = 80)? First, as indicated above, the old Moderato 𝄴 had evolved in its tempo and notation from M.M. ♩ = 80 to M.M. ♩ = 130, leaving Haydn without a means to notate the former, which was evidently one of his favorite tempos. But then, why could Haydn not have simply reverted to the old formulation described above, Allegro di molto

Example 1

a) String Quartet Op. 9, No. 1 in C major, i, 29–30

b) String Quartet Op. 64, No. 1 in C major, i, 59–60

Example 2

a) String Quartet Op. 9, No. 2 in E-flat major, i, 10–12

b) String Quartet Op. 55, No. 1 in A major, i, 65–69

c ♩♩♩, since its tempo, M.M. ♩ = 80, seems to be equivalent to the newly developed Allegro ¢ ♩♩♩ , at M.M. ♩ = 160? In my opinion it was because the old notation implied and expressed four beats in the measure, the new notation only two; the old had sixteenths as the fastest values, the new only triplet eighths.

The important and unique harbinger of this new style was Op. 33, No. 3 in C major, i, Allegro moderato ¢ ♩♩♩. This combination of a tempo mark characteristic of the older period and a rhythmic scheme whose time signature was characteristic of the newer one was not to recur until the first movement of the very last completed quartet, Op. 77, No. 2 in F major. Just as Op. 33 foreshadowed in its "Scherzi" of 1781 the Presto minuets of the 1790s, so too a significant development of the last period is here presented in but a single precocious example.

The Haydn ¢ ♩♩♩ . ♩♩ . ♩♩♩♩ displays three shades of tempo: Allegro (for example, Op. 50, No. 1 in B-flat major, i), Allegro moderato or ma non troppo (Op. 64, No. 1 in C major, i), and Allegro spiritoso, Vivace, or Presto (Op. 74, No. 2 in F major, i). The rhythmic scheme of the first of these is characteristically ¢ ♩♩♩, of the second ¢ ♩♩♩ . ♩♩, and of the third ¢ ♩♩♩♩. Thus if in Allegro ¢ ♩♩♩, M.M. ♩ = 80, then perhaps in Allegro moderato ¢ ♩♩♩ . ♩♩ (i.e., the *"alla breve* march") M.M. ♩ should = 70. It is within the latter realm that our most valuable clues to tempo evolution and its notation lie. In this group are to be found the most characteristic "marches" such as Op. 64, No. 1 in C major, i, and Op. 77, No. 1 in G major, i.

The Mozart c ♩♩♩, on the other hand, while definitely retaining its four beats to the bar, had no modification of tempo to the slower side: it appears either as Allegro (Op. 50, No. 6 in D major, i) or as Allegro con brio (Op. 54, No. 1 in G major, i) or as Allegro con spirito (Op. 76, No. 4 in B-flat major, i). For this tempo, having evolved out of the Moderato

c 𝅘𝅥𝅯𝅘𝅥𝅯𝅘𝅥𝅯 , with its quasi eight beats to the bar, any attempt to slow it or reintroduce subdivisions smaller than the sixteenth note would have been a confusion with an earlier style of notation. This was perhaps another reason for creating the new two-beat Allegro ¢ notation: to avoid confusion with the four-beat bar of the Mozart c , also called Allegro.

Having used the rhythmic scheme ¢ 𝅘𝅥𝅯𝅘𝅥𝅯𝅘𝅥𝅯 only once, in Op. 33, No. 3, Haydn thereafter kept these two distinct tempos and notational styles strictly separate through Op. 77, No. 1 (see Table 1, p. 314). Thus it is surprising to come upon an apparent anomaly: In Op. 77, No. 2 in F major, i, we find dotted rhythms and the tempo mark Allegro moderato, familiar to us from our study of the "marches," *combined* with passage-work in sixteenths characteristic of the Mozart c . Actually the two styles are not mixed; they simply succeed one another. The "march" prevails for some thirteen bars (including a little flourish in sixteenth notes, mm. 4, 5, reminiscent of the snare drum), but in m. 14 the sixteenth-note passages begin, and the dotted rhythms disappear until the recapitulation. Nevertheless the tempo connotations seem unmistakable: if Allegro moderato ¢ as in perhaps Op. 64, No. 1, i, implies M.M. $\downharpoonright$ = 70, then the Mozart quarter note with its sixteenth notes has been speeded up to M.M. $\downharpoonright$ = 140.

It seems clear that the Allegro moderato in Op. 77, No. 2 derives from the *"alla breve* march" and refers to the half note, because the Mozart was never modified to the slower side, only to the faster. We thus see that the two styles had fallen together: under the influence of the *"alla breve* march" the Mozart c became a Haydn-Mozart ¢ 𝅘𝅥𝅯𝅘𝅥𝅯𝅘𝅥𝅯 , in which,

despite the sixteenth notes, there are only two beats, not four, to the bar. This accentual distinction was, by the end of the eighteenth century, either too self-evident, widespread, and generally understood, or else too subtle for those editors and publishers who were beyond Haydn's control, to understand; for many of them changed ¢ to c . Once the Mozart quarter note had, in performance, speeded up to M.M. $\downharpoonright$ = 140, the sign c seemed sufficiently fast to represent all types of "Classical" allegros. Since the tempos of two previously distinct genres seemed thus to have become identical, one of the signs, ¢ , formerly used by Haydn to distinguish the one from the other, seemed to have become superfluous. It was therefore removed by various editors and publishers from numerous Haydn quartet first movements, including Op. 64, No. 6 in E-flat major, and Op. 77, Nos. 1 and 2, as well as from slow ¢ movements such as those

*Table 1   Haydn's Normal Tempos
in the 1780s and 1790s*

The Haydn ₵

The Normal Allegro ₵

Op. 50, No. 1, i	Allegro
Op. 54, No. 3, i	Allegro
Op. 55, No. 1, i	Allegro
Op. 55, No. 2, ii	Allegro
Op. 64, No. 6, i	Allegro

The Slower Shade

Op. 33, No. 3, i	Allegro moderato
Op. 64, No. 1, i	Allegro moderato
Op. 64, No. 5, i	Allegro moderato
Op. 76, No. 1, iv	Allegro ma non troppo
Op. 76, No. 4, iv	Allegro ma non troppo
Op. 77, No. 1, i	Allegro moderato
Op. 77, No. 2, i	Allegro moderato

The Faster Shade

Op. 54, No. 2, i	Vivace
Op. 55, No. 1, iv	Vivace
Op. 74, No. 2, i	Allegro spiritoso
Op. 76, No. 1, i	Allegro con spirito
Op. 76, No. 3, iv	Presto
Op. 76, No. 4, iv	Presto

The Mozart ₵

The Normal Allegro ₵

Op. 50, No. 6, i	Allegro
Op. 71, No. 1, i	Allegro
Op. 71, No. 2, i	Allegro
Op. 74, No. 1, i	Allegro
Op. 76, No. 2, i	Allegro

The Faster Allegro ₵

Op. 54, No. 1, i	Allegro con brio
Op. 64, No. 2, i	Allegro con spirito
Op. 64, No. 4, i	Allegro con brio
Op. 74, No. 3, iv	Allegro con brio
Op. 76, No. 4, i	Allegro con spirito

in Op. 9, No. 6, Op. 33, Nos. 5 and 6, and Op. 77, No. 1. In the latter examples, if ₵ did not signify two beats to the bar, it implied a moderating influence on the tempo word Largo or Adagio; that is, a somewhat faster tempo than if the time signature had been C , but not a doubled tempo. This would have followed a widespread early-eighteenth-century practice concerning the meaning of the *alla breve* sign.

The Identification and Interpretation of Sign Ornaments in Haydn's Instrumental Music

CHRISTIE TOLSTOY

The identification and interpretation of Haydn's instrumental sign ornaments is a problem whose difficulty is often underrated. Compared to the tangle intricacy of late Baroque ornamentation, Haydn's sign ornaments seem a relatively simple matter: he uses fewer sign ornaments; a greater proportion of his ornamentation is written out in notes; and realizations for those signs he does use are readily available in eighteenth-century German instrumental tutors.[1] In fact, however, the problems posed by sign ornaments of the Classic period are not simpler than those of the Baroque but more complex. For one thing, by Haydn's time the sign ornament repertoire had expanded to include embellishments culled from several countries and several eras, and this heterogeneous repertoire brought with it a hybrid notation. For another, the Classic sign ornament notation system represents a transitional stage between the notation of the late Baroque, which often indicated a part of a melodic line by symbols, and that of the Romantic period, which usually wrote almost everything out in notes, so that Classic composers tended to replace traditional ornament symbols with new and unstandardized conglomerations of large notes, small notes, and signs. The result was notational confusion such as that which drove the normally courteous Haydn to write Artaria & Co. on December 10, 1785, in the following terms:

I received the pianoforte sonatas [Trios], and was greatly astounded to have to see such bad engraving, and so many glaring errors. . . . Everyone who buys them will curse the engraver and have to stop playing. . . . You should put instead of the sign *tr:* the following:✹ , for the first one, as the engraver has done it, means a trill, whilst mine is a half-mordent. If therefore, the Herr Engraver doesn't know signs of this sort, he should inform himself by studying the masters, and not follow his own stupid ideas.[2]

As it happens, the unfortunate engraver's mistake was due less to stupidity than to an ambiguity typical of the hybrid sign ornament notation of the Classic period: the symbol Haydn had chosen to represent his half-mordent (✹)—often called the "Haydn ornament" today (♧)—was almost indistinguishable from one of the traditional signs for the turned trill (✹). In the face of a heterogeneous and transitional notation system, even eighteenth-century engravers occasionally came to grief over the identification and interpretation of Haydn's instrumental sign or-

[1] For example, Bach, *Versuch*; L. Mozart, *Violinschule*; Quantz, *Versuch*; Marpurg, *Anleitung*; Türk, *Klavierschule*.
[2] Haydn, CCLN, 51 (*Briefe*, 148–49).

naments. Twentieth-century interpreters would do well to approach the matter with caution.

Since the interpretation of Haydn's ornament signs may be more perilous than it seems, it might be the better part of valor to start with a careful categorization of the problem. From the point of view of the modern musician, the principal hazards are: 1) that signs may be replaced by musical notes—and these may be either "large" notes or "small" ones, and these notes may replace the sign completely or only in part; 2) that signs may be incomplete; and 3) that signs may be ambiguous. (The first difficulty is aggravated by the transitional nature of Classic sign ornament notation, the last two by its hybrid nature.) As examples of the four varieties of signs replaced by notes one might cite the half-mordent (see Example 1a), the trill from below (1b), the appoggiatura (1c), and the prepared trill (1d). Small notes replacing signs may be misinterpreted, while large notes replacing signs may not even be recognized as ornaments, particularly when the embellishment is not grouped under a slur (1e) or begins before the beat (1f). Examples of signs whose meaning is incomplete are provided by Haydn's two most frequent symbols for the trill (1g), which specify neither the trill's beginning nor its ending, though contemporary performance practice recommended that a prefix and/or suffix be appended to the majority of trills (1h).[3] As for signs whose meaning is ambiguous, the outstanding examples in the instrumental works of Haydn are undoubtedly the various symbols for the half-mordent. The symbol quoted by Haydn in his letter, for example, might quite reasonably have been interpreted by the unlucky engraver as a half-mordent, a turned trill, a short mordent, or a long mordent (1j).[4]

Example 1

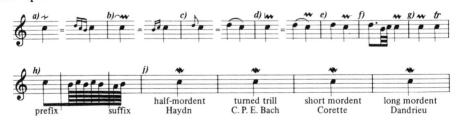

	half-mordent	turned trill	short mordent	long mordent
	Haydn	C. P. E. Bach	Corette	Dandrieu

prefix   suffix

Such lapses in the logic of the Classic sign ornament notation system pose a considerable problem for the interpreter of Haydn's instrumental works. In addition, a second series of problems results from an understandably inconsistent use of this inadequate notation by eighteenth-cen-

---

[3] For example, L. Mozart, *Violinschule,* 220 (transl., 188); Quantz, *Versuch,* 85 (transl., 103).
[4] Haydn, CCLN, 51 (*Briefe,* 148–49); Bach, *Versuch,* 72 (transl., 101); Michel Corrette, *1er livre de pièces de clavecin* (Paris, 1735), ornament table; François Dandrieu, *Pièces de clavecin* (Paris, 1724), ornament table.

tury copyists and by Haydn himself. Despite his lecture to Artaria's engraver, for example, Haydn was so inconsistent in his use of symbols for the half-mordent that musicologists have been unable to determine with any certainty whether ∞ , ⋰⋰ , and ⋰⋰ have three separate meanings, one meaning for which the signs were used interchangeably, or several such meanings. Haydn's habits of sign ornament notation alter with time, but he is also inconsistent within a single work, within a movement, or in parallel passages. Nonautograph copies share in these disconcerting traits, and in addition they disagree among themselves. The several categories of the problem may all be summed up in one central question: when are the inconsistencies in Haydn's use of sign ornament symbols due to notational difficulties of one sort or another, and when do they indicate a real difference in intent?

The usual approach to this unwieldy problem is to appeal to the authority of the primary sources. Any one source, however, may be individualistic, peripheral, or outmoded, while no two sources, as almost every writer on ornamentation since the seventeenth century has had occasion to note, are ever in complete agreement as to the names, symbols, and interpretations of sign ornaments. Nevertheless, primary sources can supply one important body of information which is of enormous help in the identification and interpretation of sign ornaments. Instrumental tutors and ornament tables of all nationalities, from the late Baroque through the Classic period, are largely in agreement upon one point: sign ornaments are embellishments of specific contexts. Each sign ornament, that is, can properly be employed in only a very limited number of melodic, rhythmic, and harmonic contexts, and this ruling principle was so consistently observed by Baroque and Classic composers that it is often possible to identify and interpret an ornament symbol from its context alone, despite inadequate notation and inconsistent usage.

One of the most extensive and detailed accounts of the contexts traditionally associated with each sign ornament is C. P. E. Bach's *Versuch,* a treatise known to Haydn.[5] In the introduction to his chapter on ornamentation Bach writes, "Embellishments . . . will be explained and their proper contexts specified. . . . Our reader . . . will learn that the nature of a passage can narrow his choice of ornament.[6] C. P. E. Bach was by no means the first to notice that choice of an ornament is contingent upon context. As early as 1698 Georg Muffat, in the preface to his *Florilegium secundum,* presented a cogent summary of the contexts proper to the principal sign ornaments, and the same precept was mentioned by scores of other late Baroque and Classic authors, including Bénigne de Bacilly, Saint Lambert, Tosi, Quantz, Mozart, Tartini, Duval, and

[5] See Schmid, "Bach"
[6] Bach, *Versuch,* 53, 55 (transl., 80, 82); cf. Chapter II, Part 1, *passim.*

Türk.[7] In addition, the ornament contexts described by theorists in their instrumental tutors are confirmed by contemporary composers, who illustrate the same contexts in their ornament tables. The principle involved is explained by Saint Lambert: "In the Ornament here called CHUTTE ET PINCÉ, the first note is not essential. It is merely there to show that one uses this ornament only when the note which precedes it is one degree lower."[8] Saint Lambert, that is, has included in his musical example not only the ornament itself but also an additional note illustrating its context. This useful habit was fairly widespread, and accounts for the extraneous notes in the ornament tables of such composers as Jean-Henry d'Anglebert, François Couperin, and Gottlieb Muffat.

Instrumental tutors and ornament tables of the most diverse provenance are surprisingly unanimous as to the contexts characteristic of or essential to each sign ornament. For the most part, however, the information is scattered and disorganized. Only a few theorists were able to formulate a complete set of rules for ornament contexts and, although eighteenth-century theorists often reminded their readers that the many individual rules for context all derived from a ruling principle known as "good taste," not one was able to define this ruling principle, verbalize its tenets, or organize them into a coherent and usable system. From the vantage point of the twentieth century, however, it can be seen that the musical system which underlies the rules for the harmonic contexts of sign ornaments is the functional harmony of the late Baroque, while melodic contexts conform to the rules for melodic construction associated with what every undergraduate music student now knows as Palestrinian counterpoint.

The influence of late Baroque functional harmony on the harmonic contexts of instrumental sign ornaments has long been familiar to modern scholars,[9] but it has not yet been sufficiently stressed that until an astonishingly late date the melodic contexts of sign ornaments were determined principally in accordance with late Renaissance ideals of beauty. In the second half of the seventeenth century, when rules for the contexts of sign ornaments were first being committed to paper, the compositional procedures of the late Renaissance were still a vital force;[10] it is not surprising, therefore, that the earliest definitions of context reflect such Renaissance precepts as on-beat consonance.[11] What is surprising is that

[7] Kolneder, *Muffat,* 77–93; Bacilly, *Chanter,* 3rd ed., 143 (transl., 67); Saint-Lambert, *Clavecin,* 50; Tosi, *Opinioni,* 29 (Eng. transl., 49); Quantz, *Versuch,* 80 (transl., 97); L. Mozart, *Violinschule,* 205 (transl., 177); Tartini, *Traité,* mod. ed., 89–90; Duval, *Méthode,* 11; Türk, *Klavierschule,* 282.
[8] Saint Lambert, *Clavecin,* 48–49.
[9] For example, Donington, *Interpretation,* 239–46; Neumann, "Appoggiaturas," 73.
[10] See, for example, the compositional procedures outlined by Berardi, *Miscellanea.*
[11] See, for example, Rousseau, *Traité.* Maintenance of on-beat consonance results in the before-the-beat appoggiaturas defended by Neumann in "Appoggiaturas" and "Ornamentation."

even as late as Haydn's time the choice of an embellishment to fit a given melodic context was still being determined not so much by the normal compositional procedures of the Classic period as by such Renaissance ideas as the concept that conjunct motion is the norm, that leaps receive different treatment, that ascending and descending motion are not synonymous, and that initial notes must be consonant, dissonance approached and left conjunctly, and leaps recovered by motion in the opposite direction. The ornament table of an early contemporary of Haydn, Dom Bedos de Celles, presents a particularly complete set of specifications for ornament contexts, and these in every case correspond to, and in fact can only be fully explained by, the Renaissance principles cited above.[12]

Although the choice of a sign ornament was primarily dependent upon the melodic context, it was also contingent upon the rhythm, and here the two most important principles were the distinction between long and short notes and on-beat and off-beat. Long notes, whether their lengths were due to note values or tempo, were more frequently and more heavily embellished than short notes. Off-beat notes could be decorated with anything which suited the melodic line, but on-beat notes had to be handled with care. As late as 1700, for example, it was considered a fault to approach an unprefixed on-beat trill from below, since this would constitute a skip to a dissonance on the beat.[13] As for the harmonic context, Renaissance-derived rules were altered by the advent of the Baroque in only one important way. Late Baroque and Classic composers preferred to enliven long, repetitiously consonant notes by the addition of ornamental dissonance.[14] Quantz suggests further that such appoggiaturas may be varied by transforming them into more complex dissonant embellishments such as the prepared trill.

In addition to melodic, rhythmic, and harmonic contexts, one or two lesser factors also affected the choice of ornament. Chief among these was the articulation. Haydn's articulation must be respected: staccato notes should be embellished only with short percussive ornaments such as the short mordent, the half-mordent ("Haydn ornament"), and the short trill, and legato notes with flowing connective ornaments such as the long mordent and trills with prefix and suffix. When Haydn has not indicated the articulation, the performer has the rather awesome responsibility of determining it himself to the best of his ability and maintaining it in his ornamentation; otherwise Haydn's sign ornamentation will lose much of its expressive meaning.

A second factor affecting choice of ornament is the *Affekt*. As Quantz points out, the gaiety of a brisk Allegro movement is best expressed by

---

[12] Compare standard precepts of late-Renaissance melodic construction, as summarized, for example, in Jeppesen, *Counterpoint,* with the table of ornaments in Bedos, *Orgues,* IV, plates CV–CXII, as given in Dolmetsch, *Interpretation,* 319–22.

[13] Kolneder, *Muffat,* 84.   [14] See, for example, Quantz, *Versuch,* 80 (transl., 97).

generally staccato ornaments, while the tender grace of a slow movement in *cantabile* style is better served by legato embellishment.[15] The ornamentation may also be adjusted to suit the character of a dance movement, the size of the performing group, the extent of the room, and the ability of the performer. A certain leeway in the choice of ornament was both permitted and expected as long as the melodic, rhythmic, and harmonic construction was properly maintained and the articulation and the *Affekt* suitably expressed.

A working knowledge of the contexts traditionally considered suitable to each embellishment, then, backed by an understanding of the harmonic and contrapuntal principles which underlie and explain them, can often be of material help in the identification and interpretation of Haydn's instrumental sign ornaments, despite inadequate notation and inconsistent usage. An example chosen from each of the three categories listed above will help to demonstrate this point. Among signs replaced by notes, for example, one of the most frequently misinterpreted ornaments is the prepared trill, an embellishment originally represented by a symbol but usually written by Haydn as a large note followed by a trilled note (Ex. 1d), often without a slur to indicate that the large note is intended as part of the ornament (1e). Whatever the notation, the harmonic context—the fact that the large note and the trilled note together add up to a long, redundantly consonant note altered to ornamental dissonance, as described by Quantz—should alert the modern performer to play these two notes not as separate entities (Ex. 2a) but as a single ornament (2b).

A similar sensitivity to context will help in the correct interpretation of Haydn's two favorite trill signs (Ex. 1g), despite their incomplete symbolism. Haydn would probably be "greatly astounded" to hear these signs rendered, as they often are today, as plain short trills without prefix or suffix (Ex. 2c), when the plain short trill is suitable only in passages of percussive brilliance. In a legato context, an ascending conjunct line demands a prefix from below if the trill is to flow smoothly from the preceding note by continuously conjunct motion and a turned suffix or added anticipation if it is to be joined to the succeeding note, while a legato descending conjunct line calls for a plain beginning to the trill or a prefix from above, as well as a turned suffix or added anticipation (2d). Omission of necessary prefixes or suffixes will alter the articulation from legato to staccato (2e).

The same method can even cast some light upon the meaning of the prime example of an ambiguous ornament, the half-mordent or "Haydn ornament." A passage taken from the early string trios will illustrate how an acquaintance with traditional concepts of ornament context can

---

[15]Ibid., 117 (transl., 134).

Example 2

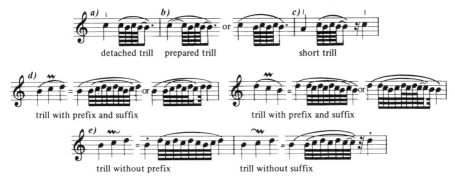

be of aid in the identification and interpretation of this enigmatic ornament, and at the same time help resolve some of the dilemmas raised by an inconsistent use of ornament symbols on the part of Haydn and the copyists. Five of the sources for Hoboken V:D3 exhibit conflicting signs for the same ornament (see Example 3). The earliest source, a copy which has some pretensions to authenticity since it is in the hand of the Fürnberg copyist No. 1,[16] calls for the "Haydn ornament" in the first violin but a trill in the second violin (Example 3a); succeeding copies substitute a trill (3b), a trill within a slur (3c), a trill at the end of a slur (3d), and a staccato tied trill at the end of a slur (3e). Such apparently meaningless variation within five otherwise closely related copies verges upon the inexplicable, but the puzzle can be neatly solved by an analysis of the context.

Example 3. String Trio Hob. V: D3
    a) Budapest, National Széchényi Library, K 1137
    b) Prague, National Museum (Pachta Archive), XXII D 31
    c) Berlin, Staatsbibliothek Stiftung preussischer Kulturbesitz, Mus. ms. 10044.5
    d) Washington, D.C., Library of Congress, Music Division, M351 A2 H43–45 (J–4)
    e) Berlin, Mus. ms. 10043.2

[16] Feder, "Überlieferung," 16.

C. P. E. Bach, Leopold Mozart, Quantz, Marpurg, and Türk make it clear that the ornament Haydn termed a half-mordent was a variety of turn.[17] The turn had several guises (see Example 4): it was usually rapid and percussive (Example 4a), but there was also a slow turn for long notes or slow tempos (4b), a snapped turn which emphasized the main note (4c), and a trilled turn for connecting descending conjunct legato lines (4d). Of this last, Emanuel Bach says,

> The turn [Example 4e] allies itself with the short trill [4f] when its first two notes are alternated with extreme rapidity. . . . The effect . . . [is] of a short trill with a suffix [4g, second illustration]. This trilled turn has no distinctive symbol. . . . It is used only in a descending second, the first note of which is drawn into [slurred to] the embellishment.[18]

Example 4

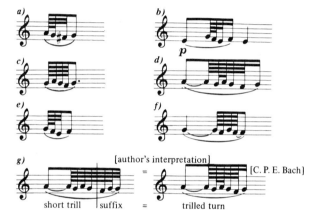

Taken together, the five variant ornament symbols in Hoboken V:D3 exactly fit this description. The Fürnberg copyist's "Haydn ornament" in this case was very probably meant to indicate not the usual staccato turn or half-mordent, but a somewhat more complex variety of turn, the trilled turn. The divergent symbols employed by the other copyists are simply a series of perfectly adequate attempts to represent the same sound in the absence of any distinctive symbol. These copyists didn't waste time examining their consciences over possible inconsistencies in their use of ornament symbols. They simply assumed that the melodic context of a descending conjunct line, the rhythmic context of an off-beat note, the harmonic context of dissonance, and the gay *Affekt* of a non-*cantabile* movement would make it obvious that the ornament in question, no matter what the symbol used to represent it, could only be a

[17] Bach, *Versuch,* 85–[98] (transl., 112–27); L. Mozart, *Violinschule,* 113–17 (transl., 106–09); Quantz, *Versuch,* 80–81 (transl., 97–98); Marpurg, *Anleitung,* 52–53; Türk, *Klavierschule,* 282–93.

[18] Bach, *Versuch,* 92–93 (transl., 121).

short turned trill or a trilled turn. The copyist of the third manuscript (3c), who indicates a legato ending to the ornament, seems to have leaned to the former, but the other four copyists apparently assumed that an implied or stated staccato articulation in such a context would be sufficient indication to the performer that a trilled turn was intended. And, despite a heterogeneous and transitional notation and inconsistent usage, most eighteenth-century performers probably would, in fact, have been able to recognize this ornament from its context alone. An awareness of context can also provide the modern performer with a very potent means to the identification and interpretation of Haydn's instrumental sign ornaments.

Indicators of Early Piano Writing in the Haydn Sonatas

LESLIE TUNG

The determination of the instrumentation for Haydn's solo keyboard sonatas written between 1766 and 1776 is complicated by the great variety of design and quality of craftsmanship found in the clavichords, harpsichords, and early pianos of the time. In addition, the ascendance of the piano was hampered by the difficulty of learning to play an instrument on which the dynamics were regulated by the force of individual finger strokes and on which the tone was beyond control once the key had been depressed. For these reasons and obvious economic motivations, keyboard works of the time were published as playable on almost any instrument available.

Our understanding of this period is also clouded by its liberal performance practice and by modern pianistic effects. For example, a sustained inner or lower part in eighteenth-century music would not necessarily have required the sustaining quality of piano tone. On the harpsichord the note would simply have been struck again or, to quote C. P. E. Bach, accepted as one of those "many things which one must imagine without really hearing"[1] (just as today we are frequently asked to imagine a crescendo on a single sustained note on our piano while knowing such a thing is actually impossible). Thus the pedal points found in the Allegro of the Sonata Hob. XVI:21 (ChL. 36), as in mm. 41–43, would not have unduly disturbed a harpsichordist and therefore cannot be taken as dependable indicators of piano writing. Equally unreliable are such modern pianistic effects as those associated with bass octaves or tremolo. The thunderous dramatics of such devices would not have been possible until later, on the larger, heavier-sounding instruments used by Clementi or Beethoven.

In Haydn's keyboard music care must also be taken in evaluating ele-

[1] Bach, *Versuch,* I, 78 (transl., 106).

ments, like frequent ornamentation, short articulation slurs, and quick, punctuated rhythms, which appear to us today as idiomatic for harpsichord. It is true that these can be observed in the "Esterházy" sonatas Hob. XVI:21–26 (ChL. 36–41), which were probably written for harpsichord. But they are also seen in the first movement of the C-minor sonata Hob. XVI:20 (ChL. 33), a work widely accepted as written for piano. Punctuated rhythms and ornamentation also can be found in Hob. XVI:19 and 33 (ChL. 30, 34). But as we shall see, more conclusive evidence suggests these sonatas were also written for piano. It is important to remember that such passages might have been quite lively and articulate on the pianos of the time, even if they sound somewhat muddled on our modern instruments. Thus ornamentation, articulation slurs, and punctuated rhythms also fail as indicators of instrumentation, since they remained consistent elements of Haydn's general keyboard style.

To identify early piano writing one must not only take into account instrument construction and capabilities but also find strong correlations among several relevant characteristics in the same works. There are several such characteristics in the Haydn sonatas written between 1766 and 1776: lengthy passages which imply a crescendo instead of terraced dynamics, harmonic texture or singing lines which would be enhanced by subtle or rapid dynamic nuances, melodic lines whose continuity depends on the use of sustained legato with subdued accompaniment, closely spaced Alberti-type accompaniments, and passages which imply an extended "open pedal" effect.

Perhaps the most significant indications of Haydn's appreciation of the new expressive potential of the piano are passages such as mm. 53–63 of the Sonata Hob. XVI:19 (ChL. 30) in D major, first movement, whose gradual dramatic intensification implies a crescendo. Such writing was part of the newer expressive style of the time, and it required an instrument responsive to gradual changes of inner feeling, not one intended for the terraced dynamics or aristocratic distance of the older style.

The sensitivity of the piano is also better suited to passages containing quick and often surprising harmonic changes, as in Hob. XVI:46 (ChL. 31) in A-flat major, 1, 31–32, 83–86; or deceptive crescendo effects, as in Hob. XVI:18 (ChL. 20) in B-flat major, i, 70–74, which would only be successful on an instrument capable of a true *subito piano*. Also, passages such as found in Hob. XVI:46, iii, 29–37 would lose much of their subtle humor without the nuance and finer control of the piano.

The new singing, sustaining style is especially evident in keyboard writing where the illusion of expressive vocal leaps seems to be intended. A well-known passage from the C-minor Sonata, i, 13–14 contains authentic dynamic indications which seem to require the piano. It is not out of the question that similar passages, even if unmarked, should be played on the same instrument, as in XVI:44 (ChL. 32) in G minor, ii, 18–22.

The piano's ability to carry a sustained melody over an accompaniment texture is a result of a combination of agogics, voicing, and the softer attack of its tone. To be effective, a passage such as Hob. XVI:33 (ChL. 34) in D major, ii, 12–16 would demand these pianistic attributes if the singing of the long melody notes is to continue uninterrupted by the faster notes of the accompaniment. (Comparison with an Adagio from the "Esterházy" set, Hob. XVI:23 [ChL. 38] in F major, shows how the melody would have to be ornamented to compensate for the poorer sustaining power of the harpsichord.) Haydn was writing such pianistic textures as early as the G-major Capriccio Hob. XVII:1 in 1765. They can also be found in the Trio of the Menuetto of Hob. XVI:43 (ChL. 35) in A-flat major, and they are prominent in the beautiful slow movements of Hob. XVI:19 and 46 (ChL. 30, 31). The Adagio of the latter is an especially complicated study in texture which demands the fine voicing and subtle shadings of the piano, particularly in such places as m. 15, where the melody must be heard through a *higher* ornamented accompaniment.

The use of Alberti bass or its variant in triplet form, as in Hob. XVI:43, i, 12ff., is also relevant in determining the instrumentation of these sonatas. Such accompaniment provides a rich, closely spaced sound that is especially effective on the piano, where the rhythmic activity would not overwhelm the resonance of the total harmony. In sonatas where other indicators suggest the use of piano, the Alberti figure is also found extensively, one example being the first movement of Hob. XVI:45 (ChL. 29) in E-flat major. In the sonatas probably intended for harpsichord, it is used only in much shorter passages, or its fuller three-pitch pattern is reduced to two notes, as in Hob. XVI:23, i, 15ff. This figuration shows a stronger interest in rhythmic activity but less concern for harmonic fullness.

Finally, an obviously unique pianistic effect is produced by playing at length without damping the accumulating sound. That Haydn was aware of such "open pedal" effects is shown definitely in a later sonata, Hob. XVI:50 (ChL. 60), first movement, where it is twice explicitly indicated. But passages in two of these earlier works could invite similar treatment: Hob. XVI:44 (ChL. 32) in G minor, i, 67–70; and the C-minor Sonata, i, 24–26.

Given the complexity of the problem we must concede that, in many cases, even apparently reliable indicators of early piano writing offer only suggestions, not definite conclusions. Indeed, the suggested instrumentation often seems to change from one movement to the next in the same work (something which Haydn surely never intended). For example, the finale of Hob. XVI:45 (ChL. 29) might sound more sparkling if played on harpsichord, but the first movement would be far more effective on piano. Similarly one could imagine that the change in texture in the

Adagio of Hob. XVI:24 (ChL. 39) in D major would be more effective on piano, even though this work belongs to the "Esterházy" set and was probably intended for harpsichord.

Nevertheless the indicators described above support Christa Landon's summary of the dynamic indications in the extant autographs which suggest the piano:

Hob. XVI:18 (ChL. 20) in B-flat major: ii, 42

Hob. XVI:20 (ChL. 33) in C minor: many indications including *f–p*

Hob. XVI:21–26 (ChL. 36–41): only two dynamic markings, one an "echo" [probably written for harpsichord]

Hob. XVI:29 (ChL. 44) in F major: return to dynamic markings[2]

In addition, the indicators suggest that all the sonatas Hob. XIV:5, XVI:45, 19, 46, 44, 20, 33, 43 (ChL. 28–35) are for piano; they are believed to date from the middle 1760s to the middle 1770s. Of the remaining sonatas from our time period, Hob. XVI:27 (ChL. 42) in G major would seem to imply the piano, but XVI:28 (ChL. 43) in E-flat major could be for harpsichord. In any case, it seems significant that this first coherent large group of Haydn's sonatas originated during the crucial third period of Haydn's development in the early 1770s.[3] They comprise an important contribution to piano literature which predates the first sonatas of Mozart.

[2] Haydn, *Sonatas,* I, foreword, pp. vi–vii.
[3] As delineated in Larsen-Landon.

PART FOUR: FORM AND STYLE

Round Table

"Classical Period" and "Classical Style" in Eighteenth-Century Music[1]

DONALD J. GROUT, *Chairman*   EUGENE HELM
BARRY S. BROOK   MILAN POŠTOLKA
BATHIA CHURGIN   CHARLES ROSEN
GERHARD CROLL   JAMES WEBSTER

Vienna and Europe: Musical Currents in the Middle of the Eighteenth Century

The Italian Symphonic Background to Haydn's Early Symphonies and Opera Overtures

CHURGIN When Haydn began composing symphonies in the late 1750s, he turned to a form that had been intensively developed for some thirty years. He could thus draw on a large repertoire providing a wide range of possibilities in both style and expression. Conspicuous in number were symphonies and overtures by Austrian, German, and Bohemian composers, and the best-known Italians of the time.

It was in Italy that the Classic symphony had its origin and where the transition from Baroque to Classic began in earnest. Already evident by the 1720s, this transition was in full swing in the thirties, a decade in which Classic traits already predominate. By the forties, when the new style reached Vienna, Paris, Mannheim, and other European centers, most Baroque traits had been eliminated in the music of the younger Italians.

[1] The text of this report was prepared by James Webster.

The Italian symphonic repertory comprises both the independent or concert symphony and the Italian overture, genres that are quite distinct, though they hold some traits in common. Most of the first symphonists were Italians active in the 1720s and 1730s. The Milanese master Giovanni Battista Sammartini was the only major Italian symphonist before Haydn.[2] Born more than thirty years earlier than Haydn, in 1700/01, he died in 1775. Of Sammartini's sixty-eight extant authentic symphonies, fifty-six—all the early and middle works—were probably composed by 1758. His earliest dated symphonies can be traced back to the year 1732, though some were undoubtedly composed before that time.

Although no other Italian symphonist could rival Sammartini's excellence, there were a number of secondary figures who produced a host of works in the new form. These composers were largely north Italian and Milanese, and a group of them constitutes the earliest symphonic school in Europe. Together with Sammartini this school consists of Antonio Brioschi, composer of some sixty extant authentic symphonies and trios, and such lesser Milanese figures as Galimberti, Giulini, and Chiesa. Other minor symphonists include Fortunato Chelleri, Tartini, and Padre Martini. Of the far more numerous composers of Italian overtures, the most notable are Leo, Galuppi, and Jommelli.

Widely disseminated in the period up to c. 1760, Italian symphonies and overtures had considerable influence on the main symphonic schools. The Fonds Blancheton in Paris, the greater part probably copied by the early 1740s, contains 300 instrumental works, most of them Italian. Among the many Milanese works are seventeen of the nineteen early symphonies by Sammartini and thirty-five compositions by Brioschi.[3] More important for the Viennese background is the Waldstein collection, now housed in Prague.[4] Containing over 1,000 compositions of all types, it is rich in Italian symphonies and overtures, including thirty-five symphonies by Sammartini, almost all of them from his middle period. Italian symphonic works, especially overtures, were also well represented in the inventory of music at Eisenstadt, 1759–61.[5]

In Vienna itself, the performance of operas by Galuppi and Gluck in the later 1740s and Jommelli's visit in 1749 brought immediate contact with the new Italian style;[6] this contact was indirectly reinforced by Wagenseil, whose symphonies up to the mid-1750s were actually opera overtures on the Italian model, though with a far stronger emphasis on development.[7] According to Giuseppe Carpani, Haydn's early biogra-

[2] See Churgin, *Symphonies,* I.

[3] See the thematic catalogue in Laurencie, *Blancheton.* Brioschi probably worked near rather than in Milan. The total number of works attributed to him in Blancheton probably includes compositions by other composers.

[4] See Rutova, "Waldstein"   [5] Larsen, "Quartbuch," 115.

[6] O. Deutsch, "Repertoire"   [7] See Kucaba, "Wagenseil"

pher, Sammartini's symphonies probably reached Viennese audiences in the 1750s and created a sensation there.[8] We know that a late Sammartini symphony was obtained in Vienna for the Bishop of Olmütz in 1759,[9] and the Eisenstadt inventory lists two Sammartini symphonies as well. The score of Sammartini's first opera, *Memet,* dated 1732, actually belongs to the collection once owned by Georg Reutter the younger, and the opera may have been performed in Vienna that year.

The early Classic Italian overture stressed brilliance of sound, rhythmic energy in the fast movements, clarity and simplicity of structure. It gave little attention to development or subtleties of harmony and form. The overture of the 1730s and early 1740s already embodies many standard features, such as the large orchestra with basic scoring of two oboes, two horns, and strings, and the three-movement cycle usually ending with a fast 3/8 minuet. First movements typically have a nonrepeating sonata form without a separate development section or with a very short development. Many first movements emphasize sharp contrast between a fanfarelike primary theme and a more lyrical secondary idea, often in minor, *piano,* and reduced texture that is sometimes imitative as well. The shorter and simpler succeeding movements utilize binary and ternary forms, or a sonata form in the finale like the first movement.

A special type of overture is the so-called da capo overture (I borrow the term from Professor Jan LaRue). Here, a large-scale A-B-A replaces the three-movement plan. A slow movement is inserted at some point in the first movement, often after the exposition, the development, or the recapitulation; then part of the first movement returns to end the overture, sometimes in coda-like fashion. Early examples occur in Leo's overture to *L'Olimpiade* (1737) and Sammartini's symphony J-C 44 (before 1747).[10]

With respect to Haydn, the Italian overture made its greatest impact, as one would think, on the overtures to his Italian operas, which Haydn accommodated to the Italian style as well. Of eleven such overtures, two have the standard three movements (*Acide* [1762; overture 1773] and *L'infedeltà delusa* [1773]); four are da capo types (*Lo speziale* [1768]; *L'incontro improvviso* [1775]; *L'isola disabitata* [1779]; *Armida* [1783]); that to *La vera costanza* (1779) has three movements of which the last is in da capo form; and four are in one movement (*Il mondo della luna* [1777]; *La fedeltà premiata* [1780]; *Orlando paladino* [1782]; *Orfeo* [1791]). The first movements and single-movement overtures are marked by nonrepeating

[8] Carpani, *Haydine,* 57–58 (2nd ed., 62–63); cf. Gotwals, Haydn, 217–18.
[9] See Sehnal, "Egk"
[10] The J-C numbers refer to Jenkins-Churgin. On the Italian overture and the da capo overture, see LaRue, "Sinfonia." (In Sammartini's symphony the slow movement is combined with the first, but the minuet finale is retained.)

sonata form, which by contrast is uncommon in the symphonies. In the overtures to *Orlando Paladino* and *Armida,* Haydn even casts the allegro movements in sonata form without a separate development section, though powerful development occurs in the recapitulation. Most of the overtures also reflect Italian overture traits in their relatively simple structure, texture, harmony, and in other aspects.

In three outstanding cases Haydn transferred the technique of inserted movements from the da capo overture to his concert symphonies: Nos. 45 and 46, both dated 1772, and No. 67, dated c. 1778. All three stem from the 1770s, when Haydn was most active as an opera composer. In the "Farewell" Symphony, No. 45 in F-sharp minor, Haydn incorporates a lyrical episode in the development of the first movement; in No. 46 in B major he recalls a varied form of the minuet in the coda of the finale. Both examples represent a transformation of the overture procedure for expressive purposes and large-scale integration. Haydn again modifies the finale of No. 67 in F major, this time strictly following the da capo scheme by interpolating an adagio between the exposition and recapitulation.

Turning to Haydn's early concert symphonies, I have used for comparison thirty-nine works dating from the start of Haydn's symphonic writing, c. 1757/59 to c. 1765.[11] The most obvious overture connections relate first to general features: the scoring for two oboes, two horns, and strings, which had become standard in the concert symphony of the 1750s; the three-movement cycle in fourteen symphonies, over one-third of this early group;[12] and the 3/8 or 3/4 minuet finale, also in fourteen symphonies.[13]

More intrinsic is Haydn's characteristic resort in the first movements to the kind of sharp thematic contrast in the secondary key area established by the overture. Even monothematic movements such as No. 30/i incorporate typical secondary theme contrasts in nonmelodic aspects. In fact, in nineteen movements of fifteen symphonies, Haydn dramatizes thematic contrast still further by introducing a theme in the secondary key area that is entirely or largely in the dominant minor, a frequent overture device.[14] These examples are telling reminders of the importance of conventional thematic contrast in these early works.

The style of the Italian concert symphony was quite different from the Italian overture, since it was conceived for performance outside the theater. Composers emphasized a greater variety and sophistication of form

[11] R. Landon's datings in Haydn, *Symphonies* have been followed. This group comprises Nos. 1–25, 27–34, 36, 37, 40, 72, and Hob. I:107 ("A") and 108 ("B").

[12] Nos. 1, 2, 4, 9, 10, 12, 16–19, 25, 27, 30, Hob. I:107.

[13] Nos. 1, 2, 4, 9, 10, 15, 17–20, 27, 30, 32, 37. In Nos. 15, 20, 32, and 37, which have four movements in all, there is a $\frac{3}{4}$ minuet as well.

[14] Haydn, Nos. 1/i, ii; 2/i; 4/i; 12/iii; 15/i; 17/iii; 18/i, ii; 20/i; 23/i; 27/i; 29/iv; 30/i; 32/i, iv; 36/i, iv; 37/i.

and other stylistic elements, and a broader spectrum of feeling. Italian concert symphonies of the 1730s already contain many features that became standard in later symphonies. In all fundamental respects, the concert symphony as an independent Classic genre was thus established by about 1740.

Unlike the overture, these symphonies call for a smaller string orchestra in three or four parts. They utilize far more variety of key and meter, such as 2/4, 3/4, and 3/8 first movements; 2/4 and 12/8 second movements; 2/4 and 3/8 nonminuet finales; and 3/4 rather than 3/8 minuet finales.

Movements are longer and richer in musical events, and nonminuet finales occur frequently. It is here that we find a preference for full sonata form, including a long development and a recapitulation beginning with the primary theme in the tonic. The first-movement form of the overture, without separate development, is avoided in the symphonic movements of this period, but it occasionally appears in slow movements and short finales. Also found occasionally is the type of sonata form with an incomplete recapitulation, beginning with material after the primary theme, a form also found in the Scarlatti sonatas and symphonies of Johann Stamitz. Thus, all the main types of sonata form can be found in the Italian concert symphony before 1740.

Though the sonata form movements thus reflect different stages of evolution, a substantial number are fully Classical in their definition of key areas, cadences, and thematic functions; organization of harmonic rhythm; and the integration of a structure based on local contrasts. Rather than the typically thin string texture of the overture, the early symphonists preferred fuller and more varied textures. Sammartini, Brioschi, and other Milanese composers may in fact be responsible for introducing into the symphony the "dialoguing" second violin that exchanges material or contrasts with the first violin in nonimitative counterpoint.

It is Sammartini's middle symphonies, the most advanced Italian examples of the period, that best represent the next stage of the Italian concert symphony, extending to the beginning of Haydn's symphonic writing. These works bear comparison with Haydn's early symphonies in several respects: in their intense rhythmic drive and continuity; irregular phrase structure; buffo elements; careful workmanship; and compact and sophisticated structure. Four symphonies in minor anticipate many "Sturm und Drang" characteristics, most of all the astonishing symphony in G minor, J-C 57, whose finale Gluck borrowed in 1749. Sammartini's textures also become more and more refined in part writing, dialoguing, and the use of imitative and nonimatative counterpoint.

Another Haydnesque feature found in Sammartini's symphonies is the type of recapitulation that is largely reformulated after the primary theme—in order and presentation of ideas, and sometimes in harmonic emphasis. As in Haydn, these sections function as a continuing development. Such recapitulations, however, are not present solely in Sammartini and Haydn, but in symphonies by many composers from the early period on, especially Brioschi and Wagenseil.

Though we should be cautious about finding specific influences of one composer on another in a period still so little known as this, I was struck by the appearance of one of Sammartini's most characteristic middle-symphony procedures in nineteen early Haydn symphonies.[15] In sonata-form movements this is a type of retransition by descending phrase sequence from the supertonic to the tonic, usually elided to the recapitulation. Though I have found scattered examples in Italian overtures, and in Monn and Wagenseil, it may be that Haydn also became acquainted with its possibilities through Sammartini's music. Typically in reduced texture and *piano,* the phrases in Sammartini are usually derived from secondary or closing themes, while Haydn varies the thematic source, tonal placement, and continuation, even introducing a sense of false re-transition.[16] A striking example in Haydn's symphony No. 15 (dated c. 1760–63) exactly parallels Sammartini's type with tutti interruption as found in his C-major symphony, J-C 4, probably composed c. 1750 (see Example 1). It is likely that this work was known in Vienna, where a copy was probably obtained for the Bishop of Olmütz in 1760. Manuscript copies can be found in the Gesellschaft der Musikfreunde and the Waldstein collection, as well as in many other sources.

Example 1

a) Sammartini, Symphony in C major, J-C 4 (c. 1750, i, 61–68 (Karlsruhe, Badische Landesbibliothek, Mus. Ms. 812)

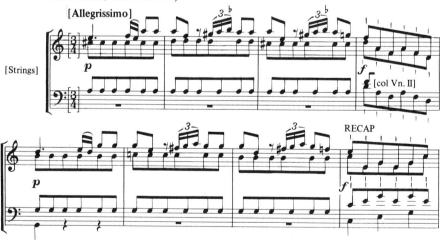

[15] Nos. 1/i, 3/i; 6/i; 8/ii; 9/i; 13/i; 14/iv; 15/i; 17/i; 18/ii; 22/ii; 23/i; 24/iv; 29/i; 33/i; 34/ii; 36/i, iv; 40/i; Hob. I:107/i, iii ("Symphony A").

[16] For example, the retransition in No. 29/i begins in the subdominant. False retransitions occur in Nos. 17/i and 36/i.

b) Haydn, Symphony No. 15 in D major (c. 1760–63), i, 74–82

The focus of attention in most of Haydn's early symphonies is already on the developmental process. While development in Sammartini is far more important and imaginative than we realize, it does not usually become the prime element. We rarely find in his middle works the Haydnesque techniques of fragmentation and developmental extension, or long passages devoted to the development of a single motive. An extreme example occurs in Haydn's Symphony No. 28 (1765), where the first movement is based almost entirely on one rhythmic motive. The emphasis in Sammartini is essentially different: it is on the invention of new phrases that incorporate variants of previous phrases and motives, and on the linking of ideas from different sources. Intervallic, rhythmic, and harmonic variation are applied with considerable subtlety within themes, in thematic derivations, and the characteristic variants of secondary themes found in recapitulations. An illustration appears in Example 2. The second phrase of the secondary theme balances the first by combining its melodic and rhythmic motives in a kind of free diminution. The basic unit is halved from four beats to two; the harmonic rhythm accelerates accordingly, and the bass drops out. So many changes occur simultaneously that the listener may at first not even perceive the connections among the phrases.

Example 2 Sammartini, Symphony in G major, J-C 52, i (Prague, National Museum, Waldstein XXXIV C404)

(m = motive; r = rhythm)

In conclusion, though Haydn's early symphonies reflect his Viennese heritage and strong individuality, they also incorporate many elements from the Italian symphonic tradition. Whether transmitted directly or indirectly, they underscore the formative role played by Italian composers in the creation of the Classic symphony.

Did Haydn "Synthesize" the Classical String Quartet?

WEBSTER The term "Classical style" appears to claim the virtues of "classic" music, in the general sense, for a particular historical period.[17] One problem with this concept is its evolutionary bias: Haydn and Mozart, it is thought, gradually perfected Classical style by means of a "synthesis" of diverse earlier "antecedents," which thus "influenced" their development. I would like to subject these hypotheses to brief critical examination. I take as my test case Haydn's string quartets.

The hypothesis that Haydn's string quartets synthesized various earlier genres appears to originate with Adolf Sandberger, writing around 1900. His "antecedents" include virtually every mid-century instrumental genre:

> [Haydn's quartets] preserve the remains of the former suite, as well as the trio-sonata and the *Quadro,* but they also number the opera overture, the keyboard sonata, and the concerto [among their ancestors]. . . . Haydn's immediate inspiration was doubtless the partita, but even in his early works the synthesis of operatic, chamber, and suite-related elements is so profound that only the historically adept can distinguish among them.[18]

This notion arises, in part, from a confusion of aesthetic quality and historical origins. As a whole, what we call Classical style developed out of many different regional and stylistic antecedents. But in its apparent perfection, Haydn's and Mozart's mature music dominates our view of the entire period. Measured against this ideal, earlier repertories seem to us imperfect; we call them "immature," "pre-Classical," mere "stages" in a "development" which was "not yet" complete. Hence the evolutionary interpretation: every common feature becomes a historical "link" between Haydn and his (clever) predecessor, and hence an "influence" on

---

[17] Blume, "Klassik"; Finscher, "Klassik."
[18] Sandberger, "Streichquartett," 59 (repr., 256).

him by that (clever) predecessor.[19] Their status as mere "links" helps us avoid careful investigation of these repertories, or of their actual historical relationship to Haydn. In this frame of mind, it is easy to believe that Haydn did "synthesize" them into Classical style—making his perfection seem all the more formidable.

This interpretation derives in part from Mozart's example. But while Mozart's undeniable assimilation of various styles depended on his continual exposure, from earliest childhood, to many different musical cultures all over Europe, Haydn never traveled as far as 100 miles from Vienna until he was almost sixty. As potential influences on Haydn, we should acknowledge only that music which he could have encountered in Vienna and at the courts where he was employed. A further reason for rejecting the "synthesis" hypothesis for the string quartet is that it was not systematically cultivated in Austria until the 1780s. Previously, Haydn and Mozart wrote quartets only occasionally, and (as far as we know) only for private use, not for publication. In this sense (not necessarily in others), their earlier production was "occasional" music, local in inspiration and perhaps in intended effect.

On the basis of their titles and groupings in the Breitkopf thematic catalogues, Sandberger (following Pohl) claimed that Haydn's early quartets were transmitted as two different groups: the North German *Quadro* and the South-German-Austrian suite.[20] But Haydn played no part in establishing Breitkopf's listings; neither their groupings nor their terminology is reflected in the authentic sources; nor do any distinctions of chronology or style correspond to them.[21] Hence Sandberger's conclusions are untenable.

Many mid-century repertories did not circulate widely in Vienna. There was no regular publication of music there until Artaria's firm was established just before 1780. Until that date, and in many cases even afterwards, the primary means of distribution was manuscript copies. Although some printed instrumental music was imported and sold by Viennese booksellers, and manuscript orchestral and operatic music was acquired for performance at court and in the theater, imported chamber music was negligible compared to local production.[22] Similarly, after 1750 there was relatively little migration into Vienna from Italy, Paris, Berlin, or Mannheim. No exposure of the Mannheim style took place in Vienna comparable to that which it enjoyed in Paris.[23]

---

[19] The most influential claim of this kind was Hugo Riemann's interpretation of the "Mannheim School," particularly Johann Stamitz, as the "link" between J. S. Bach and Haydn. See Larsen, "Mannheim."

[20] Sandberger, "Streichquartett," 44 (repr., 228–29).

[21] Feder, JHW XII:1, foreword; Webster, "Chronology," 42–43.

[22] Weinmann, *Verleger;* Gericke, *Musikalienhandel.*

[23] Gericke, *Musikalienhandel,* 28; Newman, *Classic,* 60–61, 66–67.

The claims made on behalf of composers like Sammartini and C. P. E. Bach as influences on Haydn's quartets must be interpreted in this context. We know through Professor Churgin and others that Italian overtures and symphonies were performed in mid-century Vienna and environs. And Carpani, who apparently originated the story of Sammartini's influence on Haydn, speaks logically of *orchestral* style. But Griesinger's later and better-known anecdote then brought this story into connection with Haydn's quartets.[24] In fact, however, the external circumstances and style of Haydn's compositional activity varied substantially from genre to genre.[25] (For example, most earlier writers on Haydn's early quartets recognized the three-movement symphony Hob. I:107 in B-flat major ["Symphony A"], which used to masquerade as Op. 1, No. 5, as an interloper.) Thus even if we were to agree that Sammartini influenced Haydn's early symphonies, it would not be proper to deduce a similar influence on his early quartets.

C. P. E. Bach's influence on Haydn *is* documented, not least by Haydn himself.[26] But this influence seems restricted primarily to Haydn's keyboard music, his mastery of compositional thinking,[27] and his sense of rhetoric.[28] Furthermore, it does not manifest itself until the late 1760s. Also, we know of hardly any ensemble music without keyboard from Bach's pen; none was available in Vienna.[29] And finally, Bach's ensemble music belongs to the conservative North German School based on the continuo and in the style of *Empfindsamkeit*. In all these respects, it is not relevant to Haydn's early quartet-divertimenti.

The historical context of Haydn's early string quartets was Austrian chamber music in the 1750s, of which there is still no systematic survey.[30] Haydn's early quartets were an intensification of one subspecies of this repertory: the *Divertimento à quattro* for four solo strings. Explanation of their origins or their external form by appealing to more remote phenomena is neither necessary nor desirable.[31] Even here, I would discard the search for "influences" and substitute the idea of compositional "models." A "model" or a specifically musical "stimulus" is closer to the actual process of composition, I believe, than broad but vague stylistic categories.

The evolutionary interpretation of Haydn's string quartets is thus in

[24] Griesinger, 14–15 (modern ed., 12; Gotwals, *Haydn,* 12–13); Carpani, *Haydine,* 57–58 (2nd ed., 62–63) (cf. Gotwals, *Haydn,* 217, n.13). See also Churgin-Jenkins, col. 1337, and Churgin's and Croll's remarks elsewhere in this Round Table.
[25] Larsen-Landon, col. 1895; Feder, "Pole"   [26] Schmid, "Bach"; Abert, "Klavier"
[27] Spitta, "Pohl," 169–73; Finscher *Streichquartett,* I *passim,* e.g., 192–97.
[28] Tovey, "Chamber," repr., 28; cf. the section "Rhetorical Performance" in Workshop 6.
[29] Schmid, *Kammermusik;* cf. Gericke, *Musikalienhandel,* 13–14, 133, and the catalogue 113–31.
[30] A recent attempt is Webster, "Chamber."
[31] Cf. Larsen, "Observations," 117–20; cf. also the balanced account by Abbé Stadler quoted in the Free Paper by A. Peter Brown elsewhere in this volume.

part the reverse of the historical truth. It was not synthesis of pre-Classical genres from all over Europe, but rather a development within a local tradition that became the central element in *later* explanations of the rise of a genre. For the notion of the "Classical string quartet" was an invention of the 1790s and early 1800s. In 1793, for example, Heinrich Christoph Koch singled out Haydn's and Mozart's recent quartets—those written after 1780—as the "classic" examples of the genre.[32] With the addition of early and middle Beethoven this judgement has persisted ever since. "Classical" chamber music could thus emerge only in the act of forgetting its own origins.

Remarks: Bohemia

POŠTOLKA In the eighteenth century, as we know, a number of Bohemian composers and performers contributed to the development of European music outside their native country. In addition, however, a remarkable music life continued inside Bohemia. I will concentrate here on church music, the most important branch. In the first half of the eighteenth century, the Baroque culminated in the music of B. M. Černohorský, Šimon Brixi (father of Fr. X. Brixi), and J. D. Zelenka, as well as many others, particularly J. C. Gayer, J. A. Görbig, G. Jacob and Č. Vaňura. Some features of their style, such as melodic motifs of folk character, syncopated and dance rhythms, and parallel progressions in sixths and thirds, suggest an affinity with the Czech pre-Classical idiom.

About the middle of the century, new trends became apparent in the works of F. Habermann and J. A. Sehling. In Habermann's later works, elements of the pre-Classical and early Classical styles predominate. The most outstanding among his pupils were Mysliveček, J. L. Oehlschlägel, and Fr. X. Dušek. Oehlschlägel and Fr. X. Brixi wrote in a mixture of pre-Classical and early Classical styles. Their music was a decisive model for a large number of minor composers.

Many other genres were cultivated in Bohemia: organ music (J. Seger, J. Kuchař), instrumental music (Dušek), stage works (J. A. Koželuch, V. Praupner), oratorios, keyboard music (Dušek). Thus when Haydn was brought to Bohemia by Count Morzin in the late 1750s, he came to a region where nearly all musical genres of the time were intensively cultivated, and where the processes leading toward Classical style were already in progress.

Remarks: Berlin

HELM In the pre-Classical period there was a kind of "brick wall" between Berlin and Vienna. During the Seven Years' War (1756–63), Frederick

---

[32] Koch, *Versuch*, III, 325–27; transl. and discussed in Webster, "Chamber," 230–31.

the Great allowed his spectacular musical establishment to decay. The composers at his court included J. G. and K. H. Graun, Quantz, C. P. E. Bach, and the two Bendas. Bach, the only truly original composer in this group, eventually fled to Hamburg (1767) to escape the oppressive atmosphere. The Berlin theorists Kirnberger and Marpurg intensify this image of retrospective pedanticism.

The social and cultural climate in Vienna was completely different. Viennese musicians were relatively free from royal interference and religious restrictions on popular stage music. Vienna was a melting pot of many different musical cultures; Berlin was not. Berlin's industrialization and militarization continued after the Seven Years' War. On the other hand, Berlin was not subject to stringent stage literary censorship; hence there was less "need" for music to become the chief form of expression there.

In all these respects, Berlin seems an unlikely fount of inspiration for mid-century Viennese composers. When we find emotional sensitivity or sudden harmonic shifts in Haydn, we may ascribe these traits to C. P. E. Bach, at least in part. But I fail to see any evidence in Haydn's music of Bach's melodic style, or systematic study of Bach's music or of his *Versuch*. And Bach studiously ignored the string quartet. He took cognizance of the Viennese style only once, in a group of "Sonatinas" for solo harpsichord and half a dozen instruments, with as many as ten movements all in the same key. But this experiment was quickly abandoned. The modest Bach correspondence with Artaria does prove that our two cities did know of each other's existence. But the degree of cultural correspondence between them was far less than we have been led to believe.

Remarks: Stage Music

CROLL In the period 1750–70 in Vienna, we don't know exactly what took place on the stage and especially in concert life. Musical activity, especially in the theaters, depended to a certain degree on royal patronage. We possess memoranda in Maria Theresa's own hand canceling works scheduled for performance in the Kärntnertortheater. Opera and ballet were influenced by political events, including the foreign policy of Count Wenzel Kaunitz, later State Chancellor. Italian influences were due to the influential Count Durazzo, who took a special interest, for example, in Traetta's *Armida* (1761). Two years later Traetta's *Ifigenia in Tauride* was produced, in which Gluck took a great interest.

On the subject of *opera buffa, Il finto pazzo* (probably not Piccinni's but Pergolesi's *Livietta e Tracollo*) and a French parody of Pergolesi's *La serva padrona* were given in December 1758. Among oratorios, in 1758 we find Galuppi's *Adame ed Eva* produced, and Porpora is represented with several choral compositions. (Italian instrumental music has been discussed by Professor Churgin.) In connection with Kaunitz's French policy, the Viennese French Theater imported French plays and, of course, *opéra comique,* assisted by Favart. As we all know, Gluck was the chief author of *opéra comique* in Vienna in the 1750s and early 1760s.

An unjustly neglected genre is the ballet, whose principal impresario was Starzer; occasionally Aspelmayr and Gluck held this office. Almost every performance of a play was followed by at least one, usually two ballets. We have the music of more than 150 Viennese ballets from the 1750s to 1780, including over twenty by Starzer.

Remarks: Influence; Paris

BROOK What constitutes "influence" on a composer of Haydn's stature, and how does it operate? First, a composer can mature. This internal, introspective process was very strong with Haydn. A second kind of style change or influence can be effectuated by the dissemination of music. This can occur not only by the circulation of printed or manuscript music, but also when a performer introduces new music on his travels. Many factors—political, religious, familial; the relations among princely houses; the ease of currency exchange; and so forth—determine how such dissemination can occur. As an example, the ties between Mannheim and Paris were very close, not only because of their proximity and lack of political conflict, but because for musicians the two cities complemented one another commercially. But Berlin and Vienna had little direct contact. The repertoire at Schloss Harburg, for example, which received Haydn's work directly from Prince Oettingen-Wallerstein's agent in Vienna, was substantially different from that of the Hohenlohe castles. This entire topic needs further study.

A third, more subtle kind of relationship is intellectual, aesthetic, social, and psychological. Haydn's *Il mondo della luna* is a characteristic reflection of the great advances in astronomical knowledge during the eighteenth century. Haydn's style changes cannot be understood in ignorance of the literary and philosophical unease that we call the Sturm und Drang. He once wrote to the Swiss theologian Lavater, for example, saying "I love and happily read your works";[33] and in his HNV we find a copy of an important work by Lavater.

What about the psychological affect of Paris on Vienna? In pre-1780 Vienna, music was disseminated primarily by manuscript copies. But in Paris, London, and Amsterdam, the chief means was printed editions. The first editions of both Haydn and Mozart appeared in Paris; four Haydn quartets and a symphony appeared in 1764. Perhaps the Prince de

---

[33] Haydn, *Briefe,* 106 (CCLN, 32–33).

Rohan, a passionate music lover who was the ambassador to Vienna in this period, was responsible for the transmission of these pieces to Paris, or at least for the news that here was a composer worth taking note of. The later commission for the Paris symphonies was also a rare opportunity. Haydn wrote these works with that distant and fabulous city in mind, where a musician could make his fortune, or at least a decent living free from noble patronage.

Discussion

GROUT   We've heard a great deal about "antecedents," "models," "influence," "stages," "development," "synthesis," and above all that great ghost of the late nineteenth century, "evolution." These concepts may be necessary in historical writing, but they should be regarded with the highest suspicion. Of course, Professor Churgin does not imply that there is anything like a mechanical transmission, as if over a telegraph line, from Sammartini to Haydn.

ROSEN   Influence may take place long before music is published: for example, Bach's *Well-Tempered Clavier* and Mozart. On the other hand, knowledge of music does not necessarily make for influence: Beethoven was not influenced by *The Well-Tempered Clavier* at all, except indirectly through Mozart, until the end of his life.

Discussion of influence often focuses merely on borrowings of detail. But from Prof. Webster's point of view, it would be almost impossible to find "real" influences on Haydn's creation of the string quartet. He defines it as a creation *sui generis*. If he admits an influence of C. P. E. Bach on the sonata, why would he refuse it for the string quartet? Haydn often transfers effects from one genre to another.

WEBSTER   Spitta is right to emphasize C. P. E. Bach's influence on Haydn's power of musical thinking, and Tovey to emphasize his influence on Haydn's "rhetoric" (or style). An aspect of form in which he may have influenced Haydn's string quartets involves *veränderte Reprisen* movements (a binary or sonata movement whose repeated sections are written out in full, the second time with ornamentation). A set of Bach's keyboard sonatas of this type apparently became available in Vienna in 1767. In Haydn's Opp. 9, 17, 20, and 33, we find slow movements whose expositions use this technique. But it's the inflated claims of influence I was reacting against. These points don't add up to a conclusion that C. P. E. Bach influenced Haydn's string quartet in any general sense, certainly not his early quartets.

ROSEN   This concept of influence seems to go into the idea of origins. But origins are largely a question of definition. It won't do to say that so-and-so originated the Viennese string quartet in 1746. You can only say where

Haydn got the idea for the string quartet by defining the Classical string quartet. But then your only assertion about origins is that it was done by Haydn at such-and-such a date.

WEBSTER If we knew any Austrian string quartets like Haydn's, but a little earlier, we could talk about influence, stylistic development, and so on. But we don't. It's quite different from the symphony or the sonata.

ROSEN We either do not know these features before Haydn, or we know too many examples. An example of the latter case comes from Professor Churgin's paper: the move to the dominant minor in the exposition is common all over Europe, as early as J. S. Bach. We can't even begin to answer the question who did it first.

CHURGIN For operas, we have dated performances. In Leo's overtures, secondary themes in the dominant minor occur as early as the 1730s, for example *Amor vuol sofferenza* (1739). In the 1740s, Jomelli used more extended, more lyrical themes. When a procedure appears so consistently, it is historically significant.

ROSEN It was a norm among Viennese composers in the 1750s.

CHURGIN Wagenseil's first major opera, *Ariodante,* was written for Venice in 1745. The overtures to this opera and others by Wagenseil contain secondary themes in the minor. Operas by the younger Italian composers were performed in Vienna starting in the 1740s. Perhaps Haydn was influenced by them, perhaps by Wagenseil. But the Italians were the leaders in the new style.

CROLL We have nearly complete programs of the fifteen concerts given in the Burgtheater in Vienna during Lent of 1758. On February 19 and 28 a "Concert de plusieurs instruments seuls de Sammartini" was performed.

ROSEN I think that the term "da capo overture" used by Professors LaRue and Churgin is not well defined. In these movements, the first A does not end in the tonic; it is like the exposition of a sonata form. The last A is like a recapitulation. In the true da capo, the first A closes in the tonic, and the two A's are exactly alike.

CHURGIN The form is very flexible; it could just as well be called ABA'. In Haydn's Symphony No. 67 in F major, finale, we find an exposition, a contrasting Adagio middle section, and a complete recapitulation. In the overture to *L'isola disabitata,* the first A is a complete sonata form; then follow transition, slow movement, return to the opening themes, and coda. Both of these types are very common.

ROSEN These are quite different forms. The former is a primitive sonata form with an inserted trio. This form is very common; it even persists into the nineteenth century. A Sammartini symphony in A major has this form; the reduced texture without basses and the *piano* dynamics make it function like a kind of trio.[34]

CHURGIN But this middle section also has developmental characteristics: change of mode and texture, and new treatment of old material. In the da capo overture, there is always a change of tempo.

ROSEN Formally speaking, the change of tempo is not essential.

GROUT I think we need new terminology for these forms.

BROOK We should be cautious about claiming "influence" merely because two repertories show close similarities. Even performances in the Burgtheater don't necessarily imply that Sammartini influenced Haydn. Stronger similarities may well exist between pre-Classical Viennese composers and Haydn.

ROSEN The Italians created certain aspects of the new style, but other aspects, like thematic development, they used poorly.

CHURGIN Thematic development isn't essential to Classical style. Perhaps it is for Haydn and C. P. E. Bach, but not for Mozart and many other composers. Many contemporary descriptions of the symphony omit the idea of development entirely.

ROSEN In Mozart it becomes essential in the 1780s.

CHURGIN We have to see Haydn's place in the total scene of the eighteenth century: we should not say that Classical style is like Haydn, but fit Haydn into the Classical style.

ROSEN If it isn't just a detail, a composer picks up traits from an entire group—a stylistic norm. It's impossible to talk about the "influence" of one composer, like Sammartini, on Haydn.

CHURGIN Sammartini's symphonies are the finest before Haydn; they would have been the most interesting to him. Since Milan was an Austrian possession, Sammartini's music became well known in Austria and Bohemia. Haydn and Sammartini have certain techniques in common. Perhaps Haydn *was* acquainted with Sammartini's music.

Carpani pointed to the little duet in dialogue between the violins after the double bar in the first movement of Haydn's String Quartet Op. 1, No. 1 in B-flat major and said, *there* is the influence of Sammartini—in the treatment of the second violin. That concerns Sammartini's role in the development of Classical texture. Carpani didn't say that it was an influence on the string quartet.

[34] Published in Churgin, *Symphonies,* I, No. 16.

WEBSTER Professor Churgin said that we should fit Haydn into the Classical style. But there may be no such thing as "the" Classical style. There were many styles between 1730 and 1800. We all have been biased by the identification of Haydn's and Mozart's mature music with Classical style. Even Haydn's and Mozart's own early music is usually criticized (unjustly) as "immature," or whatever. We ought at least to say "Classical styles" or "Classical style as I conceive it."

HELM Perhaps we shouldn't try so hard to relate the isolated cultural pockets in the eighteenth century.

BORIS SCHWARZ[35] There are string quartets of Tartini called "Sonata à quattro" predating 1750, whose fast movements show an advanced style of quartet writing.

ØIVIND ECKHOFF[36] Haydn himself said that everybody who knew him would acknowledge that he was indebted only to C. P. E. Bach.

HELM Dies and Griesinger and Rochlitz must have heard Haydn say that C. P. E. Bach influenced him. But I believe that he meant "influenced" in Fux's sense: he made a craftsman out of him.

EVA BADURA-SKODA[37] The Seven Years' War made Berlin into an enemy of Vienna. And Haydn was upset about the Berlin critics' dislike of his music. That is not a "brick wall" any longer.

ROSEN If you are going to discuss influences, you should eliminate the idea of style altogether. The concept "style" is not historical; it is critical, and it always arises after the fact. Haydn was not creating "Classical style"; he never heard of it. Insofar as Classical style exists (and of course it does not exist at all), it was invented by people like Koch in the 1790s. The concept of genre also ought to be eliminated. If somebody got the idea of a five-movement piece and Haydn then wrote a five-movement piece, you can talk about the relationships between the two pieces. But the leap from these to "Classical string quartet" is problematic.

WEBSTER What could we substitute for the concepts "style" and "genre"? One possibility is the concept "repertory"; that is, music with a continuous, closely knit history in a given place, and so on. We can write histories of repertories without methodological difficulties. One can also concentrate on scorings. The synthesis of a repertory and one or more related scorings often constitutes what we call a genre.

JAN LA RUE[38] Another term is "procedure." The Classical period is a collection of different procedures, used variously in different centers at different times. A style is not a unity, it's many unities.

---

[35] From the audience.   [36] From the audience.   [37] From the audience.
[38] From the audience.

ROSEN It is a unity, but it's *post facto*. Classical style was a style for Brahms; he knew what he was imitating or recreating.

LA RUE There were many procedures that he didn't take up.

GROUT People who talk about the history of music should analyze the procedures of language in regard to words like "problem," "style," and "influence." If we use these metaphors long enough and become fond enough of them, we endow them with a kind of artificial life, as though they existed somehow separately from our mental activity. The difficulty—and I say this meaning no disrespect to anyone—is one to which languages that capitalize nouns are particularly subject. We can't talk without using metaphors, but we must handle them with the caution that is necessary in handling any other kind of dangerous materials.

Round Table

Changing Concepts of Musical Form and Their Relation to Changing Approaches to Haydn's Music

GEORGE J. BUELOW, *Chairman* JANET M. LEVY
DÉNES BARTHA   ALFRED MANN
BATHIA CHURGIN   LEONARD G. RATNER
JAN LA RUE   HOWARD SERWER, *Secretary*

BUELOW In his public lecture, Dr. Larsen called for a new approach to the definition of form in Haydn's music, based not on various nineteenth-century concepts, but on the musical processes to be observed in Haydn's works. Our discussions will touch upon some of the work being carried forward in this direction.

Theories of Form: Some Changing Perspectives

RATNER Musical form can be viewed either as a plan or as a process. For analysis, the emphasis is upon plan; the features of a work are measured against a series of norms to determine conformities and deviations. In composition, the emphasis is upon process; lines of action are joined to create an organic whole. Plan and process interact in both analysis and composition, but the differing emphases lead to markedly different views of form. I should like to consider some aspects of these two approaches in eighteenth- and nineteenth-century theory.

Eighteenth-century theory of musical form was concerned with how things were being done at the time—how to put a piece together. Nineteenth-century theory was concerned with what eighteenth-century composers had done years before; it summarized and codified decades of practice. Thus, nineteenth-century theory was retrospective, while eighteenth-century theory was prescriptive. The perspective shifted from process as the guiding principle in the eighteenth century, to plan in the nineteenth century.

In the eighteenth century, the only forms dealt with in detail were dances, simple rondos, and fugues. For the nineteenth century, if we take A. B. Marx's *Komposition* as representative, we find comprehensive consideration of many forms, among them two- and three-part song forms, variations, chorale, fugue, five rondo forms, sonatina form, sonata form, and sonata-rondo form, with detailed instructions for the placement of themes, transitions, and returns.

347

In contrast to these detailed blueprints, eighteenth-century instructions for composition were concerned principally with rhetorical parameters, processes by which coherence could be established and eloquence achieved. First in importance among the form-building processes was harmony.[1] The shape of a composition was seen as a trajectory moving to and from keys, with a strong framing of the tonic to open and to close. Key schemes included the circular or solar tour of related keys in earlier eighteenth-century concertos and fugues; this solar plan was retained in later eighteenth-century fugues. But by far the most important scheme, already used in dances and arias of the earlier eighteenth century, and prescriptive in Classic music, was I–V; x–I. This polarity of tonic and dominant created lines of harmonic tension that sustained the entire form.

Another basic parameter was rhythm.[2] This included *meter,* with indications that certain meters could be linked to certain affective stances; *accent,* the "grammatical" ordering of weak and strong pulses (also called *quantitas intrinsica*); *poetic accent,* the groups of long and short notes in various patterns; *"oratorical" or "pathetic" accents* on specific notes; *groups of beats and measures,* laid out in symmetrical or complementary groups, but constantly subject to disturbance; *cadences,* points of punctuation to define larger rhythmic units; and finally a sense of *macro-rhythm,* in which broad phases of action linked to create a rhythmic contour that helped to shape the entire form.

Melody furnished local contour. When it harnessed rhythm and harmony, it became the principal carrier of musical action. For the eighteenth century, the essential element in melody was the *figure,* a short, characteristic pattern, rarely more than a measure or two in length, with a clearly defined harmonic identity and a sharply chiseled rhythmic profile. The documentation of melodic rhetoric in eighteenth-century music theory is both ample and precise. Much more attention was given to the juxtaposition of melodic figures than to the placement of different melodic ideas within a movement.

For the placement of salient thematic material, eighteenth-century theory refers only to da capo forms (rondeau and aria); to "rhyme" (the restatement of material in the recapitulation); and to the availability of a cantabile section, as Koch puts it, or a *passo caratteristico,* as described by Galeazzi, or Vogler's reference to thematic contrast.[3] Except for Vogler, these references to what would eventually become an important form-defining element in the nineteenth century—that is, the "second," the "song," the "feminine" theme—appear only in the last decade of the

[1] See Ratner, "Form." On the general topic of this paper, see also Newman, *Classic,* 26–35; Ritzel, *Sonatenform.*
[2] See Ratner, "Period."
[3] Koch, *Versuch,* III, 306; Churgin, "Galeazzi," 185, 193; Vogler, *Betrachtungen,* II, 62.

eighteenth century. Melodic contrast in Classic music occurred, as Fischer puts it, on the smallest dimensions, often from figure to figure, without disturbing the essential unity arising from the affect established by the principal theme of a movement.[4] Something of the Baroque sense of thematic unity is retained in Classic music, either through intensive manipulation of the principal subject or by highlighting the main theme with judiciously placed accessory ideas.

Apart from the prescriptive I–V; x–I tonal plan for first movements, and often for finales, arias, minuets, and slow movements, events along the way could be arranged optionally. Here we sense the spirit of the *ars combinatoria,* the game in which a given number of units could be arranged, combined, and permuted.[5] The *ars combinatoria* was used frequently in the teaching of composition, from Mersenne to Galeazzi. It bespeaks the presence of paraphrase as a resource in composition, which runs through music theory and practice from before Bach onward.

Haydn's place in the context of eighteenth-century formal practice as described above is central. In his youth he was the legatee of techniques, styles, and forms of the early eighteenth century, and his early training is evident throughout his entire oeuvre. Let us touch upon three aspects of this influence. The first was composition in the strict style of counterpoint upon a cantus firmus of long notes, a technique he acquired in part from the study of Fux's *Gradus*. This technique was the basis not only for many passages in which he employed it openly, but in thousands of places where he laid ornamental figures upon a structural melody in longer notes. The second was the mid-century *style galant,* in which the play of short, pithy figures characterized the melodic rhetoric. To the end of his life Haydn retained his unbelievable dexterity and invention in the manipulation of short melodic motives. Thirdly, in this short-thrust melodic style, the *ars combinatoria* constantly came into play. Haydn could take a simple progression and so elaborate it that the familiar cliche would take on a surprising and grateful freshness and vitality. He would rearrange the order of figures in a recapitulation so that the listener would be on the alert to grasp the new twists of rhetoric, giving the recapitulation the effect of a melodic peroration rather than a straight melodic rhyme or recall.[6]

This melodic style had a strong effect upon Haydn's sonata forms. Instead of reaching for new themes for each succeeding phrase or period, as Mozart did, Haydn explored many arrangements and combinations of a few main figures, sometimes laying them out in different phrase patterns, sometimes introducing local contrast to stage a new combination

---

[4] Fischer, "Entwicklungsgeschichte."   [5] See Ratner, "Combinatoria."
[6] The concept "peroration" was applied to Haydn's free recapitulations by Tovey (e.g., "Chamber," repr., 55–56; "Sonata," repr., 217). [Ed.]

of the salient thrusts, so that the principal harmonic objectives—the end of the exposition, the recapitulation, and the close of the movement— became grand perorations, triumphant areas of arrival.

I should like to demonstrate Haydn's application of these principles in his String Quartet in D major Op. 76, No. 5, composed in 1797. The finale of this work is laid out harmonically according to the prescriptive I–V; x–I plan of eighteenth-century sonata form. But Haydn elects a striking option; he establishes the tonic clearly but very briefly in only sixteen measures of alternating tonic and dominant. In mm. 17–24 we enter the orbit of the dominant; this appears to be contradicted in mm. 37–42; but the following measures, contradicting the contradiction, lead to V of V in m. 46. From here, a digression to B minor (ii of V) and a deceptive cadence to the minor mode broaden the harmonic trajectory. From m. 76 onward, confirmation of A major is the principal harmonic business, with strong cadences at measures 90 and 116. Thus, the harmonic action in this exposition has a very powerful end-oriented quality, a true peroration in the rhetorical sense.

Rhythmically, Haydn maintains a sense of four-measure groups throughout the exposition, reflecting the regularity of the *contredanse* style that is the topic of the finale. But on the macro-rhythmic level, there is a wonderful manipulation of this four-measure grouping. Until m. 63, the four-measure basis is maintained fairly consistently, but in mm. 64–107 it is disturbed; groups of 2, 3, and 6 bars intermingle with the 4's, creating a subtle sense of rhythmic imbalance. As might be expected, the peroration, at m. 112, reestablishes the four-measure regularity to secure the effect of rhythmic arrival comparable to that effected in the harmony. On the micro-rhythmic level, Haydn uses very simple patterns. The opening figure is iambic; its complement (upbeat to m. 8) is anapestic. These two figures constitute the principal rhythmic material of the movement. Occasionally a subtle shift to trochaic takes place, as in the steady eighth-note motion at m. 46. The only interruption, a powerful one, is the spondee half notes at m. 70.

Melodically, Haydn matches his two simple rhythmic figures with two short motives. The first, on the iamb, is an irreducible cadence figure; the second, on the anapest, is a three-note descending *tirata,* of the type used in many *contredanses,* which makes good counterpoint with the first. Both figures are conjunct, setting the stepwise melodic action for the entire movement. In the exposition, disjunct melodic incisions occur only at critical places: the interchange of mode at measure 70, and the cadential figures, measure 116 *et seq.,* that put a rein to the headlong momentum.

The terseness of the principal figures and the rhythmic squareness they promote provide a foil for extensions by means of repetition, variation, and parenthesis, so that the exposition, which could easily run its course in about 32 measures without loss of coherence, attains a length of 120 measures. To secure an effect of peroration at the end, Haydn introduces (as he often does) a new melodic idea, m. 112; this levels off the action and leads to the final cadence. In Haydn's forms, such a new theme often serves to secure the final arrival in the dominant; its presence and its place in the movement are optional, not prescriptive.

The view of Classic form sketched here is based on the coordination of theoretical comments and analysis of the music itself. The fixed element for sonata form was the I–V; x–I plan; this plan required cadential harmony as well as clearly defined phrase and period structure. Another prescriptive element was the restatement in the recapitulation of material presented in the first part, especially that material which closed the first reprise. The optional elements were the relative length and inner structure of harmonic areas, and the paths between them; and the number, nature, and placement of melodic figures.

Implied in this relationship between fixed and optional elements is the sense of form as process. When Marx and those who later subscribed to his bithematic, contrast view of sonata form have nineteenth-century forms in mind, they are on solid ground. When they extrapolate this view backward to eighteenth-century forms, and especially to Haydn, they are out of touch with the generating forces of Classic form, the sense of process and play.

Discussion

LA RUE As early as 1760, many *Kleinmeister* had a very clear hold on a plan such as A. B. Marx described. For example, Leopold Hofmann's Symphony in D major is, I think, the first symphony with a slow introduction, an exposition with full key contrast, a complete recapitulation; and a slow movement, minuet and trio, and finale.[7]

The other point that bothers me is giving the *galant* period credit for late Haydn. For me, the difference is that the motives control the *galant* composer, but late Haydn controls the motives. In the *galant,* the motive is overtly stabilized at the end. That is exactly the point at which Haydn takes hold of things and removes the stability.

RATNER I still think Haydn absorbed his techniques of manipulation of motives from the sources I quoted. The mark of the short motive is still in his music, because this is the only way he can develop thrust, just as the short thrust of a piston in a motor generates more power than the long thrust. The definition of "galant" which I have taken from eighteenth-century theory is: "everything that is not strict."[8] I would consider defining the later eighteenth century as a late Franco-Italian *galant* style.

[7] Dated 1762 in the Göttweig monastery music catalogue; also falsely attributed to Haydn (Hob. I:D27). Cf. MGG, XII, 1812–13; "Enlightenment," 401–02. [Ed.]
[8] Cf. Newman, *Classic,* 44–46, 119–23, and the references given there.

JENS PETER LARSEN[9]   I do not agree about the "Franco-Italian *galant* style." I wish
that the term *galant* could be thrown on the dungheap together with
"Sturm und Drang." I find it in Couperin and in Watteau paintings, but I
do not think there was very much *galant* in Viennese culture at that time.
In the music of those composing just before Haydn, you have the mannerism of *galant* style (or as I call it, mid-century style) in which all the
small sections end; the tension is relaxed every two or four bars, and then
something new begins. But in the mature Haydn, there is a single tension. Take as an example Symphony No. 43 in E-flat major. The beginning may seem a little like that in Symphony No. 35 in B-flat major,
where the phrases run 4 + 4, 4 + 4, 4 + 4, etc., and every time the music is
closed off. But in No. 43 there is a development in which the harmonic
tension continues to m. 31. It is a different world. It is true that many of
the same elements are in the Hofmann symphony, which apparently is
like Haydn, but actually the spirit and the whole development are completely different.

CHURGIN   Haydn had a genius for continuity and drive, but no composer is completely isolated. Many fine composers gave Haydn the stimulation that
every great artist must have. I also agree with Professor Ratner's use of
the term *galant,* as opposed to its modern association with the ornamental
melodic style found particularly in keyboard and chamber music of the
earlier Classic period. As explained by Koch, it is the opposite of the
older learned style; it is the homophonic Classic style, freer and simpler
in harmony, richer in contrasts, more ornamental in melody, and more
sectional.[10] These are fundamental distinctions which historians can use
meaningfully.

   I would like to add some remarks about thematic function. The term
passo caratteristico was used by Francesco Galeazzi, who was the first, I
believe, to describe what we call sonata form in terms of thematic function.[11] Thus he describes the "First Part" as consisting of the Introduction (optional), the Principal Motive, the Second Motive, the Departure
to the most closely related keys, the Characteristic Passage (*passo
caratteristico*), the Cadential Period, and the Coda. I believe that this description reflects what had happened in Classic music by about 1760, as
Professor LaRue implied. Composers did develop "characteristics" for
the different thematic functions, because we feel in a Classic form a sense
of where we are and where we are going. One of the most wonderful
things in Haydn's music is his play on our expectations. Galeazzi's concepts can help in understanding Haydn's formal organization—how he
treats expectations, and whether he does or does not fulfill them.

[9] From the audience.   [10] Koch, *Lexikon,* 1453.
[11] See Churgin, "Galeazzi"

Song Form and the Concept of "Quatrain"

BARTHA My purpose is to investigate a long-neglected type of Haydn's formal structure (which also appears in Mozart, Beethoven, and elsewhere): the so-called song form (binary or ternary), and its use in minuets, trios, themes for variations, rondo-ritornellos, and also in independent sections of many slow movements. The obvious lack of logic in the common term "three-part song form" for the construction A:‖ B + A:‖ was recognized long ago by Tovey;[12] yet until now musical analysis has notably failed to take his argument to heart.

Examining a great bulk of eighteenth-century popular tunes (including their relations to the poetic texts), I found that the overwhelming majority of them fell into the familiar pattern of a basic *four-part structure:* 4-line stanzas in the text, correlated with four musical phrases or sections. Both can conveniently be termed *Quatrain* (symbol: Q). The Q-concept can be applied on different levels, from the 8-bar period upward to extended structures consisting of 24, 32, or 48 measures. Although a substantial majority conform to symmetrical "periodicity" of 4, 8, 12, 16 . . . measures (especially in the initial line-units 1 and 2), a deviation from strict symmetry is a favorite tool of sophistication, for example in Haydn's minuets. A common variant of the Quatrain adds a refrain-type repetition of the second half (units 3 and 4). This results in a 6-unit pattern, 1–2–3–4–3–4, appropriately termed Quatrain + Refrain (symbol: Q-R).

Most of these melodies exhibit a characteristic artistic pattern, which appears to assign to each of the four "lines" a specific function.

Line 1—Initial Statement: mostly symmetrical (4, 8, 16 bars), built on simple harmonic progressions (I–V alternating), dynamics typically restrained.

Line 2—Restatement: either identical to Line 1 (in this case usually notated simply by repeat signs), or written out and minimally varied by first and second endings; in more sophisticated examples with changes in pitch and/or scoring; in length always equal to Line 1.

Line 3—Contrast: articulative changes in smaller motives, increased dynamic-melodic-harmonic activity, faster harmonic rhythm, modulations—a sort of mini-development. This section is open-ended, like a retransition in character; I borrow the term *enjambement* from poetry for this effect; in diagrams of form, its symbol is the asterisk ★.

Line 4—Restatement: codetta-type end-effects; often, repetition of Line 2, producing what German folklorists term "Reprisenbar," and English theorists "Rounded binary songform" (A, A, B + A′), which in Classical style appears chiefly in minuets and trios, dance-related rondo-ritor-

---

[12] Tovey, "Sonata," repr., 208–09.

nellos, and variation themes; in art music, even when this line recalls motivic material from Lines 1–2, it usually introduces subtle changes in dynamics, rhythm, pitch, or total length. Contrary to Lines 1–3, the harmony often emphasizes the subdominant region. Taken together, these features produce an effect of final rounding off; in the extended refrain type, some of these special effects may be reserved for the concluding Line 6.

A paradigmatic example of Q–R is Beethoven's "Ode to Joy" melody, with the pattern A, A^2, B★A^2, B★A^2. By introducing repeat signs, we cannot help but recognize the so-called ternary song form of countless Classical minuets, trios, and variation themes: A1:‖ B★A^2:‖. In addition, this pattern provides an ideally rounded structural concept, coming "full circle," in contrast to the conventional binary (antecedent–consequent period), which typically encompasses a mere half (or third) of a complete Q (Q–R). My "full circle" Quatrain-stanza concept, especially in its extended Q–R variety, provides the preferred building block not only for simple melodies, but also for highly artful large structures of up to eighty measures. This defies the narrow, conventional textbook definitions of "song form."[13]

As a basis for further discussion, I offer, from among hundreds more, the following analyses of complex themes and independent sections which are based on this structural principle.

Symphony No. 92 in G major ("Oxford"), ii

Overall form: Maggiore—Minore—Maggiore—Coda
Thematic pattern of the first Maggiore (mm. 1–40): Q–R

$$A \quad A^2 \quad B★A^3 \quad B★A^3$$

$$8 \quad 8 \quad \underbrace{6 \quad 6} \quad \underbrace{6 \quad 6}$$

In this diagram, the term A^2 stands for the purely coloristic, reorchestrated variation; A^3 for a more refined, metrically "telescoped" variation of A. The return of the Maggiore after the Minore follows the pattern of the return of a minuet after the trio, omitting the repetitions, and with additional varied extensions in A^3.

String Quartet Op. 77, No. 2 in F major, iii

Overall form: theme and free variations
Motivic pattern of the theme (2 × 22 = 44 measures): Q–R

$$‖: \begin{matrix} A^1 \\ 8 \end{matrix} :‖ : \begin{matrix} B★A^2 \\ 4 \quad 10 \end{matrix} :‖$$

[13] Earlier versions of this analytical method are described in Bartha, "Liedform"; Bartha, "Thematic."

Piano Sonata Hob. XVI:49 (ChL. 59) in E-flat major, ii

Overall form: Maggiore—Minore—Maggiore
Structure of the first Maggiore section (mm. 1–56): Q-R
"mit veränderten Reprisen" (varied repetitions):

$$A \quad A^2 \quad B \star A^3 \quad B' \star A^{3'}$$

$$8 \quad 8 \quad \underbrace{10 \ 10} \quad \underbrace{10 \ 10}$$

Piano Sonata Hob. XVI:48 (ChL. 58) in C major, i

Overall form: free alternation of Maggiore and Minore sections
Structure of the first Maggiore (2 × 26 = 52 measures): Q-R

$$\left\| {\raise1pt\hbox{$\cdot$}} \ {A \atop 10} \ {\raise1pt\hbox{$\cdot$}} \right\| {\raise1pt\hbox{$\cdot$}} \ {B \ A' \atop 7 \ \ 9} \ {\raise1pt\hbox{$\cdot$}} \right\|$$

Gesture, Form, and Syntax in Haydn's Music

LEVY Generally speaking, gestures in eighteenth-century music have been discussed primarily in terms of affective character—for example, pathos—and specific mimetic qualities such as those of the hunting call or characteristic dance types. These aspects of compositional gestures are certainly important. But here I should like to call attention to the syntactic significance of gestures, the role of gestural syntax in our understanding of musical processes and form. Many gestures not only have their own internal syntax but themselves function syntactically, often as "signs" to tell us where we are and where we may be going—or, perhaps wittily, where we "ought" to be—in the form of a given movement. Some of the richest and most engaging examples are to be found in the oeuvre of Haydn.

Rather than attempt an abstract explanation of "gesture" here, let me give a few examples of what I mean by gestures which, through conventional association, function as signs in the language of late-eighteenth-century composers. The clearest and most archetypal of these are closing gestures; for instance, the type found at the end of the opening theme in the String Quartet Op. 50, No. 5 in F major, mm. 7–8 and at "No, no, no, non voglio più servir" in Leporello's opening grumble in *Don Giovanni* (No. 1, mm. 29–32, etc.); or that found in mm. 66–67 in the Largo of Op. 33, No. 2 in E-flat major; yet another type is shown in Example 1. Other broad classes are, rather obviously, introductory, opening, middle, and transitional gestures. Such general types encompass many specific subtypes and functions—for example, within the general class of closing gestures some, typically, might read "close of first key area" in a sonata-form movement, others are typical coda gestures; within certain categories of closing gestures, too, may be found a variety of kinds of pedal-point action for various formal moments. In each case, it is the particular interaction among parameters that creates the gestural types, subtypes, and their functions. In what follows, I hope to stimulate thought along these lines via a somewhat tangential route: by exploring how the very conventionality of a gesture allows it to be turned topsy-turvy—or, to borrow a felicitous description from Leonard Ratner, to be put "out of countenance."

Example 1. Symphony No. 89 in F major, iv, 199–211

Example 1 contains the final bars from the rondo finale of Haydn's Symphony No. 89 of 1787, a movement borrowed and expanded from the Concerto for Two *Lire Organizzate* (hurdy-gurdies) Hob. VIIh:5 (1786). This material has not previously been heard in the movement. Haydn can, nonetheless, be sure that his audience will understand its function, because it is drawn from the common stock of conventional closing gestures for movements; precisely because the new material is stereotyped it does not disturb the listener's sense of coherence. Now compare Example 2, the opening of the String Quartet Op. 50, No. 1 in B-flat major, also 1787. The patterning of mm. 1–4 is clearly similar to mm. 199–201 in Example 1. The implication is that what follows "should be" precisely analogous to mm. 202–03 in Example 1. Obviously, the very beginning of the quartet is a pun on the function of a closing gesture.

Yet by virtue of its immediate continuation—see Example 2—the gesture is *not* quite a closing one. Contradicting the implied descent to a tonic cadence, via repetition a third lower, Haydn opens the action at measure 5 by transposing the gesture upward and then extending it with contrasting material to the end of the first period at measure 12. This "improper" continuation of such a clearly implicative gesture is the first

Example 2. String Quartet Op. 50, No. 1 in B-flat major, i, 1–12

in a long series of postponements and playful distortions of the "proper" continuation of the gesture.

The rhetoric of the movement is at least partly dependent on the fact that the strongly implied closing gesture is not merely an indivisible cadential figure—as in the example from Op. 50, No. 5 referred to earlier—but, in its archetypal form, consists of two parts, the first of which (mm. 3–4) clearly implies the second. Indeed, the whole movement can be conceived of as a subtle play on ways of avoiding the conventional conjunction of the second phrase of the closing gesture with the first phrase—i.e., the avoidance of the complete gesture in its archetypal or normative form until it occurs in the appropriate formal context, the very close of the movement.

When the closing gesture which begins the movement is next heard, at the beginning of the second period, it is intensified and slightly varied (see Example 3). Its immediate continuation is once again "improper," but this time the normal melodic completion soon follows, and it is heard not once, but four times. In mm. 20–21 and mm. 24–25, there is a kind of propriety owing to the gesture's rhythmic regularity in relation to its antecedent phrases (mm. 18–19 and mm. 22–23); the third and

Example 3 String Quartet Op. 50, No. 1, i, 12–27

fourth times it breaks the two-plus-two measure pattern in insistent reiteration. The gesture itself takes on pantomimic qualities—almost as if a character in a dumb show—where, as if in recompense for its previous absence, there are too many occurrences of the right thing at the wrong moment.

Syntactically, despite the quadruple reiteration, the archetypal form of the gesture is still not realized. For first, and most importantly, the second part of the normative gesture (mm. 20–21) is separated in time from the first part (mm. 14–15)—i.e., though linked by register and instrument (first violin), the components of the gesture are not heard contiguously. Retrospectively, what intervenes between the components may be heard as a kind of parenthesis, despite the fact that mm. 20–21 are also heard as some kind of proper response to mm. 18–19, and the same is, of course, true for mm. 24–25 in relation to 22–23. Second, the ostinato tonic pedal is not quite "right"; not only is it moved gradually from the cello to the second violin and then to the first violin—a kind of textural pun on the role of a pedal-point ostinato, as Charles Rosen has pointed out[14]—but in mm. 20–21 and 24–25 it moves to a^2 at the cadence for the sake of dominant harmony, and it is completely abandoned on the third and fourth repetitions of the gesture. Third, in the immediate context the reiterations are a response to the new emphasis on the subdominant (mm. 19 and 23). Paradoxically, the presence of the subdominant prevents the conjunction of the first and second phrases of the archetypal gesture at the same time that it strengthens the close of the first key area by providing the definitive progression IV–V–I. The pantomimic qualities mentioned earlier arise partly because the completeness of the cadence makes the third and fourth repetitions (mm. 25 and 26) seem almost gratuitous.

The complete archetypal gesture, as implied at the beginning of the movement, is once against *almost* present in basic outline in the dominant at the end of the exposition (Example 4), where a rhythmic variant of the basic melodic patterning (mm. 56–58) occurs over a tonic pedal. (Here the melodic contour of the first gesture is fused with the triplet pattern

Example 4. String Quartet Op. 50, No. 1, i, 55–60

----

[14] Rosen, *Style,* 123.

that followed it in mm. 6–11.) But the melodic outline is 4–3–2–<u>3</u>, instead of 4–3–2–1.

As we would expect, it is in the development that the opening gesture of the movement is most extensively reinterpreted. It begins the development and is actually the focus of intensive and extensive instability—primarily harmonic and textural—for more than the first half (27 measures); the gesture returns again as the material of the immediate retransition to the recapitulation (Example 5).[15]

Example 5. String Quartet Op. 50, No. 1, i, 103–12

The recapitulation enters virtually unnoticed. Indeed, we are in the midst of it before we are quite aware of it and wonder if we may have missed the correspondence with the beginning of the exposition. Surely this is one of the most understated returns in Haydn's oeuvre. That the precise moment of the return to the tonic is not dramatized or underlined but, rather, treated as part of an ongoing process can now perhaps be explained in terms of gestural syntax. Evidently Haydn wanted to save the archetypal patterning of the gesture for the close of the movement. Its appearance at the beginning of the recapitulation would have robbed its appearance at the end of the movement of much of its force. (Of course, the minimal return of material of the first part of the exposition may also be related to its extensive use in the development.) The ostinato pedal point and the melodic figure with which it was associated for the first 27 measures of the exposition are completely abandoned after the briefest reference at the moment of the return to the home key.

After a reordering of the material of the exposition Haydn presents the long-awaited closing gesture with utter syntactic propriety—as a close (Example 6). Here, for the first time in the movement, the tonic pedal is

---

[15] The traditional reading in the first violin, m. 108, is corrupt. Cf. JHW XII:4, from which these excerpts from Op. 50, No. 1 are adapted. [Ed.]

maintained as an ostinato for the entire melodic gesture (mm. 152–55). And instead of a simple varied repetition, as in the comparable gesture of Symphony No. 89, the quartet gesture transcends its expected dimensions and is extended to include an intensification of dominant harmony and a full-scale ii⁶–V–I progression, making a close that is not merely twice four measures but a more integrated statement of (2 + 2) + 4 measures. The way in which Haydn stages the appearance of this gesture has all the qualities of prestidigitation in a magic show: from the start the ingredients are added bit by bit; after various diversions, and seemingly effortlessly, the magician produces the whole object, just as it should be.

Example 6. String Quartet Op. 50, No. 1, i, 150–64

In terms of syntax: because the implications of the first four measures of the movement are formulaic in the style and because of the avoidance of their formulaic continuation—i.e., the completion of the closing gesture—we recognize the double formal impropriety at the beginning. We know from the outset that the gesture will receive special treatment. Mattheson wrote: "One can make use of many ordinary and well-known devices. Cadences, for example, are quite common . . . and may be found in every piece. When, however, they are used at the beginning of a piece, they become something *special,* since they normally belong at the end."[16] We can infer that Haydn expected his audience to understand the opening gesture of the quartet as being "out of countenance" and to attend to when and how it would be shown in its proper countenance—reach its proper conclusion. And Haydn does something more than set up a cadence whose formal structure is discrepant with its syntactic context. In addition to the tension intrinsic to the gesture itself—i.e., the tension between the ostinato pedal point and the melodic figure beginning on the fourth degree of the scale—two things are wrong: not only does a closing gesture begin the movement, but the gesture itself is patently incomplete—an incompleteness all the more tantalizing because we can so clearly imagine how it should be. Had the gesture been completely realized as a closing gesture at the outset, the compositional problem and, consequently, the composition itself would have been quite different.

Discussion

RATNER This example demonstrates my point about species-contrapuntal technique in Haydn's music. The principal motive is simply E♭–D, with the first note ornamented by a decorative figure. Therefore, it can be placed in any kind of harmonic context. It is typical of Haydn to take a tired figure of this sort and make it come alive.

JAMES WEBSTER[17] In Example 5 from Professor Levy's paper, the at-first-glance surprising reading in the first violin, m. 108, with the apparent parallel fifths with the cello (cf. n. 15), means that the melody in mm. 108–9 is a repetition of mm. 3–4. This seems to me to strengthen her interpretation of these measures (and to make it clear that m. 108 is the entry of the recapitulation). Haydn reinterprets his opening gesture—which had something of the character of a closing gesture—as a closing gesture of a different sort. It unexpectedly "closes" the development *into* the recapitulation. That is, it has become a retransition.

But I am skeptical about the assertion that these motives in Examples 1 and 2 have the "inherent" character of closing motives. I should think it would be a question of how they were used in the piece.

LEVY Although the recapitulation begins formally at m. 108, in terms of process—reaching the tonic—it does not arrive until m. 109 (cf. the similar situation at the reprise in the first movement of Mozart's G-minor Symphony).

About your second point, it is not simply the melodic nature of the gesture in Op. 50, No. 1 but its concatenation with the tonic pedal and the motion from the fourth degree of the scale down. Also, my point hinges on the prevalence of the motive as a closing gesture in the Classic repertory.

[16] Mattheson, *Capellmeister*, 123; as transl. Lenneberg, "Mattheson," 70.
[17] From the audience.

RATNER I should like to speak to my point of being "out of countenance." I was relating it to a particular kind of "ungrammatical" syntax, at the beginning of the Trio of Mozart's "Jupiter" Symphony, where the cadence is "out of countenance" because there is no tonic to precede it. So it has movement and arrival, which is a closing gesture rather than a departure movement; therefore an arrival can sound like the end, and on the other hand the piece sounds as if it has been under way before it has started. The important thing is that the motive does not have a tonic to precede it; therefore you have to *end* it to find some kind of limit.

The Interpenetration of Form and Style

LA RUE These sessions are described as sessions on form *and* style. Of all composers, Haydn is the one who must be approached by putting form and style together, not by separating them. The following remarks, then, are an outline of the reasoning behind my conviction that these aspects must be joined together.

Background

The form/style dichotomy, which was implied as early as the Baroque *Affektenlehre* and became explicit at the end of the nineteenth century, combined two currents of thought. 1) It followed the form/content dichotomy of art and literature, a false analogy, since much of music has no specific content. 2) It resulted from an obviously incomplete view of the formal process, often relying on little more than thematic structure, sometimes even passing over tonal movement. (Other typical omissions were texture, harmonic rhythm, phrase module.) Such one-sided thinking easily led to an unusual separation of form from its sources in all the basic elements of music.

Argument

1. Style in music derives from the manner in which each composer handles and combines the musical elements (which can be generalized as sound, harmony, melody, and rhythm).
2. To discuss musical form adequately we must consider all musical elements; and in distinguishing the action of these elements, of course, we inevitably must observe the style of the composer.
3. We cannot discuss musical style adequately without reference to form, since the interactions of musical elements in producing a musical shape yield many of the most vital insights into a composer's creative process.

Conclusion

Any dichotomy between form and style risks misrepresentation of the essentially integrated nature of music, leading to incomplete and potentially distorted understanding. While every detail of music may have important implications, our understanding grows most soundly from a perception of each movement as an emergence from all its elements. Form separated from style is like a portrait without eyes—or ears.

Round Table

Melodic Style Traditions and Haydn's Personal Style

EVA BADURA-SKODA, *Chairperson*   EUGENE HELM
GERHARD CROLL   ALFRED MANN
STEPHEN CUSHMAN   WALTER PASS
GEORG FEDER   JAMES WEBSTER
LUDWIG FINSCHER   HOWARD BROFSKY, *Secretary*

BADURA-SKODA   The panel has agreed to avoid lengthy discussions of terminological problems. Therefore the question "What is a melody?" will not
be discussed. We are more concerned with historical than systematic investigation of melodies and melodic style. Our first concern, the
similarities and differences among various melodic styles around 1750,
we have organized according to the traditional division of music into
chamber, church, and theater styles. Professor Webster will speak on
Haydn's relation to Austrian chamber music around 1750; Dr. Feder on
his relation to Neapolitan operatic traditions; and Dr. Pass on the
melodic style of his early church compositions.

Remarks on Early Chamber Music

WEBSTER   I would like to present a set of melodies from the chamber music of
Haydn and his Austrian and Bohemian contemporaries (Examples 1–4).
The Haydn melodies date from the second half of the 1750s; those by the
other composers date, at the latest, primarily from the 1760s; some may
be earlier. As a contrast, Example 5 illustrates a type not characteristic of
Haydn.

Example 1. a) attr. Burcksteiner (no later than 1763), Hob. II:F3, [i,] 1–4

b) Haydn, String Quartet Hob. III:2 ("Op. 1," No. 2) (late 1750s), i, 1–4

365

Example 2. a) Albrechtsberger, Divertimento, Viola, Cello, Violone (1767), i, 1–2 (from Somfai, "Albrechtsberger," Part 2, No. 58)

b) Haydn, String Quintet Hob. II:2 (1750s), ii, 1–3

Example 3. a) Albrechtsberger, Divertimento, 2 Violins, Viola, Violone (?) (1764), iv, 1–4 (from Somfai, "Albrechtsberger," Part 1, No. 27)

(with variations)

b) Albrechtsberger, Divertimento, 2 Violins and Bass (1759), iv, 1–4 (from Somfai, "Albrechtsberger," Part 2, No. 43)

c) Haydn, String Quartet Hob. III:12 ("Op. 2," No. 6), i, 1–4

(with variations)

d) Haydn, Sextet Hob. II:1 (1750s?), i, 1–4

Example 4. a) Albrechtsberger, Divertimento, 2 Violins and Bass (1759), i, 1–4 (from Somfai, "Albrechtsberger," Part 2, No. 44)

b) attr. Fr. X. Dušek, String Quartet, [i,] 1–4 (publ. 1774) (quoted from Hob. III:G4)

c) Haydn, String Quartet Hob. III:10 ("Op. 2," No. 4) (late 1750s), i, 1–4

Example 5. Albrechtsberger, Divertimento, 2 Violins, Viola, Violone (?) (1760) (from Somfai, "Albrechtsberger," Part 1, No. 25)

The similarities within Examples 1–4 are so obvious that comment would be superfluous. Haydn's "popular" melodic ideas in this period were typical of the repertory in which his early chamber music originated. Despite a few publications in DTÖ (and compare Feder, "Urteil"), this repertory is still largely unknown. We do not know to what extent ideas of this kind were "in the air" when Haydn began writing music; we cannot yet say whether Haydn himself was the first to use them in formal compositions (in which case the other melodies quoted here might already represent early imitations of his style). Similar strictures would apply to melodic similarities between Haydn and other composers in symphonies, Masses, operas, or any other genre, as long as our knowledge of mid-century repertories remains as deficient as it is today. Until this necessary documentary and—especially—chronological knowledge has been achieved, we can hardly hope to speak authoritatively about the development of Haydn's melodic style, or for that matter about any other aspect of his style.

A Special Feature of Neapolitan Opera Tradition in Haydn's Vocal Works

FEDER It is common knowledge that eighteenth-century *opera seria* was a highly stylized genre. Its stereotypes influenced Haydn's vocal music, as shown by the da capo form of several arias in the little "festa teatrale" *Acide* (1762), the Italian secular cantatas of the 1760s, the allegorical Latin cantata *Applausus* (1768), and the large Italian oratorio *Il ritorno di Tobia* (1775), all of which are more or less conventionally shaped works. The same influence is apparent in the extensive use of coloratura in these and other vocal compositions by Haydn. However, it is not always clear what should be ascribed to such influence, and what was Haydn's own invention.

One kind of melody was documented in the operas of Johann Adolf

Hasse by Rudolf Gerber as long ago as 1925.[1] Gerber considers these melodies, characterized by triple meter, the tempo Andante or Allegretto, and the expression of tender emotion ("affetto amoroso"), to be the most beautiful in Hasse. The first bars of three arias, shown here as Examples 6–8, may serve as examples for the similarities between Hasse and the young Haydn, who greatly admired the famous opera composer. Without knowing, it would be difficult to say which is Haydn and which is Hasse.

Example 6. Hasse, *Attalo* (1728) (from Gerber, *Hasse,* 72)

Example 7. Hasse, *Didone abbandonata* (1742) (from Gerber, Hasse, 77)

Example 8. Haydn, *Le pescatrici* (1769) (JHW XXV/4, 244)

Such common patterns were used not only in melodic-rhythmic but perhaps more often in rhythmic-metric structure. Gerber describes as Type I of Hasse's arias a thematic construction built of three sections of normally equal length, the third usually repeating the words, and more or less the music, of the second: a–b–b'. It is this repetition of a melodic cadence that Tovey criticizes when speaking of a "recipe made fashionable all over Europe by composers of the Neapolitan school."[2] Arias constructed in this way often abound with syncopation and normally show a typical cadence for the third section. Gerber gives two examples: in Example 9, the cantabile effect of the syncopations is made more effective by introducing embellishments; in Example 10, the division into three sections of two bars each is emphasized by the almost identical motifs of the second and third sections. The bass uses a typical formula.

Many more examples could be shown from the time of the Neapolitan school and its German followers Hasse and Carl Heinrich Graun. Different variants of this model can also be found. The ratio of the three sections is not necessarily 2:2:2; it can also be 1:1:1 or 3:3:3 or 4:4:4 or 2:3:3

[1] R. Gerber, *Hasse*   [2] Tovey, "Chamber," repr., 15.

Example 9. Hasse, *Atalante* (1737) (from Gerber, *Hasse,* 47)

Example 10. Hasse, *L'asilo d'amore* (1743) (from Gerber, Hasse, 46)

or 3:2:2, and so forth. In the literature on Haydn I have found no reference to this kind of melodic construction, but it is quite common in his operas and early cantatas or oratorios. Examples 11–14 illustrate this type of melody.

Many more examples and different variants of this melodic type occur

Example 11. Haydn, *Il ritorno di Tobia* (1775) (JHW XXVIII:1, Vol. 1, 107)

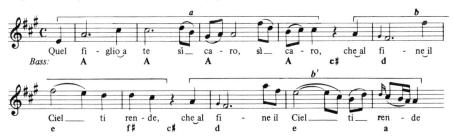

Example 12. Haydn, *Il mondo della luna* (1777) (JHW XXV:7, Vol. 1, 135)

Example 13. Haydn, *Orlando paladino* (1782) (JHW XXV:11, Vol. 1, 71)

si____ scon-vol - ge il ne - ro a-bis-so
e   f   g   c

Example 14. Haydn, *Armida* (1783–84) (JHW XXV:12, 39)

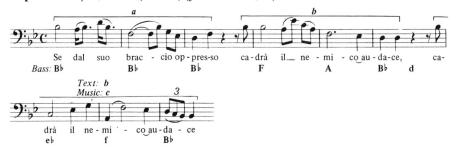

Se dal suo brac - cio op - pres-so ca-drà il__ ne - mi - co au - da-ce, ca-
Bass: Bb   Bb   Bb   F   A   Bb   d

Text: b
Music: c   3

drà il ne - mi ' - co au - da - ce
eb   f   Bb

in Haydn's vocal music. To illustrate the difference between this type and the Classical style of melodic writing, it will suffice to compare another melody from Haydn's *Armida,* Example 15, with Examples 11–14. We have eight bars, constructed however not a–b–b', but in four sections, 2:2:2:2; the melody is divided a–b–a–c (a Classical type of thematic construction described by Dénes Bartha as characteristic of Haydn's instrumental music; cf. the Round Table on *Changing Concepts of Musical Form*). We can also divide this melody into two parts, 4:4, that is, into antecedent and consequent. By either interpretation it is different from the Neapolitan type described above.

Example 15. Haydn, *Armida* (1783–84) (JHW XXV:12, 56)

Se__ pre - ta - de a-ve - te, o Nu - mi, del mio duol, del - le mie pe-ne, voi ren -
Bass: A   e   a   e   a   a f#   e   g#   a   e

Text: c   *Text: d*
Music: a   *Music: c*

de - te - mi il mio__ be - ne, voi ser - ba - te a me quel cor
A   e   a ,   e   a   d   e   e   e   A

Even more revealing is an example from Haydn's last opera, *Orfeo ed Euridice* (1791), Example 16. Example 16a shows the main theme in F minor; it is a clear offspring of the Hasse style. Text: a–b–b; melody: a–b–c; bars: 4:4:4; one syncopation; Neapolitan cadence. Example 16b, the second theme in A flat, immediately following a short orchestral interlude, is constructed in the Classical manner. Text: a–b; melody: a–b; bars: 4:4 (antecedent–consequent).

Example 16. Haydn, *Orfeo ed Euridice* (1791) (JHW XXV:13, 130–131)

I would like to add that Hasse's Type I is not quite absent from Haydn's instrumental music where, however, it seems to have undergone considerable change. An example is the opening theme of Haydn's String Quartet Opus 17, No. 4 in C minor (Example 17). Melody: a–b–b'; bars: 4:2:2; two syncopations; typical bass formula; varied Neapolitan cadence. It is hardly necessary to point out that the middle parts provide much of the individual color and character. This theme becomes personal by the variants Haydn applies rather than by its type.

Example 17. Haydn, String Quartet Op. 17, No. 4 in C minor, i, 1–8

Melodic Construction in Haydn's Two *Salve Regina* Settings

PASS The following remarks concern the melodic construction of Haydn's two authenticated settings of the *Salve Regina:* Hob. XXIIIb:1 in E major, from 1756; and XXIIIb:2 in G minor, from 1771. The former dates from the end of Haydn's studies with Porpora, one of the most important singing teachers of his time and an exponent of the Neapolitan School; the latter, from the revolutionary experimental years around 1770, the years of minor-key symphonies, the string quartets Op. 20, and the piano sonata in C minor, Hob. XVI:20 (ChL. 33). Both works fall within a single phase of development in church music, characterized by a change in aesthetic values from the Baroque doctrine of the affections, the so-called *Nachahmungsästhetik,* to an early Romantic style, the

Empfindungsästhetik. This change was part of a larger social and political evolution, in which Haydn finally became an individualistic artist almost in the modern meaning of the word.

A brief glance at the melodic construction—without doubt the most important factor in these compositions—will show immediately the different stylistic intentions. (See Examples 18 and 19.) The early *Salve Regina* is full of Neapolitan melodic patterns and coloratura passages (rarely found in the G minor work), which probably betray the influence of Porpora.[3] Haydn's melodic figures show the sureness and the ease with which he handled, as early as 1756, the musical grammar inherited from the past. They reveal a strong connection with the aesthetic views Schiller was to call "naive." This is, in fact, a traditional form of melodic construction, a *Fortspinnungstypus,* as Wilhelm Fischer calls it.[4]

Example 18.   *Salve Regina* in E major, Hob. XXIIIb:1, 16–24

Example 19.   *Salve Regina* in G minor, Hob. XXIIIb:2, 18–24

When writing in the tradition of the Neapolitan school, Haydn used virtuoso-coloratura figures. However, to a certain extent, this kind of writing tends to paint individual words in a stereotyped manner, thereby pushing the meaning of the whole text into the background. Later, as a result of the Enlightenment, Haydn increasingly treated his texts more individually, more according to their content. One may compare, for instance, the settings of the words "spes nostra, salve" (mm. 35–41 in the E major, 47–52 in the G minor). The first is rhetorical; the second is more personal in feeling. In the earlier *Salve Regina* we can observe closer re-

[3] Brand, *Messen,* 26.   [4] Fischer, "Entwicklungsgeschichte"

semblance to the formal structure of the antiphon in Gregorian chant. Although not of primary concern in our discussion, it nevertheless clarifies the difference between the types of melodies in the two compositions.

About 1750 the traditional melodic construction began gradually to change to the eight-bar period, in which rhythm and meter achieved a new kind of independence. Rhetorical figures and coloratura were pushed into the background in favor of tunes and "more natural melodies" (Rousseau). The G-minor *Salve Regina* obviously reflects this tendency more than the first one. But it is still full of traditional elements, such as the many Neapolitan triplets (Allegro, mm. 32 ff.; Allegretto, mm. 30 ff.; Adagio, mm. 39, 43), the stereotyped figures in the Allegro, mm. 65 ff. and 10 ff.; and the unison runs in sixteenth notes (Allegretto, mm. 26 ff.)—typical characteristics of the church music of Caldara and Georg Reutter. More modern is the organ solo which opens this work; it has a powerful persuasiveness of construction. The chromaticism (Adagio, mm. 69 ff.) and the orchestration are still rather traditional. Thus we have a connection to the past as well as to a new kind of musical expression and textual setting.

An interesting sign of this development is Haydn's response to the loss of Neapolitan decoration as a primary element. To fill this void and, at the same time, to be able to emphasize certain parts of text, Haydn begins to alter the word-order. He turns away from a straight setting of the text and twice hints at a strictly Christological interpretation of the antiphon: first in the third part, "Et Jesum benedictum fructum ventris tui . . ." (Largo), to which he attached the words "Jesum ostende nobis" (mm. 11–12); secondly in the middle of the last movement (Allegretto), when the text is changed to read "nobis Jesum ostende fructum ventris tui" (mm. 131–42). In this way, the setting of the text differs decidedly from the earlier composition, in which emphasis on the word "Maria" alone forms the culmination. The religious affect now receives a new and personal form of interpretation: the accent given to "Per Mariam et Jesum" as the way to Salvation is as it was in the Counter-Reformation.[5] Compared with the earlier work, this composition is therefore far more dramatic, like an "Oratio in angustiis," a prayer in time of need, while that of 1756 is light and playful, although in no way irreligious, and perhaps easier to understand around 1760.

The differences in character of the two compositions reflect much more than mere changes in musical style. They should be seen in the light of changes taking place in the Austrian Church during this period, discussed in Workshop 1, and reflect in fact a need for a new expression. This change of style, especially of melodic style, made possible the indi-

[5] See Pass, "Bearbeitungen"

vidualistically formed work of 1771. Like other church composers, Haydn no longer wrote in simply conceived molds. Creativity is necessary in order to produce something new. Haydn's genius had understood this: we do not yet find the *Liedtypus* of the mature Classical style, but we do find an approach to it. We see old musical idioms, or "speech symbols," receive a new value (for example the individually formed "Seufzer," Adagio, mm. 63 ff.). Thus a comparison of Haydn's two *Salve Regina* compositions not only shows Haydn's personal development toward maturity in his "adaptation" of this rather special liturgical antiphon text, but it also reflects the *Zeitgeist* of the Enlightenment in Catholic church music.

Haydn's Relationship to the *stile antico*

MANN My remarks are concerned not so much with the general tradition of Austrian church music as with Haydn's approval of the traditional melodic rules of the *stile antico*.

Having been trained as a choirboy on the *solfeggiamenti* of Fux, Haydn absorbed melodic principles of the *stile antico* long before he took up his systematic exploration of Fux's *Gradus ad Parnassum*. Thus the traditions of vocal polyphony represent an essential element in the synthesis of Haydn's melodic style.

As examples characteristic of this orientation in Haydn's writing, three passages from his corrections of Beethoven's contrapuntal exercises are quoted below, written in the course of Beethoven's studies with Haydn and preserved in the Gesellschaft der Musikfreunde.[6] (In each case, Haydn's correction is concerned merely with the part written in quarter notes.)

In Example 20, his change was obviously prompted by the parallel fifths between alto and bass. Yet in rewriting the passage, Haydn not only restored the independence of part writing, but strengthened the melodic progression. In Beethoven's version, a downward step is followed by a downward leap, emphasized by the interval of the diminished fifth

Example 20.

[6] See Mann, "Beethoven"

from which the leap occurs, and dividing the group of quarters into two similar fragments. Haydn, outlining the same melodic compass with the first two notes, avoids the stress of the diminished fifth and transforms the same group of notes into an unbroken melodic entity.

Example 21 illustrates not a correction of part writing, but a change from the same type of disjunct melodic progression Beethoven had written in Example 20. Haydn eliminates the lowest tone f¹ through which a break in the melodic cohesion is caused. Substituting d², he places it between a' and b', thus tightening and at the same time varying and balancing the melodic line.

Example 21.

Haydn's most interesting corrections of Beethoven's third contrapuntal species exercises are illustrated in Example 22. The change is prompted once again by a flaw in part writing—the progression from a perfect to an imperfect fifth, doubly obvious since it involves an outer voice. The sequence of tones represents the same melodically disjunct pattern that Haydn had corrected in the two previous examples, and it is given further weight by the use of the highest tone d² (occurring for the third time) on a light beat on which the upward skip is less well placed than it would be on the accented beat (cf. Haydn's corrections in Examples 20 and 21). Haydn widens the total compass by using the tone e² (removing the emphasis on the melodic diminished fifth), closes the gap in the descending line, and on a wider scale than in Example 20 transforms a pair of fragments into one linear entity.

How methodically Haydn concerned himself with the melodic study arising from the discipline of placing four notes against one is shown in

Example 22.

his *Elementarbuch* (1789), an abstract of Fux's rules. Here Haydn corrects and intensifies Fux's explanations, and enlarges the vocabulary of melodic formulae suggested by Fux's examples to exhaust all possible combinations of consonant and dissonant sounds within a well-designed melodic flow.[7]

Discussion

BADURA-SKODA   Beethoven apparently was not satisfied with Haydn as a teacher, but it is interesting to see *how* Haydn taught Beethoven and what he found necessary to correct.

PASS We should not take too seriously Nottebohm's idea that Haydn wasn't a good teacher.

BADURA-SKODA   Yes, but we know from Johann Schenk that Beethoven looked for a different teacher.[8]

MANN The important point is the quality of Haydn's teaching. Beethoven was not satisfied because he was impatient. He wanted to cover more ground.[9]

BADURA-SKODA   We all have a tendency to speak of "melodic figures" or "patterns" rather than "melody" as such. This difficulty concerns not only the definition of melody, but the difference between our modern technical concept and the much broader, traditional eighteenth-century meanings.

Another point of interest is a possible influence on Haydn of the French airs and vaudeville melodies which came to Vienna when the *opéra comique* was fashionable during the 1750s. "Haydn and Gluck" could be the theme of a book. When Gluck settled in Vienna and collaborated with Durazzo, Haydn was probably eager to hear as much of Gluck's music as possible. On the other hand, Professor Croll has pointed out that Haydn and Gluck were quite different; their goals, their whole conception of opera, and—last but not least—their musical talents differed.

CROLL Dr. Badura-Skoda has clarified Haydn's relationship to the German *Singspiel* in the 1750s, but what is known about his interest in French music? It is a problem because the Viennese wanted composers who knew French to transcribe the imported French music. Gluck did such things very powerfully. Haydn would have had a possibility of doing this since he was in contact with the Kärntnertortheater.

[7] See Haydn, *Elementarbuch*, transl.; on his corrections of Fux see also Mann, "Critic."
[8] Schenk, "Skizze"
[9] Haydn may nonetheless have decisively influenced Beethoven's development in free composition. See Solomon, *Beethoven*, Ch. 7. [Ed.]

BADURA-SKODA   Not a single document in the Hofkammerarchiv has been found hinting that Haydn was actively involved as a composer in any of the court-commissioned French or Italian operas. Unlike Starzer or one of the Italian *buffo* composers, Giuseppe Scarlatti, he probably had nothing to do with them. At the beginning of the 1750s the Burgtheater was a court theater, but the Kärntnertortheater was a city theater, managed by Kurz-Bernardon, where the performances were in German and open to the public, and were very popular. Impresarios such as Kurz could invite whomever they wanted as composers. The subsidized French operas were usually performed in the Burgtheater, or in one of the castle theaters such as Favoriten or Laxenburg. Knowledge of French must have been a prerequisite for getting one of these commissions.

BROFSKY   In addition to Hasse and Gluck, I want to mention the name of Jomelli, who had a very big year in Vienna in 1749, when Haydn was at a most impressionable age. I wonder if Haydn heard these operas?

BADURA-SKODA   An interesting question. Who had access to Italian opera performances in the Burgtheater? Haydn might have heard them in standing room or by substituting in the orchestra.

What was "Austrian music" in the 1750s? Music composed by Austrian composers with a German or Bohemian name? But was it not often at least half Italian in style? It is said that under Karl VI approximately 11 percent of Vienna's population was Italian. Even if Haydn later denied an influence by Sammartini, he must have heard some of his works when they were performed in Vienna (cf. the Round Table "Classical Period and Classical Style"). Many Italians lived and composed in Vienna. For many decades in the eighteenth century *commedia dell'arte* was still played in Italian at market places in Vienna; it didn't have to become *comédie italienne* as it did in Paris. It is even said that Salieri, who lived in Vienna for more than fifty years, never bothered to learn German.

FINSCHER   I think it is not so much a question of nationalities as a question of styles.

Sources of Haydn's Melodic Material

CUSHMAN   Haydn's melodic indebtedness to the *Ohrenvergnügendes und gemüthergötzendes Tafelconfect* of Valentin Rathgeber (Augsburg, 1733/37/46) seems likely.[10] One important feature of Haydn's melodic uses that is related to the *Tafelconfect* is an assimilation process that may be associated with aspects of parody technique.

Large-scale assimilation of *prius factus* material into Haydn's music is rare. But when it occurs, it usually maintains the source as an entity,

[10] Published in EdM, 19, ed. Hans Joachim Moser (1942). Abbreviated *Tafelconfect*. Discussed in detail in Cushman, "Materials."

with retention of its segmental, phraseological, rhythmic, and figural properties. More interesting is that even when specific internal transformations occur, the ordering of the elements is usually preserved. (This feature contrasts with Haydn's more common technique of borrowing only head motives or gestural elements.) Haydn's treatment of consequent phrases or segments also deserves attention: delayed completion of an antecedent is articulated by specific methods of rhythmic division or elaboration, as well as by pitch and motivic continuity. His transfer of melodic resemblances occurs on a large-scale basis, in which discrete elements of the model recur in the same order; but the intervening passages disintegrate the resemblances to varying degrees. When the points of resemblance are spread over a wide area of interactive phrase structure, the result is a valuable example of compositional development of a model.

Of the two examples offered here, the first relates to the *Tafelconfect* (see Example 23). The prototype consists of a 4-bar period (Example 23a, mm. 9–12), which is a delayed consequent of the antecedent period in mm. 3–5. The period mm. 9–12 may be regarded as two segments, $(x + x)$ $(y + y^1)$. The material in mm. 6–8 functions as an extension of the consequent (m. 5) of the antecedent period, and as a retransition to m. 9. The final form is a double period, mm. 3–8, 9–12, with the first period extended sequentially to six bars: $(x + x)$ (y + extension); $(x + x)$ $(y + y^1)$.

Example 23.   a) *Tafelconfect,* "Stultorum plena sunt omnia" (from EdM, Vol. 19)

b) Haydn, String Quartet Op. 71, No. 1 in B-flat major, iv, 1–12

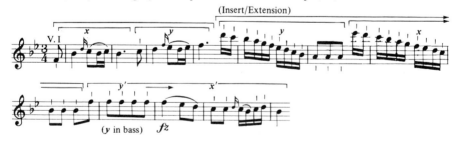

This kind of structure makes up the main theme of the finale of Haydn's String Quartet Op. 71, No. 1 in B-flat major (Example 23b). Important differences remain: the repeated antecedent phrase (mm. 1–2,

3–4; cf. Example 23a, mm. 3–4) has no immediate consequent corresponding to m. 5 of Example 23a, and there is no reprise of this antecedent corresponding to m. 9. This theme therefore appears as a single eight-bar period (1–4, 9–12), with an extension of the antecedent (5–8) proceeding directly from its own internal segmentation. (In Example 23a the extension comes from the consequent, m. 5.) Haydn's structural principles of truncation, extension, and fragmentation of period relationships find points of origin in this brief piece of vocal *Derbheit* of 1733.

In Example 24, we confront structural and textural evidence of interlocking source materials of the seventeenth and eighteenth centuries.[11] Once again, Haydn incorporates a complete fragment in Symphony No. 30 (and it is amusing to note its recurrence in the spurious "Op. 3"). The possible origin of this melodic grouping within seventeenth-century Hungarian sacred melody makes the minuet of Symphony No. 30 (Example 24a) an additional example of Haydn's liturgical borrowings. (This fits well with Landon's restriction of such borrowings largely to the years before 1770.)[12]

Example 24.   a) Haydn, Symphony No. 30 in C major, ii, 1–8

b) Hoffstetter(?), String Quartet (formerly attr. Haydn as "Op. 3," No. 2), ii, 1–8

c) MS Stark (No. 41), "Salomon" (17th century) (Bónis, "Tänze")

d) *Cantus Catholici* (1674), 18/19/1 (Bónis, "Tänze")

Aaron vesz-je

---

[11] On MSS Stark and Vietoris, see Bónis, "Tänze"; Abelmann, "Vietoris." MS Heck is discussed in W. Krabbe, "Heck."

[12] R. Landon, *Symphonies,* 254–66, 285–93.

e) MS Vietoris (1680), 126v–127r, clarino melody 14 (Abelmann, "Vietoris")

f) MS Vietoris, 24v–25r, "Polidora" (Bónis, "Tänze")

g) MS Heck (1679), pp. 50–51, No. 27, "Polidora du schöne" (W. Krabbe, "Heck")

h) *Philomela Mariana* (1713), No. 30, "Salomon . . ." (Harvard University Library)

Sal-o-mon dich bil-lich prey - sen . . .

The international migration of this group of melodies is at present one of the strongest substantiations of my hypothesis that Austro-Hungarian, Bavarian, and French popular melody of the seventeenth and eighteenth centuries formed the basis of the so-called folk melody that was one source of Haydn's melodic creativity. If there is a still earlier context, it appears to lie within the circle of Melchior Franck and the associated *Tafelmusik* and *quodlibetica.* One may now assume an extension of this tradition into the popular religious plays of the Jesuits, the Latin schools and cloister schools of the Benedictines, and the pseudo-cantatas, arias, *quodlibetica,* and "gibberish" or grammatical-joke songs of the Augsburg *Tafelmusik* repertories. This tradition seems to function as an identifiable underpinning of the "tunes" in Haydn's melodic style.

Discussion

FINSCHER   Dr. Cushman and I are thinking along similar lines. We must remember, however, that Haydn's somewhat "popular" instrumental idiom, whose origins you have so persuasively described, is only one of many highly differentiated melodic styles in his output as a whole. I think it would be premature to acknowledge the process you have described as the one most fundamental aspect of the change from late Baroque to early Classical style. But what is especially important in your approach is that you go beyond the mere quotation of similar melodies and begin to talk about compositional structure.

BADURA-SKODA   Regarding Haydn's connection with folk songs, the publications of Walter Deutsch deserve special attention.[13] He and Bartha have shown

---

[13] Especially W. Deutsch, "Volkslied"; also "Wirkungen."

that to search for complete folk melodies in Haydn's music meets with little success. Instead, we must look for folkloristic elements integrated into his melodies.

CUSHMAN Bartha's remarks are especially valuable because he includes poetical structure as a factor in his analysis.[14]

FINSCHER Professor Webster's examples permit one to show exactly where there is a juxtaposition of styles, where a synthesis, and where a new style is formed from very different traditions.

BADURA-SKODA   Around 1750, the leading music in Vienna was still in the Italian tradition, which had also become a genuine Viennese tradition: Caldara, Conti, Porsile, Predieri, Bonno—these composers all lived in Vienna. Dr. Feder's remarks on Hasse show how closely Haydn was related to it.

FINSCHER That is vocal music. We need not be so interested in the Italian tradition transplanted to Vienna, as in what happens when one tradition of melodic style is transplanted to different surroundings. Here Dr. Cushman's work comes in very handy. We know from Professor Geiringer's lecture that the Viennese nobility, bourgeois, artisans, and lower classes lived together, with chiefly Italian or Bohemian servants. This created the opportunity for a fusion of national styles.

In Professor Webster's examples, I find it suggestive that some of the melodies juxtapose different things a little mechanically. Examples 1a, 3b, and 4b are closely linked to South German folk music; these traditions undoubtedly stem from the collections of popular songs that Dr. Cushman discussed. But Examples 2a and 3a are different. In Example 2a, the stereotyped Neapolitan cadence is preceded by something like the sequential construction typical of folklike melodies; in Example 3a, the first bar is folklike, but the continuation reverts to a modified Neapolitan tradition. The latter tune is actually commonplace, save for its mixture of traditions. Another contrast is between the quotation of a folk tune, as in the Dušek Example 4b, and the stylization in Haydn's Example 4c. Here the melodic phrase develops out of variations of a germ cell, which may or may not actually derive from popular music.

MANN Example 4b actually resembles Bach's *Coffee Cantata*. This reinforces the idea of a quotation from common property.

WEBSTER There are differences within the repertory, however. You would search in vain in Haydn's early instrumental music for the stiff *Fortspinnung* in a moderate tempo that we see in Example 5.

FEDER There are great similarities between many of Haydn's and Albrechtsberger's early divertimenti. It is no accident that a string quartet by

---

[14]Cf. the Round Table *Changing Concepts of Form.* [Ed.]

Albrechtsberger, Hob. III:D3, was long supposed to be by Haydn. Another Albrechtsberger divertimento quotes the posthorn signal which occurs in Haydn's Symphony No. 31; in the same work, he combines that with the Night Watchman's Song which Haydn quotes several times in early compositions.[15] Is that an integration of style, or is it merely the addition of heterogeneous materials to an otherwise conventional composition?

FINSCHER I think the latter is usually the case. It is the same as the Biber serenade with the Night Watchman's Song that Geiringer quoted in his lecture— they are mere genre pieces produced for amusement. But it is different in Haydn's "Posthorn" symphony; he uses the signal as a structural element.

FEDER In that case, we can speak of a synthesis of styles. The new element becomes integrated in a work of art.

BADURA-SKODA   If the term "synthetic" is understood in this way, I can agree to its use in connection with Haydn. But it is essential to guard against the misconception that his style is merely a compilation of different features drawn from all sides.

To Haydn from C. P. E. Bach: Non-tunes

HELM We have reason to believe that C. P. E. Bach influenced Haydn's music in certain ways well into the 1770s and possibly longer. Where Haydn gives us instrumental recitative or "Sturm and Drang" or *empfindsamer Stil,* we might well decide that he is consciously or unconsciously carrying a bit of Bach's style into his own. But if we are to limit ourselves to C. P. E. Bach's melodic influence on Haydn, perhaps we should concentrate on those works which originated in proximity to identifiable C. P. E. Bach works. We understand from Griesinger, Dies, and Rochlitz that the young Haydn had what might be called an "encounter" with Bach's music or his *Versuch* or both—according to Griesinger—most importantly, with "the first six sonatas." It has long been assumed that this referred to Bach's first published set of keyboard sonatas, the "Prussian" Sonatas of 1742. Of course, as A. Peter Brown points out in his Free Paper elsewhere in this volume, reliable chronology is not among the strong points of Haydn's earliest biographers, and the "Prussian" Sonatas are not designated "Opus 1," whereas both the unauthorized Huberty collection of the 1760s and the Sonatas for "Ladies" published in 1770 are so designated.

But I don't think we need to rummage through C. P. E. Bach's sonatas of three decades to illustrate the relation of his melodies to those of

---

[15]Cf. Chew, "Watchman" [Ed.]

Haydn. Griesinger fairly well convinces me that the encounter did take place when Haydn was quite young, probably in the early 1750s. And in any case the melodic styles of C. P. E. Bach and Haydn remained so grossly different during Haydn's youth, middle age, and old age that exact chronology hardly seems to matter. Still, for the purpose of illustration, it is better to restrict the time period here to the "Prussian" and "Württemberg" Sonatas of the early 1740s.

Where in Haydn should we look for the influence of such Bach sonatas? If we are going to limit ourselves to melody in the strictest sense, perhaps we should concentrate on the first half-dozen or so of Haydn's certifiably genuine keyboard sonatas, forgetting about the delights that Bach passed on to composers of symphonies, concertos, and chamber music in Haydn's generation. Furthermore, we must compare similar types of movements. Comparing a minuet in an early Haydn sonata, for instance, with any movement in the "Prussian" or "Württemberg" Sonatas would be about as informative as comparing apples with oranges. Bach wrote delightful minuets by the yard, but he considered most of them to be miniatures unworthy of the kind of formal setting given them by Haydn. Similarly, the *empfindsam* Adagios in the Bach sonatas have no real counterparts in this early group of Haydn sonatas, and the Presto themes in the finales of the Haydn sonatas have a *volkstümlich* derivation foreign to the aesthetic of the North German sonata. As an example of such a presto theme, we might consider the opening of the finale of Haydn's Sonata in E major Hob. XVI:13 (ChL. 15), probably from the early 1760s at the latest (Example 25). Fetching, folksy, witty, Haydnesque; but quite foreign to the introspective makeup of a certain Berliner—not to mention the fact that triadic themes were anathema to him.

Example 25. Sonata Hob. XVI:13 (ChL. 15) in E major, iii, 1–8

After such apples and oranges are removed from consideration, what is left? Primarily the first movements. In both groups of sonatas the first movements are uniformly marked Allegro or Moderato, they evoke no particularly local or ethnic styles, and they follow an established form and mode of address.

Haydn's movements generally contain tunes; C. P. E. Bach's are replete with "non-tunes." This statement is not intended to put Bach in a bad light; in fact, his seem to me by far the better of the two groups of sonatas. The main basis on which the Haydn melodies can be called tunes is their return, within a few bars, to the motive which begins the melody. (This was hardly an original device.) After this return, the melody is free to move on to new thoughts. The beginning of the aforementioned Sonata in E illustrates this point (Example 26, mm. 1–2, 5–6). The main basis on which Emanuel's melodies can be called "non-tunes" is the absence of that little return. The sixth "Prussian" Sonata opens with a similar melody (Example 27), but the little return is missing. Emanuel Bach was not averse to repetition, especially if it was varied; but within a single melody he typically avoided repetition or anything else that might be easily remembered.

Example 26.   Sonata Hob. XVI:13 (ChL. 15) in E major, i, 1–8

Example 27.   C. P. E. Bach, "Prussian" Sonatas, Wq. 48 (publ. 1742), No. 6, i, 1–7

Haydn's and C. P. E. Bach's melodies are also often differentiated by their phrase lengths, not as marked in number of measures, but by number and relative weight of pulses. Even where Haydn writes a phrase whose length is an odd number of measures, we generally feel the end of the phrase. But even where Emanuel Bach writes a 2- or 4- or 8-bar phrase, he seems quite consciously determined to obscure all of it by presenting the greatest heterogeneity of note values in the shortest possible time, or to obscure the end of it with a phrase extension, a rest, an inserted figure, a metrical shift of a motive, or a fresh start on a new phrase before the old one sounds finished. He will do anything to ensure that nobody is going to go around humming his melodies.

How are the melodies alike? Primarily in their common rejection of Baroque *Fortspinnung* in a single *Affekt,* and in their common adherence to the idea of structuring melody in more or less discrete segments. Haydn makes the segments easily divisible; Emanuel Bach prefers to avoid obvious divisibility.

I believe that the young Haydn fell upon C. P. E. Bach's sonatas eagerly as the work of a master craftsman in a style then startlingly new to him. By his own testimony, these sonatas expanded his horizons dramatically. But Haydn's melodies kept on marching to a different drummer.

BADURA-SKODA   Haydn's inclination to use more tunelike melodies than Emanuel Bach could be related to his having been born eighteen years later. Also, the greater proximity of Vienna to Italy and the influence of Italian *buffo* composers must have been a contributing factor. I find more obvious "tunes" in his early comedy arias and *Singspiel* music than in his early keyboard works. An early example would be the *Aria di Dorina* (Hob. XXIVb:1; Example 28). This melody contains a variant of the second half of *America* (*God Save the Queen*).[16]

Example 28.   Aria Hob. XXIVb:1, 25–32

Co-stret-ta pian-ge-re   do-len-te e mi - se-ra   non veg - go un ter -mi-ne   al   mio pe-nar

---

When did Haydn Begin to Write "Beautiful" Melodies?

WEBSTER   A distinguishing feature of much of Haydn's early instrumental music is the absence therein of certain kinds of melodies which we may call "beautiful." An example of what I mean is the second theme in the first movement of Mozart's G-minor Symphony K. 550. It is cantabile, without distinctive ornamental figuration, excessive leaps, or marked rhythmic complexity; it is in a single key (at least until m. 55); it has clear phrase structure; and it is a *Gestalt,* that is, the expression of a single, integrated idea or gesture. In addition to these intrinsic features, this melody owes much of its effect to its role as a contrast to what has preceded it: it is in the major; *piano;* it moves almost entirely by step; it lacks the insistent eighth-note motion of the preceding passages; and so forth.

  Few of Haydn's symphonic second themes, especially in his earlier works, fit this supposedly "normal" pattern. In many first movements, there is no contrasting second theme at all.[17] More surprising, even when Haydn writes what sounds like a well-formed second theme, he does not follow the pattern described above. In most of these cases the effect of contrast is achieved exclusively by devices such as *piano,* reduced instrumentation, and new material, but not by "singable" melodies or clear period structure. An excellent example occurs in Symphony No. 6 in D major, "Le Matin" (1761), mm. 21–27: it sounds at first like a "second theme." But it is only six measures long; it is jumpy, motivic rather than melodic, with wide leaps of a seventh in "Scotch snap" rhythm; it is not cantabile; it has no firm period structure, but moves in sequential steps downwards; it is not tonally stable, but begins off the root-position

---

[16] See Badura-Skoda, "Comedy," 194.
[17] R. Landon, *Symphonies,* describes Haydn's symphonic second themes, without focusing on the issue raised here.

tonic on I⁶ and moves to V, further complicated by touches of the minor; and the bass undermines the apparent relaxation by maintaining the restless tension of Haydn's characteristic repeated eighth notes. Similar second themes in triple meter may be found in other early Haydn symphonies.[18] Movements in duple meter often turn to the minor mode, to nervous, imitative eighth-note motion, or both.[19] Haydn's closest approach to a real contrast in the early symphonies probably occurs in No. 38 in C major (c. 1766), but even here we find nothing resembling Mozart's cantabile.

In the "Sturm und Drang" period we begin to encounter "beautiful" second themes. But even the famous D-major melody from the "Farewell" Symphony, No. 45 in F-sharp minor (1772), finds no place in Haydn's stormy exposition; it must be postponed until the second half of the development. The closest approach to the cantabile type in an exposition seems to occur in No. 56 in C major (1774).[20] Many other symphonies from the 1770s have clear second themes.[21] Symphony No. 67 in F major (c. 1775–76)[22] is especially noteworthy in this regard, for it not only has periodic contrasting second themes in both the first movement and the finale, but the latter movement also breaks off into an Andante which is based on as "beautiful" a melody as one could wish. But this procedure is noteworthy precisely for its exceptional features. The fast–slow–fast form of this finale derives from the opera, not the world of autonomous instrumental music,[23] on its first presentation it is played by a solo string trio, and the continuation in B flat quotes the opening of the *Missa Sti. Nicolae* (1772). The first symphony whose second theme seems clearly to adumbrate Mozart's type may well be No. 77 in B-flat major (1782). For once Haydn even dispenses with the characteristic eighth-note motion. And from this point on we find numerous equally clear examples of second themes in Haydn's symphonies.[24]

[18] E.g., Nos. 5 (second movement), 17, and 40.
[19] E.g., Nos. 1, 2, 4, 10, 12, 15, 20, 24, 25, 27, 30, 32, and 37.
[20] Those in Nos. 42, 57, and 61 lack the clear periodic structure. Indeed in No. 42 in D major (1771), the *closing* theme of the first movement (mm. 66–73) is closer in style to our ideal than the actual second theme (mm. 26–42). This feature recalls the type of exposition structure that Larsen describes in "Sonatenform."
[21] Including Nos. 48, 51, 53, 62, 63, 65, 69, 71, 74, and 76.
[22] The dates given here for Symphonies Nos. 64, 67, 74, and 75 are taken from Gerlach, "Ordnung"; they are more accurate than those in R. Landon, *Symphonies* or Haydn, *Symphonies*.
[23] This new proximity of symphony and opera is characteristic of Haydn's music after the "Sturm und Drang," that is after 1774 or so. The question whether the specifically melodic style of these symphonies—or, more generally, the changes of style in the orchestral music of the 1770s—can be attributed to this rapprochement still awaits a thorough investigation of these repertories.
[24] E.g., in Nos. 82, 83, 86, 88, and 90; and, if one also accepts closing themes, Nos. 80 and 92.

Haydn's early symphonic slow movements also are not characterized by "beautiful" melodies. The majority of Haydn's early slow-movement melodies fall into one or another of several well-defined types, including the Siciliano in 6/8 meter;[25] several types of sprightly Andante themes in 2/4 meter;[26] and a third type which consists of a long-held note over figured accompaniment, eventually "dissolving" into more rapid melodic activity.[27]

Among these early slow-movement themes, only two contexts tend to exhibit "beautiful" melodies. When the slow movement is the *first* movement, Haydn often writes serious Adagio melodies with tight phrase structure. The first movement of Symphony No. 21 in A major (1764) opens with one of the finest orchestral melodies in any early Haydn symphony.[28] The other "beautiful" themes in Haydn's early slow movements are written for solo concertante instruments. Classic examples here are the concerto slow movement in Symphony No. 7 in C major, "Le Midi" (1761), after the recitative; and the cello melody in the slow movement in Symphony No. 13 in D major (1763).

Once again, the "Sturm und Drang" offered Haydn new opportunities. In this period, Haydn's slow movements are almost all Adagio and *con sordini.* "Beautiful" melodies are found, at least, in Symphonies Nos. 44, 47, 54, and 56; once again, the latter is closest in style to later Classical themes.

But Haydn's most characteristic types of late slow melodies do not appear until after the "Sturm und Drang." One type is outwardly a reversion to the Andante style of the 1760s, but imbued with new depth of feeling. This unmistakably Haydnesque mood of sprightly profundity appears for the first time, perhaps, in the "Farewell" Symphony. One of the most characteristic examples appears in Symphony No. 74 (1780?).[29] Another type is the hymnlike Adagio in 3/4 meter with clear period structure. It seems to occur for the first time in one of the strangest movements Haydn ever wrote, the slow movement of Symphony No. 64 (c. 1771–73). The first thoroughly characteristic example is found in No. 75 (1779?).[30] A third type is the serious, lyric Andante in 6/8 with

[25] As in Nos. 12, 27, 31, 46, and Hob. I:108 ("Symphony B").

[26] An upbeat in short notes, followed by eighth-note motion, as in Nos. 1, 19, 30, and 41; an eighth-note upbeat followed by eighth notes grouped in twos, as in Nos. 23, 35, 37, 40, 43, 53, 55, 60, 82, and 90; without upbeat, as in Nos. 8, 9, 14, 28, and Hob. I:107 ("Symphony A").

[27] E.g., Nos. 4, 10, 33, 34, and 38.

[28] A similar, if less deeply felt melody in the same key is found in the opening slow movement of Symphony No. 5 (c. 1760).

[29] Comparable melodies appear in Nos. 55, 67, 68, 71, 74, 76, 78, and 79.

[30] It also occurs in Nos. 61, 66, 87, and 98; and, varied in Nos. 83, 86, 88, 99, and 102. The opening theme of No. 21, cited above, is similar in mood, but it lacks the regular period structure of the later works.

short phrases including thirty-second notes, and often with dotted rhythms. It first appears in Symphony No. 81 (1783–84). This type recurs not only in later symphonies,[31] but also in other genres, for example the string quartets Op. 50, No. 1 (1787) and Op. 76, No. 5 (1797). It also lived on after Haydn's death: one of its purest examples is the slow movement of Schubert's Symphony No. 5 in B-flat major.

We may summarize these results by saying that Haydn uses "beautiful" melodies but rarely in his early symphonies, and then only in first-movement Adagios and in movements for concertante soloists. In the "Sturm und Drang" period he wrote them more often, deepening and refining them in content. But both quantitatively and in terms of the types which dominate Haydn's late instrumental music, "beautiful" melodies did not become a normal resource of his symphonic style until the late 1770s and early 1780s.[32]

It is hardly necessary to point out that the cantabile melody was an essential aspect of Mozart's style from the beginning. This is attributable at least in part to his early exposure to Italian opera and musical culture in Salzburg and Italy, and to its instrumental descendants such as J. C. Bach. In this respect, then, melodic usage in early Classical style is highly differentiated. An investigation of Haydn's Viennese contemporaries might tell us to what extent the absence of "beautiful" melodies in early and middle Haydn was his own personal peculiarity, to what extent it was a general Viennese characteristic. In any case, Haydn's symphonies suggest that, until 1780, Viennese orchestral music got along very well without "beautiful" melodies at all.[33]

BADURA-SKODA   There are differences between Haydn's vocal and instrumental style throughout his life. It seems likely that in Haydn's operas and Masses "beautiful" melodies (in Professor Webster's sense) are to be found earlier than in his instrumental works. This topic is one that deserves to be pursued in the future.

[31] E.g., Nos. 84 and 95; perhaps also in Nos. 89 and 96.

[32] Here we have one indication—and it is by no means the only one—of the inadequacy of Landon's criticism of Haydn's stylistic changes in the late 1770s and early 1780s. This subject too deserves a fundamental reappraisal.

[33] For a fruitful early formulation of the topic discussed here, I am indebted to Daniel R. Brown.

Round Table

Turning Points in Haydn's Stylistic Development

JAN LA RUE, *Chairman*   KARL GEIRINGER
BARRY S. BROOK   DENNIS MONK
A. PETER BROWN   LÁSZLÓ SOMFAI
LUDWIG FINSCHER   JUDITH SCHWARTZ, *Secretary*

LA RUE Our four topics are intended to illustrate a progression from large-dimension to small-dimension "turning points" in Haydn's style.

Haydn's London String Quartets

SOMFAI The tremendous changes in style in Haydn's London symphonies, sonatas, and piano trios have often been discussed. In his string quartets the differences are less striking. The quartet was not to be a central genre for him in London, because of the circumstances of London concert life. He went to London in 1791 with the very fine set of six string quartets Op. 64, composed in 1790, some of which were performed in concerts there. These affairs were big public concerts with mixed programs, including symphonies, concertos, and arias. He prepared himself for the second London journey by writing the six quartets Opp. 71–74 in Vienna in 1793, with the specific purpose of scoring a triumph in London.[1]

The difference between the two quartet styles was that the pre-London quartet was "chamber music" in the original meaning of the term, in that it was to be played in a small or medium-sized room; the London quartets, however, were written for a mixed public concert in a larger hall. As happened now and then, Haydn used very nearly the same opening theme in two of these quartets, one each from Op. 64 and Opp. 71–74, and this allows us to describe the change in style precisely. (See Example 1.) Op. 64, No. 6 is in a typical Haydn chamber-music style, written at Eszterháza for Vienna or for those unknown chamber music groups in Paris, Amsterdam, and London, where his string quartets were published. Op. 74, No. 1, on the other hand, represents idiomatic writing for London, in particular for Salomon's violin style. It is a most impressive concertante style.

The main thematic material and the constructions of the two entire expositions are also related. Another interesting parallel appears in the reca-

[1] This hypothesis also appears in Pohl-Botstiber, 311.

Example 1.

a) String Quartet Op. 64, No. 6 in E-flat major, i, 1–12

b) String Quartet Op. 74, No. 1 in C major, i, 1–18

pitulation: shortly after the presentation of the first half of the theme, both works continue with a fugato development (Op. 64, No. 6, m. 102; Op. 74, No. 1, m. 105). The stylistic discrepancies, however, are more characteristic. For example, the main theme in Op. 64, No. 6 is a very concentrated statement, with great economy, control of the tessitura, and homogeneous rhythmic growth from the larger rhythmic unit to the smaller ones. This whole exposition goes in the direction of diminution; one theme unfolds after another, not so much in the sense of *Fortspinnung* as with real directional growth typical of Haydn. The second theme (m. 31) is characteristic (that is, "thematic") only in its rhythm: it does not unfold in a single direction, but is put together out of various contrasting motives.

Op. 74, No. 1 does not begin with the *piano* primary subject, but the famous "instant noise-killer" (mm. 1–2) which is typical of the London string quartets. It can be just one chord (Op. 71, No. 3 in E-flat major), or a very brief introduction (Op. 71, No. 2 in D major), or, as here, two loud chords without tempo indication (which really kill the noise of a big audience). The primary subject is built up on contrast: *piano* and *forte,* small tessitura and full tessitura, homogeneous and contrasting rhythmic action.

As far as the whole exposition is concerned, Op. 64, No. 6 is a concentrated, chamber-style development, whereas Op. 74, No. 1 establishes a strong concertante trend, continuing to alternate solid thematic areas (mm. 18–34, 42–44) with figurative-virtuoso areas (35–41, 45–54).

Discussion

FINSCHER The differences between Vienna and London go a little further. Viennese chamber music had usually been performed privately. And the repertory had never gone beyond the confines of "chamber music." The string quartet had become the most important genre. This is quite different from performing a quartet in the context of the public orchestral and vocal concerts in London. From this perspective, I'm surprised how *small* the stylistic change is between Op. 64 and Opp. 71–74. I don't think Op. 74, No. 1 was a rewarding task for a man like Salomon; if you compare the Lyre Notturno No. 7 (Hob. II:31) that Haydn rewrote for one of his London concerts, you can see a really concertante part that was intended for Salomon. There are elements of the *quatuor concertant* in Haydn's later quartets, but they are integrated into his traditional texture. They are not true *quatuors concertants*.[2]

SOMFAI It is not just whether the violin solo is demanding, but the character of the primary theme itself. The first theme of Op. 64, No. 6 is a fully sophisticated musical statement in which each step is the logical outcome of the preceding one, and the homogeneous tessitura of the first-violin part is calculated for idiomatic performance. Whereas in Op. 74, No. 1, first we have a *piano* cantabile melody on the A string, next the full tessitura with *spiccato,* then the first idea intensified, then a new phrasing (m. 15), and finally in m. 18 a real *dolce*—at least four contrasting ideas in sixteen bars. It certainly gave an opportunity to a violinist like Salomon to present a number of impressive, personal violinistic styles, instead of concentrating on the musical idea.

FINSCHER This "noise-killer": I still doubt whether one should interpret it as specifically intended to quiet the large London audience; quite a number of Haydn quartets begin in this way.

SOMFAI Not many. It is interesting to see which elements of the London style are missing from the later quartets. This "noise-killer" recurs only in the two quartets in G major, Op. 76, No. 1 and Op. 77, No. 1. Everything that comes before London—see earlier quartets in G major, Op. 33, No. 5 and Op. 64, No. 4—has thematic value. The two chords in Op. 74, No. 1 are "outside" the piece; they have no tempo indication, no rhythm, no characteristic line, no characteristic sound. They're just to make the audience be quiet.

[2] On the *quatuor concertant,* see Trimpert, *Quatuor.*

LA RUE Apart from the "noise killer," each quartet opens with two four-bar phrases, seemingly parallel structures; but Op. 74, No. 1 projects a larger-scale impression because of the pedal underneath mm. 3–6. And mm. 11–18 confirm the eight-bar dimension: range and dynamics are expanded, rhythm accelerates, the melodic line takes a more active part, and the "fourth" bar, m. 14, is poised on V/V so we can't stop.

Another difference: the violin line of Op. 64, No. 6 reaches a ceiling on b♭² and hardly exceeds it until the end of the exposition. In Op. 74, No. 1, bars 7, 24, 39, and 50 reach successive peaks of e³, f³, g³, and b³, an impressive long-range effect.

Stylistic Change in Haydn's Oratorios: *Il Ritorno di Tobia* and *The Creation*[3]

GEIRINGER The first part of the overture to *Il Ritorno di Tobia* (1775) and the prelude to *The Creation* (1799) resemble each other in many respects. Both pieces are in C minor, 4/4 meter, Largo, and begin with a *forte* of the full orchestra in a unison C. The prevailing mood is dark.

On the other hand, there are sizable differences in *The Creation* compared to the earlier work. First, the harmonic language is even bolder. Observe the imaginative use of chromatic progressions, appoggiaturas, augmented and diminished intervals, and chords of the seventh and ninth. Such details as the ambiguities of mm. 5 and 6, the surprising modulation in 19–21, and the harmonic clashes in 50–55 induced Tovey to compare Haydn's harmonic technique to Wagner.[4] Second, the orchestra is augmented by two flutes, two clarinets, three trombones, and double bassoon. Third, it is used in a more imaginative and colorful manner. The predominance of the solid body of string instruments is broken. The texture is transparent, with flutes, clarinets, and bassoons making significant contributions. Occasional cadenzas, for instance m. 31, further enliven the sound picture. The Largo is more than four times as long, and its mysterious grandeur is not destroyed, as in *Tobia,* by soon turning to a rather conventional Allegro di molto. The *Tobia* overture appears like a kind of preparation for the first chorus; *The Creation* prelude appears as an imposing structure in its own right and is followed by a recitative of transitional character.

Fourth, the *Creation* prelude does not quote a vocal number from the following work; its music is freely invented and only poetically connected with the rest of the oratorio. Haydn outlines a highly Romantic program in the title he gives to this piece, but he describes it with purely

---

[3] Professor Geiringer's introductory remarks to this section were read in his absence by Professor Brook.
[4] Tovey, *Essays,* V, 116, 118.

instrumental means. It is a stage preceding the story, in a way the basis for the whole vocal work.

Fifth, the spirit of *Empfindsamkeit* is noticeable in the initial Largo of *Tobia* only as a quickly passing episode. The prelude to *The Creation,* on the other hand, enlarges and deepens this mood to a pervading Romantic feeling which foreshadows developments in nineteenth-century music.

Discussion

BROOK I don't believe that this comparison really indicates a stylistic "turning point." *Tobia* is an Italian oratorio on a Metastasian libretto by Giovanni Gastoni Boccherini, the brother of the composer. It is not dramatically successful. The poem upon which *The Creation* is based is very different indeed. That creates two very different kinds of pieces. I feel that Haydn was cutting his dramatic teeth with *Tobia.* It is his first large dramatic work; until he added the two great additional choruses in 1784, it was practically an *opera seria* with three choruses. Its powerful plot, which comes from the Apocrypha, is vitiated in Boccherini's text into a parable. *The Creation* is more in a Handelian tradition, with nine or ten choruses. It's more creative.

The overtures reflect some aspects of the oratorios as a whole. The overture to *Tobia* is a fairly typical Italian overture of the time: a slow introduction and a sprawling sonata-allegro. The overture to *The Creation,* on the other hand, based on a concept with specific dramatic purpose, is unique. On the whole, *Tobia* is similarly sprawling. It has great and powerful moments, but many find it much too long performed without cuts. *The Creation,* on the other hand, was written in full consciousness of the kind of audience that could appreciate it; it's compact and beautifully structured. There is also a sociological difference, in that *Tobia* was written with two possible objectives—performance at the imperial court or membership in the Tonkünstler-Societät. *The Creation* was intended for the public.

Despite its resemblance to *opera seria, Tobia* exhibits a gradual progression toward Anna's aria in the minor, "Come in sogno," about two-thirds of the way through the work. There is an intensification at that point, represented by the remarkable chorus 13c.

MONK Tovey relates this representation of Chaos to the eighteenth-century nebula hypothesis,[5] which makes this first number of the *Creation* certainly very much a part of the piece rather than just an overture. Haydn was aware of the moon in *Il mondo della luna;* here he's aware of the creation of the earth out of Chaos.

[5] Ibid., 114–19.

BROWN   I was also surprised by the choice of *Tobia* and *The Creation*. To take a parallel example, the well-known oratorio by Dittersdorf, *Esther*, was written for the same series of concerts; but its conservative prelude could hardly serve as a turning point in Dittersdorf's output.

BROOK   *Tobia* is highly underrated. It may be too long, but there are some extraordinary things in it, such as fantastic dramatic accompanied recitatives, with five voices. Nor is it only the two added choruses that make it great; note, for example, some of the wonderful instrumental accompaniments, the inventive use of English horns, and so on. Also the sections in the minor represent not *Empfindsamkeit* but "Sturm und Drang" textures or procedures.

LAWRENCE TAYLOR[6]   Did not Haydn later think that the work was somewhat old-fashioned?

BROOK   The "old-hat" idea came about in 1808, when his former pupil Neukomm rewrote the oratorio, added various instruments, cut substantial sections, and in particular removed the coloraturas. He was attempting the impossible: to turn an Italian oratorio into a new-style oratorio à la *Creation* and *Seasons*. It's not certain, but it seems that Haydn was not completely pleased.

ROBERT N. FREEMAN[7]   We should be careful not to refer to *Tobia* and Haydn's big early Masses simply as "Italian" works. The Viennese *Hof-Stil* was an important and unique style in its own right. When Caldara came to Vienna, his style changed; he adopted this *Hof-Stil*.[8] Haydn's *Tobia* belongs to this genre. It has more counterpoint; the first chorus is not typical of a slow chorus in the contemporary Italian oratorio; that style was more homophonic—more modern, in that sense.

BROOK   The model is Italian, the texts and the construction are Italian, but there is a great difference in depth and mood. Actually, there isn't a great deal of counterpoint, except for the three choruses at the beginning and end of the first part and the end of the second part. This reflects traditional Italian practice in oratorios with chorus.

Realization of an Idiomatic Keyboard Style in Sonatas of the 1770s

BROWN   We know from both tradition and documents that Haydn had access to and probably used the full gamut of keyboard instruments—clavichord, organ, harpsichord, and fortepiano—throughout a large part of his life.[9] The question of when he began to write his solo sonatas for the piano has

---

[6] From the audience.   [7] From the audience.

[8] See U. Kirkendale's excellent *Caldara*.

[9] See Walter, "Klavier," and Walter, "Tasteninstrument." [The term "fortepiano" is used here to designate eighteenth-century pianos, in distinction to the modern pianoforte. On

elicited many different opinions: Geiringer states that "from sonata No. 6 on, the pianoforte seems to have been in Haydn's mind"—though Feder dates this sonata not later than 1760;[10] Parrish feels that "beginning with sonata 18 [c. 1768] [Haydn's] writing is more completely of the character one finds in 18th-century compositions that are avowedly for the piano";[11] Newman writes that with No. 20 in C minor Haydn "may have started to compose for the piano . . . to judge by the first appearance of dynamic signs as well as by the character."[12]

However, even if we could answer this question, it would not necessarily signify a crucial point in Haydn's development. Rather, a turning point should be located by searching for the "crystallization" of an idiomatic keyboard style in the music itself. Considering two chronologically neighboring sonata first movements, I would like to argue that Hob. XVI:26 (ChL. 41) in A major of 1773 exemplifies the crystallization of a style for the harpsichord, while Hob. XVI:29 (ChL. 44) in F major of 1774 exemplifies a fortepiano style.

The appearance of dynamics in a reliable source for Sonata No. 29 and the lack of them in Sonata No. 26 suggest that only the former was conceived for the fortepiano. I would prefer to look at these two movements from the viewpoint of compensatory activity: the availability or nonavailability of certain elements having a distinctive effect on the behavior of others. Thus, the limited dynamic and coloristic capabilities of the harpsichord are compensated for by shifts of texture, figuration, and tessitura at the level of the phrase and subphrase. In the opening measures of Sonata No. 26 (see Example 2), note the transfer of material from one octave to another in m. 1, the subsequent contrapuntal texture (mm. 11–13), and the active three-voice texture beginning in m. 14. The result is a series of well-defined, short-lived ideas, underlined by beat-marking and the relatively quick harmonic rhythm. In addition, rhythmic stress is often created by ornaments or dissonance. Compared to the neutral style of writing found in many of Haydn's keyboard works, this movement indicates a clearly articulated harpsichord idiom.

Example 2. Sonata Hob. XVI:26 (ChL. 41) in A major, i, 1–2, 11–12, 14–15

---

this point, as well as the topics discussed in the following pages, cf. numerous contributions in the section Performance.—Ed.]

[10] Geiringer, *Haydn* 2, 2nd ed., 227. The datings given here are taken from Feder, "Klaviersonaten."

[11] Parrish, "Piano," 33.   [12] Newman, *Classic,* 465.

Although the exposition in No. 29 is approximately the same length, activity here occurs at the middle rather than the small dimension. In fact, some of the same musical elements which in No. 26 provided activity merely at the small dimension now define the structure of the entire exposition (mm. 1–14, 15–26, 27–31; see Example 3). Although a contrast of register is again found at the beginning, the effect is "streamlined," and the surface and harmonic rhythms are less erratic. Particularly idiomatic is the manner in which dynamics are employed, both locally and structurally. For example, in mm. 7–10 the lack of coordination between dynamics and sonority—the *forte* is always on the single note; the *piano* on the chords—is in opposition to harpsichord style; the structural crescendo beginning in m. 22 contributes to the resolution of the tonal conflict in mm. 26–27. Furthermore, the repetitions without change of register in mm. 15–20 actually imply dynamic nuances possible only on the newer instrument. In sum, the functional divisions of the exposition (primary, transition, and closing sections) clearly emerge from elements of fortepiano style itself.

Example 3. Sonata Hob. XVI:29 (ChL. 44) in F major, i, 1–2, 9–10, 15, 21–27

A musical idiom is not as narrow a concept as the historians who adopt an evolutionary or chronological approach to the problem of medium usually imply. Rather, Haydn's realization of a fortepiano style demands reexamination of conventional notions of harpsichord idiom. Perhaps this explains why in these two chronologically neighboring sonatas Haydn temporarily departed from a more neutral approach to keyboard composition.

Discussion

SCHWARTZ Is the "clearly articulated harpsichord idiom" you describe for Sonata No. 26 necessarily limited to the harpsichord? The characteristics you cite remind me of C. P. E. Bach's sonatas, which we generally associate with the clavichord. Also the contrapuntal textures, small-dimension shifts in texture, textural contrast within the movement, small-dimension orientation, the beat marking, and so on—are these features really specific to any keyboard idiom? Such textural and registral contrasts are common to mid-century chamber styles. Likewise the small-dimension focus: in comparing string quartets and symphonies by Gassmann, for example, one of the most striking differences is in the dimension of activity and the arrangement of the texture in the string quartet: short, fussy ideas, shifting up and down through the texture from one register to another, small contrasts giving a great deal of vertical flexibility, not necessarily typical of a symphony. Are these characteristics then really inherent in a keyboard idiom, or merely part of a more general style change?

As for the shift in focus from small to middle dimensions: does it really define a difference in instrumental idiom? The broader contours, the longer range of contrasts in Sonata No. 29, represent a more mature handling of Classic elements than finely detailed oppositions in No. 26. But aren't these types to be found in other genres too? (For example, Symphonies No. 15 in D major and Hob. I:107 ["Symphony A"] in B-flat major are built on very short motivic ideas, but No. 24 in D major unfolds in broad 4- and 8-bar periods.) Haydn's keyboard crescendo also has a familiar ring: it appears in the exposition at a critical point, that is, just before stabilization of the dominant key; it appears again in the development, and once again in the recapitulation. At least two symphonies by Johann Stamitz, written at least twenty years earlier, are similar. This procedure of using dynamics to define large structural sections is usually associated with orchestral style. So again, the new dynamics may not be so much a keyboard characteristic as a general Classic feature that has begun to infiltrate the keyboard idiom, which then becomes less chamber-like and more symphonic. The idea of a general stylistic turning point also fits well with Horst Walter's conclusion that the development of piano style in Haydn's keyboard music seems to have taken place independently of whichever instrument he might have been using at the time.[13]

BROWN   The comment about C. P. E. Bach and the clavichord certainly has some validity. But the prominent eighth-note beat marking in the A-major Sonata, with dissonance and ornamentation giving rhythmic emphasis, still suggests the harpsichord; with the clavichord, it is possible to make these kinds of metric differentiations dynamically. And my notion of compensatory activity applies: whenever Haydn brings an active melody to rest, he compensates with activity of texture or rhythm. The A-major Sonata is so full of idiomatic harpsichord figuration, that it could not conceivably be done in any other medium. Therefore the comparisons with rapid shifts of tessitura and the Italian overture style don't seem to apply.

Did this change take place in 1773 or 1766 or 1784? We should recall a comment that Haydn is said to have made during the last years of his life, that now that he had finally learned how to write for wind instruments, he was too old to make use of this knowledge.[14] Haydn was considering the problem of idiom in a number of genres. The 1770s were the crucial years in the development of a really idiomatic quartet style. The "Capriccio" Piano Trio in A major (Hob. XV:35), which Feder dates in the middle 1760s, exhibits a totally different approach to the problem of texture from that of his earlier keyboard trios. At about this time Haydn's symphonies start to move away from various kinds of set Viennese styles into a more constant type of relationship between movements; for instance, after 1768 the "church sonata" idea seems to drop out. So the 1760s and 1770s are a turning point in this respect.

[13] Walter, "Klaviere," 264.
[14] Apparently first transmitted by Pohl, in his article on Haydn in the first edition of *Grove's Dictionary*.

FINSCHER Two points on method. If your aim is to relate the change of musical texture to the change of instrument intended, you must recall that, unlike Mozart, Haydn was not a virtuoso pianist. Even in his keyboard music, a level of "abstract" compositional thinking would be required.

Second, in the late 1760s and early 1770s Haydn apparently shifted constantly among different models of composition. These two sonatas are a case in point: in the A-major Sonata C. P. E. Bach's influence is very strong, while in the second sonata there are influences from Mannheim or thereabouts, from J. C. Bach, and so on. It's much more complicated than just a step in a continuous development.

BROWN Haydn composed at different keyboard instruments. (Tovey pointed out that in certain string quartet textures Haydn has preserved a kind of keyboard texture, especially figurations in the inner parts.)[15] Also, Haydn had a great deal of ability and facility at the keyboard.

Concerning models: I think this type of composition is similar to C. P. E. Bach only in the control of small-dimension orientation. In Vienna, the Italian overture was a much more direct influence than the Mannheim style. And finally, although J. C. Bach is mentioned in the *Wienerisches Diarium* and the HNV, this doesn't create a valid precedent for Haydn's keyboard style.

SOMFAI The Esterházy set (from which the A-major Sonata was drawn) was intended to be a representative kind of court sonata: its style is certainly for harpsichord. The F-major Sonata belongs to the 1774–76 set, delivered to Vienna in copies without direct indication of harpsichord or piano. The A-major stands last in the autograph. It has a marvelous first movement, not really typical of the whole set. But the two other movements are an arrangement of the "al rovescio" minuet from Symphony No. 42 in G major, and a tiny presto. These are not really the court harpsichord style.

CHRISTIE TOLSTOY[16]   Professor Brown mentioned repetition without change of register as characteristic of piano music. But what about the *petite reprise* in French music, or Bach's *Echo,* in which *forte* and *piano* are written in with no change of register? It is perfectly possible to change volume on a two-manual harpsichord. Also, the criterion that harpsichord music is necessarily more heavily ornamented assumes that the only function of ornamentation is to supply "missing" accents. But ornaments also have rhythmic, melodic, and harmonic functions. Is there any difference in the functional use of ornamentation in these particular examples?

BROWN I think so; and also with dissonance. When we discuss harpsichord and harpsichord color, we cannot apply generalizations regarding French composers to South German and Austrian practice. If you look at

---

[15] Tovey, "Chamber," repr., 56–57.   [16] From the audience.

Haydn's sonatas up to the A-major work (1773), the style is quite neutral.

CHRISTA LANDON[17]   Sonata Hob. XVI:46 (ChL. 31) in A-flat major is earlier. I think the Esterházy sonatas go backwards in style.

BROWN I agree. But it would make little difference for my approach if the A-major work had been written later. Haydn seems to have been thinking about an idiom for the Italian type of harpsichord at the Esterházy court.

MONK As Brown has structured his evidence, the whole is greater than the sum of the parts. Individual points of style may be appropriate to different genres, but taken together, they contribute to the establishment of certain idioms. In the 1770s, Haydn was evolving more idiomatic styles, as opposed to neutral styles.

GEORG FEDER[18]   When one uses stylistic arguments in authenticity problems, one is soon criticized for being too selective. But such skepticism is seldom applied when Haydn's stylistic development or "turning points" are discussed. It would be easier for me to agree with these suggested turning points if they were worked out on a broader statistical basis, rather than merely comparing two works from different periods.

LA RUE Our purpose is not to produce such generalizations, but to show approaches by which they can be evolved. Professor Brown's approach suggests to me that Haydn's musical style was not a fixed entity at a particular time, but an enormous language with tremendous but partly unknown potentialities, any of which could emerge at any time. For example, this A-major Sonata, which sounds somewhat tinkly at the beginning, contains an advanced procedure: from bar 24 (fermata on the dominant), going backwards we can trace a preparation for the dominant all the way to bar 14.

BROWN The cadences do this all the time. In m. 2 you have a weak tonic cadence, in m. 4 a strong one, and in m. 8 an open (half) cadence. This keeps the whole flow of structure moving.

Stylistic Changes within Op. 20

MONK Ludwig Wittgenstein has characterized history not as a chain of successive events, but as a hemp rope, with many strands and fibers of varying strengths and lengths intertwined together to make the whole. This is how I see Haydn's style development: many different influences overlapping and coexisting in time. In the compositions of the 1760s and early 1770s we can see clear examples of North German, Italian, and Austrian styles—plural—some new, some old, being combined in a vari-

---

[17] From the audience.   [18] From the audience.

ety of ways in different works and in different parts of individual works. The older styles have lost none of their vitality. The newer styles are sometimes experimental. But we have nevertheless a combination or synthesis of these styles. Haydn did not revert or regress to older styles, as is so often suggested. Both Baroque and mid-century styles are clear throughout his development up to Op. 20. After that point they are somewhat less common, but they never really disappear.

To speak of a turning point within a single opus is to push a generalization an improbable distance. Only if we can accept "turning point" as a metaphor denoting the stylistic dualism found in Op. 20 can we use this concept to explain Haydn's style at this point in his development. The C-major Quartet, No. 2, offers a summary of Baroque style elements, while the D-major Quartet, No. 4, demonstrates many more modern elements. A brief comparison should illustrate this; owing to limitations of space, it will be presented in outline form.

I. The general affect or mood of the quartets

No. 2: Serious, at times intense and even dramatic in mood, largely as the result of the following Baroque features:

Fugal-sounding thematic announcement of the first movement with its moderate tempo, unusual texture, harmonic structure, and dissonances;

Development section with wide-ranging sequences in several minor keys;

Unusual form, harmony, and dramatic quality of slow movement, cadentially linked to the minuet;

Extreme concentration of musical activity in the fugal finale.

No. 4: Far less serious, often characterized by humor and surprise, reflecting the rationality of Classical style:

Elements of humor (especially in the "Menuet alla Zingarese" and the finale), dependent on a logical and predictable style, notably in symmetrical phrases, harmonic stability, rhythmic regularity, and thematic development (cf. i, 1–50);

Humorous mood, often comic (sudden dynamic, harmonic, and rhythmic surprise); false recapitulation in (i).

Rationality: second-movement theme and variations.

II. Texture

No. 2: Textures most often associated with late Baroque and early mid-century styles, viz. trio sonata, melody-accompaniment, and polyphony of the sort that emphasizes the linear independence of individual voices:

Contrapuntal trio texture, with voice crossings and parallel thirds (i); in many four-part passages one part could be omitted without harming the texture;

Unison and melody-accompaniment textures in (ii);
Baroque polyphony in the finale.

No. 4: True quartet texture—each voice potentially bears primary material; primary and subordinate roles exchanged among the players as
various textures blend into shifting patterns:

Primary roles shift from part to part; types of texture alternate freely
(iv, 19–37, 55–67);

Variations in (ii) bring each instrument into prominence; *thematische Arbeit* in the first variation.

III. Harmony

No. 2: Opening marked by sudden change to the dominant (without
modulation), followed by sudden return to the tonic, followed yet again
by the dominant, still without functional transition. Partly Baroque in
technique. Conservative idiom emphasized by harmonic sequences (i,
48–60; iii, 57–79) and bifocal cadence in the exceptionally unstable (ii,
28–35).

No. 4: Opening 30 bars in the tonic, with five tonic cadences (one deceptive). The next 12 bars a transition, set in motion by a dramatic dynamic
and harmonic shift to vi, followed by a logical modulation to V. Establishes a highly stable harmonic idiom, later reinforced by brief contrasting passages or ornamental harmony (ii, 89–109) and bimodality and
harmonic surprise (iv, 19–37).

IV. The sonata-form movements

No. 2: Unclear structure of exposition due to alternations of tonic and
dominant, absence of functional transitions, and inconsequential thematic ideas in the dominant. Development begins with long sequence
based on a motive whose relationship to the main theme is so vague that
it sounds almost like new material. Recapitulation extremely abbreviated, particularly in first group. Irregular even for Haydn.

No. 4: More regular: principal theme clearly establishes tonic; transition,
second group, and closing section use motives from this theme. Development (fully one-third of the movement) is more stable harmonically
than that of No. 2, at the same time developing the motives. After three
false recapitulations, the true recapitulation omits only the part of the
principal theme used for the preceding false recapitulations.

Last movement of No. 4: Also in sonata form. Transition, second-
group, and closing material are drawn from the main theme. The motivic unity continues in the development, the most advanced among
these three movements.

V. Small formal aspects: thematic construction

No. 2: Much of the material Baroque; the opening theme suggests a Baroque fugue theme (head, *Fortspinnung,* cadence). Second-movement
material Baroque in character and structure.

No. 4: Thematic material more modern:

Main theme of first movement five balanced 6-bar phrases;

Second-movement theme periodic;

Finale theme analogous to many in Op. 33: clear, distinct, related motives suitable for development. Its functional quality is enhanced by its derivatives in the transition, second group, codetta, and development.

Discussion

FINSCHER   Can we really talk of "Baroque polyphony" in the fugal finales in Op. 20? I think there is a quite distinct development (possibly independent of the chronology of the individual quartets) from a true Baroque-type fugue, namely the F-minor fugue, to this so-called "fuga a quattro soggetti" in the C major, which is a kind of capriccio, quite contrary to Baroque tradition; in texture, too, it is quite different.[19] Op. 20, where Haydn experiments so wildly, transforms the Baroque tradition into something really new.

SOMFAI   The rhythmic-metric organization of the D-major opening movement is fascinating: it has three different "speeds" of large-scale meter. The real metric intent is a *tre battute* structure: 1|2 3 4|5 6 7|8 9 10|11 12 13, and so on. The harmonic and textural plan confirms the upbeat bar and then the grouping by threes. At bar 31, however, this changes to *due battute,* and finally at bar 41 we arrive at *una battuta.* There is an amazing concinnity between the diminution of the metric grouping and the decrease in surface values from quarter note to triplet eighths. Of course later on there is a much freer style; only the primary subject area is *tre battute,* but it's a fascinating new phenomenon.

LA RUE   Haydn's fugues confirm his lifelong attempts to be different. When everyone else was writing in a clearly articulated style, Haydn was looking for ways to bridge over obvious points of punctuation. But now, where everybody else's fugues are unpunctuated music, all bridged over, Haydn writes an unbridged, punctuated fugue! As in so many questions of style, Haydn finds a true but personal Classic solution.

[19] See W. Kirkendale, *Fuge*

Round Table

Haydn and Mozart

GERHARD CROLL, *Chairman*   LUDWIG FINSCHER
EVA BADURA-SKODA   CHARLES ROSEN
GEORG FEDER   LÁSZLÓ SOMFAI
KARL GUSTAV FELLERER   JAMES WEBSTER
    SHELLEY DAVIS, *Secretary*

Introductory Remarks

CROLL We will focus mainly on the problem of Haydn's and Mozart's mutual influence, because the facts concerning their personal contacts have already been well summarized.[1]

Haydn's and Mozart's artistic personalities were quite different. Compare Mozart's most familiar remark about himself, "I am able to imitate all kinds of style," to Haydn's, "Therefore I had to become original."

In their lectures, both Professor Larsen and Professor Geiringer have mentioned that Haydn remained close to the Baroque tradition, while Mozart, a generation younger, grew up in a changing world. Nevertheless their relation was not one-sided but in a certain sense mutual. Strictly speaking, mutual influence presupposes only a continual or lasting give and take, not necessarily continual personal contact. Mozart was concerned with Haydn's music long before they became acquainted. Thus the questions of dating and chronological relationship are relevant. First, we should try to establish for which compositions it can be documented that one composer knew those of the other; second, which compositions they must have known (even though we cannot document it); third, which compositions of each man could have influenced the other; and finally, which compositions were definitely *not* known by the other.

Haydn and Mozart had their first personal contact, I suppose, as late as the summer of 1784 or the winter of 1784–85, the year 1785 being most important in several respects.

A special problem for "mutual contact" concerns Mozart's influence on Haydn after his death. For example, many of us have noticed the similarity of the "Quam olim Abrahae" fugue from Mozart's *Requiem* to the chorus "Sei nun gnädig" from *The Seasons*. Mozart gained popularity very rapidly after his death. As early as 1793, Johann Friedrich Reichardt took note of "gemozarte" in music everywhere in Austria and Germany.[2]

---

[1] See especially Schmid, "Mozart"; Larsen, "Mozart."
[2] In the *Musikalische Zeitung* (Berlin) in 1793.

Therefore we should look for certain "Mozartisms," in Reichardt's sense, in the 1790s, in fashionable pieces *à la Mozart* of varying quality, and in the so-called elaborated Mozart style.

Concerning Haydn's compositions after Mozart's death, I was interested to hear Professor Geiringer's example from the dances for the Redoutensaal which Haydn composed in 1792. He composed them as Mozart's successor; Mozart had been employed as chamber musician and court composer to compose such dances beginning in the 1787–88 season. Perhaps the sketches for these dances that Professor Geiringer mentioned reveal some kind of relation to Mozart's dances.

Systematic specifications of thematic relations or connections between works of Haydn and Mozart have been made for several decades.[3] It is not our task to enlarge this repertory of borrowings, although a critical reexamination of previous specifications of thematic influences is necessary. Not all of these are persuasive. For example, it is well known that Mozart's famous motet *Exsultate, jubilate,* K. 165, at the last cadence moving to "Alleluja . . . ," anticipates the climax of Haydn's famous *Kaiserhymne.* But we must be very careful how we handle such quotations. This one is a simple sequence of two downward fourths, which can be found from Haydn's *Mariazellermesse* and *Seven Last Words* to Wagner's *Parsifal.* Furthermore, *Exsultate* is an early work (1773), and Haydn's hymn dates from 1797.

Mutual Influence—Primarily in Chamber Music

Remarks on a Mozart Quartet Fragment

CROLL Let me begin our discussion with one example which shows true mutual influence between Mozart and Haydn—Haydn's influence on Mozart. Example 1 shows the opening bars of two movements for string quartet in E major. Mozart's "composition"—only these eight bars plus two (incomplete) ones were written—might at first suggest a slow movement (similar to certain second movements in Haydn's symphonies), since E major is rare in Mozart's instrumental music. But if we perform these bars in a slow tempo, we feel that they do not have the character of a slow movement.

Of course, most of us will recognize the similarity to the beginning of Haydn's Quartet Op. 17, No. 1 in E major, composed in 1771. The first question is, when did Mozart compose these bars, adapting Haydn's six-bar opening to an eight-bar opening? The second question concerns the musical relationships between them.

[3] See Köchel, *passim,* and the references in Schneider-Algatzy; most recently, Flothuis, "Groeten."

Example 1

a) Mozart, Fragment for string quartet, K. deest (NMA VIII:20/1, Vol. 3, critical report, pp. 90–91)

b) Haydn, String Quartet Op. 17, No. 1 in E major, i, 1–9

To locate Mozart's sketch, we have to consider the context and, even more important, his handwriting. To judge by Wolfgang Plath's studies of Mozart's handwriting,[4] the sketch is not earlier than 1780—many years after the first edition of Op. 17 (1772). The context of the sketch even points to the spring of 1782, because in the autograph it is followed by a transposed and rescored transcription of the B-flat-minor fugue from Volume 2 of *The Well-Tempered Keyboard*. The latter draft must date from April or May 1782, when Mozart made the arrangements K. 405. This implies that the adaptation of Haydn's string quartet originated between 1780 and 1782 (very probably in spring 1782).

Comparing the two compositions, we notice that Haydn's m. 5 recurs nearly identically as Mozart's m. 5. Even the scoring is nearly the same (Mozart changing the unisono leading of the viola and violoncello into contrary motion). But this next-to-last bar of Haydn's six-bar theme apparently was the very point where Mozart felt the need for an alteration. Reaching a certain "crescendo" quality in this bar, Mozart uses it twice, completing an eight-bar period. Other noteworthy details are that Haydn's first phrase begins and closes with the tonic, followed by a rest dividing bars 1 and 2; but Mozart begins on b′, and he joins bars 1 and 2 by a connecting phrase.

ROSEN Mozart returned to this fragment. If you compare mm. 5–8 of K. 428 in E-flat major—written shortly afterwards—you can see that he borrowed from himself.

FEDER In Augsburg there is a manuscript of Op. 17 with performing marks in Mozart's hand.[5]

Mozart's Indebtedness to Haydn: Some Remarks on K. 168–173

FINSCHER In their preface to the first volume of string quartets in NMA, the editors state that the relationship of Mozart's K. 168–173 to Haydn's Opp. 9, 17, and 20 is a familiar topic which requires no further discussion in that context. But I am convinced that these relationships are not well known, and that they ought to be thoroughly investigated. Within this framework, however, I must confine myself to a few preliminary remarks.

The NMA editors reflect a common view. Mozart already knew Opp. 9, 17, and 20, or he came to know them when the Mozarts visited Vienna in the summer of 1773. Abert assumes that the works were written "under the fresh impression of Viennese chamber music, especially Haydn's . . . Op. 17 . . . and Op. 20. . . . [They are] Mozart's first quartets in four movements [i.e., with minuets]. . . . Fugal finales likewise can be credited to Haydn . . . the older sequential techniques still can be

---

[4] Plath, "Autographie," II.   [5] See Senn, "Heilig Kreuz," 352.

discerned. . . ." On the other hand, Abert was too good a musician not to find something unsatisfactory: "One often receives the impression that Mozart felt inhibited by his great model, that he attempted to compensate for his lack of assurance by careful workmanship."[6] Similarly, Barrett-Ayres finds evidence of Haydn's influence in the four-movement form, the fugal finales, the opening theme and variations in K. 170, and the use of irregular phrase lengths.[7]

Moreover, the thematic relations occasionally come close to outright borrowings on Mozart's part. These have been listed more or less completely by Abert, Barrett-Ayres, and others: the slow movement of K. 168 and the fugue subject of Haydn's Op. 20, No. 5 (in the same key); the first movement of K. 170 and the slow movement of Haydn's Op. 17, No. 3; the slow movements of K. 170 and Haydn's Op. 9, No. 4; the minuets of K. 173 and Haydn's Op. 9, No. 4. From all these details, it is evident that Mozart consciously and laboriously tried to imitate Haydn, and that his models were indeed Haydn's Opp. 9, 17, and 20. To what extent was this imitation successful?

The two fugal finales in these quartets are placed first and last in the series (which was obviously designed as a coherent opus). Mozart tried to give it more weight by adopting the Viennese fugal tradition. But either he was attempting a departure from Haydn, rather than an imitation, or he completely misunderstood the fugal finales in Op. 20. Haydn tried to solve his finale problem by systematically working out fugues "a due," "a tre," and "a quattro soggetti"; at the same time he tried to change the conventional Viennese serious fugue into a kind of "scherzando" fugue, better adapted to the requirements of the sonata-cycle finale.[8] But Mozart reverts to the most conventional subjects and types of fugue writing and, moreover, occasionally handles them rather clumsily.[9] His model seems to be not Haydn so much as the special Viennese tradition of fugues for string ensembles, mostly for string quartet, by Gassmann, Albrechtsberger, and others. Mozart's strategy is the more understandable in that this Viennese fashion had always been linked with the Viennese imperial court.

But Haydn also seems to have been only one model among many with regard to types and genres of first movements, slow movements, and finali. The first movement of K. 171 is a kind of "French Overture" which has nothing to do with Haydn, and the slow movement is fashioned after the obsolete model of the trio sonata. The first movement of K. 172 is an Italian sinfonia of quite unabashed simplicity—a type of first movement that Haydn had abandoned long before. The finales of K. 169 and 170 are French "Rondeaux" in a style which Haydn hardly ever utilized, and K. 170 has a strong flavor of the divertimento (compare the

---

[6] Abert, *Mozart*, I, 394 ff.   [7] Barrett-Ayres, *Quartet*, 145 ff.

[8] See W. Kirkendale, *Fuge;* Finscher, *Streichquartett,* I, 218 ff.

[9] Barrett-Ayres, *Quartet*, 149.

first movement of K. 247). In all these examples, Mozart openly copied established models. This and the equally frank mixture of French and Italian traditions constitute a stylistic orientation which in these respects is quite different from Haydn and from Vienna, and much nearer to Mozart's primary artistic background: Salzburg, especially the chamber music of Michael Haydn.

Abert's and Barrett-Ayres's descriptions of Mozart's sonata movements read as if Mozart had really succeeded in approaching Haydn's concept of sonata form and musical form in general—perhaps without the elegance of Op. 17 or the emotional impact of Op. 20. But the opposite is the case. Much more important than the so-called thematic development (Abert) and the sometimes asymmetrical subdivision of symmetrical thematic phrases (Barrett-Ayres) is Mozart's pervasive technique of building musical form by addition, repetition, and rearrangement of one- and two-bar units, four- and eight-bar periods, and whole sections. While conforming to the general compositional standard of the 1770s and to what we might reasonably expect from a seventeen-year-old composer, this remains far behind everything Haydn had achieved in Opp. 9 and 17.

In K. 168 the exposition of the first movement is built out of mostly irregular periods (9, 9, 9, 5, 5, 7 bars), but the overall impression is of the addition of tiny phrases and of mostly unconnected musical events, the unconnectedness being emphasized by decisive cadences (mm. 9, 18, 26–27, 30–31, 34–35, 41). The development begins with a slightly varied repetition of mm. 13–17, again repeated at 46–50. Two bars of conventional contrapuntal material and two cadential bars lead to a new theme (53–57), which is repeated with the order of entries reversed. After two more bars, the recapitulation begins. Bars 79–83 are inserted, but otherwise the recapitulation is literal; after m. 83 everything goes on as if nothing had happened in between.

The same mechanical insertion of new material (in this case sequential) within the recapitulation and the same mechanical continuation of the "verbatim" repeat occurs in K. 169. Moreover, the development section of this movement attempts to emulate Haydn's "false recapitulation." After 21 bars of contrapuntal development the principal theme returns for 10 bars, in F major instead of A major but otherwise literally reproduced; after 5 more bars of development the recapitulation begins again with the principal theme. The difference between ingenious technical and formal device and clumsy imitation are clear if one compares this movement with the first movement of Haydn's Op. 20, No. 4.

The theme and variations of K. 170 are obviously fashioned after the corresponding movement of Haydn's Op. 17, No. 3. But whereas the underlying two-bar symmetry and motivic correspondence are very cleverly disguised in Haydn's theme, they are obvious in Mozart's; and Haydn's variations never leave the sphere of sophisticated chamber music. Mozart's third and (quite openly) fourth "alla marcia" variations return to his familiar Salzburg divertimento tradition.

The minuet of K. 173—one of the most ambitious movements of the whole opus—is inspired by the minuet from Haydn's Op. 9, No. 4, in the same key. But whereas Haydn develops his opening motive into a highly rhetorical melody *à la* C. P. E. Bach, in rich harmonic setting, Mozart builds the same motive into a conventional four-bar phrase with conventional accompaniment, in an astonishingly simple harmonic framework. Again, whereas Haydn's short trio functions as contrast and relief after the rhetorical and complex minuet, Mozart's trio develops along the same broad lines as his minuet, the only differences being that the conventional cadences stand out even more clearly (bars 9–10 and 27–28 of the trio against 19–20 of the minuet), and the phrase structure is completely regular (4, 2, 2, 2, 2, 2, 4, 4, 2, 2, 2). Mozart's ambition seems to aim at formal expansion alone, but even this expansion is realized by quite conventional means.

To sum up: Mozart reacted to Viennese musical fashion (probably hoping to gain access to the Court) and to the challenge which Haydn's quartets must have posed for him. But his reactions were comparatively superficial, chiefly copying details; apparently he understood neither Haydn's use of the fugue nor his concept of form which, even in these early years, was already close to the mature Classical concept of form as the result of thematic development. Mozart's concept of form, most clearly seen in his handling of sonata form, remained closer to pre-Classical concepts: a highly conventionalized frame that was to be filled with original musical invention. The reason Mozart succeeds again and again, even in these quartets, is that his invention was so much more original, rich, and diversified than that of most of his contemporaries. His Viennese quartets are therefore far from being "abominable,"[10] but often their beauty is achieved in spite of their conventional handling of musical form. (Even some of Mozart's greatest late chamber music does not escape this concept of form which, seen from Haydn's point of view, is indeed a weakness.) To see Mozart's indebtedness to Haydn in K. 168–173 is valuable, not so much in itself, as in its suggestion that the difference between the two composers in their approach to musical form is a fundamental one, which requires careful and systematic investigation in the future.

Mozart's and Haydn's Mutual Borrowings: Levels of Plausibility

WEBSTER In considering any pair of passages by different composers, of which we believe that one may have been borrowed from or modeled on the other,

---

[10] Keller, "Chamber," 94–95.

we must answer two questions.[11] First, we must show that the borrowing was possible: that Composer B could have known the given work of Composer A, and that it is likely that he did know it. Secondly, we must establish a high level of musical plausibility. The passages must be sufficiently similar, and sufficiently distinct in character, to persuade us that the resemblance is not merely incidental, and that both passages do not merely reflect musical ideas which were "in the air."[12]

Mozart's quartet fragment which Professor Croll has just discussed (Example 1) is an excellent example. Both the "external" and the "internal" evidence linking this fragment to the opening of Haydn's Op. 17, No. 1 is very strong. In particular, we have no mere vague stylistic similarity, but Mozart's *recomposition* of Haydn: every relevant aspect of Haydn's theme—melody, bass line, harmonic progression, relation of antecedent and consequent—recognizably recurs in Mozart's version. Another very plausible borrowing from the first half of the 1780s has been described by Joshua Rifkin.[13]

A different kind of relationship exists between the slow movements of Haydn's Quartet Op. 20, No. 1 and Mozart's Quartet K. 428. Here we have neither direct thematic quotation nor paraphrase nor overt recomposition. On the other hand, both movements are scored for string quartet; both are in A-flat major and in related meters and tempos; both function as slow movements in E-flat-major works; both emphasize the middle and low registers; both are highly chromatic; both are somewhat elegiac in tone. Nor need we doubt that Mozart knew Op. 20. Finally, the special atmosphere of these two movements is unique, as far as I know; this kind of music was *not* "in the air" in the early 1780s. Hence Tovey seems justified in his belief that Mozart borrowed the compositional premise of this movement from Haydn.[14]

My next two examples are apparent quotations, but nevertheless they are problematic. In Mozart's "Hunt" Quartet in B-flat major, K. 458, the first four bars of the second theme in the finale (mm. 82–97) are almost identical to the first four bars of a countersubject (mm. 9–16) in the first movement of Haydn's Quartet Op. 2, No. 2 in E major. We also have the same genre, meter, tempo, phrase lengths, and—with the displacement of but a half-step—the same pitch level. If the Haydn passage were from Op. 33, the case would be complete. But Haydn wrote this work before 1761, and we have no evidence that Mozart ever heard it.

In *Die Zauberflöte,* in the quintet from the first act (No. 5), mm. 196–203, Mozart once again quotes Haydn almost literally, this time in

---

[11] No comprehensive account of Haydn's and Mozart's mutual borrowings is attempted here. Cf. Prof. Croll's introductory remarks, especially at nn. 1 & 3; cf. also Prof. Rosen's remarks below.

[12] LaRue, "Resemblances"   [13] Rifkin, "Zitat"

[14] Tovey, "Chamber," repr., 41.

the same key; and the theme in question does appear in Op. 33 (No. 4 in B-flat major, first movement, mm. 7–11). But in this case we not only have a ten-year time lag to contend with, but a transfer from instrumental chamber music to opera.

Two familiar examples show Haydn, after Mozart's death, apparently modeling his music on that of his younger colleague. One is the second theme of the slow movement of Symphony No. 98 in B-flat major, mm. 15–22; although there is no thematic quotation, this passage is in the same key, meter, genre, and scoring as the analogous passage from Mozart's "Jupiter" Symphony, K. 551; it reproduces virtually the entire substance of Mozart's theme, right down to the "punctuating" offbeat wind chords. We must remind ourselves that we have no direct evidence that Haydn had ever heard Mozart's last three symphonies before his departure for England in 1790. But the paraphrase is so striking—and unique—that it is tempting to reverse customary scholarly procedure and to argue that it "proves" that Haydn *did* know them before 1791! (Symphony No. 98 was the first he composed after hearing of Mozart's death.)

The second example is the reflection of the fugue "Quam olim Abrahae" from Mozart's *Requiem* (*Hostias,* mm. 55–62) in the chorus "Sei nun gnädig" from Haydn's *The Seasons* (mm. 74–82), to which Professor Croll referred. The stylistic evidence here is perhaps less compelling, because musical "tags" like this one were common in choral fugues.

Finally, consider one *weak* example. The minuets of Haydn's Quartet Op. 20, No. 3 in G minor and Mozart's Quintet K. 516 in the same key are outwardly similar: chamber music for strings, second position in the four-movement cycle, trios in the major mode, prominent use of E-flat major as a related key, and—depending on one's liberality—certain motivic connections at analogous points in the form, for example between m. 40 of the Haydn and m. 35 of the Mozart. But it was fifteen years from Op. 20 to K. 516; and these musical relationships are general, rather than specifically thematic or compositional. Hence nothing compels us to take the hypothesis of Mozart's borrowing seriously. On the other hand, we might still argue that both works belonged to a coherent tradition of G-minor minuets in Viennese chamber music.[15]

Remarks on "Influence"

ROSEN Mozart could also borrow a procedure, a "gimmick," from Haydn. The fugue of Op. 20, No. 2 in C major is a jig in 6/8, chromatic in texture. At m. 83, Haydn astonishingly rephrases the rhythm in groups of four eighth notes (two legato, two detached); the 6/8 rhythm is completely

[15] For an example of this kind of argumentation, see Webster, "Beethoven."

contradicted. Mozart does the same in the only jig he wrote in fugal style (and it is equally chromatic): K. 574 of 1789, mm. 20–23.

But the trouble with these borrowings—Haydn's and Mozart's in particular—is that the more evident the borrowing, the more superficial it is. (I remember Oliver Strunk's remark about Haydn's Symphony No. 98, which sounds, he said, as if Haydn were trying to remember what the "Jupiter" was like, but couldn't quite get it right.) If it's exact, it's not an influence at all, but simply plagiarism, the appropriation of another's property (which every composer indulges in, consciously or unconsciously). But the more profound forms of influence are not verifiable in that way. In particular, Mozart's and Haydn's styles are so different in many respects, their procedures are so often diametrically opposed, that a really interesting example of influence is likely to be completely absorbed and leave little trace.

Let me give a couple of tentative examples. One common procedure in Haydn's sonata-form movements is to introduce a single harsh dissonance very early in the piece, and later to insist on the same dissonance, sometimes to produce the modulation to the dominant.[16] I do not find this technique in Mozart. Mozart deals generally with much larger areas, and his introduction of dissonance is of a different nature. He may have a highly chromatic opening section, so that no particular dissonance stands out, as we find at the beginning of the E-flat major String Quartet K. 428, or the Trio in E major K. 542.

However, in the "Prague" Symphony Mozart uses this technique of Haydn's. (J. P. Larsen has already noted the Haydnesque use of ritornello in this movement.[17] Compare the use of a tonic ostinato followed immediately by the appearance of the flatted seventh degree in both this work and Haydn's Symphony No. 81 in G major). Furthermore, when the opening theme of the "Prague" reappears in m. 72 (on a dominant pedal, but not yet in the dominant key), Mozart adds another dissonance by changing E to E sharp; and *this* dissonance helps to produce the modulation. This reappearance of the main theme at the dominant and these uses of dissonance derive from Haydn, I believe.

As far as Haydn's borrowings from Mozart are concerned, many of the pieces that used to be thought to show an influence have now been dated earlier, when no such influence was possible. The Sonata Hob. XVI:46 (ChL. 31) in A-flat major, whose slow movement was often cited as an example of Mozart's influence on Haydn, was actually written around 1770, apparently.

One further example of the difference in the treatment of dissonance: Haydn's remote modulations occur in the development section, never, so far as I can remember, in the exposition. But the exposition of Mo-

---

[16] Cf. Rosen, *Style,* 120–32.   [17] Larsen, "Symphonies," 188–89.

zart's Trio K. 542 has a very powerful modulation to G minor in the second group. However, I think there may be a relationship between this trio and Haydn's Trio Hob. XV:28 in the same key, because Haydn, quite exceptionally, introduces pervasive chromaticism in the second phrase (mm. 5–7). But these kinds of adaptation from one style to another are necessarily difficult to trace, because the transformation of the influence is likely to be almost complete with two such different composers.

There is no way to sum up what they were doing by the concept of a common style. This illusion has been foisted upon us by Beethoven, who combined the procedures of both composers. Without Beethoven's middle period in particular, we would never discuss Haydn and Mozart as if they were writing the same sort of thing at the same time.

Keyboard Music

A Comparison of Haydn's and Mozart's Keyboard Music

FEDER Mozart the pianist, Haydn the Kapellmeister or music director—these two cliches are perhaps not wholly misleading. I need not comment on the greater pianistic demands of many of Mozart's compositions for the piano, especially in his concertos, compared to Haydn's keyboard style. Some passages in Haydn's late piano trios have the virtuoso touch, and almost all of Haydn's keyboard works reveal his interest in sonority, in the timbre of keyboard instruments; but a different attitude remains. I would like to deal very briefly with the genres of keyboard music found in the output of Haydn and Mozart.

Two groups of works stand in the center of Haydn's writing for the keyboard: the solo sonata and the trio for piano, violin, and violoncello. Mozart did not especially favor either of these, although the sonatas are among his most familiar keyboard works. Mozart favored, as you know, the concerto for piano and orchestra. Only one Haydn piano concerto, Hob. XVIII:11 in D major, can be compared to them. Two other concertos are earlier, and another group is considered to comprise organ concertos rather than cembalo works. The number of Haydn's concertos is small, and they center around the earlier years of his career, whereas the majority of Mozart's numerous concertos belong to his mature masterworks. Mozart's lesser interest in the piano trio was balanced by his liking for other kinds of chamber music with piano. The sonatas for piano and violin have no counterpart in Haydn's oeuvre. The same is true of the two great quartets for piano, violin, viola, and cello and of several works with accompanying wind instruments. There is only one comparable early composition by Haydn (Hob. XIV:1).

To summarize my first hypothesis: Haydn was more specialized and rarely composed in other genres than the solo sonata and the piano trio. Mozart's oeuvre is more diversified, though with a special accent on the concerto.

The smaller pieces for piano solo reveal other differences. Whereas Mozart liked to write solo variations, Haydn favored the variation as a movement in a cycle rather than as an independent solo work. Most characteristic are his double variations with alternating minor and major sections. Mozart preferred stricter variation forms, not only in his independent variations, but also as a movement within a cyclic chamber composition. Most conspicious among Mozart's solo works outside the sonatas are the preludes and fugues, the jig, and the Suite in C major. These pieces were old-fashioned forms of the Baroque period. There is nothing comparable in Haydn; I believe that even the fugue in the String Quartet in C major, Op. 20, No. 2, is something different. When Haydn used old forms, it was in traditional genres where they were still used, as in the motet or Mass. But he did not imitate old styles just for the sake of imitation, as Mozart occasionally did.

Both Haydn and Mozart used several cyclic forms. Their keyboard music seldom exhibits the four-movement cycle of their string quartets and symphonies. It was apparently Beethoven who, in Opp. 1 and 2, transferred the four-movement cycle from the string quartet and the symphony to the piano trio and the piano sonata. Haydn's and Mozart's keyboard sonatas normally have three movements, occasionally two. In the cycle of three movements, the order Fast–Slow–Fast, which is the regular one in both masters' concertos, also characterizes their most developed and mature works. But Haydn also used this cyclic form with a minuet in place of a slow movement. The minuet could be the second or the third movement. This three-movement form without a slow movement but with a minuet is regularly found in Haydn's early keyboard music.

To summarize my second hypothesis: Mozart's cyclic forms center around the concerto type Fast–Slow–Fast, while Haydn changes the different types of cyclic forms more often.

Further Comparisons

SOMFAI We generally believe that most of Haydn's and Mozart's music was *Gebrauchsmusik,* meant for a particular public or composed for a particular occasion. When we take their solo keyboard music, of course, the basic difference is that, although Mozart may have had some external influences, his solo piano sonatas were basically written for himself, with the purpose of presenting his way of playing the piano, to give an idea of what solo piano music could be.

Mozart's solo piano output (probably excluding the very early pieces) can be placed in three groups. To the first one belong the Salzburg sonatas from 1774 (K. 279–283/189d–h), which represent the cantabile sonata type, not a distinctly concert-style sonata. Much more concertlike are the solo piano pieces of the second group, written in Munich, Mannheim, and Paris in the mid-1770s. One or two of these pieces (K. 309/284b and 311/284c) may have been influenced by a particular person, like the famous "Cannabich" Sonata, written "nach dem Charakter der Mademoiselle Rose Cannabich." But at the same time it is one of Mozart's strongest concert sonatas. And finally we have a very small number of interesting sonatas from the Viennese epoch, all quite different in style and technique.

We have only a very few documents which show any direct relationship between Haydn's and Mozart's solo piano works, or suggest that they knew each other's solo sonatas. The Salzburg and Paris Mozart sonatas were published by Artaria and Torricella around 1784. But Haydn had achieved such maturity in his solo piano style by that time that one need hardly consider Mozart's influence on Haydn's pianistic style, nor Haydn's influence on Mozart's sonatas. (The one exception in Haydn might be certain features in the "Genzinger" Sonata, Hob. XVI:49 [ChL. 59] in E-flat major.) Probably the only late Viennese Mozart sonata which has many similarities to Haydn's mature style, as represented by the "Genzinger" Sonata, is K. 570 in B-flat major, at least in its first movement.

Vocal Music

Text and Music in Mozart's and Haydn's Masses

FELLERER Mozart wrote his Mass compositions between 1768 and 1783, Haydn between 1750 and 1802. Both masters stopped writing Masses after 1782 or 1783 for several years. After this break, Mozart was to write only one more Mass, the *Requiem;* while Haydn, in a second period of church music, wrote his six great Masses from 1796 to 1802.[18]

Their break in composing church music was the result of the church-music reforms of the Enlightenment in 1782, represented by the Em-

---

[18] On these subjects, see also Workshop 1 and the Free Papers by Karl Gustav Fellerer and Walter Pass.

peror Joseph II and the Archbishop Hieronymus Colloredo of Salzburg, in accordance with the church-music encyclical of Pope Benedict XIV in 1749. Mozart wrote his Mass compositions during Haydn's first period of church-music compositions; Haydn's later Masses were, of course, unknown to Mozart. Both masters grew up in local Austrian traditions, and these local traditions were united with the local musical traditions of Vienna in which Haydn participated throughout the 1740s.

The accentuation, comprehension, and interpretation of the liturgical text are significant for Mozart's and Haydn's church music. In his instructions for the performance of *Applausus* (1768), Haydn stressed the importance of correct and clear accentuation and declamation. Musical form and style are shaped by the interpretation of the text. Common to both composers is the distinction between the *Missa brevis* (short Mass) and the *Missa solemnis* (sometimes called "cantata Mass" in English). Unlike Schubert, Mozart omitted some words, for example, in the Gloria and Credo of K. 65, 259, and 275. Haydn followed the text strictly, except for a small omission in the Gloria of the *Theresienmesse* ("et in unum dominum . . ."). But the simultaneous performance of different passages by different voices, for example in the Gloria of Haydn's *Missa brevis* in F major, makes the text almost incomprehensible. The Gloria consists of only twenty-nine measures, of which the Amen alone occupies eleven.

Here, as well as in the Credo, the brevity of the text is combined with simultaneous declamation. The period from "Et incarnatus est" to "sepultus est" is comprehensible only because of the homophonic declamation. The Credo concludes with the same Amen as the Gloria. In Haydn's *Great Organ Mass,* the three-part division of the Credo is developed in musically independent sections. The first movement declaims the complete text chiefly homophonically with a vigorous orchestral accompaniment, up to "de coelis." The "Et incarnatus," a slow solo, leads into the "Crucifixus" with its contrapuntal opening. The third movement, beginning with "Resurrexit," brings the complete text, Allegro, with word-painting effects, specifically on "descendit," "vivos et mortuous," and the emphatic repetition of the "non" of "non erit finis." The movement ends with a fugal Amen, Presto. Descriptive music and word repetition are also found in Mozart's Masses. The repetition of the word "Credo" in Mozart's *Missa brevis* K. 192 and in Haydn's *St. Caecilia Mass* is particularly effective.

This three-part construction is very common in Credos of Haydn's and Mozart's time. The Credo of K. 192 is the only case in which Mozart has no change of tempo. The words "Et in spiritum" are often set off as a solo, for example in K. 49, 66, and 139; K. 65 uses four solo voices. The final movement begins with the words "Et unam sanctam" in K. 220, 262, 258, 275; with "Et vitam venturi" in K. 115, 194, and 259. In K. 66,

139, 167, and 262 it is written in fugal style. The musical form and phrase
structure are clearly determined by the liturgical text, which is separated
into three sections according to the Gregorian melody. The separation is
articulated by solo vs. chorus, by tempo and key, and by homophony vs.
imitation. Longer sections are marked off by short instrumental interludes. Mozart unites "Et vitam venturi" and the "Amen," while
Haydn separates the "Amen" in the Gloria and Credo, except in the
Great Organ Mass and the *St. Caecilia Mass.* In the Gloria of Haydn's
Missa Sti. Nicolai an "Amen," beginning in imitation, follows the homophonic "Quoniam."

With the exception of the solo parts and the fugal movements, the
texts of the Gloria and Credo are declaimed mostly homophonically,
with a lively orchestral accompaniment. Haydn includes more extended
separate instrumental periods, even in movements with long texts. (His
Masses are longer.) If he strives for brevity, he reaches it by simultaneous
declamation, which means neglecting the text in favor of concentration
on the sound. This neglect of the text remained foreign to Mozart, even
though he juxtaposed different texts in the counterpoint. But he sought
to organize the text more clearly, by contrasting the different segments
of the liturgical text, and by punctuation with short instrumental passages. Haydn emphasizes formal unity and symphonic completeness
more than Mozart, who emphasizes the text phrases by clear declamation.

In the "Benedictus," the long instrumental introduction is based li-
turgically on the practice of playing music during the elevation of the
Host. This event is effectively expressed in all of Haydn's and Mozart's
Masses. Mozart omits it only in K. 49, 65, 192, and 337. In the "Benedictus" of K. 259 he emphasizes the organ concertante in the same manner
as Haydn in his "organ" Masses. Besides the "Et incarnatus est," the
"Benedictus" is the most expressive movement in Mozart's and Haydn's
Masses. The Kyrie, Sanctus and Agnus are constructed in similar fashion
not only by Haydn and Mozart, but by all church-music composers of
the time.

It is questionable whether reciprocal influences between Haydn and
Mozart took place, although their mutual knowledge of the same church
music can be assumed. Mozart left Salzburg for Vienna in 1781, but
Haydn did not move from Eszterháza to Vienna until 1790. Neapolitan
Mass compositions were not without influence on the local traditions of
Salzburg and Eszterháza. But the correct treatment of the liturgical text
according to the demands of the Encyclical of 1749 determined the compositions of both masters. (Haydn's *Missa brevis* in F major and *Little
Organ Mass* do not fulfill the demand for the intelligibility of the text,
because of their compression in the different voices.) The formation of
the text and its distribution between solo and choir, homphony and

counterpoint, slow and fast movements are common to both masters, based on the liturgical conception. In general, we may speak of clear stylistic similarities current within these church-music traditions.

Haydn's Masses after 1796 are determined by the great symphonic form, which also led to Beethoven's Mass in C major, Op. 86. Haydn must have heard Mozart's Masses performed in Vienna, but his personal tradition and his rejection of Neapolitan art—contrary to Mozart—established a different mood in his liturgical music. The solo virtuoso is neglected in favor of the solo quartet, and the expression of the text is deepened. The motivic parallels in the "Gratias agimus" of Haydn's *Theresienmesse* and in Mozart's *Requiem* may be the product of direct influence, or mere cliches found in many church compositions of the period.

Personal Contacts and Mutual Influence in the Field of Opera

BADURA-SKODA   We have no documentary evidence of personal contacts between Haydn and Mozart before January 22, 1785. On that date father Leopold, in a letter to Nannerl, reported an encounter between Wolfgang and Joseph Haydn. But I doubt that this was really their first contact. In a lost letter whose contents Leopold reported on January 22, Wolfgang had mentioned that he had performed his six new quartets for his "dear friend Haydn."[19] Does one speak in this manner of a person one has met for the very first time?

If Mozart had met Haydn in Vienna after 1781 for the first time, it would have been strange if he had not mentioned this in letters to his father. Father and son shared a lively common interest in Haydn's music. A personal link to Haydn's brother had existed since 1763, when Michael became a colleague of the Mozarts in Salzburg. Michael was apparently on good terms with both father and son. Wolfgang composed duos for him in 1783. Why do we not read anything about a new friendship with Joseph Haydn in the Mozarts' correspondence from 1781 to 1784? Perhaps they had met in the 1760s or in 1773; perhaps one or more letters are lost. Many more letters were exchanged between Leopold and Wolfgang than are extant today. Deutsch deduced the existence of eleven letters of Wolfgang to his father and one to Nannerl, and forty-five letters by Leopold to his son, all from 1781–84, which are lost.[20] Many other letters by Wolfgang may have left no trace.

Although the question of personal contact before 1785 can hardly be solved at present, there must have been musical contact and mutual influence between the two great masters in the field of opera. Haydn must

[19] W. Mozart, *Briefe* III, 367–68.
[20] Those of Wolfgang and Nannerl are registered in W. Mozart, *Briefe,* Nos. 628, 676, 694, 711, 769, 798, 800, 807, 812, 818, 821, 839.

have heard at least one Mozart opera, if not two, before writing his famous letter to Roth in Prague in praise of Mozart.[21] We do not know whether Mozart heard Haydn's operas. But we find obvious hints not only in Mozart's last and most Viennese opera, *Die Zauberflöte,*[22] but in the three great Italian operas of the 1780s. Despite the similarities of the libretti, it seems unlikely that Mozart knew *L'incontro improvviso* when composing *Die Entführung;* the differences are too pronounced. In addition, Haydn's peculiar wit in *L'incontro improvviso* (for example JHW XXV:6, vol. 1, 120, m. 66) would never appear in Mozart. Mozart's opera shows a more mature and dramatically more convincing rendering of the story. Its overall superiority cannot be explained merely on the basis that he composed his opera several years later than Haydn and had become the more experienced opera composer. Some passages in *L'incontro* may remind us of *Die Zauberflöte* (for example the terzet Rezia-Balkis-Dardana, vol. 1, 84), but these features may have common roots in the Viennese *Singspiel.*

An opera by Haydn which Mozart probably heard (or at least knew in score) was the German version of *La vera costanza.* Most likely Mozart saw one of the performances presented by the troupe of Kumpff & Schikaneder in Vienna in 1785–86. When composing his *Kriegslied,* "Ich möchte wohl der Kaiser sein," K. 539, it seems that he had the German text of Masino's aria "Spann deine langen Ohren" in mind.[23] The song K. 539, with its otherwise rather un-Mozartian melody and form, makes sense only in this way, and it may reflect the typical kind of humor with which Mozart always tried to overcome bitterness. Emperor Joseph II and the wars he led in these years became rather unpopular in Vienna and were widely criticized.[24] For the *Kriegslied* Mozart chose a text by Gleim which had appeared under the title "Meine Wünsche an unseren deutschgesinnten grossen Kaiser." The explanation for the parody which lies in the texts of K. 539 thus seems to have been Mozart's personal revenge, subtle enough, at having been passed over by the Emperor for a position at the imperial court.

Another resemblance between a passage in *La vera costanza* and a Mozart aria brings *Don Giovanni* into the picture. In the famous "Catalogue Aria," Leporello sings the excerpt shown as Example 2a. This motive had appeared almost literally in the second act finale of *La vera costanza* (Example 2b). But above all it is Mozart's *Figaro* which seems to have been inspired by *La vera costanza.* These two operas are quite distinct from other Italian operas of the time. The relationship is established through the large scope of the finali, the density of texture, the unusually rich instrumentation, the harmonic rhythm, and the lyrical quality of the

[21] Haydn, *Briefe,* 185–86; CCLN, 73–74.   [22] Flothuis, "Groeten"
[23] The original of Masino's aria is now available in JHW XXV:8, 62.
[24] See E. Wangermann, "Nulla Salus Bello," *Literatur und Kritik,* V (1966), 48.

arias, especially uncommon for "lower class" characters such as Rosina and Susanna. Although all these qualities place Haydn's opera very near to Mozart's, still one understands why the older master, after having heard *Figaro,* renounced the commission from Prague in Mozart's favor.

Example 2

a) Mozart, *Don Giovanni,* No. 4 (NMA II:5/17, 83–84)

b) Haydn, *La vera costanza* (JHW XXV:8, 291)

Free Papers

Style

Haydn and the London Pianoforte School

Haydn's last three piano sonatas, Hob. XVI:50–52 (ChL. 60–62) are undeniably among his most impressive contributions to that genre. Indeed, those last sonatas tend to confirm a more general notion concerning Haydn's development—that his style continued to change and to grow in refinement and sophistication until the last stages of his rather lengthy career. All interpretive studies of the three sonatas are nevertheless limited in two significant respects: our documentary knowledge of the origin of the works is less than secure and our appreciation of the stylistic milieu in which they were created is incomplete.

The ambiguities in the sources have led to a shaky assumption that the three sonatas constitute a coherent group, or "opus." Even Oliver Strunk's valuable essay of 1934 has added weight to this assumption.[1] In the second problem area, the unusual style characteristics of the three sonatas have stimulated a preoccupation with their novelty and the extent to which they anticipate techniques later associated with Beethoven or Schubert. While such comparisons clearly may be useful, they also may tend to distort the nature of Haydn's originality and to underestimate his responsiveness to the artistic environment of London in the 1790s, where the three sonatas were presumably written.

During the period of Haydn's visits, London was the setting for an unprecedented flowering of pianistic activity. Neither Haydn nor any other composer could long remain unaware or unaffected as the language of the pianoforte became so strikingly enriched. There is certainly no insult to Haydn in the hypothesis that he may have learned something from the music he heard during these ambitious journeys. Still, all questions of influence in music are hazardous, so an assessment of the relationship between Haydn's last solo sonatas and the music of other composers then active in London must first include a reexamination of the documents that bear on the chronology and original purposes of those Haydn compositions.

The most useful current information concerning Haydn's last sonatas derives largely from Abert's ground-breaking essay from the 1920s, the source studies of Strunk and Larsen, and the recent editions by Georg

[1] Strunk, "Autograph"

Feder and Christa Landon.[2] Since the known sources leave an incomplete picture of the origin of the works, each scholar has been forced to speculate to some degree. The solutions offered have varied somewhat, although Strunk's essay has been especially influential and is adopted without significant challenges by Hoboken and Feder. For this reason, his conclusions in particular require fresh scrutiny.

A brief summary of the documentary evidence concerning composition and publication will dramatize the need for caution and skepticism. The Sonata Hob. XVI:50 (ChL. 60) in C major is known through an edition by J. & H. Caulfield from around 1800, but the middle movement was published in 1794 by Artaria. No edition of the Sonata Hob. XVI:51 (ChL. 61) in D major is known before the Breitkopf & Härtel edition of 1805. For the Sonata Hob. XVI:52 (ChL. 62) in E-flat major there exists an autograph manuscript, dated 1794 and dedicated to Therese Jansen, in the Library of Congress. The first authentic edition of this sonata may be the Longman & Clementi edition from about 1800, although it was first published in 1798 by Artaria, with a different dedication. The sonatas in C and E flat were both written for Therese Jansen, the gifted London pianist who was married in 1795 to Gaetano Bartolozzi, with Haydn himself serving as a witness.[3] These two sonatas, then, have demonstrable links to Haydn's London visits. Sonata No. 51 is tied to England by two bits of indirect evidence. When the Breitkopf & Härtel edition appeared in 1805, a note in the *Allgemeine musikalische Zeitung* suggested that it had been written much earlier, perhaps as an occasional piece for someone with only a modest proficiency on the piano.[4] A letter from Griesinger tells us further that it was put forward by Haydn to satisfy Clementi's urgent requests for additional sonatas, although Haydn apparently decided to send it first to Härtel. According to Griesinger, the sonata was written for a woman in England who still possessed the manuscript.[5] Can we therefore regard all three sonatas as a kind of group, all written in England and all dedicated to Therese Jansen Bartolozzi? The evidence does not support such a conclusion.

If Mrs. Bartolozzi owned the manuscripts for the two sonatas in C and E flat dedicated to her, then she apparently permitted their publication in England during a two-year period around 1800, perhaps because she and her husband were in some financial difficulty at the time.[6] But the D major work was never published in England during Haydn's lifetime (despite Griesinger's remark), and if that sonata was designed for an En-

---

[2] Abert, "Klavier"; Strunk, "Autograph"; Larsen, HÜb; JHW XVIII:3; Haydn, *Sonatas,* Vol. 3.

[3] Cf. the account in Strunk, "Autograph," 171–81.   [4] Quoted in Hoboken I, 778.

[5] Pohl-Botstiber, 233; Thomas, "Griesinger," 95.

[6] This is one possible explanation suggested by the evidence, but the details of their financial situation are not entirely clear. Cf. Strunk, "Autograph," 178–79.

glish woman of modest accomplishments, it could hardly have been intended for Mrs. Bartolozzi. Haydn himself recognized Therese as one of the most gifted performers in London, and among Haydn's less talented acquaintances Mrs. Schroeter (to whom he dedicated a set of trios) would be a more plausible possibility. If the dedication of No. 51 must remain in question, some association with London is nevertheless safe to assume.

The final documentary issue that has shaped our perception of the last three Haydn sonatas is the presence in Haydn's own catalogue of his London works of a set of two or three "sonatas" for Miss Jansen. (The confusion in number exists because Haydn's original list is lost, and although Dies and Griesinger both copied the list individually, their records differ in certain important details.) Nearly every scholar who has addressed this question has concluded that Haydn's entry refers to the three solo sonatas from the London years. However, since the designation "sonata" was at that time applied readily to various species of composition, and to duos and trios in particular, Haydn's list should be reassessed with a completely open mind.

Summarized in Table 1 are all of the "sonata" entries included in Haydn's catalogue.[7] This chart follows Dies; the differences in Griesinger's list are given in brackets. I have also indicated the compositions to which each entry may refer. The chart is similar to that included in Strunk's essay, but my interpretation differs on certain crucial points. Strunk and other writers have long believed that each entry of three sonatas except the set for Miss Jansen refers to piano trios. But why should an exception be made for the Jansen item? Why would Haydn ignore the trios that he wrote for her? If we assume that the entry refers to those trios, then the list contains *all* of the trios Haydn is believed to have written in London. Still, since all of the trios carried dedications, why should Miss Jansen be identified when the other entries mention publishers? The answer again is straightforward: the other three collections were already published or in the process of publication at the end of Haydn's second visit, but the Jansen set was not published by Longman & Broderip until 1797. Since the two entries for single "sonatas" also apparently identify works that would no longer be so labeled today, the catalogue appears to contain no solo sonatas whatever. This destroys the supposed link between Sonatas Nos. 50–52 and Therese Jansen.

Without additional documentary evidence, the only conclusions that can be justified are that Haydn probably did write his last three solo sonatas in London, though that is less certain for the D major sonata, and that two of them were written for Miss Jansen. Aside from the certainty

---

[7] Based on Gotwals, *Haydn,* 32 (Griesinger, 53–55; modern ed., 31–32), 209 (Dies, 219–20; modern ed., 217–18).

Table 1 "Sonatas" in Haydn's London Catalogue

Dies [Griesinger]	3 Sonates for Broderip	3 Sonates for P—— [Preston]	3 Sonates for Ms. Janson [2]	1 Sonate in F minore	1 Sonate in g	3 Sonates for Broderip [lacking]
Probable work(s) concerned	Trios Hob. XV:18–20	Trios Hob. XV:21–23	Trios Hob. XV:27–29	Variations Hob. XVII:6	Trio Hob. XV:32	Trios Hob. XV:24–26
Probable 1st ed.	Longman & Broderip	Preston	Longman & Broderip	Artaria	Preston	Longman & Broderip
date	1794	1795	1797	1799	1794	1795
dedicatee	Princess Esterházy née Hohenfeld	Princess Esterházy née Lichtenstein	Therese Jansen Bartolozzi	Baroness von Braun	none	Mrs. Schroeter
Remarks	Ent. Sta. Hall, 15 Nov. 1794	Ent. Sta. Hall, 23 May 1795	Ent. Sta. Hall, 27 April 1797	called "Sonate" in aut. ms.	"Letter A"	Ent. Sta. Hall, 31 Oct. 1795

that the E-flat sonata was finished in 1794, the chronological sequence of the sonatas is open to question. Strunk argued that the sequence of the sonatas must have been 52, 51, then 50, since No. 50 uses the widest range (up to a³), and pitches above f³ were not available on older five-octave instruments. This cannot be regarded as conclusive; pitches above f³ can be found in Clementi works from 1790 (Op. 25/1) and Dussek works from 1793 (cf. esp. Op. 23).

For confirmation and clarification of the issues raised by the sources, we must probe the more dangerous questions of style characteristics and stylistic influence. If the idiosyncracies of the London manner of keyboard writing can be detected in the last sonatas of Haydn, then their association with England will be made more tangible and more significant. During Haydn's two visits to London the most prominent active pianist-composers included, by his own account, Clementi, Dussek, and J. B. Cramer.[8]

Among those composers, Dussek enjoyed perhaps the most advantageous position for cultivating Haydn's interest. He appeared regularly in the Salomon concerts, usually playing his own concertos, and the high mutual regard that developed between the two men is demonstrated by a letter from Haydn to Dussek's father written in 1792 in which Haydn praises the younger Dussek's abilities highly.[9] In the summer of 1791, when Dussek left for a tour of Scotland, he even loaned his piano to Haydn.[10]

The young Clementi student J. B. Cramer also became a close acquaintance of Haydn, despite the fact that he was primarily associated with the rival Professional Concerts. There were, after all, numerous benefit concerts in which the artists associated with all of the prominent series intermingled freely. When Haydn moved to a suburban residence in Lisson Grove, Cramer reportedly visited him almost daily.[11] Both Cramer and Dussek dedicated collections of sonatas to Haydn, providing further evidence of friendly relations.

Muzio Clementi occupied the foremost position among London pianists at that time, but his relationship to Haydn submits less easily to a simple characterization. In the first place, Haydn had known some of Clementi's most precocious works since the early 1780s. In a letter from 1783, Haydn had thanked Artaria for sending him a collection of Clementi sonatas (either Op. 7 or Op. 9), and he described the works as "very beautiful."[12] However, the relationship between the men during Haydn's London visits was distinctly chilly. Clementi was then trying

---

[8] Haydn, CCLN, 262–63 (*Briefe,* 497–99).   [9] Haydn, CCLN, 130–31 (*Briefe,* 278–79).
[10] Craw, "Dussek," 60.   [11] Hughes, *Haydn,* 72.
[12] Haydn, CCLN, 42 (*Briefe,* 128). For further study of the early links between Clementi and Vienna see Tyson, "Clementi."

desperately to establish himself as a composer of symphonies for the Professional Concerts, and the isolated example of a reaction by Haydn is an abrupt notation in his journal: "Mr. Clementi sat at the pianoforte, and conducted his new grand symphony, without success."[13] All the same, Clementi presented Haydn with a gift upon his departure, and several years later they enjoyed a fruitful business relationship when Clementi became Haydn's English publisher.

There was clearly sufficient contact between Haydn and the most prominent London pianoforte composers to permit Haydn to know their music well. While all of the composers in London must have learned much from Haydn's example, he also may have learned from the strengths and novelties that he perceived in their music. To the extent that Haydn's late sonatas reveal "English" characteristics, the impact of Dussek and Cramer may be the easiest to assess, since they were young men of limited renown. Clementi's music may have worked upon Haydn's imagination for a considerably longer period, and it is consequently more difficult to identify particular Clementian techniques with Haydn's London residence.

Although there is no way to discover all of the specific compositions that Haydn saw or heard in London, we can now determine which works by Dussek, Cramer, and Clementi had been published before Haydn's departure in 1795. I cannot hope to explore here all of the similarities that exist between that repertoire and Haydn's works, but perhaps I can point out enough details to indicate the character and extent of the general relationship.

The most exceptional and the most tantalizing single relationship is the similarity in the openings of the first movements of Haydn's Sonata in D major and the Sonata Op. 4, No. 3 in F minor by Cramer (Example 1). The Cramer sonata was probably written around 1790, and the marked similarity to Haydn's opening suggests that in this single instance the master may have created an unconscious imitation of the younger man. If this example is something more than an astonishing coincidence, it provides perhaps the most conclusive link between the Haydn sonata and his London visits.

Example 1

a) Cramer, Sonata Op. 4, No. 3 in F minor, i, 1–2

[13] Haydn, CCLN, 288 (*Briefe,* 530).

b) Haydn, Sonata Hob. XVI:51 (ChL. 61) in D major, i, 1–2

Nearly all of the other relationships pertain to details of style, especially to passage-work and the handling of sonorities, that Haydn could easily have adopted without any fundamental change in his compositional approach. As tempting as it may be to find a kinship between the motivic concentration of Haydn's C-major sonata and the more closely knit of Clementi's works, for example, such an argument is unnecessary and would probably be specious. All of the relationships in question here involve compositions written before the end of Haydn's second London visit.

Aside from the most general relationships that resist easy description, most of the similarities between Haydn's works and the music of other London composers fall into two broad classes: 1) mannerisms associated with specific structural functions, and 2) sonority effects that are essentially flexible in function. Within the first category, the most easily detected details concern the manner of beginning a movement. The Cramer example already cited must be regarded as exceptional, but there are additional similarities. The forthright beginning of Haydn's Sonata in E flat also has numerous English counterparts. In every early piano concerto by Cramer and Dussek available for study, the first solo entrance is an impressive, full, chordal passage. Even the rolled chord of Haydn's sonata can be found in Cramer's Sonata Op. 4, No. 2, in the same key (i, mm. 5–6). The use of a high, lyrical melodic line as the registral peak of a section, a prominent feature of Haydn's Sonata in C major, was another common mode of expression for London composers. In the example given (Example 2) Dussek's arrangement is clearly close to Haydn's.

Example 2

a) Dussek, Sonata Op. 24, No. 2 in G major, iii, 105–11

b) Haydn, Sonata Hob. XVI:50 (ChL. 60) in C major, i, 66–67

The lyrical octave melody near the beginning of Haydn's D-major sonata is one of the most frequently cited Schubertian touches in the work,
but it could be more accurately described as Dussekian. Clementi and
Cramer had also cultivated this vein, but it was an especially characteristic element of Dussek's style (for example, his Sonata Op. 23, i, 25–29).
Dussek also corresponds to Haydn in perhaps the most striking instance
of a parallel structural mannerism that I have detected. The London composers frequently used the warm middle range of the instrument for closing passages, but Dussek in particular showed a tendency to include
some chromatic alteration in closing material. The first movement of
Haydn's Sonata in D major ends with a passage in which B flat is introduced into the left-hand figure. A Dussek sonata in the same key (Op.
25, No. 2) ends with precisely the same chromatic addition to the left-
hand figure in the closing material (Example 3).

Example 3

a) Dussek, Sonata Op. 25, No. 2 in D major, iii, 213–18

b) Haydn, Sonata Hob. XVI:51 (ChL. 61) in D major, i, 108–10

An even greater profusion of similarities can be found in the second
general category—effects that have no specific structural associations.
Some tendencies were so widespread in keyboard music of that time in
London that they do not require illustration individually. A penchant for

consecutive thirds and sixths in allegro movements, a tendency to use much of the piano's available range within a short time span, or the frequent use of hand crossing to present an idea in contrasting registers all represent aspects of Haydn's late sonatas that repeatedly occur in the music of other London composers. To this list we might add some effects that characterize the relationship between the two hands: octaves in one hand opposing rapid figuration in the other, and syncopated dialogue such as occurs in one of the famous "open pedal" passages in Haydn's Sonata in C major, i, 120–23. An instructive final illustration for this class of relationships can be found in one of the variants of the opening idea in Haydn's Sonata in D. This dialogue pattern between the hands (Example 4) exists in a suggestively similar form in a Dussek sonata in the same key, Op. 31, No. 2. As distinctive as the relationship appears to be, there is one major difficulty in assessing its importance. The Dussek work was probably published in 1795, during Haydn's last year in London, so the direction in which the impulse moved (if indeed it existed in a particular sense) is impossible to determine. Yet even if this particular similarity is merely a coincidental by-product of a generally shared stylistic vocabulary, it serves to affirm the existence of that common language of pianoforte effects.

Example 4

a) Dussek, Sonata Op. 31, No. 2 in D major, i, 96–98

b) Haydn, Sonata Hob. XVI:51 (ChL. 61) in D major, i, 44–45

Several general conclusions should be added to the details already mentioned. The relationships between Haydn and the London composers are more frequent in the first movements of the sonatas than in the slow movements or finales. The Sonatas in C and D represent closer approaches to a London style than the E-flat sonata. The Sonata in D major, by virtue of its two-movement plan, its predominantly two-voiced texture, and its generally loose structure, is in fact a fair approximation of the kind of light sonata that was fashionable in London. The works of Dussek and Clementi seem to have made a stronger impression on Haydn than the young J. B. Cramer's music, but some of Clementi's influence may have existed considerably earlier than Haydn's London visits.

These observations do not imply that Haydn's last sonatas were written in conscious imitation of a London manner. Rather, they demonstrate that his conception of pianoforte style was strongly conditioned by the music he encountered in England and that his own idiom was enriched by his new experiences. While some of the traditional documentary arguments must be revised or discarded, the sum of stylistic evidence reinforces the links between London and all three of the Haydn sonatas. Only the discovery of manuscript sources for all the sonatas could make their English origin appear more certain. Haydn's apparent receptiveness to the fresh impulses of a foreign culture testifies eloquently to his intellectual vigor at an advanced age and to his unfading artistic curiosity.

Stylistic Features of Haydn's Symphonies from 1768 to 1772

CAROLYN D. GRESHAM

The period from 1768 to 1772 represents a unique, isolated phase in Joseph Haydn's symphonic development. (I shall refer to it as the Expansive Period rather than the "Strum und Drang" in order to avoid the issue of the literary movement of the same name and the controversy over its influence on Haydn's compositions.) Many writers attempt to explain this period from a subjective viewpoint only, as a period displaying intense emotion and passion, but these dramatic elements are seldom dealt with from a musical standpoint. The term "expansive" refers to the increased variety of musical techniques to create tension and expressiveness, and to their increasing use in combination with each other. Exactly what techniques does Haydn use to create this feeling of drama and expansiveness? What musical characteristics determine the uniqueness of these symphonies?

These unique dramatic qualities appear most strongly in No. 39 in G minor, No. 44 in E minor, No. 45 in F-sharp minor (the "Farewell"), No. 46 in B major, No. 49 in F minor, and No. 52 in C minor. The most obvious characteristic of this period is the use of the minor mode. Only ten of Haydn's symphonies are in minor; six of these originated during this one period (No. 26 in D minor and the five listed above). The other four (Nos. 78, 80, 83, and 95) were written between 1783 and 1791; they begin in minor but modulate quickly to major keys, remaining in major much of the time, and they exhibit few of the unique qualities of the earlier six.[1] Prior to the Expansive Period, Haydn's only important instrumental work which uses the minor key as its principal tonality is the Piano Trio Hob. XV:f1 in F minor, which Feder dates before 1760.[2] During this period, Haydn uses minor tonality to create a dark, somber atmosphere that becomes a foundation for other dramatic techniques.

One method of achieving greater intensity is the use of a longer, continuously unfolding phrase—a *Fortspinnung* phrase—which creates tension and suspense by avoiding cadences. The tension is often achieved by a combination of techniques—a repetitive rhythmic figure, recurring syncopation, sequences, and the use of contrapuntal materials. An increase in dynamics, instrumentation, and a rising pitch level also aid in this tension-building process. Melodically, the phrases are often disjunct and asymmetrical, as opposed to the use of simple, folklike melodies in many of Haydn's other symphonies.

Abrupt dynamic contrasts, constantly shifting the dynamic level as well as the rhythmic and melodic content, abound in the opening and closing movements, for example Nos. 44/iv, 45/i, 46/i, and 49/iv. A greater use of harmonic resources is another feature. The emphasis is often on a sudden unexpected change, with frequent use of diminished seventh chords, abrupt modulation, deceptive cadences, and strongly emphasized dissonances. Rhythm is closely bound to harmony, melody, and a continuous phrase structure. Often it is the surging rhythmic drive in combination with *Fortspinnung,* increase in dynamics, and higher pitch level that contribute to the drama of these symphonies. Other characteristics of this period—tremolo, abrupt timbre change, use of silence—will not be discussed in detail because of their obvious dramatic effectiveness. Table 1 summarizes the appearance of many of these characteristics in the symphonies of this period.

Two symphonies can serve to illustrate several of these points. Symphony No. 52 opens with an initial bold, dramatic unison. This type of opening can also be seen in Nos. 49/i and iv and in No. 46/i. The disjunct staccato melody in No. 52 expands with increasingly wider intervals in mm. 1–3. Beginning with m. 4 the repetitive rhythmic accompaniment aids the melody in its expanded surge to the end of the phrase in m. 8. This cadence is followed by silence and then by an abrupt contrast. The impact of this opening can be attributed to the tightly concentrated combination of these elements into an eight-measure *Fortspinnung* phrase in a minor tonality.

Symphony No. 45 exhibits similar dramatic elements in its opening: the descending disjunct, nonlegato melody; the syncopated accompaniment in the second violins; the driving eighth-note rhythmic repetition in the lower strings; the quickening pace of sixteenth-note groups in

---

[1] See Brook, "Sturm und Drang," 279.   [2] See Feder, "Klaviertrios," 311–14.

Table 1   Expressive Characteristics in the Symphonies of Joseph Haydn, 1768–1772

Dynamics—Abrupt Contrasts
45/i, 108; iii, 1–40
46/i, 35–36
47/iii
49/i, 34–37; ii, 13–14; iv, 1–8
52/i, 14; iii, 42–45

Continuous *Fortspinnung* Phrases
44/i, 20–42
45/i, 25–38, 38–55
46/iv, 187–98
49/ii, 1–13, 52–71, 111–26; iv, 1–50
52/i, 1–8, 50–64

Expressive Appoggiaturas
44/iii
49/i, 11–14; iii, 41–45

Disjunct Melody
44/i, 1–4; ii, 1–16
45/i, 1–18
46/i, 1–18
49/iii, 41–44

Dramatic Repeated Notes
45/i, 1–16
46/i, 13–20
47/iv, 1–16
49/iv

Suspensions
44/iv, 120–25 (oboes)
45/iv, 25–40 (oboes)
46/iv, 136–46
49/ii, 58–69

Syncopation
44/i, 48–51; iv, 151–57
46/i, 36–40
49/ii, 4–5

Pedals for Phrase Extension
46/i, 7–10, 36–41; iv, 201–10
47/iv, 186–94
49/i, 1–4; iv, 1–6, 7–10, 57–65

Silence
46/iv, 195–200
49/i, 32–33
52/i, 32, 158; iv, 156–63, 164–71

Timbre Contrasts
49/ii, 13–14; iv, 78–79

Tremolo
39/iv, 1–13
52/i, 27–31

Deceptive Cadences
49/i, 46–47
52/i, 7–8

mm. 13–15; the two-beat period of silence followed by a sudden contrast of dynamics in mm. 16–17; and in the following sections the sequential use of materials at higher pitch levels. These techniques create a continually expanding phrase to heighten the drama.

A truly unique example of the expansion principle is found in the end of the first movement of Symphony No. 52. The material of the second group is presented in extended form beginning at m. 140, until it arrives at a standstill in m. 158. The melody becomes increasingly disjunct in mm. 148–52. The tied notes in the lower strings support the melody and create an unusual feeling of suspension and expansion, which contrasts effectively with the *forte* driving force to the end (mm. 159–63).

Many of these features can also be found in earlier and later Haydn symphonies. What then accounts for the unique characteristics of those from the period 1768–72? In general, the earlier symphonies lack the imagination and power of these maturer works. They have more clearly delineated sections, so that no feeling of continuously unfolding phrases can arise. The music is more predictable, and it stays within traditional harmonic and rhythmic frameworks. The unexpected, whether it be a shift in rhythm, accent, dynamics, texture, or theme, is less likely to occur, and if it does occur, it produces a weaker effect than is seen in the symphonies of the Expansive Period. Following 1772, the most obvious change is Haydn's return to the restricted tonality of the pre-1768 period. Most of his symphonies are now in the major again, which is associated with bright, cheerful melodies and humorous effects. Instead of the powerful rhythmic drive, motivic impulses, abrupt contrasts, and contrapuntal developments, Haydn reverts to a simpler, more straightforward approach. These post-1772 symphonies are not necessarily inferior to those of the Expansive Period, but rather they represent a shift of emphasis from a concentrated, dramatic style to a lighter, more popular style.

In the Expansive Period we find a greater concentration of the dramatic, "Romantic" elements described above. It is this unified, tightly woven combination of elements that gives these symphonies their unique qualities. In the earlier and later symphonies this intensity is lacking; only isolated examples of these expressive, dramatic elements occur.

Why did these stylistic experiments essentially stop in 1772? Did Haydn choose to refine these radical ideas because of his listeners' demands? Are the later symphonies a refinement of these expansive principles, or do they represent a rejection of these experiments? Whatever the answers, the symphonies from the years 1768–72 represent a unique, significant phase in Haydn's development. In many ways they seem closer to Beethoven and the Romantic tradition than Haydn's own later symphonies.

The Enlightenment and Haydn

CARSTEN E. HATTING

The problem of the Enlightenment has been faced by almost as many historians as have written about the music of the eighteenth century, be it in monographs of the great composers of the century, general views of the development of musical style, or descriptions of the change in the relations between music and society. Different approaches have, as a rule, led to different points of view not only concerning musical matters, but also regarding the designation and possible influence of the idea or ideas represented by the term "enlightenment."

It is perhaps possible to see two main tendencies among the various conceptions of the functions of the Enlightenment in European history. One stresses the coherence between rationalistic philosophy and the ideas of the Enlightenment. Important here is that the great metaphysical systems of thought in the seventeenth century are the foundation for the way of thinking in the following century, an age in which philosophy was less distinctive, but in which moral, political, journalistic, educational, and critical literature increased immensely. In recent musicological literature this tendency can be felt, for example, in Paul Henry Lang—though he also uses as a special term "the Enlightenment of the eighteenth century"[1]—and Eberhard Preussner.[2] The latter describes a corresponding continuity in the literature of aesthetics. The *Affektenlehre* of Athanasius Kircher (1650) develops without a break into Batteux's *Traité des beaux arts* (1743), just as rationalism from the time of Descartes develops into Immanuel Kant's *Sapere aude,* "venture to know."[3]

Another tendency appears in the chronologically more limited approach to the Enlightenment in Donald J. Grout[4] and in Georg Knepler.[5] Though they disagree fundamentally about where the creative powers of history are to be found, they both find correlations between the ideas of the Enlightenment and the development of musical style in the eighteenth century, that is to say, the development away from the Baroque and toward Classicism and Romanticism. The New Oxford History of Music even titles its relevant volume *The Age of Enlightenment 1745–1790,*[6] thus defining to a certain degree the general notion of "enlightenment" by a chronological limitation. But regretably the volume offers little, apart from Gerald Abraham's spirited preface, to explain a possible relation between music and nonmusical ideas.

Why this regret? Would it only disturb our understanding of the history of music to contaminate it with philosophical, moral, or political ideas? Ever since Wölfflin's "Begriffspaare,"[7] attempts to discover "inherent" general principles in the arts have given rise to endless discussions about the proper way to label historical periods. It is evident that a further widening of the scope of historical investigation will almost automatically place new hindrances in the path of a broad consensus. Still, the difficulties in handling a more complex conception of history are hardly greater than those connected with the defense of the conception of an independent development of musical style. As in any other period, music was not composed in the eighteenth century merely to demonstrate a stage of stylistic development, but rather in order to fill a practical purpose—or demand—and as a means of human expression.

One may question whether, despite its obvious respect for philosophy

---

[1] Lang, *Civilization,* 430–32.   [2] Preussner, "Aufklärung"

[3] Immanuel Kant, "Beantwortung der Frage: Was ist Aufklärung?" *Berlinische Monatsschrift,* December 5, 1783; quoted from *Werke in sechs Bänden,* ed. Wilhelm Weischedel, VI (Frankfurt am Main. Insel-Verlag, 1964), 53.

[4] Grout, *History,* 411–16.   [5] Knepler, *Musikgeschichte,* I, 24–110.

[6] See "Enlightenment"

[7] As developed, for example, in Heinrich Wölfflin, *Renaissance und Barock* (Munich: Ackermann, 1888; 4th ed., Munich: Bruckmann, 1926), transl. Kathrin Simon, *Renaissance and Baroque* (Ithaca: Cornell Univ. Press, 1966).

and philosophers, especially French ones, the Englightenment of the
eighteenth century was primarily a philosophical movement. But the ob-
jects of philosophy in the eighteenth century were less metaphysical than
they had been in the seventeenth, and rather more secular, physical, and
practical. If the intellectualism, the belief in human thought and reason,
were inherited from rationalism (as indeed they were), they were used
for an attack on the inherited reality, on all religious, moral, and political
values, aiming optimistically at an improvement of human conditions
through fundamental alterations, thus leading up to the French revolution.

That music was connected with the development of society has been
shown through a social approach to music history. Important musical institutions were conditioned by the appearance of the "public," as a growing, anonymous consumer of music. Public concerts, following the same
routes as the social evolution and the "enlightened" way of thinking,
spread from England and France to the German-speaking countries.
Music publishers' houses were established, with early centers in France
and the Netherlands. Music now also became an object of trade, and
musical criticism soon became a feature in magazines, of which,
again, the first were published in England.

In the nineteenth century these musical institutions were part of a
musical life in which, as Carl Dahlhaus has suggested, they were related
to 1) aesthetic ideas (the idea of the autonomy of music, the conception of
the genius); 2) theoretical thinking (the "logic" of music); and 3) the idea
of "classical" works, meaning works regarded as valuable independent
of any historical context, resulting in the formation of an established concert repertoire.[8] Dahlhaus regards nineteenth-century musical life as a
structure combining compositional standards, aesthetic ideas, and the
function of musical institutions.

The fundamental question elicited by a broader conception of history
concerns the nature of historical relations. It must be acknowledged that
empirically provable—or refutable—relationships between different historical processes (and a "structural" conception of history must be concerned with processes rather than with events) can hardly be discovered.
In presenting his design for a structural history of music of the nineteenth
century, Dahlhaus referred to Max Weber's concept of the *Idealtypus*.
This "ideal model" should be understood as a construction formed by
the historian on the basis of empirical results, to be sure, but not necessarily shaped by any specific historical mold. As Dahlhaus uses it, it
forms a structure whose elements are not causes or consequences of each
other. There is no distinction between foundation and superstructure,
and even if it should be possible to fix starting points or to eliminate one

[8] Dahlhaus, "Strukturgeschichte"

or another of the elements, this result should not be used to impose a "causality" upon the structure. Dahlhaus defends this principle and the term "correlation" (*Entsprechung*) in place of causality by showing that more or less comprehensive categories had been in general use in music history (such as conceptions of musical genre, of national or personal styles), and by stating, pragmatically, that the gain in insight will compensate for the slight inaccuracies between the construction and the historical facts. The essential and inspiring point in Dahlhaus's use of Weber's model is that it not only is applied in the field of social history, as might be evident from its origin in the social sciences, but it includes theoretical and aesthetic views. Although he applies it only to the history of music, and to a time-span which is traditionally regarded as a single style period, it may illuminate the eighteenth century as well and, perhaps, the relations between strictly musical ideas and extramusical ones. On the other hand the historical structure of an age in which great changes took place, or were prepared, will undoubtedly appear more complex and contain a greater number of paradoxical details.

The establishment of public concerts arose out of the use of music in clubs and salons. There, the new sense of "publicity" (*Publizität*) developed first as a literary movement, then as a political one in "the area between the spheres of privateness and state authority" (in Jürgen Habermas's formulation).[9] It was formed by means of discussions (public use of human reason)[10] and socio-cultural activities—of which one was public music making.[11] Admission to these circles depended on property and refinement.[12] The function of music was to act as a medium for unification and socialization of the middle class, whereas earlier it had been primarily to illuminate the representation of power at court or in the church—functions that persisted, but with decreasing importance.

Corresponding to these social changes was a change in musical style. But this change should not be interpreted merely as a simple movement from the mature Baroque to mature Classicism, bridging over a "transitional" period comprising many different trends of style. The historical nature of the style shift appears most clearly in the second quarter of the century, the initial phase when the desire for change was most intense. Far more important than the convergence of styles in Viennese Classical style, which is so tempting to use as a norm for earlier production, was the diffusion of different styles in many places in Europe at about the same time, all representing a move *away* from Baroque style.[13] Still, some habits of composition were preserved. Reaction and opposition were

---

[9] Jürgen Habermas, *Strukturwandel der Öffentlichkeit,* 5th ed. (Neuwied and Berlin: Luchterhand, 1971), 45.
[10] Kant's definition of the function of enlightenment (op. cit., 55).
[11] Habermas, op. cit., 55–56.   [12] Ibid., 108.   [13] See Newman, *Classic,* 59.

more or less inhibited by tradition, resulting in a diversity of styles.

The various trends have been labeled in different ways; recently they have been combined again in Larsen's conception of "mid-century style."[14] From the perspective of the Baroque traditions, this style can be generally characterized by the concept *simplification.* The logically developed contrapuntal texture and the careful voice leading of most early eighteenth-century music did not disappear. But now the texture frequently consists of hints instead of fullness of detail, as when, for example, Telemann in his *Sept fois sept et un Menuet* (1728) leaves it to the performer to decide where to add middle voices to the two-part texture.[15] The omission of melodic details emphasizes the triadic character of the motives, and in harmony as well as in tonality dominant–tonic relationships tend to predominate and to force the more colorful chords and regions of mediant relationship into the background. Metrically, the music moves essentially in regular four-bar periods, even during sequential sections of traditional cast, and many features of dance movements, being the least complicated, characterize the new standard patterns.

From Scheibe onward,[16] simplicity of style has frequently been connected with the "natural" or nonartificial. It seems less important to decide whether this simplification is to be correlated with the folk music of the time (though the investigations of Szabolcsi and others concerning Haydn's use of folk tunes in his works suggest that it actually was so in many cases)[17]—than to acknowledge that composers deliberately chose to compose in a simple, "natural," popular style. The features of simplification mentioned above might almost comprise a modern conception of eighteenth-century style, were it not that almost the same style is found in such genres as *opera buffa, opéra comique,* and *Singspiel,* in which even the plots and characters bear witness to the concern for popularity.

A most striking, although late, example of this intentional simplicity of style occurs in the A-major chorus toward the beginning of Haydn's *The Creation,* at the significant words "Und eine neue Welt entspringt auf Gottes Wort" (A new-created world arises at God's command). As Martin Stern has shown, this work stands in intimate relation to the dominant literary and theological thoughts of German Enlightenment.[18] Although Stern does not enter into a technical analysis of the music, he persuades us that Haydn regarded his music as a worthy equivalent to van Swieten's libretto and considered his work a unity of words and music.

Up to about 1768, Haydn's works represent a mixture of traditional and experimental styles and hardly exceed the limits of "mid-century

[14] Larsen, "Observations," 123.   [15] Provided that soloistic performance is chosen.
[16] Scheibe, *Musicus,* 62.   [17] See, for example, Szabolcsi, "Ungarisch."
[18] Stern, "Schöpfung"

style." the early symphonies, quartets, and divertimenti clearly reveal the simplicity which, whether Haydn recognized it or not, corresponds to the social changes of the period. But a problem arises in applying this concept to the vastly changed structure which gradually emerged around 1770. Karl Geiringer seems to accept this change as merely another expression of the Enlightenment in music, pointing out the line of development from Rousseau to the German "Sturm und Drang," whose spirit he perceives in the expressive works from these years.[19] This view has become widely accepted, supported by the existence of similar works by Vanhal and Mozart.

But Haydn's works from these years may also represent a more specifically musical evolution. He may have felt a personal need for increased expressiveness (not to be understood or interpreted as a *crise romantique*),[20] and he may have determined to achieve this through a concentration of style, an extended use of traditional polyphonic procedures (never quite forgotten in Vienna), and greater differentiation in dynamics. It may have been a personal musical inventiveness of this type to which he referred, in telling Griesinger that he had "had to become original."[21] But the spiritual power in these works should not blind us to their closer relations to "mid-century style" than to the fashions of the Baroque.

While these works mark a personal achievement, at the same time they are the first examples of a music that defends its own existence by reason of what it is, an autonomous music to be listened to for its own sake, rather than because of or in terms of its social function. The stream of musical events is determined by an "inner logic," which was substantiated by Forkel in 1788.[22] Here another element of Dahlhaus's structure emerges.

There are evident paradoxes in the picture of Haydn as a musician of the Enlightenment. He held a traditional appointment as Kapellmeister at a princely court—an appointment which he is never known to have opposed—and yet he incorporated the new structure of musical life through his commercial negotiations with publishers, his responses to commissions from Paris, Cadiz, and Naples, and his acceptance of Salomon's invitations to London. Furthermore, most of his music up to 1790 indisputably served the function of courtly diversion, and yet his personal style adopted, and eventually refined, a wealth of features from the simple and popular style in which composers addressed themselves to the

---

[19] Geiringer, "Protagonist"

[20] As in the influential interpretation by Wyzewa, "Centenaire."

[21] Griesinger, 24–25 (modern ed., 17; Gotwals, *Haydn,* 17).

[22] Forkel, *Geschichte,* I, "Vorrede" and 49–52. The historical importance of Forkel's view is stressed in Dahlhaus, "Strukturgeschichte."

middle class. That Haydn apparently never thought of these as paradoxical tells us something about his personality, but it does not affect their pertinence as clues to his position in an age of great change.

The case of *The Creation* is different. In this work Haydn consciously devotes his powers to words expressing the ideas of an optimistic, nonconfessional Christianity, deeply in tune with the thinking of the Enlightenment. His letter to the Bohemian schoolmaster Karl Ockl,[23] also quoted by Stern, must be read as a personal affirmation of the "message" in the libretto of this work. In 1801, if not earlier, Haydn acknowledges himself as an artist of the Enlightenment.

But rather than this confession, it is Haydn's musical style, regarded as part of human activity in a changing world, that determines his place in history. After all, style is not only a medium of expression: it is expression itself.

"Sturm und Drang" and Haydn's Opera

JOEL KOLK

In the late 1760s and early 1770s Haydn produced a series of compositions in minor keys that seem to breathe a strange new spirit, one often described as tragic, sombre, violent. Afterwards, he seems to have reverted to a less dramatic style. The earlier phase, Haydn's so-called "Sturm und Drang" period, has interested scholars because it is thought to have anticipated the Romantic period and, presumably, because a solution to the mystery of its birth may help us to understand how major shifts in style take place. The attempt to discover the cause of this phenomenon has produced conflicting points of view. This may be attributed in part to a lack of authentic source information;[1] in part to an aesthetic issue underlying the controversy that has since arisen. This paper will attempt to define this issue and to submit a hypothesis based on a characteristic of Haydn's opera.

A classic disagreement exists between those who regard Haydn's "Sturm und Drang" style as a manifestation of extramusical influences and those who regard it as a purely musical development. The former idea has apparently undergone an evolution of its own. Théodore de Wyzewa, who first mentioned the possibility of a "crise romantique chez Haydn" in 1909, may have initiated a trend of thought which, according to Jens

[23] Haydn, *Briefe,* 373 (CCLN, 186–87).
[1] The extant letters from this period contain no reference to Haydn's craft or to his artistic beliefs.

Peter Larsen, "has been reproduced in countless books and articles since
then."[2] In 1946, for example, Karl Geiringer wrote:

If anything in Haydn's personal life was responsible for these unrestrained out-
bursts, it was not the excess, but rather the starvation of his emotional life. Here
lay the danger in his existence at Eszterháza. His wife meant nothing to him;
friends like Tomasini, Weigl, and Friberth . . . were receivers rather than givers
in their relation to him. So all the emotional forces of which he was capable inun-
dated his music, sometimes almost marring its artistic quality.[3]

A decade later, H. C. Robbins Landon reiterated this idea in substance,
though with greater qualification.

Very little is known about Haydn's personal life during these critical years. This
almost total absence of concrete facts about his early years as *Capellmeister* of the
Esterhazy court renders it difficult to explain the extraordinary change which
began to take place during the latter half of the sixties. We have no evidence that
this was the result of any event in his personal life; and it seems more likely that
the compositions of this time are the reflection of some inner disturbance of
which we can only perceive the result and not the cause.[4]

Jack A. Westrup seems to have reversed his views on this subject. In
1967, he dismissed Haydn's "Sturm und Drang" style as "a popular
legend."[5] However, in a subsequent article he repeated the Wyzewa-
Geiringer-Landon theme: "The violence of the symphonies to which the
label is applied is clearly an expression of his own state of mind. The
reasons for this are obscure; but at least there is no need to look for external causes."[6]

The untenability of this explanation may have prompted a movement
to broaden its foundations. Geiringer indicated that manifestations of a
larger unrest were to be found in the music of other composers.[7] Landon
also assented to "a curious kind of collective crisis that was not by any
means limited to a single composer."[8] Though allowing the possibility
of physical illness as a cause, but rejecting the possibilities of an emotional crisis or the influence of the German literary movement, Rosemary
Hughes attributed this "volcanic eruption of Haydn's genius" to "an unconscious attunement to the spirit of the time."[9] Barry S. Brook maintains that concepts of style periodization that place the start of the Romantic period early in the nineteenth century do not allow for the earlier
appearance of several anti-Classical trends in the arts. The latter represent
the disaffection engendered by an oppressive social order:

By 1750, the revolt against rationalist thought, which sought to organize not
only all knowledge but all society by reason alone, was well under way. Rous-

[2] Wyzewa, "Centenaire"; Larsen, "Observations," 129.
[3] Geiringer, *Haydn*₂, 75–76.   [4] R. Landon, *Symphonies,* 273.
[5] Westrup, *"Editorial,"* 1–2.   [6] Westrup, "Aspects," 172–73.
[7] Geiringer, *Haydn*₂, 75.   [8] R. Landon, "Crise," 32.
[9] Hughes, *Haydn,* 3rd ed., 45–46.

seau led the attack with his *Discours sur les sciences et les arts* (1750), and with his *Discours sur l'inégalité* (1754). The battle, which continued throughout the rest of the century, was fought on political, social, philosophical and aesthetic grounds, and often within the minds of single individuals.

The two main streams of thought ran side by side and often ran together. In sum, the one favored the divine right of princes, the uncritical acceptance of the dogma that reason can explain everything and that the world could not be better than it was. It preferred an art that was *précieux,* decorative, serene, well-ordered. The other, responding to the aspirations of the rising bourgeoisie, proclaimed the individual's right to independence of action and freedom of thought and society's need for a return to the simplicity of nature; it held that feelings had priority over reason and it preferred an art that was sombre, intense, introspective, impassioned. . . . This duality so readily recognized in the other arts, is fully paralleled, if insufficiently recognized, in music.

There may be no evidence that Haydn read Rousseau . . . Mercier or Goethe, but I find it impossible to believe that he could have been insensitive to the widespread distress, disenchantment and melancholy that were in the air of Europe at that time.[10]

Brook offers statistical evidence to show that this flourishing of compositions in minor keys by Haydn, Mozart, Vanhal Gassmann, and others around 1770 was indeed an extraordinary trend.

The various forms of the preceding hypothesis all stress the milieu and its effects on the artist's personality and his work. (It actually makes little difference whether Haydn's "Sturm und Drang" style originated in a malaise of his own spirit or the spirit of the age in which he lived; both points of view tend to minimize Haydn's own creative purposes.) The second hypothesis, however, represents an important and influential trend of thought: L. D. Ettlinger tells how it came into being:

As far as the treatment of art history is concerned, from the curious alliance of Winkelmann, the Romantic antiquarian, and Hegel, the determinist philosopher of history, was born that preoccupation with the general problem of "styles"— both national and period—which has become so pronounced a characteristic of art historical studies right up to our own day. The individual work of art and all its qualities became submerged in something larger. Instead of being apprehended as the result of a concrete task and a personal creative act, it became the expression of an inescapable, super-individual force.[11]

Monroe C. Beardsley points out that formalists were the most vigorous opponents of Hegel's theory:

Hegel also worked out, in great detail, a theory of the dialectical development of art in the history of human culture. . . . These categories were to prove very influential in nineteenth-century German aesthetic thought, in which the Hegelian tradition was dominant, despite attacks by the "formalists" (such as J. F. Her-

---

[10] Brook, "Sturm und Drang," 271, 278.
[11] "Art History Today" [Inaugural Lecture, University College, London, 1961], 10. See Peter Murray's introduction to Heinrich Wölfflin, *Renaissance and Baroque,* transl. Kathrin Simon (Ithaca: Cornell University Press, 1966), 4–5.

bart), who rejected the analysis of beauty in terms of ideas as an overintellec-
tualization of the aesthetic and a slighting of the formal conditions of beauty.[12]

Modern formalists continue to reject Hegel's assumption. George
Boas, for example, bases his criticism on the fact that more than one ambience may be present in a given era and that the effects of an ambience
can only be inferred. Boas observed, "How one can be influenced by a
'time' is too mysterious to be treated rationally."[13] Karl Aschenbrenner's
statement to that effect shows even greater partiality.

From alone does not determine the aesthetic impact of a work, which is also
composed of elements, but only form can be analyzed adequately, and is, therefore, alone fit to be the subject of aesthetic theory.[14]

That Haydn's "Sturm und Drang" style was but one manifestation of the
ills besetting eighteenth-century Europe emerges, therefore, as both
Hegelian in concept and as one side of an enduring controversy in aesthetics.

Before turning to the evidence that seems to contradict this hypothesis, it should be noted that a number of authorities have identified
Haydn's "Sturm und Drang" style with eighteenth-century opera.[15] The
search for the origins of this style has, nevertheless, bypassed Haydn's
own operas. But they are pertinent: 1) Haydn's opera production for the
Esterházy court began, coincidentally, with the appearance of his first
"Sturm und Drang" symphonies;[16] 2) Haydn's opera resembled the
comic opera of his contemporaries in its limited use of the minor mode, a
practice which seems to parallel the dearth of instrumental compositions
in minor keys at that time; 3) in time, as the dimensions of Haydn's
operas broadened, this restriction remained in effect. Further investigation, including comparisons of Haydn's operas with those of other composers, suggests that Haydn's "Sturm und Drang" style may have emanated from an earlier operatic convention.

Haydn's earliest surviving opera, *Acide* (1762), is a brief composition
consisting essentially of four arias, one "accompagnato," and one en-

[12] Monroe C. Beardsley, "Aesthetics, History of," *The Encyclopedia of Philosophy,* ed. Paul
Edwards, 8 vols. (New York: Macmillan, [1967]), I, 29.
[13] George Boas, "In Search of the Age of Reason," *Aspects of the 18th Century,* ed. E. R.
Wasserman (Baltimore: Johns Hopkins University Press, 1965), 1–19.
[14] Quoted in W. Tartarkiewicz, "Form in the History of Aesthetics," *Dictionary of the History of Ideas,* ed. Philip P. Wiener, 4 vols. (New York: Scribner, 1973), II, 219.
[15] Adler, "Haydn," 200, for example, alludes to this possibility: "Haydn's 'tempests,' despite an intensity of expression that is due to Gluck's example, are contrived after the fashion of his day." See Larsen, "Observations," 129; Marks, "Rhetoric," 51; Heartz,
"Opera," 168.
[16] *La canterina* may have been performed at Eszterháza in 1766, prior to its premiere (February 1767) in Pressburg; see Bartha-Somfai, 385–86. Haydn's earliest "Sturm und Drang"
symphony, No. 26 in D minor ("Lamentatione"), is dated c. 1767–68, and Nos. 39 in G
minor and 49 in F minor c. 1768.

semble.[17] Its formal resemblance to Baldassare Galuppi's *Il mondo della luna* (c. 1750) can be demonstrated by the following table (Galuppi's designations appear in parentheses):

1. Aria (Aria)	Allegro molto (Allegro)	C (C)
2. Aria (Aria)	Andantino (Allegro)	A (C)
3. Aria (Aria)	Allegro molto (Allegro)	G (G)
4. Accompagnato (Aria)	— (Allegretto)	G (G)
5. Aria (Aria)	Allegro moderato (Largo)	G (E flat)
6. Quartetto (Duetto)	Allegretto (Largo)	D (D)

Although these concordances may not be significant in themselves, they indicate that Haydn's earliest extant opera followed a pattern of major keys typical of his time.

Galuppi's *Il filosofo di campagna* (c. 1754) and Niccolò Piccinni's *La buona figliuola* (c. 1760) are also alike in this regard. The former consists of twenty-one arias; the latter of an overture in three movements, nineteen arias, and a concluding "duetto." Both exhibit a trait that shows up consistently in Haydn's later operas: a single minor-key aria in an overall context of major-key solos and ensembles. In both, the fourth aria is in the minor, and though musically dissimilar they are alike in tempo (Larghetto) and in the sentiments they express. *La canterina* (c. 1767), Haydn's first full-length opera, displays this characteristic. However, in contrast to the preceding examples, its one minor key aria (II, No. 10) employs typical "Sturm und Drang" devices such as the tempo Allegro di molto, driving rhythms, and an angular melody built on wide skips. A comparison of its opening with that of Gluck's "Che fiero momento" (*Orfeo*, III.i) reveals distinct similarities in melody, harmony, and texture. Gluck's aria represents an early use (1762) of "Sturm und Drang" effects.

This pattern is continued in Haydn's subsequent operas. The one minor-key aria in *Lo speziale* (I, No. 9) employs "Sturm und Drang" effects as an accompaniment to sentiments of disdain and resignation. In Nanni's well-known F-minor aria from *L'infedeltà delusa* (I, No. 9), such effects accompany sentiments of anger and vengefulness. Lindoro's D-minor aria in *Le pescatrici* (I, No. 14), however, represents a departure from these apparent norms of pathos and revilement. In this case, the "Sturm und Drang" effects depict an actual storm, an idea that Haydn repeated in the opening chorus of his marionette opera *Philemon und Baucis*.

A related use of the minor mode can be found in F. L. Gassmann's *La contessina* (c. 1770). Except for a G-minor Andantino in the finale of the

---

[17] Consideration of *recitativo secco* in Haydn's operas is excluded here.

second act, all twenty-nine of its solos and ensembles originate in major keys.[18] However, in the finale of Act I, an outburst of invective is accompanied by a shift to the dominant minor. Charles Rosen has noted a similar passage in *Le Nozze di Figaro*'s "sextet of recognition" in Act III, where Susanna's rage at seeing Figaro kiss Marcellina is accompanied by a shift to the dominant minor.[19]

This evidence suggests that around 1770, opera composers reserved the minor mode and an accompanying repertory of musical effects for rhetorical accompaniments to moments of heightened emotion and occasionally for the representation of storms.[20] Since Haydn used the minor mode in this way in his operas, it seems unlikely that his use of similar materials in instrumental music represented an involuntary response to extramusical influence. Haydn's "Sturm und Drang" style appears to involve the carryover of an older, operatic convention to the instrumental sphere. Why this transfer occurred, and why it flourished so briefly, is still unknown. Perhaps adaptations of this kind were in vogue for a while; perhaps in anticipation of his new responsibilities, Haydn used these instrumental compositions as a means to develop his skills as an opera composer. It has been said that Symphonies Nos. 26 in D minor ("Lamentatione") and 49 in F minor ("La Passione") suggest the suffering of the Crucifixion.[21] Haydn may have simply considered these effects appropriate to the mood he wished to convey. This formalistic interpretation runs counter to many prior solutions to this problem.

The Significance of Haydn's Op. 33

ORIN MOE, JR.

Haydn rarely spoke about his compositional intent. Therefore, his statement that the string quartets Op. 33 were written in a "new and special way" must indicate something significant.[1] Many historians have concluded that the "new and special way" means that Op. 33 contains Haydn's first mature string quartets. With this, I cannot agree. Op. 50 is the first set to contain all the essential elements of his mature style.

[18] Antonio Sacchini's opera *L'isola amore* (c. 1766) is similarly disposed.
[19] Rosen, *Style*, 292.
[20] Schubart, *Ästhetik*, 261–63, seems to support this contention. A chapter entitled "Charakteristik der Töne" (377ff.) describes specific affects of several major and minor keys.
[21] Cf. R. Landon, *Symphonies*, 285–86, 297.
[1] The familiar viewpoint concerning Op. 33 was first presented by Sandberger, "Streichquartett." The only subsequent author to argue this position thoroughly and persuasively is Finscher, *Streichquartett*, I, 238–75. Dissenting opinions have not been absent, however: Larsen, HÜb, 83 and n. 59; R. Landon, *Symphonies*, 382–83; Bartha in Haydn, *Briefe*, 108; Moe, "Texture," 236–47; Webster, "Chronology," 44–46.

In what does the supposed maturity of Op. 33 consist? It is not texture, since this had already been brought about in Opp. 9, 17, and 20. Op. 9 is Haydn's first essay in the genre of the concertante-quartet, as evidenced by the frequent display of the first violin. Some attention is given to the other members of the quartet, however; they assume increasing importance in Op. 17; with Op. 20, a true quartet texture has been achieved. This texture, perhaps best described as equal-voice, is accomplished in two ways—by *simultaneous* or *successive* independence of the four players. The former, of course, is counterpoint: each voice is distinguished by melodic and/or rhythmic means. Counterpoint is occasionally present in the earliest of Haydn's quartets, and it reaches an extraordinary level of technique with Op. 20. Its most obvious manifestation is the fugue, but it may also appear in other contexts. Example 1 is essentially a melody and accompaniment texture, but each of the voices is distinct in rhythmic pattern and melodic shape—features associated with counterpoint.

Example 1. String Quartet Op. 20, No. 5 in F minor, ii, 72–77

Successive independence involves the exchange of textural roles between instruments, a very effective procedure in a style governed by homophony. Each instrument may take any role in any texture, from leading melodic line to accompanimental line, from secondary melodic line to bass. A cumulative impression of equality is conveyed by continually changing the function of the four instruments. The opening of Op. 20, No. 2 in C major illustrates this procedure (mm. 1–14). The viola and the cello alternate as the bass voice, the cello and the first violin as the leading melody. The second violin remains in a subsidiary melodic role. A further, brilliant example may be taken from the development (Example 2). There is an unusual exchange of the function of the bass between the second violin, first violin, and cello. Equally interesting is the sharing of an important motive between the viola, second violin, and first violin; at one point the viola is on top of the texture. All the instruments, then, are freed from previously stereotyped functions and may share the same register to the extent that it is technically possible.

These two ways of achieving an equal-voice texture are not mutually exclusive, however. A touch of counterpoint helps to enliven the subsidiary parts when only one or two voices have an important line, and in a fugal exposition there is obviously a free exchange of roles among the instruments.

Example 2. String Quartet Op. 20, No. 2 in C major, i, 60–64

If the maturity of Op. 33 consists in things other than texture, then it is safer to stress its importance. Indeed, a large number of significant stylistic changes occur in this set, some of importance for the quartets alone, others affecting numerous genres. Pertaining mainly to the string quartets is the first appearance of a balanced movement-sequence. This balance is found in both a fluent use of equal-voice texture and an appropriate, fully-formed style in all movements. Texturally, Haydn had his greatest problems with slow movements. They tended to remain in one simple texture, frequently melody and accompaniment, or a "dialoguing" violin pair over doubled viola and cello reminiscent of the trio sonata. Only with Op. 33 do the slow movements consistently show changing textures of reasonable complexity, with some emphasis on all the members of the quartet. No such problem existed with the other movements. Opening movements quickly showed some interest in equality between the instruments and adopted the textural variety typical of the period. Finales followed suit, and the minuets had a long tradition of counterpoint. Haydn had his most serious difficulties in finding the right finale. The famous fugues of Op. 20, however fascinating, are a symptom of this difficulty. The problem was to balance the first movement without duplicating its character, to provide a light, but emphatic, conclusion. Haydn's solution in Op. 33 and the later sets was to differentiate the finale from the opening movement by the use of simpler textures, more regular phrasing and harmonic rhythm, more emphasis on soloistic passages for various instruments, and the frequent use of timbre as a thematic element. Form may enter into this differentiation—for instance, Haydn favors the rondo in Op. 33—but it need not. In the later quartets, the sonata-form finale is very frequent.

Many of the movements of this set have a formal complexity not found in the previous quartets. A fine sense of detail exists in many of the earlier works, but Op. 33 finds Haydn aware of the larger aspects of structure and the possibilities of their manipulation. In the exposition of the opening movement of No. 3 in C major, instead of the usual tonal pattern tonic—transition—dominant, there is the more complex pattern tonal instability (mm. 1–17)—tonic (mm. 18–26)—transition (mm. 27–42)—dominant (mm. 43–59). A firm statement of the tonic is delayed by opening the movement with what is essentially an extended I (mm. 1–6)—ii (7–12)—V (13–17)—I (18–26) progression. Emphasis on the initial tonic is avoided by first stating the chord in first inversion and then by having the cello enter with the root on the *second* beat of m. 4. The tonic section (18–26) is the only part of the exposition not associated with the central anapestic motive of the movement, a most unusual disjunction of tonic and theme. Haydn's sense of the larger structure of the exposition is evident in his giving a partial sense of resolution by placing that motive in a context of relative tonal stability. His sense of the whole movement is revealed in his alteration of the pattern of the exposition, to tonal instability (mm. 109–38)—tonic (mm. 139–67) in the recapitulation. This is accomplished by collapsing the first two sections of the exposition into the first section of the recapitulation, by avoiding any conclusive cadence onto the tonic, and by omitting the transition. This compression compensates for the tonal sameness of this section. The style elements discussed so far occur much earlier in the symphony, the nearest relative to the string quartet, so there is the possibility that the one genre learned from the other.

Of future importance for genres besides the string quartet are *thematische Arbeit* and metric, rhythmic, and harmonic irregularities. The former involves the construction of themes in such a way that particles or motives may be broken off and reassembled to form material for other parts of the movement. This technique adds an important dimension to equal-voice texture, because each instrument can share directly in the constructive matter of the movement. *Thematische Arbeit* can be found in some of the quartets of Op. 20, but only in Op. 33 does it become a transparent and consistent stylistic feature.

Metric, rhythmic, and harmonic irregularities occur in Haydn's earlier works, but the strong emphasis given to them in Op. 33 approaches mannerism. These irregularities involve abrupt tonal shifts, the conflict of harmonic and metric accent, and changing metrical placement of the cadences, particularly onto weak beats. Related factors include asymmetry both within and between phrases, placement of phrase beginnings at any point in the measure, and the insertion of a rest between a chord and its appropriate resolution.

Some of these devices and motivic work may both be observed at the opening of Op. 33, No. 1 in B minor (mm. 1–17). The principal motive is in the first violin in mm. 1–2. Its presence in both tonic and dominant areas and its permeation of the four-part texture is clear. More complex is the fluid and unpredictable handling of the phrase structure. The first two measures are tonally ambiguous; the second two are tonally emphatic, placing strong emphasis on the dominant of B minor, but resolving deceptively to VI on the fourth beat of m. 4. One might reasonably expect a cadence onto the tonic on the third beat of that measure or on the first beat of m. 5. Instead, rests in m. 5 abruptly intrude and the whole process is repeated (mm. 5–9). The twice-delayed resolution to the tonic finally occurs in m. 11, but it is promptly undercut by the new theme which appears at that point. No conclusive tonic cadence appears in mm. 11–17. The tonality then turns abruptly to the relative major. This extraordinary passage shows little trace of conventional antecedent–consequent phrase structure. Haydn's playfulness in attaining his goal of B minor and its quick relinquishment when reached is characteristic of his exceptional freedom of movement in these quartets.

The features described here are by no means limited to the string quartet. They are perhaps more familiar to most listeners from the symphonies. Nevertheless, their most intense application occurs in the string quartets from Op. 33 on.

When Haydn spoke of the "new and special way," he could have been referring to any or all of the above stylistic changes, but in comparing Op. 33 to Opp. 9, 17, and 20, we notice something new. They have a light, popular touch, something not heard since Opp. 1 and 2. The themes are folklike, the formal outlines clear. The outward simplicity, however, frequently conceals an inward complexity. All this might be said about the many symphonies with which Op. 33 has much in common. These quartets are both the summation of the popularizing tendencies found in certain symphonies of the preceding decade and the first clear anticipation of a style that will be especially characteristic of the late symphonies, a style which will not make a mature appearance in that genre until 1785.

However important Op. 33 is, it is not the first to present all the characteristics of Classical style as we conceive it. This honor belongs to Op. 50. To a large extent, Op. 33 reduces the intense concern of Op. 20 with equal-voice texture, elaborate counterpoint, and soloistic display. Opus 50 revives this concern and unites it with the accomplishments of Op. 33. The look back to the quartets of the 1770s is evident in the fugal passages of many of the developments and the fugal finale of No. 4 in F-sharp minor—the last such occurrence in Haydn's string quartets. The lightness of Op. 33 does not disappear entirely, but it yields much to learning and complexity. A fine example of the best of both approaches is the finale to No. 1 in B-flat major.

The development of Haydn's Classical quartet style spans many years, from the attainment of equal-voice texture in Op. 20 and the *thematische Arbeit* and irregularities of Op. 33 to their combination in Op. 50. Nor does the succession stop there. The string quartet was Haydn's workshop; his experimenting never ceased. The late quartets are particularly remarkable for a refined sense of timbre, for unusual forms, and for harmonic color. No single set of quartets should distract from the fascination of the whole.

Comedy, Wit, and Humor in Haydn's Instrumental Music

STEVEN E. PAUL

Throughout the vast literature on Joseph Haydn, one characteristic of his music—its wit and humor—is frequently mentioned. Yet surprisingly, no thorough study of this important aspect of his style has been made.[1] The humor of other composers, however, has been treated extensively, and in Beethoven's case there is even an entire work on the subject.[2]

The wit and humor in Haydn's instrumental music were clearly recognized by his contemporaries, however, some of whom acknowledged him to be an innovator in this field. In 1782, Reichardt wrote in a review of Hummel's editions of six symphonies "Op. 18" and of the String Quartets Op. 33 that "these works are full of thoroughly original humor and the liveliest wit,"[3] and Mozart himself summed things up perfectly when he said that Haydn could "amuse and shock, arouse laughter and deep emotion, as no one else."[4]

[1] Of 2,285 entries in Brown, "Bibliography," only nine deal with Haydn's humor.
[2] Veidl, *Humor*
[3] Reichardt, *Magazin,* 205: "Diese beiden Werke sind voll der originalsten Laune, des Lebhaftsten Witzes."
[4] AmZ, I (1798–99), 116.

Haydn's humor, however, was not merely designed to entertain, amuse, or even fool musical performers and audiences. It also played an important role in the form and structure of his music by providing elements of relaxation, comic relief, and variety. Charles Rosen has observed that with the growing use of humorous devices in the instrumental music of the second half of the eighteenth century, "the comic becomes not only the characteristic mood of a work but often, particularly with Haydn, an essential technique."[5]

Most of the examples of wit and humor in music can be explained in terms of the element of surprise. Haydn is well known for his humorous and witty use of the unexpected. Indeed, the many devices and techniques for creating humor in music, such as understatement, overstatement, incongruity, and ambiguity are all manifestations of this basic principle of surprise, and they were integral parts of Haydn's musical language. He frequently used pauses and silences, false reprises and false endings, delayed cadences, and extreme or abrupt changes of dynamics, timbre, harmony, and range. He constantly endeavored to play upon the expectations of the listener through formal, rhythmic, harmonic, and dynamic surprises.

Philosophers have long held that the interjection of the unexpected into a routine course of thought or action is a major component of humor. One of the first known applications of this concept to musical aesthetics appeared in an important article by Haydn's contemporary C. F. Michaelis in the AmZ for August 12, 1807; it deserves to be quoted at length:

Music is humorous when the composition accords with the mood of the artist rather than strictly adhering to an artistic system. The musical thoughts are then of a completely original, unusual kind; they do not follow each other in a way one would expect, but they surprise by totally unexpected turns and transitions. . . . The humorous composer distinguishes himself by his unusual ideas, which tempt one to smile. . . . His imagination plays such an entertaining game with melody and accompaniment that one is surprised by the new, the novel, the unexpected. . . . The more recent music is for the most part humorous, especially since Haydn, the greatest master in this field, took the lead in his original symphonies and quartets.[6]

[5] Rosen, *Style,* 97.

[6] Michaelis, *Humor,* 725–29: "Die Musik ist humoristisch, wenn die Komposition mehr die Laune des Künstlers, als die strenge Ausübung des Kunstsystems verräth. Die musikalische Gedanken sind dann von einer ganz eigenen, ungewohnten Art; sie folgen nicht so auf einander, wie man etwa nach einem gewissen Herkommen, oder nach dem natürlichen Gange der Harmonie und Modulation vermuthen sollte, sondern überraschen durch ganz unerwartete Wendungen und Uebergänge. . . . Der humoristische Komponist zeichnet sich durch sonderbare Einfälle aus, die zum Lächeln reizen. . . . Seine Imagination [treibt] ein so unterhaltendes Spiel mit der Melodie und Begleitung, dass man sich über das Neue, Eigne, Unerwartete verwundert. . . . Ist unsere neueste Musik grossentheils humoristisch, besonders seitdem Joseph Haydn, als der grösste Meister in dieser Gattung, vorzüglich in seinen originellen Sinfonieen und Quartetten, den Ton dazu angab."

Throughout the long span of his creative activity, Haydn always seemed to delight in confounding the expectations of his audience. Georg Feder notes that Haydn loved surprise as an artistic device, and that he was perhaps the first to make it an essential category of expression.[7]

Like any art, music has its conventions, rules, and standard practices which, within the context of a given style or period, tend to gain unquestioned acceptance and to produce expectations in the listener. Wit is the power and ability to *invent* within an existing style. Hence a deliberate deviation from established norms of the style—a breach of the "contract" between the composer and his audience—could be interpreted as a mockery of convention and result in the production of a striking, unexpected effect. Strunk observes:

> Only when the rules of the game are well established is it feasible for the composer to play on the expectation of his listener. And even then, to play on expectation he must first arouse it. To secure emphasis he must first exercise self-control. He cannot afford to be continually surprising his listener. He must be simple before he is complex, regular before he is irregular, straightforward before he is startling. The composer of the "Surprise" Symphony understood the working of these first principles.[8]

Of course, the famous *Paukenschlag* in Symphony No. 94 in G major is the most familiar example of Haydn's technique of dynamic surprise, although it may be found in many other works, for example Symphonies Nos. 60/i, 80/ii, 83/ii, 84/iv, 89/iii, 93/ii, and 100/ii, iv. This joke works on three levels: first, it shatters the tranquility of the quiet, almost-too-innocent theme; secondly, it deceives our expectation of an exact repeat of the first 8 bars; and finally it comes in the slow movement, the least likely section of a symphony to expect musical jokes and surprises.[9] The result is a masterly surprise within a surprise, a practical joke, the musical equivalent of the punchline. Because the repetition ends in a manner totally different from our expectations, it is amusing in this simple, non-dramatic context. The convention of the exact repeat is rendered comic through the exaggerated and extreme change in both dynamics and timbre. Of course, sudden loud interjections occur elsewhere in Haydn (often in a serious, dramatic context), but they are usually an integral part of the music and logically connected to what has gone before (the shocking moment is found to be part of a larger plan). But the "Surprise" is a gratuitous addition, because the theme would not only be complete without it, but it continues uninfluenced by it in any way.[10] It is superimposed upon the structure, yet prepared in advance with great care and

---

[7] Feder, "Paukenschlag," 6.   [8] Strunk, "Haydn," 79.

[9] For example, Meyer, *Ideas,* 11n., states that fast movements offer a greater possibility for surprise or wit. But some of Haydn's most effective displays of wit and humor occur in the slow movements, notably those of Symphonies Nos. 93 and 94.

[10] I am indebted to Walter Gerboth for this suggestion.

attention to details. Also, there is the question of taste: Haydn had the good judgment not to repeat the joke.

A perhaps even more striking, if crude, comic effect appears in another slow movement from a London symphony, No. 93 in D major. Sixteen bars before the end of the movement, the principal theme resolves itself into a delicate exchange of alternating strings and winds until, as Landon describes it, "the bassoons let out a most obscene and ridiculous ff note, C_1 (2 octaves below middle c), which is one of the few times that Haydn ever indulged in Rabelaisian humor."[11] Here Haydn, a master of timing, uses several elements of surprise to ensure the success of the amusing effect: the extreme shift in range from the high flutes to the bassoons, the sudden change from *pp* to *ff*, the reversal of the alternating string and wind patterns, and, of course, the extraordinary timbre of the *doubled* bassoons in their lowest register. This is perhaps the supreme example of Tovey's "Great Bassoon Joke."

It is interesting to contrast this rather obvious comic effect, an example of musical overstatement, with the subtly witty understatement in m. 210 of the Finale of Symphony No. 94. Here, the music goes abruptly from *loud* to *soft*. More significant is the intervention of a bar of silence (m. 209), which delays the expected cadential resolution of the four chords in mm. 207–08 and breaks up the musical continuity.[12] Instead of the expected resolution to a G-major chord, on the first beat of m. 209, a single note G is sounded in the following bar (210). This ushers in the next section, but it only peripherally fulfills the expectation of the previous cadential resolution. Haydn provides the minimum amount of sound possible—a mere "shadow" of what is expected. Once again, several parameters guarantee the success of the effect: instead of a chord, a single note; instead of g^2 in the violins, G three octaves below in the cellos; instead of m. 209, m. 210; instead of *forte,* it is *piano;* and it is pizzicato. The same delayed cadence device appears in several other works, including the Menuet of Symphony No. 104 in D major ("London"), mm. 43–49; the Scherzo of the String Quartet Op. 33, No. 5 in G major, mm. 9–10; the first movement of the Sonata Hob. XVI:40 (ChL. 54) in G major, mm. 71–72; and the finale of the Quartet Op. 76, No. 1 in G major, mm. 179–80.

Haydn also makes witty use of silence to create musically ambiguous situations.[13] Probably the most fertile ground for his use of ambiguity is

---

[11] R. Landon, "Notes," 14.

[12] In a discussion of implicative relationships in connection with the Minuet of Symphony No. 104 in D (m. 45), Meyer, *Explaining,* 114–15, observes that in this use of a pause, "A compellingly goal-directed process is abruptly broken off." Haydn's witty use of silence represents the antithesis of the Baroque conception of continuity, a strikingly original departure from that period's *horror vacui.*

[13] Silbert, "Ambiguity," 573, notes the connection between Haydn's ambiguity and his witty effects.

the "false ending," by which he deceives the listener into thinking that a work has come to an end and then—possibly just at the point where someone might be caught clapping—the piece resumes. The Finale of Symphony No. 90 in C major, with its extraordinary four bars of silence at what appears to be the final cadence, is a case in point. (This "ending" would be more credible if the bass went *down* to c in bar 167, and, perhaps, if the tutti were chordal rather than in unison.) The surprising and humorous effect of the continuation is enhanced by the abrupt jump to D-flat major, and by the transformation of the triumphant eighth- and sixteenth-figure into a mocking echo. This type of wit thus also depends on reinterpretation, the placing of the same material in a new context. A similar moment occurs in the Andante of Symphony No. 101 in D major ("Clock"), mm. 96–98. Of course, the most famous example is at the close of the String Quartet Op. 33, No. 2 in E-flat major, the so-called "Joke" quartet.

Let me describe some other techniques of musical wit and humor in Haydn's work more briefly. Rhythmic ambiguity is found in the opening of the Finale of Symphony No. 80 in D minor, as well as in the Trio of Symphony No. 92 in G major ("Oxford"), where the winds and strings appear to have different downbeats and, later on, shifts of accent and rests cause even more confusion. The "surprise return"[14] can be found in the finales of Symphonies Nos. 79, 88, and 89, as well as several of the London symphonies, including Nos. 93, 94, 98, 100, and 102. Haydn deliberately designs themes (usually with upbeats) which are easily capable of fragmentation. Then he manipulates this material, suggesting and delaying the return of the theme until nobody can tell just when it will come (an excellent example is No. 93 in D major, iv, 165–72). By systematically exploiting this technique in the London Symphonies, Haydn elevated it to a structural principle. Related to the surprise return is the false reprise, which appears in several symphonies and quartets, from about 1770 right up to Symphony No. 102 in B-flat major.

Wit can also be found in the understated "throw-away" pizzicato endings of Symphony No. 23 in G major and the Quartet Op. 33, No. 4 in B-flat major. The quiet, understated ending to close a movement or a work appears in all genres and periods of Haydn's *oeuvre,* including the Sonatas Hob. XVI:39/iii, 40/ii, 42/ii (ChL. 52, 54, 56); Symphonies Nos. 23/iv, 31/ii, 55/iii, and 91/ii; and especially in the quartets, where no fewer than eighteen works end *pianissimo.*[15] Last, but far from least, Haydn indulged in what seems to be thought of alternately as either the highest or the lowest form of wit and humor—the pun—which, in musical terms, can be seen in the context of reinterpretation. For example, it appears in his use of an opening phrase as a closing one, as in the last movement of the Quartet Op. 17, No. 5 in G major, the first movement of the Quartet

[14] Rosen, *Style,* 337–39.   [15] Somfai, "Kvartett," 329, 418.

Op. 33, No. 5 in G major, the last movement of Symphony No. 35 in B-flat major, and the second movement of Symphony No. 57 in D major. He also transforms melody and accompaniment, as in the String Quartets Op. 33, No. 1/i and 64, No. 5/i and the Symphonies Nos. 68/iii and 101/ii. These techniques involved new principles in music and were among his most original inventions.[16]

Finally, there is extramusical, that is to say, theatrical and visual humor. The best-known example, of course, is the Symphony No. 45 in F-sharp minor ("Farewell"), which depends upon the staging of the performance for its effect. Another kind of extramusical device—in the sense that it is outside the range of normally used musical material—is the surprisingly incongruous tuning of the strings after the beginning of the last movement of Symphony No. 60 in C major ("Il distratto").

The last two examples suggest that Haydn may have inspired humor and wit in other composers. The connection in this area between Haydn and Beethoven has often been described.[17] The Czech composer Pavel Wranitzky (1756–1808), who was a student and friend of Haydn and probably knew Symphonies 45 and 60, wrote a "Sinfonia Quodlibet" (Prague, National Museum, Lobkowitz Archives), which not only ends with a "farewell" movement, but also opens with an "arrival" movement, each player entering one at a time on cue. In addition, the four string soloists begin the work by tuning up: the first violin enters and tunes his instrument (written out in open fifths) and is followed in rapid succession by the second violin, viola, and cello, who all begin by "tuning" their respective instruments as well (see Example 1)—a device straight out of "Il distratto". In a superb display of wit Wranitzky integrates the four players' tuning up (in turn) into the actual opening of the movement—a structural, delightful, and even beautiful musical device.

Example 1. Wranitzky, "Sinfonia Quodlibet," Opening (c. 1798)[18]

["ANKUNFT"]

---

[16] Cf. Rosen, *Style,* 78–79, 95–98, 116–18.
[17] For example, Busoni, "Beethoven"; Feder, "Stilelemente."
[18] LaRue, "Hail," 257.

Of course, Mozart created a similar effect at the end of the first act of *Don Giovanni;* perhaps "Il distratto" had been a model or inspiration for this as well. In any case, it can safely be argued that Haydn's innovation and originality in the sphere of wit, comedy, and humor must have provided the basic impetus by setting the mood and "tone" for this important aspect of Classical style.

Alessandro Scarlatti: A Predecessor of Joseph Haydn in the Genre of the String Quartet

RUDOLF PEČMAN

Up to now the prehistory of the string quartet still has not been sufficiently elucidated. Naturally even Joseph Haydn, the true founder of the genre, did not create it at a single stroke as we find it in his later works. His first ten quartets (Op. 1, Nos. 1–4 and 6; Op. 2, Nos. 1, 2, 4, 6; Hob. II:6), intended for performance at Baron Fürnberg's country home in Weinzierl (before 1759), were in five movements, including two minuets in second and fourth position, in the manner of the Austrian and Bohemian traditions of cassation and divertimento which reach back to before 1750. Moreover, the publisher Breitkopf had advertised these works in 1765 under the alternative titles of "Quadri" and "Cassationes." However much the details of the composition and the form of these first quartets may anticipate later Haydn works,[1] there exists nonetheless an unmistakable relationship with the predecessors of this genre, such as the three-section *canzone* for two violins, viola, and cello by Gregorio Allegri (1582–1652),[2] the four-part pieces by Austrian composers of the seventeenth century,[3] the Italian trio sonata, and the so-called "Orchester-Trios," including those of Jan Václav Stamic (Stamitz, 1717–57) composed around 1755.

When we look into the genesis of four-part quartet writing, we are struck by the fact that it by no means originated by simply adding a fourth part; that is, not by the introduction of an independent viola part into the structure of the trio sonata or other genres in which the thoroughbass principle predominates. On the contrary, quartet writing could only be created on the precondition that thoroughbass was suppressed in favor of Classical compositional procedures; and it could fully develop only by coupling the idea of contrast with that of thematic dualism. Interestingly, quartet forms by other European composers originated at about the same time, or only a little bit later than Haydn's. We see this most clearly in the case of Luigi Boccherini (1743–1805) and a few Parisian composers.[4] This is doubtless one of the clearest indications

---

[1] Georgiades, "Sprache," 92.   [2] Hull, "Quartet"
[3] Geiringer, *Haydn*₃, 173–200.   [4] "Streichquartett," 911.

that the string quartet evolved in response to objective historical tendencies. In any case, Haydn deserves the credit for having elevated the new genre to the pinnacle of art.

Fausto Torrefranca has already indicated that from the end of the seventeenth century names such as "Concertino a quattro," "Concerto," "Sinfonia," or "Quadro" were often attached to four-part concertante compositions for string instruments, and that these could be played solistically or orchestrally.[5] Frequently the obbligato viola was entrusted with thematically important and characteristic materials in the four-part texture. All these works, which, however, were not yet called string quartets, represent an important chapter in the developmental period preceding Haydn's quartets. They have one thing in common: their inner and lower parts, long treated as subordinate, gradually begin to strive towards equality. To be sure, a chamber-music style of quartet composition had not yet crystallized, because these works could not entirely free themselves from an orchestral style; but it is characteristic that solistic elements relating back to the concerto grosso became prominent.[6] The string quartet in pure chamber style could not be born until the stylistic change around the middle of the eighteenth century,[7] although tendencies towards simplicity of expression in the pre-Classical manner were to be found fifty years earlier in Corelli.[8] Haydn, especially in the slow movements of his symphonies, began to intensify the solistic character of many instrumental parts, but always maintaining their function as obbligato components of the orchestral structure.

The sonatas of Alessandro Scarlatti (1660–1725) represent a most interesting transitional stage on the path to the string quartet. Scarlatti's role in the evolution of instrumental music has apparently not yet been fully evaluated, but it was he who, even in the period before Haydn's string quartets, foresaw the potential in that form of instrumental composition in which the continuo was replaced by freely developing melodic parts. For example, even in his orchestral symphonies (which served as operatic overtures) Scarlatti let the melodic parts play an essential role. But his *sonate à quattro* engaged directly in the development of the "proto-quartet."[9] Allessandro Scarlatti's *Quattro Sonate à quattro* were published in London around 1740 along with Scarlatti's *VI Concertos in Seven Parts.* The title page reads as follows:

[5] Torrefranca, "Avviamento."
[6] See, for example, the four-voice concertos of Giuseppe Torelli from the years 1687–98, Albinoni's *Sinfonie à 4,* as well as works by Galuppi, Pergolesi, Sammartini, Giardini, Tartini, and the quartet-symphonies of Zach and Holzbauer, compositions by Monn, Filz, Starzer, etc.
[7] Larsen, "Stilwandel"   [8] Pečman, "Rokoko"
[9] See the excellent recent monograph Pagano-Bianchi; concerning the *Sonata à Quattro,* see 534.

> Publish'd by His Majesty's[10] Royal License,
> London,
> Printed for & Sold by
> BENJ:N COOKE
> at the Golden Harp in Newstreet Cov/t Garden.

These *Quattro Sonate*[11] by Scarlatti are scored for two violins, a "violetta," and a violocello.[12] The harpsichord, the indispensible element for basso continuo, is lacking. The "violetta" is the notable feature in the instrumentation. It seems to imply not the viola or the already-outmoded viola da braccio, but Scarlatti's intention of allowing the middle part to be performed by any appropriate instrument in the viola range.[13] Unfortunately, the date of composition of the four sonatas cannot be determined exactly, but the fact that they were printed some fifteen years after Scarlatti's death indicates their unusual popularity. Assuming that they were composed around 1700 or in the first two decades of the eighteenth century, it is clear that in these pieces we have a bold anticipation of compositional procedures that became normal only in the 1740s or around mid-century. The term "violetta" indicates that in Scarlatti's day—and even later[14]—the employment of the instruments in general was by no means unequivocally settled. Besides, Italian musicians of the eighteenth century appear not to have understood the proper function of the viola, which was clear in Germany from the 1680s on.[15]

In what sense, then, are Scarlatti's *Quattro Sonate à quattro* forerunners of Haydn's string quartets?

In the first place, the anticipation of the principle of Haydn's quartets is to be seen in the omission of the harpsichord. Scarlatti could make do with real musical parts from which he spun his harmonic and melodic fabric. Naturally it is possible that the omission of the harpsichord was dictated by practical considerations; instrumental music for small ensembles was often performed even in situations where a harpsichord was not always available. In any case, a musical texture without harpsichord was usually satisfying only if there was real three-part writing, to which the

---

[10] George II (1683–1760).

[11] This is a kind of concerted composition for which the term "sonata" is not really suitable—yet another demonstration of how imprecisely instrumental works were titled in the eighteenth century.

[12] The complete score is found in Münster, Bibliothek des Bischöflichen Priesterseminars and in the Santini Collection. It comprises Sonatas No. I (F minor), II (C minor), III (G minor), IV (D minor. An incomplete set is to be found in Dresden in the Sächsiche Landesbibliothek, and the British Library owns a fragment.

[13] In fact, "violetta" seems usually to have designated the viola in English prints of this period. [Ed.]

[14] The name "violetta" appears in Italian music as late as the 1770s.

[15] See Speer, *Unterricht;* Sachs, *Handbuch,* 200.

fourth voice—say, the viola—was added. At first it was not independent, but written in unison with the bass part, something that still often happens even in Haydn's early quartets. The viola's road to freedom and equality was a long one, and it was not Haydn who opened the gates, but Alessandro Scarlatti. His four sonatas differ from those of Haydn, however, in that they were composed in the manner of a concerto grosso. He did not succeed in bridging the gap between soli and tutti. In an age when antiphonal performance by instrumental groups and the "combative" nature of compositions were important elements of expression and form, this could never have happened. Haydn already works on a completely different basis; he employs the principle of thematic dualism, which only began to appear modestly in Scarlatti's time. We know that even Haydn had to struggle for a relatively long time to free himself of the baggage of orchestral style in the quartet. Scarlatti's instrumental music—including his *Quattro Sonate à quattro*—do not yet reflect the difference between orchestral and chamber style. Moreover, Haydn only really perfected his pure quartet style when he consistently reserved the quality of all four instruments and turned away from the tendency to favor the first violin at the expense of the remaining instruments. So this master took an unusually advanced position for his time.

It is regrettable that Haydn achieved little fame with his string quartets in that Italian milieu from which his great forerunner Alessandro Scarlatti came. "The string quartets of Haydn . . . remained as good as unknown in Italy and in any case had no influence."[16]

Stylistic Influence in the Early Haydn Piano Trios

MARIE ROLF

Research regarding the early piano trios of Joseph Haydn has been restricted until recent years by the lack of any published complete edition. These early trios are now available in JHW XVII:1 and in an edition by H. C. Robbins Landon.[1] However, many research problems involving authenticity and chronology still confront the Haydn scholar today.

Georg Feder has investigated possible solutions to questions of authenticity and chronology of these works.[2] His conclusions concerning authenticity are based on early editions, manuscript copies, EK and HV, and publishers' catalogues;[3] his criteria for establishing a chronology include investigation of various notational idiosyncrasies in the manu-

[16] Finscher, "Italienische," 25.
[1] See R. Landon, *Trios*   [2] Feder, "Klaviertrios"
[3] Most of the early piano trios are conspicuously absent from EK and HV. Perhaps Haydn did not consider them "important" enough to be included; perhaps those composed after 1761 were intended for another private party, and he did not want Esterházy to know of their existence.

scripts, copyists' handwriting, the keyboard ranges of the works, appearances of works in the Breitkopf catalogues and so on. These results are summarized in Table 1. Specific stylistic features of the music itself are treated only in a general manner. The chief intention of this paper is not to attempt a new chronology of Haydn's piano trios based on style, but to provide a more thorough examination of style and compositional procedure than has previously appeared.

Table 1   *Haydn's Early Piano Trios*

Date	*Work*	*JHW XVII:1*	*Landon*	*Keys of Movements*
—1760	Hob. XV:36	No. 1	No. 12	E♭–c–E♭
	Hob. XV:C1	No. 2	No. 2	C–C–C
	Hob. XV:37	No. 3	No. 1	F–F–F
	Hob. XV:38	No. 4	No. 13	B♭–B♭–B♭
	Hob. XV:34	No. 5	No. 11	E–E–E
	Hob. XV:f1	No. 6	No. 14	f–f–f
	Hob. XV:41	No. 7	No. 7	G–G–C–G
	[Hob. XV:33	Anhang 1	No. 8	D–D–G–D–D–D]
c. 1760	Hob. XV:40	No. 8	No. 6	F–F–F
c. 1760–62	Hob. XV:1	No. 9	No. 5	g–g–g
c. 1764–65	Hob. XV:35	No. 10	No. 10	A–A–A
c. 1767–71	Hob. XV:2	No. 11	No. 17	F–F–F
[—1771	Hob. XV:D1	Anhang 2	No. 9	D–D–D]

Haydn was exposed to many different musical styles in his early compositional development, from ecclesiastical influences at St. Stephen's in Vienna to his private studies of Fux, Mattheson, and Kellner and his work with the Italian composer Porpora. These influences stem from both the immediate and the more distant past; they include features of both the more progressive Classical innovations and the older Baroque style. In addition, some of Haydn's unique qualities as a composer are already revealed even during this early period of his development. Later in his life, Haydn himself alluded to these qualities in his remark on his situation at the Esterházy court, "I was cut off from the world, there was no one around to mislead and harass me, and so I was forced to become original."[4] In Haydn's piano trios, Baroque, early Classical, and Haydn's own compositional features are juxtaposed, overlapped, and intertwined. In this study, however, it will sometimes be necessary to sacrifice the clarity of the overall stylistic picture in order to focus on individual influences.

Some of the Baroque idioms found in Haydn's early piano trios stem from the older forms of trio sonata, suite, concerto, and aria with accompaniment. Many of Haydn's compositional procedures of Baroque an-

---

[4] From Griesinger, 24–25 (modern ed., 17; Gotwals, *Haydn,* 17); quoted in translation from Grout, *History,* 2nd ed., 478.

cestry are manifested in key schemes among movements, monothematic principles, contrapuntal devices, variation procedures, and the "motor" rhythms characteristic of the mid-eighteenth century. Early Classical influences are found in the period structure, the tonal plan within a movement, new approaches to ornamentation, and texture. This presentation will concentrate on the Baroque elements in Haydn's early trios, since Classical features are generally expected in this period and have been discussed at length elsewhere.

In the Baroque trio sonata, the cembalo and cello realize the thorough bass while the upper parts incorporate parallel and similar motion or contrapuntal interplay. Similarly, in Haydn's early piano trios the cello doubles the lowest line of the cembalo part, in effect providing a continuo. The right hand of the cembalo functions like the second upper voice of a trio sonata, imitating the violin or doubling it in thirds or sixths. This texture is evident in the first movement of Hob. XV:37 in F major (Example 1). The figured bass in mm. 5 and 6, like the figured and unfigured basses elsewhere in the early piano trios, have Baroque ancestry. The evenly pulsating eighth notes of the bass line are also Baroque in nature. The four-bar phrases are typical of the Classical era; Haydn, however, overlaps these four-bar phrases, creating an irregular phrase structure of seven measures. The recapitulation of this movement is characteristic of

Example 1. Piano Trio Hob. XV:37 in F major, i, 1–8

Haydn in that the thematic material is not presented in the same manner as in its exposition; the first three measures are a drastically truncated version of the first thematic group, which proceeds immediately into the secondary thematic material. This movement concludes with certain devices that originated in the Baroque concerto grosso and were expanded and became standardized in the Classical solo concerto form (Example 2): the concerted idea between the violin and the cembalo in mm. 61–64, the quasi-orchestral "tutti" unison effect, and the fermata indication for a cadenza.

Example 2. Piano Trio Hob. XV:37 in F major, i, 61–68

Each of the three movements of this trio are in F major—a key scheme that follows that of the Baroque suite. Of the extant early trios, all but Hob. XV:36 in E-flat major and XV:41 in C major likewise place all three movements in the tonic. Haydn actually incorporates Baroque binary suite forms in Hob. XV:36 with its "Polones," and in the lost Hob. XV:33 with its six-movement structure.

The third movement of the only four-movement early piano trio, Hob. XV:41 in G major, is similar to Example 1. The movement is in a rounded binary form, where the A section returns at the end of the second reprise, cadencing in the tonic. The pulsating eighth-note bass line in a slow tempo and the highly embellished melody once again suggest an aria with accompaniment. The chord progression at the beginning of this movement establishes the tonality with I–ii$_2^4$–V$_6$–I. This harmonic cliche is heard over and over again in music of the Baroque; an excellent example is found in Bach's *Well-Tempered Clavier,* Prelude No. 1, Vol. I.

The opening movement of Hob. XV:35 in A major features pedal points, "motor" rhythm, and *Fortspinnung* techniques, resulting in a single basic affection. In the process of this continuous growth, the melody is passed between the violin and cembalo parts in Baroque dialogue fashion. In contrast to the first movement, the Menuet and Trio reflects a more Classical approach. (Haydn generally employs a more progressive style in the Menuet and Trio movements. The thinner two-part texture in which the cembalo merely doubles the violin part, the simpler harmonies, and the abundance of ornaments in these movements were becoming more fashionable.[5] In this case Haydn contrasts the phrase structures; the Menuet has regular four-bar phrases, while the Trio displays a more sophisticated grouping: ‖:4 + 6 :‖: 6 + 6 + 6:‖ —the six-measure groups being achieved by inner repetition of two measures. The Finale of the A-major Piano Trio (Example 3) begins with a canon between the cembalo and violin, a rather unusual contrapuntal device for the early Classical period, though perhaps not for Haydn. These two instruments spin out the material in dialogue sequence so that the first cadence is delayed until m. 10, again resulting in an irregular phrase pattern.

Example 3. Piano Trio Hob. XV:35 in A major, iii, 1–7

The first movement of Hob. XV:2 in F major contains a number of indications that Haydn has assimilated both older and more progressive elements into a personal style (Example 4). Here the irregular phrase groupings of 7 + 7 are attained through a rhythmic contraction of the last two measures. The repetition of the melody in m. 8 is transferred to the cembalo and is noticeably ornamented. This variation process is found throughout the early piano trios; other techniques for variation include a

[5] The Menuet and Trio form appears as a middle movement in the great majority of the early piano trios, and occasionally as the final movement.

change of register, mode, and/or texture.[6] This variation process has its roots in the Baroque forms such as *doubles* and the chorale prelude, and it culminates in the later Classical works of composers like Beethoven. The first movement of Hob. XV:2 is a sonata form in which the second thematic group is derived from the first; this is foreshadowed in the transition section, which begins at m. 15 (see Example 5). The textural shift into triplets at this point is a typical "Haydnism." At the same time, the Alberti bass texture of the Classical era is assimilated into Haydn's style.

Example 4. Piano Trio Hob. XV:2 in F major, i., 1–7

Example 5. Piano Trio Hob. XV:2 in F major, i, 15–18

This study of style in the early piano trios supports the remark of H. C. Robbins Landon that "Haydn's mentality . . . was by instinct baroque, by conviction classical."[7] Further study of stylistic elements in the early trios should include a comparison between the piano trios and other genres, such as divertimenti in Hoboken's Group XIV, the baryton trios, and the piano sonatas; an attempt should be made to discern general trends (for instance, the relative density of Baroque, Classical, and Haydn's own compositional procedures). These trends must be evaluated together with the results of nonstylistic research before an accurate chronology of the early piano trios can be established.

[6] The variation as a *form* occurs only in Hob. XV:C1, iii and XV:2, iii.
[7] R. Landon, *Symphonies,* 82.

Form and Analysis

The Submediant in Haydn's Development Sections

HAROLD L. ANDREWS

The basic organizing force of tonal harmony in eighteenth-century "sonata form" has often been stressed in recent years. However, discussions of tonal procedures in the development section of a sonata movement are usually limited to general statements about instability and rapid modulations. This paper is an effort to contribute specific information which will help clarify the logic of tonal organization in that part of the movement which may be most complex and evasive.

The composer who contributed most to the maturation of the Classic development section was Joseph Haydn. In order to define Haydn's approach at all stages of his career, I have analyzed the first quick movements (in all but a few it is the first movement) of his symphonies, string quartets, keyboard trios, and solo keyboard sonatas.[1] Of 279 movements, 248 may be considered to be in sonata form. This paper deals with the development sections of the 219 of these movements which are in the major mode.

The ultimate tonal function of the development section is to return from the second main key of the exposition to the tonic key for the recapitulation. In Haydn's major-mode movements this second key is the dominant, and the simplest way to return is to extend the harmony of the last cadence of the exposition directly into the tonic without intervening cadences. This procedure, common to any number of smaller binary forms of the eighteenth century, is found in a few early Haydn movements. In the usual development section, however, intermediate modulations interrupt and delay the return to the tonic, thus enlarging the tonal framework and increasing the tension before the recapitulation.

While there is no one consistent scheme, the great majority of Haydn's major-mode movements modulate into the submediant and cadence in that key at some point before the final approach to the tonic begins. This emphasis on the relative minor, which compensates somewhat for the overwhelming predominance of the major mode in the rest of the movement, is found in both early and late movements, in both simple and complex ones. In fact, of the 219 development sections of this study, only forty-three—one fifth—fail to have an important part, including at

[1] A grant from the University of North Carolina Research Council made possible the assistance of Jeannine Ingram and Jane Pierce with the preliminary analysis.

465

least one significant cadence, in the submediant key.[2] The basic tonal movement of dominant to submediant to tonic half-cadence is often elaborated, perhaps disguised by additional tonal maneuvers, including transient modulations or even subsections in other intermediate keys. When several keys are given internal emphasis, the decision as to which is the most important can be at times subjective and difficult to make. However, ruling out all questionable cases, there still remains a clear majority which emphasize the submediant.

The particular route of approach to the submediant as well as the eventual return to the tonic may be comparatively direct and simple, or it may be marked by evasions and puzzling turns before its final logic becomes evident. It may rather prosaically follow its course, or it may exhibit the composer's greatest skill and imagination.

Before 1766 Haydn's development sections typically begin with a continuation of the dominant key, and with a statement in that key of the thematic material which began the movement. About half of them remain in the dominant long enough to cadence in that key. A good example is found in Symphony No. 6 in D major ("Le matin"). The statement of the principal theme in the dominant ends with an authentic cadence, and is followed by a section of soft, chromatic sequences which lead via an augmented-sixth chord to the dominant of the submediant and the subsequent full orchestral confirmation of that key. Then a short circle-of-fifths passage moves into the tonic and preparation for the recapitulation.

About as frequent in the earlier works is the procedure of Symphony No. 9 in C major. Here the development begins in the dominant, but moves to the submediant before cadencing.

The internal emphasis on the submediant was described in 1787 by Heinrich Christoph Koch. According to Koch a typical development section in a major-mode movement begins with brief passages in the dominant and the tonic before modulating into the submediant. It may then remain in this key until recapitulation; or it may continue, after a cadence, with a transition to the tonic, this transition often being made by way of several intermediate modulations.[3]

Koch's mention of brief passages in the tonic leads us to a small but significant group of Haydn development sections from around 1760, most of them in symphonic first movements, for example that of Symphony No. 19 in D major. In these, the statement of opening material in the dominant is followed immediately by a more or less complete statement in the tonic before further tonal maneuvers lead to the submediant.

---

[2] As stated above, a few of these are direct transitions. The others seem to turn elsewhere, mostly to the supertonic or the mediant, for the main intermediate key.
[3] Koch, *Versuch,* II, 224.

H. C. Robbins Landon has suggested a relationship between these opening thematic statements on dominant and tonic and the later Haydn false recapitulation.[4] In Symphony No. 41 in C major the development begins with a 17-measure transition to the tonic and what appears to be the recapitulation. But after two pauses the whole development procedure begins again and cadences strongly in the submediant before returning to the tonic for the real recapitulation.

A major challenge for Haydn in the 1760s and 1770s was to work out ways of expanding his material and his tonal design to sustain the broader scale of longer movements. The false recapitulation is one rather dramatic means for expanding the development section. Any logically added subsection, as for example a modulation through an intermediate key, serves the same purpose. On a smaller scale are many devices, including varied repetition of phrases, cadence prolongations and evasions, pedals, addition of units in the opposite mode, and in particular many kinds of sequences, including circle-of-fifths progressions such as those in Symphony No. 41. Many of these devices appear in the keyboard Sonata Hob. XVI:23 (ChL. 38) in F major, in which the underlying structure and tonal procedure are the same as in Symphony No. 6.

This sonata is perhaps a little too predictable with its many sequences and lack of tonal surprises. Haydn's growing ability to expand the tonal scheme by intermediate maneuvers through other keys can be seen as early as the Symphony No. 31 in D major. Its development section modulates very soon into the submediant. But after the half-cadence, rather than continue in the submediant, it moves deceptively into the subdominant, restates its material sequentially on the dominant, and even hints at the supertonic before returning at the cadence point to the submediant.

In the String Quartet Op. 9, No. 2 in E-flat major the expansion is the kind suggested by Koch; that is, the transition from the submediant to the tonic is made by way of intermediate keys, with emphasis given, in this case, to the mediant. This development section is also one of the earliest to begin immediately in the submediant, without any continuing reference to the dominant key. In fact, it begins on the dominant of the submediant, emphasizing a tertial harmonic contrast which Haydn employed fairly often in the early 1770s.[5]

Haydn continued to experiment with other ways of opening the development section. In the Quartet Op. 20, No. 6 in A major he begins with dominant harmony of the supertonic key. In just a few measures the

[4] "By lengthening the time between V and I and by omitting the announcement of the principal subject in V, Haydn is able to create the erroneous impression that the recapitulation is at hand." R. Landon, *Symphonies*, 320.

[5] See, for example, the beginning of the development in Symphonies Nos. 54, 55, 56, and 57, all written in 1774.

music is poised *sotto voce* on an augmented sixth chord in that key. But the harmony resolves deceptively, and the bass line leads up gradually through thirteen measures of chromatic harmonies into the submediant, which is then diatonically confirmed for most of the rest of the section. This fine control of the means of modulation is but another bit of evidence for the accomplishment of this set of quartets.

In the Quartet Op. 33, No. 5 in G major Haydn both delays the approach to the submediant and also later moves into another key and back before the transition to the tonic. As in three other major-mode quartets of this outstanding opus, the movement from the end of the exposition into the first part of the development involves the progression dominant to tonic to subdominant. In No. 5 the end of the exposition already prepares for the tonic beginning of the development, but we are surprised when it is the tonic minor. That surprise assures us that this is development, not repetition of the exposition, and the major mode returns for the second phrase. It is the latter which is extended into the subdominant. The next cadence is a submediant half-cadence. An expansion into the supertonic is eased back into the submediant by a descending bass line.

In the second half of the 1780s, beginning with the Paris symphonies and the Quartets Op. 50, Haydn wrote some of his most ingenious and sophisticated development sections. They include a great variety of internal tonal maneuvers, which show his most imaginative manner of organization and at the same time provide an important means of expanding the scope and the intensity of this part of the movement. This expansion of scale, this ability to sustain tonal arches over longer periods of musical time, is a vital aspect of the development of the mature Classic style.

Let us consider first the development of Symphony No. 85 in B-flat major. It begins with dominant harmony of the submediant, but, after a rest, continues "deceptively" in the subdominant key and moves further toward the flat side to a half-cadence in the subtonic ($\flat$ VII). The next part of the development section continues in this key, the relative of the minor dominant, and then passes through the supertonic before finally reaching the submediant. However once the submediant is confirmed, it is strongly emphasized by an extended half-cadence. This harmony, dominant of the submediant (with which this development section both begins and ends), leads then directly into the tonic of the recapitulation.

This possibility of moving directly from submediant into recapitulation, which was also mentioned by Koch, is used only rarely in early Haydn, but it occurs rather frequently in works from around 1790.[6] In other first movements from this period, for example in the Quartet Op.

---

[6] For example, the String Quartets Op. 54, No. 3 in E major and Op. 64, No. 6 in E-flat major, Symphony No. 90 in C major, and the *Sinfonia Concertante* (Hob. I:105). For further discussion of unusual harmonic approaches to the recapitulation, see Schwarting, "Reprise."

55, No. 1 in A major, the preparation of the tonic may be no more than a single chord. In most of these movements Haydn avoids the submediant in the earlier parts of the development, so that it becomes in a way the goal of the section, reached just before recapitulation.

Symphony No. 85 has given us an example of a development section opening toward the submediant, but expanding in other directions before confirming it. Expansion can take place, of course, at any point. In the Quartet Op. 50, No. 2 in C major the main expansion takes place in forty-five measures of shifting harmonies between the dominant opening and a submediant half-cadence. After the cadence is emphasized by an eight-measure extension, the return to tonic recapitulation, however, takes only seventeen measures.

In the Piano Sonata Hob. XVI;49 (ChL. 59) in E-flat major the proportions are almost reversed. A submediant half-cadence is reached in sixteen measures, and the greatest expansion falls between this point and the recapitulation fifty-one measures later. From the submediant a series of sequences by descending thirds takes us slowly into the supertonic and an intermediate half-cadence in that key. Then a move into the minor dominant provides a brief opening into more remote keys before we are led back to the tonic for recapitulation.

In the late 1780s Haydn began to use "bimodal" tonal schemes much more extensively.[7] (The minor dominant key had appeared in major-mode movements throughout Haydn's career, and occasionally, as in the previous example, it leads to brief passages in other keys which "belong" to the minor mode.) The bimodal orientation is extensive, for example, in Op. 55, No. 1. The development begins as though in the minor tonic but cadences first on the dominant of the minor dominant. Then a sudden "deceptive" progression leads into the major key on the lowered mediant, in other words the relative of the minor tonic, for a kind of "false recapitulation in the wrong key"[8] before a series of ascending sequences leads finally to the usual submediant, which is well established before the quick turn into recapitulation mentioned above.

In the Quartet Op. 71, No. 3 in E-flat major Haydn goes a step further in the use of more remote keys. The first part of the development section consists of sequential statements in minor keys related by descending major thirds. The first statement is in the tonic minor, so the second follows in the lowered submediant minor.[9] The third key, another major third lower, is the mediant G minor, which soon leads (with a faster pace

---

[7] So that, in terms of C major, for example, related keys include not only A minor, G major, and E minor, F major, and D minor, but also C minor and E-flat major, G minor and B-flat major, F minor and A-flat major, and perhaps also the Neapolitan D-flat major. See Cuyler, "Tonal," 138.

[8] This might also be called a ritornello. See Tutenberg, "Durchführungsfrage," 90–94.

[9] Written enharmonically as B minor rather than C-flat minor. For explanation of the way Haydn handles the problems of intonation in this passage, see Somfai, "Model," 373–74.

of thematic treatment) into the submediant. Having thus chromatically stretched out the approach to the submediant, Haydn is, however, still not ready to turn toward the tonic; instead he first descends a major third again and in the subdominant gives us another "false recapitulation in the wrong key," before returning via sequences to submediant emphasis, and at the last moment quietly preparing the tonic.

Sometimes the use of the opposite mode of a related key depends more simply upon the nature of the thematic material. So, for example, in the Piano Trio Hob. XV:28 in E major, after the opening submediant key yields to a half-cadence in the mediant, it is the mediant-made-major (written enharmonically) in which the main theme of the movement is heard briefly before the submediant returns.

Bimodality also offers Haydn the option of using the submediant of the minor mode; in other words, the major key on the lowered sixth degree of the major scale. In a few works of the 1790s he includes both major-mode and minor-mode submediants in the same development section. In the sonata, Hob. XVI:50 (ChL. 60) in C major, for example, the main internal cadence is an extended half-cadence in A-flat major. After a pause, the harmony gradually shifts to the dominant of A minor (accompanied by a dynamic and rhythmic crescendo) and then proceeds in more usual fashion.

Tonal organization does not, of course, exist independently of the other elements of the composition. In fact, one of the beauties of the Classic style often mentioned is the interrelationship and coordination of changes among elements. Nor is the organization of the development section independent of the rest of the movement. There is no space here for more than an occasional short reference to other aspects of the music, but each example obviously needs to be considered in context.

Not all of Haydn's mature first movements include expanded tonal schemes in the manner of the last examples. The tonal organization of the Quartet Op. 76, No. 4 in B-flat major, for example, is simple and straightforward. It is also clearly coordinated with the treatment of thematic material and the patterns of contrasting textures and dynamics. The first part of the development section softly presents a variant of the movement's gentle opening theme over mediant harmony, which leads to the submediant in the next part. This slightly longer second part, based thematically on the vigorous principal contrasting thematic material of the movement, remains essentially in the submediant. A third part, developing what might be called the closing theme of the exposition, modulates smoothly, *decrescendo,* to the tonic for a quiet recapitulation. The division of the whole section into three parts, each marked by different thematic material, clearly supports the three phases of the tonal scheme: first, movement away from the dominant toward the submediant; second, extension and emphasis of the submediant; and, finally, modulation toward the tonic, which, evaded for a while, is reached at the point of recapitulation.

These few examples provide only a glimpse into the variety of Haydn's procedures. Each development section is unique. Yet, whether simple or complex in its particular details, it is likely to be organized around a basic scheme which depends upon the evasive movement of dominant to submediant in expanding the scope and increasing the tension of this part of the sonata movement.

Modulation in Haydn's Late Piano Trios in the Light of Schoenberg's Theories

ROGER E. CHAPMAN

The piano trios of Joseph Haydn, especially those written in the 1790s, reveal an extensive use of changes of key signature. The changes are partly found in movements where major and minor modes are juxtaposed. But they are also found in sonata and rondo movements where exceptional modulations occur.

A few years ago László Somfai described how in several of his string quartets Haydn anticipated the type of modulations introduced on the well-tempered piano by Schubert and Chopin. "In these modulations Haydn does not employ chords allowing enharmonic interpretations; in the course of the modulations there only occur diatonic or obvious chromatic progressions, and the tonal connection between the succeeding keys is clearly noticeable."[1]

The success of these modulations leads us then to ask: if Haydn succeeds so in his harmonic experiments within the confines of the "pure" string quartet texture, how expansive do his ideas for modulatory development become in his writing that includes the well-tempered piano? The piano trios of the 1790s give us evidence that his harmonic experimentation continues and that the modulatory expansion into wider key areas anticipates habits common in the music of the Romantic era.

To develop a perspective of the expanded key areas used in the trios it is helpful to review them in terms of the concept of monotonality put forward by Arnold Schoenberg.[2] Schoenberg's concept of monotonality considers that there is only one tonality in a piece. What might be called other tonalities he called "regions," that is, "harmonic contrasts within [the] tonality."[3] Within a tonality Schoenberg classified five different regions: 1) Direct and Close; 2) Indirect but Close; 3) Indirect; 4) Indirect and Remote; 5) Distant. These five regions he explained in a chart, showing the tonics in the related regions. The tonics of the regions in C major

[1] Somfai, "Model," 370.

[2] Schoenberg, *Structural* (an outgrowth of Schoenberg, *Harmonielehre*).

[3] Schoenberg, *Structural*, 57.

are presented in Example 1. Capital letters represent tonics of the major mode; lower-case letters, minor mode tonics. To the left or right of any major mode tonic are its minors, related and parallel, respectively. Within the area enclosed by the broken line are Regions 1, 2, and 3. Region 1, Direct, comprises keys that have many chords in common with the tonic; Regions 2 and 3 include third-related mediant and submediant chords that can interchange major and minor modes by secondary dominants.

Example 1. Schoenberg's System of Key Relationships

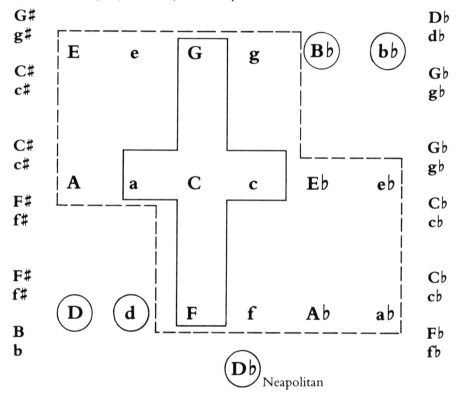

The remaining Regions 4, Indirect and Remote (circled), and 5, Distant (those remaining), customarily appear in development sections of nineteenth-century sonata-allegro movements. Their appearance earlier is rare, but Mozart's Piano Trio K. 442 in D minor moves easily in its first movement to C minor (Region 4). In Beethoven's piano trios, movement into remote and distant regions becomes more frequent. The movements from Haydn's piano trios making use of Regions 4 and 5 are, generally, in sonata form or a variation-rondo form; it is in these movements that extensive changes of key signature appear.

The modulations of Classes 1, 2, and 3 involve common chords and secondary dominants that strengthen the modulatory direction. In Region 4, which has fewer chords in common with the central tonic, altered chords produce seemingly sudden changes of key. Common triads occur in the second inversion to weaken the forward movement of the harmony; dominant seventh chords in various inversions appear. The augmented sixth chord and the dominant seventh chord are often interchanged, surprising the listener as the progression moves in unexpected directions. Example 2 shows a succession of dominant sevenths, in which (at the asterisk) B flat fails to move downward as expected but instead rises (as if it were A sharp in an augmented sixth chord) and leads to an unexpected E-minor chord. The harmonies of these remote regions are loosened by occasional altering of a chord tone. And at times the chords rock back and forth until the harmony, having lost its previous orientation, leaps forward into a fresh region.

Example 2. Piano Trio Hob. XV: 26 in F-sharp minor, i, 47–49

A trio that introduces enharmonic changes within a movement—that is, changes key signature and penetrates to Region 3 or 4—also tends to use Indirect but Close relations between the keys of its several movements. In Hob. XV:14 in A-flat major, the middle movement is in the flat submediant, notated as E major rather than as F-flat. In the first movement, a modulation leads away from A flat and back via the key signature of B major rather than C flat. In Hob. XV:22 in E-flat major, the middle movement is in the unusual mediant major, G major. In the sonata-form finale, the signature changes from three flats to three sharps and back. Thus enharmonic freedom appears both between the movements and within a single movement. Schoenberg points out such contrasts in Beethoven's Trio Op. 97 in B-flat major (third movement in D major), Schumann's Symphony No. 3 in E-flat major (second movement in C major), and Schubert's String Quintet (first movement, second theme, in E-flat major).[4]

[4]Ibid., 57.

Another aspect of enharmonic modulations involves the relationship between the well-tempered piano and the two stringed instruments. This can lead to unusual freedom in enharmonic changes. In Example 3, the cello is renotated A flat to G sharp, that is, from the dominant of D-flat major to the leading tone of the following key, A major. The reinterpretation as a leading tone encourages the feeling of chord change. The cello's underlying continuity is important, for the violin must move by double stops through a violent enharmonic change. At the other extreme, in Hob. XV:14, i, 114, movement with the signature changing from four flats to five sharps, the piano proceeds as a solo in the new key for six measures, and the string instruments join after the new key has been established.

Example 3. Piano Trio Hob. XV:22 in E-flat major, iii, 63–68

In his later trios, Haydn was much attracted to the use of key signatures of three and four sharps and three and four flats. This meant that the more distant regions required notation of double flats and double sharps. For example, in A-flat major the flat submediant F flat (Indirect but Close) requires the note b♭ ♭; from E major, one must introduce an extensive number of double sharps.

When the key of the movement is in three or four flats, an enharmonic section will be notated in several sharps; when the key is in three or four sharps, the interpolated change of key will be expressed in a number of flats. This kind of enharmonic notation—which, of course, is not necessarily the same as a true enharmonic modulation—sharply reduces the number of double sharps and double flats which would otherwise be required. For example, the development of Hob. XV:28 in E major contains a key change to A-flat major, avoiding the introduction of G-sharp major while modulating to a key four steps higher in the circle of fifths. Other trio movements in sharp keys which move enharmonically to flat key signatures also move three or four steps higher in the circle of fifths (Hob. XV:26 in F-sharp minor, i; XV:29 in E-flat major, ii). On the other hand, movements in flat keys move down three or four steps in the circle of fifths (Hob. XV:14 in A-flat major, i; XV:31 in E-flat minor, ii).

In his piano trios Haydn thus explores key regions far afield, but he simplifies the notational signposts of his travels.

Sonata-Exposition Procedures in Haydn's Keyboard Sonatas

MICHELLE FILLION

This paper presents the results of an analytical study of the tonal organization of the sonata expositions in all the sonata-form first movements of Haydn's solo keyboard sonatas. The point of departure has been Jens Peter Larsen's discussion of two-part $\overline{[T-(D)}$, D] and three-part $\overline{[T}$; $\overline{T-(D)}$; $\overline{D]}$ exposition forms.[1] The aim has been to discover the extent to which each of these two types is in fact representative of these works and, in so doing, to identify the formal procedures in Haydn's keyboard sonata expositions.

Forty-six expositions have been considered, of which at least three are of very questionable authenticity: Hob. XVI:5 (ChL. 8) in A major and the two Raigern sonatas Hob. deest XVI:Es2 and Es3 (ChL. 17–18). One must also keep in mind the generally poor state of the sources of the sonatas composed before 1766. Of the sixteen early works under examination here, only Hob. XVI:3,4,6,14 (ChL. 14, 9, 13, 16) can be established as authentic on the grounds of an autograph or a citation in EK. One should therefore be wary of making unqualified style judgments on the basis of these unauthenticated works.[2]

Although tonal events constitute the basis of these observations, one cannot regard tonal organization in isolation from the other important and more or less related bases of formal articulation: phrase and period structure, harmonic rhythm, thematic material, and figurational style.

---

[1] Larsen, "Sonatenform," 226–28.
[2] On the authenticity of the early keyboard sonatas, see Feder, "Klaviersonaten"; Haydn, *Sonatas,* I, xvi–xvii; Hatting, "Haydn"; see also the Round Table on the Raigern Sonatas elsewhere in this volume.

These factors have been taken into consideration in determining the following formal classifications:[3]

I. Clear examples of:
    A. Two-part exposition with modulating transition
        XVI:3 (before 1766); 18,45,46,44 (c. 1766–70); 23,25 (1773); 28,29,31,32 ("von Anno 1776"); 35,37 (pub. 1780) [ChL. 14; 20,29,31,32; 38,40; 43,44,46,47; 48,50]

        With main theme transposition (MTT)
        XVI:G1 (before 1766); 36 (pub. 1780); 34 (c. 1781–82?); 49 (1789–90); 51,52 (1794–95) [ChL. 4; 49; 53; 59; 61,62]

    AA. Two-part exposition, without transition
        XVI:8,Es3, 47 [E minor] (before 1766); 27 ("von Anno 1776") [ChL. 1,18,19; 42]

        With MTT
        XVI: 10, 1 (before 1766); 50 (1794–95). [ChL. 6,10; 60]

    B. Three-part exposition with expansion section
        XVI:9,4,2,12,13 (before 1766); 19 (1767); 20 (1771); 22 (1773) [ChL. 3,9,11,12,15; 30; 33; 37]

        With MTT
        XVI: 26 (1773) [ChL. 41]

II. Ambiguous works
    A. MTT without transition
        XVI: 33,43 (c. 1771–73?); 21,24 (1773); 38 (pub. 1780); 41 (pub. 1784) [ChL. 34,35; 36,39; 51; 55]

    B. Exceptions
        XVI:5,6,14,Es2 (before 1766); 30 ("von Anno 1776") [ChL. 8,13,16,17; 45]

The results of this examination show that the distinction of two basic exposition types, the two-part and the three-part, is valid for at least a large percentage of these movements. The essential difference between the two- and three-part expositions lies in the degree of importance placed on the modulation from tonic to secondary tonic. The two-part exposition may either make use of a relatively short modulating transition growing out of the first group (I.A), or it may dispense with transition altogether, juxtaposing first and second groups without tonal preparation (I.AA). The resulting bisectional form resembles the traditional textbook account of sonata form, defined, however, according to tonal rather than thematic criteria.

---

[3] Within each category, the sonatas have been arranged in approximate chronological order. Works for which no precise date of composition is available have been assigned the date of first publication, when publication is believed to have followed within a few years of composition. The remaining sonatas are dated according to C. Landon in Haydn, *Sonatas*.

The first main section of the two-part exposition is occupied by the first group, the area which presents one or more thematic units in the tonic, usually in a form of periodic phrase structure. If there is a modulating transition, it is short and subsidiary to the first group. The second main section of this exposition type stands firmly in the secondary tonic; it comprises a second group with or without a closing group, ending with cadential figuration. The second group is distinguished from the first not so much by its degree of thematic contrast as by its new tonality and structure. Sentence formations are particularly characteristic of the second group, especially in the sonatas from the later 1760s (Hob. XVI:18 [ChL.20]) to the early 1780s (Hob. XVI:34 [ChL. 53]). Although the "sentence" (*Satz*) is a formal concept of great importance in analysis of the music of the classical period, it has not yet received sufficient exposure in the English-language literature.[4] In its most regular form $\overline{(2 \times 2} + 4)$ the sentence consists of a two-measure phrase, its repetition, and a four-measure continuation. In the second groups of Haydn's two-part sonata expositions, this continuation is often expanded to some length; the second group of Hob. XVI:44 (ChL. 32) in G minor furnishes an excellent example of this expanded sentence structure $\overline{(2 \times 1} + 7)$:

Example 1. Sonata Hob. XVI:44 (ChL. 32) in G minor, i, 13–20

[4] For a description of this structure in Beethoven's piano sonatas, see Ratz, *Formenlehre,* 3rd ed., 21–24.

Here the sentence ends with a perfect authentic cadence, and is thus "closed"; "open" sentences ending with a half-cadence are also frequently found in the second groups.

The closing group is the second thematic unit in the secondary tonic area, and is set off from the second group proper by a perfect authentic cadence. Its closing effect is usually created by the balanced construction of a phrase followed immediately by its literal or varied repetition.

All of these characteristics may be found to a more or less regular degree in all the two-part expositions listed above under category I. Hob. XVI:23 (ChL. 38) in F major of 1773 may be regarded as a model of the two-part exposition with transition. This exposition is divided clearly into two sections roughly equal in length. The first group (mm. 1–12), a closed period, is followed by the transition in open sentence form (mm. 13–20). The second part of the exposition consists of a second group (mm. 21–39) constructed as a closed sentence with a long expansion, a regular closing group (mm. 39–44), and cadential figuration (mm. 44–46).

The three-part exposition, particularly characteristic of Haydn, has no counterpart in traditional theory. It revolves around a central "expansion section" (in Larsen's term, *Entwicklungspartie*), a dramatic area of directional tonal activity whose purpose is the establishment of the new secondary tonic. In its most representative examples (XVI:13,19,20,22,26 [ChL. 15,30,33,37,41]) the expansion section makes use of most or all of the following devices: long-range avoidance of strong root-position cadence and root-position tonic triads in the new tonality until the end of the expansion section; sequences; vast extension of phrase length; introduction of the dominant minor; long dominant prolongations; deceptive cadences; and fantasialike keyboard figuration. The expansion section is preceded by the first group and followed by the closing group, both of which display basically the same features as the corresponding parts in the two-part exposition. The expansion section of XVI:19 (ChL. 30) in D major of 1767 is one of the best examples of this structure, displaying all the above-mentioned features:

Example 2. Sonata Hob. XVI:19 (ChL. 30) in D major, i, 19–33

On a rather objective basis, therefore, thirty-five of the forty-six expositions may be assigned to either the two-part or three-part models. The remaining works pose problems of one kind or another. The works listed under category II.B present difficulties because of their lack of clear demarcation points between sections or other irregularities of form. Sonatas XVI:6 and 14 (ChL. 13,16) are particularly subtle examples in which the first few measures of the closing group function at the same time as the closing measures of the preceding section.

Apart from these ambiguous works, specific problems of interpretation arise in a group of sonatas displaying Haydn's common procedure which is popularly, and misleadingly, known as "monothematicism." In these works the secondary tonic area begins with a clearly recognizable transposed variation of the opening of the main theme. Since this quotation usually occupies only a small proportion of the secondary tonic area, and in no way results in "monothematicism" in the strict sense of the term,[5] the more neutral term "main theme transposition" (MTT) has been substituted here.

Sixteen keyboard sonata first movements, extending from the very earliest (XVI:G1 and 10 [ChL. 4, 6]) to the three late sonatas of the mid-1790s (XVI: 50–52 [ChL. 60–62]) display this procedure. The main theme transposition may be a mere recollection of the opening motive of the first group (as in XVI:33 and 41 [ChL. 34,55]), but more frequently it is a quite literal repetition of the opening of the first group, expanded to

---

[5] A. Peter Brown voices similar reservations in "Exposition," 108.

two or more measures in length (XVI:43, 36, 49 [ChL. 35,49,59]). With the exception of the early XVI:G1, all the sonatas using this device prior to XVI:36 (ChL. 49) in C-sharp minor from the Artaria set of 1780 and a few after this date have no modulating transition. In these ten works without transition, the first group is an open structure, ending with a half-cadence. The main theme transposition enters directly in the new to-nality without tonal preparation.

The sonatas with main theme transposition preceded by a modulating transition are uniformly two-part expositions (see group I.A). Among the works without transition (group I.AA), several are also unam-biguous because of the clear establishment of the new tonality by the MTT. Problems of interpretation arise, however, in the six works lack-ing transition (category II.A). Here the short MTT establishes the secon-dary tonic, but is followed immediately by an extension that shows to a greater or lesser extent the earmarks of an expansion section. In all six of these sonatas there remains a doubt whether the main theme transposi-tion has defined the new tonality emphatically enough to bear the strain of the tonal play that follows. Accordingly, these six works cannot be as-signed to a precise formal category without doing an injustice to their ambiguity.

From the preceding one may draw the following conclusions:

1. On the basis of the analytical method sketched at the beginning of the paper, thirty-five of the forty-six expositions may be regarded as ex-amples of either two-part or three-part form. Of these, two-part exposi-tions outnumber three-part twenty-six to nine.

2. Before 1766 Haydn showed about equal preference for the two- and three-part forms. While the most paradigmatic examples of three-part form fall in the period between the mid-1760s and the early 1770s, Haydn seems to have abandoned the pure three-part exposition in the first movements of the keyboard sonatas following XVI:26 (ChL. 41) of 1773, in favor of the two-part form. Nevertheless, features of the expan-sion section persist in the second group areas of the large-scale two-part works.

3. The two-part exposition, corresponding at least in tonal clarity and overall proportions to the so-called "Classical sonata form," becomes common in the works of the later 1760s and is used throughout the 1770s. After the mid-1770s, Haydn uses this form in conjunction with the main theme transposition.

4. The main theme transposition is found throughout the body of keyboard sonatas and is used without exception in all the first-movement sonata expositions after XVI:41 (ChL. 55), published 1784. Moreover, Haydn's use from about 1780 of modulating transitions in the sonatas displaying

this device introduces a new level of structural clarity not found in the earlier works without transition.

In closing, it must be added that these results apply only to the first movements of the keyboard sonatas. A comparable study of other Haydn instrumental genres might lead to conclusions quite different from these.

Sonata Procedures in Haydn's Symphonic Rondo Finales of the 1770s

STEPHEN C. FISHER

In his pioneering study of the Haydn symphonies, H. G. Robbins Landon states that Haydn's first symphonic finale in sonata-rondo design appears in Symphony No. 77 in B-flat major, composed in all likelihood in 1782.[1] Since Mozart, who may have originated the usual type of sonata-rondo, employs the form in works written as early as 1773,[2] it has been suggested—most notably by Malcolm Cole—that Haydn adopted the concept in the early 1780s as a result of his acquaintanceship with the music of the younger man.[3]

Attractive though this hypothesis may seem at first glance, it presents difficulties when considered closely. It is true that the earliest known composer to use the sonata-rondo regularly is Mozart, but what is not so certain is whether Haydn acquired his own sonata-rondo concept from the younger man. If this last were accepted, it would substantiate the widely held theory that Mozart played a role in the formation of Haydn's late style, a concept that has been debated at some length but never fully proved or disproved. As Cole admits, however, there are difficulties in calling the finale of Symphony No. 77 a sonata-rondo;[4] both the repetition scheme and the tonal structure of the movement suggest not a sonata-rondo but a sonata design. Furthermore, Cole finds more differences than similarities in the sonata-rondo procedures employed by Mozart and Haydn in the 1780s. Most important of all, there is a group of symphonic finales from the 1770s that shows Haydn already experimenting with elements of the sonata-rondo, at a time when it was not likely that he knew any of Mozart's works.

The first Haydn finale to show sonata-rondo elements is that of Symphony No. 64 in A major, probably written about 1773, or just when

[1] Landon, *Symphonies,* 389–90.
[2] In the String Quartet in C major K. 157 (late (1772 or early 1773) and the Symphony in D major K. 181 (19 May 1773). This suggestion was apparently made first in Tobel, *Formenwelt,* 181–83.
[3] Cole, "Rondo," 87–91, 127–28; Cole, "Evidence."   [4] Cole, "Rondo," 170–72.

Mozart was first using the design himself. The other two movements to be discussed, the finales of Symphonies Nos. 69 in C major and 66 in B-flat major, date from a few years later, probably composed, in that order, by 1777.[5] All three finales show several differences from Haydn's previous rondo movements, where the episodes were closed blocks of new material. Here, the episodes are developmental in nature and use material derived from the rondo theme. Even more important, the first episode moves to the dominant in the same fashion as the transition of a sonata-form movement. Haydn had previously avoided the dominant for rondo episodes, preferring the relative minor, the subdominant, and, above all, the tonic minor. In Symphony No. 66, the transitional passage merely touches on the dominant before the return to the tonic for the second appearance of the rondo theme. The transition in No. 69 is longer and leads to a substantial closing passage, suggesting the type of sonata exposition in which the second theme and closing material are compressed into a single brief area following the principal cadence in the dominant. Jens Peter Larsen has stressed this design as characteristic of Haydn.[6] Even more strikingly, the transition in Symphony No. 64 leads to a partial restatement of the main theme in the dominant, a procedure that suggests the "monothematic" sonata design Haydn so often uses.

After the first episode comes a complete return of the main theme; the following episode has developmental features. The second episode in Symphony No. 64 works with an idea from the transition, taking it into the relative minor, with an extensively prepared return to the tonic at the end. The corresponding sections in Nos. 66 and 69 both use material from the main theme; in No. 69 this part of the movement is in the tonic minor, while in No. 66 it begins in the relative minor but quickly settles into the subdominant. The tonic minor and the subdominant are areas that Haydn does not use very extensively in the development sections of sonata-form movements; in movements in major keys, Haydn usually emphasizes the supertonic, the relative minor, or the mediant. The regions used in these three middle sections seem, on the whole, more characteristic of rondo than sonata procedures.

The three movements begin to diverge from each other in their latter stages. In Symphony No. 64, only the first strain of the theme returns

[5] On the dating of Nos. 66 and 69, see Gerlach, "Ordnung," 58. For No. 64, see ibid., 36, n. 18: it probably dates from no later than 1773, because the sole extant authentic copy, Frankfurt, Stadt- und Universitätsbibliothek, Mus. Hs. 1499, shows Bartha-Somfai's watermark No. 192, which occurs in dated manuscripts from 1769 to 1773. My examination of this source also located No. 193, the usual companion watermark to 192; this supports the dating at 1773 or earlier. On the other hand an earlier date than c. 1773 seems improbable on stylistic grounds.

[6] Larsen, "Sonatenform"; cf. Larsen, "Observations," 137–38. [See also the Free Paper by Michelle Fillion elsewhere in this volume. —Ed.]

after the second episode, and there follows a short developmental episode in the tonic minor. The rondo theme returns in full, and there is a developmental coda. In No. 69, the theme returns intact after the second episode, with a coda following. The third statement of the main theme in No. 66 leads to a short episode in the tonic and a fourth thematic statement to conclude the movement; this procedure is made possible by the fact that the returns of the theme in the movement are varied.

There are two possible objections to calling these three finales sonata-rondos. First, none of these movements exhibits a second theme that is melodically distinct from the main theme. This objection can easily be answered, since Haydn so often reintroduces first-theme material in the dominant as part of the second theme of a sonata-form movement. The only sonata-rondos in the Haydn symphonies with contrasting second themes appear in the London symphonies Nos. 93, 94, 100, and 102. If Haydn's sonata-rondo procedures owe any great deal to Mozart's, it would be odd for him to begin using such an important feature of the younger man's style as thematic contrast only in works written some ten years after their first meeting.

A second, more substantial objection to calling our three movements sonata-rondos is the absence of a recapitulation of the material heard in the dominant. (This is probably the reason why these movements, up to now, have not been seen as steps in Haydn's evolution of sonata-rondo design.) In the case of Symphony No. 64, one might attempt to overcome this objection with a certain amount of gerrymandering. The principal element heard in the dominant is a transposition of the first strain of the main theme (m. 41), and this same idea appears again by itself in the tonic after the development (m. 113). One could call this partial return of the theme the beginning of the recapitulation, since the remainder of the movement is in the tonic. The result would be a type of sonata-rondo recapitulation common in Mozart's late works, such as the Piano Concerto in B-flat major K, 595, discussed by Cole, in which the second theme returns in the tonic before the third statement of the main idea. This structure would not be at all characteristic of Haydn, however; Haydn prefers to begin the recapitulations of his sonata-rondo movements with the main theme. This difference in procedure between Mozart and Haydn is one of the difficulties Cole faces in his attempt to show a mutual influence between the two men. I do not really think that Haydn intended us to hear any part of the finale of Symphony No. 64 as a return of material from the secondary area.

On the other hand, several points can be made to weaken the objection I have just raised. Eugene K. Wolf has suggested that, for Haydn, the transition may have been the most important section of the exposition, the one that carries out the basic function of this part of the movement by establishing the basic tonal tension.[7] Recent thinking about the nature of Classical form has emphasized the role of tonality over and above that of thematic material. There is no composer whose works support this interpretation better than Haydn's, given his penchant for reintroducing familiar ideas in just the places where one would expect new thematic material. More significant than the precise distribution of melodic ideas in a Haydn movement is the tension created by the secondary harmonic region and its resolution with the return of the tonic later in the movement. This resolution is most often accomplished by recapitulating some or all of the material heard in the secondary region. Haydn will often omit parts of this secondary material in the recapitulation, or bring it back only in a paraphrased or abridged form in which the connection with the exposition is weakened. This is particularly likely when this material either is derived from the first theme or is cadential in nature. Thus, in the first movement of Symphony No. 70 in D minor Haydn omits the second theme, which is closely related to the first theme; and in that of No. 82 in C major he omits the closing idea in the recapitulation, replacing it with a concluding peroration based on the first theme. In the three rondo movements under consideration, as I have indicated, the material heard in the dominant is based on the main theme, and in two cases it is purely cadential. The lack of recapitulation of this material later in the movement is thus perfectly consistent with Haydn's practice in sonata-form movements. There is no compelling structural reason for it to return. Each movement concludes with substantial enough a section in the tonic to settle the tonal tension of the structure. (The return of the main theme in the tonic between the secondary area and the development section reduces this tension to a lower level than one would normally find in a sonata design.) Further, in each case most of the material in the last part of the movement consists of restatements of the main theme or of developmental work derived from it and thus is closely related to the material that was heard in the dominant.

Of the three finales under discussion, that of Symphony No. 69 seems to have been the one that Haydn found most useful as a model for later rondo movements. The finale of No. 85 in B-flat major, which Cole discusses, resembles it rather closely. The second episode is in the relative minor rather than the tonic minor, which makes it sound a bit more like a normal Haydn development section. More important is that the cadential passage in the dominant from the first episode does return in the tonic. (That of No. 69 does not.) The question could be raised, however, as to whether this is the crucial point in determining the form of the entire movement. The passage in question is not particularly distinctive,

[7] Wolf, "Stamitz," 573; cf. the extended-transition and compressed-second-group expositions mentioned above.

and it is only fourteen measures long. It is entirely different from the lyrical second theme of a Mozart movement like the finale of K. 595; the difference in the types of material used by the two composers at this point in the movement further weakens Cole's argument on behalf of mutual influence between Haydn and Mozart.

The last movement of Symphony No. 88 in G major appears at first to be a satisfactory example of a textbook sonata-rondo. Here a passage in the dominant, set off by a point of articulation, sounds more like a theme than the corresponding segments of Nos. 69 and 85, despite its clear derivation from the main theme. The development is again in the relative minor. The recapitulation, however, shows the same feature encountered in the three works from the 1770s: there are hints of the second theme, but nowhere as much as four measures together.

The same is true of the three finales from the London symphonies. In No. 97 in C major, the basic plan is much like that of No. 69, with the second episode in the tonic minor. Again, the material from the first episode does not return in the same form. Symphonies No. 95 in C minor and 101 in D major show a mixture of fugal procedure with the kind of rondo we have been examining; the passages in the dominant in these works resemble fugal episodes, and they do not recur.

The issues raised by examining these three finales are thus of greater importance than might have first appeared. One might dismiss a single movement with the peculiarities shared by these three as an anomaly. (Although Nos. 64 and 66 resemble the later rondos I have mentioned in their large structure as shown by a diagram, they do not sound quite the same.) But three movements with similar procedures are more difficult to explain away, and inasmuch as the finale of Symphony No. 69 clearly initiates a series of movements composed over the next twenty years of Haydn's career, one must consider them seriously. If one insists on some recapitulation of second-theme material as a criterion, there are at most seven sonata-rondos in the Haydn symphonies—the finales of Nos. 85, 93, 94, 99, 100, 102, and 103. Yet seven other movements exhibit sonata-rondo procedures without recapitulation of second-theme material: the finales of Nos. 64, 66, 69, 88, 95, 97, and 101. Whether one also wishes to call these movements sonata-rondos will depend on which elements one considers vital to the design. Cole does not commit himself on the issue. I find it hard to distinguish between the two groups in a meaningful way; it is difficult to find more than two works in either group that do not differ in some potentially significant feature. I would therefore call all fourteen movements sonata-rondos, and say simply that the proportion of sonata to rondo elements varies from work to work.

This implies that there is reason to question the use of the term "sonata-rondo" in its conventional meaning with respect to Haydn. This is one aspect of a familiar problem in dealing with mature Haydn. It was noted long ago that his earliest works were his most conventional ones, by and large; but it becomes nearly impossible to reconcile much that goes on in his late works with textbook formal schemes.[8] In particular, a major factor in Haydn's stylistic evolution is a continuing tendency to replace square-cut thematic statements with developmental material. This trend appears early in his tendency to extend the transition of his sonata designs and to compress the second theme and closing material. In the later works, he rewrites his recapitulations so thoroughly that the term "recapitulation" sometimes hardly seems appropriate. The rondo and variation movements, and to some degree the minuets, become less sectional in character. The finales of Symphonies Nos. 64, 66, and 69 would seem to be attempts to create a new type of final movement that had some of the lighter quality of the rondo but that was more continuous in nature. In so doing, Haydn would naturally have turned to the procedures he normally used in writing in the more continuous forms, those we describe in terms of the sonata, although they are equally characteristic of the concerto first movement or the aria. Evidently, one of the most important of these features is the establishment of a basic tonal polarity near the beginning that gives the movement a quality of tension that is only resolved near the end.

If this redefinition of Haydn's sonata-rondo is accepted, it becomes possible to dismiss the notion of Mozart as a major influence on his rondo procedures. Haydn's interest in combining sonata and rondo elements in a final movement dates from nearly a decade before his first meeting with the younger man. It may be significant for the history of Classical style that they seem to have hit upon the sonata-rondo idea at almost the same time, around 1773. No good earlier precedent is known, and it would be difficult to imagine a single movement that could have served as the model for the early sonata-rondos of both men. It therefore seems likely that there are two types of sonata-rondo, which we may call the Mozart and Haydn varieties. Mozart's type encompasses a series of forms that begins with a primarily strophic design and gradually takes on a more continuous character; in his mature output it appears largely in soloistic and chamber works, not at all in his late symphonies. Haydn's sonata-rondo type begins as a more continuous movement and serves from its origin as a symphonic finale, spreading into the finales of other genres after 1780.[9] Mozart's sonata-rondo type seems to have been the

[8] See, for example, Tovey, *Essays,* I, 139.
[9] Examples without return of second-theme material include the keyboard concerto Hob. XVIII:11 in D major; the Sonata Hob. XVI:43 (ChL. 35) in A-flat major; the String Quartet Op. 55, No. 1 in A major; and the Sinfonia Concertante. The type with return of second-theme material includes the Sonata Hob. XVI:48 (ChL. 58) in C major; the String Quartets Op. 64, No. 6 in E-flat major, Op. 74, No. 2 in F major, and Op. 76, No. 2 in D minor; the

more influential historically, since his designs are easier to imitate and codify. It is probably for this reason that the forms used by Mozart, or perhaps more accurately those used by his imitators, have served as the basis for the textbook definition of the sonata-rondo, leaving Haydn's type to be considered an anomaly. On the contrary, Haydn's sonata-rondo design is not historically dependent on Mozart's, and it represents the creation of a very different personality working toward a distinct artistic purpose.

A Critical Review of Fritz Tutenberg's Theory of First-Movement Form in the Early Classical Symphony

NIELS KRABBE

The value of Fritz Tutenberg's study of the symphonies of J. C. Bach has long been recognized, and it is considered a pioneer study of mid-eighteenth-century style.[1] Some scholars have even placed it on the same level as the writings of Wilhelm Fischer, Rudolf von Tobel, and Kurt Westphal.[2] (One must bear in mind that when it appeared, the repercussions of the Mannheim-Vienna dispute had not yet quite faded away. Nevertheless it seems to be one of the few works of the time that avoided the prejudices that resulted from Hugo Riemann's launching of Stamitz and his school as "the" model for Haydn's early works.[3]) Tutenberg attempted a broad survey of symphonies and overtures written from 1750 to 1780 as a basis for comparison with the symphonic output of J. C. Bach. Hence more than one third of the book deals with other composers, especially C. P. E. Bach, Jomelli, Wagenseil, Monn, Haydn, and the Mannheim symphonists.

An aspect of Tutenberg's book which, even today, scholars may be able to use to advantage is his contribution to the theory of sonata form. No serious attempt to describe and analyze Classical style can get around the question of sonata form, which still seems to be one of the most controversial issues in eighteenth-century studies. Just as eighteenth-century composers and critics knew nothing of a ready-made plan for the first movement of a symphony or a sonata, Tutenberg tries to go behind the "textbook" sonata scheme of the nineteenth century and make the music itself his starting point. One of his great merits is that he introduced an original and useful terminology and method which were then, and are

---

Trumpet Concerto; and the orchestral movement Hob. Ia:4 in D major (probably Haydn's first movement of this type, and possibly intended as a symphonic finale; cf. Gerlach, "Ordnung," 36, 57–59, 61–62).

[1] Tutenberg, *J. C. Bach.* A brief version of his typology can be found in Tutenberg, "Durchführungsfrage."

[2] Fischer, "Entwicklungsgeschichte"; Tobel, *Formenwelt;* Westphal, *Form.*

[3] On these subjects see Larsen, "Mannheim."

still today, rather unique. Instead of making the music fit the standard terms of sonata form by means of modifications and "missing" parts, he created a vocabulary that was based directly on the music it was intended to illuminate.

The question whether sonata form is bipartite or tripartite is one of the standard topics in twentieth-century sonata theory. Seen in historical perspective, however, there seems to be no doubt that it was originally conceived and understood as a bipartite form. One need only refer to J. A. Scheibe's *Critischer Musikus,* where the description of first movement form clearly emerges in two parts (or "Clauseln," as Scheibe puts it).[4] The same is true of H. C. Koch's detailed description of first movement form half a century later in his *Versuch einer Anleitung . . .* of 1793, even though Koch divides the second part in two, thus admitting a secondary structure in three parts within the main bipartite division.[5] (Koch uses the terms "Theil" and "Hauptperiode," and accordingly speaks of first movement form in two "Theilen," of which the first consists of a single "Hauptperiode," the second of two.)

Another main point of discussion in present-day sonata form theory is the status of thematic dualism. Most scholars now agree that a much more important dualism—to many *the* constituent dualism—is that of key areas. (One need only recall Colles's famous attempt at a "definition" of sonata form in Grove's Dictionary: "a movement built round a contrast of key subsequently reconciled."[6]) Furthermore, Fred Ritzel claims that the thematic dualism which is actually found in mid-century symphonies has no formal significance;[7] in this connection he quotes Charles Burney's words referring to J. C. Bach as "the first composer who observed the law of *contrast* as a principle,"[8] adding that this is no reference to any contrast of *theme,* but only to the principle. As far as Burney is concerned, this may be so, although he might also be interpreted in other ways. But analysis of J. C. Bach's symphonies—which inspired Burney to his remarks—shows unambiguously that when, as is often the case, there is a well-defined and self-contained contrasting theme, it certainly contributes to the formal design of the movement as a whole. This is not to advocate a return to the old concept of sonata form, but merely to show that one should not go to the other extreme and deprive the interplay of two contrasting thematic ideas of any formal significance. The lack of a concept of thematic dualism in eighteenth-century theory of form does not in itself justify disregarding the actual existence of such dualism in the music.

I have dwelt on these controversial aspects of sonata form in order to provide a suitable background for Tutenberg's ideas. After calling atten-

---

[4] Scheibe, *Musikus,* Das 68. Stuck, Dienstag, den 15. December, 1739, 623ff.
[5] Koch, *Versuch* III, 304, 307.   [6] Colles, "Sonata"
[7] Ritzel, *Sonatenform,* 103–04.   [8] Burney, *History* IV (1789), 483 (mod. ed., II, 866).

tion to the very scarceness of references to form problems in contemporary musical criticism, Tutenberg sets up four standard types of first-movement form, each with a different historical background, and in his analyses of a hundred or more symphonies he constantly uses these four categories, though not necessarily in as strict a form as they appear below. This typology served a double purpose: partly as a useful means of classification, offering a much more varied tool for analysis than the "textbook" sonata scheme; and partly to illuminate the history of the sonata principle.

Tutenberg takes as his starting point the well-known diagram of a binary movement in two parts, with two thematic groups (not necessarily contrasting) in each part:[9]

a b a b

(The italics indicate the dominant or the fifth degree.) His main concern, then, is to find out how this scheme, or rather how this principle, contributes to the development of Classical sonata form. After analyzing a large number of Italian and German pre-Classical symphonies, Tutenberg arrives at the following standard forms (see Example 1).[10]

Example 1

Suite-symphony, the overture of *opera seria*
a   *b*   /V/   a   b   [from   a   *b*   a   b]

Song-symphony, the overture of *opera buffa*
a   *b*   *c*   a   b   [from   A   *c*   A]

Mannheim Ritornello Symphony, the symphony derived from the Tessarini concerto
a   *b*   *a*   b   a   [from   a . . . a . . . a]

Vienna Ritornello Symphony, the symphony derived from the Tartini concerto
a   *b*   *a*   b   (VI)   a   b   (a)   [from   R   *S*   *R*   S   R   S   R]

There is no space to go into the designations of these four types and their historical background. Instead I would like to comment on the diagrams themselves and on some of the music on which they are based. On one rather important point it is necessary to modify Tutenberg's terminology: he uses the letters a and b to refer to *themes;* such a purely thematic interpretation of mid-century form does not agree with the music. But if we let the letters represent *either* themes *or* parts, or even

[9] The distinction between thematic and nonthematic parts of the music under consideration might be replaced by a distinction between tonally stable and tonally unstable parts.

[10] Tutenberg's terminology for these four types reads, respectively: "Suitensinfonie, die Sinfonie der Seria; Liedsinfonie, die Sinfonie der Buffa; Mannheimer Ritornell Sinfonie, die Sinfonie in Anlehnung an das Tessarinische Konzert; Wiener Ritornell Sinfonie, die Sinfonie in Anlehnung an das Tartinische Konzert."

tonal areas, they not only make sense, but they also express something important about the music. In considering the effect and the actual place of the thematic recapitulation in the early Classical symphony, for instance, we must remember that more often than not mid-century critics, such as Scheibe and Riepel (*Anfangsgründe,* Vols. 1–3, 1752–57), place it at the *beginning* of the second part (the beginning of the development section, in modern terminology). Thus they implicitly distinguish between a thematic return there, and a tonal return later in the movement. This quotation of the opening theme (*Hauptgedanke*) at the beginning of the second part is one of the most common formal characteristics of the early symphony. The result is that the main theme often appears three times during the movement: at the beginning in the tonic, at the beginning of the second part in the dominant, and somewhere in the middle of the second part, again in the tonic.

Tutenberg's four diagrams show that he interprets this as a reminiscence of the Baroque concerto. In fact, the conclusion that emerges from his book as a whole, which is also mirrored in the four types, is that Classical sonata form resulted from union of 1) binary form, known from the suite, with a short intermediate period between the two parts (that is, his "Suite-symphony [*Suitensinfonie*]"); and 2) the Baroque concerto with its alternating ritornellos and solos. This deliberate addition of the concertato and ritornello principles of the Baroque to Classical sonata theory gives Tutenberg's analyses their value.

One aspect of his typology, however, seems a little theoretical and divorced from the actual music: the strict distinction between the Mannheim and the Vienna versions of the "ritornello symphony." According to Tutenberg, one of the main characteristics of mid-century Viennese form is the section in the middle part of the movement in the relative minor, and he implies that this episode in the minor was a special Viennese phenomenon. But one need only glance at Koch's description of the symphony allegro movement, where a modulation to the minor is recommended ("in die weiche Tonart der Sexte, oder auch in die weiche Tonart der Secunde oder Terz"),[11] to disprove this idea. Neither Koch's biography nor the broad outlook that manifests itself in his writing indicate that he particularly favored a Viennese state of affairs.

In the last part of this paper I shall deal briefly with Tutenberg's application of his typology and give a few examples of his analyses. Of course the methodological problem of his approach is that the various diagrams, if taken too literally and not merely as *principles* of form, tell us very little about the actual music.

Two composers will be discussed here: Haydn and J. C. Bach. Tuten-

[11] Koch, *Versuch* III, 308.

Example 2 Haydn, Symphony No. 1 in D major, i

[Exposition]			[Development] Middle Part	Recapitulation		
1ˢᵗ section ("1ˢᵗ theme") Mannheim cresc.	2ⁿᵈ section (Development or expansion, based on 1ˢᵗ theme)	3ʳᵈ section (Second, Closing themes)		(1)	(2)	(3)
I — Iⱽ [half cadence]	I — vi — V	v — V	V — ii — Iⱽ [half cadence]	I	I	i — I
1 —— 9	10 23	28 ¦ 29 39	40 58	59	68	76 86
"a"	"b" ("Nebensatz")	"Fortspinnung"	"d"	"a"	"b"	

["second theme"]

[Tutenberg: a b d a b]

berg analyzes Haydn's Symphonies Nos. 1, 2, 3, 9, 11, 13, 23, and 27, all supposed to have been written earlier than 1765. Except for No. 1 in D major, they all have a formal design that more or less obviously corresponds to Tutenberg's Vienna ritornello form. But No. 1 stands apart, and to my mind Tutenberg gives a somewhat inadequate analysis of its first movement (see Example 2). Tutenberg's formal diagram (see the lower section of Example 2) does not indicate any change to the dominant key whatsoever. This is explained by his placing the second theme (*Nebensatz*) in m. 10 and its "Fortspinnung" in mm. 23–39, that is, for the rest of the first part. The serious flaw in this analysis (apart from its tonal defects) is that the G. P. in m. 22 is invested with formal implications. In my view (cf. the upper section of Example 2), the period beginning in m. 10 is not brought to a logical conclusion until m. 28. (We see here the well-known Haydn exposition with an introductory part in the tonic, a long and unstable intermediate part leading from the tonic to the dominant, and then, shortly before the double bar, a structured and stable part in the dominant.)[12]

In the second part of his book Tutenberg describes and analyzes forty-one symphonies proper (and six concerted symphonies) by J. C. Bach.[13] His analyses distribute the first movements of these works as shown in Table 1 (see p. 492). All forty-one have been reexamined here. In quite a few cases a work does not fit as neatly into one of the categories of Table 1 as Tutenberg would seem to think. On the other hand a clear tendency emerges: even if the dating of J. C. Bach's symphonies is uncertain and only approximate, most of the eight ritornello symphonies are late

[12] Larsen, "Sonatenform"; Brown, "Exposition." [See also Michelle Fillion's paper elsewhere in this volume.—Ed.].

[13] At least eight genuine and twenty doubtful or spurious further symphonies by J. C. Bach are known today. See Krabbe, "J. C. Bach," 233–54.

works, written after 1770, whereas most of the "modern sonata form" or "suite" symphonies are relatively early. There seems to be a clear correlation between form and texture in Bach's first movements: a development from a more complex formal design to a simpler one. His contribution to the evolution of Classical sonata form should therefore be sought in his early rather than in his late symphonies. Together with this formal simplification, an increase in purely melodic power can be felt. Finally, the advanced motivic development and *thematische Arbeit* of the early development sections yields to a more concerto-like texture.

Table 1   Formal Types in J. C. Bach's Symphonies

Type	Number of Symphonies
Suite symphony	11
Song symphony	7
"Modern sonata form"	5
Vienna ritornello symphony	4
Mannheim ritornello symphony	2
Ritornello symphony as such	2
Indeterminate	10

To repeat: the most important aspect of Tutenberg's typology is the introduction of the ritornello symphony, which, apart from the ritornello-solo alternation, accounts for the inclusion of material from the second theme in the middle part. (This goes for both the Mannheim and the Vienna versions.) On the other hand, it seems to be of little consequence whether, in the recapitulation, the second theme or the first theme comes first, or whether they are both present at all. Therefore there seems no need to acknowledge two different types of ritornello symphony, as Tutenberg does: the "Mannheim" form is found but rarely in the mid-century symphonies that have been accessible for investigation (one or two symphonies by Johann Stamitz, one by Franz Beck, and two by J. C. Bach). This is not a sufficiently large repertory to justify an independent designation giving Mannheim as its provenance.

The single important feature that distinguishes the Mannheim form from the Vienna one is the "mirror" recapitulation, with b before a. As already hinted, this is not very common even among Mannheim composers. Moreover, in the case of J. C. Bach, we find that the second theme, which in this form is supposed to be recapitulated (in the tonic) *before* the first theme, does not introduce the third part of the movement at all; rather it rounds off the *middle* part. This changes the whole formal design. An illustration is provided by Example 3, showing an E-flat major symphony by J. C. Bach.[14] Although not included in Tutenberg's

---

[14] "Ouverteur a piu Stromenti obligati con Corni di Caccia obligate. Del Sig:r Gio: Bach," manuscript in Kungl. Musikaliska Akademien, Stockholm.

Example 3. J. C. Bach, Symphony in E flat first movement

I	**a** (1st theme)	**x**	**b** (2nd theme)
	Ritornello	**Solo with tutti-elements**	**Solo**
	I	**I—I^V [half cadence]**	**V—v**
	1–7	8–23	23–31
"Mannheim rit. form":	**"a"**		**"b"**

II	**a**	**y**〰〰〰〰 **b**	
	Ritornello	**Solo with tutti-elements**	
	V	**vi — iii — I — V [of i]**	
	32–39	40 – (53)–62	
	"a"	**"b"**	

(?)

III	**a**	**x$_1$**	**Coda Tutti**
	Ritornello	**Solo, with brilliant horn passages**	
	I	**I**	**I**
	63–68	69–91	91–96
	"a"		

book, it has been claimed as an example of Mannheim ritornello form.[15] In other words we have not another example of the Mannheim "mirror recapitulation," but a much less dramatic and more common example of a recapitulation that omits the second theme. This omission is perfectly justifiable, since it has just been present as part of the development.

Even though one may disagree with Tutenberg's individual analyses, his general approach to this music, and especially to the problems of first-movement form, are worth studying. This is true not only in connection with J. C. Bach's symphonies, but for the entire repertoire of mid-century symphonies—including those by Haydn, who probably more than anyone else has been the "problem child" of modern theory of sonata form.

Unifying Elements in Haydn's Symphony No. 104

ERNEST F. LIVINGSTONE

Unifying elements in a work can be classified under a variety of headings; space allows dealing with only the two most important of them, namely thematic unity and structural unity.

---

[15] Blomstedt, "J. C. Bach."

I Thematic Unity

1. Basic ideas presented in the Introduction

The work opens with an upward leap of a fifth, D–A, and a downward leap of a fourth, D–A. These are later filled in: A–B–C♯–D–E (Vc., B.)—the E being taken over by Va. (mm. 9–12), and C–D–E–F (–E) in Bsn. In contrast to the open fifths and fourths in mm. 1, 2, 7, 8, 14, 15, we have whole-step and half-step figures, mm. 3–6 (strings), 9–13 (upper strings), 16 with upbeat. The high B♭ and the G♯ in mm. 10, 11, 16 introduce the idea of the neighboring tone to the prominent thematic tone A; E and C♯ in mm. 3, 4, 5 have already been neighbors to the other prominent tone D. The neighboring second scale degree—which is most important throughout the work—is emphasized by E♭ in the last beat of 15 and the rest after the (unresolved) E in 16, a device for emphasis also used in other movements.

There is a strong emphasis on the third, the center of the thematic 5th in m. 1, through motivic development: F–C up, F–C down at the center of the Introduction, mm. 7–8. This idea reappears at the center of each movement. Finally, there is a descent of a minor 9th from D to C♯ and of a minor 7th from D to E in the first violin in mm. 12–13 and 15–16, respectively, an expansion of the idea of the major and minor seconds in mm. 3–5.

2. Specific application of these ideas

The first measure of the Allegro theme F♯–G–E(–D) comes from the last three half notes of the first violin in the Introduction and the dotted half note D in the second violin, now rearranged in the form of a "hook"; this hook idea has been prepared in m. 6 in the bassoon: E–F–D–C. Measures 18–19 come from m. 1, the 5th D–A now filled in; 19–20 come from 10, 11, V.I; 21–22 from 2, the fourth D–A now filled in; 23 again from 10–11, V.I, the turn around A. The octave range D–D of the theme reflects that of A–A in mm. 1–2, while the range D–E (minor 7th down) is derived from mm. 15–16 and the range F♯–G (minor 9th in mm. 25–30) is derived from mm. 12–13. Similar relationships to the Introduction can be pointed out for all themes in all movements.

II Structural Unity

1. Development sections

These emphasize the neighboring tone not only in the melody but also in the middleground. In the bass of i 124–38 we have a turn around B (instead of A), then an octave span made up of a 5th- and a 4th-span from B to B: $\hat{8}$ = B Vla. 140, $\hat{7}$ in 142, $\hat{6}$ and $\hat{5}$ in 144, $\hat{4}$ in 145, then $\hat{4}$ = E with its upper neighbor F♯ in 145–49, then $\hat{4}$ in 149, $\hat{3}$ in 150, $\hat{2}$ in 152, and $\hat{1}$ in 154; this is followed by an octave span E–E with its lower neighbor D♯ in 159–66; then, in preparation for the recapitulation, comes an ascent from D to A, 183 to 185 ff. In the finale, which in many respects is a reversal of the first movement, the above situation is also reversed: in the bass we first have an ascent from E to B in 128–43, then a triadic descent from B to E in 143–47, then a turn around F♯, the upper neighbor of the upper neighbor (culmination of the neighboring-tone idea), and finally the octave span from B in 178–93, but with the expected B at the end of the span replaced by D, since here the recapitulation begins (*not* in 195).

The form of the Andante is ambiguous. It is sometimes called a rondo, but it is basically only A–B–A'. The B section has many traits of a development section: the beginning in the parallel minor; change of key to the relative major, prepared by the melodically accented B♭ in m. 6; statement and variation of part of the main theme in B-flat major in m. 57 ff.; and the section from 42 to 55 is a prolonged version of i 7–8 and 10–11 (VI). Most interesting is the return of an octave span on the upper neighbor A in first violins and flute: $\hat{8}$ (m. 42), $\hat{7}$ (44–45), $\hat{6}$ (46), $\hat{5}$ (E♭, 47), $\hat{4}$ (48), $\hat{3}$ (50), $\hat{2}$ (51–53), $\hat{1}$ (turn around A, 53–55). The Trio also has traits of a development and recalls the corresponding section of the Andante in its key, B-flat. Here the middleground once again is a span on B♭ with its corresponding 5th, F: octave span F–F 53–79 in oboe and flute, followed by octave span B♭–B♭ 84–94 in flute and oboe (with first violin). It is as if Haydn had raised each development section one scale degree, thus reinforcing the basic idea of the neighboring tone.

2. Introductions and codas

The introduction is 16 bars. The coda of the first movement is 11 bars, of the Andante 11 with upbeat, of the minuet $4 \times 3 = 12$ bars (since mm. 49–52 are played a total of three times). This sum of 50 measures is balanced by the two measures of introduction and the 48 measures of coda (287–334) in the finale; the latter can be considered a coda to the whole work, since it restates ideas from all movements, especially in mm. 287–309. The most interesting feature is the combination of the main themes of i and iv: the melody in the flute has C♯–D–B–A mostly in whole notes (mm. 304–07), which is a transposition and augmentation of the hook idea from 1, 17; then clarinet and first violins have F♯–G–E–D, with the violins leaping up to A two measures later (307–11), while in 311 ff. the main theme of iv is restated.

3. Climax points

Main climax in i is at m. 228 ff. with emphasis on the upper neighbor E; main climax of iv is at 232 ff., emphasizing the other important upper neighbor, B; it comes almost exactly at the analogous point as in i.

Main climax of ii is at m. 129 f., again with emphasis on E with its upper neighbor F♯.

Main climax in iii is at m. 20 ff. on the repeated high D, but again with emphasis on E as the highest note in the phrase (m. 25 in flute and violins).

4. Midpoints

These always emphasize the third, just as the middle of the Introduction stresses F at mm. 7 and 8.

Midpoint of i is at mm. 146–56, where the lower parts stress F♯–E, while the center of the descent in the melody is F♯, stressed by upper neighbor G♯ and lower neighbors E♯ and E.

Midpoint of ii is the return of the main theme, B as third in G major, m. 74.

Midpoint of iii is the Trio with emphasis on F, minor third above fundamental key of D.

Midpoint of iv is around m. 167 ff., with great emphasis on F♯ in the measures immediately preceding, in the flute line from 167 to 181 ff., and in V.I in mm. 173 and 193 (beginning of the recapitulation).

Much has been said about the monothematic character in many of Haydn's sonata-form movements. In this symphony—and some others—the same thematic and structural ideas appear in all four movements. Since the middle parts of ii and iii also have something of a developmental character, this work might be called not only monothematic but also "monoformal" and "monostructural."

Haydn's Sonata Hob. XVI:52 (ChL. 62) in E-flat Major: An Analysis of the First Movement

LAWRENCE K. MOSS

Like Beethoven after him, Haydn seems in this work to generate a massive structure from a single simple idea (see Example 1). The simplicity is somewhat deceptive, however. Note that there are at least three different levels on which clearly defined ideas are expressed in the opening two measures. There is first of all the prominent dotted rhythm, occurring on both weak and strong beats. From a harmonic standpoint, there is a striking movement to the subdominant, followed by a return to the tonic through the dominant. And finally, considered purely melodically, one may isolate a basic motive of the minor third articulated by successive whole and half steps. Although embedded within the inner voices, its importance can perhaps be inferred by its doubling at the octave, visually reinforced in Haydn's manuscript on the separate staves.[1]

[1] Cf. the composer's autograph in the Library of Congress, Washington, D. C.; facs. of the opening bars in JHW XVIII:3, frontispiece.

Example 1. Sonata Hob. XVI:52 (ChL. 62) in E-flat major, i, 1–3

Measures 3 through 5 are relatively uneventful, being a phasing out of the last measure of the theme. This half is itself reduced by half, leading to a series of running sixteenths, which will serve the rest of the movement as a basic accompaniment pattern. Perhaps more important is the abrupt change of register and harmony (essentially V–I), which pave the way for the resumption of the opening register and subdominant harmony on the downbeat of m. 6.

Here, on the opening E♭ (see Example 2), we have a first surprise: IV instead of the expected I. This example shows the presence of our motive here as well as the relation of mm. 6 and 7 to m. 1. The phrasing in m. 6, leading to emphasis on D♭, is my reading of Haydn's autograph, and would seem to stress the subdominant even more than in m. 1. The fall from C to E♭ in the bass, mm. 6–8, duplicates the same thing two octaves higher in the soprano, mm. 3–6.

Example 2. Ibid., 6–8

At the cadence in m. 9 we have another surprise, achieved through fresh means. The harmony is "correct," but the register is a dramatic shift to the upper octave, which had been abandoned during the course of m. 5. Also, a slight but telling change, the repeated g^1 of the theme is changed to g^1–$e♭^1$ giving the sixteenth-note upbeat more of a push. When it reaches the previously heard high c^3 (note again the E♭—C gamut!), the sixteenth notes are transformed into a downward rush of thirty-seconds, eventually reaching the low E♭ with which the bass line began.

Now the play of registral shifts begins once more, with the last beat of m. 10 resuming the climatic c^3 abandoned in the previous measure. A kind of repeat of m. 6 ensues, obscured by the reversal of the voices. Soon, Haydn takes us to more distant regions, emphasizing in particular the dominant of the minor V of E-flat (of B-flat minor). By m. 14 a strong cadence in this key is set up, with dominant pedal in the bass and the characteristic augmented second G♭–A of B-flat minor emphasized in

the soprano. Haydn could have chosen the more conventional rising melodic minor F–G♮–A♮–B♭ but this would have spoiled the dramatic announcement of B-flat major in m. 17.

Here Haydn, typically, opens the B section of his exposition with the
A theme transposed to the dominant. But even more momentum is
generated in this repetition by the subtle shift of the thirty-second-note
cascade to an upbeat position, combined with the change noted in m. 9
(see Example 3). In looking back, one might note also how the dominant
proper has been reserved for this point. It is used in the opening section
mm. 1–10 as a sort of "corrective" to the prominent subdominant, while
immediately thereafter it emerges only in its functionally weak minor
form. But from m. 17 on we find B-flat major firmly established, even to
the point of attracting *its* subdominant, E-flat: a first outburst at the end
of m. 22, emphasized by the striking change of register, and a more sustained excursion in mm. 25–26. These latter two measures slow down
the harmonic motion in order to set off the new theme proper in m. 27,
with its pattern of rapid change.

Example 3. Ibid., 9, 17

This theme seems wholly new, though we can recognize the dotted
rhythm accompanying the imitations of horn calls as a diminution of the
second beat of the main theme. Perhaps a more important link is its underlying bent towards the subdominant (see Example 4). Another surprise: the expected B-flat major cadence in m. 29, as well as the conclusion of our *Urmotiv,* crumble before our eyes (the dashed lines in the
example) to B-flat minor. This neat switch to minor exactly reverses that
of m. 17, while the shift of register (Example 4b) is now a familiar device
at dramatic junctures. Example 4 also draws a relationship between the
themes of mm. 29b and 27 (see the dashed lines).

Measure 29b condenses eventually into octaves in the left hand, which
swiftly plunge down to a new, lowest register at m. 32. As previously,
B-flat minor is emphasized by the augmented second A♮–G♭. (The latter
pitch will come to have a special importance in m. 38.) Meanwhile, by
the now-familiar switch of register, we have what could stand as a closing theme (m. 33), which recalls melodic and rhythmic material from the
main theme. There is also a similar emphasis on the subdominant,
though it is not as strong and is counteracted by a more powerful thrust
to the dominant in mm. 34–35.

Example 4. Ibid., 27–32

a) m. 27f.

b) mm. 29–30

The most dramatic registral shift so far occurs in m. 38. It is reinforced by a long pause as well as a shift in dynamics and, most tellingly, texture. Haydn himself seems to have been subliminally aware of this dramatic break. The autograph, which up to this point has busily filled out the staves, shows a gap just where this measure would have been. One turns the page and finds it heading the next system.

Attention has already been called to the low F in m. 38 as a continuation of the register from mm. 31–32. Similarly, mm. 39–40 move up to the register of m. 33. A series of cadential V–I chords innocuously closes the exposition in the bright upper register of the "horn call" theme of m. 27.

The somewhat ominous movement toward C minor with which the development begins, with its abrupt change in texture and register, is really not as different as it seems. Example 5 shows the link with m. 38, just before the shift to brighter registers which concluded the exposition. Moreover, we even have the same notes: f–f♯–g are an enharmonic retrograde of g–g♭–f in m. 38. And to complete the tie-in with the past, the accompanying voices give us our original descending motive from m. 1, doubled in thirds (the added voice is marked with its own stems in Haydn's autograph).

Example 5. Ibid., 38–39, 44–45, 61–65, 73–74, 76

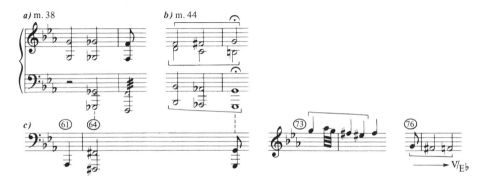

a) m. 38   *b)* m. 44

c)

Having thus marked off the beginning of the development, Haydn returns to the "horn call" theme for a series of sequential harmonies which eventually reach the dominant of G minor in m. 51. The harmonic rhythm slows down now in a quasi-imitative passage moving from G minor to C minor, F minor, and, finally breaking the circle of fifths, to A-flat major in m. 61. The surprise of the latter key is enhanced by the octave shifts in the chromatically descending bass mm. 58–60. These phrases thus isolated contain our familiar *Urmotiv*. The low A♭ reached in m. 61 links up, through its isolation from the succeeding three measures, with the low F♯ octave in m. 64, as well as the register of the beginning of the development, while the low F♯ octave can be heard as an echo of the low G♭ octave just before the end of the exposition (see Example 5c).

Now that these loose ends are so neatly tied, we have the most astonishing of registral and harmonic surprises so far. For in place of the expected C minor (or even a direct move to the recapitulation), we have our "horn call" theme, in the vastly remote key of E major, and two octaves higher as well! Charles Rosen writes, "the surprise of the distant new tonality is much admired."[2] I share his admiration and surprise, but I would attempt in retrospect to find some sort of preparation for it. Perhaps this lies in the A♭s of the left hand in mm. 65–66, which could be reinterpreted as G♯ after the break. Likewise, a slight emphasis in performance on the B♭ in m. 67 would help associate it with m. 68. But Haydn turns this freaky interruption into something more substantial. E major brings A major in its train, and then B minor. We are heading toward home, but we are still five sharps away from E-flat major. The dénouement comes in mm. 73–75 with a chromatic slide in the top voice from D down to A♯, accompanying a similar slide in the bass from A♯ to F♯. In m. 76, Haydn makes us hear A♯ and F♯ as B♭ and G♭, and we are suddenly jolted back enharmonically to home base. The recapitulation follows swiftly. An interesting detail is the appearance at the beginning and end of this brief transition section of the critical pitches G and F♯ (Example 5c). To these is added a pivotal E♯ (m. 73) = F (m. 76). These are the same pitches which ended the exposition and began the development (Example 5a).

The recapitulation is routine up to the point where our mysterious motive makes a final appearance, in mm. 109–10 (see Example 6). Note its extension via its own modified inversion. These successive appearances of the motive bracket a central B♭, surrounded as it were by a cluster of leading tones. Without making unhistorical deductions, it is interesting to see this particular technique expanded into a formal principle in the late quartets of Béla Bartók. A more immediate relationship for Haydn might have been to the mysterious key of E major, which is

---

[2] Rosen, *Style*, 111.

Example 6. Ibid., 109–11

enharmonically implied by Example 6, and which will recur again in the second movement. Not every eighteenth-century composer could write two measures that look forward not only to another movement, but to another era two centuries away.

Thematic Asymmetry in First Movements of Haydn's Early Symphonies

JUDITH L. SCHWARTZ

In describing the first movements of Haydn's symphonies from 1771 to 1774, H. C. Robbins Landon cited as an important milestone in the development of Haydn's style the composer's adoption of the regular period, specifically "the eight measure period, which is capable of being broken down to four or combined to make sixteen measures, as required. This unifies and concentrates his thematic material, imposing a sense of symmetry on the symphonic form. Having mastered this important principle, he is free to alter it as the occasion arises; his frequently uneven structures are by now no longer the outgrowth of the baroque 'spinning-out' principle but a deliberate and carefully thought-out refinement of the basic period technique."[1]

Listening to Haydn's earliest symphonies, one quickly notices not only the lack of a larger sense of symmetry, but also the highly variable and often elusive continuity created by successions of irregular phrases and sentences. Can this effect be entirely attributed to the "baroque spinning-out principle" (or *Fortspinnung*)? The structural characteristics of asymmetrically growing themes, such as frequent cadences, short rhythmic-melodic patterns, and the prevalence of repetition, variation, and reciprocal phrase relationships over Baroque motivic development often suggest a model other than the motivic development frequently cited as the source of thematic asymmetry in the early classic period.

A survey of Italian, German, and Austrian symphonies composed between 1720 and 1765 reveals a striking variety of formal growth processes at the phrase level.[2] In addition to gradual emergence of the eight-bar period, there is continual use of periodicity based not on multiples of

[1] R. Landon, *Symphonies*, 319.   [2] See Schwartz, "Phrase"

two, but of three. Specifically, three-bar phrases capable of being broken down into one-bar or combined into six-bar units, and six-bar periods divisible into two-bar or combinable to form twelve-bar units, appear with sufficient frequency to rival the developing four- and eight-bar standard. Units such as the six-bar period divisible by both two and three provided the opportunity for continual rhythmic variety at the phrase level. Often units of two and three bars combine into statements five, seven, eight, nine, or more bars in length, in a manner perhaps suggesting the rhythmic flexibility of *galant* themes, in which alternating duplet and triplet patterns enhance the rhythmic surface of the music with a supple grace.

While eighteenth-century writers on musical composition increasingly stressed a preference for a thematic hierarchy based on two, four, eight, and sixteen bars, centering on the four-bar phrase,[3] they did not fail to discuss phrases of odd length. Indeed, odd phrases and irregular thematic construction were described with greater respect and articulateness by Koch in 1787 than by Riepel in 1752. Riepel, Marpug, and Kirnberger regarded three-bar phrases as inferior to four-bar phrases, though least offensive if repeated, or heard as a subordinate member of a six-bar unit. Koch, however, no longer felt the need to hear odd phrases only in pairs. Furthermore, he detailed three principal ways of creating odd phrases and irregular periods: *Erweiterung* (extension, for example by repeating the final bar of a two-bar subphrase, resulting in a three-bar subphrase), *Ausdehnung* (expansion, for example lengthening some note values, consequently stretching the two-bar unit over three bars), and *Verkürzung* (abridgement, especially by means of elision, making one bar serve simultaneously as the culmination of one subphrase and beginning of the next).[4]

In light of widespread usage and theoretical recognition of asymmetrical phrasing, it is not surprising to find that the young Haydn followed the practice of his contemporaries in symphonies he composed between 1757 and 1765. In thirty-four of his beginning fast movements probably composed before 1765,[5] the total number of bars devoted to periodic structures based on a hierarchy of two-, four-, and eight-bar units is less than half that given over to units of one, three, and six bars, units of five and ten bars, and other asymmetrical constructions—despite the prevalence of two-bar over three-bar units at the lowest structural levels.

[3] Riepel, *Anfrangsgründe*, I, 35; Marpurg, *Handbuch*, 222; Kirnberger, "Einschnitt"; Koch, *Versuch*, II, 346–47.

[4] Koch, *Versuch*, II, 427, 374. Cf. Massenkeil, *Symmetrie*, 33–36.

[5] For the chronology of Haydn's symphonies I rely on the dates given by R. Landon in his prefaces to Haydn, *Symphonies*, as modified by his later commentary to the complete recordings of Haydn's symphonies on London records. The symphonies examined in this study, in presumed rough chronological order, were Hob. I:107 ("A") and 108 ("B"), and Nos. 37, 1–5, 10, 11, 15, 18, 27, 32, 33, 19, 20, 6–8, 16, 17, 25, 36, 9, 14, 12, 13, 40, 72, 21–24.

Thus, periodicity based on odd multiples of a subordinate unit appears to have been a strong alternative to regular periodicity at this time.

At least three different types of construction provided early Classic composers with an alternative to regular periodicity based on even-numbered multiples of a basic metrical unit. First comes regular periodicity in which the symmetrically recurring phrase length is based on an odd-numbered multiple of the basic metrical unit, for instance 3 + 3 or 5 + 5. This type occurs frequently in symphony first movements by Italian, Mannheim, Viennese, and North German composers. The several instances of 1½ + 1½-bar phrasing in Haydn find counterparts in symphonies by Vinci, Sammartini and Holzbauer (see Example 1); 3 + 3-bar phrasing notable in modulatory transitions of Haydn symphonies finds parallels in overtures by Conti, Caldara, Monn, Sammartini, Jommelli, Brioschi, Graun, Hasse, Benda, Gluck, and Wagenseil (see Example 2).

Example 1

a) Haydn, Symphony Hob. I:108 ("B") in B-flat major (c. 1757–61), i, 14–16

b) Holzbauer, Symphony in A major, i, 1–3 (Vienna, Gesellschaft der Musikfreunde, XIII 8472)

Example 2

a) Haydn, Symphony No. 13 in D major (1763), i, 1–6

b) Wagenseil, Symphony in E (Kucaba, "Wagenseil," No. 36) (before 1764), i, 1–6 (Prague, National Museum, XXVII B 15)

Example 3

a) Haydn, Symphony No. 16 in B-flat major (c.1761–62), i, 43–52

b) Galuppi, Sinfonia, *La calamità de' cuori* (1752), 5–14 (London, British Museum, Add. 31645)

Haydn's periods of 5 + 5 were anticipated by Sammartini and Galuppi (Example 3).

The second type presents phrases of equal length, whether of an odd or even number of bars, in odd-numbered groupings. Most striking here is the 2 + 2 + 2-bar period used in at least ten Haydn symphonies, particularly in No. 27 in G major, where it occurs in primary, modulatory, and secondary themes (see Example 4a). This triple grouping of a duple unit was used widely in Italian, Mannheim, North German, and Viennese symphonies, representing the entire spectrum of current phrase relationships for connecting two-bar units, e.g. sequence, *aaa, aab, abb, aba, abc* (Example 4b).

Example 4

a) Haydn, Symphony No. 27 in G major (c.1760), i, 1–6

b) Wagenseil, Symphony in B-flat major (Kucaba, "Wagenseil," No. 63) (before 1757), i, 1–6 (Prague, National Museum, XXVII B 18)

In the third type, phrases of unequal length, usually one of odd and one of even length, combine to form asymmetrical periods. Most frequently heard here are 2 + 3 (sounding like 2 + 2 with a one-bar extension) and 4 + 3 (sounding like an elided would-be eight-bar unit that cadences into the first bar of the following phrase). Included in this class are eight-bar periods with unequal subdivisions, apparently a specialty of Haydn's (see Example 5), and periods in which either the antecedent or consequent phrase is extended by motive repetition or development.

Example 5. Haydn, Symphony No. 36 in E-flat major (c. 1761–65), i, 1–9

Not only the ultimate shape of Haydn's periods but also the processes involved in their internal shaping correspond to those in contemporary Italian overtures and concert symphonies. As Koch indicated, processes used to create odd phrases often involve modification of an even phrase unit. Haydn's most common techniques are 1) harmonic extension or cadential resolution; 2) motivic extension or development; 3) motivic repetition (as in *xxy* or *xyy* or *xyx*); 4) elision or overlap, leaving one bar to serve as both an ending and a beginning for two adjacent units; or 5) truncation, when upon repetition of a phrase, a portion is simply omitted. But these techniques do not account for themes in which phrasing in three or other odd rhythms arises naturally as a result of a complete harmonic or melodic contour, independent of larger metric implications, as illustrated in Examples 2a and b.

And what of phrases and sections that do not fall into these classes of not-so-regular periodic construction? There are many of them in Haydn's early symphonies, normally sounding more individual than the conventional periodic themes. Some issue from periodic origins, such as those characterized by abrupt modular shifts to the next larger or smaller dimension, in which the initial phrase-unit length either doubles or divides in half. An example from Haydn's Symphony No. 9 in C major (see Example 6) shows an opening two-bar announcement—the hammerstrokes or *coups d'archet* so popular in the Italian overture and the French concerto—followed by a repeated two-bar phrase, answered in turn by a four-bar consequent. The initial modular length, established in the first two bars, thus doubles to become four bars within the subsequent eight-bar period.

Example 6. Haydn, Symphony No. 9 in C major (1762) i, 1–10

Dividing a previously established phrase length in half creates a much livelier effect. In Example 7a, Haydn dissolves the period structure of his opening theme by echoing and developing motives from it, cutting the module size down from a two-bar phrase to a series of one-bar motives. Jommelli anticipated this device in his opera overtures (Example 7b).

Example 7

a) Haydn, Symphony Hob. I:107 ("A") in B-flat major (c. 1757–61), i, 1–15

b) Jommelli, Sinfonia, *Didone abbandonata* (1746), 7–19 (Paris, Conservatoire, D. 6234)

Carrying modular division a step further, Haydn created highly developmental themes by twice halving the initial modular length, successively fragmenting a phrase into subphrases and motives. In Symphony No. 20 (see Example 8), he follows the opening eight-bar period (*ab*) with a four-bar phrase (*c*), repeating the last two-bar subphrase (*y*), then extracting the last one-bar eighth-note motive (*m*) for development in the succeeding bars. A similar ratio prevails in Symphony No. 21 in A major, ii, in which an established two-bar module breaks down to one and then to a half bar.

Modular compression of this sort creates a curious hybrid between Classic periodicity and Baroque motivic development, since the motivic recurrences at the end add up to an irregular and unpredictable number of bars—unlike later usage by Haydn and Beethoven, according to which

Example 8

a) Haydn, Symphony No. 20 in C major (c. 1761), i, 1–20

Allegro molto

b) Hasse, Sinfonia in D, *Egeria* (1764), 1–9 (Vienna, Austrian National Library, 18280)

Allegro con spirito

the motivic fragments spin themselves out within the larger periodic framework. This theme type appeared in overtures by Hasse (see Example 8b) and symphonies by C. P. E. Bach.

Motivic focus in the Baroque permitted the growth of lengthy themes from small motives without prominent periodic articulation. Such themes depended upon one or a few strongly directional elements—such as a broad melodic contour or harmonic pattern—to counter the uniform motivic repetition. The sequences used mainly in modulatory sections of Haydn's early symphonies illustrate this type, often resembling the beat-marking style of many North German works. So does the Italian-overture crescendo theme beginning Haydn's Symphony No. 1 in D major (Example 9a), in which a chain of one-bar motives fuses into a nine-bar theme by virtue of the unity provided by a dynamic crescendo, melodic rise, tonic pedal point, and increasing rhythmic agitation. Any one of a number of Jommelli or Galuppi overtures might have provided a model for this rousing opening idea (for example, Example 9b).

Example 9

a) Haydn, Symphony No. 1 in D major (c. 1759–60), i, 1–9

Presto

b) Jommelli, Sinfonia in D, *Attilio regolo* (1753), 1–10 (London, British Museum, Add. 31690)

In citing the works of mid-eighteenth-century composers other than Haydn, I have tried to show that the asymmetrical thematic construction in Haydn's early symphonies resulted not merely from Fortspinnung techniques, but from a variety of periodic and nonperiodic thematic processes in wide current usage among the most fashionable practitioners of the early Classic style, including many composers whose works Haydn could have known. The question of antecedents for these thematic patterns is a hard one. While thematic symmetry is often traced to song and dance types, the kinds of asymmetry and nonregular symmetry considered here cannot be so easily associated with a genre or type. Is it possible to find functional antecedents for the asymmetrical phrase rhythms that so naturally integrated themselves into the symphony—perhaps in folk music and dance, as examples of odd phrasing in Weber's *Theorie* suggest? Or must one conclude that these were simply a part of instrumental vocabulary in general, an alternative result of the breaking up of Baroque lines by *galant* articulation? The occurrence of three-unit phrasing in Beethoven suggests what a tenacious hold this type of asymmetry had on the musical mind of the eighteenth century, at least for purpose of obtaining variety in instrumental music.

There seems to be no correlation between the degree and type of thematic asymmetry that Haydn employs and other elements of his style. Symphonies with Italian overture traits such as tremolo themes, minor-mode secondary themes, or *opera buffa* rhythmic patterns (for example, Nos. 1, 32, 9), those with Mannheim leaps, slides, sighs, and dialogue themes (Nos. 33, 10), and those with North German "sewing machine" rhythms, rapid harmonic rhythm, or C. P. E. Bach's dramatic leaps (Nos. 15, 13) or with Viennese "learned" quasi-contrapuntal themes (No. 16) show no consistent differences with regard to favoring either symmetry or asymmetry, or favoring one type of asymmetry over another. What differences there are seem to result from differences in the size of the characteristic module, that is, the most consistently recurring phrase length in the movement. Movements based on half-bar and one-bar motives (for example, Hob. I:107 ["A"], No. 15) tend to be more erratic in thematic construction, unpredictably running the gamut of possibilities from isolated motivic statements to full eight-bar sentences (often sequences), without establishing a larger modular rhythm, while movements wholly committed to the two-bar and four-bar phrase (Nos. 17, 24) tend to avoid dangling bars and half bars, effectively combining one-, two-, and three-bar units into a larger rhythm that transcends the barline. To this extent, the date of the work may relate to the type of asymmetry employed, since modular length tended to increase over the years, but even this tendency is not directly continuous in Haydn's works.

If questions about the roots of Haydn's asymmetry remain unanswered, it is because the inquiry has not yet acquired sufficient scope. The nature of asymmetry in Baroque music, particularly as it survived in Austrian church and chamber music of Haydn's time, has to be clarified before the extent of transfer can be determined. Furthermore, phrase rhythm in music of various regions (Italy, Mannehim, Vienna, North Germany, and France) must be more carefully differentiated—if indeed this is possible—to see whether there may be regional, functional, or stylistic origins for particular phrase rhythms. The position of Vienna as the musical melting-pot of the eighteenth century perhaps may make the task of separating the influences upon Haydn ultimately impossible, but it at least partly explains the seemingly endless variety in Haydn's musical imagination.

Haydn's Hybrid Variations

ELAINE R. SISMAN

Haydn's variations, never studied in their entirety, have traditionally been placed in a number of categories that emphasize superficial differences. Actually, a division into two broad categories—here termed strophic and hybrid—is most appropriate. And although a few subtypes of the latter are apparent, I hope to demonstrate that the principles underlying all of Haydn's hybrid variations are the same.[1]

A set of strophic variations may be likened to a row of boxes. The theme, the first box, has a certain structure which is retained in each successive box, or variation. Elements of the theme, particularly period structure, harmony, and melody, can always be recognized. The basic constructive principle is one of *repetition.* Hybrid variations, on the other hand, are dominated by *recurrence* of the initial structure after intervening, contrasting material. Here the succession of theme and variations is interrupted by couplets or episodes with different structures, or it may even alternate with another theme and its own variations.

Haydn combines variation form with rondo and ternary (ABA) designs. He also varies alternately a major and minor theme. These hybrids may be termed "rondo-variation," "ternary variation," and "alternating

---

[1] Some of this material appears in Sisman, "Variations," Ch. 3, 5.

variation." Common to all of them, however, are two essential ideas. One is the varied return of the theme. The other is contrast of mode: only a few exceptional rondo- or ternary variations do not contain a section in the opposite mode.

The terminology and formal concepts used in this paper reflect those of eighteenth-century writers wherever possible. Koch defines variations as "multiple immediate repetitions of a short piece."[2] While so concise and accurate a term as "strophic variation" is not used by the theorists, Walther's reference to "the second *verse* of an air, varied," is one good precedent.[3] Rondo-variation is described by Koch as an option for a symphony finale: ". . . sometimes it contains variations on a characteristic dance melody or on a short Allegro: these variations, however, are usually mixed with short interpolated episodes in closely related keys, after the fashion of the rondo."[4] Clearly, the form is considered a set of variations with "rondo-like" interpolations, rather than a rondo form with varied returns of the theme. Hence, "rondo-variation" is a better term than the traditional "variation rondo."

Alternating variations on a major and a minor theme are described by Reicha.[5] The term "double variation," often used to designate these movements, will be avoided here for two reasons: first, it overlaps with the term *Double,* which not only refers to the older improvised or composed embellishment practice for suite movements, but is often a synonym for "variation" itself in many eighteenth-century treatises; and second, it has been used to describe variations in which, within a given variation, the repeats are written out and varied further.[6] "Alternating variation" is more consistent with Reicha's discussion and with Haydn's practice.

Haydn's hybrid variations illustrate an important point about his style: he was most interested not in arrangements of "boxes" or sections in each piece, but rather in underlying principles through which interesting hybrids could be made: varied recurrence and contrast of mode or tonality. An examination of his hybrids from this standpoint shows that rondo-variation and alternating variation are two sides of the same coin; ternary variation is related currency.

The most striking examples of this relationship are found in the Sonatas Hob. XVI:36 in A major and XVI:39 in G major (ChL. 49,52), from the "Auenbrugger" set published in 1780. The Scherzando second movement of the former and the Allegro con brio first movement of the latter open with almost exactly the same theme. Haydn's often-quoted letter to Artaria of February 25, 1780 purports to explain:

[2] Koch, *Lexikon,* s.v. "Variazionen, Variazioni."   [3] Walther, *Lexicon,* s.v. "Double."
[4] Koch, *Versuch,* III, 314.   [5] Reicha, *Traité,* II, 303–04.
[6] Nelson, *Variation,* 85–88 uses the term in this way and cites similar applications by other writers.

Incidentally, I consider it necessary, in order to forestall the criticisms of any hecklers, to print on the reverse side of the title page the following sentence, here underlined:

Avertissement:
Among these 6 Sonatas there are two single movements in which the same subject occurs through several bars: the author has done this intentionally, to show different methods of treatment. For of course I could have chosen a hundred other ideas instead of this one; but so that the whole opus will not be exposed to blame on account of this one intentional detail (which the critics and especially my enemies might interpret wrongly), I think that this avertissement or something like it must be appended, otherwise the sale might be hindered thereby.[7]

Was Haydn covering up for a memory lapse? Abert champions him, claiming that even the change in key from A major to G major was a distinct "difference in treatment," since it affected the listener's sensibilities.[8] Other writers, notably Feder and Newman, doubt Haydn's sincerity.[9] We can make no further judgment here on Haydn's motives. More relevant to our purpose is the way in which each movement continues. The identity of the two themes affords a good opportunity to compare each movement's structure and to judge the categories "alternating variation" for Hob. XVI:36 and "rondo-variation" for Hob. XVI:39.

The second movement of Hob. XVI:36 comprises a theme and two variations, alternating with two couplets in the parallel minor. At first, we perceive the second couplet as a more highly figured variation of the first one, because the initial material and the key are the same. But they have different harmonic structures; even though they are identical in length, only the final cadences actually coincide.

The theme and the two variations in Hob. XVI:39 are set off by two couplets in different minor keys, the parallel and the relative minor. Their thematic material is entirely different, despite relations to the main theme in both cases, and both variations end on a half cadence. This movement is the prototype for the first movement of the Piano Trio in G major, Hob. XV:25.

Two important similarities exist between these two sonata movements. First, the principle of contrast in mode dominates the structure as a whole. The major themes and their variations are thrown into relief by the *minore* couplets. That the first episode in each is in the parallel minor heightens the closeness of this relationship.

Second, and most telling, is the reprise of the *theme* between the end of each couplet and the next variation proper. Haydn here requires that we recognize the theme before it is varied. Indeed, in the vast majority of variation movements that contain one or more themes, couplets, or vari-

[7] Haydn, CCLN, 25 (with slight alterations) (*Briefe* 90–91).
[8] Abert, "Klavier," Part 2, 843–44.
[9] Feder, "Similarities," 187; Newman, *Classic,* 466.

ations in the opposite mode, he includes a partial or total reprise of the main theme after the intervening material. (This is quite different from the procedure, common before 1775 but rare thereafter, of rounding off a set of strophic variations with an unadorned repetition of the main theme.)

It thus appears that the five-part alternating variation is a specific form of rondo-variation, with the Sonatas Hob. XVI:36 and 39 the paradigm cases. This type may therefore be termed "alternating rondo-variation." What then of the alternating variation in six parts, which consists of three double strophes? Movements of this type, like the Andante of Symphony No. 103 in E-flat major ("Drum Roll"), always begin in minor, so that the desired conclusion in major is assured.[10] These movements actually combine repetition with recurrence: the initial structure in each mode recurs after contrast, but the pattern is also a higher-level repetition. While still a hybrid form, this "alternating strophic-variation" is more distantly related to the rondo-variation, since the first theme does not recur at the end. Table 1 lists all of Haydn's hybrid variations.

Haydn's alternating rondo-variation has a direct predecessor and possible model in a one-movement "Sonata" by C. P. E. Bach. This piece, the sixth of the *Sonaten mit veränderten Reprisen* (1760, H. 140), has a C-minor theme with two varied restatements which are separated by two related C-major couplets. In fact, the second couplet varies the first. Departing from the form of the other sonatas in the set, it nonetheless retains the varied reprise idea by repeating with further variation each segment of the piece. Six different versions of each part of the minor theme are thus created, and four of each part of the major "theme." (Constant repetition and varying occur also in the finales of Sonatas II and III.) Significantly, the *veränderte Reprisen* sonatas were circulating in Vienna in 1767 and 1769, immediately preceding Haydn's first experiments with the varied reprise in the Op. 9 string quartets (c. 1769–70); it was also advertised in 1773.[11] Haydn's first datable rondo-variation is from 1767, in the Sonata Hob. XVI:19 (ChL. 30) in D major, and the first datable alternating rondo-variation belongs to 1773, in the Sonata Hob. XVI:22 (ChL. 37) in E major—both in keyboard sonatas. The evidence certainly suggests a connection between Bach's sonatas and Haydn's applications of variation techniques to a hybrid form.[12]

---

[10] Reicha, *Traité,* II, 304 prescribes an ending in the major, basing his remarks on Haydn's "andantes variés." But his suggested model begins in the major, has four variations on each theme, and concludes with a "development and coda" on the major theme.

[11] Gericke, *Musikalienhandel,* 61, 72. In addition, Bach's *Kurze und leichte Clavierstücke mit veränderten Reprisen,* first collection (1766; H. 193–203, Wq. 113) were advertised in 1769. (Gericke, 51, incorrectly identifies this as the second collection [1768; H. 228–238, Wq. 114], because what was in circulation was the 1768 Augsburg edition of the earlier set.)

[12] Bach even has a ternary variation movement in his Sonata H. 158 (Wq. 52,3), from 1762, considerably before Haydn's first use of this form. But there is no evidence that it circulated in Vienna.

Table 1 *Haydn's Hybrid Variations*

Key

RV	Rondo-variation
ARV	Alternating rondo-variation
ASV	Alternating strophic-variation
ABA	Ternary
★	Unusual structure

Symphonies (Hob. I)

42, iv	RV		82, ii	ARV
51, iv	RV		88, ii	RV★
55, iv	RV		89, ii	ABA
53, ii	ARV		90, ii	ARV
70, ii	ARV		92, ii	ABA
63, ii	ASV		101, ii	RV
74, ii	RV		103, ii	ASV
76, ii	RV		104, ii	ABA
78, iv	ASV★			

String Quartets

Op. 33, No. 2, iii	RV		Op. 64, No. 5, ii	ABA
Op. 33, No. 4, iv	RV		Op. 64, No. 6, iii	ABA
Op. 33, No. 6, iv	ARV		Op. 71, No. 2, iv	ABA
Op. 50, No. 3, ii	RV		Op. 71, No. 3, ii	ARV★
Op. 50, No. 4, ii	ARV		Op. 74, No. 3, ii	ABA
Op. 54, No. 2, iv	ABA★		Op. 76, No. 2, ii	ABA
Op. 55, No. 2, i	ASV		Op. 76, No. 5, i	ABA
Op. 64, No. 3, ii	ABA		Op. 77, No. 2, iii	RV
Op. 64, No. 4, iii	ABA			

Piano Trios (Hob. XV)

6, ii	ABA		20, iii	ABA
8, ii	ABA		23, i	ASV
11, ii	ABA		25, i	RV
13, i	ASV		31, ii	ABA
15, ii	ABA		30, ii	ABA
18, ii	ABA		27, ii	ABA
19, i	ASV★		29, i	ABA

Keyboard Sonatas (Hob. XVI [ChL.])

19 (30), iii	RV		34 (53), iii	ARV
44 (32), ii	ASV★		40 (54), i	ARV
22 (37), iii	ARV		40 (54), ii	ABA
33 (34), iii	ARV		41 (55), ii	ABA
36 (49), ii	ARV		48 (58), i	ARV★
39 (52), i	RV		49 (59), ii	ABA

Independent Set

Hob. XVII:6	ASV★

Haydn rarely labeled his variation and rondo movements. None of the hybrid variation movements carries the term "Variation." In fact, with a few special exceptions,[13] none of the variation movements of any type past the mid-1770s is so labeled. On March 29, 1789, Haydn wrote to Artaria concerning the Piano Trio Hob. XV:13 in C major: "I send you herewith the 3rd Sonata, which I have newly composed [*ganz neu verfertigte*] with variations, to suit your taste." The first movement of the trio is an alternating strophic-variation set in C minor. And terminological confusion also results from Haydn's titles "Sonata" and "Un piccolo Divertimento" for the F-minor piano variations, Hob. XVII:6. This piece is the only example of a seven-part alternating variation set; most probably, Haydn originally intended it to be the first movement in a sonata. The short original ending in F major, placed after the second major variation, was replaced—and (inadvertently?) not crossed out in the autograph—by a reprise of the theme and long coda in minor. With the original ending, the movement would have been a more common six-part alternating strophic-variation set, such as those in the first movements of the Piano Trios Hob. XV:13 and XV:23 in D minor, and the String Quartet Op. 55, No. 2 (also in F minor). The evidence of the autograph supports the idea that the movement's present form as well as its existence as an independent set was an afterthought.[14]

Before about 1780, when the Sonatas Hob. XVI:36 and 39 appeared, the rondo-variation form had developed in Haydn's presto or allegro finales of sonatas and symphonies. The alternating rondo-variation appeared more sporadically, in minuet finales of piano sonatas and slow movements of symphonies. After about 1780, both types of hybrid variation remained for the most part in andante or adagio first or second movements.

The theoretical dicta of Koch again serve to illuminate the relationship of these movements. The third volume of his *Versuch* discusses possible spots in the symphony for a variation movement. He explains that an ordinary strophic variation series, based by definition on a non-character piece, may be used for the slow movement; a ritornello-like use of the theme modifies the repetitive structure, thus introducing the principle of recurrence. And the last allegro of a symphony, as cited above, may con-

[13] For example, String Quartet Op. 76, No. 3 in C major, ii (the "Emperor" variations)—labeling was common when using a borrowed melody. Or the first piano variation in "Dr. Harington's Compliment," Hob. XXVIb:3—following the practice of the suite or sonata *double*, common in Wagenseil. Or the independent piano variations Hob. XVII:5—labeling was common in independent sets. In all contexts, Haydn labeled only the first few strophic sets; that such headings recur in the slow movement of Symphony No. 75 in D major may be due to its "hymn-like" theme.
[14] The autograph has a separate title page bearing the heading "Sonate," the rewritten ending placed after a blank page, and da capo markings and instructions overlaid in red pencil.

tain variations on a characteristic piece, with rondo-like interpolations.[15]

Surely this contemporary comment links the minuet "alternating rondo-variation" finale with the allegro/presto "rondo-variation," and brings slow-movement variations into the realm of the hybrid forms.

A Numerical Approach to Activity and Movement in the Sonata-Form Movements of Haydn's Piano Trios

LESTER S. STEINBERG

In tracing the evolution of sonata form in Haydn's piano trios, one is confronted almost immediately with a most puzzling problem: how does the composer manage to maintain continuous musical flow in a formal structure characterized by strongly articulated thematic areas that naturally tend to fragment it? It appears that Haydn also concerned himself with this problem. In his conversations with Griesinger, he described his method of composing as follows:

> Once I had seized upon an idea, my whole endeavor was to develop and sustain it in keeping with the rules of art. Thus I sought to keep going, and this is where so many of our new composers fall down. They string out one little piece after another, they break off when they have hardly begun. . . .[1]

Although Haydn developed many harmonic and melodic devices for "keeping the music going," he also succeeded in creating musical flow or movement in another, perhaps intuitive, manner by establishing patterns of fluctuating activity.

One effective approach to understanding activity and movement has been developed by Jan LaRue.[2] He calls attention to an inherent stratification: movement is created by changes in the activity of one or more of the basic elements—harmony, melody, or rhythm. Since overall activity results from the interaction of all three elements, a pattern in which this overall activity continuously rises and falls would generate continuous musical flow. However, describing and comparing activity levels *verbally* in a large number of samples presents a formidable problem. Terms such as "very active," "slightly active," or "moderately active" soon become inadequate, and one is forced to seek some method for converting activity to more precise numerical terms. The aim of this discussion is to suggest such a method and to report on some of the results obtained with it.

The process of measuring activity consists, fundamentally, of attaching a numerical value to each basic element, then combining all of

[15] Later, Koch suggests the rondo-variation for concerto finales (*Versuch,* III, 341) and the strophic variation for sonata finales (319). His aim, he states, is not to account for every possibility, but only the usual ("das Gewöhnliche") (III, 381n).

[1] Gotwals, *Haydn,* 61. (Griesinger, 114; modern ed., 61).

[2] LaRue, *Guidelines,* 12 ff.

the values to determine the quantitative effect of their interaction. At the outset the dimension of the areas to be considered must be established so that the aspects of each basic element which are pertinent to that dimension can be determined. Comparison of small-dimension areas require more detailed and refined observations, while large areas can be observed in broader terms. For example, one unusual chord may create a great difference between motives, but would probably have little effect when comparing large thematic areas or sections of a sonata-form movement. Since our concern is with large areas, we can disregard many details and observe the method in its most basic form.

Harmonic activity in large- or middle-dimension areas is measured simply by counting the number of chord changes within the sample. Here the effective component is frequency of change; small-dimension considerations, such as the kinds of chords or the types of harmonic progressions, have little or no effect upon large-dimension harmonic activity. *Melodic* activity is determined by totaling the intervals between each pair of notes. Differentiation of steps, skips, and leaps, an important factor in small-dimension calculations, becomes relatively unimportant in large or middle dimensions where the fundamental consideration is the cumulative effect created by the melodic line. *Rhythmic* activity can be measured by counting the number of impacts in the sample. In this element, note values, syncopation, and metrical shifts such as hemiola are essentially small-dimension considerations and have little effect upon large-dimension activity.

Thus three numerical values can easily be established that reflect the total amount of activity contributed individually by each element. Each of these numbers is now divided by the length of the sample to arrive at the *density* of each element, or the average rate of activity per measure. In Example 1 a four-bar phrase contains four chord changes, an interval count of sixteen, and twelve impacts. It thus has a harmonic density of 1, a melodic density of 4, and a rhythmic density of 3.

Example 1

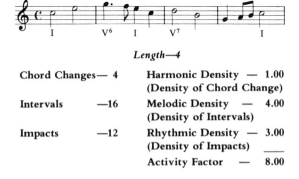

Length—4

Chord Changes— 4   Harmonic Density — 1.00
                     (Density of Chord Change)

Intervals   —16   Melodic Density — 4.00
                     (Density of Intervals)

Impacts   —12   Rhythmic Density — 3.00
                     (Density of Impacts)   ____

                     Activity Factor — 8.00

Since each density figure represents the average number of activity events contributed by one element in one measure, it is clear that we can now add these numbers together to determine the average number of events contributed by all of the elements per measure. This figure will be called the *activity factor* and becomes the basis for comparing and evaluating large- or middle-dimension activity.

Although computation of the activity factor is relatively simple, the musical considerations obviously are much more complex. Throughout the process musical decisions must be made and consistently maintained. For example: is the I_4^6–V–I cadence to be counted as three chords, or is the I_4^6 chord simply an appoggiatura to V and I_4^6–V therefore not a chord change at all? (In our calculations it is convenient to consider I_4^6 as an independent chord.) How are ornaments to be read? One must determine the difference between a grace note which is merely ornamental and an appoggiatura which involves an additional impact. Does chromaticism play an important part in the style? If so, melodic activity must be measured in chromatic rather than diatonic intervals.

The most complex problems, however, are those created by texture. In order to evaluate the effect of texture upon activity it is necessary to reexamine how we actually hear music in terms of its basic components of harmony, melody, and rhythm. The opening phrase of Mozart's Piano Sonata K. 545 in C major represents a situation in which the accompaniment obviously contributes to the activity. In order to determine the extent of this contribution it is necessary to compare the original with a version in which the accompaniment is omitted. Example 2a represents the phrase as Mozart wrote it, Example 2b illustrates what we actually hear in terms of interaction, and Example 2c is a version of the phrase in which the Alberti accompaniment is replaced by simple chords. By comparing the activity factor of Example 2a with that of Example 2c we find that the accompaniment contributes almost one third of the total activity of the phrase.

We are now prepared to examine a complete sonata-form movement and to compare the activity of its thematic areas and its sections. For this purpose I have chosen the second movement of Haydn's Piano Trio Hob. XV:13 in C minor, completed in 1789 (see p. 519).

After determining the lengths of the sections under consideration, the statistical data for each is then systematically assembled—the number of chord changes, the intervallic count, and the number of impacts. From this we calculate the densities by dividing each statistical element by the length of the section. Finally the activity factor for each section is determined by adding all of the density figures in that section.

The results, displayed in Table 1, show that activity does indeed fluctuate in Haydn's expositions. In this particular movement the activity

Example 2. Mozart, Sonata K. 545 in C major, i, 1–4

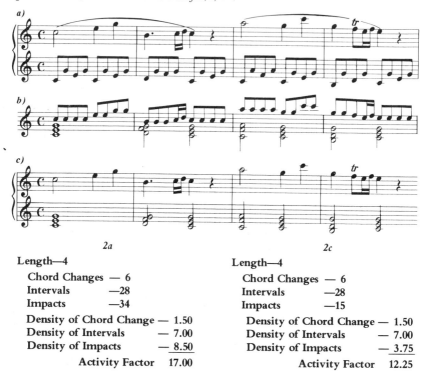

Length—4		Length—4	
Chord Changes — 6		Chord Changes — 6	
Intervals	—28	Intervals	—28
Impacts	—34	Impacts	—15
Density of Chord Change — 1.50		Density of Chord Change — 1.50	
Density of Intervals	— 7.00	Density of Intervals	— 7.00
Density of Impacts	— 8.50	Density of Impacts	— 3.75
Activity Factor	17.00	Activity Factor	12.25

factor drops in the transitional area (T),[3] increases in the secondary theme (S), and drops again in the closing theme (K). The *activity range,* or the difference between the least active and the most active thematic area, is 43%. This figure may bear a relationship to the dramatic quality of the movement, since music of strong dramatic impact is usually characterized by broad differences in activity.

The secondary thematic area (S) appears to be the most active of the exposition, a typical Haydn characteristic. On the other hand, the low activity level of the closing theme (K) is rather uncharacteristic; although many of Haydn's closing themes are somewhat less active than the secondary themes, they are rarely the least active of the entire exposition. We also find the secondary key area (S and K combined) to be slightly more active than the primary key area (P and T), while the activity factor of the development increases somewhat over that of the exposition as a whole. Contrary to what one might expect, in these works the developments do not appear to be large-scale climactic areas. In fact, as we shall soon see, many of Haydn's developments are actually less active than the preceding expositions.

---

[3] The symbols used here are those suggested by LaRue, *Guidelines,* 154.

Table 1   *Haydn, Piano Trio Hob. XV:13 in C minor, ii*

	P	T	S	K	Exp.	Dev.
Length	23	20	31	26	100	52
Chord Changes	26	31	32	40	131	68
Intervals	213	160	272	161	826	444
Impacts	141	128	299	153	719	387
Density of Chord Changes	1.13	1.55	1.03	1.54	1.31	1.31
Density of Intervals	9.26	8.00	8.77	6.19	8.26	4.44
Density of Impacts	6.13	6.40	9.65	5.88	7.19	7.44
Activity Factor	16.52	15.95	19.45	13.61	16.76	17.29

Primary Key Area—16.24   Activity Range of Exposition—43%
Secondary Key Area—16.53   (13.61 to 19.45)

While these observations may be significant in their own right, they gain considerably in importance as a basis for comparison with other works. In Tables 2, 3, and 4 the activity factors for all the sonata-form movements in the piano trios that appear either as opening movements or allegro second movements have been tabulated chronologically.

Table 2 confirms that fluctuating activity characterizes Haydn's expositions even in the earliest works. The sequences of activity changes, however, do not conform to any single pattern. Thus, for example, in Hob. XV:C1 in C major activity increases from P to T and from T to S, then decreases to K, while in XV:1 in G minor activity drops from P to T, increases to S, and drops again to K. S themes remain highly active; in fact, in at least half of the trios of this period they are the most active sections of the exposition. Activity ranges vary considerably in these works, averaging a moderate 41%. Secondary key areas are more active than primary key areas with only two exceptions, XV:35 in A major and XV:38 in B-flat major.

Table 2   *Activity Factors: Early Trios c. 1755–1765*

Trio	P	T	S	K	Range %	Prim. Key Area	Sec. Key Area	Exp. Length	Exp. A.F.	Dev. Length	Dev. A.F.
37/1	20.67	23.00	25.01	28.40	37	21.84	26.71	23	24.78	26	20.58↓
C1/i	30.66	32.67	39.50	28.00	41	31.67	33.75	20	32.90	23	38.57
1/i	36.00	28.85	46.50	44.28	61	32.43	45.39	28	42.93	21	36.00↓
40/i	19.15		24.46	16.36	50	19.15	20.41	43	19.81	28	19.71↓
41/i	13.08	15.14	21.03	18.43	61	14.11	19.73	40	18.05	42	18.50
35/i	25.64	22.04	24.06	20.83	23	23.84	↓22.45	63	23.49	39	23.88
34/i	18.16	15.60	16.01	19.63	26	16.88	17.82	36	17.64	31	15.61↓
36/i	23.16	22.16	23.19	25.20	14	22.66	24.20	38	24.00	34	28.21
38/i	29.63	42.80	38.60	32.00	44	36.22	↓35.30	23	35.61	19	37.15
f1/i	32.34	28.20	43.46	42.40	54	30.27	42.93	27	38.45	16	36.57↓
Ave.	24.85	25.61	30.18	27.55	41	24.91	28.87	34	27.77	28	27.48↓

Table 3   Activity Factors: Middle-Period Trios 1784–1789

Trio	P	T	S	K	Range %	Prim. Key Area	Sec. Key Area	Exp. Length	Exp. A.F.	Dev. Length	Dev. A.F.
5/ii	20.14		24.96	23.11	24	20.14	24.04	59	23.36	41	24.29
6/i	24.15	23.01	21.67	23.68	10	23.58	↓22.81	59	23.24	51	23.49
8/i	18.40	17.69	21.43	20.13	21	18.05	20.78	60	19.50	44	19.67
9/i	15.67	11.52	13.27	15.07	36	13.60	14.17	77	15.26	58	17.62
10/i	16.00	25.00	23.08	17.14	56	20.50	↓20.11	51	21.18	47	23.28
11/i	14.73	21.12	19.31	18.82	43	17.93	19.07	79	18.98	74	20.47
12/i	15.53	19.09	20.53	19.88	32	17.31	20.21	70	19.30	21	22.57
13/i	16.52	15.95	19.45	13.61	43	16.24	16.53	100	16.76	52	17.29
14/i	18.51	15.88	16.53	18.00	17	17.20	17.27	82	17.46	79	17.47
Ave.	17.74	18.66	20.03	18.83	31	18.28	19.44	71	19.46	52	20.68
3/i	14.87	19.60	13.36	16.79	48	18.24	↓15.11	130	14.86	58	14.56↓
4/i	23.38	19.97	25.77	13.20	95	21.68	↓19.49	90	21.02	64	16.61↓

An unexpected aspect of Haydn's earliest experiments with sonata form is the generally low activity level of his development sections. In half of the early trios the development is actually less active than the exposition, and in some of the remaining works differences between the two sections are so slight as to be practically negligible, for example in Hob. XV:40 in F major and XV:41 in G major.

By 1784, the beginning of the middle period, significant changes occur in Haydn's sonata-form structure, accompanied by a marked increase in the length of the movement and a general reduction in activity and activity range (Table 3). Average activity factors are now approximately one third lower than those of the early period, and the activity range of the expositions has been reduced by about 25%, indicating perhaps that Haydn was now more concerned with structural considerations than with dramatic change. Secondary key areas remain more active than principal key areas but to a somewhat lesser degree than those of the early period.

The relationship between the exposition and the development has now become more consistent. Every middle-period development is, to some degree, more active than its exposition. Although in some of the works the activity factors are too close to indicate a real difference, we find no sonata-form movements comparable to those of the early period in which an unmistakable drop occurs in the development.

In the 1790s, Haydn's late period, his sonata-form structure appears to have undergone further change (Table 4). The movements are somewhat shorter than those of the middle period, but not as short as those of the early works. Activity factors have become higher, and the dramatic quality of these works is reflected in the unusually high activity ranges, averaging 86%. Secondary key areas are now frequently less active than the primary key areas by appreciable amounts. Similarly, activity factors

Table 4 Activity Factors: Late Trios 1790–1796

Trio	P	T	S	K	Range %	Prim. Key Area	Sec. Key Area	Exp. Length	A.F.	Dev. Length	A.F.
16/i	20.58	16.40	22.13	15.07	47	18.49	18.60	61	18.69	65	19.62
15/i	12.82	15.35	15.17	16.23	27	14.09	15.70	95	15.19	55	16.09
17/i	36.75	33.36	34.78	23.17	59	35.06	↓28.98	32	33.21	30	34.13
18/i	15.19	21.12	16.79	18.13	39	18.16	↓17.46	77	18.39	47	16.26↓
20/i	32.51	18.75	30.94	25.43	73	25.63	28.19	40	29.76	28	20.82↓
21/i	22.63	17.86	18.00	18.41	27	20.25	↓18.20	52	19.00	33	20.24
22/i	13.07	22.20	15.00	17.08	70	17.64	↓16.04	86	17.80	63	18.57
24/i	16.96	12.43	27.91	11.43	144	14.70	19.67	69	16.91	51	17.60
26/i	13.63	26.23	47.71	30.55	243	19.93	38.63	37	28.51	25	41.56
30/i	19.09	13.67	17.78	24.27	78	16.38	21.03	91	19.03	45	19.11
27/i	22.36	48.15	45.22	34.57	115	35.26	39.90	43	38.43	35	31.40↓
28/i	18.40	29.36	33.65	37.69	105	23.88	35.67	38	30.29	21	35.85
Ave.	20.33	22.91	27.01	22.67	86	21.62	24.84	60	23.77	42	24.27

of late-period development sections are more likely to be lower than those of the expositions.

Thus we see that activity factors provide us with a profile of the composer's style that can vary from one period to the next as significant changes occur. If these profiles are truly individual and distinctive, they should also be useful as tools for determining authenticity. An opportunity for testing this possibility presents itself in these Haydn trios.

In 1785, three piano trios were published by William Forster in London as Haydn's Op. 40. Although doubts arose concerning the authenticity of two of these works shortly after their publication, they appear in Hoboken as XV:3 and XV:4 and in modern editions such as Peters.

Alan Tyson has established that only one of the Op. 40 trios is actually by Haydn and that the remaining two are most probably by Pleyel, who had been his student.[4] The publication date 1785 places the Pleyel trios squarely in Haydn's middle period. At the bottom of Table 3 the activity factors for both works have been computed and can now be compared with the Haydn trios of the same period.

The most striking aspect of XV:3 is that its exposition is considerably longer than that of any Haydn trio. Another unusual feature is the comparatively low activity factor of S, in this case the lowest of the entire exposition. This uncommon situation occurs in only one Haydn trio, XV:6 in F major, and even there the activity factor of S is only slightly lower than that of the surrounding areas. The decisive drop in activity at S in this Pleyel trio never seems to occur in Haydn's middle period. Also, the sequence of activity fluctuations in this exposition—an increase to T, a decrease to S, followed by another increase to K—does not occur in any Haydn trio of this period. Although the development section also repre-

[4] Tyson, "Trios"

sents a drop in activity, unusual in a Haydn trio of this period, the difference is very small and probably well within the acceptable margin of error. More important, however, are the extremely low activity factors of both the exposition and the development, considerably lower than those of any Haydn trio in any period.

The activity factors of XV:4 also indicate marked differences from those of Haydn's authentic works. S has now become the most active area of the exposition. Although this is commonplace in Haydn, here the activity factor appears to be excessively high, higher than that of any Haydn middle-period trio. K on the other hand, is less active than any comparable closing section. As a result, the activity range of XV:4 soars to 95%, more than three times the average of Haydn's authentic works in the middle period. The appreciable drop in the secondary key area and particularly the large drop in the development are also highly uncharacteristic of Haydn's middle-period works.

It is now apparent that each of the Pleyel trios deviates in many ways from the profile established for Haydn's middle period. Had it not already been established that these are not authentic works, this method would certainly have aroused strong suspicions.

Preliminary computations indicate that the sonata-form movements of Mozart and Beethoven can also be delineated by means of highly distinctive activity profiles. Although the method is still in its early stages and much remains to be done, the information that has already emerged appears to be valid. This system has many practical possibilities and can be adapted to music of many types and periods.[5]

Freedom of Form in Haydn's Early String Quartets

JAMES WEBSTER

A serious problem with the analytical literature on Haydn is its inadequate treatment of his early music. To an extent, this omission is understandable. Until recently, relatively little of his early music was known, and almost none in accurate texts. Furthermore, the principal historical accounts of Classical style tend to dismiss it as immature, tentative, and stereotyped; at best, it is damned with faint praise, as in the view that it represents Haydn's promising "first steps" towards eventual "maturity." But in fact Haydn's early music is a treasure-trove of miniature delights. From a methodological point of view, its small dimensions and relatively simple textures make it easier to analyze than most of his later music—no mean advantage in the struggle with Haydn's individual and heterogeneous formal procedures. Finally, and most important, there are striking continuities between Haydn's early music and almost all of his

[5] The method of activity analysis is also used by Jan LaRue in the Round Table on "Opus 3." [Ed.]

later production. In turning to it with an unbiased and sympathetic ear, we will also gain important new perspectives on Haydn's development as a composer.

Conventional descriptions of form are no more adequate as explanations of Haydn's early music than of the London symphonies. In invoking the concept "freedom" I naturally do not mean to suggest that a composition which happens to exemplify conventional notions of form is somehow "unfree," or that a work which does not exemplify them is necessarily better than one which does. My point is rather that even before 1760 Haydn can never be assumed to have composed by scheme or by rote. Even here, one finds the kind of imaginative, resourceful, varied responses to artistic situations that characterize mature artists in full command of their powers. I would like to document this freedom in two formal contexts: the return to the main theme in the second half of minuets, and the reorganization of material in the recapitulation of sonata-form movements. For this discussion I have chosen my examples from Haydn's early string quartets.

Even in Haydn's earliest works, many minuets are constructed like miniature sonata-form movements: a statement in the tonic leading eventually to a cadence in the dominant; a quasi-development section or dominant pedal leading to a return of the first idea in the tonic; and a close in the tonic paralleling the earlier close in the dominant.[1] A clear example is the second movement of Op. 2, No. 2 in E major (see Example 1). Here,

Example 1. String Quartet Op. 2, No. 2 in E major, ii, 1–8, 17–24

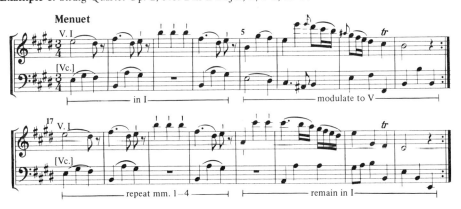

[1] Though not often recognized in conventional writings on form, the formal identity of minuets of this structural type and sonata form is consonant not only with Schenkerian analysis, but the best traditional analysis as well. Tovey often described sonata forms as expansions of the relations within a single melody. And Charles Rosen (*Style*, 83–88) offers a brilliant analysis of just this relation between a binary theme and its expansion, in the first movement of the Piano Trio Hob. XV:19 in G minor.

mm. 17–20 repeat the "first group" mm. 1–4; and mm. 21–24 recompose mm. 5–8—note the high register, the descending sixteenths, and the cadence—in such a way as to end in the tonic.

Often, Haydn varies or rewrites the reprise (the point where the main theme returns in the tonic). In the fourth movement of Op. 2, No. 6 in B-flat major, the motive corresponding to mm. 1–2 is inverted in mm. 21–22, and similarly in succeeding measures; and the harmonic contents are altered (see Example 2). Although mm. 21–28 clearly function as a recapitulation of mm. 1–8, no two corresponding bars are the same except for the two-bar cadential phrases.

Example 2. String Quartet Op. 2, No. 6 in B-flat major, iv, 1–8, 17–28

An even more thoroughgoing process of recomposition appears in the second minuet of Op. 2, No. 4 in F major (Example 3). The first half of this tiny binary movement comprises two contrasting four-bar phrases (a) and (b). The second half is a disguised repetition: mm. 9–12 transfer (a) into the bass and state it twice; mm. 15–16 and 17–18 both end with the lilting motive (b), in the same harmonic position; and the close in the tonic parallels the cadence in the dominant, mm. 7–8. Thus all the important events of the first half return, in the same order, and with the appropriate tonal orientation; but none of them is literally repeated.

These variations show that the young Haydn was already possessed by his irrepressible urge to vary and develop his material. The most striking

Example 3. String Quartet Op. 2, No. 4 in F major, iv, 1–20

example of this tendency in the early minuets is the fourth movement of Op. 2, No. 1 in A major (see Example 4). The two-bar idea of mm. 1–2 dominates the entire movement. It consists of an upbeat e^2; a stepwise descent of a third, from d^2 to b^1, in dotted rhythm; and a skip of a third, $c\#^2$–a^1. The following phrase varies this idea by compressing the thirds d^2–b^1 and $c\#^2$–a^1 into a single measure. The third phrase places the idea the inner parts, and it inverts both components based on the third: the dotted-rhythm move from b to d^1 in m. 5, and the skip in m. 6. The fourth phrase, still under the pedal, returns to the original register and contour. In the second half of the minuet, mm. 11–12 repeat mm. 1–2, inflected towards the subdominant. At the reprise (mm. 17–18), the purely harmonic support in the lower parts of mm. 1–2 is replaced by obbligato writing in all four instruments—that is, the scoring is already

Example 4. String Quartet Op. 2, No. 1 in A major, iv, 1–26

analogous to mm. 3–4. Though mm. 21–22 are analogous to mm. 5–6 in placing the motive in the inner parts, they differ considerably in other respects. And in mm. 23–24 the motive is inverted in a new sense: it skips up a sixth from f♯² to the climax on d³, creating a connection in register between the preparations for the two final cadences. Except for those two cadences and mm. 13–16, every phrase is based on mm. 1–2, and yet the only exact repetition among these nine statements is that of mm. 3–4 in 19–20. A more convincing example of Haydn's facility in building an entire movement out of a single idea could hardly be found in any later work.

The sonata-form movements in Haydn's early quartets exhibit a similar variety of formal procedure. One of these betrays the influence of binary form on early sonata form, and it may also have been a progenitor of the "false recapitulation": it consists of bringing the main theme back in the tonic shortly after the double bar—usually the second half will have begun with the main theme in the dominant—*before* the development proper.[2] In the first movement of Op. 1, No. 2 in E-flat major the first group consists of a twofold statement of the main theme: first homophonically, answered by a more active five-bar phrase (mm. 1–9); then

[2] Cf. R. Landon, *Symphonies*, 206–08, 320. I am grateful to Professor Rosen for clarifying the difference between this procedure and a "true" false recapitulation.

accompanied by a descant in the first violin (10–17), leading to a half-cadence in m. 21. Following the double bar, eight measures of dominant transition lead directly to a repetition of mm. 1–9 in the tonic (mm. 56–64). The true development follows, leading eventually to the recapitulation in m. 85. Quite logically, Haydn ignores mm. 1–9 here, beginning instead with the second statement of the main theme, corresponding to m. 10. (Similar returns to a counterstatement of the main theme often occur in later works.)

Occasionally, Haydn rewrites the main theme upon its reprise (its return in the tonic at the beginning of the recapitulation).[3] In the first movement of "Op. 0" (Hob. II:6) in E-flat major, the main theme consists of a fourfold imitative presentation of the main idea, followed in mm. 9–10 by a new eighth-note motive in the first violin, leading to a full cadence in m. 14. In the reprise (m. 54), the original main idea is stated only in the inner parts; the eighth-note motive appears simultaneously in the first violin, as a descant; and the cadence from m. 14 becomes a half-cadence (m. 67). (In the second group, the measure-by-measure harmonic contents of the busy passage mm. 15–23 are reversed in mm. 68–76.)

Another of Haydn's common techniques is to rearrange the material from the exposition in the recapitulation. An excellent example occurs in the first movement of Op. 2, No. 2 in E major. The first group consists of two different themes: mm. 1–8 are based on contrasting alternations between solo violin and unison lower strings; mm. 9–16 comprise a homophonic melody in two four-bar phrases. In the recapitulation (m. 80), the first theme appears as expected, but before closing it detours into a sequence over a dominant pedal; the theme from mm. 9–16 is nowhere to be heard. But Haydn has not forgotten it: it returns at the very end of the movement, functioning as a brief coda.

The most drastic recomposition of a recapitulation in the early quartets occurs in the Presto of Op. 2, No. 4 in F major (see Example 5, p. 528ff). The first group consists of a first theme (*a*), a vigorous sixteenth-note motive (*b*), an eighth-note figure (*c*) alternating several times with (*b*), and finally a transition to V of V on a new motive (*d*). As Tovey pointed out, the development is remarkable for its wide-ranging modulations and unexpected tonal resolutions.[4] Following the preparation for the reprise, however, we hear at m. 65 not the characteristic dotted-rhythm motive (*a*), but a simpler eighth-note rhythm in the lower strings under an eighth-note pedal descant. The contour in the second violin, emphasizing c^2 and f^2, and its metrical placement relate it to (*a*). But the key to this reprise lies in the bass, which states, not its original plain I–V–I

[3] Haydn's irregular reprises are described in Schwarting, "Reprisen," and Wolf, "Recapitulations." Characteristically, both writers focus on the late music; I know of no comparable discussion of Haydn's earlier music from this point of view.
[4] Tovey, "Chamber," repr., 18–19.

roots, but a more fluid motive based on (*c*). In mm. 69–71 the latter motive takes over completely, in a powerful unison passage leading directly to the dominant preparation for the return of the second group, on (*d*). Of the original first group and transition, (*a*) appears only in disguise, the important sixteenth-note (*b*) is entirely lacking, and even (*c*) is present primarily in varied form. Yet the tonal structure and formal function of this passage are so clear that we receive the impression of a complete recapitulation of the first group.

These are but a few of the many examples of formal freedom and variety in Haydn's early string quartets. And the same resourcefulness can be found in the solo keyboard sonatas, keyboard trios, and symphonies from this period. The procedures in question—false recapitulation, variation of material upon its return, continual variation of a theme throughout a movement, and rearrangement and recomposition of the recapitulation—suggest that many of Haydn's later "unconventional" formal devices were integral components of his style from the very beginning. In the presence of such imaginative and vital compositional technique, it seems difficult to maintain the myth of the young Haydn's "immaturity" any longer.

Example 5. String Quartet Op. 2, No. 4 in F major, i, 1–22, 65–74

List of Works Cited

This bibliography lists all the works cited in the present volume, and only those, in a single alphabetical ordering keyed to the short titles used in the notes. (For a recent comprehensive Haydn bibliography, see Brown, "Bibliography.") Omitted from this list are works of music (except in the case of scholarly editions with prefaces or critical reports), modern general encyclopedias of music and the like, works dealing with other subjects, and ephemera such as modern newspaper articles. These items are cited in detail in the notes.

The listings include translations, recent editions, and facsimile reprints, especially of works dating from before 1800. (No completeness is claimed in this respect. The original edition and relevant historical reissues are always cited. But recent works, and later and modern editions and translations of works from Haydn's time, are restricted to certain widely available publications and to those actually cited by the contributors.) When more than one original edition is cited, reprints or facsimiles of a given version are listed immediately following—i.e., preceding the next original edition. In the notes, the absence of a qualifying remark such as "2nd ed." or "repr." or "trans." indicates that the reference is to the first edition cited here.

Full bibliographic particulars are given for articles from congress reports, *Festschriften,* and the like, except in the case of a few frequently cited volumes, for which cross-references are supplied. A complete listing of such volumes up to 1972 can be drawn from Brown, "Bibliography," pp. 176–79.

Abelmann, "Vietoris"	Abelmann, Charlotte. "Der Codex Vietoris: Ein Beitrag zur Musikgeschichte des ungarisch-tschechoslowakischen Grenzgebietes." 3 vols. Ph.D. diss., Univ. of Vienna, 1946.
Abert, "Klavier"	Abert, Hermann. "Joseph Haydns Klavierwerke." *Zeitschrift für Musikwissenschaft* 2 (1919–20), 553–73; 3 (1920–21), 535–52. [Second installment bears the title "Joseph Haydns Klaviersonaten."]
Abert, *Mozart*	———. *W. A. Mozart.* 2 vols. 6th ed. Leipzig: Breitkopf & Härtel, 1922. [Revision of Jahn, *Mozart.*]
Adler, "Haydn"	Adler, Guido. "Haydn and the Viennese Classical School." *The Musical Quarterly* 18 (1932), 191–207.
Adler, *Methode*	———. *Methode der Musikgeschichte.* Leipzig: Breitkopf & Härtel, 1919.
Albrechtsberger, *Composition*	Albrechtsberger, Johann Georg. *Gründliche Anweisung zur Composition.* Leipzig: Breitkopf & Härtel, 1790.
ALz	*Allgemeine Literatur-Zeitung.*
AmZ	*Allgemeine musikalische Zeitung* [Leipzig].
AmZ (Berlin)	*Allgemeine musikalische Zeitung* [Berlin].
AmZ (Vienna)	*Allgemeine musikalische Zeitung* [Vienna].
Angermüller, "Neukomm"	Angermüller, Rudolph. "Neukomms schottische Liedbearbeitungen für Joseph Haydn." *Haydn-Studien* 3 (1973–74), 151–53.

Anon., "Haydn"   "An Account of Joseph Haydn, a Celebrated Composer of Music." *European Magazine, and London Review,* October, 1784, 252–54.

Anon., "Moravian"   "The Moravian Contribution to Pennsylvania Music." In National Society of the Colonial Dames of America, Pennsylvania. *Church Music and Musical Life in Pennsylvania in the Eighteenth Century,* II, 116ff. Philadelphia: The Society, 1927.

Bach, *Versuch*   Bach, Carl Philipp Emanuel, *Versuch über die wahre Art das Clavier zu spielen.* . . . 2 vols. Berlin: Author, 1753–62.

—Facs. repr. ed. Lothar Hoffman-Erbrecht. Leipzig: VEB Breitkopf & Härtel, 1957.

—2nd ed. 2 vols. Leipzig: Schwickert, 1780.

—3rd ed. 2 vols. 1787–97.

—*Essay on the True Art of Keyboard Playing.* Transl. William J. Mitchell. New York: W. W. Norton & Co., 1949.

Bacilly, *Chanter*   Bacilly, Bénique de. *Remarques curieuses sur l'art de bien chanter.* . . . Paris: Author (Ballard), 1668.

—2nd ed. 1671.

—3rd ed. 1679. Facs. repr. Geneva: Minkoff, 1971.

—*A Commentary upon the Art of Proper Singing.* Trans. Austin B. Caswell. Brooklyn: Institute of Medieval Music, 1968.

Badura-Skoda, "Comedy"   Badura-Skoda, Eva. "The Influence of the Viennese Popular Comedy on Haydn and Mozart." *Publications of the [Royal] Musical Association* 100 (1974), 185–99.

Badura-Skoda, "Comoedie-Arien"   ———. " 'Teutsche Comoedie-Arien' und Joseph Haydn." In *Der junge Haydn* [q.v.], pp. 59–73.

Badura-Skoda, "Opera"   ———. "Reflections on Haydn Opera Problems." In *Haydnfest* [q.v.], pp. 27–31.

Bär, "Basso"   Bär, Carl. "Zum Begriff des 'Basso' in Mozarts Serenaden," *Mozart-Jahrbuch,* 1960–61, 133–55.

Barrett-Ayres, *Quartet*   Barrett-Ayres, Reginald. *Joseph Haydn and the String Quartet.* London: Barrie & Jenkins, 1974.

Bartha, "Liedform"   Bartha, Dénes. "Liedform-Probleme." In *Festskrift Larsen* [q.v.], pp. 317–37.

Bartha, "Repertory"   ———. "Haydn's Italian Opera Repertory at Eszterháza Palace." In *New Looks at Italian Opera: Essays in Honor of Donald J. Grout,* ed. William W. Austin, pp. 172–219. Ithaca: Cornell Univ. Press, 1968.

Bartha, "Thematic"   ———. "On Beethoven's Thematic Structure." *The Musical Quarterly* 61 (1970), 759–78.

—Repr. *The Creative World of Beethoven,* ed. Paul Henry Lang, pp. 257–76. New York: W. W. Norton & Co., 1971.

Bartha-Somfai   Bartha, Dénes, and László Somfai. *Haydn als Opernkapellmeister: Die Haydn-Dokumente der Esterházy-Opernsammlung.* Budapest: Verlag der Ungarischen Akademie der Wissenschaften, 1960.

Becker, "Orchester"   Becker, Heinz. "[Orchester. B.] Das neuere Orchester." *Die Musik in Geschichte und Gegenwart,* vol. 10 (1962), cols. 172–94.

Becker-Glauch, "Haydn"   "Haydn, Franz Joseph." In International Musicological Society—International Association of Music Libraries. *Répertoire*

International des Sources Musicales, vol. A/I/4, pp. 140–279. Kassel: Bärenreiter, 1974.

Becker-Glauch, "Kirchenmusik"
———. "Neue Forschungen zu Haydns Kirchenmusik." *Haydn-Studien* 2 (1969–70), 167–241.

Becker-Glauch, "Te Deum"
———. "Joseph Haydns 'Te Deum' für die Kaiserin: Eine Quellenstudie." In *Festschrift Joseph Schmidt-Görg zum 70. Geburtstag,* ed. Siegfried Kross and Hans Schmidt, pp. 1–10. Kassel: Bärenreiter, 1967.

Bedos, *Orgues*
Bedos de Celles, Dom François. *L'Art du facteur d'orgues.* 4 vols. Paris: L. F. Delatour, 1766–78.
—Facs. repr. 3 vols. Kassel: Bärenreiter, 1963–66. (Documenta musicologica, first series, vols. 24–26.)

Berardi, *Miscellanea*
Berardi, Angelo. *Miscellanea Musicale.* . . . Bologna: Giacomo Monti (Marino Silvani), 1689.
—Facs. repr.   Bologna: Forni, 1970.

Bertuch, *Reise*
Bertuch, Carl. *Bemerkungen auf einer Reise aus Thüringen nach Wien im Winter 1805 bis 1806.* 2 vols. in 1. Weimar: Verlag des Landes-Industrie-Comptoirs, 1808–10.

Biba, "Kirchenmusik"
Biba, Otto. "Die Wiener Kirchenmusik um 1783." In *Beiträge zur Musikgeschichte des 18. Jahrhunderts,* ed. Gerda Mraz, pp. 7–79. (Jahrbuch für österreichische Kulturgeschichte, vol. 1, part 2.) Eisenstadt: Institut für österreichische Kulturgeschichte, 1971.

Blomstedt, "J. C. Bach"
Blomstedt, Herbert T. "Till Kännedomen om J. C. Bachs Symfonier." *Svensk Tidskrift för Musikforskning* 33 (1951), 53–86.

Blume, "Klassik"
Blume, Friedrich. "Klassik." *Die Musik in Geschichte und Gegenwart,* vol. 7 (1958), cols. 1027–90.
—Repr. *Syntagma Musicologicum: Gesammelte Reden und Schriften,* vol. 1, ed. Martin Ruhnke, pp. 123–86. Kassel: Bärenreiter, 1963.
—"Classic Music." In Friedrich Blume, *Classic and Romantic Music,* trans. M. D. Herter Norton. New York: W. W. Norton & Co., 1970.

Blume, "Streichquartette"
———. "Josef Haydns künstlerische Persönlichkeit in seinen Streichquartetten." *Jahrbuch Peters* 38 (1931), 24–48.
—Repr. in *Syntagma Musicologicum: Gesammelte Reden und Schriften,* vol. 1, ed. Martin Ruhnke, pp. 526–51. Kassel: Bärenreiter, 1963.

Bónis, "Tänze"
Bónis, Ferenc. "Die suitenmässigen Tänze des Codex Vietoris." *Zenetudományi Tanulmányok* 6 (1957), 290–336, 755–56.

Boyden, "Geigenbogen"
Boyden, David D. "Der Geigenbogen von Corelli bis Tourte." In *Violinspiel und Violinmusik in Geschichte und Gegenwart: Bericht über den Internationalen Kongress am Institut für Aufführungspraxis der Hochschule für Musik und darstellende Kunst in Graz, vom 25. Juni bis 2. Juli 1972,* ed. Vera Schwarz, pp. 295–310. (Beiträge zur Aufführungspraxis, 3.) Vienna: Universal-Edition, c1975.

Brand, *Messen*
Brand, Carl Maria. *Die Messen von Joseph Haydn.* Würzburg: Triltsch, 1941.
—Facs. repr. Walluf: Sändig, [1973].

Brantley, "Authorship"
Brantley, Daniel Lawrence. "Disputed Authorship of Musical

Works: A Quantitative Approach to the Attribution of the Quartets Published as Haydn's Opus 3." Ph.D. diss., Univ. of Iowa, 1977.

Breitkopf   [Breitkopf, Johann Gottlob Immanuel, *comp.*] *Catalogo delle Sinfonie [dei Soli . . . per il Violino. . . ; de' Soli . . . per il Flauto . . . ; de' Soli . . . per il Cembalo . . .; de' Quadri . . .; delle Arie . . .] che si trovano in manuscritto. . . .* 6 vols. Leipzig: Breitkopf, 1762–65.

    —*Supplemento I. . . . XVI. . . .* Leipzig: Breitkopf, 1766–87.

    —Facs. repr. [6 vols. and 16 supplements]. *The Breitkopf Thematic Catalogue.* Ed. Barry S. Brook. New York: Dover Books, 1966.

Brion, *Vienna*   Brion, Marcel. *Daily Life in the Vienna of Mozart and Schubert.* New York: Macmillan, 1962.

Bröcker, *Drehleier*   Bröcker, Marianne. *Die Drehleier: Ihr Bau und ihre Geschichte.* 2 vols. Düsseldorf: Gesellschaft zur Förderung der systematischen Musikwissenschaft, 1973.

Brook, "Sturm und Drang"   Brook, Barry S. "Sturm und Drang and the Romantic Period in Music." *Studies in Romanticism* 9 (1970), 269–84.

Brook, *Symphonie*   ————. *La Symphonie française dans la seconde moitié du XVIIIe siècle.* 3 vols. Paris: Publications de l'institut de musicologie de l'université de Paris, 1962.

Brown, "Biography"   Brown, A. Peter and James T. Berkenstock, with Carol Vanderbilt Brown. "Joseph Haydn in Literature: A Bibliography." *Haydn-Studien* 3 (1973–74), 173–352.

Brown, "Biography"   Brown, A. Peter. "The Earliest English Biography of Haydn." *The Musical Quarterly* 59 (1973), 339–54.

Brown, "Exposition"   ————. "The Structure of the Exposition in Haydn's Keyboard Sonatas." *The Music Review* 36 (1975), 102–29.

Bryan, "Horn"   Bryan, Paul R. "The Horn in the Works of Mozart and Haydn: Some Observations and Comparisons." *The Haydn Yearbook* 9 (1975), 189–255.

BUC   Schnapper, Edith E., ed. *The British Union-Catalogue of Early Music Printed Before the Year 1801.* 2 vols. London: Butterworths Scientific Publications, 1957.

Burney, *History*   Burney, Charles. *A General History of Music from the Earliest Ages to the Present Period. . . .* 4 vols. London: Author, 1776–89.

    —Modern ed. Frank Mercer. 2 vols. London: G. T. Foulis & Co.; New York: Harcourt Brace & Co., 1935.

Burney, *State*   ————. *The Present State of Music in Germany, the Netherlands and United Provinces.* 2 vols. London: Becket, Robson & Robinson, 1773.

    —2nd ed. 2 vols. 1775.

    —Facs. repr. 2 vols. New York: Broude Brothers, 1969.

    —Trans. C. D. Ebeling and J. J. C. Bode. *Carl Burney's der Musik Doctors Tagebuch seiner musikalischen Reisen . . . ,* vols. 2–3. Hamburg: Bode, 1773 Facs. repr. ed. Richard Schaal. *Tagebuch einer musikalischen Reise. . . .* Kassel: Bärenreiter, 1959. (Documenta musicologica, first series, 19.)

—Modern ed. Percy A. Scholes. *Dr. Burney's Musical Tours in Europe,* vol. 2. London and Toronto: Oxford Univ. Press, 1959.

Busoni, "Beethoven" Busoni, Ferruccio. "Beethoven and Musical Humour." In *The Essence of Music and other Papers,* trans. Rosamond Ley, pp. 134–37. London: Rockliff, 1957.

Carpani, *Haydine* Carpani, Giuseppe. *Le Haydine, ovvero lettere su la vita e le opere del celebre maestro Giuseppe Haydn.* Milan: C. Buccinelli, 1812.

—2nd ed. Padua: Tipografia della Minerva, 1823. Facs. repr. Bologna: Forni, 1969.

Carse, *18th Century* Carse, Adam. *The Orchestra in the XVIIIth Century.* Cambridge: W. Heffer & Sons, 1940.

—Facs. repr. New York: Broude Bros., 1969.

Carse, *Orchestra* ———. *The Orchestra from Beethoven to Berlioz.* Cambridge: W. Heffer & Sons, 1948.

CCLN [See Haydn, CCLN.]

CE [See Haydn, CE.]

Chew, "Watchman" Chew, Geoffrey. "The Night-Watchman's Song Quoted by Haydn and its Implications." *Haydn-Studien* 3 (1973–74), 106–24.

ChL. [See Haydn, *Sonatas.*]

Chrysander, "Concertwesen" Chrysander, Friedrich. "Eine Geschichte des Wiener Concertwesens." AmZ, 3rd series, 4 (1869), Nos. 28–40, pp. 217–20, 225–38, 233–35, 241–44, 249–52, 257–61, 265–66, 273–75, 283–85, 291–93, 299–300, 307–10, 316–19. [Review of Hanslick, *Concertwesen.*]

Churgin, "Galeazzi" Churgin, Bathia. "Francesco Galeazzi's Description (1796) of Sonata Form." *Journal of the American Musicological Society* 21 (1968), 181–99.

Churgin, *Symphonies* ———. *The Symphonies of G. B. Sammartini.* Vol. 1, *The Early Symphonies.* Cambridge, Mass.: Harvard Univ. Press, 1968.

Churgin-Jenkins Churgin, Bathia, and Newell Jenkins. "Sammartini." *Die Musik in Geschichte und Gegenwart,* vol. 11 (1963), cols. 1336–43.

Cole, "Evidence" Cole, Malcolm S. "The Rondo Finale: Evidence for the Mozart–Haydn Exchange?" *Mozart-Jahrbuch,* 1968–70, 242–56.

Cole, "Rondo" ———. "The Development of the Instrumental Rondo Finale from 1750–1800." 2 vols. Ph.D. diss., Princeton Univ., 1964.

Colles, "Sonata" Colles, H. C. "Sonata." *Grove's Dictionary of Music and Musicians,* 5th ed., vol. 7, pp. 886–908.

Craw, "Dussek" Craw, Howard Allen. "A Biography and Thematic Catalog of the Works of J. L. Dussek (1760–1812)." Ph.D. diss., Univ. of Southern California, 1964.

Cripe, *Jefferson* Cripe, Helen. *Thomas Jefferson and Music.* Charlottesville: Univ. of Virginia Press, [1974].

Croll, "Schwarzenberg" Croll, Gerhard. "Mitteilungen über die 'Schöpfung' und die 'Jahreszeiten' aus dem Schwarzenberg-Archiv." *Haydn-Studien* 3 (1973–74), 85–92.

Cudworth, "Cadence" Cudworth, Charles L. "Cadence Galante: The Story of a Cliché." *Monthly Musical Record* 79 (1949), 176–78.

Cushman, "Materials" Cushman, David Stephen. "Joseph Haydn's Melodic Materials: An

Exploratory Introduction to the Primary and Secondary Sources Together with an Analytical Catalogue and Table of Proposed Melodic Correspondence and/or Variance." Ph.D. diss., Boston Univ., 1973.

Cuyler, "Tonal" — Cuyler, Louise E. "Tonal Exploitation in the Later Quartets of Haydn." In *Festschrift Geiringer* [q.v.], pp. 136–50.

Dahlhaus, "Strukturgeschichte" — Dahlhaus, Carl. "Gedanken zu einer Strukturgeschichte der Musik des 19. Jahrhunderts." [Paper read at the colloquium "Česka hudba," Brno, 1974.]

Daube, *Dilettant* — Daube, Johann Friedrich. *Der musikalische Dilettant.* . . . 2 vols. Vol. 1. Vienna: Kurtzböck, 1771 (originally published 1770–71 as a weekly journal). Vol. 2. Vienna: Trattner, 1773.

Davis, "Lang" — Davis, Shelley G. "The Keyboard Concertos of Johann Georg Lang (1722–1798)." Ph.D. diss., New York Univ., 1972.

O. Deutsch, "Kanons" — Deutsch, Otto Erich. "Haydns Kanons." *Zeitschrift für Musikwissenschaft* 15 (1932–33), 112–24, 172.

O. Deutsch, "Repertoire" — ———. "Das Repertoire der höfischen Oper, der Hof- und Staatsoper." *Österreichische Musikzeitschrift* 24 (1969), 392–93.

W. Deutsch, "Volkslied" — Deutsch, Walter. "Volkslied und Geniemusik: Ein Beitrag zur Darstellung ihrer Beziehungen im Werke J. Haydns." *Jahrbuch des österreichischen Volksliedwerkes* 8 (1959), 1–9.

W. Deutsch, "Wirkungen" — ———. " 'Volkstümliche' Wirkungen in der Musik Joseph Dies Haydns." *Musikerziehung* [Vienna] 14 (1960), 88–92.

Dies, Albert Christoph. *Biographische Nachrichten von Joseph Haydn*. . . . Vienna: Camesinaische Buchhandlung, 1810.

—Modern ed. Horst Seeger. Berlin: Henschel, 1959, 2nd ed., 1962. [For trans., see Gotwals, *Haydn*.]

Dittersdorf, *Lebensbeschreibung* — Dittersdorf, Karl Ditters von. *Lebensbeschreibung: Seinem Sohne in die Feder diktirt*. Leipzig: Breitkopf & Härtel, 1801.

—English trans. 1896 (reprint 1970).

—Modern ed. Norbert Miller. Munich: Kosel, 1967.

Dlabač, *Lexikon* — Dlabač, Jan Bohuma [Dlabacž, Gottfried Johann]. *Allgemeines historisches Künstler-Lexikon für Böhmen, und zum Theil auch für Mähren und Schlesien*. 3 vols. Prague: G. Haase, 1815.

Dolmetsch, *Interpretation* — Dolmetsch, Arnold. *The Interpretation of the Music of the XVIIth and XVIIIth Centuries Revealed by Contemporary Evidence*. London: Novello, 1915

—2nd ed. London: Oxford Univ. Press, 1946.

Donath, "Gassmann" — Donath, Gustav. "Florian Leopold Gassmann als Opernkomponist." *Studien zur Musikwissenschaft* 2 (1914), 34–211.

Donington, *Interpretation* — Donington, Robert. *The Interpretation of Early Music*. London: Faber & Faber, 1963.

—New Version. New York: St. Martin's Press, 1974; London: Faber & Faber, 1975.

Drummond, *Philadelphia* — Drummond, Robert B. *Early German Music in Philadelphia*. New York: Appleton, 1910.

—Facs. repr. New York: Da Capo Press, 1970.

DTÖ — *Denkmäler der Tonkunst in Österreich*

Duval, *Méthode*   Duval, Pierre. *Méthode agréable et utile pour apprendre facilement à chanter juste.* . . . Paris: Author; Lyon: Castaud, 1775.
      —Facs. repr.   Geneva: Éditions Minkoff, 1972.

EdM   *Das Erbe deutscher Musik*

Edwall, "Lira"   Edwall, Harry R. "Ferdinand IV and Haydn's Concertos for the 'Lira Organizzata.' " *The Musical Quarterly* 48 (1962), 190–203.

"83"   [See Haydn, "83."]

Eineder, *Watermarks*   Eineder, Georg. *The Ancient Paper-mills of the Former Austro-Hungarian Empire and their Watermarks.* Hilversum: The Paper Publications Society, 1960.

Eitner, *Musikalienhändler*   Eitner, Robert. *Buch- und Musikalien-Händler . . . die Musik betreffend.* . . . Leipzig: Breitkopf & Härtel, 1904.

EK   [See Haydn, EK.]

"Enlightenment"   Abraham, Gerald. Introduction to *The New Oxford History of Music,* vol. 7, *The Age of Enlightenment,* ed. Egon Wellesz and Frederick Sternfeld, pp. xv–xx. London: Oxford Univ. Press, 1973.

Erbe   *Musikalisches Erbe und Gegenwart: Musiker-Gesamtausgaben in der Bundesrepublik Deutschland,* ed. Hanspeter Bennwitz et al. Kassel: Bärenreiter, 1975.

Eszterházy   Eszterházy, János [Gróf]. *Az Eszterházy család oldanágainak leírása: Kézirat gyanánt kiadja herceg Eszterházy-Miklós.* Budapest: Athenaeum r.-tars, 1901.

Feder, "Datierung"   Feder, Georg. "Zur Datierung Haydnscher Werke." In *Anthony van Hoboken: Festschrift zum 75. Geburtstag,* ed. Joseph Schmidt-Görg, pp. 50–54. Mainz: B. Schotts Söhne, 1962.

Feder, "Dramatiker"   ———. "Einige Thesen zu dem Thema: Haydn als Dramatiker." *Haydn-Studien* 2 (1969–70), 126–30.

Feder, "Editoren"   ———. "Bericht über das Symposion musikwissenschaftlicher Editoren in der Herzog August Bibliothek Wolfenbüttel vom 5.–7. Juni 1974." In *Wolfenbütteler Beiträge: Aus den Schätzen der Herzog August Bibliothek,* ed. Paul Raabe, vol. 3, pp. 337–57. Frankfurt a.M.: Vittorio Klostermann, 1978.

Feder, "Eingriffe"   ———. "Die Eingriffe des Musikverlegers Hummel in Haydns Werken." In *Musicae Scientiae Collectanea: Festschrift Karl Gustav Fellerer zum 70. Geburtstag,* ed. Heinrich Hüschen, pp. 88–101. Cologne: Arno Volk, 1973.

Feder, "Hoffstetter"   ———. "Aus Roman Hoffstetters Briefen." *Haydn-Studien* 1 (1965–67), 198–201.

Feder, "Klaviersonaten"   ———. "Probleme einer Neuordnung der Klaviersonaten Haydns." In *Festschrift Friedrich Blume zum 70. Geburtstag,* ed. Anna Amalie Abert and Wilhelm Pfannkuch, pp. 92–103. Kassel: Bärenreiter, 1963.

Feder, "Klaviertrios"   ———. "Haydns frühe Klaviertrios: Eine Untersuchung zur Echtheit und Chronologie." *Haydn-Studien* 2 (1969–70), 289–316.

Feder, "Opern"   ———, ed. "Ein Kolloquium über Haydns Opern." *Haydn-Studien* 2 (1969–70), 113–31.

Feder, "Orgelkonzerte"   ———. "Wieviel Orgelkonzerte hat Haydn geschrieben?" *Die Musikforschung* 23 (1970), 440–44.

Feder, "Paukenschlag" ———. "Haydns Paukenschlag und andere Überraschungen." *Österreichische Musikzeitschrift* 21 (1966), 5–8.

Feder, "Pole" ———. "Die beiden Pole im Instrumentalschaffen des jungen Haydn." In *Der junge Haydn* [q.v.], pp. 192–201.

Feder, "Similarities" ———. "Similarities in the Works of Haydn." In *Festschrift Geiringer* [q.v.], pp. 186–97.

Feder, "Stilelemente" ———. "Stilelemente Haydns in Beethovens Werken." In Gesellschaft für Musikforschung. *Bericht über den Internationalen musikwissenschaftlichen Kongress Bonn 1970,* ed. Carl Dahlhaus et al., pp. 65–70. Kassel: Bärenreiter, 1973.

Feder, "Streichquartette" ———. "Apokryphe 'Haydn'-Streichquartette." *Haydn-Studien* 3 (1973–74), 125–50.

Feder, "Überlieferung" ———. "Die Überlieferung und Verbreitung der handschriftlichen Quellen zu Haydns Werken (Erste Folge)." *Haydn-Studien* 1 (1965–67), 3–42.

——"Manuscript Sources of Haydn's Works and Their Distribution." Trans. Eugene Hartzell. *The Haydn Yearbook* 4 (1968), 102–39.

Feder, "Urteil" ———. "Die Bedeutung der Assoziation und des Wertvergleichs für das Urteil in Echtheitsfragen." In International Musicological Society. *Report of the Eleventh Congress Copenhagen 1972,* ed. Henrik Glahn et al., vol. 1, pp. 365–77. Copenhagen: Wilhelm Hansen, 1974.

Feder, "Zwei Sonaten" ———. "Zwei Haydn zugeschriebene Klaviersonaten." In Gesellschaft für Musikforschung. *Bericht über den Internationalen musikwissenschaftlichen Kongress Kassel 1962,* ed. Georg Reichert and Martin Just, pp. 181–84. Kassel: Bärenreiter, 1963.

Feder-Gerlach Feder, Georg, and Sonja Gerlach. "Haydn-Dokumente aus dem Esterházy-Archiv in Forchtenstein." *Haydn-Studien* 3 (1973–74), 92–105.

Festschrift Geiringer *Studies in Eighteenth-century Music: A Tribute to Karl Geiringer on his Seventieth Birthday.* Ed. H. C. Robbins Landon and Roger E. Chapman. New York: Oxford Univ. Press, 1970.

Festskrift Larsen *Festskrift Jens Peter Larsen 14. VI. 1902–1972.* Ed. Nils Schiørring et al. Copenhagen: Wilhelm Hansen, 1972.

Finscher, "Italienische" Finscher, Ludwig. "Joseph Haydn und das italienische Streichquartett." *Analecta Musicologica* 4 (1967), 13–37.

Finscher, "Klassik" ———. "Zum Begriff der Klassik in der Musik." *Deutsches Jahrbuch der Musikwissenschaft* 9 (1966), 9–34.

Finscher, Streichquartett ———. *Studien zur Geschichte des Streichquartetts.* Vol. 1, *Die Entstehung des klassischen Streichquartetts: Von den Vorformen zur Grundlegung durch Joseph Haydn.* Kassel: Bärenreiter, 1974.

Fischer, "Entwicklungsgeschichte" Fischer, Wilhelm. "Zur Entwicklungsgeschichte des Wiener klassischen Stils." *Studien zur Musikwissenschaft* 3 (1915), 24–84.

Flothuis, "Groeten" Flothuis, Marius. "Groeten van Joseph, Groeten van Wolfgang." *Mens en Melodie* 30 (1975), 2–4.

Forkel, Almanach Forkel, Johann Nicolaus. *Musikalischer Almanach für Deutschland.* 4 vols. Leipzig: Schwickert, 1782–89.

—Facs. repr. Hildesheim and New York: G. Olms, 1974. 4 vols.

Forkel, *Geschichte* ———. *Allgemeine Geschichte der Musik.* 2 vols. Leipzig: Schwickert, 1788–1801.

—Facs. repr. ed. Othmar Wessely. 2 vols. Graz: Akademische Druck- und Verlagsanstalt, 1967.

Framery, *Haydn* Framery, Nicolas Étienne. *Notice sur Joseph Haydn.* . . . Paris: Barba, 1810.

Freeman, "Melk" Freeman, Robert N. "The Practice of Music at Melk Monastery." Ph.D. diss., Univ. of California at Los Angeles, 1971.

Fux, *Gradus* Fux, Johann Joseph. *Gradus ad Parnassum, sive manuductio ad compositionem musicae regularem, methodo nova.* . . . Vienna: Johann Peter van Ghelen, 1725.

—Facs. repr. New York: Broude Bros., 1966.

—Modern ed. Graz: Johann-Joseph-Fux-Gesellschaft. *Sämtliche Werke.* Series 7, Theoretische und pädagogische Werke, vol. 1, *Gradus ad Parnassum,* ed. Alfred Mann. Kassel: Bärenreiter, 1967.

—*Gradus ad Parnassum oder Anführung zur regelmässigen musikalischen Composition.* Trans. Lorenz Christoph Mizler. Leipzig: Mizler, 1742.

—*The Study of Counterpoint.* . . . Trans. Alfred Mann. New York: W. W. Norton & Co., 1943. Repr. 1965. [Sections on counterpoint.] —*The Study of Fugue,* trans. and ed. Alfred Mann, pp. 78–141. New Brunswick: Rutgers Univ. Press, 1958; repr. New York: W. W. Norton & Co., 1965. [Sections on fugue.]

GA [See Haydn, GA.]

Galeazzi, *Elementi* Galeazzi, Francesco. *Elementi teorico-pratici di musica.* 2 vols. Rome: Cracas, 1791; Puccinelli, 1796.

Geiringer, *Catalogue* Geiringer, Karl. *A Thematic Catalogue of Haydn's Settings of Folksongs from the British Isles.* (Studies in Musicology, Series A, 2.) Superior: Research Microfilm Publishers, 1953.

Geiringer, *Haydn*₁ ———. *Joseph Haydn.* (Die grossen Meister der Musik.) Potsdam: Akademische Verlagsgesellschaft Athenaion, 1932.

Geiringer, *Haydn*₂ ———. *Haydn: A Creative Life in Music.* New York: W. W. Norton, 1946; London: G. Allen & Unwin, 1947.

—2nd ed. rev. in collaboration with Irene Geiringer. Garden City, N.Y.: Doubleday, 1963.

—3rd ed. Berkeley: Univ. of California Press, 1968.

Geiringer, *Haydn*₃ ———. *Joseph Haydn: Der schöpferische Werdegang eines Meisters der Klassik.* Mainz: B. Schotts Söhne, 1959.

Geiringer, "Protagonist" "Joseph Haydn: Protagonist of the Enlightenment." *Studies on Voltaire and the Eighteenth Century* 25 (1963), 683–90.

Georgiades, *Sprache* Georgiades, Thrasybulos. *Musik und Sprache: Das Werden der abendländischen Musik dargestellt an der Vertonung der Messe.* (Verständliche Wissenschaft 55.) Berlin: Springer, [1954].

E. L. Gerber, "Haydn" Gerber, Ernst Ludwig. "Haydn." In Gerber, NL [see following item], vol. 2, cols. 535–605.

E. L. Gerber, NL   ——. *Neues historisch-biographisches Lexikon der Tonkünstler.* . . . 4 vols. Leipzig: A. Kühnel, 1812–14.

    —Facs. ed. *Ernst Ludwig Gerber: Historisch-biographisches Lexikon der Tonkünstler und Neues historisch-biographisches Lexikon der Tonkünstler . . . ,* ed. Othmar Wessely, vols. 2–3. Graz: Akademische Druck- und Verlagsanstalt, 1966–67.

R. Gerber, *Hasse*   Gerber, Rudolf. *Der Operntypus Johann Adolf Hasses und seine textlichen Grundlagen.* Leipzig: Kistner & Siegel, 1925.

    —Facs. repr.   Hildesheim: G. Olms, 1973.

Gericke,   Gericke, Hannelore. *Der Wiener Musikalienhandel von 1700 bis 1778.*
Musikalienhandel   (Wiener musikwissenschaftliche Beiträge, 5.) Graz and Cologne: Hermann Böhlaus Nachfolger, 1960.

Gerlach,   Gerlach, Sonja. "Haydns Orchestermusiker von 1761 bis 1774."
"Orchestermusiker"   *Haydn-Studien* 4 (1976–80), 35–48.

Gerlach, "Ordnung"   ——. "Die chronologische Ordnung von Haydns Sinfonien zwischen 1774 und 1782." *Haydn-Studien* 2 (1969–70), 34–66.

Glöggl,   Glöggl, Franz Xaver. *Kirchen-Musik-Ordnung: Erklärendes Handbuch*
Kirchenmusikordnung   *des musikalischen Gottesdienstes.* Vienna: Wallishausser, 1828.

Gluck, *Correspondence*   Gluck, Christoph Willibald von. *The Collected Correspondence and Papers of Christoph Willibald von Gluck.* Ed. E. H. and Hedwig Müller von Asow. Transl. Stewart Thomson. London: Barrie & Rockliff, [1962].

Goldoni, *Opere*   Goldoni, Carlo. *Tutte le opere di Carlo Goldoni.* Ed. Giuseppe Ortolani. 14 vols. Verona: Mondadori, 1935–56.

Gombosi, *Herbst*   Gombosi, Marilyn. *Catalog of the Johannes Herbst Collection.* Chapel Hill: Univ. of North Carolina Press, 1970.

Gotwals, *Haydn*   Gotwals, Vernon, transl. and ed. *Joseph Haydn: Eighteenth-century Gentleman and Genius.* Madison: Univ. of Wisconsin Press, 1963. Repr. as *Haydn: Two Contemporary Portraits,* 1968. [Translations of Dies and Griesinger.]

Grider, *Bethlehem*   Grider, Rufus A. *Historical Notes on Music in Bethlehem, Pa., from 1741 to 1841.* Philadelphia: John L. Pile, 1873.

    —Facs. repr. ed. Donald L. McCorkle. Winston-Salem: Moravian Music Foundation, 1957.

Griesinger   Griesinger, Georg August. *Biographische Notizen über Joseph Haydn.* Leipzig: Breitkopf & Härtel, 1810. [Expanded repr. of articles originally publ. AmZ, 1809.]

    —Modern ed. Franz Grasberger. Vienna: Paul Kaltschmid, 1954. [For trans., see Gotwals, *Haydn.*]

Grout, *History*   Grout, Donald J. *A History of Western Music.* New York: W. W. Norton & Co., 1960.

    —2nd ed., 1973.

Haas, "Komödie"   Haas, Robert. "Die Musik in der Wiener deutschen Stegreifkomödie." *Studien zur Musikwissenschaft* 12 (1925), 3–64.

Hanslick, *Concertwesen*   Hanslick, Eduard. *Geschichte des Concertwesens in Wien.* 2 vols. Vienna: Braumüller, 1869–70.

    —Facs. repr.   Farnborough: Gregg, 1971.

Hárich, "Dokumenta"   Hárich, János. "Haydn Documenta." *The Haydn Yearbook* 2

(1963–64), 2–44; 3 (1965), 122–52; 4 (1968), 39–101; 7 (1970), 47–168; 8 (1971), 70–163.

Hárich, "Fideikommiss"   ———. "Das fürstlich Esterházy'sche Fideikommiss." *The Haydn Yearbook* 4 (1968), 5–38.

Hárich, "Inventare"   ———. "Inventare der Esterházy-Hofmusikkapelle in Eisenstadt." *The Haydn Yearbook* 9 (1975), 5–125.

Hárich, "Librettos"   ———. "Szövegkönyvgyüjtemény." Typescript. Budapest: National Széchényi Library, 1941. ["The librettos of the Esterházy opera collection."]

Hárich, "Opernensemble"   ———. "Das Opernensemble zu Eszterházá im Jahr 1780." *The Haydn Yearbook* 7 (1970), 5–46.

Hárich, "Orchester"   ———. "Das Haydn-Orchester im Jahr 1780." *The Haydn Yearbook* 8 (1971), 5–69.

Hárich, "Repertoire"   ———. "Das Repertoire des Opernkapellmeisters Haydn in Eszterházá (1780–1790)." *The Haydn Yearbook* 1 (1962), 9–110.

Hárich, *Textbücher*   ———. *Esterházy-Musikgeschichte im Spiegel der zeitgenössischen Textbücher.* . . . (Burgenländische Forschungen, 39.) Eisenstadt: Burgenländisches Landesarchiv, 1959.

Hase   Hase, Hermann von. *Joseph Haydn und Breitkopf & Härtel.* . . . Leipzig: Breitkopf & Härtel, 1909.

Hatting, "Haydn?"   Hatting, Carsten E. "Haydn oder Kayser?—Eine Echtheitsfrage." *Die Musikforschung* 25 (1972), 182–87.

Hatting, "Satz"   ———. "Obligater Satz versus Generalbass-Satz: Einige Betrachtungen zur Satzfaktur in Klaviersonaten aus der Mitte des 18. Jahrhunderts, insbesondere zu Haydns Sonaten aus der Zeit vor 1770. In *"Festschrift Larsen* [q.v.], pp. 261–74.

Haydn, "Autobiography"   Haydn, Joseph. [Autobiographical sketch, 1776.] MS. Budapest, National Széchényi Library, Esterházy Archives (Theater Collection), Acta musicalia, Fasc. 68, No. 4225.
    —Facs. repr. Valkó II [q.v.], following p. 560, Pl. 2–5; Somfai, *Bilder* [q.v.], pp. 68–71.
    —Ed. Ibid; Haydn, *Briefe* [q.v.], pp. 76–82.
    —Trans. Haydn, CCLN [q.v.], pp. 18–20.

Haydn, *Briefe*   ———. *Joseph Haydn: Gesammelte Briefe und Aufzeichnungen.* Ed. Dénes Bartha. Kassel: Bärenreiter, 1965.

Haydn, CE   *Joseph Haydn: Gesamtausgabe—Complete Edition.* Ed. Jens Peter Larsen. 4 vols. published. Boston and Vienna: The Haydn Society, 1950–51.

Haydn, CCLN   *The Collected Correspondence and London Notebooks of Joseph Haydn.* Ed. H. C. Robbins Landon. London: Barrie & Rockliff, 1959.

Haydn, "83"   *Collection complette des Quatuors d'Haydn.* . . . 4 installments. Paris: Pleyel, 1801–02.

Haydn, EK   Haydn, Joseph. [Entwurf-Katalog.] Berlin, Deutsche Staatsbibliothek, Mus. ms. Kat. 607.
    —Facs. repr. in Larsen, DHK [q.v.].

Haydn, *Elementarbuch*   [Haydn, Joseph.] "Elementarbuch der verschiednen Gattungen des Contrapuncts. Aus den grössern Werken des Kappm Fux, von Joseph Haydn zusammengezogen." MS, copied by F. C. Magnus. Budapest, National Széchényi Library, Ha. I. 10.

—Modern ed. and trans. by Alfred Mann. "Haydn's Elementar-buch: A Document of Classic Counterpoint Instructions." *The Music Forum* 3 (1973), 197–237.

Haydn, GA   *Joseph Haydn Werke: Erste kritisch durchgesehene Gesamtausgabe.* 11 vols. Leipzig: Breitkopf & Härtel, 1907–33.

Haydn, HBV   "J. Haydns's Verzeichniss musicalischer Werke theils eigner, theils fremder Comp[o]sition." MS, written by Johann Elssler. London, British Library, Add. 32070.

Haydn, HNV   [Haydn-Nachlass-Verzeichnis.] MS. Vienna, Archiv der Stadt Wien, Persönlichkeiten, 4/1–4.

Haydn, HV   [Haydn, Joseph.] "Verzeichniss aller derjenigen Compositionen welche ich mich beyläufig erinnere von meinem 18ten bis in das 73ste Jahr verfertiget zu haben." MS, copied by Johann Elssler; now lost.
—Facs. repr. in Larsen, DHK [q.v.].

Haydn, JHW   *Joseph Haydn: Werke.* Ed. by the Joseph Haydn-Institut, Cologne, under the direction of Jens Peter Larsen (1958–61) and Georg Feder (1962–   ). Munich & Duisburg: G. Henle Verlag, 1958–.

Haydn, "Librettos"   [Haydn, Joseph. Catalogue of librettos.] MS, Vienna, Stadt-bibliothek.

Haydn, "Oeuvres"   *Oeuvres Complettes de J. Haydn.* 12 vols. Leipzig: Breitkopf & Härtel, 1800–06.

Haydn, *Sonatas*   *Joseph Haydn: Sämtliche Klaviersonaten—The Complete Piano Sonatas.* Ed. Christa Landon. 3 vols. Vienna: Universal-Edition, [c. 1964–66]. (Wiener Urtext-Ausgabe.)

Haydn, *Sonaten*   *Joseph Haydn: Sämtliche Klaviersonaten.* Ed. Georg Feder. 2 vols. Munich: G. Henle, 1972.

Haydn, *Symphonies*   *Joseph Haydn: Kritische Ausgabe sämtlicher Symphonien—Critical Edition of the Complete Symphonies.* Ed. H. C. Robbins Landon. 12 vols. Vienna: Universal-Edition—Verlag Doblinger, 1965–68.

Haydnfest   *Haydnfest: Music Festival . . . International Musicological Conference.* [Ed. Jens Peter Larsen and Howard Serwer. Washington, D. C.: The John F. Kennedy Center for the Performing Arts, 1975.]

HBV   [See Haydn, HBV]

Heartz, "Opera"   Heartz, Daniel. "Opera and the Periodization of Eighteenth-century Music." In International Musicological Society. *Report of the Tenth Congress Ljubljana 1967,* ed. Dragotin Cvetko, pp. 160–68. Kassel: Bärenreiter; Ljubljana: Univ. of Ljubljana, 1970.

Heussner, "Konzert"   Heussner, Horst. "Joseph Haydns Konzert (Hoboken XVIII:5): Marginalien zur Quellenüberlieferung." *Die Musikforschung* 22 (1969), 478–80.

HNV   [See Haydn, HNV.]

Hob.   [See Hoboken.]

Hoboken   Hoboken, Anthony van. *Joseph Haydn: Thematisch-bibliographisches Werkverzeichnis.* 3 vols. Mainz: B. Schotts Söhne, 1957–78.

Hoboken, *Discrepancies*   ———. *Discrepancies in Haydn Biographies.* Trans. Donald Mintz. Washington, D. C.: The Library of Congress, 1962.

Holschneider, "Bibliothek"   Holschneider, Andreas. "Die musikalische Bibliothek Gottfried van Swietens." In Gesellschaft für Musikforschung. *Bericht über den*

Internationalen musikwissenschaftlichen Kongress Kassel 1962, ed. Georg Reichert and Martin Just, pp. 174–78. Kassel: Bärenreiter, 1963.

Hopkinson-Oldman, "Haydn"   Hopkinson, Cecil, and C. B. Oldman. "Haydn's Settings of Scottish Songs in the Collections of Napier and Whyte." *Edinburgh Bibliographical Society Transactions* 3, pt. 2 (1949–51), 85–120. [A continuation of the following item.]

Hopkinson-Oldman, "Thomson"   ———. "Thomson's Collections of National Song with Special Reference to the Contributions of Haydn and Beethoven." Ibid. 2, pt. 1 (1938–39), 1–64.

———"Addenda et Corrigenda." Ibid. 3, pt. 2 (1949–51), 121–24.

HÜb   [See Larsen, HÜb.]

Hughes, *Haydn*   Hughes, Rosemary. *Haydn.* London: Dent; New York: Pellegrini and Cudahy, 1950.

———[3d] rev. ed. London: J. M. Dent, 1962.

Hull, "Quartet"   Hull, Arthur Eaglefield. "The Earliest Known String Quartet." *The Musical Quarterly* 15 (1929), 72–76.

HV   [See Haydn, HV.]

Jahn, *Mozart*   Jahn, Otto. *W. A. Mozart.* 4 vols. Leipzig: Breitkopf & Härtel, 1856–59. [Cf. Abert, *Mozart.*]

Jahrbuch   *Jahrbuch der Tonkunst von Wien und Prag.* [Vienna:] Schönfeld, 1796.

———Facs. repr. ed. Otto Biba. Munich and Salzburg: Katzbichler, 1976.

Jenkins-Churgin   Jenkins, Newell, and Bathia Churgin. *Thematic Catalogue of the Works of Giovanni Battista Sammartini: Orchestral and Vocal Music.* Cambridge, Mass., and London: Harvard Univ. Press, 1976.

Jeppesen, *Counterpoint*   Jeppesen, Knud. *Kontrapunkt (vokalpolyfoni).* Copenhagen: Wilhelm Hansen, 1930.

———*Kontrapunkt: Lehrbuch der klassischen Vokalpolyphonie.* Transl. Julie Schulz. Leipzig: Breitkopf & Härtel, [c. 1935].

———*Counterpoint: The Polyphonic Vocal Style of the Sixteenth Century.* Trans. Glen Haydon. New York: Prentice-Hall, 1939.

JHW   [See Haydn, JHW.]

Johansson, *Catalogues*   Johansson, Cari. *French Music Publishers' Catalogues of the Second Half of the Eighteenth Century.* 2 vols. Stockholm: Almqvist & Wiksell, 1955.

Johansson, *Hummel*   ———. *J. J. and B. Hummel Music-Publishing and Thematic Catalogues.* 3 vols. Stockholm: Almqvist & Wiksell, 1972.

Johnson, *Boston*   Johnson, H. Earle. *Musical Interludes in Boston, 1795–1830.* New York: Columbia Univ. Press, 1943.

Der junge Haydn   Graz. Hochschule für Musik und darstellende Kunst. Institut für Aufführungspraxis. *Der junge Haydn: Wandel von Musikauffassung und Musikaufführung in der österreichischen Musik zwischen Barock und Klassik: Bericht der internationalen Arbeitstagung des Instituts . . . 29. 6.–2. 7. 1970.* Ed. Vera Schwarz. (Beiträge zur Aufführungspraxis, 1.) Graz: Akademische Druck- und Verlagsanstalt, 1972.

Junker, *Componisten*   [Junker, Karl Ludwig.] *Zwanzig Componisten: Eine Skizze.* Berne: Typographische Gesellschaft, 1776.

Karajan, *Haydn*   Karajan, Theodor Georg, Ritter von. *Joseph Haydn in London, 1791 und 1792.* Vienna: K. Gerolds Sohn, 1861.

Keller, "Chamber"   Keller, Hans. "The Chamber Music." In *The Mozart Companion,* ed. H. C. Robbins Landon and Donald Mitchell, pp. 90–137. London: Barrie & Rockliff; New York: Oxford Univ. Press, 1956. Repr. New York: W. W. Norton & Co., 1969.

Kellner, *Kremsmünster*   Kellner, Altman. *Musikgeschichte des Stiftes Kremsmünster.* Kassel: Bärenreiter, 1956.

Kelly, *Reminiscences*   Kelly, Michael. *The Reminiscences of Michael Kelly.* 2 vols. London: Colburn, 1826.

    —Modern ed. Roger Fiske. London: Oxford Univ. Press, 1975.

U. Kirkendale, *Caldara*   Kirkendale, Ursula. *Antonio Caldara: Sein Leben und seine venezianisch-römischen Oratorien.* Graz: H. Böhlau, 1966.

W. Kirkendale, *Fuge*   Kirkendale, Warren. *Fuge und Fugato in der Kammermusik des Rokoko und der Klassik.* Tutzing: Hans Schneider, 1966.

Kirnberger, "Einschnitt"   [Kirnberger, Johann Philipp.] In Sulzer, *Theorie* [q.v.], s. v. "Einschnitt."

Knepler, *Musikgeschichte*   Knepler, Georg. *Musikgeschichte des 19. Jahrhunderts.* 2 vols. Berlin: Henschel-Verlag, 1961.

Koch, *Lexikon*   Koch, Heinrich Christoph. *Musikalisches Lexikon. . . .* Frankfurt am Main: Hermann jüng., 1802.

    —Facs. repr.   Hildesheim: G. Olms, 1964.

Koch, *Versuch*   ——. *Versuch einer Anleitung zur Composition.* 3 vols. Rudolstadt & Leipzig: A. F. Böhme, 1782–93.

    —Facs. repr.   Hildesheim: G. Olms, 1969.

Köchel$_{1,3,6}$ Köchel, Ludwig Ritter von. *Chronologisch-thematisches Verzeichnis sämtlicher Tonwerke Wolfgang Amadé Mozarts.* Leipzig: Breitkopf & Härtel, 1862.

    —3rd ed. by Alfred Einstein, 1937.

    —6th ed. by Franz Giegling et al. Wiesbaden: Breitkopf & Härtel, 1964.

Kolneder, *Muffat*   Kolneder, Walter. *Georg Muffat zur Aufführungspraxis.* Strasbourg: P. H. Heitz, 1970.

N. Krabbe, "J. C. Bach"   Krabbe, Niels. "J. C. Bach's Symphonies and the Breitkopf Thematic Catalogue." In *Festskrift Larsen* [q.v.], pp. 233–54.

W. Krabbe, "Heck"   Krabbe, Wilhelm. "Das Liederbuch des Johann Heck." *Archiv für Musikwissenschaft* 4 (1922), 420–38.

Kucaba, "Wagenseil"   Kucaba, John, Jr. "The Symphonies of Georg Christoph Wagenseil." 2 vols. Ph.D. diss., Boston Univ., 1967.

Lahee, *America*   Lahee, Henry C. *Annals of Music in America.* Boston: Marshall Jones, 1922.

C. Landon, "Dokument"   Landon, Christa. "Ein Dokument zur 'Schöpfung.' " *Haydn-Studien* 4 (1976–80), 113.

R. Landon, "Authenticity"   Landon, H. C. Robbins. "Problems of Authenticity in Eighteenth-century Music." In *Instrumental Music: A Conference at Isham Memorial Library, May 4, 1957,* ed. David G. Hughes, pp. 31–56. Cambridge, Mass.: Harvard Univ. Press, 1959.

R. Landon, "Crise"   ———. "La crise romantique dans la musique autrichienne vers

1770." In *Les influences étrangères dans l'oeuvre de W. A. Mozart,* ed. André Verchaly, pp. 27–46. Paris: Centre national de la recherche scientifique, 1956.

R. Landon, *Haydn*   Landon, H. C. Robbins, in association with Henry Raynor. *Haydn.* New York: Praeger; London: Faber & Faber, 1972.

R. Landon, "Haydniana"   Landon, H. C. Robbins. "Haydniana (I)." *The Haydn Yearbook* 4 (1968), 199–206.

R. Landon, "JHW"   ———. "Joseph Haydn: *Werke.*" *The Haydn Yearbook* 1 (1962), 224–27.

R. Landon, "Marionette"   ———. "Haydn's Marionette Operas and the Repertoire of the Marionette Theatre at Esterház Castle." *The Haydn Yearbook* 1 (1962), 111–97.

R. Landon, "Mondo"   ———. Preface to Joseph Haydn. *Die Welt auf dem Monde (Il mondo della luna).* Kassel: Bärenreiter, 1958. [Piano-vocal score.]

R. Landon, "Notes"   ———. "Notes on Symphonies 93–104." Decca HDNJ, 41–46. [Liner notes.]

R. Landon, "Quartets"   ———. "Doubtful and Spurious Quartets and Quintets Attributed to Haydn." *The Music Review* 18 (1957), 213–21.

R. Landon, "Sonatas"   ———. "Haydn's Piano Sonatas." In *Essays on the Viennese Classical Style,* pp. 44–67. New York: Macmillan, 1970.

R. Landon, *Symphonies*   ———. *The Symphonies of Joseph Haydn.* London: Universal Edition, Rockliff, 1955; New York: Macmillan, 1956.

R. Landon, *Trios*   ———. *Die Klaviertrios von Joseph Haydn: Vorwort zur ersten kritischen Gesamtausgabe.* Vienna: Doblinger, 1970.

Lang, *Civilization*   Lang, Paul Henry. *Music in Western Civilization.* New York: W. W. Norton & Co., 1941.

Larsen, "Bildnisse"   Larsen, Jens Peter. "Zur Frage der Porträtähnlichkeit der Haydn-Bildnisse." *Studia Musicologica* 9 (1970), 153–66.

Larsen, DHK   ———. *Drei Haydn Kataloge in Faksimile mit Einleitung und ergänzenden Themenverzeichnissen.* Copenhagen: Einar Munskgaard, 1941. [Includes Haydn, EK and Haydn, HV.]
    —Facs. repr., with additions. New York: Pendragon Press, 1979.

Larsen, "Echtheitsbestimmung"   ———. "Über die Möglichkeiten einer musikalischen Echtheitsbestimmung für Werke aus der Zeit Mozarts und Haydns." *Mozart-Jahrbuch,* 1971–72, pp. 7–18.
    —Repr. "Über Echtheitsprobleme in der Musik der Klassik." *Die Musikforschung* 25 (1972), 4–16.

Larsen, HÜb   ———. *Die Haydn-Überlieferung.* Copenhagen: Einar Munksgaard, 1939.

Larsen, "Interpretation"   ———. "Handel Traditions and Handel Interpretation." *Dansk Årbog for Musikforskning* (1961), 38–50.

Larsen, "Mannheim"   ———. "Zur Bedeutung der 'Mannheimer Schule.' " In *Festschrift Karl Gustav Fellerer zum sechzigsten Geburtstag am 7. Juli 1962,* ed. Heinrich Hüschen, pp. 303–09. Regensburg: Gustav Bosse Verlag, 1962.

Larsen, "Mozart"   ———. "Haydn und Mozart." *Österreichische Musikzeitschrift* 14 (1959), 216–22.

Larsen, "Observations" ———. "Some Observations on the Development and Characteristics of Viennese Classical Instrumental Music." *Studia Musicologica* 9 (1967), 115–39.

Larsen, "Quartbuch" ———. "Haydn und das kleine Quartbuch." *Acta Musicologica* 7
(1935), 111–23.

Larsen, "Revisit" ———. "Evidence or Guesswork: The 'Quartbuch' Revisited."
Acta musicologica 49 (1977), 86–102.

Larsen, "Revival" "Haydn Revival." In *Haydnfest* [q.v.], pp. 39–43.

Larsen, "Sonatenform" ———. "Sonatenform-Probleme." In *Festschrift Friedrich Blume
zum 70. Geburtstag,* ed. Anna Amalie Abert and Wilhelm Pfann-
kuch, pp. 221–30 Kassel: Bärenreiter, 1963.

Larsen, "Stilwandel" ———. "Der Stilwandel in der österreichischen Musik zwischen
Barock und Wiener Klassik." In *Der junge Haydn* [q.v.], pp. 18–30.

Larsen, "Symphonies" ———. "The Symphonies." In *The Mozart Companion,* ed. H. C.
Robbins Landon and Donald Mitchell, pp. 156–98. London: Barrie
& Rockliff; New York: Oxford Univ. Press, 1956. Repr. New
York: W. W. Norton & Co., 1969.

Larsen-Landon Larsen, Jens Peter, and H. C. Robbins Landon. "Haydn." *Die
Musik in Geschichte und Gegenwart,* vol. 5 (1956), cols. 1857–1916.

LaRue, "Gniezno" LaRue, Jan. "The Gniezno Symphony Not by Haydn." In *Festskrift
Larsen* [q.v.], pp. 255–60.

LaRue, *Guidelines* ———. *Guidelines for Style Analysis.* New York: W. W.
Norton & Co., 1970.

LaRue, "Hail" ———. "A 'Hail and Farewell' Quodlibet Symphony." *Music and
Letters* 37 (1956), 250–59.

LaRue, "Mozart" ———. "Mozart or Dittersdorf—KV 84/73q." *Mozart-Jahrbuch*
(1971–72), 40–49.

LaRue, "Resemblances" ———. "Significant and Coincidental Resemblances Between
Classical Themes." *Journal of the American Musicological Society* 14
(1961), 224–34.

LaRue, "Sinfonia" ———. "Sinfonia." *The New Grove Dictionary of Music and Musicians.* London: Macmillan, 1980.

Laurencie, *Blancheton* Laurencie, Lionel de la. *Inventaire critique du Fonds Blancheton.* 2
vols. Paris: Société française de Musicologie, 1930–31.

Lenneberg, "Mattheson" Lenneberg, Hans. "Johann Mattheson on Affect and Rhetoric in
Music." *Journal of Music Theory* 2 (1958), 47–84, 193–236.

Loewenberg, *Annals* Loewenberg, Alfred. *Annals of Opera, 1597–1940. . . .* Cambridge:
W. Heffer & Sons, [1943].
—2d ed. Geneva: Societas Bibliographica, [1955].

McCorkle, "Antes" McCorkle, Donald M. "John Antes, 'American Dilettante.' " *The
Musical Quarterly* 42 (1956), 486–99.

McCorkle, *Moravian* ———. *The Moravian Contribution to American Music.* (Moravian
Music Foundation Publications, 1.) Winston-Salem: Moravian
Music Foundation, 1956. [Repr. from *Notes* 13 (1956–57),
597–606.]

MacIntyre, "Seminar" MacIntyre, Bruce C. "The City University of New York: An
Unusual Haydn Seminar." *Current Musicology,* 20 (1975), 42–49.

Mahling, *Orchester* — Mahling, Christoph-Hellmut. "Orchester und Orchestermusiker in Deutschland von 1700 bis 1850." *Habilitationsschrift,* Univ. of the Saar, 1972.
—Rev.   Kassel: Bärenreiter, [in press].

Mahling, "Orchesterpraxis" — ———. "Mozart und die Orchesterpraxis seiner Zeit." *Mozart-Jahrbuch* (1967), 229–43.

Mahling, "Volksinstrumente" — ———. "Verwendung und Darstellung von Volksmusikinstrumenten in Werken von Haydn bis Schubert." *Jahrbuch des österreichischen Volksliedwerkes* 17 (1968), 39–48.

Manferrari, *Opere* — Manferrari, Umberto. *Dizionario universale delle opere melodrammatiche.* 3 vols. Florence: Sansoni, 1954–55.

Mann, "Beethoven" — Mann, Alfred. "Beethoven's Contrapuntal Studies with Haydn." *The Musical Quarterly,* 61 (1970), 711–26.
—Repr. *The Creative World of Beethoven,* ed. Paul Henry Lang, pp. 209–24. New York: W. W. Norton & Co., 1971.

Mann, "Critic" — ———. "Haydn as Student and Critic of Fux." In *Festschrift Geiringer* [q.v.], pp. 323–32.

Marks, "Rhetoric" — Marks, Paul F. "The Rhetorical Element in Musical *Sturm und Drang:* Christian Gottfried Krause's *Von der musikalischen Poesie." International Review of the Aesthetics and Sociology of Music* 2 (1971), 49–63.

Marpurg, *Anleitung* — Marpurg, Friedrich Wilhelm. *Anleitung zum Clavierspielen.* . . . Berlin: Haude & Spener, 1755.
—2nd ed. 1765.
—Facs. repr. New York: Broude Bros., 1969; Hildesheim: G. Olms, 1970.

Marpurg, *Handbuch* — ———. *Handbuch bey dem Generalbasse und der Composition.* . . . 3 vols. Berlin: Johann Jacob Schützens Witwe, 1755, 1757, 1758.
—2nd ed. of vol. 1:   Berlin: G. A. Lange, 1762.
—Facs. repr. [1762, 1757, 1758]. Hildesheim: G. Olms, 1971.

Marpurg, *Tonkunst* — ———. *Kritische Briefe über die Tonkunst.* . . . 3 vols. Berlin: F. Wilhelm Birnstiel, 1759–60, 1761–63, 1764.
—Facs. repr. Hildesheim: G. Olms, 1971.

Marrocco, "Franklin" — Marrocco, W. Thomas. "The String Quartet Attributed to Benjamin Franklin." *Proceedings of the American Philosophical Society* 116 (1972), 477–85.

Marx, *Komposition* — Marx, Adolf Bernhard. *Die Lehre von der musikalischen Komposition, praktisch-theoretisch.* 4 vols. Leipzig: Breitkopf & Härtel, 1837–47.

Massenkeil, *Symmetrie* — Massenkeil, Günther. *Untersuchungen zum Problem der Symmetrie in der Instrumentalmusik W. A. Mozarts.* Wiesbaden: F. Steiner, 1962.

Mattheson, *Capellmeister* — Mattheson, Johann. *Der vollkommene Capellmeister.* Hamburg: Christian Herold, 1739.
—Facs. repr. ed. Margarete Reimann. Kassel: Bärenreiter, 1974. (Documenta musicologica, first series, 5.)

Meier, *Kontrabass* — Meier, Adolf. *Konzertante Musik für Kontrabass in der Wiener Klassik.* Giebig über Prien am Chiemsee: Katzbichler, 1969.

Meyer, *Explaining*   Meyer, Leonard B. *Explaining Music.* Berkeley: Univ. of California Press, 1973.

Meyer, *Ideas*   ———. *Music, the Arts and Ideas.* Chicago: Univ. of Chicago Press, 1967.

Michaelis, "Humor"   Michaelis, C. F. "Ueber das Humoristische oder Launige in der musikalischen Komposition." *AmZ* 9 (1806–07), cols. 725–29.

Moe, "Texture"   Moe, Orin, Jr. "Texture in the String Quartets of Haydn to 1787." Ph.D. diss., Univ. of California, Santa Barbara, 1970.

Mooser, *Annales*   Mooser, R.-Aloys. *Annales de la musique et des musiciens en Russie au XVIIIe siècle.* 3 vols. Geneva: Mont-Blanc, 1948–51.

Mörner, "Haydniana"   Mörner, C.-G. Stellan. "Haydniana aus Schweden um 1800." *Haydn-Studien* 2 (1969–70), 1–33.

L. Mozart, *Violinschule*   Mozart, Leopold. *Versuch einer gründlichen Violinschule.* Augsburg: Lotter, 1756.

—Facs. repr. ed. Bernhard Paumgartner. Vienna: Stephenson, 1922.

—3rd ed. 1787.

—Facs. repr. ed. Hans Joachim Moser. Leipzig: VEB Breitkopf & Härtel, 1956.

—*A Treatise on the Fundamentals of Violin Playing.* Trans. Editha M. Knocker. London: Oxford Univ. Press, 1948. 2nd ed. 1951.

W. Mozart, *Briefe*   *Mozart: Briefe und Aufzeichnungen.* Ed. Wilhelm A. Bauer and Otto Erich Deutsch for the International Stiftung Mozarteum, Salzburg. Commentaries and Indices by Joseph Heinz Eibl. 7 vols. Kassel: Bärenreiter, 1962–75.

W. Mozart, NMA   *Wolfgang Amadeus Mozart: Neue Ausgabe sämtlicher Werke.* Ed. Internationale Stiftung Mozarteum, Salzburg. Kassel: Bärenreiter, 1956–.

MRz   *Musikalische Real-Zeitung* [Speyer].

J. Mueller, *Orchestra*   Mueller, John H. *The American Symphony Orchestra.* Bloomington: Indiana Univ. Press, 1951.

K. Mueller, *Orchestras*   Mueller, Kate Hevner. *Twenty-seven Major American Symphony Orchestras.* Bloomington: Indiana Univ. Press, 1973.

NBMz   *Neue Berliner Musikzeitung.*

Nelson, *Variation*   Nelson, Robert U. *The Technique of Variation.* Berkeley and Los Angeles: Univ. of California Press, 1949.

NMA   [See W. Mozart, NMA.]

Neumann, "Appoggiaturas"   Neumann, Frederick. "Couperin and the Downbeat Doctrine for Appoggiaturas." *Acta Musicologica* 41 (1969), 71–85.

Neumann, "Ornamentation"   ———. "A New Look at Bach's Ornamentation." *Music and Letters* 46 (1965), 4–15, 126–33.

Newman, *Classic*   Newman, William S. *The Sonata in the Classic Era.* Chapel Hill: Univ. of North Carolina Press, 1963.

—2nd ed. New York: W. W. Norton & Co., 1972.

Nottebohm, *Studien*   Nottebohm, Gustav. *Beethoven's Studien: Erster Band: Beethoven's Unterricht bei J. Haydn, Albrechtsberger und Salieri nach den Original-Manuscripten dargestellt.* Leipzig and Winterthur: J. Rieter-Biedermann, 1873.

—Facs. repr. Niederwalluf: Sändig, [1971].

NrMZ   *Niederrheinische Musik-Zeitung* [Cologne].

Odell, *Annals*   Odell, George C. D. *Annals of the New York Stage.* 15 vols. New York: Columbia Univ. Press, 1927–49.

"Oeuvres Complettes"   [See Haydn, "Oeuvres."]

Olleson, "Griesinger"   Olleson, Edward. "Georg August Griesinger's Correspondence with Breitkopf & Härtel." *The Haydn Yearbook* 3 (1965), 5–53.

Olleson, "Patron"   ———. "Gottfried van Swieten, Patron of Haydn and Mozart." *Publications of the [Royal] Musical Association* 89 (1962–63), 63–74.

Olleson, "Swieten"   ———. "Gottfried, Baron van Swieten, and his Influence on Haydn and Mozart." Ph.D. diss., Oxford, 1967.

Olleson, "Zinzendorf"   ———. "Haydn in the Diaries of Count Karl von Zinzendorf." *The Haydn Yearbook* 2 (1963–64), 45–63.

Pagano-Bianchi   Pagano, Roberto and Lino Bianchi. *Alessandro Scarlatti: Catalogo generale delle opere a cura di Giancarlo Rostirolla.* Turin: Edizione RAI radiotelevisione italiano, 1972.

Päsler, "Sonatas"   Päsler, Karl. Forewords to Haydn, GA [q.v.], Series 14: *Klavierwerke.* 3 vols. 1918.

Pandi-Schmidt   Pandi, Marianne, and Fritz Schmidt. "Musik zur Zeit Haydns und Beethovens in der Pressburger Zeitung." *The Haydn Yearbook* 8 (1971), 165–293.

Parrish, "Piano"   Parrish, Carl. "Haydn and the Piano." *Journal of the American Musicological Society* 1, No. 3 (Fall, 1948), 27–34.

Pass, "Bearbeitungen"   Pass, Walter. "Zu den Salve Regina-Bearbeitungen von Georg Prenner und Jacob Vaet in Joanellis Sammelwerk von 1568." In *De ratione in musica: Festschrift Erich Schenk zum 5. Mai 1972,* ed. Theophil Antonicek et al., pp. 29–49. Kassel: Bärenreiter, 1975.

Pečman, "Rokoko"   Pečman, Rudolf. "Zum Begriff des Rokokostils in der Musik." *Muzikološki zbornik* 9 (1973), 5–34.

Petri, *Anleitung*   Petri, Johann Samuel. *Anleitung zur praktischen Musik. . . .* Lauban: Johann Christoph Wirthgen, 1767.

—2nd ed.   Leipzig: Breitkopf, 1782.

—Facs. repr.   Giebig: Katzbichler, 1969.

Phelps, "Chamber"   Phelps, Roger Paul. "The History and Practice of Chamber Music in the United States from Earliest Times up to 1875." Ph.D. diss., Univ. of Iowa, 1951.

Planyavsky, *Kontrabass*   Planyavsky, Alfred. *Geschichte des Kontrabasses.* Tutzing: Hans Schneider, 1970.

Plath, "Autographie"   Plath, Wolfgang. "Beiträge zur Mozart-Autographie: I: Die Handschrift Leopold Mozarts." *Mozart-Jahrbuch* (1960–61), 82–117.

—"II: Schriftchronologie 1770–1780." *Mozart-Jahrbuch* (1976–77), 131–73.

Pohl   Pohl, Carl Ferdinand. *Joseph Haydn.* Vol. 1. Berlin: A. Sacco, 1875; Leipzig: Breitkopf & Härtel, 1878. Vol. 2. Leipzig: Breitkopf & Härtel, 1882.

—Facs. repr. Wiesbaden: Sändig, 1970–71.

[For continuation, see Pohl-Botstiber.]

Pohl, *London* — ———. *Mozart und Haydn in London.* Vol. 2. *Haydn in London.* Vienna: Carl Gerold's Sohn, 1867.
—Facs. repr. London: Gregg; New York: Da Capo, 1971.

Pohl-Botstiber — ———. *Joseph Haydn: Unter Benutzung der von C. F. Pohl hinterlassenen Materialien weitergeführt von Hugo Botstiber: Dritter Band.* Leipzig: Breitkopf & Härtel, 1927.
—Facs. repr. Wiesbaden: Sändig, 1971.
[Continuation of Pohl.]

Poštolka, *Haydn* — Poštolka, Milan. *Joseph Haydn a naše hudba 18. století.* (Hudební rozpravy, 9.) Prague: Státní Hudební Vydavatelství, 1961. [Joseph Haydn and our 18th-century Music.]

Preussner, "Aufklärung" — Preussner, Eberhard. "Aufklärung." *Die Musik in Geschichte und Gegenwart,* vol. 1 (1949–51), cols. 810–22.

Quantz, *Versuch* — Quantz, Johann Joachim. *Versuch einer Anweisung die Flöte traversière zu spielen.* Berlin: Voss, 1752.
—*On Playing the Flute.* Trans. Edward R. Reilly. New York: Free Press, 1966.

Radant, "Rosenbaum" — Radant Else. "Die Tagebücher von Joseph Carl Rosenbaum 1770–1829." *The Haydn Yearbook* 5 (1968), 7–159.

Ratner, "Combinatoria" — Ratner, Leonard. "Ars Combinatoria: Chance and Choice in Eighteenth-century Music." In *Festschrift Geiringer* [q.v.], pp. 343–63.

Ratner, "Form" — ———. "Harmonic Aspects of Classic Form." *Journal of the American Musicological Society* 2 (1949), 159–68.

Ratner, "Period" — ———. "Eighteenth-century Theories of Musical Period Structure." *The Musical Quarterly* 42 (1956), 439–54.

Ratz, *Formenlehre* — Ratz, Erwin. *Einführung in die musikalische Formenlehre.* Vienna: Österriechische Bundesverlag, 1951.
—3rd ed. Vienna: Universal-Edition, 1973.

Reicha, *Traité* — Reicha, Anton. *Traité de haute composition musicale.* 2 vols. Paris: Zetter et cie, 1824–26.

Reichardt, *Magazin* — Reichardt, Johann Friedrich. *Musikalisches Kunstmagazin.* 8 vols. in 2. Berlin: Author, 1782–91.
—Facs. repr. Hildesheim: G. Olms, 1969.

Reichardt, *Studien* — Reichardt, Johann Friedrich, and Friedrich Ludwig Aemilius Kunzen. *Studien für Tonkünstler und Musikfreunde . . . fürs Jahr 1792. . . .* 2 vols. in 1. Berlin: Verlag der neuen Musikhandlung, 1793.

Reinhard, "Schwerin" — Reinhard, A. E. "Eine Haydn-Uraufführung in Schwerin." *Allgemeine Musikzeitung* [Berlin] 59 (1932), 194.

Reuther-Orel — Reuther, Hermann, and Alfred Orel. *Katalog der Haydn-Gedächtnisausstellung Wien 1932.* Vienna: Österreichische Kunst, 1932.

Riedel-Martiny, "Oratorien" — Riedel-Martiny, Anke. "Das Verhältnis von Text und Musik in Haydns Oratorien." *Haydn-Studien* 1 (1965–67), 205–40.

Riepel, *Anfangsgründe* — Riepel, Joseph. *Anfangsgründe zur musikalischen Setzkunst. . . .* 5 vols. Frankfurt am Main, etc., 1752–68. Vol. 1. *De rhythmopoeia oder Von der Taktordnung. . . .* Regensburg and Vienna: Emerich Felix Bader; Augsburg: J. J. Lotter, 1752.

Rifkin, "Zitat" — Rifkin, Joshua. "Ein unbekanntes Haydn-Zitat bei Mozart." *Haydn-Studien* 2 (1969–70), 317.

Ripin, "Devices"   Ripin, Edwin M. "Expressive devices Applied to the Eighteenth-century Harpsichord." *The Organ Yearbook* 1 (1970), 64–80.

RISM   International Musicological Society—International Association of Music Libraries. *Répertoire international des sources musicales.* Munich: G. Henle; Kassel: Bärenreiter, 1960–.

Ritzel, *Sonatenform*   Ritzel, Fred. *Die Entwicklung der "Sonatenform" im musiktheoretischen Schriftum des 18. und 19. Jahrhunderts.* Wiesbaden: Breitkopf & Härtel, 1968.

Rochlitz, *Tonkunst*   Rochlitz, Friedrich. *Für Freunde der Tonkunst.* 4 vols. Leipzig: Cnobloch, 1824–32.

Rosen, *Style*   Rosen, Charles. *The Classical Style.* New York: The Viking Press, 1971. Repr. New York: W. W. Norton & Co., 1972.

Rousseau, *Traité*   Rousseau, Jean. *Traité de la viole.* . . . Paris: Ballard, 1687.
—Facs. repr. Amsterdam: Antiqua, 1965.

Rudnicka, *Lessel*   Rudnicka-Kruszewska, Hanna. *Wincenty Lessel: Szkic biograficzny na podstawie listów do snya.* Cracow: Pol. Wydawn. Muzyczne, 1968. (Krak. Zakl. graf. 6, XII, 1968.)

Rutová, "Waldstein"   Rutová, Milada. "Valdstejnská hudební sbírka v Doksech." ["The Waldstein Music Archive from Doksy Castle."] 3 vols. Ph.D. diss., Charles Univ., Prague, 1971.

Sachs, *Handbuch*   Sachs, Curt. *Handbuch der Musikinstrumentenkunde.* 2nd ed. Leipzig: Breitkopf & Härtel, 1930.

Sachs, *Lexikon*   ———. *Real-Lexikon der Musikinstrumente.* Berlin: Julius Bard, 1913.

Saint Lambert, *Clavecin*   Saint Lambert, Michel de. *Les principes du clavecin.* . . . Paris: Ballard, 1702; Amsterdam: Roger, c. 1710.
—Facs. rep.   Geneva: Éditions Minkoff, 1971.

Sandberger, "Haydniana"   Sandberger, Adolf. "Neue Haydniana." *Jahrbuch Peters* 40 (1933), 28–37.

Sandberger, "Streichquartett"   ———. "Zur Geschichte des Haydnschen Streichquartetts." *Altbayerische Monatsschrift* 2 (1900), 41–64.
—Repr. *Ausgewählte Aufsätze zur Musikgeschichte,* vol. 1, 224–65. Munich: Drei Masken Verlag, 1921.

Saslav, "Tempos"   Saslav, Isidor. "Tempos in the String Quartets of Joseph Haydn." D. Mus. diss., Univ. of Indiana, 1969.

Scharnagl, *Sterkel*   Scharnagl, Augustin. *Johann Franz Xaver Sterkel: Ein Beitrag zur Musikgeschichte Mainfrankens.* Würzburg: K. Triltsch, 1943.

Scheibe, *Musicus*   Scheibe, Johann Adolph. *Der critische Musicus.* 2 vols. Hamburg: Thomas von Wierings Erben, 1738; Rudolf Benecke, 1740.
—Rev. ed. Leipzig: Breitkopf, 1745.
—Facs. repr. Hildesheim: G. Olms, 1970.

Schenk, "Skizze"   Schenk, Johann Baptist. "Autobiographische Skizze." [Ed. Guido Adler.] *Studien zur Musikwissenschaft* 9 (1924), 75–85.

Schiedermair, "Kapelle"   Schiedermair, Ludwig. "Die Blütezeit der Öttingen-Wallerstein'schen Hofkapelle." *Sammelbände der internationalen Musikgesellschaft* 9 (1907–08), 83–130.

Schmid, "Bach"   Schmid, Ernst Fritz. "Joseph Haydn und Carl Philipp Emanuel Bach." *Zeitschrift für Musikwissenschaft* 14 (1931–32), 299–312.

Schmid, "Drehleier" ———. "Haydns Werke für die Drehleier." *Die Musik* 24 (1931–32), 451–52.

Schmid, "Flötenuhr" ———. "Joseph Haydn und die Flötenuhr." *Zeitschrift für Musikwissenschaft* 14 (1931–32), 193–221.

Schmid, "Funde" ———. "Neue Funde zu Haydns Flötenuhrstücken." *Haydn-Studien* 2 (1969–70), 249–55.

Schmid, *Haydn* ———. *Joseph Haydn: Ein Buch von Vorfahren und Heimat des Meisters.* 2 vols. Kassel: Bärenreiter, 1934.

Schmid, *Kammermusik* ———. *Carl Philipp Emanuel Bach und seine Kammermusik.* Kassel: Bärenreiter, 1931.

Schmid, "Mozart." ———. "Mozart and Haydn." *The Musical Quarterly* 47 (1956), 145–61.

—Repr. The *Creative World of Mozart,* ed. Paul Henry Lang, pp. 86–102. New York: W. W. Norton & Co., 1963.

Schneider-Algatzy. Schneider, Otto and Anton Algatzy. *Mozart-Handbuch: Chronik, Werk, Bibliographie.* Vienna: Gebrüder Hollinek, 1962.

Schoenberg, *Harmonielehre* Schoenberg, Arnold. *Harmonielehre.* Vienna: Universal-Edition, 1911. 7th ed., 1966.

—*Theory of Harmony.* Trans. Robert D. W. Adams. New York: Philosophical Library, [1948].

Schoenberg, *Structural* ———. *Structural Functions of Harmony.* New York: W. W. Norton, 1954. Rev. ed., 1969.

—*Die formbildenden Tendenzen der Harmonie.* Trans. Erwin Stein. Mainz: Schott, 1957.

Schreiber, *Kraus* Schreiber, Karl Friedrich. *Biographie über den Odenwälder Komponisten Joseph Martin Kraus.* Buchen: Verlag Bezirksmuseum, 1928.

Schubart, *Ästhetik* Schubart, Christian Friedrich Daniel. *Ideen zu einer Ästhetik der Tonkunst.* Vienna: J. V. Degen, 1806.

Schwarting, "Reprise" Schwarting, Heino. "Ungewöhnliche Repriseneintritte in Haydns späterer Instrumentalmusik." *Archiv für Musikwissenschaft* 17 (1966), 168–82.

Schwartz, "Phrase" Schwartz, Judith L. "Phrase Structure in the Early Classic Symphony (c. 1720–c. 1765)." Ph.D. diss., New York Univ., 1973.

Schwarz, "Cembalo" Schwarz, Vera. "Die Rolle des Cembalos in Österreich nach 1760." In *Der junge Haydn* [q.v.], pp. 249–58.

Schwarz, "Missverständnisse" ———. "Missverständnisse in der Haydn-Interpretation dargestellt an Beispielen aus seiner Klaviermusik." *Österreichische Musikzeitschrift* 31 (1976), 25–35.

Scott, "83" Scott, Marion M. "Haydn's 'Eighty-Three': A Study of the Complete Edition." *Music and Letters* 11 (1930), 207–29.

Scott, "Op. 2–3" ———. "Haydn's Opus Two and Opus Three." *Publications of the [Royal] Musical Association* 61 (1934–35), 1–15.

Sehnal, "Egk" Sehnal, Jiří. "Kapela Olomouchéko Biskupa Leopolda Egka (1758–60) A Její Repertoár." *Acta Musei Moraviae* 50 (1965), 203–30. ["The Kapelle of Leopold Egk, Bishop of Olmütz 1758–60, and its Repertory."]

Senn, "Heilig Kreuz" Senn, Walter. "Die Mozart-Überlieferung im Stift Heilig Kreuz zu

Augsburg." *Zeitschrift des historischen Vereins für Schwaben,* vol. 62/63 (= *Neues Mozartbuch*), pp. 333–68.

Šetková, Štěpán   Šetková, Dana. *Klavírní dílo Josefa Antonína Štěpána.* Prague: Státnín Hudební Vydavatelství, 1965.

Silbert, "Ambiguity"   Silbert, Doris. "Ambiguity in the String Quartets of Joseph Haydn." *The Musical Quarterly* 36 (1950), 562–73.

Silverstolpe, Återblickar   Silverstolpe, Fredrik Samuel. *Några återblickar på rygtets, snillets och konsternas verld.* Stockholm: Norstedt, 1841. [*Some Reminiscences of the World of Fame, Genius, and the Arts.*]

Silverstolpe, *Kraus*   [———.] *Biographie af Kraus, med bilagor af femtio bref ifrån honom.* Stockholm: Hörberg, 1833.

Sisman, "Variations"   Sisman, Elaine. "Haydn's Variations." Ph.D. diss., Princeton Univ., 1978.

Solomon, *Beethoven*   Solomon, Maynard. *Beethoven.* New York: Schirmer Books, 1977.

Somfai, "Albrechts-berger"   Somfai, László. "Albrechtsberger-Eigenschriften in der National-bibliothek Széchényi, Budapest." *Studia musicologica* 1 (1961), 175–202; 4 (1963), 179–90; 9 (1967), 191–220.

Somfai, *Bilder*   ———. *Joseph Haydn: Sein Leben in zeitgenössischen Bildern.* Buda-pest: Corvina; Kassel: Bärenreiter, 1966.

—*Joseph Haydn: His Life in Contemporary Pictures.* Trans. Mari Kuttna and Károly Ravasz. London: Faber & Faber; New York: Taplinger, 1969.

Somfai, "Kvartett"   ———. "A klasszikus kvartetthangzás megszületése Haydn von-ósnégyeseiben." *Zenetudományi tanulmányok* 8 (1960) (*Haydn-Emlékére*), 295–420. ["The Evolution of Classical Quartet Style in Haydn's Quartets."]

Somfai, "Model"   ———. "A Bold Enharmonic Modulatory Model in Joseph Haydn's String Quartets." In *Festschrift Geiringer* [q.v.], pp. 370–81.

Somfai, "Op. 3"   ———. "Zur Echtheitsfrage des Haydn'schen 'Opus 3.'" *The Haydn Yearbook* 3 (1965), 153–65.

Sonneck, *Concert*   Sonneck, Oscar G. T. *Early Concert-Life in America, 1731–1800.* Leipzig: Breitkopf & Härtel, 1907.

Sonneck, *Librettos*   ———. *Catalogue of Opera Librettos Printed Before 1800.* 2 vols. Washington, D.C.: U.S. Government Printing Office, 1914.

Speer, *Unterricht*   Speer, Daniel. *Grund-richtiger . . . Unterricht der musicalischen Kunst. . . .* Ulm: G. W. Kühne, 1687.

Spitta, *Bach*   Spitta, Philipp. *Johann Sebastian Bach.* 2 vols. Leipzig: Breitkopf & Härtel, 1873–80.

—*Johann Sebastian Bach: His Work and Influence on the Music of Germany.* Trans. Clara Bell and J. A. Fuller-Maitland. 3 vols. Lon-don: Novello, Ewer, 1884–85. Facs. repr. 2 vols. New York: Dover Books, [1951].

Spitta, "Pohl"   ———. "Joseph Haydn in der Darstellung C. F. Pohls." In *Zur Musik: Sechzehn Aufsätze,* pp. 151–76. Berlin: Paetel, 1892. Facs. repr. Hildesheim and New York: G. Olms, 1976.

Stadler, "Geschichte"   "Materialien zur Geschichte der Musik unter den österreichischen

Regenten." MS. Vienna, Austrian National Library, S.n. 4310.

—*Stadler, Maximilian: Seine Materialien . . .: Ein Beitrag zum musikalischen Historismus im vormärzlichen Wien.* Ed. Karl Wagner. (Schriftenreihe der Internationalen Stiftung Mozarteum, 6.) Kassel: Bärenreiter, [1974].

Steinpress, "Oratorien"   Steinpress, Boris. "Haydns Oratorien in Russland zu Lebzeiten des Komponisten." *Haydn-Studien* 2 (1969–70), 77–112.

Stern, "Schöpfung"   Stern, Martin. "Haydns 'Schöpfung': Geist und Herkunft des van Swietenschen Librettos: Ein Beitrag zum Thema 'Säkularisation' im Zeitalter der Aufklärung." *Haydn-Studien* 1 (1965–67), 121–98.

"Streichquartett"   *Riemann Musik Lexikon.* 12th ed. Vol. 3, *Sachteil,* s.v. "Streichquartett."

Strunk, "Autograph"   Strunk, Oliver. "Notes on a Haydn Autograph." *The Musical Quarterly* 20 (1934), 192–205.

—Repr. *Essays on Music in the Western World,* pp. 171–87. New York: W. W. Norton & Co., 1974.

Strunk, "Baryton"   ———. "Haydn's Divertimenti for Baryton, Viola and Bass." *The Musical Quarterly* 18 (1932), 216–51.

—Repr. op. cit., pp. 126–70.

Strunk, "Haydn"   ———. "Haydn." In *From Bach to Stravinsky: The History of Music by its Foremost Critics,* ed. David Ewen, pp. 78–87. New York: W.W. Norton & Co., 1933.

—Repr. op. cit., pp. 114–25.

Sulzer, *Theorie*   Sulzer, Johann Georg, et al. *Allgemeine Theorie der schönen Künste.* 2 vols. Leipzig: Weidmann, 1771–74.

—2nd ed. 4 vols. 1778–79.

—3rd ed. ["neue vermehrte zweyte"]. 4 vols. 1792–94.

Szabolcsi, "Ungarisch"   Szabolcsi, Bence. "Joseph Haydn und die ungarische Musik." *Beiträge zur Musikwissenschaft* 1 (1959), 62–73.

—Repr. *Bericht über die internationale Konferenz zum Andenken Joseph Haydns, Budapest, 17.–22. September 1959,* ed. Bence Szabolcsi and Dénes Bartha, pp. 159–75. Budapest: Akadémiai Kiadó, 1961.

Tartini, *Traité*   Tartini. Giuseppe. *Traité des agrémens de la musique. . . .* Paris: Author, 1771. [Original: MS, Italian.]

—Modern facs. ed. Erwin R. Jacobi, trans. Cuthbert Girdlestone. Celle and New York: H. Moeck, 1961.

—2nd ed. Paris: Chevardière, 1775.

Thomas, "Griesinger"   Thomas, Günter. "Griesingers Briefe über Haydn: Aus seiner Korrespondenz mit Breitkopf & Härtel." *Haydn-Studien* 1 (1965–67), 49–114.

Thomas, "Mondo"   ———. "Zu 'Il mondo della luna' und 'La fedeltà premiata': Fassungen und Pasticcios." *Haydn-Studien* 2 (1969–70), 122–26.

Tobel, *Formenwelt*   Tobel, Rudolf von. *Die Formenwelt der klassischen Instrumentalmusik.* Bern: P. Haupt, 1935.

Tomaschek, "Memoirs"   [Tomaschek, Johann Wenzel.] "Excerpts from the Memoirs of J. W. Tomaschek." Trans. Abram Loft. *The Musical Quarterly* 32 (1946), 244–64.

Torrefranca,   Torrefranca, Fausto. "Avviamento alla storia del quartetto ita-
"Avviamento"   liano." Ed. Alfredo Bonaccorsi. *L'Approdo musicale* 12 (No. 23,
    1966), 5–181.

Tosi, *Opinioni*   Tosi, Pierfrancesco. *Opinioni de' contori antichi, e moderni.* . . . Bo-
    logna: Lelio dalla volpe, 1723.
    —Facs. repr. Bologna: Forni, 1968.
    —*Observations on the Florid Song.* . . . Trans. Mr. Galliard. Lon-
    don: J. Wilcox, 1742.
    —2nd ed. 1743.
    —Facs. repr. New York: Johnson Reprint, 1968.
    —*Anleitung zur Singkunst.* . . . Trans. Johann Freidrich Agricola.
    Berlin: Winter, 1757.

Tovey, "Chamber"   Tovey, Donald Francis. "Franz Joseph Haydn." In *Cobbett's Cyclo-
    pedic Survey of Chamber Music,* ed. W. W. Cobbett, vol. 1, 515–45.
    London: Oxford Univ. Press, 1929.
    —Repr. *The Main Stream of Music and Other Essays* [also titled
    Essays and Lectures on Music], ed. Hubert J. Foss, pp. 1–64. London:
    Oxford Univ. Press, 1949. Repr. New York: Meridian, 1959.

Tovey, *Essays*   ———. *Essays in Musical Analysis.* 6 vols. and one supplementary
    vol. London: Oxford Univ. Press, 1935–44. Repr. 1972.

Tovey, "Sonata"   ———. *Encyclopedia Brittanica.* 11th ed. (1910), s.v. "Sonata
    Forms." Repr. 12th–14th eds.
    —Repr. *Musical Articles from the Encyclopedia Britannica,* ed. Hu-
    bert J. Foss, pp. 208–32. London: Oxford Univ. Press, 1944. Repr.
    The Forms of Music. New York: Meridian Books, 1956.

Traeg, *Verzeichnis*   Traeg, Johann. *Verzeichniss alter und neuer sowohl geschriebener als
    gestochener Musikalien.* . . . Vienna: Traeg, 1799.

Trimpert, *Quatuor*   Trimpert, Lutz. *Die quatuors concertants von Giuseppe Cambini.*
    Tutzing, Hans Schneider, 1967.

Türk, *Klavierschule*   Türk, Daniel Gottlob. *Klavierschule.* . . . Leipzig and Halle: Author
    (Commission: Schwickert; Hemmerde & Schwetschke), 1789.
    —Facs. repr. ed. Erwin R. Jacobi. Kassel: Bärenreiter, 1962.
    (Documenta musicologica, first series, 23.)

Tutenberg, *J. C. Bach*   Tutenberg, Fritz. *Die Sinfonik Johann Christian Bachs: Ein Beitrag
    zur Entwicklungsgeschichte der Sinfonie von 1750–80.* Wolfenbüttel:
    Kallmeyer, 1928.

Tutenberg,   ———. "Die Durchführungsfrage in der vorneuklassischen Sin-
"Durchführungsfrage"   fonie." *Zeitschrift für Musikwissenschaft* 9 (1926–27), 90–94.

Tyson, "Clementi"   Tyson, Alan. "Clementi's Viennese Compositions, 1781–82." *The
    Music Review* 27 (1966), 16–24.

Tyson, "Leonore"   ———. "The Problem of Beethovens 'First' *Leonore* Overture."
    Journal of the American Musicological Society 28 (1975), 292–334.

Tyson, "Trios"   ———. "Haydn and Two Stolen Trios." *The Music Review* 22
    (1961), 21–27.

Tyson-Landon   Tyson, Alan, and H. C. Robbins Landon. "Who Composed
    Haydn's Op. 3?" *The Musical Times* 105 (1964), 506–07.

Unverricht, *Hoffstetter*   Unverricht, Hubert, in collaboration with Adam Gottron and Alan
    Tyson. *Die beiden Hoffstetter: Zwei Komponisten-Porträts mit Werk-*

verzeichnissen. (Beiträge zur mittelrheinischen Musikgeschichte, 10.) Mainz: B. Schotts Söhne, 1968.

Unverricht, *Streichtrio*   Unverricht, Hubert. *Geschichte des Streichtrios.* Tutzing: Hans Schneider, 1969.

Valkó I–II   Valkó, Arisztid. "Haydn magyarországi müködése a levéltári aktak tükrében." *Zenetudonmányi tanulmányok* 6 (1957) (*Kodály Zoltán 75. születésnapjára*), 627–67; 8 (1960) (*Haydn-Emlékére*), 527–668.

Veidl, *Humor*   Veidl, Theodor. *Der musikalische Humor bei Beethoven.* Leipzig: Breitkopf & Härtel, 1929.

Vieira, *Portuguezes*   Vieira, Ernesto. *Diccionario Biographica de Musicos Portuguezes.* . . . 2 vols. Lisbon: Moreira & Pinheiro, 1900.

Vogler, *Betrachtungen*   Vogler, Georg Joseph. *Betrachtungen der Mannheimer Tonschule.* 3 vols. Mannheim: n.p., 1778–81.

—Facs. repr. Hildesheim and New York: G. Olms, 1974. 3 vols. in 4.

VZ   *Berlinische Nachrichten von Staats- und gelehrten Sachen* (*Vossische Zeitung*)

Walter, "Beziehungen"   Walter, Horst. "Die biographischen Beziehungen zwischen Haydn und Beethoven." In Gesellschaft für Musikforschung. *Bericht über den Internationalen musikwissenschaftlichen Kongress Bonn 1970,* ed. Carl Dahlhaus et al., pp. 79–83. Kassel: Bärenreiter, [1973].

Walter, "Klaviere"   ———. "Haydn's Klaviere." *Haydn-Studien* 2 (1969–70), 256–88.

Walter, "Tasteninstrument"   ———. "Das Tasteninstrument beim jungen Haydn." In *Der junge Haydn* [q.v.], pp. 237–48.

Walter, "Textbücher"   ———. "Gottfried van Swietens handschriftliche Textbücher zu 'Schöpfung' und 'Jahreszeiten.'" *Haydn-Studien* 1 (1965–67), 241–77.

Walters, *Choir*   Walters, Raymond. *The Bethlehem Bach Choir: An Historical and Interpretive Sketch.* Boston: Houghton Mifflin Co., 1918.

Walther, *Lexicon*   Walther, Johann Gottfried. *Musicalisches Lexicon.* . . . Leipzig: Wolfgang Deer, 1932.

—Facs. ed. Richard Schaal. Kassel: Bärenreiter, 1968. (Documenta musicologica, first series, 3.)

Weber, *Theorie*   Weber, Gottfried. *Versuch einer geordneten Theorie der Tonsetzkunst.* . . . 3 vols. Mainz: B. Schott, 1817–21.

—2nd ed. 4 vols. 1824.

—3rd ed. 1830–32.

Webster, "Bass Part"   Webster, James. "The Bass Part in Haydn's Early String Quartets." *The Musical Quarterly* 63 (1977), 390–424.

Webster, "Beethoven"   ———. "Traditional Elements in Beethoven's Middle-period String Quartets." In *Beethoven, Performers, and Critics,* ed. Robert Winter and Bruce Carr, pp. 94–133. Detroit: Wayne State Univ. Press, 1980.

Webster, "Chamber"   ———. "Towards a History of Viennese Chamber Music in the Early Classical Period." *Journal of the American Musicological Society* 27 (1974), 212–47.

Webster, "Chronology"   ———. "The Chronology of Haydn's String Quartets." *The Musical Quarterly* 61 (1975), 17–46.

Webster, "Quartets"   ———. "Haydn's String Quartets." In *Haydnfest* [q.v.], pp. 13–17.

Webster, "Violoncello"   ———. "Violoncello and Double Bass in the Chamber Music of Haydn and his Viennese Contemporaries, 1750–1780." *Journal of the American Musicological Society* 29 (1976), 413–38.

Weinmann, *Verleger*   Weinmann, Alexander. *Wiener Musikverleger und Musikalienhändler von Mozarts Zeit bis gegan 1860.* Vienna: [Rudolf M. Rohrer], 1956.

Wendschuh, *Opern*   Wendschuh, Ludwig. *Über Joseph Haydns Opern.* Halle a. S.: C. A. Kaemmerer, 1896.

Westphal, *Form*   Westphal, Kurt. *Der Begriff der musikalischen Form in der Wiener Klassik: Versuch einer Grundlegung der Theorie der musikalischen Formung.* Leipzig: Kistner & Siegel, 1935.

Westrup, "Aspects"   Westrup, Jack A. "Aspects of the 18th Century." *Current Musicology* 9 (1969), 169–73.

Westrup, "Editorial"   ———. "Editorial." *Music and Letters* 48 (1967) 1–12.

Wr. Ztg.   *Wiener Diarium* [= *Wienerisches Diarium* / *Wiener Zeitung*].

Wirth, *Dramatiker*   Wirth, Helmut. *Joseph Haydn als Dramatiker: Sein Bühnenschaffen als Beitrag zur Geschichte der deutschen Oper.* (Kieler Beiträge zur Musikwissenschaft, 7.) Wolfenbüttel: Kallmeyer, 1940.

Woldemar, *Méthode*   Woldemar, Michel. *Grande Méthode ou étude élémentaire pour le violon.* . . . Paris: Cochet, 1798.
          —2nd ed. 1800.

Wolf, "Recapitulations"   Wolf, Eugene K. "The Recapitulations in Haydn's London Symphonies." *The Musical Quarterly* 52 (1966), 71–89.

Wolf, "Stamitz"   ———. "The Symphonies of Johann Stamitz: Authenticity, Chronology, and Style." Ph.D. diss., New York Univ., 1972.

Wurzbach, *Lexikon*   Wurzbach, Constantin von. *Biographisches Lexikon des Kaiserthums Oesterreich.* . . . 60 vols. Vienna: K. k. Hof- und Staatsdruckerei, 1856–91.

Wyzewa, "Centenaire"   Wyzewa, Théodore de. "A propos du centenaire de la mort de Joseph Haydn." *Revue des deux mondes* 79th year, 5th series, vol. 51, May–June 1909, pp. 935–46.

Zaslaw, "Orchestra"   Zaslaw, Neal. "Towards the Revival of the Classical Orchestra." *Publications of the [Royal] Musical Association* 103 (1976–77), 158–87.

Appendix A

Program of the Conference

Saturday, October 4, 1975

Opening Session
  Jens Peter Larsen, Chairman
  Roger L. Stevens, Chairman, The John F. Kennedy Center for the
    Performing Arts
  Martin Feinstein, Executive Director, Kennedy Center
  Karl Gustav Fellerer, President, German Musicological Society;
    Chairman, Joseph Haydn-Institut, Cologne
  Ludwig Finscher, Vice President, International Musicological Soci-
    ety
  Jens Peter Larsen, Musicologist-in-Residence
  Janet M. Knapp, President, American Musicological Society
Section I: Performance Problems
  Round Table I. Performance Problems in Haydn's Music, I:
  Historical Performance Conditions and Traditions
    Barry S. Brook, Chairman
  Workshop 1. Church Music
    Alfred Mann, Chairman
  Workshop 2. Keyboard Sonatas
    William S. Newman, Chairman

Sunday, October 5, 1975

Public Lecture. Haydn and his Viennese Background
    Karl Geiringer
Workshop 3. String Quartets
    Ludwig Finscher, Chairman
Workshop 4. Symphonies
    Boris Schwarz, Chairman

Free Papers

Monday, October 6, 1975

Workshop 5. Opera
    Barry S. Brook, Chairman
Free Papers

Round Table II. Performance Problems in Haydn's Music, II:
Problems of a Present-Day Haydn Performance
    Jens Peter Larsen, Chairman

Tuesday, October 7, 1975

Section II: Documentation
  Public Lecture. A Survey of Haydn Research in Our Time:
  Solved and Unsolved Problems
    Jens Peter Larsen
  Round Table III. Haydn Documentation, I:
  Background, Biography, Iconography
    Dénes Bartha, Chairman
  Workshop 6. Piano Trios
    Donald J. Grout, Chairman
  Round Table IV. Classical Period and Classical Style in Eighteenth-
  Century Music
    Donald J. Grout, Chairman
  Free Papers

Wednesday, October 8, 1975

  Round Table V. Haydn Documentation, II:
  Source Problems, Authenticity and Chronology, Lists of Works
    Georg Feder, Chairman
  Round Table VIa. "Opus 3": Haydn or Hoffstetter?
    László Somfai, Chairman
  Round Table VIb. Authenticity and Chronology Problems in Haydn's
  Early Sonatas
    William S. Newman, Chairman

Thursday, October 9, 1975

  Public Lecture. The Collected Works of Joseph Haydn
    Georg Feder, Chairman
Section III: Form and Style
  Round Table VII. Changing Concepts of Musical Form (Historical vs.
  Systematic Approach) and their Relation to Changing Approaches to
  Haydn's Music
    George J. Buelow, Chairman
  Free Papers
  Round Table VIII. Melodic Style Traditions and Haydn's Personal
  Style
    Eva Badura-Skoda, Chairperson
  Free Papers

Friday, October 10, 1975

  Round Table IX. Style and Style Changes in Haydn's Music:
  Suggested Turning Points in His Development
    Jan LaRue, Chairman

Free Papers

Round Table X. Haydn and Mozart
Gerhard Croll, Chairman

Free Papers

Saturday, October 11, 1975

Public Lecture. Haydn in America
Irving Lowens
Concluding Session
Jens Peter Larsen, Chairman

Appendix B

Participants

Note. The institutional affiliations provided are those obtaining at the time of the Conference. When a participant's affiliation has changed in the meantime, the latest known affiliation is appended in parentheses.
   Graduate student participants are indicated by asterisks.

Harold L. Andrews, University of North Carolina at Chapel Hill
Eva Badura-Skoda, Vienna
Reginald Barrett-Ayres, University of Aberdeen
Dénes Bartha, University of Pittsburgh (Budapest)
Irmgard Becker-Glauch, Joseph Haydn-Institut, Cologne
Malcolm Bilson, Cornell University
David D. Boyden, University of California, Berkeley
Howard Brofsky, Queens College, City University of New York
Barry S. Brook, City University of New York
A. Peter Brown, Indiana University
Paul Bryan, Duke University
George J. Buelow, Rutgers University (Indiana University)
Roger E. Chapman, University of California, Santa Barbara
Bathia Churgin, Bar-Ilan University
Gerhard Croll, University of Salzburg
Stephen Cushman, Wheaton College
Shelley Davis, University of Maryland
Ellwood Derr, University of Michigan
Antal Dorati, National Symphony Orchestra, Washington, D. C. (Detroit Symphony Orchestra)
Georg Feder, Joseph Haydn-Institut, Cologne
Michael Feldman, City University of New York (St. Luke's Chamber Ensemble, New York)
Karl Gustav Fellerer, Joseph Haydn-Institut, Cologne
* Michelle Fillion, Cornell University (McGill University)
Ludwig Finscher, J. W. Goethe University, Frankfurt am Main
* Stephen E. Fisher, University of Pennsylvania
Robert N. Freeman, University of California, Santa Barbara
Karl Geiringer, University of California, Santa Barbara
Sonja Gerlach, Joseph Haydn-Institut, Cologne

Vernon Gotwals, Smith College

Jerald C. Graue, Eastman School of Music

★ Carolyn D. Gresham, Eastman School of Music

Donald J. Grout, Cornell University

Carsten E. Hatting, University of Copenhagen

Eugene Helm, University of Maryland

Newell Jenkins, The Clarion Music Society, New York

J. Merrill Knapp, Princeton University

★ Joel Kolk, City University of New York

Dina Koston, Theater Chamber Players, Washington, D. C.

Niels Krabbe, University of Copenhagen

Christa Landon, Vienna (deceased)

Paul Henry Lang, Columbia University

Jens Peter Larsen, University of Copenhagen

Jan LaRue, New York University

Robert Levin, State University of New York at Purchase

Janet M. Levy, City College of New York

Ernest F. Livingstone, Rensselaer Polytechnic Institute

Irving Lowens, Music Critics Association, Reston, Va. (Peabody Institute)

★ Bruce MacIntyre, City University of New York

Christoph-Hellmut Mahling, University of the Saar, Saarbrücken

Alfred Mann, Rutgers University (Eastman School of Music)

Eduard Melkus, Akademie für Musik und darstellende Kunst, Vienna

Orin Moe, Jr., Georgia State University (Vanderbilt University)

Dennis C. Monk, Central Michigan University

Sonya Monosoff, Cornell University

C.-G. Stellan Mörner, Swedish Radio, Stockholm (deceased)

Lawrence K. Moss, University of Maryland

William S. Newman, University of North Carolina at Chapel Hill

Makoto Ohmiya, Ochanomizu University, Tokyo

★ Stephen E. Paul, Kings College, Cambridge (Polydor International GmbH, Hamburg)

Walter Pass, University of Vienna

Rudolf Pečman, University of Brno

Zdeňka Pilková, Prague

Andrew Porter, New York

Milan Poštolka, Music Division, National Museum, Prague

★ Jane Bostian Price, Eastman School of Music

Leonard G. Ratner, Stanford University

Robert Ricks, The Catholic University of America

Edwin M. Ripin, Musical Instrument Collection, The Metropolitan Museum of Art, New York (deceased)

★ Marie Rolf, University of Indiana (Eastman School of Music)

Charles Rosen, State University of New York at Stony Brook

Isidor Saslav, Baltimore Symphony Orchestra and Peabody Institute

Judith L. Schwartz, Northwestern University

Boris Schwarz, Queens College, City University of New York

Vera Schwarz, Institut für Aufführungspraxis, Hochschule für Musik und darstellende Kunst, Graz (deceased)

Howard Serwer, University of Maryland

Charles Sherman, University of Missouri

★ Laurie Shulman, Cornell University (Central Michigan University)

★ Elaine R. Sisman, Princeton University (University of Michigan)

László Somfai, Bartók Archive, Budapest

★ Lester S. Steinberg, New York University

★ Jeannette Taves, Eastman School of Music

Günter Thomas, Joseph Haydn-Institut, Cologne

★ Christie Tolstoy, City University of New York

★ Leslie Tung, Eastman School of Music

Alan Tyson, All Souls College, Oxford

Hubert Unverricht, Johannes Gutenberg University, Mainz

Horst Walter, Joseph Haydn-Institut, Cologne

James Webster, Cornell University

Mogens Wöldike, Copenhagen

Neal Zaslaw, Cornell University

Index of Haydn's Works

References to musical examples are indicated by **boldface** type.

565

Index of Doubtful and Spurious Works

(composers, as far as can be determined, are given in parentheses)

General Index

References to illustrations are indicated by **boldface** type. Published books and the like are cited according to the short titles used in List of Works Cited.

Abert, Hermann, 118, 407–8, 422
Adler, Guido, *Methode,* 17
Albrechtsberger, Georg
 divertimento by, 382
 fugues, 408
 Haydn's friend, 163
 musical examples from, **366, 367**
 as organist, 193, 194
 scoring by, 239
 string quartet by, attributed to Haydn, 77–78, 381–82
Allegri, Gregorio, 456
Allgemeine musikalische Zeitung, 66, 71, 423
Allgemeine Literatur-Zeitung, 153
American musical scene (1782–1810)
 concerts, 36, 40–42
 documentation of performances, 37–38
 Haydn societies, 48
 Haydn's works performed, 42–43
 Moravian musical societies, 43–45
 publications of Haydn's works, 36–37, 40
 see also collections; Jefferson, Thomas
Anfossi, Pasquale, 254, 256, 257, 259
 setting of *La vera costanza,* 155, 261
Annereau, Madame, 96–98
Ansermet, Ernest, recording by, 246
Antes, John, 45
Arbesser, Ferdinand, 9
Artaria & Co., 10, 104
 editions by, 29, 76–77, 225
 establishment of, 337
 Haydn's letters to, 216, 288, 315, 426, 510–11, 514
 as Haydn's publisher, 137
 overture (*La vera costanza*) published by, 157
 sonatas published by, 142–43, 216, 306, 423

articulation
 accents, 274
 autograph changes in, 219–20, 233
 on fortepiano, 219
 markings, 227, 230–31, 272–73
 by "original" violin bow, 224
 and ornaments, 319
 and phrasing, 231
 portato, 230–32
 and rhythm, 274
 slurs, 228–32, 272
 staccato, 230, 231, 319
 in Symphony No. 85, 247
Aschenbrenner, Karl, 443
Asplmayer, Franz, 7
Austrian music
 chamber music melodies (c. 1750), 365–67
 for the church
  encyclical concerning, 164–65, 168, 417
  Josephinian reforms, 168–70
  orchestration, 204, 205
  restoration of instrumental music, 166, 171
  restrictions on, 165–67
  traditions, 203–4
 and imperial family, 3, 5
 and Italian style, 377
 for organ, 192–94
 and social classes, 3, 5
 symphonies (1720–65), 501–5
authentication
 degrees, 79
 difficulties in, 119
 direct, 75–76
 indirect, 76–77
authenticity
 doubtful works, 77–78, 99–102